Lecture Notes in Computer Science   10324

Commenced Publication in 1973
Founding and Former Series Editors:
Gerhard Goos, Juris Hartmanis, and Jan van Leeuwen

More information about this series at http://www.springer.com/series/7412

Lucio Tommaso De Paolis · Patrick Bourdot
Antonio Mongelli (Eds.)

Augmented Reality, Virtual Reality, and Computer Graphics

4th International Conference, AVR 2017
Ugento, Italy, June 12–15, 2017
Proceedings, Part I

 Springer

Editors
Lucio Tommaso De Paolis
University of Salento
Lecce
Italy

Antonio Mongelli
University of Salento
Lecce
Italy

Patrick Bourdot
University of Paris-Sud
Orsay
France

ISSN 0302-9743   ISSN 1611-3349   (electronic)
Lecture Notes in Computer Science
ISBN 978-3-319-60921-8   ISBN 978-3-319-60922-5   (eBook)
DOI 10.1007/978-3-319-60922-5

Library of Congress Control Number: 2017943083

LNCS Sublibrary: SL6 – Image Processing, Computer Vision, Pattern Recognition, and Graphics

Printed on acid-free paper

This Springer imprint is published by Springer Nature
The registered company is Springer International Publishing AG
The registered company address is: Gewerbestrasse 11, 6330 Cham, Switzerland

Preface

Virtual Reality (VR) is a simulation in which computer graphics is used to create a realistic-looking where the feeling of immersion and realistic presence is very high.

Augmented Reality (AR) technology allows for the real-time fusion of computer-generated digital contents with the real world with the aim of enhancing the users' perception and improve their interaction or assist them during the execution of specific tasks.

Human–Computer Interaction technology (HCI) is a research area concerned with the design, implementation, and evaluation of interactive systems that make more simple and intuitive the interaction between user and computer.

This book contains the contributions to the 4th International Conference on Augmented Reality, Virtual Reality and Computer Graphics (SALENTO AVR 2017) that has held in Ugento (Italy) during June 12–15, 2017. We cordially invite you to visit the SALENTO AVR website (http://www.salentoavr.it) where you can find all relevant information about this event.

SALENTO AVR 2017 intended to bring together researchers, scientists, and practitioners to discuss key issues, approaches, ideas, open problems, innovative applications, and trends on virtual and augmented reality, 3D visualization, and computer graphics in the areas of medicine, cultural heritage, arts, education, entertainment as well as industrial and military sectors.

We are very grateful to the Program Committee and local Organizing Committee members for their support and for the time spent to review and discuss the submitted papers and doing so in a timely and professional manner. We would like to sincerely thank the keynote and tutorial speakers who willingly accepted our invitation and shared their expertise through illuminating talks, helping us to fully meet the conference objectives.

In this edition of SALENTO AVR, we were honored to have the following keynote speakers:

- Mariano Alcañiz, Universitat Politècnica de València, Spain
- Vincenzo Ferrari, Università di Pisa, Italy
- Fabrizio Lamberti, Politecnico di Torino, Italy
- Roberto Scopigno, ISTI-CNR, Pisa, Italy
- Fabrizio Nunnari, German Research Center for Artificial Intelligence (DFKI), Germany

We extend our thanks to the University of Salento for the enthusiastic acceptance to sponsor the conference and to provide support in the organization of the event.

We would also like to thank the EuroVR Association, which has supported the conference since its first edition, by contributing each year to the design of the international Program Committee, proposing the invited keynote speakers, and spreading internationally the announcements of the event.

SALENTO AVR attracted high-quality paper submissions from many countries. We would like to thank the authors of all accepted papers for submitting and presenting their works at the conference and all the conference attendees for making SALENTO AVR an excellent forum on virtual and augmented reality, facilitating the exchange of ideas, fostering new collaborations, and shaping the future of this exciting research field.

For greater readability of the two volumes, the papers are classified into five main parts that include contributions on:

- Virtual Reality
- Augmented and Mixed Reality
- Computer Graphics
- Human–Computer Interaction
- Applications of VR/AR in Medicine
- Applications of VR/AR in Cultural Heritage

We hope the readers will find in these pages interesting material and fruitful ideas for their future work.

June 2017   Lucio Tommaso De Paolis
                                                              Patrick Bourdot
                                                              Antonio Mongelli

Organization

Conference Chair

Lucio Tommaso De Paolis   University of Salento, Italy

Conference Co-chairs

Patrick Bourdot   CNRS/LIMSI, University of Paris-Sud, France
Marco Sacco   ITIA-CNR, Italy
Paolo Proietti   MIMOS, Italy

Honorary Chair

Giovanni Aloisio   University of Salento, Italy

Scientific Program Committee

Andrea Abate   University of Salerno, Italy
Giuseppe Anastasi   University of Pisa, Italy
Selim Balcisoy   Sabancı University, Turkey
Vitoantonio Bevilacqua   Polytechnic of Bari, Italy
Monica Bordegoni   Politecnico di Milano, Italy
Pierre Boulanger   University of Alberta, Canada
Andres Bustillo   University of Burgos, Spain
Massimo Cafaro   University of Salento, Italy
Bruno Carpentieri   University of Salerno, Italy
Marcello Carrozzino   Scuola Superiore Sant'Anna, Italy
Pietro Cipresso   IRCCS Istituto Auxologico Italiano, Italy
Arnis Cirulis   Vidzeme University of Applied Sciences, Latvia
Lucio Colizzi   CETMA, Italy
Mario Covarrubias   Politecnico di Milano, Italy
Rita Cucchiara   University of Modena, Italy
Matteo Dellepiane   National Research Council (CNR), Italy
Giorgio De Nunzio   University of Salento, Italy
Francisco José Domínguez   University of Seville, Spain
  Mayo
Aldo Franco Dragoni   Università Politecnica delle Marche, Italy
Italo Epicoco   University of Salento, Italy
Vincenzo Ferrari   EndoCAS Center, Italy
Francesco Ferrise   Politecnico di Milano, Italy
Emanuele Frontoni   Università Politecnica delle Marche, Italy
Francesco Gabellone   IBAM ITLab, CNR, Italy

Damianos Gavalas	University of the Aegean, Greece
Osvaldo Gervasi	University of Perugia, Italy
Luigi Gallo	ICAR/CNR, Italy
Viktors Gopejenko	ISMA University, Latvia
Mirko Grimaldi	University of Salento, Italy
Sara Invitto	University of Salento, Italy
Fabrizio Lamberti	Politecnico di Torino, Italy
Leo Joskowicz	Hebrew University of Jerusalem, Israel
Tomas Krilavičius	Vytautas Magnus University, Kaunas, Lithuania
Salvatore Livatino	University of Hertfordshire, UK
Silvia Mabel Castro	Universidad Nacional del Sur, Argentina
Luca Mainetti	University of Salento, Italy
Andrea Martini	CETMA, Italy
Antonio Mongelli	University of Salento, Italy
Sven Nomm	Tallinn University of Technology, Estonia
Roberto Paiano	University of Salento, Italy
Andrea Pandurino	University of Salento, Italy
Giorgos Papadourakis	Technological Educational Institute (TEI) of Crete, Greece
Gianfranco Parlangeli	University of Salento, Italy
Gianluca Paravati	Politecnico di Torino, Italy
Nikolaos Pellas	University of the Aegean, Greece
Roberto Pierdicca	Università Politecnica delle Marche, Italy
Sofia Pescarin	CNR ITABC, Italy
James Ritchie	Heriot-Watt University, Edinburgh, UK
Jaume Segura Garcia	Universitat de València, Spain
Robert Stone	University of Birmingham, UK
João Manuel R.S. Tavares	Universidade do Porto, Portugal
Daniel Thalmann	Nanyang Technological University, Singapore
Nadia Magnenat-Thalmann	University of Geneva, Switzerland
Carlos M. Travieso-González	Universidad de Las Palmas de Gran Canaria, Spain
Antonio Emmanuele Uva	Polytechnic of Bari, Italy
Volker Paelke	Bremen University of Applied Sciences, Germany
Krzysztof Walczak	Poznań University of Economics and Business, Poland
Anthony Whitehead	Carleton University, Canada

Local Organizing Committee

Ilenia Paladini	University of Salento, Italy
Silke Miss	Virtech, Italy
Valerio De Luca	University of Salento, Italy
Pietro Vecchio	University of Salento, Italy

An Introduction to Unity3D, a Game Engine with AR and VR Capabilities (Tutorial)

Paolo Sernani

Università Politecnica delle Marche, Ancona, Italy

Games, Augmented Reality, and Virtual Reality are capturing the attention of the research community as well as the industry in many application domains with purposes such as education, training, rehabilitation, awareness, visualization, and pure entertainment.

From a technical perspective, scientists, researchers, and practitioners need tools and integrated frameworks that allow them running a fast prototyping as well as an accurate development and production of applications and gaming experiences.

The tutorial presents the Unity3D game engine, describing its main features (cross-platforms applications, cloud build, the asset store, and the wide community of users). Moreover, the tutorial introduces the integration of Unity3D with AR and VR tools.

Keynote Abstracts

The Future Fabrics of Reality: Socio-psychological Aspects of Human Interaction in Advanced Mixed Reality Environments

Mariano Alcañiz

Universitat Politècnica de València, Valencia, Spain

In the last two years, technological tools known as Mixed Reality Interfaces (MRIs) have appeared on the market, which not only allow user interaction with a virtual environment, but also allow the physical objects of the user's immediate real environment to serve as elements of interaction with the virtual environment. That is, MRIs are perfect tools to introduce into our reality new virtual elements (objects and virtual humans) that will generate a new reality in our brain. Today, MRIs are the most technologically advanced tools that human beings have used to date to improve their reality and generate artificial realities that improve the reality they live. In the last year, there is an unusual interest in MRI in the ICT industry. That means that MRI will be a revolution in human communication mediated by new technologies, as in the moment was the irruption of the mobile phone. Therefore, the central question that motivates the present talk is: what capacity will MRIs have to alter the reality that we are going to live in a few years and hence alter the social communication between humans? To date, only a very basic aspect of MRIs is being investigated, its ability to simulate our current reality. However, the above question calls for a paradigm shift in current MRI research. It is necessary to advance towards this new paradigm by proposing a basic research scheme that will allow to analyse the influence of individual personnel variables and MRI interaction aspects will have on basic aspects of human behaviour, like decision making. In this talk, we present several examples of how MRI can be used for human behaviour tracking and modification, we describe different research projects results and we conclude with a discussion of potential future implications.

Potentialities of AR in Medicine and Surgery

Vincenzo Ferrari

Università di Pisa, Pisa, Italy

Patient safety and the surgical accuracy can be nowadays significantly improved thanks to the availability of patient specific information contained in particular in medical images. AR is considered an ergonomic way to show the patient related information during the procedure, as demonstrated by the hundreds of works published in the last years. To develop useful AR systems for surgery there are many aspects to take into account from a technical, clinical and perceptual point of view. During the talk particular attention will be posed to the using of HMD for surgical navigation describing also current doubts related to the using of this kind of technologies to perform manual tasks under direct view.

AR offers also the possibility to improve surgical training outside the surgical room. Surgical simulation based on AR, mixing the benefits of physical and virtual simulation, represents a step forward in surgical training. In this talk the last advancements in visual and tactile AR for surgical simulation will be showed.

Phygital Play: Where Gaming Intersects Mixed Reality, Robotics and Human-Machine Interaction

Fabrizio Lamberti

Politecnico di Torino, Turin, Italy

Developments in Virtual Reality (VR) and Augmented Reality (AR) technologies are dramatically changing the way we perform many of our everyday activities. One of the fields that is expected to be more profoundly influenced by this technological revolution is entertainment and, especially, gaming. With VR and AR, players will be able to fully immerse in computer-generated environments and become part of them, while gaming elements will be allowed to enter the real word and interact with it in a playful way. The physicality ensured by the possibility to move in open spaces as well as to touch, move and, in a word, feel both real and virtual objects will make gaming more engaging, as it will bring players' experience to a more primordial level. The "physicalization" of gaming is a process that will encompass a number of other fields. For instance, ways to make players interaction with computers and computer-generated contents ever more concrete, e.g., by exploiting haptic, tangible or hand and body tracking-based interfaces will have to be experimented. Similarly, the contribution of non-technical research fields will have to be taken into account. As a matter of example, according to behavioural studies, robotic elements could be introduced in the playing area, e.g., as players' avatars, artificial companions, etc. to strengthen the relation between the digital and physical worlds. By leveraging the above considerations, the aim of this talk is to present the activities that are being carried out to create a cloud-based platform supporting a systematic use of VR/AR technologies, robotic components and human-machine interaction paradigms with the aim to further push the transformation of real-world settings in ever more amazing gaming environments.

VR/AR: Success Stories and Opportunities in Cultural Heritage and Digital Humanities

Roberto Scopigno

ISTI-CNR, Pisa, Italy

Virtual and Augmented Reality have already a quite long story and a consolidated status. There are a number of projects and installations specifically developed for presenting or navigating Cultural Heritage (CH) data. But CH or, more broadly, Digital Humanities are domains with specific needs and constraints. Previous projects have selected these domains either to assess new technologies or to provide new tools and navigation experiences. The users in this domain belong to two well differentiated classes: ordinary public (museum visitors, web surfers) or experts (scholars, archaeologists, restorers). The talk will present in a comparative manner some selected previous experiences, aiming at deriving a critical assessment and suggest issues and open questions.

Populating Virtual Worlds: Practical Solutions for the Generation of Interactive Virtual Characters

Fabrizio Nunnari

German Research Center for Artificial Intelligence (DFKI),
Saarbrücken, Germany

Creating a state-of-the-art virtual character is a job which requires the employment of many professionals–dedicated artists do modeling, texturing, and rigging. However, since few years it is possible to find some software tools allowing nonskilled users to generate fully functional virtual characters quickly. The characters, which feature a compromise between quality and creation speed, are ready to be employed for either movie production or in real-time applications. In this tutorial, I will give an overview of some modern virtual character generators, and I will show how to use them to populate with characters real-time interactive applications.

Contents – Part I

Augmented and Mixed Reality

Contents – Part II

Application of VR/AR in Cultural Heritage

Computer Graphics

Human Computer Interaction

Virtual Reality

Cognitive Control Influences the Sense of Presence in Virtual Environments with Different Immersion Levels

Boris B. Velichkovsky[(⊠)], Alexey N. Gusev, Alexander E. Kremlev,
and Sergey S. Grigorovich

Moscow State University, Moscow, Russia
velitchk@mail.ru

Abstract. Presence is an important subjective aspect of interacting with virtual environments. In this study, the influence of cognitive control on presence was investigated. A battery of cognitive control tasks was used (measuring inhibition, switching, and working memory updating). The virtual scenario consisted in collecting objects in a virtual space. The virtual scenario was presented either in a full-immersion CAVE environment, or in a low-immersion display environment. Presence was assessed with the ITC-SOPI inventory. Cognitive control is related to various aspects of presence, most notably spatial presence, negative somatic effects, and virtual scenario naturalness. The influence of cognitive control on presence is not straightforward, as strong cognitive control may be detrimental to presence. Elaborated control was more important for the emergence of presence in the low-immersion setting. Mechanisms through which control influences presence are discussed as are implications for developing virtual environments with more presence potential.

Keywords: Virtual reality · Presence · Cognitive control · Interference · Task switching · Working memory · Situation model · Emotions

1 Introduction

The illusion of presence is an important aspect of interacting with virtual environments [1, 2]. Presence is experienced when there is "a perceptive illusion of non-mediation" [3], that is, when the user experiences the virtual scenario without the awareness of its being mediated by some technology. While a direct relationship between presence and successful operation of a virtual environment has not been proven yet [4], the creation of virtual environments with increased sense of presence is an important goal for VR applications developers. The study of presence is thus a lively research area. This paper is devoted to the study of psychological determinants of presence, namely cognitive control.

Presence is not unitary but a multi-dimensional construct. This is evidenced in the empirically derived structure of instruments used to measure presence [3], as well as in recent attempts to build an overarching theory of presence [5]. Questionnaires used to assess presence usually discern aspects of presence like spatial presence, naturalness of

© Springer International Publishing AG 2017
L.T. De Paolis et al. (Eds.): AVR 2017, Part I, LNCS 10324, pp. 3–16, 2017.
DOI: 10.1007/978-3-319-60922-5_1

a virtual scenario, emotional involvement, controllability of a virtual scenario, and other [1, 3]. The determinants of presence may be divided into technological and psychological. Initially, studies concentrated on the technological determinants of presence [1, 6]. It was shown, that increasing the fidelity of VR presentation, adding several modalities, and the possibility of natural interaction with virtual objects increases the illusion of presence. However, a technologically advanced presentation system alone cannot guarantee optimal sense of presence. And vice versa, a rudimentary presentation medium can under some circumstances produce a pronounced sense of presence (like in reading an interesting book). Presence occurs at the user's side; it is a psychological phenomenon and is thus at least partly determined by psychological factors. These findings cause a redirection of attention towards psychological characteristics related to presence [6–8].

The research on the psychological determinants of presence led to the identification of many such factors. Presence has been related to demographic factors (gender, age) and experience with computers and VR [9, 10]. More important, presence was associated with several individual differences variables. Specifically, presence has been linked with impulsivity, openness to experience, extraversion, introversion, psychological absorption, locus of control and other personality characteristics [11–14]. Interestingly, a suggested link with spatial abilities was not found [15]. It is to note that the studies of psychological determinants of presence have led to mixed results. While presence was found to be relatively independent of low-level cognitive abilities, its links with personality level variables are not straightforward and somewhat contradictory. For instance, a positive relationship of presence was fond with both extraversion and introversion [16], which are opposite constructs. This forces to look for the psychological determinants of presence at different levels of individual organization. One alternative is cognitive control.

Cognitive control is a system of cognitive processes which regulate the working of the cognitive system. The function of cognitive control is to fine-tune specialist cognitive processes (like attention, perception, memory, etc.) for the achievement of the current goal respecting the limitations of the current context [17, 18]. Cognitive control is thus crucially involved into the regulation of any kind of complex goal-directed behavior [17], providing for the adaptation of human's cognitive system to the changing conditions. Failures of cognitive control are always associated with severe failures of adaptation. Cognitive control in humans is extremely flexible allowing for the quick acquisition of any forms of behavior adaptive in the current setting [19]. As such, cognitive control may also be responsible for the (un)successful adaptation to a virtual environment. Thus, cognitive control may be a powerful determinant of presence which has not been studied yet.

Cognitive control may modulate the sense of presence through several mechanisms. First, cognitive control processes may influence the distribution of attention toward the virtual environment. This involves perception amplification for task-relevant virtual objects, as well as inhibition of task-irrelevant stimuli from the virtual environment. The modulation of attention toward a virtual environment may underlie the distribution of focused attention as an objective index of presence [20]. Second, cognitive control is responsible for a flexible switching of task sets [19], which may underlie the task-appropriate adaptation of cognition when confronted with a virtual environment.

Indeed, such flexible adaptation may be needed because the interaction with virtually environments differs a lot from the interaction with real situations. Third, the illusion of presence may be mediated by working memory, which may be used for the under-standing of a virtual scenario. Working memory and the manipulation of its content is assumed to be a part of cognitive control [21], which again suggests a role of control processes in presence. There are also other possible routes of influence for cognitive control on presence like the influence of conflict monitoring (criticality) [18]. In sum, cognitive control as the system responsible for goal-directed adaptation to specific situations may influence various aspects of presence.

In the present study, we check whether aspects of cognitive control are related to aspects of experienced presence in a simple virtual scenario. The virtual scenario was presented either in a full-immersion CAVE system (high immersion condition) or with a standard computer display (low immersion condition). This allowed for additionally assessing the influence of physical immersion level on the relationship between cog-nitive control and presence. In the cases that links between cognitive control and the level of subjective presence will be found, it will help to describe the mechanisms of presence and may have consequences for the practice of VR application development and user selection for VR.

2 Method

2.1 Subjects

Forty subjects, aged 18–23, 26 females, were recruited for the study among the students of the department of psychology at Moscow State University in exchange for a course credit.

2.2 Cognitive Control Tests

Three basic cognitive control functions – interference control, switching, and working memory updating [22] were assessed via computerized tests. Inhibition of distractor stimuli, irrelevant representations and motor responses (interference control) is the most basic control function which is responsible for the realization of task-appropriate cognitions and behaviors in dynamic contexts. Switching is the function responsible for the flexible change of task sets – collections of sensory-motor mappings ("task rules") which underlie the achievement of goals. For a task to be accomplished a corre-sponding task set must be activated and irrelevant task sets must be de-activated with task switching referring to the easiness with which an individual changes task sets (cognitive flexibility). Working memory updating is a control function responsible for task-appropriate changes in the content of working memory which is responsible for task-relevant on-line storage and processing of information. While these three cognitive control functions are not the only control function, they usually considered to be very important for the realization of goal-directed behavior adaptive to changes in the context [22].

Interference control was assessed via the antisaccade task, the Eriksen flanker task, and the Go-NoGo task (tapping different aspects of interference control [23]). Switching ability was assessed via the letter-digit task [24] in two variants: one with a predictable and one with a random switching sequence. Working memory updating was assessed via the n-back task [25]. Details on the control tasks are given below.

Eriksen Flanker Task. Five horizontally arranged arrows were presented either congruently (i.e., <<<<<) or incongruently (i.e., <<><<) with respect to the central arrow. The task of the subject is to identify the direction of the central arrow via keypress. There was a training series of 36 trials, and four experimental blocks of 216 trials each. The most important variable of interest is the differences in RTs and errors between incongruent and congruent trials.

Go-NoGo Task. Atarget stimulus (letter X) was presented embedded in a series of distractors stimuli (14 Cyrillic letters) with 80% probability. The task of the subject is to press a button upon the presentation of the target stimulus, and to withhold the reaction if a distractor was presented. There was a training block of 20 trials, and an experimental block of 200 trials. The variables of interest are the RT for correct responses, the number of hits and false alarms.

Antisaccade Task. The subject fixates the center of the screen, and a distractor is presented at a randomly selected half of the screen which the subject is instructed to ignore. After 200 ms, an arrow is presented for 125 ms in the other half of the screen, and the subject is required to identify its direction with a keypress. A visual mask follows the presentation of the arrow. If the subject is not able to inhibit the imperative saccade to the distractor, the identification of arrow's direction is very hard. The main variable of interest it the number of corrects responses.

Letter-Digit Task (Predictable). The screen is divided in four quadrants. In a trial, a letter-digit pair (four odd digits, for even digits, four vowels, and four consonants) is presented in a quadrant. The task of the subject is to judge the parity of the digit (odd/even, the digit task) or the kind of the letter (vowel/consonant, the letter task) via a keypress depending on the quadrant. The presentation starts in the right upper quadrant and proceeds clockwise, the order of the tasks is letter-letter-digit-digit. There are thus an equal number of switch trials (the current task is different from the previous task) and non-switch trials (the current task is the same as the previous task). There is a training series of 24 trials, and an experimental series of 128 trials. The main variables of interests are the RT and error switch costs (the differences between switch and non-switch trials).

Letter-Digit Task (Random). The same as the predictable letter-digit task, but the stimuli are presented in the center of the screen, and the order of the tasks is random. On the average, there are still an equal number of switch and non-switch trials. The current task is announced by a color cue to the user.

N-Back Task. Arandom series of digits is presented to the subject in the middle of the screen. The task of the subject is to indicate via a keypress, if the current digit is equal to the digit presented two positions before (the 2-back task). There is a training series of

40 trials, and three experimental series of 48 trials. The signal probability is 16%. The main variables of interest are correct response RT and the number of hits and misses.

2.3 Presence Assessment

A Russian version of the ITC-SOPI questionnaire [3] was used. The inventory consists of 44 items measuring different aspects of presence on a 5-point Likert scale. The study of the questionnaire's structure [3] revealed four factors – Spatial Presence, Virtual Scenario Naturalness, Emotional Involvement, and Negative Effects. Spatial Presence refers to the illusion of being transferred to a virtual location which is an important component of presence. Virtual Scenario Naturalness refers to the feeling of realism associated with the interaction with a virtual scenario which is grounded in scenarios coherence, understandability, and predictability. Emotional involvement is associated with positive emotions stemming from the interest in the virtual scenario. Finally, Negative Effects refer to negative somatic feelings (e.g., nausea) associated with the presentation of the virtual stimulation (which are reciprocally related to the sense of presence). A general index of presence (General Presence) was computed by summing the scores on all four scales.

2.4 Virtual Scenario

The virtual task was presented either in a high-immersion CAVE system or with the low-immersion standard computer display (21"). The virtual task was to traverse a set of digits (1–9) randomly placed within a homogenous 20×20 m virtual space in the correct numerical order (Fig. 1). Upon reaching the next digit in the sequence the subject had to select it with the flystick. A digit could not be selected out of order.

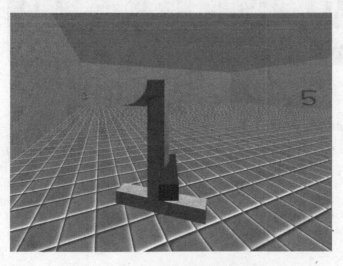

Fig. 1. A screenshot of the virtual scenario.

Upon the selection of the last digit, the scenario was terminated. There was a training scenario (with digits 1–5) and two experimental scenarios (with the full range of digits) in each of the immersion conditions (CAVE/display). The total exposure to VR lasted about 20 min.

2.5 CAVE System

The MSU CAVE system (Fig. 2) has four large flat screens (Barco ISpace 4), which were connected into one cube consisting of three walls and a floor. The length of each side was about 2.5 × 2.2 m. Shutter glasses were made by Volfoni. Projection system was based on BarcoReality 909. The projector's matrix resolution was 1280 × 1024 with 100 Hz update frequency. Tracking system produced by ArtTrack2, include Flystick, Fingertracking, Motion Capture. Graphic Cluster for five PCs was based on Quadro FX 5800. 3Dvia Virtools was used for software developing.

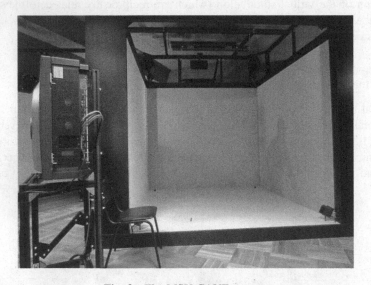

Fig. 2. The MSU CAVE system.

2.6 Procedure

The subjects first completed a computerized cognitive control test battery in a group session. After the completion of the computerized test battery, the subjects individually completed the virtual scenario in either immersion conditions (the individual session in VR started about one week after the completion of the tests). The order of the immersion conditions was counterbalanced across participants. After either immersion condition, the subjects completed the presence inventory.

3   Results

As some of the measures were distributed non normally (Kolmogorov-Smirnov test), non parametric Spearman correlations were computed between cognitive control and presence measures. The results are presented for each basic control function (interference control, task switching, working memory updating) separately broken by the immersion condition (high-immersion – CAVE, low-immersion – standard display). Given the exploratory nature of the study, ps < 0.1 were considered as significant and no alpha level correction was employed.

3.1   Interference Control

The results about the link between interference control (inhibition) and presence are presented in Table 1. The data shows that there is some relationship between interference control and presence. The antisaccade accuracy is inversely related to spatial presence and to general presence (in the low-immersion condition). The error-related interference effect in the Eriksen flanker task is positively related to the general presence, spatial presence, and somatic negative effects (in the high-immersion condition). Go-No Go performance is inversely related to virtual scenario naturalness and to general presence and spatial presence (in the low-immersion condition). The inverse links mostly suggest that elaborated interference control is related to less presence.

Table 1. Correlations between interference control and aspects of presence (here and below: GP – general presence, SP – spatial presence, EI – emotional involvment, VSN - virtual scenario naturalness, NE – negative effects. AS RT – antisaccade reaction time, AS ACC – antisaccade accuracy, FT RT –interference effect in flanker task, time, incongruent minus congruent trials, FT ACC - interference effect in flanker task, accuracy, incongruent minus congruent trials, GNG RT – Go-NoGo reaction time, GNG ACC - Go-NoGo accuracy)

Interference control	Presence				
	GP	SP	EI	VSN	NE
High immersion					
AS RT	−0.010	0.012	−0.008	−0.127	0.205
AS ACC	−0.048	**−0.261***	0.196	−0.164	0.038
FT RT	0.106	0.148	0.035	−0.021	0.080
FT ACC	**0.213***	**0.215***	−0.037	0.182	**0.281***
GNG RT	0.009	0.173	−0.089	−0.133	0.039
GNG ACC	−0.172	−0.100	−0.098	**−0.311***	−0.140
Low immersion					
AS RT	−0.006	0.074	−0.094	0.126	0.167
AS ACC	**−0.236***	**−0.225***	−0.102	0.019	−0.113
FT RT	0.002	−0.057	0.13	0.001	−0.071
FT ACC	0.168	0.123	0.095	0.082	0.141
GNG RT	0.138	**0.293***	−0.033	0.077	0.055
GNG ACC	**−0.222***	−0.132	**−0.231***	**−0.213***	0.115

3.2   Switching

The results about the link between task switching efficiency and presence are presented in Table 2. The data show a specific relationship between the efficiency of switching and the intensity of negative somatic effects. Low switching efficiency as reflected in high RT-related switch costs is related to increased negative effects. A detailed analysis of the components of switch costs revealed that this correlation is driven by the correlation of between RT during switch trials and negative effects intensity ($r = 0.330$, $p < 0.05$). RT on switch trials is also positively related to general presence ($r = 0.280$, $p < 0.1$). The link between switching efficiency and negative effects (as well as general presence) is evident for random switching task while it fails short of reaching significance for the predictable switching task.

Table 2. Correlations between switching ability indices and aspects of presence (RND RT – time-related switch cost, random sequence, RND AC – error-related switch cost, random sequence, PRED RT - time-related switch cost, predictable sequence, PRED AC - error-related switch cost, predictable sequence)

Switching	Presence				
	GP	SP	EI	VSN	NE
High immersion					
RND RT	**0.223***	0.130	0.064	0.129	**0.328**
RND AC	−0.092	0.025	−0.106	−0.069	−0.007
PRED RT	0.205	−0.02	0.138	**0.225***	**0.222***
PRED AC	0.007	0.055	−0.122	0.135	0.052
Low immersion					
RND RT	**0.367***	**0.451**	0.07	0.210	**0.378***
RND AC	−0.013	0.021	−0.017	0.063	−0.097
PRED RT	0.142	0.030	**0.238***	−0.004	0.174
PRED AC	0.124	0.185	−0.004	0.126	0.075

3.3   Working Memory Updating

The results on working memory and presence are presented in Table 3. The data show that there is a relationship between working memory functioning and aspects of

Table 3. Correlations between working memory updating and aspects of presence (NB RT – n-back reaction time, NB ACC – n-back accuracy)

Updating	Presence				
	GP	SP	EI	VSN	NE
High immersion					
NB RT	0.079	0.080	0.126	0.025	0.070
NB ACC	**−0.227***	**−0.262***	0.017	**−0.337**	−0.112
Low immersion					
NB RT	**−0.277***	−0.154	**−0.306***	−0.045	−0.112
NB ACC	−0.197	**−0.245***	−0.086	−0.019	−0.159

presence. Notably, n-back speed (which is related to the efficiency of information processing in working memory) was related to general presence and emotional involvement (in the low-immersion condition). N-back accuracy (which is more related the storage capacity of working memory) is systematically related to spatial presence and visual scenario naturalness and general presence (in the high-immersion condition).

4   Discussion

The above results indicate that individual differences in cognitive control influences the experienced sense of presence while interacting with a virtual scenario in a full-immersion CAVE system. Significant correlations were observed for each basic control function (interference control, switching, and updating) and subjective presence measures. It is to note that different control functions were associated with different aspects of presence. Such differentiation of results suggests that there may exist several causal mechanisms through which the subjective feeling of presence is linked to cognitive control. We will consider these mechanisms in turn.

Efficient interference control is probably the most obvious determinant of presence given its relationship with the control of attention. Accordingly, most correlations with presence were obtained for this function. It is to note, however, that interference control (or inhibition) is a heterogeneous construct [23], which suggests several possible control/presence relationships in this category. First, the ability to control eye-movements and, accordingly, overt attention distribution (the antisaccade task) was shown to be inversely related to spatial presence and to general presence. This may indicate that the susceptibility to automatic attention capture is an important determinant of presence, especially in low-immersion settings. Second, the extent of interference produced by visual distractors (the flanker task) was related to somatic negative effects, spatial presence, and presence in general. This result corroborates the first result in that susceptibility to attention capture by visual distractors originating from the virtual environment contributes to spatial presence (the user being "drawn" to the virtual world). This may, however, have detrimental effects in that attention capture may induce uncomfortable vestibular feelings. Third, the decreased efficiency of response inhibition is related to increased virtual scenario naturalness. Such disinhibition may benefit presence by being the mechanisms through which the personality characteristic of impulsiveness leads to greater presence [16, 26]. It is interesting that disinhibition is specifically related to the perceived naturalness of the virtual scenario. This may be related to the easiness with which response tendencies associated with the virtual scenario overtake the control over the cognitive-motor system in the user. Susceptibility to attention capture and impulsivity may be closely related and form a basis of an "impulsive", "thrill-seeking" personality profile related to presence. It is to note that our results indicate that (for interference control) elaborated cognitive control is detrimental for the emergence of the sense of presence, as it prohibits attention capture by VR distractors and impulsive reactions to VR events.

For the task switching control function, three main results were observed. First, switch costs were systematically related to the somatic negative effects. That is, users who are less able to quickly adapt their current task-set to the virtual environment experience more uncomfortable somatic symptoms. Given that task sets are usually understood as perceptual-motor mappings needed to solve the current task [19], it is easy to see how the rigidity of perceptual-motor mappings can lead to negative somatic effects produced by sensory-motor incongruencies. Thus, to diminish negative effects and consequently increase general presence, one can (1) select VR users on the basis of cognitive flexibility and (2) apply interventions which increase cognitive flexibility. These include, for instance, increasing the preparatory intervals during which task sets are changed [16] and brain stimulation (tDCS) at lateral prefrontal cortex [27]. Second, larger switch costs were strongly associated with spatial presence in the low-immersion condition. This is at odds with the previous result as larger switch costs indicate less cognitive flexibility. A possible explanation for this result is that less cognitive flexibility means less distractibility [19] which is important for the emergence of the sense of presence and prevention of breaks in presence, especially in low-immersion environments. That is, given the user successfully adapted his/her cognitive system to the requirements of the virtual environment, cognitive inflexibility will support user's immersion into the virtual environment. Third, switch costs during predictable task switching were related to the perceived naturalness of the virtual scenario. This relationship may be driven by involvement of working memory which is assumed in predictable but not random task switching (via the monitoring of the task sequence). Working memory may in turn be related to the construction of the mental model of the virtual scenario (see below). In sum, a clear conclusion from these results is that cognitive flexibility is an important determinant of presence. Selecting users according to cognitive flexibility and applying interventions which modulate cognitive flexibility may predictably increase the sense of presence while interacting with high- and low-immersion virtual environments.

A set of significant correlations was observed for the working memory task (the n-back task) and aspects of presence. It was, first, found that n-back accuracy is systematically inversely related to spatial presence. N-back accuracy is related to working memory capacity (the ability to store information available for processing). Thus, low capacity is related to greater spatial presence. This may be related to the fact that the feeling of spatial presence is mediated by the situation model of the virtual environment held in working memory [5]. It may be speculated that spatial presence is promoted by the virtual environment situation model totally replacing the default situation model of the real environment in working memory for the guidance of perception and action. Such replacement of situation models is clearly supported by user's working memory being able to incorporate only a single situation model at once (low capacity). This conclusion is supported by the fact that n-back accuracy is strongly inversely related to virtual scenario naturalness (at least in the high-immersion condition). As virtual scenario naturalness may strongly depends on the ability to construct a comprehensible situation model of the virtual scenario, this may indicate a role for working memory which is directly involved in the construction of situation models in narratives' comprehension [28]. Another interesting finding is that in the low-immersion setting, presence (general presence and emotional involvement) is related to the speed of the n-back task, which relates to the efficiency of processing in working memory. It seems that in low-immersion setting in which the potential for automatic attention capture and situation model replacement by the virtual environment is diminished, the controlled construction of a meaningful and subjectively enjoyable situation model for the virtual scenario is one of the most important ingredients of the sense of presence. In sum, these results indicate a role of working memory in presence experience (especially for situation model construction) which matches with the results of a recent individual differences study [29].

Overall, the results indicate that cognitive control may be related to different aspects of the sense of presence in virtual environments and that the level of cognitive control functions may be more appropriate than the level of personality for the study of the psychological determinants of presence. These results corroborate recent finding about the role of prefrontal cortex (the site of cognitive control) in the emergence of the sense of presence [31]. It seems, however, that the relationship between cognitive control and presence is not straightforward. This is because strong cognitive control may promote presence, but it may also diminish presence (for instance, see the results for interference control). It is interesting that in real world adaptation a similar ambivalence about the adaptability of stronger/weaker cognitive control also exists [30]. Cognitive control determinants of presence obtained in the present study are as follows: relaxed interference control for easier attention capture; cognitive flexibility; and working memory capacity/processing efficiency as related to the construction of situation models for virtual scenarios. Thus, cognitive control may influence the sense of presence via different mechanisms. The common idea is that users' selection for work with VR may be based on cognitive control assessment, and that the development of virtual environments with high presence-eliciting potential should target cognitive control functions of the potential users. A more advanced development is brain stimulation of cognitive control areas of users before/during VR exposure with the aim of presence amplification. Converging evidence indicates that lateral prefrontal cortex may be an appropriate locus for such stimulation [26, 27].

Our results also suggest that the high- and low-presence conditions differed with respect to the influence of cognitive control on the experienced sense of presence. This is not surprising, given that both conditions differ with respect to the demands placed on the cognitive system during the interaction with the virtual scenario. Generally, we assume that low-immersion conditions are more dependent on cognitive control for the emergence of the sense of presence as they provide less opportunity for users to be "drawn away" by the stream of virtual stimulation automatically creating an appropriate situation model dominating the content of user's working memory. In the case of low immersion settings, such situation models are to be created and guarded against distractors in a controlled mode of operation. Another finding is that emotional involvement was the aspect of presence least often associated with cognitive control. This may (1) because our virtual scenario was extremely non emotional, but also (2) because cognitive control refers more to the "cold" aspects of cognition and less to the "hot" (affective) aspects of cognition. In this respect it should be noted that cognitive control was most related to spatial presence and negative somatic effects, which are rooted in basic cognitive abilities. The associations to emotional involvement and scenario naturalness, which are much more rooted in the content and motivational-affective factors, are more sporadic. It follows that cognitive control may influence presence via the influence on "cold" cognitive functions, while there is additionally a considerable influence on presence from the affective and motivational variables mainly related to the content of a virtual scenario. The exact proportion of cognitive and affective influences on presence remains to be estimated in future work.

5 Conclusions

The present study was aimed at explicating the influence of cognitive control on the sense of presence in virtual environments. Cognitive control is a set of meta-cognitive processes responsible for the fine-tuning of cognitive system with respect to the accomplishment of a current goal in a given context. As a system responsible for adaptation to given conditions, cognitive control was thought to be responsible to the adaptation to the interaction with a virtual environment. It was shown that cognitive control was indeed related to various aspects of presence, most notably spatial presence, negative somatic effects, and virtual scenario naturalness. Cognitive control influences the sense of presence via different mechanisms: control of attention, change of task sets, and situation model construction in working memory. It was found that the influence of cognitive control on presence is not straightforward, as strong cognitive control may be detrimental to presence. It was also found that the influence of cognitive control on presence may differ under different immersion conditions with elaborated control more important in low-immersion settings. Finally, it was concluded that cognitive control may primarily affect the cognitive components of presence (spatial presence, sensory-motor coordination) but that presence may independently be influenced by emotional factors. Cognitive control is an important psychological determinant of presence. Interventions should target cognitive control in order to increase presence in existing and new virtual environments.

References

1. Witmer, B., Singer, M.: Measuring presence in virtual environments: a presence questionnaire. Presence 7, 225–240 (1998)
2. Slater, M., Usoh, M.: Presence in immersive virtual environments. In: IEEE Virtual Reality Annual International Symposium (VRAIS), 18–22 September, Seattle, Washington, pp. 90–96 (1993)
3. Lessiter, J., Freeman, J., Keogh, E., Davidoff, J.: A cross-media presence questionnaire: the ITC-Sense of presence inventory. Presence: Teleoperators Virtual Environ. 10, 282–297 (2001)
4. Barfield, W., Zeltzer, D., Sheridan, T.B., Slater, M.: Presence and performance within virtual environments. In: Barfield, W., Furness, T.A. (eds.) Virtual Environments and Advanced Interface Design, pp. 473–541. Oxford University Press, Oxford (1995)
5. Wirth, W., Hofer, M., Schramm, H.: The role of emotional involvement and trait absorption in the formation of spatial presence. Media Psychol. 15, 19–43 (2012)
6. Sacau, A., Laarni, J., Ravaja, N., Hartmann, T.: The impact of personality factors on the experience of spatial presence. In: Slater, M. (ed.) Proceedings of the 8th International Workshop on Presence, pp. 143–151. University College, London (2005)

7. Laarni, J., Ravaja, N., Saari, T., Hartmann, T.: Personality-related differences in subjective presence. In: Alcaniz, M., Ray, B. (eds.) Proceedings of the Seventh Annual International Workshop Presence, pp. 88–95. UPV, Valencia (2004)
8. Sas, C., O'Hare, G.: Presence equation: an investigation into cognitive factors underlying presence. Presence: Teleoperators Virtual Environ. 12, 523–537 (2003)
9. Kober, S.E.: Effects of age on the subjective presence experience in virtual reality. In: Challenging Presence: Proceedings of the International Society for Presence Research, pp. 149–157. Facultas, Vienna (2014)
10. Felnhofer, A., Kothgassner, O.D.: Does gender matter? Exploring experiences of physical and social presence in men and women. In: Riva, G., Waterworth, J., Murray, D. (eds.) Interacting with Presence: HCI and the Sense of Presence in Computer-Mediated Environments, pp. 152–163. De Gruyter, Amsterdam (2014)
11. Baños, R., Botella, C., Garcia-Palacios, A., Villa, H., Perpiña, C., Gallardo, M.: Psychological variables and reality judgments in virtual environments: the role of absorption and dissociation. Cyberpsychol. Behav. 2, 135–142 (1999)
12. Jurnet, I.A., Beciu, C.C., Maldonado, J.G.: Individual differences in the sense of presence. In: Slater, M. (ed.) Proceedings of the 8th International Workshop on Presence, pp. 133–142. University College, London (2005)
13. Laarni, J., Ravaja, N., Saari, T., Hartmann, T.: Personality-related differences in subjective presence. In: Alcaniz, M., Ray, B. (eds.) Proceedings of the Seventh Annual International Workshop Presence 2004, pp. 88–95. UPV, Valencia (2004)
14. Murray, C., Fox, J., Pettifer, S.: Absorption, dissociation, locus of control and presence in virtual reality. Comput. Hum. Behav. 23, 1347–1354 (2007)
15. Thornson, C., Goldiez, B., Huy, L.: Predicting presence: constructing the tendency toward presence inventory. Int. J. Hum. Comput. Stud. 67, 62–78 (2009)
16. Kober, S.E., Neuper, C.: Personality and presence in virtual reality: does their relationship depend on the used presence measure? Int. J. Hum.-Comput. Interact. 29(1), 13–25 (2012)
17. Botvinick, M.M., Braver, T.S., Barch, D.M., Carter, C.S., Cohen, J.D.: Conflict monitoring and cognitive control. Psychol. Rev. 108, 624–652 (2001)
18. Lorist, M.M., Boksem, M., Ridderinkhof, K.: Impaired cognitive control and reduced cingulate activity during mental fatigue. Cogn. Brain. Res. 24, 199–205 (2005)
19. Rubinstein, J., Meyer, D., Evans, J.: Executive control of cognitive processes in task switching. J. Exp. Psychol. Hum. Percept. Perform. 27, 763–797 (2001)
20. Draper, J., Kaber, D., Usher, J.: Telepresence. Hum. Factors 40, 354–375 (1998)
21. Engle, R.W.: The role of working memory in cognitive control. Curr. Anthropol. 51(Suppl. 1), S17–S25 (2010)
22. Miyake, A., Friedman, N.P., Emerson, M.J., Witzki, A.H., Howerter, A., Wager, T.D.: The unity and diversity of executive functions. Cogn. Psychol. 41(1), 49–100 (2000)
23. Friedman, N.P., Miyake, A.: The relations among inhibition and interference control functions: a latent-variable analysis. J. Exp. Psychol. Gen. 133(1), 101–135 (2004)
24. Monsell, S.: Task switching. Trends Cogn. Sci. 7(3), 134–140 (2003)
25. Owen, A.M., McMillan, K., Laird, A.R., Bullmore, E.: N-back working memory paradigm: a meta-analysis of normative functional neuroimaging studies. Hum. Brain Mapp. 25, 46–59 (2005)
26. Beeli, G., Casutt, G., Baumgartner, T., Jäncke, L.: Modulating presence and impulsiveness by external stimulation of the brain. Behav. Brain Funct. 4, 33 (2008). doi:10.1186/1744-9081-4-33
27. Leite, J., Carvalho, S., Fregni, F., Boggio, P.S., Gonçalves, O.F.: The effects of cross-hemispheric dorsolateral prefrontal cortex transcranial direct current stimulation (tDCS) on task switching. Brain Stimul. 6(4), 660–667 (2013)

28. Zwaan, R.A., Radvansky, G.A.: Situation models in language comprehension and memory. Psychol. Bull. **123**(2), 162–185 (1998)
29. Rawlinson, T.G., Lu, S., Coleman, P.: Individual differences in working memory capacity and presence in virtual environments. In: Zhang, H., Hussain, A., Liu, D., Wang, Z. (eds.) BICS 2012. LNCS, vol. 7366, pp. 22–30. Springer, Heidelberg (2012). doi:10.1007/978-3-642-31561-9_3
30. Goschke, T., Bolte, A.: Emotional modulation of control dilemmas: the role of positive affect, reward, and dopamine in cognitive stability and flexibility. Neuropsychologia **62**, 403–423 (2014)
31. Jäncke, L., Cheetham, M., Baumgartner, T.: Virtual reality and the role of the prefrontal cortex in adults and children. Front. Neurosci. **3**(1), 52–59 (2009)

Defining an Indicator for Navigation Performance Measurement in VE Based on ISO/IEC15939

Ahlem Assila[1(✉)], Jeremy Plouzeau[1], Frédéric Merienne[1],
Aida Erfanian[2], and Yaoping Hu[2]

[1] LE2I, Arts et Métiers, CNRS, University of Bourgogne Franche-Comté,
71100 Chalon-sur-Saône, France
{ahlem.assila, jeremy.plouzeau,
frederic.merienne}@ensam.eu
[2] Department of Electrical and Computer Engineering,
Schulich School of Engineering, University of Calgary, Calgary, Canada
{aerfania, huy}@ucalgary.ca

Abstract. Navigation is a key factor for immersion and exploration in virtual environment (VE). Nevertheless, measuring navigation performance is not an easy task, especially when analyzing and interpreting heterogeneous results of the measures used. To that end, we propose, in this paper, a new indicator for measuring navigation performance in VE based on ISO/IEC 15939 standard. It allows effective integration of heterogeneous results by retaining its raw values. Also, it provides a new method that offers a comprehensive graphical visualization of the data for interpreting the results. The experimental study had shown the feasibility of this indicator and its contribution to statistical results.

Keywords: Virtual Environment (VE) · Measure · Performance · Navigation · Evaluation

1 Introduction

Virtual reality is a technology that allows users to immerse in a virtual environment and enable them to navigate in order to explore it and to interact with its objects [1, 2]. This technology is realized, usually, via 3D real-time computer graphics and advanced display devices (e.g. head mounted displays (HMDs) or Caves) [3]. Generally, a virtual environment (VE) can be infinite and can afford numerous possibilities. To explore it, navigation interfaces and metaphors are necessary [2]. Undoubtedly, navigation in the virtual environment differs from the real world. It presents a main common task between virtual reality applications whatever if its goals are focused or not on moving [2].

As in all fields of application, evaluation is very crucial phase after designing a virtual reality application. Navigation performance is one of criteria to be considered when evaluating VE [4]. In literature, there are several measures proposed for making navigation performance evaluation (e.g. Task completion time [2], percentage of errors of path [5], navigation time [6], etc.). The choice between these measures differs from

L.T. De Paolis et al. (Eds.): AVR 2017, Part I, LNCS 10324, pp. 17–34, 2017.
DOI: 10.1007/978-3-319-60922-5_2

one study to another. It can depend, usually, on the application to be evaluated. For examples, in the two studies [7, 8], authors have included only the measure of task completion time to evaluate navigation methods. In the study proposed by [9], authors have used mainly task completion time with the measure of error per task. However, analyzes and results reported are presented separately. Otherwise, Bliss et al. [6] have been focused on the two measures of navigation time and wrong turns. Working in the same direction, we have been interested, in our previous work [10], to measure navigation performance when evaluating a guidance method in a VE. Thus, we have based on the two measures of trajectory precision and the completion time of navigation. We have firstly started by analyzing results separately which conduct us to some confusing results. These difficulties led us to think about aggregating both measures in one quantifiable value by dividing trajectory precision with the completion time of navigation. Although this formula is standard, we have found different other difficulties, mainly, in the analysis and interpretation of the huge amount of results in order to get a global conclusion. Also, the aggregation of the data into an overall score may ignore some important results that may be very useful in the analysis.

To that end, we propose in this paper another way for measuring navigation performance in VE by adapting indicator concepts defined by the ISO/IEC 15939. This standard allows defining a measure called "indicator" which combines heterogeneous data and specifies the procedure for interpreting the results. Our contribution bears on defining an indicator for navigation performance in VE, based on ISO/IEC 15939, with keeping the raw data. It includes not only the procedure for interpreting the results but also offers a clear graphical visualization to facilitate interpretation.

This article is organized as follows. Section 2 presents the related works about measurement concepts and the existed measures used in VE. Section 3 describes the motivation of our research and the proposed indicator of navigation performance, defined for evaluating a VR environment based on ISO/IEC 15939. Section 4 presents the experimental study by applying the proposed indicator for evaluating a VR application. Section 5 introduces significant discussions about threats of validity of our study and the raised limitations. Finally, Sect. 6 draws some conclusions and outlines some future works about more research proposals.

2 Related Works

2.1 Measurement Concepts Based on ISO Standards

Before using measure, we should think firstly about its definition and their main concepts. From literature and standards, several methodologies for measures definition have been proposed (e.g. Software Quality Measure [11], Practical Software Measurement [12], Systems and software engineering—Measurement process [13]). Based on standards, we distinguished heterogeneity in terminologies adopted. Some standards (such as ISO/IEC 14598 [14] and ISO 9126 [15]) refer to the term "Metric", whereas other standards such as ISO/IEC 25022 [16] adopt the term "Measure". The distinction between the different terminologies of the measurements has been well explored in the field of software engineering. Indeed, the term "Metric" has been published in the two sets of ISO/IEC 14598 (1999–2001) and ISO/IEC 9126 (2001–2004) standards that correspond to the first international consensus on terminology for quality characteristics for the evaluation of the software product. Based on these two standards, a metric is defined as follows: "*a measurement scale and the method used for measurement*".

In the new sets of standards, a new generation of quality standards for the software product has been proposed. It named "Systems and software Quality Requirements and Evaluation" (SQuaRE) [17]. This series of standards has replaced the two sets of ISO/IEC 14598 and ISO/IEC 9126 standards with ensuring uniformity and coherence between its terminologies. Nevertheless, SQuaRE avoided the use of the term "Metric" adopted in ISO/IEC 9126 and ISO/IEC 14598 and replaced it with the term "measure" in accordance with ISO/IEC 15939 (2007) [18]. This term has been adopted in the SQuaRE series of standards (such as (ISO/IEC 25000, [19], ISO/IEC 25021, [20], ISO/IEC 25022, [16]). The ISO/IEC 15939 (2007) has defined a measure, in general, as "*a variable to which a value is assigned as the result of measurement*" [13]. This standard distinguished it compared to the measurement term which is defined as "*a set of operations having the object of determining a value of a measure*".

Based on the ISO/IEC 15939, we distinguished three kinds of measures as follows: base measure, derived measure and indicator. While, a base measure is defined as "*a measure defined in terms of an attribute and the method for quantifying it*", a derived measure is defined as "*a function of two or more values of base measures*" [13]. The third kind concerned indicator is defined for responding to specific goals to be achieved called Information needs. Based on the ISO/IEC 15939, this concept is defined as "*a measure providing estimation or evaluation of specified attributes*" [13]. These attributes are quantified using objective or subjective methods. Generally, an indicator is structured around a measurement information model defined as "*a structure linking the needs to the relevant entities to the attributes of concern*" [13]. This model illustrates quantification and conversion process of the relevant attributes to indicators using measures that provide a basis for decision making [13]. Further, the definition of indicator requires the specification of an analysis model that responds to the information needs to be achieved. Following the ISO/IEC 15939 standard this model describes as "*an algorithm or calculation combining one or more base and/or derived measures with associated decision criteria*" [13]. In turn, these decision criteria are used as a tool for ensuring the interpretation stage of indicator results. It consists on "*numerical thresholds or targets used to determine the need for action or further investigation or to describe the level of confidence in a given result*".

2.2   Using Indicators Based on ISO/IEC 15939 Standard

Since the specification of this measurement standard, the use of indicator concept has been more explored in the software engineering field. One advantage of use it is the fact that it can be considered as the most recent standard which provides a comprehensive measurement construction process (i.e. the measurement information model) ranging from the specification of its attributes to the establishment of indicators that meet the specific requirements of stakeholders and their information needs [13]. In literature, several works have been focused on defining indicators which bear on the quality evaluation of software process (e.g. [21–23]). Other works have been used indicators to perform quality evaluation of software products and systems (such as, [24, 25]). In these works, authors have proposed some interpretations for supporting the analysis of indicators results.

Another prime specificity provided by indicator is its capability to combine various heterogeneous base and/or derived measures together considering a predefined information need. Based on ISO/IEC 15939, this combination can be made through the analysis model following two ways. The first is via mathematical calculations in order to have an overall score.

The second way deals with the definition of an algorithm or a model which specifies the measures associated of the indicator without effective aggregation of data and by keeping the raw data. In this same direction and based on ISO/IEC 15939, a more recent proposal about the specification of usability indicators in the field of Human-Computer Interaction has been proposed [26, 27]. These indicators mainly allow evaluating the quality of user interfaces of interactive systems, applied into traffic supervision field, with integrating effectively measures results extracted from both subjective and objective evaluation tools. Their main purpose is to prove how these indicators can support evaluators in the detection of usability problems considering effectively both the two sides of the evaluation (subjective and objective). In fact, this proposal describes how to define an indicator that performs effective integration with complementary and consistent manner [26, 27]. Furthermore, it proposed a strong basis for interpreting indicator results and supporting the decision-making in the evaluation via predefined decision criteria. In turns, it includes a set of recommendations for enhancing more the quality of user interfaces.

In this approach, the specification of a usability indicator involves three main steps [26]. The first is to identify the information need which bears on the main objective using the indicator. The second step concerns the specification of the base and derived measures associated to the indicator, with taking into account its intended purpose. The third step concerns the specification of the indicator via the specification of an analysis model that responds to the specified information need. This analysis model is defined by identifying the measures concerned and their associated decision criteria. Firstly, considering the objective of integration, the indicator is instantiated as a combination of measures for subjective and objective evaluation. The association of these measures was defined on the basis of a mapping model which combines the measures in a complementary and coherent way with respect to the same criterion to be evaluated. Secondly, for ensuring interpretation of indicator results, the decision criteria have been defined based on a set of simple rules that take into account each chosen analysis model. A rule consists in interpreting the values related to the combined measures of the indicator on the basis of predefined thresholds for each measure. The definition of a threshold has been used as a useful means of data analysis. This threshold allows indicating the acceptable results, which can be either above or below it [26, 27].

In addition, an indicator is represented graphically on the basis of the scatter plots (2D, 3D) graphs to effectively and concretely illustrate the integration between the combined measures. Figure 1 illustrates an example of a hypothetical indicator (instantiated as a pair of two measures M1 and M2) with the defined rules for the decision criteria (see [26]).

In this work, as presented in the Fig. 1, three levels of quality have been identified as follows [26]:

- Very bad (when all indicator measures have unacceptable/bad results);
- Bad (when at least one of the measures has an unacceptable/bad result);
- Good (in the case where all measures have acceptable/good results).

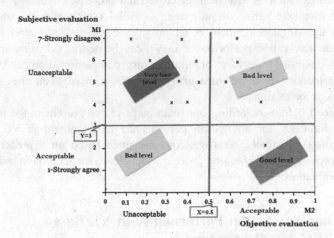

Fig. 1. Example of a hypothetical indicator with its decision criteria [26].

Considering the difficult phase of the selection of measures thresholds, this approach emphasizes the importance of involvementof a user expert in the evaluation during the experiments. His role is to select thresholds based, mainly, on the context of use of the evaluation [26].

2.3 Using Measures for Evaluating VE

For making evaluation of any designed interactive system, regardless of its field of application, the use of measures is very essential. In the Human-Computer Interaction (HCI) field, the evaluation of user interfaces covers, generally, a set of quality factor (such as usability) that in turns depend on criteria to be evaluated (for example usability can be measured in terms of effectiveness, efficiency, etc. [28]). These criteria can be evaluated using measures.

As in HCI domain, in virtual reality, the evaluation depends on the parameters/ criteria to be evaluated (such as the sense of presence, navigation performance, cyber-sickness, etc.) [29]. Indeed, several other works have been interested in more specific criteria for defining indicators/measures in specific domains of VR. For instance, Thubaasini et al. [30] have been focused on three main criteria (frame rate, image quality and mouse motion)for the evaluation of two operating systems in the field of VR. In other example related to concurrent engineering domain [31], different criteria have been proposed for measuring the VR systems performances (such as, design cycle, product quality, etc.). Thus, the use ofmeasures to make evaluation in VR environment is very significant. In literature, several measures have been proposed. Those allow ensuring subjective or objective evaluation respectively with or without involving user perceptions [26]. For example, many authors have proposed presence questionnaires as a measure for performing subjective evaluation of the sense of presence in order to take an overall score [32, 33]. Others have been focused to define objective measures (such as heartbeat, electrodermal processes, reactions of the eyes, etc. [29]) for assessing sense of presence. Asvirtual reality allows measuring any parameters in the simulation, there is an infinity of parameters/criteria that can be measured. Thus, navigation performance in VE can be performed using several measures (such as position, trajectory, orientation, task completion time [2, 10]). Nevertheless, the selection of these measures depends, primarily, on the application/simulator/tasks to be evaluated.

As introduced before, regarding our main purpose, we present in the next section the proposed indicator for navigation performance measurement in VE. It mainly allows integrating effectively heterogeneous measures based on a predefined information need, providing interpretation process and a clear visualization in order to better support the evaluation.

3 Measuring Navigation Performance in VE Based on ISO/IEC 15939 Standard

As explained in the Sect. 2.2, Assila et al. [26] have proposed, recently, a generic process to be applied for constructing indicators based on ISO/IEC 15939 standard. Those are aimed to evaluate interactive systems based on predefined quality criteria with the integration of heterogeneous measures. This approach has been applied in the field of Human-computer Interaction and it has proved its feasibility. Believing the strength of this proposal and considering our goal, we propose to apply this process for defining a navigation performance indicator used in evaluating a specific application for navigation guidance in a VR environment. This section comprises two parts. In the first subsection, we introduce our motivation for specifying the proposed indicator. In the second subsection, we describe the measurement information model proposed for evaluating navigation in aVE.

3.1 Motivation

For our knowledge, in the field of virtual reality the use of indicator concepts defined by ISO/IEC 15939 standard is not yet proposed. In this paper, we argue that the exploitation of this concept is very promising, regarding, firstly, that it is a standard characterized by its applicability and adoption in industry [26, 34]. Secondly, its capability to define a complete procedure for specifying, collecting and interpreting measures that respond to our goal [13]. Thus, our contribution is to apply indicator-concept for evaluating navigation performance in aspecific VR environment for effective integration of heterogeneous findings in a way that offers a simple way and quick understanding of results through the use of visual metaphors (in our case the scatter chart). Further, this approach allows supporting evaluators in the analysis of their heterogeneous results and provides a basis for making interpretation via the decision criteria proposed. As a result, it provides a comprehensive and visual conclusion to better manage the navigation performance in virtual reality environments. Also, it is beneficial for detecting and fixing the causes of problems detected. In addition to that, it could be used to create matrix of choices for decision support.

3.2 Proposed Indicator of Navigation Performance for Evaluating a VE

By following the process of defining indicators proposed by Assila et al. [26], we start first by identifying information need using the proposed indicator. As we explained before, our main goal for defining this indicator is to evaluate navigation performance in a virtual environment by integrating heterogeneous data. This indicator can be used in two ways, for assessing one pattern in a VE or to compare several patterns together.

The second step consists on identifying base and/or derived measures to be used when specifying the indicator. To that end, we started firstly by specifying the entities and their attributes which are the most suitable with our information need. In our case, we identified the pattern to be evaluated as the entity from which we considered the path as the main attribute.

Subsequently, considering both our goal and the attribute to be considered we have focused on some existing measures, defined in literature [10], for measuring navigation performance in virtual environment. For base measures, we have considered: Length of trajectory followed, Total length of the trajectory, Time of arrival and Time of departures. As for the derived measures, we have selected the Trajectory precision and the Path time measures.

The third step consists on specifying the indicator itself. We called it as "*Navigation performance indicator in VE*". Considering our information need, we enounced this indicator as a pair of the two following derived measures: the trajectory precision and the path time.

The measure of Trajectory precision allows measuring the precision for following the right trajectory. It is calculated as follows [10]: **Trajectory precision = Length of trajectory followed/Total length of the trajectory.**

For the Path time which measures the completion time of navigation, we adopted this formula [10]: **Path time = Time of arrival – Time of departures.**

Since the visualization of the measures data generated by the indicator is a primordial phase to illustrate the effective integration of the results, we decided to represent our indicator by a scatter chart.

For interpreting indicator results, we have adopted the same principle proposed by [26] based on the definition of decision criteria. Those bear on specifying a set of rules associated to both combined measures. Each rule consists on checking if measures results are acceptable or not based on predefined thresholds. As proposed by the ISO/IEC 15939 standard, the use of thresholds is a useful technique for analyzing results. In turn, the selection of these thresholds should be made by a user expert considering, mainly, the context of use of the evaluation [26]. Thus, in our case, we decided to involve a user expert in the evaluation of VE when selecting thresholds of measures. He/her should take into account the following aspects of the context of use according to the ISO 9241-11 standard which are: users, tasks, equipment (hardware, software and materials), and the physical and social environments [28]. In addition, following the approach of [26], the user expert should consider in our instance users' experiences with virtual reality technology and also their experiences with the system to be evaluated.

We present in Table 1 the detailed description of the measurement information model for our proposed indicator. As illustrated in this Table (see Decision criteria), we have proposed four rules for interpreting indicator results as follows:

- **Rule 1:** If (Path time is Acceptable) & (Trajectory precision is Acceptable) => Good level of navigation performance: No problem.
- **Rule 2:** If (Path time is Unacceptable) & (Trajectory precision is Acceptable) => Bad level of navigation performance caused by Path time.
- **Rule 3:** If (Path time is Acceptable) & (Trajectory precision is Unacceptable) => Bad level of navigation performance caused by trajectory precision.
- **Rule 4:** If (Path time is Unacceptable) & (Trajectory precision is Unacceptable) => Very bad level of navigation performance caused by the two measures.

In other words, through our indicator, we have identified three levels of performance described as follows: good, bad and very bad, represented by three colors respectively: green, yellow and red.

Table 1. Specification of the measurement information model for the navigation performance indicator

Information need	Evaluate the performance of navigation in VE for one or more patterns.
Indicator	The navigation performance indicator in VE
Analysis model	The model is enunciated as a pair of the two measures (*Path time of a user* and *the trajectory precision by a user*) represented by a scatter chart.
Decision criteria	**Interpretation of each measure**

- For the *Path Time* measure named T: The smaller the value the better the performance.
  $0 \le T \le N$ where N is the maximum value obtained.
  The results are divided into two subranges according to the threshold X specified by an expert:
  - Acceptable: for values ϵ [0 ; X[
  - Unacceptable: for values ϵ [X ; N]
- For the *trajectory precision by a user* measure named P: The higher the value the better the performance.
  $0 \le P \le M$ where M is the maximum value obtained.
  The results are divided into two subranges according to the threshold Y specified by an expert:
  - Unacceptable: for values ϵ [0 ; Y[
  - Acceptable: for values ϵ [Y ; M]

  Note: The user expert specifies thresholds X and Y taking into account the context of use of the evaluation and users' experiences.

Decision criteria of the indicator

		Path time	
		[0 ; X[: *Acceptable*	[X ; N] : *Unacceptable*
Trajectory precision	[Y ; M] *Acceptable*	Good level of performance No problem.	Bad level of performance caused by Path time.
	[0 ; Y[*Unacceptable*	Bad level of performance caused by trajectory precision.	Very bad level of performance caused by the two measures.

Derived measures	*Trajectory precision*: measures the rate of the well-traced trajectory.
Measurement Function	*Trajectory precision* (P) = Length of trajectory followed / Total length of the trajectory. $0 \le P \le 100\%$
Base measures	*Path time* (T): measures the total time between departures and arrivals. $0 \le T \le 1000s$
Measurement method	*Path time* (T) = Time of arrival – Time of departures

During the analysis phase, the indicator results are represented by a scatter chart. Those will be distributed on the four areas identified by the indicator rules and will be grouped into clusters. Two cases are represented here. If the indicator is used to evaluate the navigation performance of one pattern, then the conclusion can be derived directly from the Table of Decision Criteria (Table 1). Otherwise, if the indicator is used to compare different patterns, the conclusion can be established through the comparison of patterns clusters.

At the end of the evaluation, a complete and visual conclusion will be established. As a result, evaluators' decisions will be made based mainly on the evaluated case study.

4   Experimental Study

In this section, we are focused, mainly, to apply our proposed indicator of navigation performance in the guidance navigation evaluation of a VE in order to check its feasibility and its contribution compared to the statistical results obtained during our previous work [10]. Indeed, the previous study was intended to compare two vibration patterns for guiding navigation in VE, which are described below in more detail. Thus, to reach our goal, we have taken the same experiment that we have already realized.

As described in [10], a VE has been created. It is composed by a grassy plain where the user could navigate using Razer Hydra game pads. In fact, a pair of shoes was displayed at the user's feet. These virtual shoes were following the user when he moved through the VE. In addition, in auditory feedback of walking steps gives the user the illusion of walking. Further, he could view both plain and shoes during his/her promenading.

When navigating, user had to follow an invisible path of navigation being guided by two different vibration patterns. Those have been called pushing and compass patterns [10]. The pushing pattern is composed by two different signals, one to tell the user to go forward and the second to tell him to turn. The compass pattern indicates the direction to follow by constant vibrations around ankles [10]. The path was configured as a sinusoidal curve with a period of 12 meters and 6 different amplitudes of 0.0 m, 0.3 m, 0.6 m, 1.2 m, 2.4 m and 4.8 m. The order of the different amplitude was randomized. The only constant was the first part and the last which was the straight line. The path ran each amplitude for two periods, corresponding 24 m (see Fig. 2).

In the following, we present the experimental protocol, the indicator results obtained and we end up by a conclusion.

4.1   Experimental Protocol

The experiment study was conducted under an ethics clearance following the Canadian Tri-Council Ethics Guidelines. It has been based on the same context of use composed by the following components:

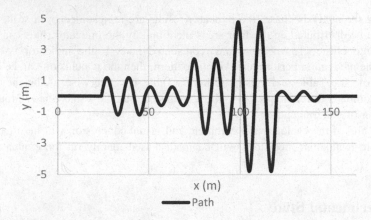

Fig. 2. Example of a generated path

- **Users:** during experiment, users' sample was involved 8 participants (5 females and 3 males), with an average age of 30 years (aged 25 to 44). There have different profiles, with no experience either in virtual reality technology or research.
- **Environment:** the experimentations were took place in a research room at the University of Calgary (Canada).
- **Equipment:** Each participant stood stationary in front of a 24" flat widescreen, which displayed the VE to minimize cybersickness for the participant. As depicted in Fig. 3, the screen was located in an arm distance from the participant and inclined at about 40° with respect to the participant. The head of the participant titled naturally forward, allowing his/her gaze line perpendicular to the surface of the screen. The height of the screen was adjustable to ensure this perpendicularity following the height of the participant. As mentioned above, participant used Razer Hydra game pads to navigate in the VE. Two Vibrotac bracelets were anchored around the ankles of the participant. The motor under the control box of each bracelet was located exterior-laterally just above the ankle joint. To eliminate the interference of any footwear, the participant was barefooted with socks during the experiment [10].
- **Tasks & experimental scenario:** As we have described in our previous work [10], the scenario followed during the experiment included six parts. The first was to perform pretests for checking the participant's color vision, handedness, footedness and their sensibility to the vibrations. Thus, participants with colorvision or vibration sensibility troubles were asked to stop the experiment. Subsequently, participants were invited to perform three learning and two testing sessions [10]. During the first learning session, the participant focused on learning navigation in the VE using only the game pads. Then he/she was to learn one of the two patterns for guiding navigation (pushing or compass pattern). Afterward, the participant underwent the first testing session; he/she had to navigate in the VE by following firstly the guidance given by the learned pattern from the bracelets. Subsequently, he/she had to perform the third learning session in order to learn the second pattern of guidance from the bracelets. Therefore, he/she executed the second testing

session which consisted on navigating in the VE based on this leaned pattern. After each testing session, participants were asked to answer a questionnaire about the simulation [10]. For information, each participant undertook the two patterns of guidance in a random order. Between any two sessions, there was a 10-minute break for each participant. Each participant was involved in the experiment for about 1.5 and 2 h, including both pre-test and experimental blocks. Regarding the captured data, the actual trajectory and path time of navigation were logged, for each participant, in real time during the experiment via our VE.

Fig. 3. The experimentation equipment

4.2 Results Obtained and Conclusion

After experimentation, we were generated in our previous work all participants results for the Path time measure and the trajectory precision measure [10]. Figure 4 illustrated the path time obtained by each participant using both patterns. Further, the results of trajectory precision measure using the two patterns, were obtained by dividing the length of trajectory followed with the total length of the trajectory (see Fig. 5).

In our previous work, when analyzing results separately with paired t-test (Figs. 4 and 5), we have noted a heterogeneity especially for results of trajectory precision measure (see Fig. 5). This made the analysis difficult although the results of path time measure have been shown that the participants have spent more time in navigation using the pushing pattern.

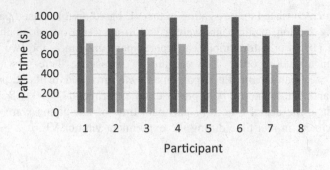

Fig. 4. Path time results [10]

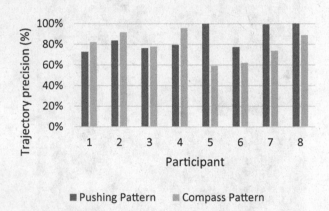

Fig. 5. Trajectory precision results [10]

Subsequently, we have calculated the performance index by aggregating the two measures by dividing the trajectory precision with the path time.

$$P = \frac{Trajectory\,precision}{Path\,time}$$

As illustrated in Fig. 6, the heterogeneity of results obtained by each participant made the interpretation task more complicated and difficult for reaching an effective conclusion. In addition to that, we have proceeded to calculate the mean performance index for the two patterns. Results obtained have been shown that the mean performance index of compass pattern is higher than those of pushing pattern. The paired t-test returned a p-value of p = 0.022, lower than the significant level α = 0.05. Observations of the results and the statistical analysis allow then to conclude that the compass pattern is more efficient to guide user through a VE.

Nevertheless, these results still insufficient and qualitative analyses can be improved by applying our proposed indicator for navigation performance.

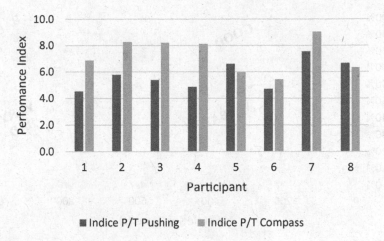

Fig. 6. Statistical results for performance index obtained in our previous work [10]

According to the results from previous article presentation, the three Figs. 4, 5 and 6 are needed to analyses data and give some early conclusions. Figure 4 shown that in every case, participants used more time to complete the path with the Pushing pattern than with the Compass pattern. Figure 5 indicated that some participants were better in precision with the Pushing pattern while others did better with the Compass pattern. Finally, Fig. 6 allows concluding that the loss of precision with the Compass pattern is compensated by the path time. As a result, the use of the compass pattern is better than the pushing pattern.

By applying our proposed indicator for navigation performance, which integrates effectively the measures of the trajectory precision and the path time, we found the same conclusion with one representation and clear analyses. Figure 7 shows the equivalent precision which is above the threshold for most participants. It also shows that participant used less time to complete the path with the Compass pattern. We have selected the two thresolds (850s for the path time and 75% for the trajectory precision) based mainly on the context of use of our experiment and users' experiences as described above. Further, indicator results indicate that the majority of users results using Compass pattern have good levels of performance compared to those using Pushing pattern. Moreover, thresholds, barycenter and standard deviation as seen in Fig. 7 allow to show that compass pattern increase performances as results are mainly located in the good level space division.

In summary, although that statistical analysis is needed to conclude that the Compass pattern is better in guiding user, we argue that our indicator shows clearly and simply the different impacts of guiding patterns with keeping the raw data. Therefore, this indicator provides a feasible method for measuring navigation performance with an effective integration of heterogeneous results.

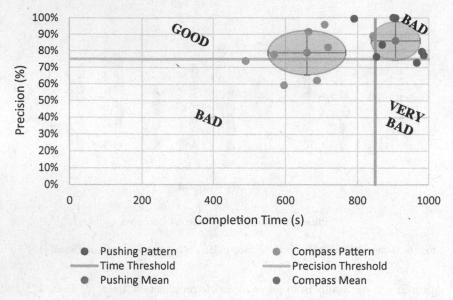

Fig. 7. Mean results of the indicator for the two patterns

5 Discussion

Usually, when performing evaluation experiments, it is necessary to study risks that can impact on the validity of the results obtained [35]. So, during our experiment, we have worked to minimize these biases. Those can be synthesized as follows. The first risk is related to the construction validity of our contribution. It consists on checking if the considered measures adequately reflect the navigation performance evaluation in VR environment. So, to overcome this risk, we have based on our work only on well known and referenced measures dedicated for measuring navigation performance in VE. The second risk deals with the conclusion validity that affect the ability to draw the right conclusion after generating indicator results. To reduce this risk, we have included statistical data (barycenter and standard deviation) in addition to thresholds that require mainly the consideration of the context of use. The third risk is associated with internal validity of our study. It concerns the influences generated by the very small sample of participants involved in the experiment. However, we assumed this risk since we have considered the same sample of our published work [10]. Also, because our main study goal is to prove feasibility of our approach. The last risk concerns limitations that affect external validity of our contribution. More precisely, it deals with the difficulty of generalization of the proposed indicator which has been developed for a specific application of navigation guidance in a VE. Thus, our indicator cannot be used for other experiences, but it can be adapted to evaluate navigation performance of other VR environments with taking into consideration the tools used for navigation, the context of use and the selected measures. Therefore, measures calculation will depend on the designed VE.

As we mentioned in the previous section, our proposed approach has been built to overcome the difficulties detected during the analysis of the results using the performance measures method. Despite the fact that our approach only deal with objective evaluation data (i.e. independently to users' opinions), case study outcomes have demonstrated its feasibility to integrate heterogeneous data compared to other evaluation methods of VR systems (such as, heuristic evaluation, questionnaire, observation, etc.). Considering that each one of these methods has its own requirements, advantages and suffers from some shortcomings, none of them allows effective integration of the heterogeneous findings generated in a way that facilitates interpretation. As a result, our approach can be used as a complementary method to ensure this benefit.

Nevertheless, we mentioned below some limitations to consider when using it. First, our proposal has been applied for a specific VR environment. This means that the selected measures of the defined indicator and their interpretation procedure have depended largely to the evaluated virtual environment. So, our approach is limited, in this paper, to this kind of technology. Further, we have not interested in this work to the issue of the selection of measures thresholds which presents a real difficulty that can impact on the obtained conclusion. We limited only to suggest the involvement of a user expert/evaluator with taken into account mainly the context of use of the VR environment. In addition, the proposed indicator has included only objective data, without the involvement of user perception and subjective evaluation data. This lack may have an impact on the conclusion obtained of the evaluation. Moreover, despite the fact that the use of the scatter chart when presenting indicator results in our approach is appropriate, this cannot be the most solution if we look to integrate more than three measures. Finally, considering the decision criteria proposed for making interpretation of indicator results, we have not proposed in this work some recommendations for facilitating interpretation when findings of patterns evaluated have the same levels of quality.

6 Conclusion and Perspectives

This study shows an innovative way to analyze heterogeneous data from virtual reality experiment in order to evaluate and compare the navigation performance in a VR environment using two different modalities. As we have demonstrated the feasibility of this contribution, this work can be considered as a preliminary phase towards the generalization of indicator concepts in the VR domain. Whereas this work has revealed a number of limitations, as we mentioned in Sect. 5, this contribution has allowed us to open up more challenging works to achieve a better evaluation. These perspectives are summarized as follows. To enable a broad exploitation of our contribution, its generalization requires to be validated to other experiences considering different types of VR domain (e.g. building, medicine, etc.) and technologies (e.g. tablet, mobile, etc.). Further, to facilitate the task of selecting thresholds for the associated measures of the indicator, we will consider in our future work the creation of a decision support system based on the recorded thresholds and results with taking into account the different evaluation contexts. In addition, to establish a more complete assessment, we will propose in our next work a new indicator that allows effective integration between the actual objective findings and subjective data relatives to navigation performance evaluation (extracted from a questionnaire tool).

Moreover, in the case of indicators that deal with more than three measures, we intend to exploit the concepts of information visualization in our future work, in particular in order to represent these indicators and analyze their results with an easy way. In other terms, we intend to represent data using projection in hyperplanes by including a geometric analysis in a mathematical way.

Finally, virtual reality is ruled by several parameters which are often needed to be evaluated, such as cyber-sickness, sense of presence, cognitive load, and more. These parameters depend on several measures and the method exposed in this paper could be used to evaluate them. Thus, it would be a tool to describe a virtual reality application through cyber-sickness indicator, sense of presence indicator and more. To go further, it would be possible to combine all data in one indicator or at least some indicator together to evaluate the virtual reality experience. Using this kind of indicator could lead to decision making in real-time to adapt the simulation parameter to increase the user's virtual reality experience.

Acknowledgments. This research work was supported by the region of Burgundy Franche-Compté.

References

1. Louka, M.N.: Augmented and virtual reality research in Halden 1998–2008. In: Skjerve, A., Bye, A. (eds.) Simulator-Based Human Factors Studies Across 25 Years. Springer, London (2010)
2. Pouzeau, J., Paillot, D., Chardonnet, J.R., Merienne, F.: Effect of proprioceptive vibrations on simulator sickness during navigation task in virtual environment. In: International Conference on Artificial Reality and Telexistence Eurographics Symposium on Virtual Environments, Japon, pp. 10–28 (2015)
3. LaViola, J.J.: A discussion of cybersickness in virtual environments. SIGCHI Bull. **32**, 47–56 (2000)
4. Walker, B.N., Lindsay, J.: Navigation performance in a virtual environment with bonephones. In: Proceedings of ICAD 2005-Eleventh Meeting of the International Conference on Auditory Display, pp. 260–263. Limerick, Ireland (2005)
5. Terziman, L., Marcal, M., Emily, M., Multon, F.: Shake-your-head: revisiting walking-in-place for desktop virtual reality. In: Proceedings of ACM VRST 2010, pp. 27–34. ACM, Hong Kong (2010)
6. Bliss, J.P., Tidwell, P.D., Guest, M.A.: The effectiveness of virtual reality for administering spatial navigation training for firefighters. Presence **6**(1), 73–86 (1997)
7. Kopper, R., NI, T., Bowman, D., Pinho, M.S.: Design and evaluation of navigation techniques for multiscale virtual environments. In: Proceedings of IEEE Virtual Reality Conference (VR 2006), pp. 175–182. IEEE Computer Society Washington, DC, USA (2006)
8. Ardouin, J., Lécuyer, A., Marchal, M., Marchand, E.: Navigating in virtual environments with 360° omnidirectional rendering. In: IEEE Symposium on 3D User Interfaces, Orlando, FL, USA, pp. 95–98 (2013)

9. Zielasko, D., Horn, S., Freitag, S., Weyers, B., Kuhlen, T.W.: Evaluation of hands-free HMD-based navigation techniques for immersive data analysis. In: 2016 IEEE Symposium on 3D User Interfaces (3DUI), Greenville, South Carolina, USA, pp. 113–119 (2016)
10. Plouzeau, J., Erfanian, A., Chiu, C., Merienne, F., Hu, Y.: Navigation in virtual environments: design and comparison of two anklet vibration patterns for guidance. In: 2016 IEEE Symposium on 3D User Interfaces (3DUI), Greenville, South Carolina, USA, pp. 263–264 (2016)
11. Suetendael, N.V., Elwell, D.: Software Quality Metrics. Federal Aviation Administration Technical Center, Atlantic City International Airport, New Jersey (1991)
12. McGarry, J., Card, D., Jones, C., Layman, B., Clark, E., Dean, J., Hall, F.: Practical Software Measurement: Objective Information for Decision Makers. Addison-Wesley, Boston (2002)
13. ISO/IEC 15939: International Organization for Standardization/International Electrotechnical Commission: Systems and Software Engineering—Measurement Process (ISO/IEC 15939: 2007(E)). Author, Geneva, Switzerland (2007)
14. ISO/IEC 14598-1: Information Technology – Software Product Evaluation – Part 1: General Overview. International Organization for Standardization, Geneva, Switzerland (1999)
15. ISO/IEC 9126-1: Software Engineering - Product Quality - Part 1: Quality Model. International Organization for Standardization, Geneva, Switzerland (2001)
16. ISO/IEC 25022: Systems and Software Engineering - Systems and Software Quality Requirements and Evaluation (SQuaRE) - Measurement of Quality in Use. International Organization for Standardization, Geneva, Switzerland (2012)
17. ISO/IEC 25010: Systems and Software Engineering — Systems and Software Quality Requirements and Evaluation (SQuaRE) — System and Software Quality Models. International Organization for Standardization, Geneva, Switzerland (2011)
18. Abran, A., Al-Qutaish, R., Cuadrado-Gallego, J.: Analysis of the ISO 9126 on software product quality evaluation from the metrology and ISO 15939 Perspectives. WSEAS Trans. Comput. 5(11), 2778–2786 (2006). World Scientific and Engineering Academy and Society
19. ISO/IEC 25000: Ingénierie des systèmes et du logiciel – Exigences de qualité des systèmes et du logiciel et évaluation (SQuaRE) – Guide de SQuaRE. International Organization for Standardization, Geneva, Switzerland (2014)
20. ISO/IEC 25021: Systems and Software Engineering – Systems and Software Quality Requirements and Evaluation (SQuaRE) – Quality Measure Elements. International Organization for Standardization, Geneva, Switzerland (2012)
21. Antolić, Ž.: An example of using key performance indicators for software development process efficiency evaluation. R&D Center Ericsson Nikola Tesla (2008)
22. Feyh, M., Petersen, K.: Lean software development measures and indicators - a systematic mapping study. In: Fitzgerald, B., Conboy, K., Power, K., Valerdi, R., Morgan, L., Stol, K.-J. (eds.) LESS 2013. LNBIP, vol. 167, pp. 32–47. Springer, Heidelberg (2013). doi:10.1007/978-3-642-44930-7_3
23. Monteiro, L., Oliveira, K.: Defining a catalog of indicators to support process performance analysis. J. Softw. Maint. Evol.: Res. Pract. 23(6), 395–422 (2011)
24. Moraga, M.A., Calero, C., Bertoa, M.F.: Improving interpretation of component-based systems quality through visualization techniques. IET Soft. 4(1), 79–90 (2010)
25. Staron, M., Meding, W., Hansson, J., Höglund, C., Niesel, K., Bergmann, V.: Dashboards for continuous monitoring of quality for software product under development. In: Mistrik, I., Bahsoon, R., Eeles, P., Roshandel, R., Stal, M. (eds.) Relating System Quality and Software Architecture, pp. 209–229. Morgan Kaufmann Publisher, Waltham (2014)
26. Assila, A., Oliveira, K., Ezzedine, H.: Integration of subjective and objective usability evaluation based on ISO/IEC 15939: a case study for traffic supervision systems. Int. J. Hum.-Comput. Interact. 32(12), 931–955 (2016)

27. Assila, A., Oliveira, K., Ezzedine, H.: An environment for integrating subjective and objective usability findings based on measures. In: IEEE 10th International Conference on Research Challenges in Information Science, Grenoble, France, pp. 645–656. IEEE (2016)
28. ISO 9241-11: ISO 9241-11, Ergonomic requirements for office work with visual display terminals (VDT) s- Part 11 Guidance on usability (1998)
29. Van Baren, J., Ijsselsteijin, W.: Compendium of presence measures. Deliverable 5 for OmniPres project: Measuring presence: A guide to current measurement approaches (2004)
30. Thubaasini, P., Rusnida, R., Rohani, S.M.: Efficient comparison between windows and linux platform applicable in a virtual architectural walkthrough application. In: Sobh, T., Elleithy, K. (eds.) Innovations in Computing Sciences and Software Engineering, pp. 337–342. Springer, Dordrecht (2009)
31. Mengoni, M., Germani, M.: Virtual reality systems and CE: how to evaluate the benefits. In: Ghodous, P. et al. (eds.) Leading the Web in Concurrent Engineering, pp. 853–862. IOS Press, Amsterdam (2006)
32. Witmer, B.G., Singer, M.J.: Measuring presence in virtual environments: a presence questionnaire. Presence 7(13), 225–240 (1998)
33. Gerhard, M., Moore, D.J., Hobbs, D.J.: Continuous presence in collaborative virtual environments: towards a hybrid avatar-agent model for user representation. In: Antonio, A., Aylett, R., Ballin, D. (eds.) IVA 2001. LNCS, vol. 2190, pp. 137–155. Springer, Heidelberg (2001). doi:10.1007/3-540-44812-8_12
34. Staron, M., Meding, W., Nilsson, C.: Framework for developing measurement systems and its industrial evaluation. Inf. Softw. Technol. 51(4), 721–737 (2009)
35. Wohlin, C., Runeson, P., Höst, M., Ohlsson, M.C., Regnell, B., Wesslén, A.: Experimentation in Software Engineering. Springer, Heidelberg (2012)

A Study of Transitional Virtual Environments

Maria Sisto[1(✉)], Nicolas Wenk[1], Nabil Ouerhani[2], and Stéphane Gobron[1]

[1] Image Processing and Computer Graphics Group, HE-Arc, HES-SO,
Neuchâtel, Switzerland
{maria.sisto,stephane.gobron}@he-arc.ch
[2] Interaction Technology Group, HE-Arc, HES-SO, Neuchâtel, Switzerland

Abstract. Due to real world physical constraints (*e.g.* walls), experimenting a virtual reality phenomenon implies transitional issues from one virtual environment (VE) to another. This paper proposes an experiment which studies the relevance of smooth and imperceptible transitions from a familiar and pleasurable virtual environment to a similar workplace as a mean to avoid traumatic experiences in VR for trainees. Specifically, the hereby work assumes that the user consciousness regarding virtual environment transitions is a relevant indicator of positive user experience during those. Furthermore, serious games taking place in purely virtual environments have the advantage of coping with various workplace configurations and tasks that the trainee can practice. However, the virtual world of serious games should be carefully designed in order to avoid traumatic experiences for trainees. The results presented stem from an empirical evaluation of user experience conducted with 80 volunteers. This evaluation shows that more than one-third of the participants did not even notice the VE global change.

Keywords: Virtual reality · Virtual environment · Head-mounted display · Health application · Musculoskeletal disorder

1 Introduction

The effect of transitions between real and virtual environment (see Fig. 1) is a subject that emerged with the renew of VR those last years. This section presents the context of this work and the reasons we needed to understand better the impact of word transitions on users.

1.1 Context

This project is a preliminary work for the project *Serious Game for Health at Work oriented towards prevention of Musculoskeletal Disorder (MSD)* that aims to reduce the MSDs occurrences in manufacturing industries. As a reminder, MSDs are lesions to muscles, articulations or nervous systems due to repetitive

© Springer International Publishing AG 2017
L.T. De Paolis et al. (Eds.): AVR 2017, Part I, LNCS 10324, pp. 35–49, 2017.
DOI: 10.1007/978-3-319-60922-5_3

Fig. 1. Context of the main question of this paper: how did the user consciously realize virtual environment transition? [1].

work in an inappropriate position. According to the INRS [2], this is one of the main work-related injuries in western countries, with costs of hundred of billions of euros per year in Europe [3]. The idea is to create a Serious Game (SG) using Virtual Reality (VR) that tracks players' gestures and gives feedback whenever a movement is potentially harmful (see Fig. 2). It has been shown that SGs using VR are a valid solution in the health field as the main trigger for users' motivation [4–6]. Furthermore, VR can be used to teach procedure sequences [7] and movement tracking devices enables ergonomic monitoring [8,9]. Considering previously described context relative to VR and the fact that SG development must include various environments, we must evaluate potential impact of virtual environment (VE) transitions on users. Results of the current study will therefore help us tweaking the VE parameters in order to change and improve the exercise context.

1.2   Literature Review

The SG domain being very specific, projects treating the same subjects are rare. Many SGs and exergames are about health and re-education domains [10] but very few cover the subject of MSD or movements and postures. We can cite three of them. The first one is an application called "Halte aux TMS" by the company daesign [11]. It is a web application explaining MSD dangers with interactive videos and scenes. The second one is a study named "A Serious Game to Improve Posture and Spinal Health While Having Fun" [12]. This game is in two phases: one passive and one active. In the first phase, the user has to correct the positions of a character portrayed working in a scene. In the second phase, the user has to stand and do stretching exercises in front of the Kinect. The application validates the exercise using the Kinect data. The third one named "Kinect-Based Virtual Game for the Elderly that Detects Incorrect Body Postures in Real Time" [13] has two aims. Firstly it helps the elderly to

Fig. 2. General idea: the user (right side) is immersed in VR and performs a manufacturing task (left side). A feedback is given about the potential dangers on the user body (white figure on the right).

maintain physical activity and sense of balance. Secondly, it uses the Kinect to give feedback on the dangerous postures. It also gives advice on the best postures to avoid harm or falls. The game is in VR and the user has to catch falling objects from the sky.

1.3 Environments and Transitions

The physical environment is an essential component, both in the working context and in knowledge acquisition. We know, for instance, that the classrooms organization impacts the student learning rate. For example, it has been shown that factors such as environmental color, personalization and light have a significant influence on this rate [14]. It has also been shown that factors such as light, noise and room layout impact the well-being of employees [15,16] and hence their productivity [17].

In order to enable optimal learning, the user should be placed in the best-suited environment for this activity. The ART theory (Attention Restoration Theory) [18] suggests that natural environments (whether immersion in nature or observation of nature images or videos) stimulate the concentration recovery ability and allows to be more relaxed. Therefore, we decided to put the user in a virtual environment representing a "calm" scene in the middle of nature. Moreover, choosing a totally different environment from the usual one contributes to motivating the user to play the SG. Actually, if the user is only placed in his work environment, it is difficult to see the VR interest. In addition, the stress linked to his being in his workplace may slow down the user's learning rate.

Once the bad habits are banned from the exercises in a calm environment, it must be ensured that those habits remain present in the workplace. In order to do this, the user is gradually transposed to a virtual environment representing his actual work environment, relative to his progression in the game: the environment will begin to change only when the user is able to correctly perform the required task. Thereby, the user will gradually become accustomed to a more and more realistic environment and eventually translate the good habits acquired through the calm environment to his work environment successfully.

1.4   Environment and MSDs

Although this is not the sole cause of MSDs, the environment is not entirely foreign to these problems. Indeed, a noisy environment, fast work pace and repetitive tasks take part in inducing stress to employees. Referring to the INRS website: "There are many stress effects related to MSDs. Clamping and supporting forces are increased, muscle tension increases, recovery time increases. Stress amplifies the pain perception and makes employees more sensitive to MSDs risk factors." [19].

1.5   Types of Environments

Keeping in mind the stress influence on MSDs, we can distinguish two environment types: the calm environment, which is the starting environment, and the working environment, which is the environment towards which the transition is heading. In order to allow a gradual evolution, a third type of environment has been defined: the intermediate environment, which must be between total decontextualization and the exact workplace reproduction. Several environments of each type can exist, allowing customization according to user preferences and actual working conditions. Thus, each personal session can be adapted according to the needs with a corresponding combination of possibilities (see Figs. 3 and 4 for an application example).

1.6   Technological Choices

For the development of 3D environments, the Unity Game Engine [20] has been chosen because it allows the rapid creation of a scene from 3D objects and it provides an efficient scripting system. Many resources are available on the Unity Asset Store [21] and the community is substantial and very active. We have chosen Blender [22] to edit 3D models because it is open source and gives us the flexibility to import and export from and to multiple formats. The selected HMD was the HTC Vive [23] because it provides a several-meters-wide tracking zone which lets the player move physically into the virtual world while walking. In addition, two special controllers (one for each hand) are provided to allow a much more natural interaction than with a conventional keyboard or game controller.

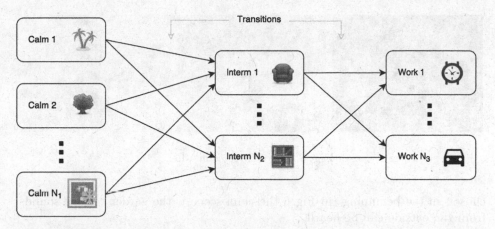

Fig. 3. Transitional concepts, three types of VEs are represented from left to right: *calm* VE (see Fig. 5), *intermediate* VE (see Fig. 6), and *work* VE. (see Fig. 7). Figure 4 illustrates the transition's impact can be on VEs.

Fig. 4. Main context transitions, from calm to workplaces.

2   Virtual Environment and Transitions

This section describes the chosen environments and their implementation. It also describes the chosen types of transitions, with one example for each type.

2.1   Virtual Environment

Three calm environments have been designed: a garden, a beach and a snowy mountain (see Fig. 5). The intermediate environment and the working environment are a living room and a watchmaker workshop.

The garden is a grassy place with trees and is very sunny. A tree and a sun umbrella are near, providing some shadow. The sound of the wind and birds can be heard in the background. The beach is sandy, has palm trees and is also very sunny. Some very large beach umbrellas shade you from the sun. The sea is calm, we can hear waves and a light wind blowing. We can also hear a seagull shrieking. The mountain is snowy, with some pine trees. Little noise, just a light wind and noises from small animals can be heard. The same round wooden table has been used in the three scenes.

The intermediate environment is a living room. It is a closed space with a large window on the quiet outside landscape, according to the EV that was

Fig. 5. Set of three *calm* VEs.

chosen in the beginning (in Fig. 6 the calm scene is the garden). Faint sounds from the outside can be heard.

Fig. 6. A living room: the *intermediate* VE.

The watchmaker workshop is a closed space, filled with workbenches and tools. Large lateral windows let the natural light enter and thus the user can see outside (see Fig. 7). Sounds from outside are no longer audible, but for work-related sounds.

2.2 Transitions

The first environment is always calm, natural, outdoors. In order to make the transitions more subtle, the intermediate scene (the living room) is indoors, but still a calm environment. A living room is familiar to everyone and is a relaxing place. A link with the calm environment is maintained by a large window showing the outside and letting the faint sound from the outside world in. Once the transition to the intermediate environment is complete, the change to the working environment is launched. The outdoor is still visible through the windows, but without the sounds of nature and with the specific sounds of the workplace. We can see this transitions in Fig. 4.

We have used different methods to change the scenes: fade in and out, scale and position change, shape and texture morphing, offscreen appearance/disappearance, fragmentation, sound transition.

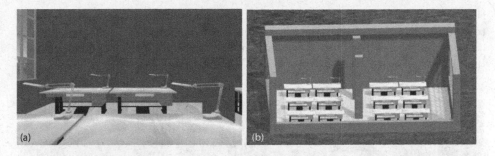

Fig. 7. A workshop: the *working* VE. – *i.e.* potentially more stressful.

Fade In/Out — The fade effect is easily achieved by changing the alpha channel in the object shader. We have used it on the ground to make the floor of the intermediate and work scene appear. The sound effects are also fades. The sound's volume slowly changes in order to make the sounds audible/inaudible.

Scale Change — The change of scale is a linear enlargement or shrinking on a given time. This transition can be very subtle if applied to small objects, or totally obvious on big objects. This effect has been used on the grass in the garden scene and on the walls of both intermediate and work scenes. It can create an illusion of movement, hence provoking motion sickness to sensitive users.

Position Change — The change of position is a linear movement in a given time period. We have used it on the tree in the garden scene and the pine in the mountain scene. The trees back slowly away from the user (see Fig. 8). If noticed, this transition has caused slight discomfort.

Fig. 8. Tree transition: the depicted tree virtually gets out of the scene not too fast, and not too slowly, nevertheless only few subjects noticed such an odd behavior for a tree.

Morphing — The morphing is the change of size and/or texture of an object. Shape morphing cannot be done natively in Unity, so we chose Blender and its KeyShapes in order to store both start and target vertex positions and import them to Unity. On import, a Unity script is generated with the necessary options to make a seamless shape transition. Texture transition has been done with a custom shader by displaying a certain amount of two textures blended together. In Fig. 9 we can see the table shape and texture transition.

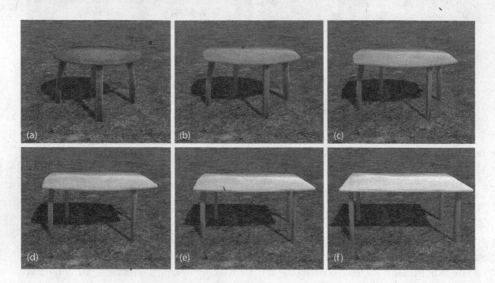

Fig. 9. Table transition: the table changes size and shape from round to rectangular and texture from dark wood to white marble. The morphing is progressive, done in a few minutes. This transition was under detected compared to our expectations (as described in Sect. 4).

Offscreen Appearance/Disappearance — In an offscreen appearance/ disappearance, an object instantly appears/disappears when it is outside the user's field of view.

Fragmentation — Fragmentation is an effect created by the breaking of an object into small pieces. This operation is not available natively in Unity, so we used Blender in order to create the pieces. We applied it on the chairs in the garden, where we wanted to apply a blow out effect (see Fig. 10). Unity provides an explosion option that generates a force applied on each object in an epicenter.

Sound Transitions — The sound transitions are all fading in or out. The sound aspect will be worked on more in a further development of the final project.

3   Task

We have created a prototype of a SG to be able to test the transitions in similar conditions to the final ones. Asking the testers to be in the environment and wait will imply they focus more on the environment than on doing a task that can

Fig. 10. Chair transition: this third example of local transition was showy as it depicted an object breaking into small pieces. Most of the people, fortunately, noticed the event – especially in the sky – but failed to understand that the chair next to them had exploded.

inhibit their attention level. Therefore, we implemented the following interaction using the HTC Vive controllers: they must build robots by assembling their limbs to the body and giving them weapons or shields. A task overview can be seen in Figs. 2 and 11.

Fig. 11. This drawing shows the general task that the participant has to do. Objects (a), (b), and (c) describe the VR hardware used in this simulation; entities (d) and (f) represent two of the main attributes that were used as local transitions; item (e) illustrates the partially built robot.

Three robot-part sets are available in different colors. The user can choose whether he respects the color while building the robot. The arms and shields are on the table, the bodies and weapons are on a shelf and the legs stand on the floor. The user can grab them by using the Vive controllers trigger buttons. When a part is grabbed, all the articulations where it can be put together glow in yellow. When this area overlaps a corresponding articulation, the color changes to green (Fig. 12a) and, by releasing the part, they are automatically set into place. When a limb is mounted, we still need to screw it in order to seal it. The user has to pick up a screw in a container and put it in the correct articulation place shown by a yellow glowing orb. Then he must screw it completely in (Fig. 12b).

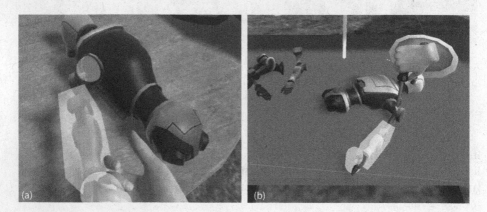

Fig. 12. Renderings of the robot building main task. Image (a) presents a selected robot arm (surrounded by a yellow sphere) and the area where it has to be fixed is highlighted by a green sphere; Image (b) depicts a user screwing a limb to the robot. (Color figure online)

The weapons and shields are immediately sealed when mounted. The sealed state is used when the robot falls or is thrown out the playing area. All the pieces that aren't sealed will be disassembled and placed back to their initial location. This also works for the screws and screwdriver. The sealed parts will appear on the floor behind the user.

Since the task was an alibi to distract the user while the transitions were taking place, it had to be longer than the overall time taken by the transitions to happen. Not a single user had finished building the three robots in the required time to do all the transitions, so the estimated time for the task was long enough. To avoid any frustration, when the transitions were over, the users were allowed to continue their task so some finished building up the three robots.

The robot assembling and screwing tasks were chosen because they seemed to be promising tasks for the final SG. They are close to the user usual work tasks and still allow various gameplay possibilities.

The weapons and shield were thought for the future SG where the goal might be to build fighting robots. This possibility was explained to the users as the potential goal of the future game. This gave them a scenario opening and a purpose to do the task even if no score or any game component were present. The implemented solution is a contextualized interactive VR experience but it was not introduced as SG. Most of the users were conscientious in doing the task successfully and enjoyed it.

4   User Test

A user test was made over five days on 80 people. They were asked to perform the robot task, which was to assemble robots limbs and screw them in place. The activity lasted 15 to 20 min, which is the time for all the transitions to occur and let the user finish his task. The environment transitions were never mentioned and the users were not aware of any environment change. After the session, the user had to fill a survey about the environment and the transitions.

4.1   Population

The sample was 40% female and 60% male, and with 84% having never tested VR or only once. The age range scaled between 12 and 73 years old, with 48% of them between 20 and 30 years old. The users had very different backgrounds, but most of them (80%) feeling at ease with the technology.

4.2   Transitions

For each transition taking place, the user was asked if he noticed it while it was happening. The results show that most of the transitions were not noticed (see Fig. 13), with only four transitions which are two walls, the table and the floor noticed by 25% people or more. The living room and the workplace walls appearing are the two biggest transitions in size, the table is the place where the task is executed and the floor is where the objects fall; so the chances the user never looked at those while they were changing are very low. The table transition is probably one of the most surprising results of this study; the user main working area was not only changing texture from dark wood to white marble, but was basically changing size and shape from round to rectangular; still few people realized such tremendous changes.

If we look at the number of noticed transitions per person, we can see that nobody remarked all the changes when they were taking place, with a maximum of 10 transitions seen out of 14 (see Fig. 14), and with 23 people not noticing any of them. In total, we have 84% of people noticing less than half of the transitions.

4.3   Environments

The results of the questions asked about the transitions show that few of them were observed. But since the final and starting environment are so different, you would expect the user to notice at least some change, even after it took place. This user test shows that it is not the case with 37% of users not noticing any environmental change at all (see Fig. 15a). As expected, most of the people that did not notice any environment change noticed zero or one transition (see Fig. 15b). However, some people noticed up to five transitions, without realizing that the whole environment was changing.

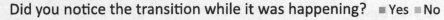
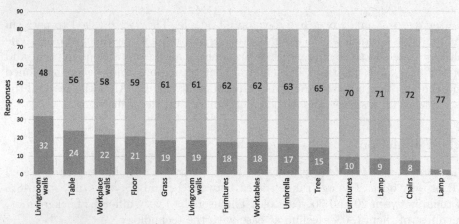

Fig. 13. Fourteen local transitions and corresponding survey results from the most noticed (left) to the least (right). The blue and red colors indicate respectively positive and negative answers. (Color figure online)

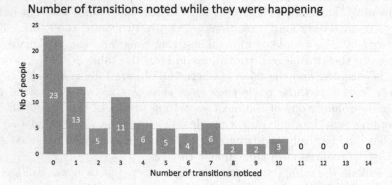

Fig. 14. This figure represents how many of the fourteen local transitions were actually noticed by participants when they occurred: surprisingly 29% of the users did not see a single of them.

4.4 Results

This test results highlight several elements. The first being that environmental changes do not bother the users in their tasks. This is an important element for the project continuation. In fact, had transitions been proved to be disturbing or too distracting, the imagined transitional principle would have had to be completely redesigned. The transitions proved to be so little disturbing that the majority was not even noticed, with only 22% of them being observed while they were taking place.

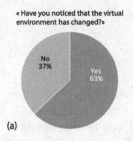

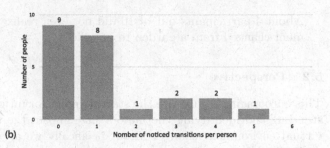

(a)   (b)

Fig. 15. (a) Considering the global virtual environment, and after an average of 20 min in VR, 37% of the candidates did not realize they moved from the middle of a garden to a working office. (b) Among those people, 25% noted from 2 to 6 transitions.

These results can be due to the fact that users were not aware of the future environment evolution, and were therefore focused solely on their task, causing a phenomenon called "Inattentional Blindness" [24], which is the fact of not noticing a new element because of the concentration on something else. Some transitions were obviously not seen because they were outside the user's field of view, but this is by far not always the case. Most of the transitions happen over a certain period of time (up to 2 min) with the only transitions that last under 20 seconds are the off-screen appearances as well as the explosion. For all the other transitions, it is unlikely that the object was never in their field of view during this time. In addition, many transitions have clearly taken place in the field of view without them noticing. This blindness phenomenon is such that 37% of users did not see that the environment had changed between the session beginning and end, when the difference was obvious and right before their eyes.

5   Discussion

5.1   Conclusion

This paper has presented an empirical study relative to the virtual environment (VE) impact and more specifically to transition from one VE to another. Indeed, due to real world room constraints, experimenting a virtual reality phenomenon implies transition issues – at least at the very beginning and end, i.e. from the real world to the virtual and vice versa.

As developed in the user test Sect. 4, the original objective was to identify how participants were consciously noticing global VE changes (i.e. from being in the middle of a garden to a closed indoor office with artificial lights) and/or local transition (e.g. a tree few meters away virtually *walking* out of the scene).

This experiment conducted over 80 participants demonstrated the following results:

– Local object transitions being noticed on an average of 20%;
– About 3 people out of 10 did not see any of the local transitions as they occurred;

– About 4 participants out of 10 did not even realize that the global environment changed from a garden to an office.

5.2   Perspective

This encouraging results are the starting point for future work related to understanding and identifying the factors that impact the user experience during a virtual environment change. More specifically we are now conducting investigations on the unconscious influence of the environment (lights, sound, voice, colors, number of objects, etc.) on manual tasks such as handling in the industrial area.

Acknowledgement. This work was supported by the EU Interreg program, grant number (contract no.1812) as a part of the *SG4H@W* project. We would like to thank all the health professionals that took part in the investigation or contributed otherwise to this project; many thanks also to the CHUV (University Hospital of Canton Vaud, Switzerland) for its help and advice.

References

1. Johansson, E.: Dreamwalking...in between worlds (2014)
2. INRS: Troubles musculosquelettiques (TMS). Statistiques. http://www.inrs.fr/risques/tms-troubles-musculosquelettiques/statistiques.html
3. Bevan, S.: Economic impact of musculoskeletal disorders (MSDs) on work in Europe. Best Pract. Res. Clin. Rheumatol. **29**, 356–373 (2015). doi:10.1016/j.berh.2015.08.002. Elsevier
4. Bartolom, N.A., Zorrilla, A.M., Zapirain, B.G.: Can game-based therapies be trusted? Is game-based education effective? A systematic review of the serious games for health, education. In: 6th International Conference on Computer Games (CGAMES), pp. 275–282. IEEE (2011). doi:10.1109/CGAMES.2011.6000353
5. Ma, M., Zheng, H.: Virtual reality and serious games in healthcare. In: Brahnam, S., Jain, L.C. (eds.) Advanced Computational Intelligence Paradigms in Healthcare 6. Virtual Reality in Psychotherapy, Rehabilitation, and Assessment, vol. 337, pp. 169–192. Springer, Heidelberg (2011). doi:10.1007/978-3-642-17824-5_9
6. Gobron, S.C., Zannini, N., Wenk, N., Schmitt, C., Charrotton, Y., Fauquex, A., Lauria, M., Degache, F., Frischknecht, R.: Serious games for rehabilitation using head-mounted display and haptic devices. In: Paolis, L.T., Mongelli, A. (eds.) AVR 2015. LNCS, vol. 9254, pp. 199–219. Springer, Cham (2015). doi:10.1007/978-3-319-22888-4_15
7. Sportillo, D., Avveduto, G., Tecchia, F., Carrozzino, M.: Training in VR: a preliminary study on learning assembly/disassembly sequences. In: Paolis, L.T., Mongelli, A. (eds.) AVR 2015. LNCS, vol. 9254, pp. 332–343. Springer, Cham (2015). doi:10.1007/978-3-319-22888-4_24
8. Martin, C.C., Burkert, D.C., Choi, K.R., Wieczorek, N.B., McGregor, P.M., Herrmann, R.A., Beling, P.A.: A real-time ergonomic monitoring system using the Microsoft Kinect. In: 2012 IEEE Systems and Information Design Symposium (SIEDS), pp. 50–55. IEEE (2012). doi:10.1109/SIEDS.2012.6215130

9. Haggag, H., Hossny, M., Nahavandi, S., Creighton, D.: Real time ergonomic assessment for assembly operations using Kinect. In: 15th International Conference on Computer Modelling and Simulation (UKSim), pp. 495–500. IEEE (2013). doi:10.1109/UKSim.2013.105

10. Johnson, D., Deterding, S., Kuhn, K.A., Staneva, A., Stoyanov, S., Hides, L.: A systematic review of the literature. In: Internet Interventions, vol. 6, pp. 89–106. Elsevier (2016). doi:10.1016/j.invent.2016.10.002

11. Daesign: La pédagogie numérique au service des apprenants, des entreprises et des professionnels de la formation. http://www.daesign.com/

12. Rodrigues, M.A.F., Macedo, D.V., Pontes, H.P., Serpa, Y.R., Serpa, Y.R.: A serious game to improve posture and spinal health while having fun. In: 2016 IEEE International Conference on Serious Games and Applications for Health (SeGAH), pp. 1–8. IEEE (2016). doi:10.1109/SeGAH.2016.7586260

13. Saenz-De-Urturi, Z., Garcia-Zapirain Soto, B.: Kinect-based virtual game for the elderly that detects incorrect body postures in real time. In: Sensors for Entertainment, Sensors (2016). doi:10.3390/s16050704

14. Barrett, P., Zhang, Y., Moffat, J., Kobbacy, K.: A holistic, multi-level analysis identifying the impact of classroom design on pupils' learning. Build. Environ. J. **59**, 678–689 (2013). doi:10.1016/j.buildenv.2012.09.016. Elsevier

15. Sakellaris, I.A., Saraga, D.E., Mandin, C., Roda, C., Fossati, S., de Kluizenaar, Y., Carrer, P., Dimitroulopoulou, S., Mihucz, G.V., Szigeti, T., Hnninen, O., de Oliveira Fernandes, E., Bartzis, J.G., Bluyssen, P.M.: Perceived indoor environment and occupants' comfort in European "modern" office buildings: the OFFICAIR study. Int. J. Environ. Res. Public Health **13**, 4:1–4:15 (2016). doi:10.3390/ijerph13050444. MDPI

16. Al Horr, Y., Arif, M., Katafygiotou, M., Mazroei, A., Kaushik, A., Elsarrag, E.: Impact of indoor environmental quality on occupant well-being and comfort: a review of the literature. Int. J. Sustain. Built Environ. **5**, 1–11 (2016). doi:10.1016/j.ijsbe.2016.03.006. Elsevier

17. Zelenski, J.M., Murphy, S.A., Jenkins, D.A.: The happy-productive worker thesis revisited. J. Happiness Stud. **9**, 521–537 (2008). doi:10.1007/s10902-008-9087-4. Springer, Netherlands

18. Kaplan, S.: Toward an integrative framework. J. Environ. Psychol. **15**, 169–182 (1995). doi:10.1016/0272-4944(95)90001-2. Academic Press Limited

19. INRS: Troubles musculosquelettiques (TMS). Facteurs de risque. http://www.inrs.fr/risques/tms-troubles-musculosquelettiques/facteurs-risque.html

20. Unity Game Engine. https://unity3d.com/

21. Unity Asset Store. https://www.assetstore.unity3d.com/en/

22. Blender. https://www.blender.org/

23. HTC Corporation. https://www.vive.com

24. Simons, D.: But Did You See the Gorilla? The Problem With Inattentional Blindness. In: Smithsonian Magazine (2012)

Walk-able and Stereo Virtual Tour based on Spherical Panorama Matrix

Yanxiang Zhang[⊠] and Ziqiang Zhu

Department of Communication of Science and Technology,
University of Science and Technology of China, Hefei, Anhui, China
petrel@ustc.edu.cn, monders@mail.ustc.edu.cn

Abstract. Photo based panoramas were widely used to make realistic virtual tour for existed scenes, but traditional panorama could only allow users to look around the scene from a fixed point where it was shot, while traditional panorama could not provide binocular stereo effect that is very common for a virtual reality head mounted display. We could walk freely in a modeling based virtual tour scene, but there are great difficulties in modeling an existed scene and making it look real.

In this paper, we developed a panorama matrix based virtual tour system which could provide freely walk through ability and binocular stereo effect, by recording an existed scene using spherical panorama camera and shot in every walkable space in the scene by rows and columns, then the panoramas will be mapped and aligned on a virtual sphere and exported to head mounted displays to provide immersive experience to users.

Keywords: Panorama · Matrix · Virtual tour

1 Introduction

Usually there are two kinds of scenes that could be used for virtual tour, geometry based and image rendering based, geometry based scenes could bring freely walk through experience to the users but it is very difficult to duplicate an existed scene. While image rendering based scenes such as spherical panoramas could record an existed scene and display it realistically, users could only observe it from a fixed point in the center of the panorama. And while there is no binocular stereo effect for a traditional panoramas.

In order to provide users with a walk through experience to photo realistic panoramas, Ying [1] uses image transformations among images to achieve continuous walkthrough between the two adjacent panoramas, Jung [2] uses panoramic-based image morphing to generate intermediate panoramic images from a few captured panoramic images. Digital Route Panoramas [3, 4] could digitally archive and visualize street scenes along a route. While [5] pre-process the datasets and render key viewpoints on pre-selected paths, and [6] present a method to reconstruct a 4D plenoptic function for an observer moving in open areas within a large, complex environment while restricting camera motion to a planet eye-height inside the dataset.

© Springer International Publishing AG 2017
L.T. De Paolis et al. (Eds.): AVR 2017, Part I, LNCS 10324, pp. 50–58, 2017.
DOI: 10.1007/978-3-319-60922-5_4

Concentric panorama [7] could synthesize the scene realistically while moving the viewpoint freely within a circular region on a plane.

On stereo panoramic technologies, most of the existed systems [8–13] generate stereo panoramic image by using circular projections from images or video taken by a single rotating camera or omnidirectionalimaging.

But existed Image-Based Rendering (IBR) researches only allow movement along a linear path in three dimensions. Also many IBR techniques [14–22] focus on rendering of relatively low resolution monocular imageries with limited viewing angel. And existed stereo panoramic technologies only allow users to look around at a fixed point without walk through experience.

In this paper we designed an image-based virtual tour system which could provide realistic walk through experience at interactive frame rate, while users could look around at all direction with binocular stereo effects at high resolution. This system combines the advantages of both geometry based virtual tour and existed IBR based virtual tour while overcoming the shortcomings of both systems.

A two-fisheye-lens spherical panorama camera LG 360CAM was used to record the scene at the cross points in arrays, thus having a spherical panorama matrix dataset, then a special virtual tour player was designed to explore the spherical panorama matrix dataset which allows walking in a scene and looking around at all directions, and when a user stops walking, he or she will be provided with stereo effects of the whole touring process by head mounted display.

2 Spherical Panorama Matrix Recording

We selected a LG 360CAMspherical panorama camera to record the scene, it has two fisheye lens on its two sides, so it could record the scene in one shot, and then generate an equirectangular panorama image automatically which could be directly used for spherical panorama rendering without extra stitching by users.

2.1 Scene Recording Method

We arranged a mini-scene on the table at the dimension of 160 cm × 80 cm as our testing scene, and designed a grid and printed on papers, then put it on the table to indicate the positions where panoramas should be shot, shown as Fig. 1.

Although we only arranged a mini-scene on the table, but every shot of the panorama photo will record the entire room but not only the mini-scene on the table.

LG 360CAM spherical panorama camera could be controlled by app on tablet, so users don't need to press the button on it and leave a large hand in the captured photos.

2.2 Stereo-Pair Panoramas Shot

Existed IBR based walk through or stereo tour usually generate interpolated frames by equation from source images, which causes extra system burden but result in low image quality.

Fig. 1. **Fig. 1.** Recording a mini-scene by using LG 360CAM spherical panorama camera

In this paper, a panorama matrix with enough frames will be recorded, then any two adjacent panoramas will be directly used as stereo image-pairs for binocular stereo viewing in the virtual tour, thus the most fluent playing experience and the highest clarity could be achieved.

Each recorded spherical panorama's orientation and direction is decided by the camera's orientation and direction, in order to avoid future adjustment of aligning the panoramas in the matrix, we created marks to indicate where and which direction the panorama should be shot, shown as Fig. 2.

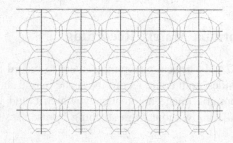

Fig. 2. Marks to indicate where and which direction the panoramas should be shot

Then panorama camera is placed on the marks and camera orientation of different shot is parallel to each other, so all the spherical panorama's orientation and direction will be aligned automatically after been recorded.

But there is a physical defect in the selected two-fisheye-lens spherical camera, which is an unavoidable seam that will appear in-between the two lens area especially when something is too close to the camera. So if something important is near to the camera, it is better to keep the camera lens directly facing it. In this situation we could rotate the camera for an angle and then offset the recorded equirectangular image to align the orientation and direction of all the panoramas.

2.3   Spacing Between Two Adjacent Shots

Because we will use two adjacent panoramas as stereo pairs, it will be very important to set a proper distance between two adjacent shots, too large distance may cause discomfort in viewing, but reducing the distance will increase the shot amount rapidly while generating dataset enormously.

We plan to set the field of view of the panorama viewing window just like our eyes, so the pupillary distance will be a very important reference for the distance between two adjacent shots.

On average the pupillary distance in an adult is usually between 60 and 66 mm. So the maximum distance between two adjacent shots should not exceed 60 mm.

In our grid of camera placement, two kinds of adjacent shot were shown as Fig. 3, in which Dmax and Dmin both could be the distance between two stereo pairs. When walk in straight directions, such as forward, backward, left and right, the distance between two stereo pairs is Dmin, when walk in tilt directions, the distance between two stereo pairs is Dmax.

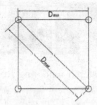

Fig. 3. Distance between two adjacent shots

Set the maximum value of Dmax as 60 mm that nearly reach the threshold of human eyes, then,

$$Dmax = Dmin * \sqrt{2}, \quad Dmin = 42.46\,mm$$

2.4   Recorded Spherical Panoramas

Figure 4 shows two recorded adjacent spherical panoramas.

Fig. 4. Two recorded adjacent spherical panoramas

3   Rendering and Interaction

3.1   Binocular Stereo Rendering

Two adjacent spherical panorama equirectangular images were retrieved from recorded datasets by mapped on two same sphere in 3D environment, and two camera were placed just inside the center of each sphere to render stereo image pairs for binocular stereo viewing, shown as Fig. 5. Two cameras in adjacent spherical panoramas will assigned the same angle and directions, also they will react to a global mouse movement with same feedback and changing.

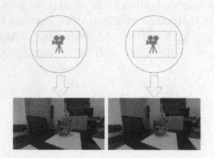

Fig. 5. Binocular stereo rendering from adjacent shots

3.2   Look Around

Users could stand at a fixed point and look around, and two adjacent panoramas will be retrieved from recorded datasets to render. The action defined for looking around is drag mouse on left button, two separate cameras in adjacent spherical panoramas will render image pairs and composite the into a side by side stereo scene, then the result could be viewed in VR head mounted display.

When users are looking around in the virtual tour, he/she stand virtually between the two adjacent panoramas, and he/she could see every direction of the scene in stereo effects, as Fig. 6.

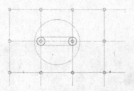

Fig. 6. Looking around in stereo rendered from two adjacent panoramas

3.3 Walk Through

There could be two kinds of walk through direction, in straight directions such as back, forth, left or right which takes the minimum distance Dmin of adjacent shots, or tilt directions which has 45° angle with straight directions and will take the maximum distance Dmax of adjacent shots, shown as Fig. 7.

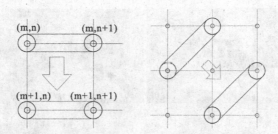

Fig. 7. Two kinds of walk through directions

Based on the above directions, the following turnings could be realized:

Turn 90°, turn −90°, turn 180°, turn −180°
Turn 45°, turn −45°, turn 135°, turn −135°

Now we define StereoPair[Left, right] as an panorama pair, And we mark pano(n, m) the panorama located at coordinate (n, m) on the matrix, and the initial panorama pair could be write as:
StereoPair[pano(m,n),pano(m,n + 1)], then,

Next pair of moving forward is: StereoPair[pano(m + 1,n),pano(m + 1,n + 1)]
Next pair of moving backward is: StereoPair[pano(m − 1,n),pano(m − 1,n + 1)]

When moving forward or backward from initial panorama pair positions, the distance between two panoramas will be D_{min} which is 42.46 mm.
If we are turning from the initial panorama pair positions
StereoPair[pano(m,n), pano(m,n + 1)], then:

Next pair of turning left is: StereoPair[pano(m,n − 1),pano(m + 1,n − 1)]
Next pair of turning right is: StereoPair[pano(m,n + 1),pano(m + 1,n + 1)]
Next pair of turning +45° is : StereoPair[pano(m,n),pano(m + 1,n + 1)]
Next pair of turning −45° is: StereoPair[pano(m,n),pano(m − 1,n + 1)]
Next pair of turning 135° is: StereoPair[pano(m,n),pano(m + 1,n − 1)]
Next pair of turning −135° is: StereoPair[pano(m,n),pano(m-1,n-1)]

If we move forward after we turned at a tilt direction, then the distance between two panoramas will be D_{max} which is 60 mm, the initial panorama pair positions could be:
StereoPair[pano(m,n),pano(m − 1,n + 1)], then:

Next pair of moving forward is: StereoPair[pano(m + 1,n + 1),pano(m,n + 2)]
Next pair of turning +45° is: StereoPair[pano(m,n),pano(m,n + 1)], And so on.

3.4 Study Something

If there is something important in the scene, we can mark it as a hotspot, then our system could retrieve panorama pairs around it to make a looking around mode. In this mode, while users walk through the side of this important thing, virtual cameras in the panorama pairs will look at it, so we could look around and study it (Fig. 8).

Fig. 8. Study an object in the scene by looking around it

As panoramas will be displayed at the same field of view as human's eye, when shooting the panoramas for studying some object, the distance between camera and the object should also obey human eye's rule that the camera should not be too near to the object, the minimum distance between camera and the object should be larger than the distance of human's distinct vision that is 25 cm. Any distance larger than 25 cm will cause discomfort.

4 Result and Discussion

4.1 Result

In our virtual tour system, users could look around at fixed point, walk through the virtual scene with 8 kinds of turning ability through controllers such as joystick, keyboard or mouse, thus they could have relatively high freedom in the virtual tour, and also users could study something important in the scene. And in the whole process of the virtual tour, users could view the scene with stereo effects.

4.2 Conclusions and Discussion

It will take much more time than normal video recording to record a scene is it covers a large range, but modeling the same scene in 3D will need much more time than the method in this paper, while 3D modeled scene can never be so real.

Before this paper, there is no existed IBR researches tackled issues of both walking through and stereo panoramic viewing in 360 * 360°. Also although some existed researched based on interpolation or plenoptic functions which could generate walking through experience, there are still some defects in these kind of systems, most of the interpolations result in distortion and low image quality, also most of these researches could only generate experience of walking through but no stereo viewing of panoramic in 360 * 360°.

In many real scenes, users usually walk in a path but not every position, so we can record only at the positions that the matrix is overlapped with the path. The dataset's amount could also be reduced by doing so.

But a defect of the research is it is very troublesome to record a large scene as we should manually move the camera to next position after each shot, also we can only record a static scene. In the future, we will try to record large scenes by using intelligent crawling robot with which to control the panorama camera shooting stereo pairs. Gyroscope data could be recorded with intelligent crawling robot at each shot, so that all the recorded panoramas could be aligned even if there are some deviation during the running of robot.

References

1. Ying, X., Peng, K., Zha, H.: Walkthrough in large environments using concatenated panoramas. In: Proceedings of the 2009 International Conference on Robotics and Biomimetics (ROBIO 2009), pp. 286–291. IEEE Press, Piscataway, NJ, USA (2009)
2. Jung, J.-H., Kang, H.-B.: An efficient arbitrary view generation method using panoramic-based image morphing. In: Huang, D.-S., Li, K., Irwin, G.W. (eds.) ICIC 2006. LNCS, vol. 4113, pp. 1207–1212. Springer, Heidelberg (2006). doi:10.1007/11816157_150
3. Zheng, J.Y.: Digital route panoramas. IEEE Multimedia **10**(3), 57–67 (2003)
4. Zheng, J.Y., Zhou, Y., Shi, M.: Scanning and rendering scene tunnels for virtual city traversing. In: Proceedings of the ACM Symposium on Virtual Reality Software and Technology (VRST 2004), pp. 106–113. ACM, New York (2004)
5. Yang, L., Crawfis, R.: Rail-track viewer an image-based virtual walkthrough system. In: Stürzlinger, W., Müller, S. (eds.) Proceedings of the Workshop on Virtual Environments 2002 (EGVE 2002). Eurographics Association, Aire-la-Ville (2002)
6. Aliaga, D.G., Carlbom, I.: Plenoptic stitching: a scalable method for reconstructing 3D interactive walk throughs. In: Proceedings of the 28th Annual Conference on Computer Graphics and Interactive Techniques (SIGGRAPH 2001), pp. 443–450. ACM, New York (2001)
7. Shum, H.-Y., He, L.-W.: Rendering with concentric mosaics. In: Annual Conference Series Computer Graphics, vol. 33, pp. 299–306 (1999)
8. Peleg, S., Benezra, M.: Stereo panorama with a single camera. In: CVPR, vol. 1, p. 1395 (1999)
9. Huang, H.-C., Hung, Y.-P.: Panoramic stereo imaging system with automatic disparity warping and seaming. GMIP **60**, 196–208 (1998)
10. Ishiguro, H., Yamamoto, M., Tsuji, S.: Omni-directional stereo. IEEE Trans. Pattern Anal. Mach. Commer. **14**, 257–262 (1992)

11. Jiang, W., Okutomi, M., Sugimoto, S.: Panoramic 3D reconstruction using rotational stereo camera with simple Epipolar constraints. In: Proceedings of CVPR, vol 1, pp. 371–378 (2006)
12. Kawanishi, T., Yamazawa, K., Iwasa, H., Takemura, H., Yokoya, N.: Generation of high resolution stereo panoramic images by omnidirectional sensor using hexagonal pyramidal mirrors. In: Proceedings of ICPR, pp. 485–489 (1998)
13. Kawanishi, T., Yamazawa, K., Iwasa, H., et al.: Generation of high-resolution stereo panoramic images by omnidirectional imaging sensor using hexagonal pyramidal mirrors. In: 1998 Proceedings of the Fourteenth International Conference on Pattern Recognition, vol. 1, pp. 485–489. IEEE Xplore (1998)
14. Gortler, S., Grzeszczuk, R., Szeliski, R., Cohen, M.: The lumigraph. In: Proceedings of SIGGRAPH 1996, pp. 43–54 (1996)
15. Zhao, Q., Wan, L., Feng, W., Zhang, J., Wong, T.-T.: Cube2Video: navigate between cubic panoramas in real-time. IEEE Trans. Multimedia **15**(8), 1745–1754 (2013)
16. Mark, W., McMillan, L., Bishop, G.: Post-rendering 3D warping. In: 1997 Symposium on Interactive 3D Graphics, pp. 7–16 (1997)
17. McMillan, L., Bishop, G.: Plenoptic modeling: an image-based rendering system. In: Proceedings of SIGGRAPH 1995, pp. 39–46 (1995)
18. McMillan, L., Gortler, S.: Image-based rendering: a new interface between computer vision and computer graphics. Comput. Graphics (ACM) **33**, 61–64 (1999)
19. Buehler, C., Bosse, M., McMillan, L., Gortler, S., Cohen, M.: Unstructured lumigraph rendering. In: Computer Graphics Annual Conference (SIGGRAPH 2001), 12–17 August 2001, pp. 425–432. Association for Computing Machinery (2001)
20. Zitnick, C.L., Kang, S.B.: Stereo for image-based rendering using image over-segmentation. Int. J. Comput. Vis. **75**, 49–65 (2007)
21. Ruhl, K., Eisemann, M., Hilsmann, A., Eisert, P., Magnor, M.: Interactive scene flow editing for improved image-based rendering and virtual spacetime navigation. In: 23rd ACM International Conference on Multimedia, MM 2015, 26–30 October 2015, pp. 631–640. Association for Computing Machinery, Inc. (2015)
22. Kawai, N., Audras, C., Tabata, S., Matsubara, T.: Panorama image interpolation for real-time walkthrough. In ACM SIGGRAPH 2016 Posters (SIGGRAPH 2016), Article no. 33. ACM, New York (2016)

Virtual Reality Applied to Industrial Processes

Víctor H. Andaluz[✉], Daniel Castillo-Carrión[✉],
Roberto J. Miranda, and Juan C. Alulema

Universidad de las Fuerzas Armadas ESPE, Sangolquí, Ecuador
{vhandaluz1, dacastillo, rjmiranda,
jcalulema}@espe.edu.ec

Abstract. The present paper shows the development of a virtual reality application through the creation of environments that allows supervision, monitoring and control of industrial processes. It has the possibility to simulate or work with live-time information, linked to existing process modules of the most important physics variables such as level, pressure, flow and temperature. The results of the application are presented to validate the project, using the functions of supervision, monitoring and control, the scopes reached in emulation, as well as the contrast between the emulation option and real interplaying with industrial processes.

Keywords: Virtual reality · P&ID · Unity 3D · Emulation · Industrial processes

1 Introduction

The constant changing of society and the technological revolution that world is living, leads to appear improvements of the techniques and methods implemented in skills training process in order to be applied in working or educational activities. The inclusion of Information and Communications Technologies (ICT's) like smart boards, videoconferences, virtual platforms, and others have allowed a speedy advance of education, creating in present generations a high dependence to digital products and services, in order to complete daily activities. Although, inside educational institutes and some industries, state-of-the-art laboratories are implemented with the objective of incrementing operators' expertise during the training process. The fact of working with high-cost equipment, makes that all elements must be manipulated carefully and considering safety standards. Similarly, for teaching purposes, it is very difficult to establish a module which includes all characteristics involved in a real industrial process. Thus, this circumstances does not allow people who uses the instruments to exploit and improve the skills and capabilities in an integral way. For that reason, the use of virtual and technological tools is essential, aiming to increase the possibilities available within training process inside industrial environments [1, 2].

In automation's field, the control pyramid [3] becomes in the central point of analysis and taking as main involved instrumentation, which acquires great importance because it is the attendant that manages every single level of the pyramid, from field components to the manage resource system implementation. Industrial processes needs constant maintenance, calibrations and adjustments of components of the system,

L.T. De Paolis et al. (Eds.): AVR 2017, Part I, LNCS 10324, pp. 59–74, 2017.
DOI: 10.1007/978-3-319-60922-5_5

where the instrumentalist is responsible for carrying out these procedures. The monitoring of this processes through acquisition data and its posterior visualization through a human machine interface (HMI), allows to keep under control the actions that are made in different stages of the system; graphics and two dimension (2D) trends, let people know the behavior of the process and at the same time it is necessary additional elements to achieve and present the results [4, 5].

Focusing on process instrumentation, some companies have been specializing in the development of tools to complement vocational training from the point of view of process analysis, structures modeling, components designing, systems simulation, and others. Nowadays, the possibility to carry out industrial tasks such as development of architectural plans is bigger, and now they can be complemented with other global use tools like electrical diagrams, pipes diagrams and tree dimensions (3D) modeling [6]. In the same way, there are tools intending to analyze and develop applications, from basic tasks, *e.g.*, math operation to the implementation of intelligent controllers for industrial plants. These tools contributes optimizing the execution time of those tasks, but the big disadvantage they present is two dimensions environment display. This fact limitates the implementation of improved techniques for tasks manipulation training, supervision and process control. Therefore, a new environment that allows to obtain the performance parameters of systems is needed, as well as alarms' status and many other alerts directly involved with process' operation.

The awakening of Virtual Reality (VR) has led researchers to find many uses and applications for virtual environments (VE). Among them we find videogames with a high immersion grade that makes users feel unique sensations [7, 8]. All of that does not finish there, due to applications in medicine's branch now are posed, especially in the way of rehabilitation [9, 10], e.g., for people with brain damage or children who has born with some kind of retardation. Another applications are virtual tours to identification institutions or hard to reach places, and more recently, this tendency is joining to educational field as projects development managers or even contributing with learning process [11–13].

For all the above, in this project the developing of a VR Application is presented. It starts with pipes and instrumentation diagrams (P&ID) that are the basis of understanding for any industrial plants. Prior to digitalization's process, with help of graphic and industrial design tools, the project is looking for the achievement of two principal objectives. [14, 15] the first one allows the *monitoring* of didactic modules placed in the laboratory of industrial processes, where physics variables, *e.g.*, level, pressure, flow and temperature are analyzed. The application enable users a live and direct interaction with modules as well as exchanging data in order to implement monitoring, supervision or any kind of control in each process without external elements. In the second part, the *emulation* of a bigger and greater complexity industrial process is developed. It has the purpose of interacting with processes that resembles to real industrial plants, where more variables are controlled as also a large data flow is processed at the same time.

This paper is divided into seven Sections, including Introduction. The second Section presents a general description of the problem, its justification and proposed solution. In the third Section environments' virtualization are illustrated. The tasks of monitoring and emulation are established in this part. The system's interaction with didactic modules is in fourth Section. The fifth Section reviews the developing of the emulation for the greater and complex process. The results of tests and its effects after the implementation in the system are analyzed in sixth Section, and finally in the seventh Section, all conclusions of the project are presented.

2   Problem Formulation

The automation pyramid helps to understand industrial process' structure, showing basically hardware and software components of systems, where communication buses allows a continuous data flow through the other levels of the pyramid. It is important to know the performance of each element part of the system, for this reason, an SCADA that belongs to the second level of the pyramid, takes on a major roll being the link between a process and users. As it can be seen on Fig. 1, devices in charge of giving information about status of a single part or the entire system are not only screens, where the dynamics of the process are shown in historical trends, but also some of the devices presents a kind of visual information by themselves. Those information, is within SCADA level of the automation pyramid.

The implementation of an application that bases on VR to present in a graphical way the behavior of a process, from the point of view of physics, *i.e.*, animations of proper characteristics of system's elements, to the possibility to find HMI's with the entire information of processes, without using additional elements. It optimizes monitoring, supervision and control tasks and attracts attention of people which works with industrial plants. By last, the application helps operators to improve their skills, because in addition of training modules they now are able to emulate the process and see a very high approximation of how it works in real world. These processes are involved generally in systems of MIMO type, where a high working complexity level, space availability inside plants and design characteristics, are more advanced as usual.

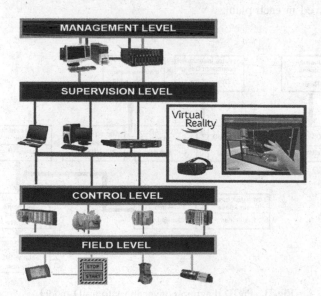

·**Fig. 1.** Characterization of the automation pyramid using VR in supervision level.

3 Environment Virtualization

A VR application should integrate some aspects that mixing each other, allows users a complete immersion into VE. For that reason, is important that every single component part of VE, present animation and functionality characteristics in order to achieve the best immersion and performance of the system. The proposed VE is shown in Fig. 2.

Fig. 2. VR application developed in unity

The base of the VR application are plants of some industrial processes. Those plants where digitized and introduced into VE using P&ID diagrams.

The technique chosen for industrial plants' digitization are based on the interaction with several specialized programs that enable the creation of equipment and instrumentation in 3D, as it seen in Fig. 3. Obtaining a representation of a real process is the main objective of virtualization, with the intention to apply on it animations and control variables involved in each plant.

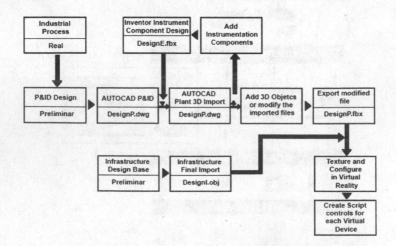

Fig. 3. P&ID diagram conversion into a 3D model.

The virtualization's process starts with references of the desired system, in this case, every industrial process has its proper P&ID diagram. Through this diagrams and using several CAD programs, the conversion from 2D to 3D is carried out, as it is seen in Fig. 4.

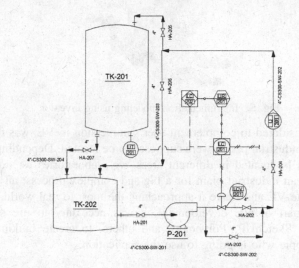

(a)   Level P&ID Diagram.

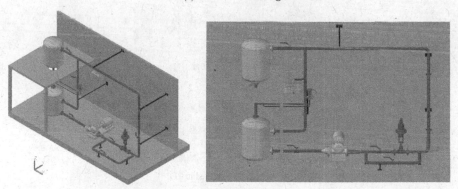

(b)   Industrial plant 3D prospects designed with AutoCAD Plant 3D.

Fig. 4. Results obtained after P&ID diagram to 3D model transformation's process.

A digitized industrial process should make user feel comfortable and familiarized with VE in the highest grade possible. For this reason, is necessary to use additional software which complements the transformation and at the same time adds a bigger immersion and credibility of the functionalities of the VR application for operators. In this case, there are some CAD software tools, *e.g.*, Inventor, Solidworks, Blender, and others, which help developers to add a high level of details in instruments' virtualization as it seen in Fig. 5. Those modifications does not represent a big change in the part of functionality, but referring to the experience given to operators, it is a really big advance, due to the reference of real world stuff in the VE.

Fig. 5. Instrumentation modeling using inventor.

An aspect considered to complement user's immersion in VE, was the creation of buildings where industrial plants were supposed to be located. Depending of industrial process, they can be located in different areas, *e.g.*, laboratories for training process modules or even an industrial plant for a big and complex process; all of this to add more reality to the VE and make it approaching the most to real world. As it seen in Fig. 6, for this part of VE development, it was necessary to use software, *e.g.*, SweetHome 3D, SketchUP, Polyboard, and others, to create buildings according necessities of people who is going to use the application.

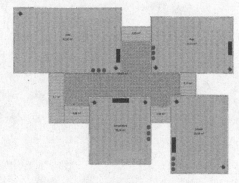

(a)   Plan of building created in 2D.

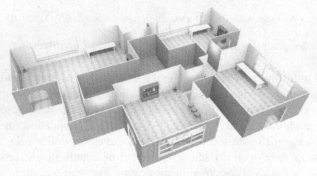

(b) Upper view of the building created using SweetHome 3D.

Fig. 6. Final building structure used in application.

One of the advantages that Unity 3D graphics engine presents, is an importing library and complements option inside application, for this reason better results are achieved due to the capacity of software to include elements which does not come originally with the program, for this case, industrial process plants and the building where they are located. Both of them were created previously with different software to complement VE.

Another important element implicated in industrial plants are control valves. They must be manipulated by operators following system's requirements, therefore, its behavior and characteristics in VR application have to be the closest to a real control valve. The import process of this kind of elements is like any other element with the difference that each control valve has its own characteristics that are going to affect the animation and as a consequence the proper performance in the application.

It is necessary to change the centroid and reference of each imported element. Related with animation in order to use them properly, as it seen in Fig. 7. All animations increase the immersion of users in the application due to the quantity of similarities with real industrial process plants included in the VE for learning or training process.

(a)   Original centroid of selected object.

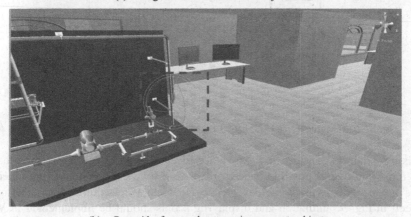

(b)   Centroid reference changes using an empty object.

Fig. 7. Changes applied in centroids and positional references of elements in Unity 3D.

4 Monitoring and Control of Industrial Processes

The VE has the same characteristics in functionality of an industrial process in real world, and for that, information is acquired and processed. These data is obtained from outputs of industrial transmitters collocated physically in processes or even from a process simulation software that generalizes the functionality of a complex industrial plant.

The link used for data exchanging between industrial processes or industrial process simulation software, both of them with VR application, is a database. It concentrates necessary variables used to modify the functionality of system on the one hand, and perform the implementation of monitoring and control on the other.

The database was created through a web server with two specific objectives; the first one is receiving the information from real industrial processes and the second one is storage data needed to manipulate emulated industrial process. The centralization of information, allows greater control in data exchanging, and at the same time an important advantage appears from the point of view of supervision. The availability of the information of all industrial processes in a web server, eliminates the fact where trainer monitors the operation of every single process in a manual way, and instead, do the same activity accessing to database remotely. For this activity is not necessary to run the VR application, because this is something that can be done by accessing database via internet, as it seen in Fig. 8.

Fig. 8. Communications established between components of VR application.

It is important to consider that experience given to users by VR application, has to be the most intuitive as possible, where processes displays real actions represented on models created with graphics engines. Hence, after data were acquired from data source as it seen in Fig. 9, animation and displaying scripts should be implemented in VE.

Some characteristics offers by scripts in VE are associated to the functioning of each element part of the system, *i.e.*, displaying the main actions executed in a real

(a)   Database chart used for industrial process emulation.

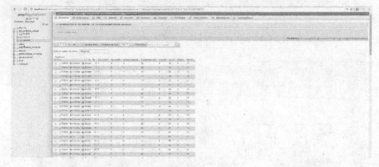

(b)   Database chart used for industrial plants monitoring.

Fig. 9. Generated files through database using phpMyAdmin and Xampp.

process, *e.g.*, opening and closing valves, filling and emptying tanks, visualization of transmitters' outputs and related to this, the response of controllers applied in each process, and finally, to have a proper displaying of plants' status, it is necessary to create historical trends where critic variables are represented as same as in a local HMI inside the control room of an industrial facility.

5   Industrial Plants Emulation

While it is true that interacting with industrial plant modules located in laboratories or training facilities generates skill's improvement in users and future operators of real processes, all of these elements are not always comparable to the real ones in real world. For that reason, an emulation of a complex industrial plant which approaches in complexity and realism, is implemented in order to complement the VR application.

The use of NI LabVIEW is not mandatory, because there are several industrial process simulation software, and for that reason new integrations of software in the application are accepted. This option would give the user the opportunity to compare results obtained with every program and select the appropriate option to be used for emulation depending of characteristics of the process.

In this case, the dynamics of the process contained in Cascade and Feed fordward Surge Tank Level LabVIEW demo [16] is used for emulation, as it seen on Fig. 10.

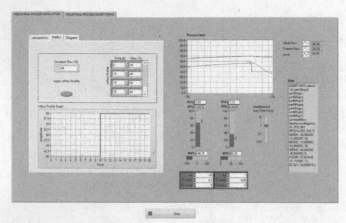

(a)   Controller process Inflow profile generation.
(b)

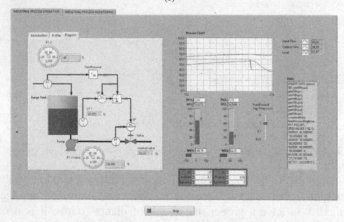

(b.1) Representation of industrial process in NI LabVIEW.

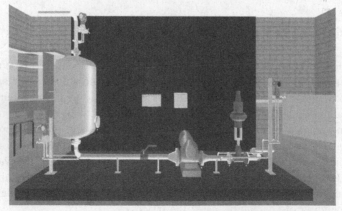

(b.2) Representation of industrial process in Unity 3D.

(c)   Comparison of the industrial process simulated using NI LabVIEW with its representation in VE.

Fig. 10.   Demo used for the emulation of a complex process.

Some changes to demo's base code included in Control and Simulation Design toolbox were applied, in order to establish data communication with Unity 3D.

The communication between emulated process and Unity 3D is vital, and to complete this activity it is necessary to process inputs and outputs of system, liberating the source code of the demo selected in order to get that information. This information is going to be exchanged through database that storages this data and at the same time it is the information's source used by Unity 3D and the emulated process.

The selected process allows users to watch and control the behavior of the emulation from the process simulation software, as same as inside of final application where VR is applied.

6 Discussion and Experimental Results

The developed application is focus on manipulation of five recreated processes using VR. Four of them are Lab-Volt didactic modules where principal variables are controlled per each, *i.e.*, pressure, level, flow and temperature.

For representation purposes, as same as for data exchanging, the principal aspect that should be considered is transmitters' outputs nature. Didactic modules delivers a standard electric current through industrial transmitters that cannot be acquired directly from any task of analysis inside the application.

6.1 Results Presentation

The final disposition of elements in application is shown in Fig. 11, where each interactive component has its own animation, *i.e.*, valves moves as they do in real world and the value of current of real industrial transmitters are presented in the corresponding virtual transmitter. In addition, some important information, *e.g.*, P&ID diagram, electric current values and process' values are displayed in a screen placed in stations acting as a HMI. All of them are intended to help users to understand in the best way possible the operation of the industrial process they are interacting with.

6.2 Experimentation

A test that shows if application is running appropriately in its monitoring stage was done by changing application input data, *i.e.*, output's values of selected transmitters in real world were modified in order to see a change in application's virtual transmitter. In this way, is proved that monitoring uses real information comes from processes as it should be.

As it seen in Fig. 12, the visualization of changes of real process is shown in transmitter, after modifying application's input data for level process plant, respecting to three different output values.

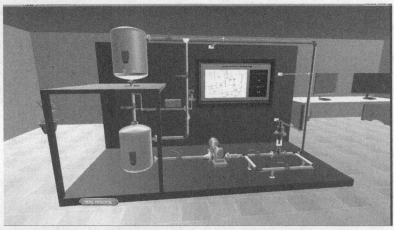

(a)   Virtual representation of level process station.

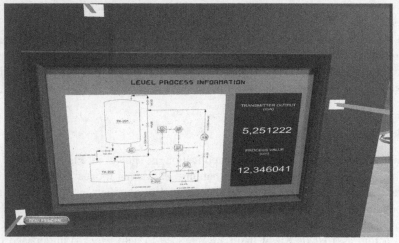

(b)   HMI displayed in screens placed in stations for plant monitoring.

Fig. 11. Application results after data interaction.

Another animation resource used to help user's visualization, are sliders located in tanks. As is can be seen on Fig. 13, the sliders show actual tank's level of both tanks. These two tanks, are filled or emptied depending on the valves that users want to open, and in this way this specific part of immersion is increased.

(a)   Results presentation of an output corresponding to 4mA.

(b)   Results presentation of an output corresponding to 7.5mA

(c)   Results presentation of an output corresponding to 12.1mA.

Fig. 12. Transmitter changes to different current input values

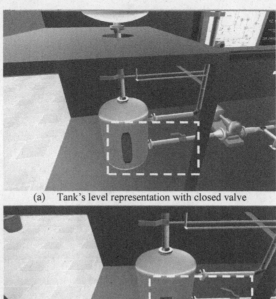

(a)   Tank's level representation with closed valve

(b)   Tank's level representation with opened valve at 50%

(a)   Tank's level representation with opened valve at 75%

Fig. 13. Tank's level changes according to valves opening

7 Conclusions

The high grade of details added in 3D models of industrial process plants, increase the immersion of users in application. The advantage of this is the capability to start familiarizing with physical connections, instrumentation and equipment as they would be in real process. Therefore, focusing on application, from the point of view of operators' training in industrial plants, it turns into a tool for students who are learning in universities following the conventional educational process.

The use of a VR application cannot be compared with real didactic modules at all. The benefits received from a safe environment where operation tests of every element in the system can be done, represents a big advance because bad connections does not cause a risk situation for operators and the rest of staff in industrial plants. It guaranties the applicability of this project, and adding to that, the development of new VR applications is opened, where the use of VR would improves production levels and performance of operators in an industrial process.

Acknowledgment. The authors would like to thanks to Universidad de las Fuerzas Armadas ESPE for all the support provided to the realization of the present paper, the one that is settled as a reference in industrial process training field, and adding to that, the same will be taken into account as previous results to the development of its engineering degree project.

References

1. Padilla Vargas, M.A., Quiroga Baquero, L.A.: The concept of linguistic modes and their application to teaching-learning processes using ICTs. J. Behav. Health Soc. Issues **6**, 9–22 (2014)
2. Andaluz, V.H., Quevedo, W.X., Chicaiza, F.A., Varela, J., Gallardo, C., Sánchez, J.S., Arteaga, O.: Transparency of a bilateral tele-operation scheme of a mobile manipulator robot. In: Paolis, L.T., Mongelli, A. (eds.) AVR 2016. LNCS, vol. 9768, pp. 228–245. Springer, Cham (2016). doi:10.1007/978-3-319-40621-3_18
3. Kumra, S., Sharma, L., Khanna, Y., Chattri, A.: Analysing an industrial automation pyramid and providing service oriented architecture. Int. J. Eng. Trends Technol. (IJETT) **3**, 1–3 (2012)
4. Yang, K., Jie, J.: The designing of training simulation system based on unity 3D. In: 2011 International Conference on Intelligent Computation Technology and Automation (ICICTA), Shenzhen, Guangdong, pp. 976–978 (2011)
5. Jing, Z., Qingyue, J.: Emotion-concerned human machine interface design. In: 2015 IEEE 19th International Conference on Intelligent Engineering Systems (INES), Bratislava, pp. 249–252 (2015). doi:10.1109/INES.2015.7329716
6. Chao, W., Zheng, X.: Secondary development of the workshop rapid simulation system based on AutoCAD, Luoyang, 2012
7. Harshfield, N., Chang, D., Rammohan: A unity 3D framework for algorithm animation. In: Computer Games: AI, Animation, Mobile, Multimedia, Educational and Serious Games (CGAMES), Louisville, KY, pp. 50–56 (2015)

8. Kim, S.L., Suk, H.J., Kang, J.H., Jung, J.M., Laine, T.H., Westlin, J.: Using unity 3D to facilitate mobile augmented reality game development. In: 2014 IEEE World Forum on Internet of Things (WF-IoT), Seoul, pp. 21–26 (2014)
9. Lloréns, R., et al.: BioTrak: análisis de efectividad y satisfacción de un sistema de realidad virtual para la rehabilitación del equilibrio en pacientes con daño cerebral. Neurología 28, 268–275 (2013)
10. Diez-Alegre, M.I., Muñoz-Hellín, E.: Empleo de sistemas de realidad virtual sobre la extremidad superior en niños con parálisis cerebral. Revisión de la literatura. Fisioterapia 35 (3), 119–125 (2013)
11. Griffin, W.N., et al.: Application creation for an immersive virtual measurement and analysis laboratory. In: 2016 IEEE 9th Workshop on Software Engineering and Architectures for Realtime Interactive Systems (SEARIS), Greenville, SC, pp. 1–7 (2016)
12. Song, S., Wang, L., Sun, H., Li, J., Wang, Q.: The studying about modeling method in development of the virtual campus. In: 2012 International Conference on Computer Science and Information Processing (CSIP) (2012)
13. Shuzhong, L., Xiaoming, C., Huilai, S.: Research on 3D online simulation system for Li/MnO2 coin cell production line based on virtual reality. In: 2010 Second Conference on Computer Modeling and Simulation, Tianjin (2010)
14. Andaluz, V.H., et al.: Immersive industrial process environment from a P&ID diagram. In: Bebis, G., et al. (eds.) ISVC 2016. LNCS, vol. 10072, pp. 701–712. Springer, Cham (2016). doi:10.1007/978-3-319-50835-1_63
15. Dobson, A.: Architectural composition in the electronic design studio: conceptual design using CAD visualisation and virtual reality modelling. In: IEEE Conference on Information Visualization, Luton (1997)
16. National Instruments: PID Setpoint Profile VI LabVIEW 2012 PID and Fuzzy Logic Toolkit Help (2012)
17. Rabbani, M.J., Ahmad, F.M., Baladi, Y., Khan, A., Naqvi, R.A.: Modeling and simulation approach for an industrial manufacturing execution system. In: 2013 IEEE 3rd International Conference on System Engineering and Technology (ICSET), Shah Alam, pp. 26–31 (2013)
18. Jiang, X., Zhang, L., Xue, H.: Designing a temperature measurement and control system for constant temperature reciprocator platelet preservation box based on LabVIEW. In: Fourth International Conference on IEEE Natural Computation ICNC 2008, pp. 48–51 (2008)
19. Fillwalk, J.: ChromaChord: a virtual musical instrument. In: 2015 IEEE Symposium on 3D User Interfaces (3DUI), Arles (2015)
20. Bogoni, T., Scarparo, R., Pinho, M.: A virtual reality simulator for training endodontics procedures using manual files. In: 2015 IEEE Symposium on 3D User Interfaces (3DUI), Arles, pp. 39–42 (2015)

Training of Tannery Processes Through Virtual Reality

Víctor H. Andaluz[1,2(✉)], Andrea M. Pazmiño[2], José A. Pérez[1],
Christian P. Carvajal[1], Francisco Lozada[2], Jeferson Lascano[2],
and Jessica Carvajal[2]

[1] Universidad de las Fuerzas Armadas ESPE, Sangolquí, Ecuador
vhandaluz1@espe.edu.ec, jlascano7178@uta.edu.ec,
chriss2592@hotmail.com
[2] Universidad Técnica de Ambato, Ambato, Ecuador
{apazmino5244,flozada0398}@uta.edu.ec,
joans11@hotmail.com

Abstract. This document presents the virtualization of an industrial process focused on the tanning of hides about bovine origin, in order to train and train the operators through a virtual environment that allows the immersion and interaction with the layout of the plant, machinery, operative elements, control and signage, referring to the productive process. The development of the virtual environment is making using computer aided software and the graphic engine Unity 3D, while for the immersion is using the virtual reality devices and hand tracking. The results one concludes obtained from the virtual experience between the operator and the environment, conclude that the proposed system allows to obtain social, economic, productive benefits and avoiding to have occupational risks.

Keywords: Tannery process · Virtual reality · Tanning · Capacitation · Industrial safety · Unity 3D

1 Introduction

Virtual Reality (VR) is defined as a group of technologies and techniques developed frequently, for integrate to the user and the developed environments [1]. Its goal is to give the user the feeling of being living in real time a virtual world through input and output devices that allow interaction with environments. Thus the VR can be seen as an experience between the user and 3D computer systems [2, 3]

Actuality the VR has a large field of applications, in the different areas of knowledge: (i) medicine, which allows to simulate or emulate treatments for burn pain and wound care, functioning as an effective or alternative complement to analgesics, [4–6], also allows the examination of physiological effects and emotional distress in adults who stutter, since they consent to manipulate and control different measures to reduce anxiety [7]; (ii) Education [8, 9], since it is taken as a methodological alternative in primary education and in higher education, since it controls and examines, not only the student's academic performance based on the degree of acceptance of the

L.T. De Paolis et al. (Eds.): AVR 2017, Part I, LNCS 10324, pp. 75–93, 2017.
DOI: 10.1007/978-3-319-60922-5_6

applications, but also aspects qualitative aspects of the academic contents, according to the curricula imposed in the different disciplines [10, 11], among them the use of emergent virtual technologies of three-dimensional prototype as a complementary tool in the teaching of cellular biology [12] Has revolutionized education in resident physicians [13], (iii) robotics presents animations of coupled and decoupled robotic mechanisms [14], creates 3D simulators applied to the area of robotics that allows analyzing the performance of different schemes of autonomous control and/or tele operated in various environments [15], (iv) industrial area, with the development of an interactive and intuitive Tridimensional Human Machine Interface to control and monitor processes of one or more variables, applying the concept of user immersion in the virtual environment, it also allows the training of officers to handle equipment during an incident at industrial site [16]; (v) the VR is taken to support the physical security of nuclear installations as it has developed environments similar possible between real installations and the virtual scenario [17], (vi) entertaining activities is another area that has grown to a great extent since it has created video games and computer simulations [18], since the objective of the simulation is to realistically represent aspects of the real world [19].

The field of immersion for training and the creation of virtual environments related to different productive processes advances as the industry and technology evolves, focusing on the complexity of the various tasks or activities carried out in the processes, to generate quality, reduce costs, apply security and improve delivery time [20]. The development a product is a complex process that requires working in the model and the functional components [21], where we are looking for new options for training, e.g. presenting works where virtualizations are performed for the interaction of the industrial training in different teams, orienting the future in training [22], is reflected the virtualization of environments in an interactive, educational and training, it allows to improve learning interest, reduce the risk of operating a real machine avoiding accidents and reduce corrective maintenance costs resulting from improper operation [16], there are dives in 3D models for factories where design problems related to human perception can be identified, such as exposing the users to heights without sufficient protection, allowing the training in industrial processes [23]. However, in the different works found in the literature the proposal is made of how to carry out the training processes oriented to industrial processes and more isn't detailed the virtualization of an environment that allows the immersion of the operators.

As described, this article presents the development based of a VR environment oriented to the training and training of personnel in a leather processing plant. For the virtualization of an industrial process, process engineering is carried executing: gathering information, identifying the production system, distributing machinery, verifying the supply chain and describing the work areas with their respective activities. Considering the 3D modeling of: the infrastructure of the plant, machinery, operative and control elements, for the creation of the virtual environment, using CAD software to create the 3D environment of the plant and machinery, followed by the characterization and change of properties of the environment using software design, Blender was used as one of the many options that exist, the next step corresponds to the virtual environment virtualization using Unity 3D, allowing immersion and interaction with (i) the different machines in the production process, (ii) the display of informative and educational messages of each work area, (iii) the visualization of Informative, preventive, obligatory and prohibitive signage; the objective of this project is to train and prepare the new staff or update the staff with new techniques and experiences in the different areas that make up an industrial process as well as prevent accidents involving the different risks to which they are exposed.

This work is divided in 6 sections, including the Introduction; Sect. 2 presents the general description of the problem, its justification and the respective solution proposed; Sect. 3 determines the productive processes of the tannery under study; Sect. 4 illustrates the virtualization of the industrial environment and interaction with processes; Sect. 5 shows experimental results and discussions to finally present the findings of the paper in Sect. 6.

2 Problem Formulation

Currently the industry is organized by hierarchy of processes. The strategic level in charge of indispensable and operational planning, the operational level that composes essential processes for the normal development of the company's activities and the third level of support processes, responsible for activities such as training and security in the company [23]. The training consists of a planned activity, based on the real needs of an organization or company, the main objective is oriented towards a change in the knowledge, skills and attitudes of the worker. Additionally, safety at the plant presents disadvantages to new applicants due to lack of knowledge of accident related procedures or evacuation protocols, so there are more than necessary reasons to apply VR in the industrial sector for training and safety, projects created in VR they allow the visualization of: work environments, necessary information of the variables of the plant, and the control of the machines as: drums, polishers, dividers, among others. In addition, it simulates risk events with the respective indications of correction, prevention.

This article presents a VR environment, which allows the worker to be immersed in the plant, the identification of instruments, machinery, processes, instructions, safety regulations, i.e. the layout of the plant, machinery maneuvering procedures and their process productive. These activities belong to the support level, which is represented in the third level of the hierarchy of processes in Fig. 1, this level focuses on training and safety. And it proposes immersive virtualization through gadgets such as: Unity 3D, Leap Motion and Oculus.

The environment created in Unity 3D presents a dive through virtual reality devices of an industrial plant where they transform bovine cattle skins, the environments that are presented reflect the tanning methods with their respective clarifications about: activities to be carried out in the positions of work, chain of the productive process of tanning and panels of technical assists. Additionally to having the appropriate signage for tanneries

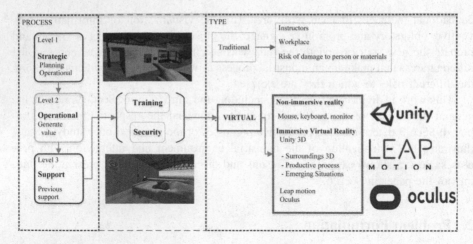

Fig. 1. Process hierarchy.

3   Tannery Process

The tanning industry is responsible for transforming goat-sheep skins, especially bovine animals, into leather indispensable for the manufacture of footwear, upholstery, clothing and special articles [24], constituting itself as the main supplier of raw material and contributing the development of the productive sector, within which it defines fur tanning as a production process that executes several sub processes that may vary according to the company, but the tannery performs four main stages, see Fig. 2. (i) Ribera comprises the cleaning of the skins and consumes more water; (ii) Tanning prepares the skin to be converted into leather by chemical products; (iii) Post-tanning removes excess moisture from the skins for softness; (iv) Finishing provides the leather with specific characteristics according to its purpose [25].

The process of leather tanning begins with the reception of skins that are treated with salt to avoid putrefaction; (i) "Ribera" stage considers sub-processes of: clean Soaking and eliminating organic matter; "Pelambre" uses large amount of water and adds sulfide and lime; "Encalado" shaves and neutralizes the skin; "Descarnado" is responsible for eliminating baits and fats; (ii) Tanning stage performs operations such as: "Desencalado" where it prepares the skin with clean water to remove lime and sulfide using natural or synthetic products; "Piquelado" modifies the acidity of the skin on rotating drums also known as drums; "Curticion" uses a wide variety of chemicals with chromium being the most important [26]; (iii) Post-tanning stage involves mostly mechanical procedures such as: "Drain" removes much of the moisture; "Divided" separates the thinner flower side and the meat side that serves to obtain gelatin; "Rasped" defines the thickness of the leather; "Dyeing" uses dyes based on anilines [27]; (iv) Finishing covers drying operations, final painting of the product either with a brush or with a torch; "Pressed" according to the requirements and purpose of the leather; "Finished" improved texture and performs leather measurement to be stored [28].

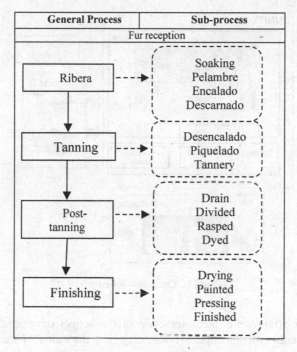

General Process	Sub-process
Fur reception	
Ribera	Soaking Pelambre Encalado Descarnado
Tanning	Desencalado Piquelado Tannery
Post-tanning	Drain Divided Rasped Dyed
Finishing	Drying Painted Pressing Finished

Fig. 2. Flowchart, process of tanning.

4   Virtualization

The virtualization of the environment allows the immersion of the personnel to be trained with the virtual installations, processes and activities regarding the processing of skins, starting from the presentation of the company, followed by the interaction with each one of the processes in a consecutive and orderly way, until the end with the presentation of security signage, in order to train the operator either in a general way or specifically in each of the jobs.

4.1   Interaction Man-Environment

In the environment of Unity 3D, each object has its animation that allows it to simulate the real operation of the processes of the tannery. For this the operating scheme is divided into four parts as shown in Fig. 3. the (i) input scenario. The Oculus Rift allows the immersion to generate a Tridimensional Environment created by the computer, being able to manipulate it by means of a gestural control that is sensed by the device Leap Motion which modifies the values of the variables related to the animations, thus giving to the user a sensation of Total interaction.

In the *(ii)* stage of Unity 3D, the entire shed in the tannery is virtually replicated, allowing the operator to associate with the installations and the different processes. The signage located according to the established in the norms allows to identify the zones of risk and the implements of protection that should be used in the delimited work areas.

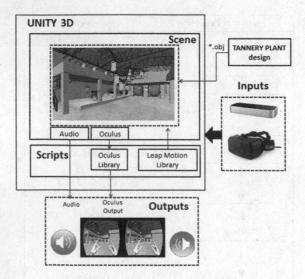

Fig. 3. Operation scheme

The *(iii)* phase represents the interaction of the scripts developed in a C# programming language with the input device, changing the value of the variables and updating the position or rotation of the machines according to their animation or modifying the properties of the animations Which Unity 3D offers us as the steam. Also scripts allow the information to be displayed in a table located in each process so that the operator has the idea of what is wanted developed, the necessary solutions, the recipe and what is obtained after each process. Finally, the *(iv)* output phase relates the feedback that the user has to perform an action in the virtual environment such as the sound of the machines and visual immersion in the virtual environment with the help of the Oculus Rift.

4.2   CAD Modeling

Is presented 3D model of the process in the bovine tanning industry used CAD software [29, 30], for the assembly of different machines, office furniture, factory structure and electrical installations expressed in Fig. 4 exemplifies the sequence of steps of design the tanning process.

Fig. 4. Diagram of 3D objects development for unity

The design of the process of tanning of skins coexists different components established in the diagram of the 3D design; (*i*) Association of actual dimensions of the plant and machinery with the design to be created, (*ii*) Creation of the design in CAD software, as an alternative SolidWorks was used for mechanical modeling in technical drawings and assembling of the different pieces in 3D with extension * .stl [31], (*iii*) Change of dimensions on a proportional scale in each element developed using MeshMagic 3D Modeling, (*iv*) Export to *.obj format and texturizing through Blender as auxiliary software for linking with Unity 3D of the industrial environment.

4.3   Virtualization

The files imported into the Unity 3D software allow to apply to the components: textures, colors, mobility to the machines, informative of each workstation, location of ignites, shutdowns of the machines, signage of the labeling in cases of emergency and restrictions of Walls on the second floor and columns of the first floor of the developing environment.

4.3.1   Factory Structure

The assembly of the factory structure is done in the Unity 3D editor by importing the objects generated in the design process with *obj extension. A 3D object "Plane" is created, which serves as the base and reference for the shed where all the created objects are located. With the transformation tools provided by the software to be able to rotate, move or extend objects according to each axis $<x, y, z>$, they are located according to the layout of the factory.

The downloaded texture graphics are stored inside the project root, the "Assets" folder. These graphics can be attached to a material created through the shaders which are scripts that contain algorithms to process the color of each pixel rendered according to the configuration of the material. This material can easily be attached to each object to give a more real appearance as shown in Fig. 5.

Fig. 5. Factory structure.

For to have a passive physical behavior, *i.e.* without movement, an object can be affected by collisions. In the physics engine that integrates Unity 3D you will find the components that handle these simulations. It adds the physical component "Mesh Collider" that generates a layer of collision according to the mesh of the object, allowing it to behave in a more realistic way.

4.3.2 Security Signage

Curtimbre's signaling is performed considering work sites where it is necessary to sectored in order to be able to clearly distinguish the existence of risks, as well as to determine patterns to follow in each place or situation of risk (prohibitions, precautions and obligations). Figures 6, 7 and 8. Under the following cases:

- When it is not possible to reduce the risk in the activity or process, through safe-guards or safety devices.
- When one could not and turns out to be necessary, protect the worker with PPE (personal protective equipment).
- As a complement to the protection given by guards, safety devices and personal protection.
- To prevent possible fires [32].

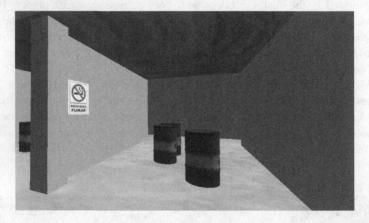

Fig. 6. Signage in the chemical storage.

4.3.3 Animation

The programming of scripts is obligatory to make animations in the virtual environment that respond to inputs of the user in order that the events are executed at the desired moment. Additionally, the scripts allow manipulating the properties of which are formed each object (*i.e.* create motion, disappear the object) or Standard Assets (*i.e.* steam animation).

The animation is developed based on the production process of the tannery for which videos are considered that illustrate the real movement of each machinery

Fig. 7. Signage in the staking process.

Fig. 8. Signage in the process of debasing.

obtaining thus the movement to be simulated, e.g., in the process of retanning the machine must rotate according to a only axis, thus creating the animation of the movement of the drum as shown in Fig. 9.

The Fig. 10 represents the script scheme used for motion animation of objects:

To perform the motion animation of the objects we need to obtain the data of their current position $<x, y, z>$, with this data we can perform an animation algorithm updating the value of the variables. In order to properly display the animation, the "Time.deltaTime" function is used, which increases or decreases the frame rate, so that it does not depend on the speed of the processor in which the application is running.

The "transform.localPosition" function updates the position of the object by generating a vertical, horizontal or diagonal motion animation by modifying the values of the variables found in a three-dimensional vector "Vector3" that contains the positions of the object; the "transform.Rotate" function allows you to rotate the object according to the $<x, y, z>$ axis at the same time or individually by setting zero to the other

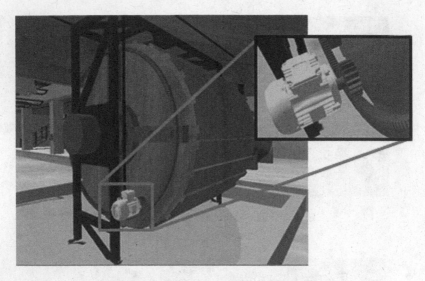

Fig. 9. Animation in the retanning process.

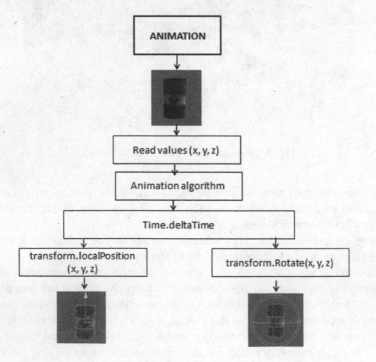

Fig. 10. Animation script.

values. The direction of the rotation depends on the sign with which the positive variable is found (schedule) or negative (anti-schedule).

Once the script is loaded to animate an object, Unity 3D allows inheriting these animations to another object, just by dragging this one inside the other already animated object in the hierarchy window which will be called child object, this was applied in the air Drying process by putting the leathers on the structure rails these acquire the same animation automatically.

The Standar Assets allow us to include animations already created as steam Fig. 11, similarly it has its own properties like "Ellipsoid Particle Emitter" (Min Energy, Max Energy), which allows us to increase or decrease the amount of steam generated being controlled using the variable "Max Energy".

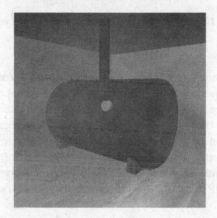

Fig. 11. Virtual environment of the cauldron, with steam simulation.

4.4 Information of the Processes Operation

For the processes of training of the operators it is necessary that previously be relations conceptually with the machinery and the process that performs. For this purpose, in this work, information panels are proposed by means of "Scroll Views", in which the following information is detailed for the process of soaking the skins:

- State that enters the leather.
- Recipe to be used according to the leather to be obtained.
- The necessary solutions.
- The time set.
- The characteristics of the leather that is obtained after finishing the process.
- The consequences of a bad process.
- Specifies the process that continues.

In the Fig. 12 showed the information displayed in a table that describe the tanning process.

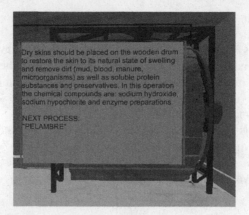

Fig. 12. Information panel of the tanning process.

Control of Machinery

The control of the machines is done by means of buttons located on the panel individually for each machine, according to their shape and actual position in the plant.

For to activate or deactivate the machines a script is created that is loaded in the buttons, which changes the value of the variables when detecting a user input, i.e., when pressing the button on or off. These variables are sent to the animation scripts comparing these values in order to start the animation or not. When the "START" button is activated, it sends the letter "a" and when it is deactivated, it sends the letter "b", so like the "STOP" button. In this case, the letters sent are "c" and "d" respectively.

In the real environment in a control panel can't be activated the two buttons "START" and "STOP" at the same time because it could damage the elements of the same, so this concept was validated exchanged the value of the variables between the two buttons also, so if the "START" button is pressed and the "STOP" button is pressed the first button is automatically deactivated Fig. 13.

 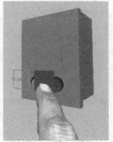

(a) Turn on machine   (b) Turn off machine

Fig. 13. Control panel of estacado process.

In the estacado process, apart from having the control panel there is also a temperature controller which handles the same logic as the "START" and "STOP" buttons; only it increases and decreases the value of a variable that represents the temperature and is displayed in the controller. This variable is also sent to the animation script to increase or decrease the steam generated by the machine Fig. 14.

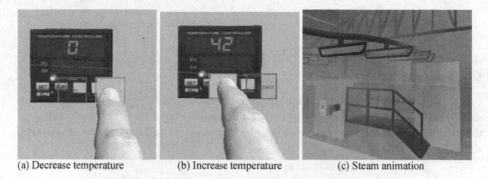

(a) Decrease temperature   (b) Increase temperature   (c) Steam animation

Fig. 14. Temperature controller of estacado process.

5   Results and Discussions

This section presents the virtualization of the "Curtiembre Quisapincha" located in the city of Ambato - Ecuador. The tannery is a microenterprise whose purpose is to obtain leather for clothing, footwear, upholstery of vehicles, accessories, among others, with an extension of 300 m², has 15 years of operation in which it has sought to extend its product to the market Internationally, for which it has increased its industrial, productive and technological development, as an option is the training of its personnel under new and modern strategies as it is the "Immersion in virtual reality", since it allows to train the personnel under safe conditions and without danger of suffering an accident at work. This innovation allows to have economic, legal benefits, technological advances, and even environmental inside and outside the organization.

To continuation is detailed the skins tannery process in sequential order, in which four wooden drums are used for the different activities such as: soaking, "pelambre", "tannery" and cutting, and the association of the other machines allows to create the environment for the immersion in the virtual reality of leather processing.

(i)   *Soaking Process*

It is the first process that the skins are subjected in which they are placed in the wood drum for the purpose of removing the salt, rehydrate the skin and remove the dirt (mud, blood, manure, microorganisms) see Fig. 15. In this operation the chemical compounds are: sodium hydroxide, sodium hypochlorite and enzyme preparations.

| (a) Turn-on the machine | (b) Wood drum for the Soaking process |

Fig. 15. Soaking process

(ii) **Pelambre Process**

This process allows hair to dissolve from the skins by adding a solution of sodium sulfide with lime and stirring for a period of one day in order to promote a swelling of the skin that promotes a loosening of the reticular structure and thus can be descarnado, see Fig. 16.

| (a) Turn-on the machine. | (b) Wood drum for the pelambre process |

Fig. 16. Pelambre process

(iii) **Descarnado Process**

This is a mechanical operation as shown in Fig. 17 in which the skins are received to remove the "carnosidades", the fat and the pieces of deteriorated skin, by means of a machine called "descarnadora". This process works with a machine that has spiral blades, which separate the adipose tissue and muscle remains, leaving the surface of the meat side of the skin clean and even.

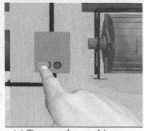

| (a) Turn-on the machine. | (b) Machine of Descanado process. |

Fig. 17. Descarnado process

(iv) **Tannery Process**

As part of the staff training, the information panels are used to detail the tanning process as shown in Fig. 18.

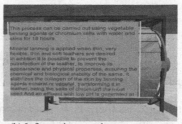

(a) Interaction of staff with the environment   (b) Information panel

Fig. 18. Tannery Process

(v) **Retanning Process**

It is the treatment of leather tanned with one or more chemicals to complete the tanning or give final characteristics to the leather that are not obtainable with the single conventional tanning, a fuller leather, with better resistance to water, greater softness or to favor the equalization of dyeing, is one of the most important operations because it would directly influence the lubrication, dyeing and finishing and will define the final characteristics of the leather see Fig. 19.

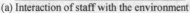

(a) Turn-on the machine.   (b) Retanning leather in the drum.

Fig. 19. Retanning process

(vi) **Drain Process**

In this area they try to prevent the edges of the skin from drying out. If this occurs, it crystallizes the salts already contained in the skin, which will lead to problems in the subsequent processes, here the skin and/or leather eliminate the Moisture by means of two rollers as shown in Fig. 20, leaving the final moisture at 20% of the dry skin weight.

(a) Turn-on the machine.   (b) Drained leather

Fig. 20. Drain process.

(vii) *Estacado Process*

In this process there is a estacado machine as shown in Fig. 21, which consists of several smooth stainless steel platforms with holes and a cover containing several systems. In addition the workers take the leather to these plates to be extended in each one and to be able to evaporate the water of the skins.

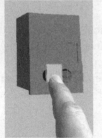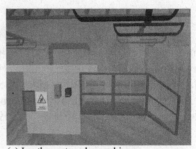

(a) Turn-on the machine.   (b) Setting the temperature   (c) Leather estacado machine.

Fig. 21. Estacado process.

(viii) *Air Drying Process*

In the Fig. 22. shows aerial drying that does not compromise the skin at all, the leather reaches the final equilibrium slowly even with the use of less heat, the absence

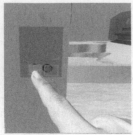

(a) Turn-on the machine.   (b) Air Drying Machine.

Fig. 22. Air drying process

of the tweezers allows the leathers to "shrink" by presenting, at the end of the drying, a remarkable softness and fluidity but, at the same time, a remarkable compactness. The disadvantage is that it takes a longer time and it requires a large outdoor space indoors.

(ix) *Leather Measurement Process*

The tanning industry markets leather by surface. The measurement of the skin depends on the state in which it is. Due to the irregular shape of the leathers to know their surface, highly accurate scanners are used as shown in Fig. 23. Once the entire process of tanning is finished, each leather passes through a scanner which captures and returns the value of the area in square feet which is displayed on the computer to which the scanner is connected.

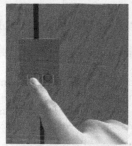 

(a) Turn-on the machine.   (b) Leather Scanner

(c) Scan result

Fig. 23. Measurement of final product.

6   Conclusions

To perform the virtualization of the process of tanning vaccines was linked several tools of 3D design; for which previously the information was collected from the respective processes of the plant with the purpose of modeling and reproducing their movements as real as possible. The proposed environment enabled the operator to be trained through immersion and interaction in the processes and their respective machines without physical, chemical, mechanical, biologic, ergonomic and psychological risks, through the visualization of: technical assistance panels, Information security, mandatory, preventive and prohibition, making staff develop their skills efficiently, improve performance with virtual immersion in work areas.

References

1. Cramer, H.S.M., Evers, V., Zudilova, E.V., Sloot, P.M.A.: Context analysis to support development of virtual reality applications. Virtual Real. **7**, 177–186 (2004). Springer, London
2. Puerta, A., Jimeno, A.: State of the art of the virtual reality applied to design and manufacturing processes. Int. J. Adv. Manuf. Technol. **33**, 866–874 (2007). Springer, London
3. Marini, D., Folgieri, R., Gadia, D., Rizzi, A.: Virtual reality as a communication process. Virtual Real. **16**, 233–241 (2012). Springer, London
4. Moore, T., Choo, J., Jones, T.: The impact of virtual reality on chronic pain (2016). Elseiver, Tokai Daigaku, JAPAN, 20 December 2016
5. Federation of State Medical Boards (FSMB): Model Policy on the Use of Opioid Analgesics in the Treatment of Chronic Pain. The Federation, Washington, DC (2013)
6. Marsch, L.A., Joseph, H., Portnoy, R.K., Rosenblum, A.: Opioids and the treatment of chronic pain: Controversies, current status, and future directions. Exp. Clin. Psychopharmacol. **16**(5), 405–416 (2008)
7. Brinton, J.M., Hancock, A.B., Brundage, S.B.: Utility of virtual reality environments to examine physiological reactivity and subjective distress in adults who stutter, 85–95 (2016). ELSEVIER, Washington DC, United States
8. Cheok, A.D., Yang, H., Zhu, J., Shi, J., Pan, Z.: Virtual reality and mixed reality for virtual learning environments. Comput. Graph. **30**(1), 20–28 (2006)
9. Tsai, J.-P., Cheng, H.-Y., Chao, C.-C., Kao, Y.-C.: Development of a virtual reality wire electrical discharge machining system for operation training. Int. J. Adv. Manuf. Technol. **54** (5), 605–618 (2011)
10. Méndez, C.L.M., de Pedro Carracedo, J.: Realidad Aumentada: Una Alternativa Metodológica en la Educación Primaria Nicaragüense. IEEE **7**(2) (2012)
11. Rambli, D.R.A., Sumadio, D.D.: Preliminary evaluation on user acceptance of the augmented reality use for education. In: Second International Conference on Computer Engineering and Applications (ICCEA), 19–21 March 2010, vol. 2, pp. 461-465 (2010)
12. Monteiro, D., Girard-Dias, W., dos Santos, T.O., Belmonte, S.L.R., Augusto, I.: Virtual reconstruction and three-dimensional printing of blood cells as a tool in cell biology education (2016). US National Library of Medicine National Institutes of Health, 15 August 2016
13. Nagasawa, D.T., Lagman, C., Tenn, S., Demos, J.V., Lee, S.J., Bui, T.T., Barnette, N.E., Bhatt, N.S., Ung, N., Bari, A., Martin, N.A., Panayiotis, I.Y., Pelargos, E.: Utilizing virtual and augmented reality for educational and clinical **35**, 1–4 (2017). ELSEVIER
14. Andaluz, V.H., Sánchez, J.S., Chamba, J.I., Romero, P.P., Chicaiza, F.A., Varela, J., Quevedo, W.X., Gallardo, C., Cepeda, Luis F.: Unity3D virtual animation of robots with coupled and uncoupled mechanism. In: De Paolis, L.T., Mongelli, A. (eds.) AVR 2016. LNCS, vol. 9768, pp. 89–101. Springer, Cham (2016). doi:10.1007/978-3-319-40621-3_6

15. Andaluz, V.H., Chicaiza, F.A., Gallardo, C., Quevedo, W.X., Varela, J., Sánchez, J.S., Arteaga, O.: Unity3D-MatLab simulator in real time for robotics applications. In: De Paolis, L.T., Mongelli, A. (eds.) AVR 2016. LNCS, vol. 9768, pp. 246–263. Springer, Cham (2016). doi:10.1007/978-3-319-40621-3_19

16. Querrec, R., Chevaillier, P.: Virtual storytelling for training: an application to fire fighting in industrial environment. In: Balet, O., Subsol, G., Torguet, P. (eds.) ICVS 2001. LNCS, vol. 2197, pp. 201–204. Springer, Heidelberg (2001). doi:10.1007/3-540-45420-9_22

17. do Espírito Santo, A.C., Marins, E.R., da Silva, M.H.: Using virtual reality to support the physical security of nuclear. Prog. Nucl. Energy **78**, 19–24 (2015). ELSEVIER, Rio de Janeiro

18. Kirkley, S.E., Kirkley, J.R.: Creating next generation blended learning environments using mixed reality, video games and simulations. TechTrends **49**(3), 42–53 (2005)

19. Brey, P.: Virtual reality and computer simulation. In: Sandler, R.L. (ed.) Ethics and Emerging Technologies, pp. 315–332. Springer, London (2008)

20. Schina, L., Lazoi, M., Lombardo, R., Corallo, A.: Virtual reality for product development in manufacturing industries. In: De Paolis, L.T., Mongelli, A. (eds.) AVR 2016. LNCS, vol. 9768, pp. 198–207. Springer, Cham (2016). doi:10.1007/978-3-319-40621-3_15

21. Mollet, N., Arnaldi, B.: Storytelling in virtual reality for training. In: Pan, Z., Aylett, R., Diener, H., Jin, X., Göbel, S., Li, L. (eds.) Edutainment 2006. LNCS, vol. 3942, pp. 334–347. Springer, Heidelberg (2006). doi:10.1007/11736639_45

22. Colley, A., Väyrynen, J., Häkkilä, J.: Exploring the use of virtual environments in an industrial site design process. In: Abascal, J., Barbosa, S., Fetter, M., Gross, T., Palanque, P., Winckler, M. (eds.) INTERACT 2015. LNCS, vol. 9299, pp. 363–380. Springer, Cham (2015). doi:10.1007/978-3-319-22723-8_29

23. Vergara, J.: Jerarquización de las actividades de un SGC. In: La gestión de la calidad en los servicio ISO 9001:2008, p. 88. Eumed - Universidad de Málaga, Málaga (2010)

24. Mijaylova, P., López, S., Ramírez, E., Cardoso, L.: Tecnología para la remoción y recuperación del cromo trivalente en efluentes de curtido de pieles. Ingeniería hidráulica en México **18**(1), 21–27 (2003)

25. Méndez, R., Vidal, G., Lorber, K., Márquez, F.: Análisis de los flujos de materia en las industrias de curtido. In: Producción Limpia en la Industria de Curtiembre. Servicio de Publicaciones e Intercambio Científico, Santiago de Compostela, pp. 63–68 (2007)

26. Colin, V., Villegas, L., Abate, C.: Indigenous microorganisms as potential bioremediators for environments contaminated with heavy metals **69**, 28 (2012). Elsevier

27. Chávez, Á.: Descripción de la nocividad del cromo proveniente de la industria curtiembre y de las posibles formas de removerlo. Revista Ingenierías Universidad de Medellín **9**(17), 41–50 (2010)

28. Téllez, J., Carvajal, R., Gaitán, A.: Aspectos toxicológicos relacionados con la utilización del cromo en el proceso productivo de curtiembres. Revista de la Facultad de Medicina de Bogotá **52**(1), 50–61 (2004)

29. Teyseyre, A., Campo, M.: An overview of 3D software visualization. IEEE Trans. Visual Comput. Graph. **15**(1), 87–105 (2009)

30. Lim, T., Ritchie, J., Louchart, S., Liu, Y., Sung, R., Kosmadoudi, Z.: Engineering design using game-enhanced CAD: the potential to augment the user experience with game elements. Comput.-Aided Des. **45**(3), 777–7795 (2012)

31. Kamarul, A., Norlida, B., Rosidah, S.: Simulation of pick and place robotics system using solidworks softmotion. In: International Conference on System Engineering and Technology, Bandung, Indonesia, 11–12 September 2012 (2012)

32. Ministerio de Relaciones Laborales: Señalización. Requisitos. Código: DSST-NT-21, 27 September 2013

Virtual Environments for Motor Fine Skills Rehabilitation with Force Feedback

Víctor H. Andaluz[1,2(✉)], Cartagena Patricio[2], Naranjo José[2],
Agreda José[2], and López Shirley[2]

[1] Universidad de las Fuerzas Armadas ESPE, Sangolquí, Ecuador
vhandaluz1@espe.edu.ec
[2] Universidad Técnica de Ambato, Ambato, Ecuador
{victorhanadaluz, cartagenapatojr,
jnaranjo0463, j.agreda4462, slopez9101}@uta.edu.ec

Abstract. In this paper, it is proposed an application to stimulate the motor fine skills rehabilitation by using a bilateral system which allows to sense the upper limbs by ways of a device called Leap Motion. This system is implemented through a human-machine interface, which allows to visualize in a virtual environment the feedback forces sent by a hand orthosis which was printed and designed in an innovative way using NinjaFlex material, it is also commanded by four servomotors that eases the full development of the proposed tasks. The patient is involved in an assisted rehabilitation based on therapeutic exercises, which were developed in several environments and classified due to the patient's motor degree disability. The experimental results show the efficiency of the system which is generated by the human-machine interaction, oriented to develop human fine motor skills.

Keywords: Rehabilitation · Unity3D · Virtual reality · Orthosis · Fine motor skills · Force feedback

1 Introduction

Virtual reality has significantly advanced in the last decade. The practical applications for the use of this technology include several fields ranging from the training of industrial machinery to medicine, where doctor and even medical interns are trained by means of VR [1]. In the las few years, there have been great advances in the application of virtual reality systems focused on the rehabilitation of several deficiencies resulting from injuries belonging to the nervous system [1, 2]. One of the main areas is the rehabilitation of stroke patients especially focused on those who have a malfunction of their upper limbs. According to the WHO about 15% of the world population live with some type of disability [3]; nevertheless, this kind of harm represents the major cause of disability worldwide with a relatively high percentage of patients experiencing long-term persistent functional disabilities [4, 5].

Physical rehabilitation is a process which is applied to people who have deficiencies and disabilities that can be permanent or temporary, it allows to recover the loss of motor skills and to prevent or reduce functional impairment. In order to achieve this

© Springer International Publishing AG 2017
L.T. De Paolis et al. (Eds.): AVR 2017, Part I, LNCS 10324, pp. 94–105, 2017.
DOI: 10.1007/978-3-319-60922-5_7

goal the patient has to accomplish the proposed tasks, in addition to being given advice and educational measures besides to technical aids and ease of adaptation to the environment [6]. In order to have a more holistic view of a person's motor damage, it is imperative to know the rehabilitation process in terms of three concepts: (i) Impairment: any loss or abnormality of psychological, physiological or anatomical structure or function [7]; (ii) Disability: any restriction or lack (resulting from an impairment) of ability to perform an activity in the manner or within the range considered normal for a human being [8]; and finally (iii) Handicap: a disadvantage for a given individual, resulting from an impairment or disability, that limits or prevents the fulfilment of a role that is normal (depending on age, sex, and social and cultural factors) for that individual [2–9].

In order to obtain a successful fine motor skills rehabilitation, it is necessary to analyze three important concepts: (i) Repetition is necessary for both motor learning and the cortical changes that produce it. However, only repetition of certain activities does not produce a motor learning, this repetition must be linked to a goal that, as it advances, will have a greater degree of difficulty [10]; (ii) Feedback allows the patient to know if the movements and exercises he is performing meet the desired goal [11]; and (iii) Motivation is the one that allows the patient to persist and to fulfill in a satisfactory way the set forth objectives [12]. The set of these three aspects allows to perform the necessary repetitions, to memorize the movements and thus to improve the fine motor skills of the user.

Several VR applications focused on motor rehabilitation have been developed using different technologies that present potential benefits of numerous proposed systems [13, 14]. For example, a two-case study using Vivid GX video capture technology demonstrates a notable improvement in the upper limb functionality of the subjects under study [15]; while another VR study focusing on fine motor recovery due to cerebrovascular damage shows that with an average of three to four intensive therapy sessions per day for two weeks, each treated patient regained most of the movement in their affected hand; in addition to improving prevailing motor skills such as their grip strength and elasticity [16].

On the other hand, service robotics like VR has a great impact in the area of fine motor rehabilitation due to the proposal of scientific community to create several systems that have as purpose to provide the patient with a tool that improves their quality of life and labor productivity. Robotics focuses on the development of devices to help the different sensory motor functions [17]; among the main developed devices are prostheses, exoskeletons and orthoses, which help in the different processes of patient recovery, for which different schemes of advanced control based on different sensing systems have been proposed in order to stimulate and promote the use of these robotic systems during the rehabilitation process [18, 19].

As described in previous paragraphs, this article proposes a bilateral rehabilitation system for fine motor with feedback of forces through an active orthosis. The proposed system allows sensing through the Leap Motion device [20] fine motor movements by means of a hand orthosis, whose ergonomic design allows different rehabilitation sessions in which objects handling tasks are considered. The designed orthosis was built with Ninjaflex filament, whose properties of thermoplastic elastomer open a world of possibilities in 3D printing, providing the necessary flexibility and comfort for the patient to carry out his rehabilitation tasks. In addition, an application developed in virtual reality using Unity 3D graphics engine is presented [21]; the interface allows the patient to visualize predetermined movements focused on his area. The movements are controlled and guided in a semi-assisted way by the built orthosis. Finally, it is presented the experimental results in which a session of movements associated to daily tasks for the patient is considered; which is why one of the advantages of the proposed system is that in addition to being comfortable and affordable for the patient, it helps in its therapeutic process of rehabilitation while immersing it in a new virtual world that stimulates and motivates to complete every single proposed task during its recovery.

This article is divided into 6 sections including the Introduction. Section 2 presents the structure of the proposed rehabilitation system; while in the graphically developed virtual reality environment is presented in Sect. 3. In Sect. 4 is shown the construction of the orthosis to be used for the feedback of forces when performing predefined tasks. The experimental results are presented in Sect. 5; and finally, the conclusions are detailed in Sect. 6.

2   Rehabilitation System Structure

The proposed system allows a feedback of fine motor movements to patients who have little or no mobility at their upper limbs. This rehabilitation system is safe and comfortable to use, in addition to entertaining the patient while rehabilitating [22, 23]. Figure 1 describes the patient's interaction with the proposed system, establishing as the main element of communication the feedback that covers the two main actions within a virtual environment, observe and act.

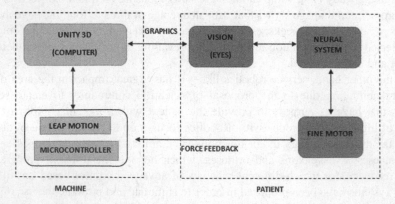

Fig. 1. Block Diagram of the Rehabilitation System

The interaction between the patient and the system is established by means of a bilateral communication, *i.e.*, first through a graphical interface the movement that the patient must execute is displayed; second the patient generates the movement trying to complete the preset exercise. Due to its motor deficiency, the movement performed by the patient is sensed through the Leap Motion device so that the hand orthosis commanded by four servos motors generates the necessary feedback of forces to reach the desired final position. The visual environment developed for this type of rehabilitation provides a systematic application which the patient first analyzes and then generates the necessary movements in order to complete the defined task.

3   Graphical Environment

The graphical environment defines the workspace where the patient manipulates environments modeled by collision regions in a real environment, thus controlling the procedures required for graphical deployment. The objective is to interact with the surfaces and environments of the interface with the purpose of generating the rehabilitation of the patient in the affected area. To improve and give more reliability to the proposed rehabilitation system, the patient's needs are identified in order to specify a suitable environment that is in accordance with the severity of its the injury [24]. Figure 2 exemplifies the programmed environment.

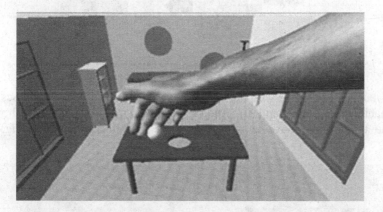

Fig. 2. Programmed environment

For the development of the rehabilitation environment, the Unity3D graphics engine is used. In the Unity3D environment the control scripts for each virtual device are programmed to respond in a real way according to the rehabilitation movements performed by the study subject. Figure 3 shows the proposed operation scheme, which is divided into 3 modules: (*i*) *Input Module* in order to control in closed loop the movement of the patient in each exercise inherent to the established therapy, it is proposed to use the device Leap Motion to sense the vectorized position of each finger that moves the patient either using the orthosis or not. In addition, it is proposed the use of the head mounting screen, HMD, Oculus Rift; device that allows the immersion of the patient in a virtual reality environment by monitoring the HMD in space, in order to modify the patient's viewing angle according to the exercise being performed.

For the (*ii*) *Interfaces Module* several virtual environments are developed so that the patient through a menu of options can select: (a) motor deficiency degree that can

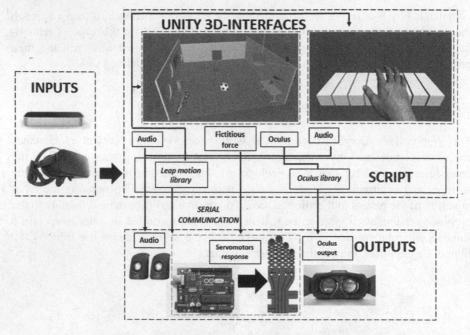

Fig. 3. Operation scheme

be mild, medium or chronic with the purpose to establish the different exercises that fit to its rehabilitation routine; and (b) virtual environment in order to motivate the patient to execute the different movements planned in the rehabilitation sessions (Fig. 4).

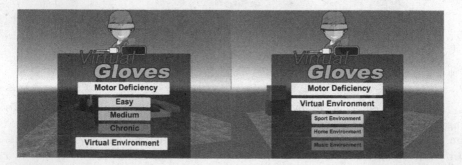

Fig. 4. Interfaces Module

This paper proposes the development of a virtual environment that allows the selection of the work environment, e.g., sports environment, office environment, fun environments, home environment, among other options, see Fig. 5. Depending on the patient's requirements, the movements incorporated in the different rehabilitation sessions are based on the task execution time, grip strength and displacement of the fingers of the upper extremities, see Fig. 6.

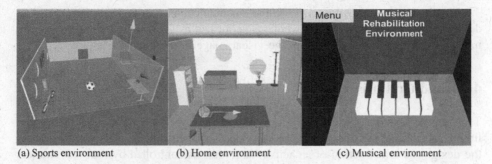

(a) Sports environment   (b) Home environment   (c) Musical environment

Fig. 5. Virtual work environments.

(a) Elongation of fan-shaped fingers

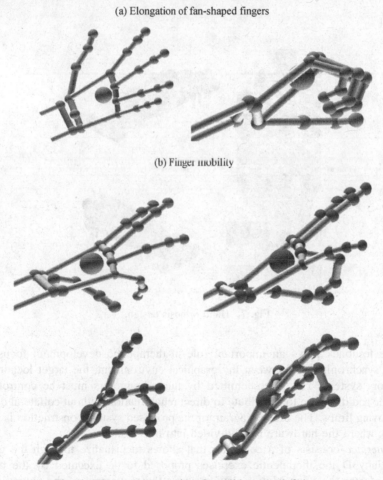

(b) Finger mobility

Fig. 6. Therapeutic exercises for mild motor deficiency.

Finally, in the *(iii) Output Module* the communication port that involves the input devices is assigned; so that the movements performed by the patient under study can be interpreted; also through this script the visual image of the interface is provided.

4   Hand Orthosis

The proposed system is exclusively focused on people with low mobility at their upper limbs, specifically the fine motor part developed by their fingers; This work proposes the design and construction of an active hand orthosis controlled by four servomotors that generate a tensile force in each one of the fingers allowing them to give greater maneuverability assisted by the rehabilitation session. Figure 7 shows the design of the ergonomic orthosis constructed and used for force feedback applied to rehabilitation therapies.

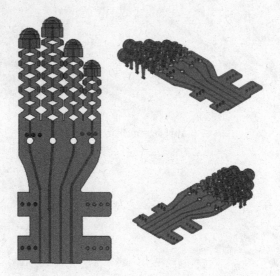

Fig. 7. Hand orthosis design.

Force feedback plays an important role in therapeutic development focused on ensuring synchronization between the graphical environment, the target location and the sensory system. The forces emitted by the servomotors must be controlled in magnitude and direction to contribute to direct rehabilitation without collateral damage to the moving limbs. The block diagram of the proposed system construction is shown in Fig. 8, where the hardware is subdivided into five modules.

(i) Interface consists of a computer that allows to visualize through the graphic engine Unity3D the therapeutic exercises proposed to be executed by the patient; *(ii) Transductor* the Leap Motion device senses the movement of the patient's hand under study in the three reference axes X-Y-Z of an inertial reference system. Sensing is done by means of an infrared light emitted through three LEDs, which produces a

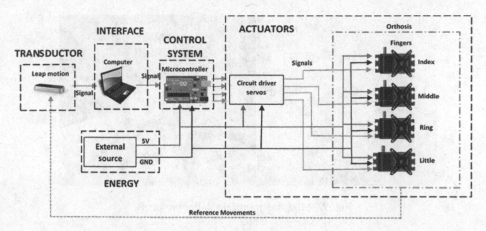

Fig. 8. Hardware Block diagram

reflection of light that reaches the device and impinges on the lenses of the two cameras it has, storing the data in the form of a matrix, digitized image (*iii*) *Control system* is composed of the microcontroller Arduino which receives the signal sent by Unity3D and performs the internal control of the actuators (*iv*) *Actuators* consist of HS-311 servomotors, which support a constant current of 7.4 [mA]; and finally (*v*) *Energy* constituted by an external source that converts 110 [v] of alternate current into 5 [v] DC in order to feed both the actuators and the microcontroller.

5   Results and Discussions

The tasks proposed to improve the fine motor skills of the subjects under study, cover a wide range of options; this is due to the motor difficulty of each patient, whether these are mild, middle or chronic injuries; so, that the rehabilitation task that most closely matches the injury can be selected, under the supervision of the physiotherapist.

The protocol to be followed for a person with mild fine motor disability is presented below: the patient sits on a chair, observing the virtual environment through the Oculus Rift device or a computer, see Fig. 9. In case that the Oculus Rift is used; the patient will have a complete immersion experience in the development of his therapy, due to the combination of the wide angle of vision and its precise low latency constellation tracking system. Once the subject under study is immersed in his therapy; he will have the possibility of interacting in a personalized way with the proposed rehabilitation exercise, observing a virtual hand in the first person that simulates the movement of his own hand, i.e., the movements made by the virtual hand correspond to the movements of the real hand.

After this task, the patient selects from the menu of options displayed on the screen the type of rehabilitation exercise that he requires, for this case opening-closing hand; once this exercise has been completed (10 min), the patient takes a rest period (3 min) and repeats his rehabilitation process three times.

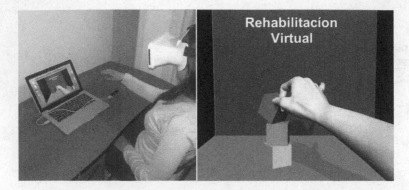

Fig. 9. Mild fine motor disability protocol

The protocol to be followed for a person with medium fine motor disability considers that the subject of study use the rehabilitation system in three stages. In the first
stage (evaluation) the patient must, without any help, perform an opening-closing
movement of his hand according to his limitations for 1 min. The second stage lasts for
5 min, the patient places the orthosis in the affected limb, and then it is placed on an
armrest, see Fig. 10.

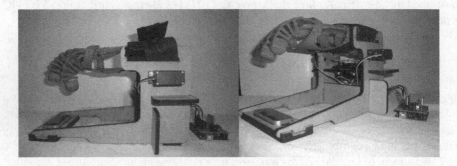

Fig. 10. Orthosis placed in armrest

In this phase the patient must perform two types of exercises: opening-closing
hand; and fingers mobility shown in Fig. 11.

The movements to be performed are completely assisted by the hand orthosis, the
objective of this task is that the patient's affected hand acquire both sensitivity and
flexibility in their joints. In the last phase (training phase, 10 min), the patient is
partially assisted by the servo motors that command the orthosis; once it has reached
the full range of its movement, the servo motors help him to complete the exercise in a
gentle and leisurely manner in order not to cause any collateral damage.

The protocol to be followed for a person with chronic fine motor disability considers
that the study subject uses the proposed system in a single stage: the physiotherapist in
charge of the rehabilitation program proceeds to place the hand orthosis in the patient's

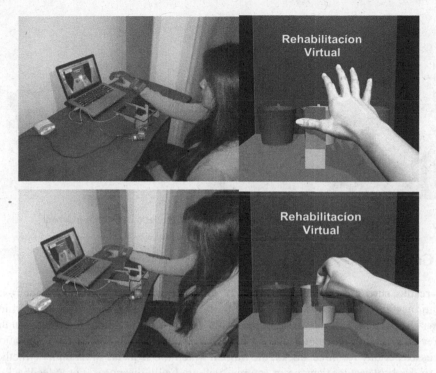

Fig. 11. Chronic fine motor disability protocol. Opening-closing hand

affected area and then locate his affected limb in the armrest. Due to the subjects considered for this stage do not have any degree of mobility in their injured limb, sessions of about 6 min of programmable movements and completely assisted by the servomotors that allow the opening-closing movement are necessary (a rest period is necessary of about 2 min between each session), i.e., movements performed autonomously by the orthosis reactive nervous memories, progressively returning the flexibility and movement of each of the fingers of the injured hand; See Figs. 12 and 13.

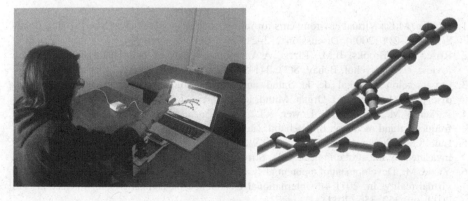

Fig. 12. Chronic fine motor disability protocol – Finger mobility

Fig. 13. Chronic fine motor disability protocol - Semi assisted movement

6 Conclusions

The results shown by the development of virtual environments for fine motor reha-bilitation with force feedback demonstrate the efficiency of proposed system, which allows the patient to substantially improve his fine motor skills, since depending on the degree of disability inherent to the patient it will be required at least two rehabilitation processes per day for three weeks, the time in which the sequelae of an injury, whether due to cerebrovascular damage or trauma, will gradually disappear. Force feedback is an alternative method to rehabilitation used in a conventional way, which aims to rehabilitate, entertain and immerse the patient in a virtual world with a wide range of possibilities for physical rehabilitation. For a future work it is proposed the imple-mentation of augmented reality, which will allow to enrich the patient's visual expe-rience by overlapping artificial realities, in addition to improving the user's interaction with his type of physiotherapy.

References

1. Holden, M.K.: Virtual environments for motor rehabilitation: review. Cyberpsychol. Behav. **8**(3), 187–211 (2005). Discussion 212–219
2. Rose, F.D., Brooks, B.M., Rizzo, A.A.: Virtual reality in brain damage rehabilitation: review. CyberPsychol. Behav. **8**(3), 241–262 (2005)
3. Organización Mundial de la Salud and Banco Mundial: Informe mundial sobre la discapacidad (Resumen), Organ. Mund. la Salud, p. 27 (2011)
4. Parker, V.M., Wade, D.T., Hewer, R.L.: Loss of arm function after stroke: measurement, frequency, and recovery. Int. Rehabil. Med. **8**(2), 69–73 (1986)
5. Lai, S.M., Studenski, S., Duncan, P.W., Perera, S.: Persisting consequences of stroke measured by the stroke impact scale. Stroke **33**(7), 1840–1844 (2002)
6. Yazid, M.: Development of a potential system for upper limb rehabilitation training based on virtual reality. In: 2011 4th International Conference on Human System Interactions HSI 2011, pp. 352–356 (2011)

7. Petersen, R.: Mild cognitive impairment **56**, 303–309 (2014)
8. WHO: International classification of impairment, disabilities and handicaps. World Health Organization, Geneva, May 1976 (1980)
9. van Swieten, J.C., Koudstaal, P.J., Visser, M.C., Schouten, H.J., van Gijn, J.: Interobserver agreement for the assessment of handicap in stroke patients. Stroke **19**(5), 604–607 (1988)
10. Krampe, R.T.: Aging, expertise and fine motor movement. Neurosci. Biobehav. Rev. **26**(7), 769–776 (2002)
11. van Vliet, P.M., Wulf, G.: Extrinsic feedback for motor learning after stroke: what is the evidence? Disabil. Rehabil. **28**(13–14), 831–840 (2006)
12. Byl, N., et al.: Effectiveness of sensory and motor rehabilitation of the upper limb following the principles of neuroplasticity: patients stable poststroke. Neurorehabil. Neural Repair **17** (3), 176–191 (2003)
13. Kizony, R., Katz, N., Weiss, P.L.: Adapting an immersive virtual reality system for rehabilitation. J. Vis. Comput. Animat. **14**(5), 261–268 (2003)
14. Deutsch, J.E., Latonio, J., Burdea, G.C., Boian, R.: Post-stroke rehabilitation with the rutgers ankle system: a case study. Presence Teleoperators Virtual Environ. **10**(4), 416–430 (2001)
15. Sveistrup, H.: Motor rehabilitation using virtual reality. J. Neuroeng. Rehabil. **1**, 10 (2004)
16. Jack, D., et al.: Virtual reality-enhanced stroke rehabilitation. IEEE Trans. Neural Syst. Rehabil. Eng. **9**(3), 308–318 (2001)
17. Alejandro, M., Cardona, C., Spitia, F.R., López, A.B.: Exoesqueletos para potenciar las capacidades humanas y apoyar la rehabilitación. Rev. Ing. Biomédica **4**, 63–73 (2010)
18. Kuhtz-Buschbeck, J.P., Hoppe, B., Gölge, M., Dreesmann, M., Damm-Stünitz, U., Ritz, A.: Sensorimotor recovery in children after traumatic brain injury: analyses of gait, gross motor, and fine motor skills. Dev. Med. Child Neurol. **45**(12), 821–828 (2003)
19. Taylor, C.L., Harris, S.R.: Effects of ankle-foot orthosis on functional motor performance in a child with spastic diplegia. Am. J. Occup. Ther. Off. Publ. Am. Occup. Ther. Assoc. **40**(7), 492–494 (1986)
20. Iosa, M., et al.: Leap motion controlled videogame-based therapy for rehabilitation of elderly patients with subacute stroke: a feasibility pilot study. Top. Stroke Rehabil. **22**(4), 306–316 (2015)
21. Unity (2004). https://unity3d.com/unity
22. Andaluz, V., Salazar, P., Silva, S., Escudero, V., Bustamante, D.: Rehabilitation of upper limb with force feedback. In: 2016 IEEE International Conference on Automatica (ICA-ACCA) (2016)
23. Andaluz, V.H., et al.: Virtual reality integration with force feedback in upper limb rehabilitation. In: Bebis, G., et al. (eds.) ISVC 2016. LNCS, vol. 10073, pp. 259–268. Springer, Cham (2016). doi:10.1007/978-3-319-50832-0_25
24. Matos, N., Santos, A., Vasconcelos, A.: ICTs for improving Patients Rehabilitation Research Techniques. Commun. Comput. Inf. Sci. **515**(97753), 143–154 (2015)

Towards Modeling of Finger Motions in Virtual Reality Environment

Sven Nõmm[1]([⊠]), Aaro Toomela[2], and Jaroslav Kulikov[1]

[1] Department of Software Science, Tallinn University of Technology,
Akadeemia tee 15a, 12618 Tallinn, Estonia
sven.nomm@ttu.ee
[2] School of Natural Sciences and Health, Tallinn University,
Narva mnt. 25, 10120 Tallinn, Estonia
aaro.toomela@tlu.ee

Abstract. Virtual reality environment with incomplete immersion is used in this paper, as a tool to alter environment, or to be more precise to alter perception of the environment, such that learning of some primitive fine motor activities would be required. Fine motor exercises and tests are not new in neurology and psychology. Nevertheless, their *digitalization* appeared to be a challenging task and up to now did not become widely accepted by practicing specialists. The present research has three distinctive novel components. First, is the way to use virtual reality environment. Namely absence of 3D glasses, changes of the objects properties and absence of the haptic feedback are used to persuade one to learn. Second, the methodology used to analyze motions and *positions* of fingers. In addition to commonly used methods, set of parameters describing motion during certain time interval is proposed. Third is the types of tests and exercises used to perform the studies. Within the present studies simple tasks of repositioning virtual cubes are used. Achieved results clearly demonstrate that proposed environment requires one to learn simple motor actions and proposed technique is able to distinguish motions in different stages of training.

Keywords: Fine motor functions · Learning process · Modeling

1 Introduction

Modeling the changes in human fine motor functions during the process of learning new motor activity constitutes the subject of the present paper. Fine motor motions usually refer to the finger movements. Therefore proper technology to capture movements of the fingers is the necessary prerequisite for any research

---

The work of Sven Nõmm and Jaroslav Kulikov was supported by Tallinn University of Technology through the direct base funding project B37.

The work of Aaro Toomela was partially supported by the Estonian Research Council through the Grant IUT3-3.

ⓒ Springer International Publishing AG 2017
L.T. De Paolis et al. (Eds.): AVR 2017, Part I, LNCS 10324, pp. 106–115, 2017.
DOI: 10.1007/978-3-319-60922-5_8

in this area. Another key issue is to find fine motor activities to learn. Note, that majority of primitive fine motor activities are learned during the first years of life. Any learning process itself is too complex to model all it nuances in the framework of just one paper. Therefore within the limits of present contributions it is targeted to demonstrate that a system consisting of relatively simple hardware and elements of Virtual Reality (VR) in its software implementation answers all the requirements necessary to create environment which will host the process of learning new motor activity. Also we will demonstrate that finger movements in the beginning of the learning process differ significantly from those observed after the completion of the learning.

Testing fine motor activities has always been a routine part for many practicing neurologists and psychologists [12]. Up to now evaluation of the test results is always done subjectively by practitioner or nurse. While such evaluation way was always in use it has few obvious drawbacks. There are many parameters naked eye could not see. It is difficult to record the test (unless time consuming video setting is in use). This lead the motivation to digitalize the tests. On the one hand such computer-aided way of conducting the tests allows to investigate more parameters. On the other hand it easiest work-flow of the practitioners and nurses and reduce influence of the subjective component into the state assessment.

Since majority of motor activities may be already learned, at least in the case of the adult individuals the idea is to change the environment such that learning would be required again. For example, by changing slipperiness and stickiness properties of the objects in 3D room one may achieve necessity to learn how to grab and release such objects. Application of the VR elements give another advantage. Absence of the physical objects reduce chances of eclipsing the sensor.

While digital tables were widely used to study drawing and hand writing motions since mid-eighties [6] of the previous century, and nowadays are mostly replaced by tablet PCs [7,9], their abilities does not allow to capture motions of individual fingers. More expensive and complicated marker based systems do provide necessary abilities and precision but require one to construct model for each particular individual, which make it impossible to apply for medical research involving large number of participants. Recently introduced Leapmotion controller was chosen as the motion capture device because of its simplicity and compatibility with Unity environment.

In spite of the fact, that Leapmotion controller is relatively new device, it has managed to attract serious attention. [13] provides evaluation of the accuracy and robustness of the Leapmotion controller. Majority of existing results either explore abilities of the controller to be used in pair with virtual reality helmets [4] or for the gesture recognition purposes, like in [3]. There are few results suggesting using leap motion controller to monitor and support children development [1]. In the best knowledge of the authors there is no available results dedicated to the modeling the process of learning fine motor activity.

To demonstrate that finger motions after the completion of the learning process differ significantly from the motions observed in the beginning of the learning process the method of statistical hypothesis testing will be used. The rest of the paper is organized as follows. Section 2 explains some necessary background information and states the problem formally. Section 3 contains formal problem statement and description of experimental setting. Main results are described in Sect. 4. Discussion of the achieved results presented in Sect. 5. Conclusions are drawn in the final section.

2   Background and Formal Problem Statement

According to [5] planning of any purposeful movement consists of three steps. On the first step decision to perform the movement (or action) is made. On the second step sequence of the orders to be send to spinal cord is generated. In [5] this sequence is referred as *motion melody*. The rough analogy is the program of low level instructions to be send to the muscles. On the third step this motion melody is send to the spinal cord. Following this paradigm one may see the process of motor activity learning as the practice in creating and implementing optimal motion melodies. Obviously the changes observable on motor level should reflect the changes occurring in generation and implementation of the motion melodies and vice verse. Learning of a new motor activity influence the second and third steps, namely generation and implementation of the motion melodies. The purpose of the movement provides a natural way to classify it. If the purpose of the movement is achieved, it is declared to be successful and failed in the opposite case. Usually the learning process targets to increase proposition of successful movements. Sometimes the part of the goal and sometimes the method to achieve it, optimization of the motions takes place during the learning process. Generation of motion melodies produce more optimal sequences. Implementation of the motion melodies performed with lesser number of corrections. Similar studies performed on a gross motor level [10] has demonstrated that parameters describing amount and smoothness of the motions demonstrate significant differences between the beginning and the ending of the learning process. Interpretation proposed in [10] suggests to relate amount of the motions to the optimality of generated motion melodies and smoothness of the motion to the quality (experience) in implementing the melody.

In [10] four parameters describing amount and smoothness of the motions were suggested, later in [11] the number of parameters grew to seven. Referred as *motion mass* these parameters describe combined lengths of trajectories (lengths of trajectories for each joint of interest), combined velocity, combined acceleration and their ratios to the shortest distance between beginning and ending points of the motion. Taking these parameters as the base one should take into account certain particularities of the fine motor motions. In addition to the different average values fine motor studies frequently utilize two more types of parameters. The first one is *jerk* which is the rate of change of acceleration [2]. The second type of parameters is based on the fact that many fine motor motions are better described in the language of angles. For example the process of grasping may be described by angular motions of fingers. Once the object is grasped static positions of the fingers are important as well. Adding jerk based and angular parameters for each finger leads relatively large set of parameters to be analyzed. The working hypothesis of the present research is that there exist two subsets of parameters. The parameters, which values vary between successful and failed movements (attempts to perform the movement), constitute the first set. The parameters, which values vary between the beginning and ending of the learning process for successful movements, constitute the second subset. Formal problem statement for the present research may be formulated as follows. Let Θ be the set of parameters describing kinematics of finger motions and their relative positions.

1. Using the method of statistical hypothesis testing find the subset $\Theta_s \in \Theta$ such that the values of its elements differ significantly for successful and failed movements.
2. Using the method of statistical hypothesis testing find the subset $\Theta_p \in \Theta$ such that the values of its elements differ significantly between the beginning and ending of the learning process for successful movements.

3   Experimental Setting and Mathematical Tools

3.1   Hardware and Software Setting

The hardware setting consists of the averagely powered laptop computer and Leapmotion controller see Fig. 1. In the frameworks of the present research the goal of the exercise is to position three virtual cubes one on top of each other. In other words one is required to build a vertical tower of the cubes. For each movement the purpose is to position one cube on top of the other without braking existing structure. The movement or more precisely the trial is defined as grasping the cube, moving it into position and releasing it. If the purpose is achieved the trial classified as successful and failed in the opposite case. Such exercise may seem a simple task in real world environment. In order to conduct the experiment 3D model of the room was created using Unity environment. Three equally sized black cubes are positioned in the room. Palm of the hand is captured by Leapmotion controller and displayed on the screen see Fig. 2. Physical properties (slipperiness and stickiness) of the cubes were slightly altered. Latest guaranteed necessity to learn activity of grasping and releasing again. Actual trials were conducted in two stages. First stage involved ten individuals. The goals of the first stage is to acquire the data to find subset Θ_s. The second stage involved lesser number of individuals. Each of them undergone learning trials of different length. The purpose of this stage is to acquire the data to find subset Θ_p. Upon completion of the exercise, acquired motion data and corresponding events are saved in CSV type file for offline processing. Kinematic and static parameters describing motions and positions of the fingers were computed in MATLAB environment for each trial.

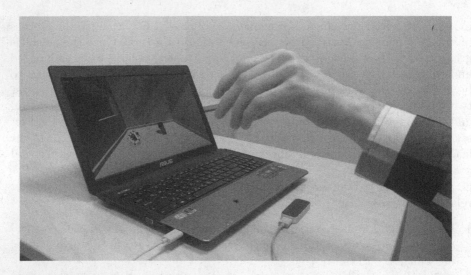

Fig. 1. Experimental setting.

Fig. 2. 3D model of the room with virtual cubes and model of the hand.

3.2   Mathematical Tools

Leap motion controller is similar by its nature to the Microsoft Kinect sensor. While Kinect was designed to model human body, Leapmotion captures motions of the human palms. With a sampling rate of sixty frames per second leapmotion returns coordinates of the joints between finger phalanges and angles describing orientation of the fingertips. These coordinates and angles are stored in the form of square matrix where each row corresponds to the certain time instance.

Based on these information parameters, describing motions and positions of the fingers were computed. By its nature, all parameters divided in to three groups. The first group consists of average values. The second group are the motion mass parameters. The third group contains ratios and indexes. While computing average values and ratios is common practice the concept of motion mass is relatively new. The idea of motion mass parameters were introduced [8,10] and later extended in [11] to model the motions of Parkinson's disease patients. Later few more parameters specific for the fine motor [7,9] parameters were added. Motion mass parameters describe combined motion of a set of joints J during certain time interval corresponding to the motion of interest. Let n be the power of the set J and k will be number of time instances recording the motion of the interest. Then *combined trajectory length* T_J and *combined Euclidean distance* are defined a follows

$$T_J = \sum_{i=1}^{n} T_i \tag{1}$$

$$E_J = \sum_{i=1}^{n} E_i \tag{2}$$

where T_i is the trajectory length of joint j_i and E_j is the distance between the locations of the same joint in the beginning and in the end of the motion. *Acceleration mass* A_J, *Velocity mass* V_J and *Jerk mass* G_j differ from the previous two parameters by the fact that computation at each observation point is required.

$$A_J = \sum_{i=1}^{n} \sum_{t=1}^{k} a_i(t) \tag{3}$$

$$V_J = \sum_{i=1}^{n} \sum_{t=1}^{k} v_i(t) \tag{4}$$

$$G_J = \sum_{i=1}^{n} \sum_{t=1}^{k} g_i(t) \tag{5}$$

where $a_i(t)$, $v_i(t)$ and $g_i(t)$ are the absolute values of acceleration, velocity and jerk along their respective directions, of the joint i at time instance t. Masses describing angular changes occurring in Pitch, Yaw, Roll angles of the fingers and overall grasping angle are computed in a similar manner. Finally different ratios like T_J/E_J and A_J/E_J compliment the list. Total number of parameters computed for each finger and palm overall is 688.

For the first stage two samples corresponding to the successful and failed attempts were formed. Then for each parameter following statistical hypothesis testing was conducted. The statement of null hypothesis is that parameter values describing successful and failed trials belong to the independent random samples drawn from normal distributions with equal means H_0: $\mu_1 = \mu_2$. The alternative hypothesis is that parameter values describing successful and failed trials belong to the random samples drawn from normal distributions with unequal means $H_1: \mu_1 \neq \mu_2$. Whereas level of significance $\alpha = 0.05$.

4   Main Results

For the group of ten untrained individuals (individuals who were conducting the exercise first time) following results have achieved. Statistical hypothesis testing has revealed that the values of 17 parameters differ between the successful and failed attempts of cube positioning. The following convention of naming the parameters is used in Tables 1 and 2. Parameter names without any specifying keywords refer to whole motion. Pitch, yaw and roll are Euler angles of finger tip directions, but word 'angle' means, that angle was computed using three points of hand: finger tip, finger basis and wrist basis. Thumb is more mobile than other angles, so it was decided to add second thumb angle: thumb to palm, which means angle between thumb tip, wrist basis and palm center. Usually, angles were computed relatively to palm, but parameters marked as 'absolute' are relative to game room. Key words 'release' and 'grasp' refer only to motion frames, when hand was grasping or releasing the object. 'Mean' and 'mass' keywords claim whether the parameter is mean arithmetical or sum of all values in vector.

Table 1 lists the parameters, which values differ significantly between the failed and successful attempts.

Table 1. Parameters which values differ significantly between the successful and failed attempts.

Parameter name	p-value	t-statistic	Parameter name	p-value	t-statistic
Time length of the motion	0.0082	2.6850	Mean velocity	0.0102	−2.6082
Mean pitch	0.0349	−2.1325	Mean yaw	0.0072	2.7290
Mean roll	0.0002	3.8355	Mean grab angle	0.0083	2.6808
Mean thumb roll	0.0368	2.1107	Mean index yaw	0.0086	2.6674
Mean index roll	0.0002	3.7853	Mean middle yaw	0.0172	2.4152
Mean middle roll	0.0001	3.9575	Mean ring yaw	0.0072	2.7333
Mean ring roll	0.0003	3.6471	Mean pinky yaw	0.0067	2.7582
Mean index roll/l	0.0219	2.3211	Mean roll/l	0.0026	3.07252
Mean pinky roll	0.0293	2.2044			

Smaller number of individuals has participated in learning process. The parameters describing successful attempts which values differ significantly between the beginning and ending of the learning process are present in Table 2. One may easily observe that grater number of parameters change their values. Also proportion of the mass parameters has increased compared to the previous case.

Table 2. Parameters which values differ significantly between attempts in the beginning and in the ending of the learning process, for the successful attempts.

Parameter name	p-value	t-statistic
Mean velocity	0.007	−2.8218
Mean pitch	0.0022	−3.2422
Mean grab angle	0.0318	−2.2153
Mean thumb pitch	0.0088	2.7348
Mean index pitch	0.0185	−2.4429
Mean middle pitch	0.0102	−2.6795
Mean ring pitch	0.0323	−2.2082
Mean pinky pitch	0.0384	−2.133
Mean thumb absolute pitch	0.0133	2.5749
Mean index absolute pitch	9.4065e−05	−4.2881
Mean index absolute yaw	0.0112	2.6431
Mean middle absolute pitch	6.7578e−05	−4.3914
Mean ring absolute pitch	0.0001	−4.1393
Mean pinky absolute pitch	8.8485e−05	−4.3073
Mean index angle	0.0102	2.6787
Mean thumb angle	0.046	2.0513
Mean thumb/palm angle	0.001	3.4751
Release velocity mass	0.0373	2.1456
Index pitch release velocity mass	0.0225	2.3629
Index roll release velocity mass	0.0443	2.0691
Middle mean pitch release velocity	0.0101	2.6836
Middle pitch release velocity mass	0.0436	2.0759
Ring mean pitch release velocity	0.0316	2.2183
Pinky mean pitch release velocity	0.0316	2.2177
Pinky pitch release velocity mass	0.0467	2.0452
Index angle release velocity mass	0.020	−2.394
Middle angle mean release velocity	0.0184	−2.4461
Middle angle release velocity mass	0.0491	−2.0217
Ring angle mean release velocity	0.0223	−2.3659
Ring angle release velocity mass	0.0443	−2.0688
Pinky angle mean release velocity	0.0281	−2.2678
Pinky angle release velocity mass	0.0337	−2.19
Thumb angle release velocity mass	0.0295	−2.2472
Index pitch release velocity mass/E	0.0437	2.0759
Index roll release velocity mass/E	0.0143	2.5476
Middle roll release velocity mass/E	0.0389	2.1271

5   Discussion

One may easily see that among parameters that differ between successful and failed trial, mean values prevail over the mass parameters and angle related parameter prevail over the kinematic parameters for the case of untrained individuals. At the same time, angle and mass related parameters change the most during the learning process. This signals importance of the finger orientation on the level of fine motor motions. In addition, this fact may describe the difference between gross and fine motor levels.

One may argue that complete immersion VR environment may lead results that are more accurate and provide better conditions for altering the environment. Most probably, this is a true claim but one should keep in mind that such approach would lead at least three serious drawbacks. First is the fact that virtual reality helmet may still be too heavy for a young children. Second is the perception of the VR helmets. In some cases, complete immersion VR system may cause severe seasickness. Finally overall cost of the systems will rise.

6   Conclusions

VR environment with incomplete immersion is proposed in this paper to capture and model the process of learning new fine motor activity. It was demonstrated that for the process of learning purposeful action one may find the set of parameters, describing fine motor movements, such for the successful trials values of the parameters vary significantly between the beginnings and ending of the learning process. Existence of such set demonstrate that proposed VR system altered environment conditions such that learning was necessary to accomplish tasks usually learned during the first years of life. Future research in this direction would be directed towards construction of dynamic models taking in to account different aspects of learning.

References

1. Caro, K., Beltrán, J., Martínez-García, A.I., Soto-Mendoza, V.: ExerCave-Room: a technological room for supporting gross and fine motor coordination of children with developmental disorders. In: Proceedings of the 10th EAI International Conference on Pervasive Computing Technologies for Healthcare, PervasiveHealth 2016, pp. 313–317. ICST (Institute for Computer Sciences, Social-Informatics and Telecommunications Engineering), Brussels (2016). http://dl.acm.org/citation.cfm?id=3021319.3021375
2. Drotar, P., Mekyska, J., Rektorova, I., Masarova, L., Smekal, Z., Faundez-Zanuy, M.: Evaluation of handwriting kinematics and pressure for differential diagnosis of Parkinson's disease. Artif. Intell. Med. **67**, 39–46 (2016)
3. Lu, W., Tong, Z., Chu, J.: Dynamic hand gesture recognition with leap motion controller. IEEE Signal Process. Lett. **23**(9), 1188–1192 (2016)

4. Lupu, R.G., Botezatu, N., Ungureanu, F., Ignat, D., Moldoveanu, A.: Virtual reality based stroke recovery for upper limbs using leap motion. In: 2016 20th International Conference on System Theory, Control and Computing (ICSTCC), pp. 295–299, October 2016

5. Luria, A.R.: Higher Cortical Functions in Man. Springer, New York (1995)

6. Marquardt, C., Mai, N.: A computational procedure for movement analysis in handwriting. J. Neurosci. Methods $52(1)$, 39–45 (1994)

7. Nomm, S., Bardos, K., Masarov, I., Kozhenkina, J., Toomela, A., Toomsoo, T.: Recognition and analysis of the contours drawn during the Poppelreuter's test. In: 2016 15th IEEE International Conference on Machine Learning and Applications (ICMLA), pp. 170–175, December 2016

8. Nomm, S., Toomela, A., Borushko, J.: Alternative approach to model changes of human motor functions. In: 2013 European Modelling Symposium (EMS), pp. 169–174, November 2013

9. Nomm, S., Toomela, A., Kozhenkina, J., Toomsoo, T.: Quantitative analysis in the digital Luria's alternating series tests. In: 2016 14th International Conference on Control, Automation, Robotics and Vision (ICARCV), pp. 1–6, November 2016

10. Nõmm, S., Toomela, A.: An alternative approach to measure quantity and smoothness of the human limb motions. Est. J. Eng. $19(4)$, 298–308 (2013)

11. Nomm, S., Toomela, A., Vaske, M., Uvarov, D., Taba, P.: An alternative approach to distinguish movements of Parkinson disease patients. IFAC-PapersOnLine $49(19)$, 272–276 (2016). (In: 13th IFAC Symposium on Analysis, Design, and Evaluation of Human-Machine Systems HMS 2016, Kyoto, Japan, 30 August–2 September 2016)

12. Tammik, V., Toomela, A.: Relationships between visual figure discrimination, verbal abilities, and gender. Perception $42(9)$, 971–984 (2013)

13. Weichert, F., Bachmann, D., Rudak, B., Fisseler, D.: Analysis of the accuracy and robustness of the leap motion controller. Sensors $13(5)$, 6380–6393 (2013)

Industrial Heritage Seen Through the Lens of a Virtual Reality Experience

David Checa[1]([✉]), Mario Alaguero[1], and Andres Bustillo[2]

[1] Department of History and Geography, University of Burgos, Burgos, Spain
{dcheca, malaguero}@ubu.es
[2] Department of Civil Engineering, University of Burgos, Burgos, Spain
abustillo@ubu.es

Abstract. 20th century industrial heritage, hardly a mainstream area of study, is rarely presented in exhibitions to the general public in Spain. Many abandoned industrial heritage sites are simply left to deteriorate with no attempt to learn from their past. In this paper, the construction and validation of three different Virtual Reality environments are reported. These Virtual Reality environments will be included in an exhibition on some of the first factories established in Burgos (Spain) in the 1960s. The environments were generated using different 3D head-mounted displays - Oculus Rift™ and card-boards, and 2D Displays running under different game engines such as Unreal Engine and Unity. Three environments were created: a 2D-virtual tour game in a small factory manufacturing steel sheets; a 3D-mobile virtual reality window to follow the expansion of a small car-component manufacturer into a leading TIER1 automotive sector company; and, a final general overview of the effect of the new companies on the development of the city using Oculus Rift displays. This research focuses on the advantages of each technology for a different objective and the analysis of the effort required to run it properly in a final application, concluding that the game engine Unreal Engine provides more photorealistic results in 3D-environments with high user-interaction capabilities, while Unity is better in 360° environments that show time evolution running on devices such as mobile phones, with low-computing power.

Keywords: Virtual reality · Industrial heritage · Immersive environments · Oculus Rift · Game engine · Exhibitions · Blender

1 Introduction

Historical built heritage has a long history of conservation, although industrial heritage is often left in a poor state of conservation and premises are rarely restored and opened to the general public for educational purposes. There is therefore less awareness of how present-day society has been shaped by its industrial past. Besides, the state of disrepair of sites is slowly destroying the physical evidence of our industrial heritage. This heritage provides one of the most important records of urban development over the last two centuries. Most of Spain's major industrial development took place during the 1960s, especially in its medium-sized cities in the interior, far from the maritime traffic of benefit to coastal zones. The city of Burgos underwent rapid growth with migration

© Springer International Publishing AG 2017
L.T. De Paolis et al. (Eds.): AVR 2017, Part I, LNCS 10324, pp. 116–130, 2017.
DOI: 10.1007/978-3-319-60922-5_9

from surrounding rural areas; economic development that was greatly assisted by the agreements to set up the first industrial zones, called a *"Polo de desarrollo* [Pole of development]" at the time. It consisted of a sort of open agreement for the construction of many large factories in the outskirts of the city. Although most of the buildings built at that time are still standing, the equipment, production processes and final products will soon be all but forgotten. Unless documented, knowledge of the industrial practices and the reality of everyday life will die with the workers who once labored in the factories.

The metalworking industry was a major activity in the *"Polo de desarrollo"* contributing to the life of the city of Burgos in the sixties. As the industry modernized and factories introduced automated production processes, so fewer jobs were available in the metalworking industry for the younger generation and interest in metalworking processes likewise diminished, although new workers and engineers are still needed nowadays and in the near future. To reduce this lack of interest, Virtual Reality (VR) can play a pivotal role in presenting these particular careers to young people at exhibitions and stimulating their interest in a variety of subjects, including contemporary history, design and engineering. Young people always feel very receptive [1, 2] to interactive techniques and VR environments that accentuate feelings of amazement, astonishment, and excitement in users [3].

Similar VR experiences have previously been presented, although most are related to historical or archaeological heritage [4]. Up until 2015, the majority of published research in Virtual Reality environments referred to very expensive solutions such as 3D caves [2, 5, 6]. Over the past few years, the launch of low-cost, high-fidelity, head-mounted displays (HMDs), such as Oculus Rift™, have opened up new horizons for the application of 3D-immersive environments in exhibition spaces; although the design of short VR experiences has been advised to prevent simulator-sickness problems [7].

Different approaches to the creation of 3D digital environments for Cultural Heritage have been proposed, each focusing on one of the main challenges that this new technology faces. First, the development of easy-to-use software to create this kind of environment has been studied and tested in digital exhibitions, such as the case of the Nefertiti bust [8]. Second, collaborative workflows between different experts, necessary to achieve the success of an exhibition with VR environments has been identified, such as the case of an old power plant in the city of Piestany (Slovakia) [9]. Third, the narrative design of such experiences, so that the final viewers would easily assimilate the information, was the objective of the researchers in the case of a VR environment of different medieval villages in Spain [7] and Italy [10]. Almost all the research in this line refers to examples of Historical [2, 7, 8, 10] and Archaeological [6] Heritage, and very few examples refers to Industrial Heritage [9], although Industrial Heritage present the advantage of the small sized virtual environment in comparison with Cultural Heritage environments; this advantage is shared with other examples of the diffusion of Industrial Heritage, such as the rendered videos of a fulling mill in Asturias (Spain) [11] for off-line viewing.

This paper reports the construction of some VR environments for inclusion in an exhibition on some of the first factories located in Burgos in the 1960s and its validation with the general public. The VR environments were set up in three rooms:

(i) a 2D-virtual tour game in a small metalworking factory producing steel sheets, providing insight into the daily life of this working environment in the 60s; (ii) a 3D-mobile virtual reality window to follow the expansion of a car-component factory in the 60s into a leading 1990s TIER1 automotive sector company; and, (iii) a final general overview of the contribution of the new companies established in the 60s to the development of the city, using 3D-displays to share up to 5 different scenes with the viewer. VR environments were created for different 3D HMDs and 2D Displays, such as Oculus Rift™, cardboards and 2D-beamers, running under different game engines such as Unreal Engine and Unity, to bring these three very different industrial stories to life. The novelty of this research is mainly drawn from the comparisons between the human effort that each solution requires and the computing time and effort related to each solution, identifying the advantages and the drawbacks of each one, depending on the message meant to be communicated to the viewers; a comparative study that has not previously been reported in the literature.

The paper is structured as follows: Sect. 2 describes the process followed to recreate the virtual environments, including both hardware and software and the process followed to create and import the 3D models; Sect. 3 discusses its real implementation in a case study: the design of three virtual reality experiences for the exhibition "*Empresas con Historia* [Firms with History]" that took place in Burgos in November 2016; Sect. 4 evaluates the efforts required to create the VR environments comparing the different technologies used in each of them. Finally, Sect. 5 presents the conclusions and future lines of work.

2   3D Reconstruction of Industrial Heritage

The following methodology was followed for the reconstruction of this industrial heritage: first, existing documentation was searched, then the 3D-models were built considering their final use and, finally, the 3D-environments were created in the game engine with the planned interaction with the end user, depending on the requirements in each case. This 3-step methodology, illustrated in Fig. 1, is based on previous Cultural Heritage reconstruction studies of medieval churches [2] and small medieval cities [12].

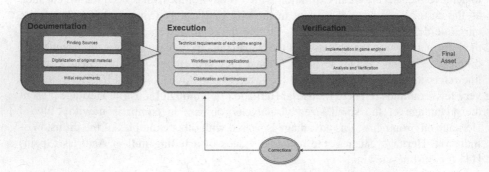

Fig. 1. Methodology for the creation of the 3D-environments in the exhibition.

The first step of the methodology, under the heading documentation, addresses three tasks. First, documentation is researched that may physically exist or may have been lost over time on the object that will be digitized. Documentary sources such as photographs, plans, etc. must be found. Second, workers from the environments in the 1960s to be recreated were interviewed to gather relevant information for the reconstruction. Finally, if the object for digitalization still exists, photogrammetry assists its reconstruction and the extraction of textures.

In the second stage, the 3D-modeling of the documented environments is performed. This 3D-modeling should be done by considering the requirements of the game engine where the 3D models will be included. We emphasize, that a low number of polygons should be maintained, while retaining photorealistic quality. To do so, Physical Based Rendering (PBR) textures were created. In the following steps, the assets were prepared for inclusion in the engine, by exporting them to a suitable format for both of the engines: in this case, Fbx. Item organization is fundamental in this sort of project, for which reason a standard of nomenclatures was set, so that all the assets followed the same naming standard.

Finally, in the verification stage, through the integration of these models in the game engines, we were able to verify that everything was running properly. For this task, several template scenes were created, where all models can be tested under the same conditions. It included checking the following points: collisions, materials and lightmaps. Following these checks, the assets were considered ready for the production stage.

3 Study Case: Design of Virtual Reality Experiences for an Exhibition

The exhibition was partitioned into two sections. A conventional section of the exhibition, with historical objects and old machinery from the three companies; and a second section, in which the three VR environments were found, where the spectator was able to participate in a guided tour through the history of these companies. This second section was structured into three parts, corresponding to the three VR experiences. In each of these subsections, an analysis of the working conditions, exploiting the advantages of this technology, recreated the following three virtual experiences.

3.1   A Virtual Tour Game to Gain Insight into the Daily Activity of a Factory in the 1960s

In this first room, the virtual experience recreates the daily activities of cutting and preparing steel sheets in a small 1960s factory, as shown in Fig. 2.

The goal was firstly to recreate the original appearance of the factory, a relatively easy task with the available graphical documentation, and the fact that the factory is still in use today, despite its modernization. In this first case, a virtual tour was designed, allowing the user to control the visit to the factory and to explore the entire manufacturing process. The feeling of viewer involvement was the main objective,

Fig. 2. First room: a small metalworking factory

while the sensation of immersiveness was secondary. Two objects were placed in the room: a recreation of a steel coil and the control panel of a cutting machine. We took advantage of the control panel to link it to the controls of the virtual tour. The experience was projected in 2D onto a white wall, allowing the interaction of large groups.

A route showing the most relevant steps in the manufacturing process was designed for the tour of the factory, conveying an idea of its daily productive activity in the 1960s. This tour was created in such a way that the user has the freedom to move around the surroundings close by, but is at the same time obliged to follow a fixed route. This is a fundamental strategy, since total freedom of movement would lead to disorientation and information would be lost in the didactic approach planned on the fixed route. The time that viewers can spend in each VR-room, due to the total capability of the program, is limited, so the visit has inevitably to be planned to some extent.

Over two-hundred unique high-quality models were generated for the virtual reconstruction of the factory, such as the control panel shown in Fig. 3, which has a mesh of 5000 polygons and for which additional PBR textures were created to give it more detail and a photorealistic appearance. As mentioned in the Introduction, despite the complexity and importance of this object, its mesh size is very small compared with objects of secondary importance included in Cultural Heritage buildings, such as small sculptures with up to ten times more polygons in their meshes [2].

The chosen game engine to build the experience was Unreal Engine 4, due to its capabilities to create photorealistic environments and the ease of use of its visual programming system. From the technical point of view, once the basic scene, which includes all the elements of the factory, is in place, the process of lighting begins. Once the desired atmosphere for the experience was created, all the illumination was pre-calculated. This action reduces the load on the CPU and means the game can run at a higher frame rate. As it is a user-controlled video game, one of the most important parts is the user interaction. For the development of this game, code was not used, but the

Fig. 3. Screen capture of the virtual tour created in Unreal engine.

visual scripting system of Unreal Engine, Blueprints. Figure 4 shows how the inter-actions with the user of the experience were established quickly and effectively, through this system; for example, when the viewer arrives near the train, the train slowly begins to move, allowing the viewer to the next part of the factory.

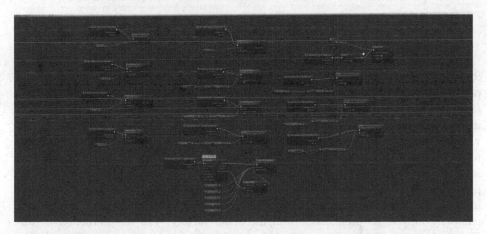

Fig. 4. Example of blueprint used for the creation of interactions in this experience

3.2 Mobile Virtual Reality to Visualize the Growth of an Automobile Company

In the second room, a 3D-mobile virtual reality experience was performed to follow the expansion of a small car-component factory into a leading TIER1 automotive sector company. The first goal was to transmit to the visitor the expansion of the production process in the automotive sector over 30 years, from almost hand-made work in small-scale industrial premises to mass production in large factories. The second goal was to transfer the physical feeling of the size of the first small factories, as opposed to the first large factories that opened at the same time in the city, as in the case of Subsect. 3.1. With these aims in mind, virtual reality means we can perceive volumes and feel the scale of space and provide quick spatial and temporal changes between the temporal scenes. Mobile phones were used to create these VR-environments, with mid-range cardboards, added handles, and a height adjustable vertical tube. This arrangement gives us an autonomous 360° virtual reality device. Five of these devices were set up, facilitating the flow of visitors and groups, as shown in Fig. 5.

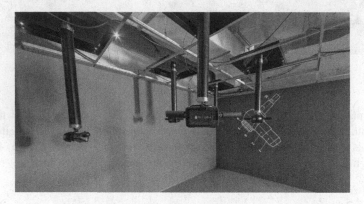

Fig. 5. 3D-mobile virtual reality room

In this second case, the documentation phase was the most time-consuming part of the project, due to the limited availability of documentary resources. Only a couple of photographs of the original workspaces still remain, with which to reconstruct the 60s factory, and the company could not guarantee the exact location of the machine-tools on the shop floor of the factory. In the investigation, the original factory was visited with an ex-employee who had worked there at the time, to gather very valuable details for the reconstruction. The original lathes are no longer available, although some very similar, newer models were found in another factory, which served, along with the photographs and plans of the originals, to rebuild quite exact copies. The second scene included the first large factory for the mass production of car-components to which the company moved its production from the small factory. The reconstruction of this factory was easier, as it still exists and plenty of documentary resources were available.

The 3D-modelling of both scenes was done with Blender software as in previous experiences [2, 12]. The modeled factory, without textures, is shown in Fig. 6. Because the user could not move around the scene, the modeling time was optimized, detailing only the parts closest to the visualization as opposed to the elements that would remain in the background. Also, only the foreground elements were detailed in the reconstruction of the first large factory, due to its dimensions, filling the rest of the factory with less detailed models.

Fig. 6. Modeled scene of the original small-scale factory

Once the models of the original small-scale factory and the first automated factory had been created in high resolution, they were exported to the game engines. An extreme optimization of the 3D models was necessary due to the use of mobile phones in this VR-environment. The game engine that obtains the best result in this field is Unity. After the first tests, the development of an app with the modeled scenes was declined, due to the large polygonal load. Since the user could not move, but simply rotate around 360°, we decided to recreate each scene separately and render a 360° image for each one, the original small factory and the first large factory. Then these images were combined and the 360° experience worked, simply by projecting them onto a sphere with the inverted normals. In order to capture the depth of the scene, stereo panoramas were chosen, so two spheres were created with separate textures for the left and right eye. Then a VR camera rig was placed in the centre and a layer culling was applied, so that each camera only sees its eye-sphere. Figure 7 shows one of these 360° panoramas that is projected onto one of the spheres. This solution provides a very light and optimized mobile application, giving a feeling of the real size of both factories.

3.3 A Virtual Reality Experience to Explain the Industrial Heritage and Its Influence in a City

The last exhibition room, unlike the previous ones that were exclusively dedicated to one company, presented an overview of all the companies participating in the exhibition and the role of industry in the development of Burgos. The room, as shown in Fig. 8, was arranged in two zones: on the one hand the HMDs and, opposite, in the form of a diorama, all the car components that are manufactured in the city.

Fig. 7. 360° panoramic view of the experience

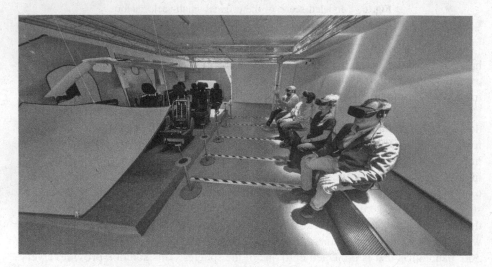

Fig. 8. Virtual reality room

This experience was the costliest, in terms of both modeling and development the virtual reality experience. It included five different scenes and the inclusion of 360° videos. The creation of the 3D-models was not problematic and the same methodology and software meant that previous VR-environments could be used. The first scene corresponded to viewing same room; in this way, the viewers had the impression that, although wearing the head-mounted display, they were still in the same room, though the car parts were levitating in front of him. The biggest challenge at this stage was the transformation of the CAD models provided by the companies and their optimization in low-polygon 3D-models to be integrated into the game engine. The second room was a recreation of the city of Burgos, which included the historic centre and the industrial area. For this, the photogrammetry technique was used with satellite images. The third room showed 360° images of the factories of the participating companies. It was decided not to record stereoscopic images, as an economy measure. In last two scenes, a modern metalworking factory producing steel sheets and a modern-day factory of a leading TIER1 automotive company are respectively shown in Figs. 9 and 10.

Fig. 9. Modern metalworking factory producing steel sheets

Fig. 10. Automated conveyor belt production line

The game engine Unreal Engine 4 was chosen for the development of the experience, again because of its ease at achieving photorealistic results and its visual programming system. The experience was designed to take advantage of the spectacular capabilities of virtual reality, so that it was maximized. The first impression of the viewer having attached the HMD was one of surprise, since it was in the same room, but with the levitating objects (Scene 1). After a little adaptation, the locution begins and after a melt, the visitors find themselves flying over the city (Scene 2). Then, again by melting, the visitors find themselves in the factories recorded in 360° (Scene 3). At the end of this sequence the visitor returns to the first room to find, not the car parts, but the final car that has now been assembled (Scene 4). Then the visitors begin to move automatically forward and, as they pass through the car door, they enter the first factory, on the assembly line of a company of the automotive sector, where large robotic arms are soldering and mounting car seats (Scene 5). Once again by melting, we switch to a metalworking factory, where steel sheets are cut on a conveyor belt. The visitors observe how a coil of steel is transformed into a sheet of steel and the final finished product (Scene 6).

The biggest technical challenge of the experience consisted in preloading these levels with their precalculated lighting, since the passage from one to another was so fast that there was no time for a load between them. So, we created a master level on which we loaded all levels from the start.

Table 1 summarizes the three experiences created for this project, focusing on the technology used for reaching the objective of each VR-experience.

Table 1. Summary of the objectives, game engines, strengths and weaknesses of each scene.

Scenes	Objective	Game engine	Type of experience	Strengths	Weaknesses
2D-virtual tour game	To gain insight into the daily factory activity of the 1960s	Unreal engine	First person game	Photorealistic and visual scripting	Needs more optimization
3D-mobile virtual reality	Visualize evolution of an automobile factory and achieve feeling of narrowness	Unreal engine	Virtual environment	Photorealistic, native 360° 3D panorama exporter	Does not accept native blender files
		Unity	Mobile app	Great mobile optimization	Needs knowledge of code
3D-HMD high end virtual reality experience	Explain the industrial heritage and its influence in a city	Unreal engine	HMD virtual reality experience	Blueprints	Difficult to stream between levels

4   Evaluation of Effort

At this stage, different characteristics of the methodology for the development of the virtual reality experience are reviewed. Tables 2, 3 and 4 show the effort in time (considered as a proportion of total time) for each step, the main tasks for every step, and the software tools in use.

Table 2 shows the time and effort required for the development of the 3D models. As expected compared with previous works of similar characteristics [2, 12], the

Table 2. Summary of time-effort in modeling

Steps	Tasks	Software tools	Time (%)
Location	Finding sources, digitalization of physical objects	Photoscan	10
Modeling	Modeling of objects and scenes	Blender	55
Game engine adaptation	Orientation of normals, collision mesh, textures (additional UV channels and PBR maps)	Blender	25
Verification of models	Implementation in game engines, analysis and verification	Unreal engine	10

Table 3. Summary of time spent on creation scenes in the game engine.

Steps	Tasks	Software tools	Time (%)
Import	Project and editor set up, classification of sources	Unreal engine	15
Placing objects	Recreation scene inside the game engine	Unreal engine	5
Materials	Creation of materials, materials instances, intelligent materials from substance designer	Unreal engine, substance designer	15
Illumination	Placing lights, creation of atmosphere, postprocess	Unreal engine	30
Animation and events	Setting up blueprints, creation custom events	Unreal engine	35

Table 4. Summary of time spent in optimization of the scenes in the game engines.

Steps	Tasks	Software tools	Time (%)
Instantiate objects	Instantiate objects	Unreal engine	25
Optimization of assets	Optimization of assets by use depending in its distance from the character	Unreal engine	20
Rendering	Balancing visuals with performance (baking light, CPU and GPU profiling, scene complexity)	Unreal engine	55

biggest expense of time in this step is taken by the modeling stage, although the time that must be spent adapting these models to the needs of a game engine is also significant. In this project, several modelers worked in parallel, but one with expert knowledge of video game engines made the adjustments. In the model verification phase, several template scenes were prepared to test all models under the same conditions and to lighten the process.

Table 3 shows the time spent on creation scenes with the game engine. As in previous work with similar characteristics [7], a good amount of time is required to import and to organize the objects in the game engine. The time dedicated to place objects in the environment is negligible, and as we move on to more artistic tasks such as creating materials or lighting, the time-effort ratio increases. Finally, the most exacting task of this step is the animation and creation of the events. It can be seen that one of the reasons for using Unreal engine in this process is its system of visual scripting, with which, with no knowledge of code, it is possible to perform complex events that drive the experience. The animation part was confronted in several ways: on the one hand, by importing those animations from the blender that needed bones, and on the other, by creating those that required simple movements or texture animation in the engine.

Table 4 collects the time spent in optimization of the different scenes inside the game engines. Like in previous work [7], the biggest expense of time in this step is taken in balancing the visual with performance. This task is slow due to the high amount of computing time and the difficulty finding the right equilibrium between quality and time spent on pre-rendering tasks.

This final stage of game optimization is critical, especially in virtual reality experiences, because despite having created a great experience, if it is not optimized correctly for the hardware in use, it can lead to the abandonment of the experience by part of the user, including severe dizziness, which will condition future use of this technology. A lot of development time was dedicated to this optimization step so that such situations would not occur.

In the first experience, the virtual tour of the factory, the optimization was clear, because it was a relatively simple game, although the scene was very large. Having decided that the light would not change at any time, after the precalculation, performance was very good. After the optimizations, using a gtx 1060, we managed to remain stable at 90 fps.

The second scene used card-board viewers and appeared to be the most complicated one, although it was easily solved with the use of panoramic 360° stereo images. The scene created in Unreal Engine, in order to capture the panorama, was not optimized. The most important aspect here was the quality of this capture. In creating the final app, it was crucial to know the exact model of mobile that would be used in all the terminals. Following that decision, the optimization was simple, adapting itself mainly to their needs.

Finally, in the last experience, virtual immersive reality, optimization was the most complicated due to its peculiarities. As we saw, several scenes should be seen in continuity, some preceded by a fade (very short, so much that it was impossible to load a level) and others that should appear instantly. The equipment used was sufficient, computers had a gtx 1070, which meets the minimum set by Oculus, but the large amount of geometry and scenes required a large optimization to reach the minimum frame rate of 90 fps. Our goal was to maintain this frame rate to avoid motion sickness. All aspects were optimized in this way, beginning with the lighting, the geometry of objects far off the camera, and their textures, as well as instantiating all possible objects to save load on the processor. No dynamic lights were used and all lighting was pre-calculated at each stage. A stable rate of 90-fps was reached throughout the experience.

5   Conclusions

In this paper, the construction has been reported of three VR-environments and their validation with the general public at an exhibition on some of the first factories located in Burgos (Spain) in the 1960s. The experience was divided into 3 rooms where different technologies were used. In the first one a 2D-virtual tour game in a metal-working factory was presented to give insight into the daily life of this factory in the 1960s; in the second room, a 3D-mobile virtual reality experience was created that showed the expansion of a small car-component factory in the 60s into a leading 1990s TIER1 automotive sector company at the same time as the narrowness of the industrial premises in the 60s is contrasted with the 3D-effect with modern-day conditions; the third room showed a general overview of the influence of the new companies founded in the 60s on the city in their development using 3D-displays to introduce the viewer to up to 6 different scenes.

All the 3D-models for the three environments were created using the Blender software tool. Related to the game engines, the first and the third VR-environments were integrated in Unreal Engine game engine, due to its photorealistic capabilities and easy to define interaction with the end-user, while Unity was selected for the second scene, due to its capabilities to produce good-quality environments for low and medium computer capabilities, such as mobile phones. In relation to the medium of visualization, the first VR-environment was projected onto a 2D-screen to allow interactivity with a group of persons together due to the reduced time to visit the exhibition, the second VR-environment was 3D projected by mobiles and cardboards because the effect of narrowness was one of the main objectives, while Oculus Rift HMD was used for the third VR-environment to produce the strongest immersion effect.

Finally, an evaluation of the time-effort ratio has been reported in a comparative way between the three VR-environments, to identify the advantages of each technology for a different objective and the analysis of the effort required to run it properly in a final application. This comparison has shown that the most time-consuming task is at the modeling stage in the development of 3D model, but the time that is required to adapt these models to the needs of a game engine is also considerable. In the creation of the scenes inside a game engine, it was clearly appreciated that the most time consuming task is the creation of the events that drive the experience. Finally, balancing the visual with performance is a critical task due to the difficulty of finding the right equilibrium between quality and time spent pre-rendering the scene.

Further research will focus on measuring the effect of these technologies and VR-environments narrating the final use of industrial heritage, considering different ages and personal interests to complete the conclusions of this work. A second-step objective will be the definition of a low-cost methodology to achieve similar visual results.

Acknowledgments. This work was partially supported through the Program "Impulso de la Industria de Contenidos Digitales desde las Universidades" of the Spanish Ministry of Industry, Tourism and Commerce and funding and documental support from Grupo Antolin, Industrias Gala and Gonvarri Steel Services. The authors would especially like to thank Dr. Gonzalo Andrés for his kind-spirited and useful advice.

References

1. Korakakis, G., Pavlatou, E.A., Palyvos, J.A., Spyrellis, N.: 3D visualization types in multimedia applications for science learning: a case study for 8th grade students in Greece. Comput. Educ. **52**, 390–401 (2009)
2. Bustillo, A., Alaguero, M., Miguel, I., Saiz, J.M., Iglesias, L.S.: A flexible platform for the creation of 3D semi-immersive environments to teach Cultural Heritage. Digit. Appl. Archaeol. Cult. Herit. **2**, 248–259 (2015)
3. Hupont, I., Gracia, J., Sanagustín, L., Gracia, M.A.: How do new visual immersive systems influence gaming QoE? A use case of serious gaming with Oculus Rift. In: 2015 Seventh International Workshop on Quality of Multimedia Experience (QoMEX), pp. 1–6 (2015)
4. Chow, S.K., Chan, K.L.: Reconstruction of photorealistic 3D model of ceramic artefacts for interactive virtual exhibition. J. Cult. Herit. **10**, 161–173 (2009)
5. Bruno, F., Bruno, S., De Sensi, G., Luchi, M.L., Mancuso, S., Muzzupappa, M.: From 3D reconstruction to virtual reality: a complete methodology for digital archaeological exhibition. J. Cult. Herit. **11**, 42–49 (2010)
6. Lucet, G.: Virtual reality: a knowledge tool for cultural heritage. In: Ranchordas, A., Araújo, H.J., Pereira, J.M., Braz, J. (eds.) VISIGRAPP 2008. CCIS, vol. 24, pp. 1–10. Springer, Heidelberg (2009). doi:10.1007/978-3-642-10226-4_1
7. Checa, D., Alaguero, M., Arnaiz, M.A., Bustillo, A.: Briviesca in the 15th c.: a virtual reality environment for teaching purposes. In: De Paolis, L.T., Mongelli, A. (eds.) AVR 2016. LNCS, vol. 9769, pp. 126–138. Springer, Cham (2016). doi:10.1007/978-3-319-40651-0_11
8. Sanna, A., Lamberti, F., Bazzano, F., Maggio, L.: Developing touch-less interfaces to interact with 3D contents in public exhibitions. In: Paolis, L.T., Mongelli, A. (eds.) AVR 2016. LNCS, vol. 9769, pp. 293–303. Springer, Cham (2016). doi:10.1007/978-3-319-40651-0_24
9. Hain, V., Löffler, R., Zajíček, V.: Interdisciplinary cooperation in the virtual presentation of industrial heritage development. Procedia Eng. **161**, 2030–2035 (2016)
10. De Paolis, L.T.: Walking in a virtual town to understand and learning about the life in the middle ages. In: Murgante, B., Misra, S., Carlini, M., Torre, C.M., Nguyen, H.-Q., Taniar, D., Apduhan, B.O., Gervasi, O. (eds.) ICCSA 2013. LNCS, vol. 7971, pp. 632–645. Springer, Heidelberg (2013). doi:10.1007/978-3-642-39637-3_50
11. Suárez, J., Rojas-Sola, J.I., Rubio, R., Martín, S., Morán, S.: Teaching applications of the new computer-aided modelling technologies in the recovery and diffusion of the industrial heritage. Comput. Appl. Eng. Educ. **17**(4), 455–466 (2009)
12. Alaguero, M., Bustillo, A., Guinea, B., Iglesias, L.: The virtual reconstruction of a small medieval town: the case of Briviesca (Spain). In: CAA2014 21st Century Archaeology, Concepts, Methods and Tools. Proceedings of the 42nd Annual Conference on Computer Applications and Quantitative Methods in Archaeology, pp. 575–584. Archaeopress (2015)

Multiple NUI Device Approach to Full Body Tracking for Collaborative Virtual Environments

Paolo Leoncini[✉], Bogdan Sikorski, Vincenzo Baraniello,
Francesco Martone, Carlo Luongo, and Mariano Guida

CIRA Italian Aerospace Research Centre, Capua, Italy
{p.leoncini, b.sikorski, v.baraniello, f.martone,
c.luongo, m.guida}@cira.it

Abstract. This paper describes the devising of a real-time full-body motion-capture system for multi-user Collaborative Virtual Environment (CVE). The idea takes advantage of some Natural User Interface devices such as the Microsoft Kinect and the Leap Motion Controller. The aim of our approach is to allow a rapid and easy access of participants to the tracked area, that is why the described system has been devised to be both wireless and markerless.

The article shows how multiple Kinect units can be used as a whole to both enlarge the tracking area and be tolerant to the shielding effect due to the overlapping of multiple participants seen by the sensors.

Further fusion strategies are presented to combine Kinect-based multi-body tracking along with head-tracking and head-mounted Leap Motion Controllers data in order to get body tracking with the full hand detail, which enables direct hand manipulation in applications such as first-person virtual maintenance training.

Although preliminary, the shown results are already encouraging. Once data will be analyzed more in depth and after a system tuning, an effective and even more reliable final multi-person tracking system is expected.

Keywords: Motion capture · Body tracking · Collaborative Virtual Environment · Virtual reality · 3D graphics · Skeleton tracking · Kinect · Leap Motion · Natural User Interface · Data fusion

1 Introduction

The ability of correctly track position and orientation of human body parts plays a key role in Virtual Reality. In particular, in the implementation of Collaborative Virtual Environments (CVE), being able to see each other in the VE as avatar mannequins moving according to the real participants' movements is key to self and mutual awareness, and to increase the sense of common presence.

During the past years, many different motion capture technologies have been developed in order to fully track human body. The most common body tracking solutions are all addressed to employ markers attached to key body parts: video-based systems utilize IR video cameras (e.g., Vicon, ART, OptiTrack), electromagnetic

© Springer International Publishing AG 2017
L.T. De Paolis et al. (Eds.): AVR 2017, Part I, LNCS 10324, pp. 131–147, 2017.
DOI: 10.1007/978-3-319-60922-5_10

systems use emitters and detectors of electromagnetic field (e.g., Ascension, Polhemus), inertial systems use trackers with accelerometers (e.g., Xsens, and several others). Altogether, these solutions are all able to track full-body motion parameters in a very accurate and reliable way, but they generally result weighty, intrusive and, above all, expensive. Furthermore, they usually require the VR user to be dressed with a body suit or by a marker, or a sensor, for each joint to be tracked, which complicates the immersion process and makes the virtual experience impractical for productive uses with high user turnover (Fig. 1).

Fig. 1. Marker-based and wireless, worn interface devices for VR and Collaborative Virtual Environment (source: Lockheed Martin).

The introduction of cheap, COTS Natural User Interface devices, such as the Microsoft Kinect for full body tracking of multiple human figures and the Leap Motion Controller for the hands, instigated lot of interest across the VR community, primarily attracted by data richness and low cost. Professional tracking systems tend to be quite expensive when compared with the price of the Kinect, and for the Leap Motion when compared to digital gloves as well. Yet the adequateness of their use for professional VR applications has still to be proven, since these devices tend to show jittering, tracking instability and false pose detection, and, for full-body, low resolution and precision.

We present our efforts of using a heterogeneous system of multiple Kinect sensors, VR HMD head trackers and Leap Motion Controllers to provide a cost-conscious, fully wireless, markerless 6-DoF tracking system for virtual reality with CVE in mind, where full body of multiple human figures must be tracked at the same time. Since the tracking system is mainly targeted at collaborative VR maintenance simulation, where the direct hand manipulation ability is a requirement, a derivative requirement for our system is the tracking of the hands of each user down to the finger/phalanxes detail.

2 Related Works

In recent years, since the introduction of low-cost high-speed depth sensor, such as Microsoft Kinect for Xbox [1], markerless human pose estimation from depth images has become a more and more active research field [2]. The use of depth data has allowed the realization of many reliable human pose estimation systems that are able to output the position of some joints in order to reconstruct the human skeleton. Anyhow, even if significant development has been achieved [3–5], pose estimation from depth images is still a challenging task.

In their research work, Shotton et al. [6] dealt the problem of pose estimation as a simpler per-pixel classification problem. As to this method, the poses estimation can be carried out without initialization even if it needs a great number of training sets and always fails when significant occlusion occurs.

Grest et al. [7] proposed an example-based approach. Their solution match the input depth map with a set of pre-captured motion exemplars to estimate the body configuration but motion capture may fail when large skinning deformation occur. Moreover, many exemplars should be tested in order to obtain the best-matched one.

Some authors [8] registered an articulated mesh model by evaluating silhouette correspondences between the assumed and observed data from monocular depth camera. In particular, Gao et al. [9] combine pose detection and tracking as a multi-layer filter to automatically evaluate accurate pose parameters from two Kinect sensors at the same time. For pose estimation of the current frame, they just use the last estimated poses instead of depth and RGB images in order to predict the pose of the next frame. This frame is used to confirm that the estimation of the current frame is consistent, at the same time, with both the estimated last pose and the predicted next pose.

Liu et al. [10] presented a markerless motion capture from multi-view video approach to the reconstruction of the skeletal motion and in depth time-varying surface geometry of two closely interacting people. They proposed a combined image segmentation and tracking approach to overcome the difficulties of ambiguities in feature-to-person assignments and frequent occlusions and demonstrated the performance of their method on several challenging multi-person actions such as dance or martial arts.

The recent introduction of innovative acquisition devices like the Leap Motion [11] allows getting a very informative description of the hands pose.

Marin et al. [12] have proposed a novel hand gesture recognition approach tailored for simultaneous acquisition of Leap Motion and Kinect data. Two ad-hoc feature sets based on fingertips positions and orientation, coming from the depth values extracted from Leap Motion and Kinect, were computed and combined in order to recognize performed gestures. Experimental results demonstrated that the combination of the two features sets allow to achieve a very high accuracy in real-time gesture recognition.

Craig and Krishnan [13] used a virtual reality game in order to demonstrate the increasing capabilities in tracking human motion due to the combination of Kinect and Leap Motion. The game users perceived the combined system to be seamless to interact with, especially when they do not need to care too much about the physical space for hand interaction.

3 Work Statement

The aim underlying the present work is to devise a real-time system for tracking multiple participants in a room-sized area for immersive VR collaborative applications leveraging direct hand manipulation. One additional requirement is to have the easiest possible access into the common tracked area, where minimal or no equipment is required to wear for interface purposes.

Hence, by listing requirements:

- room-sized tracking area ($\sim 3 \times 3$ m);
- multiple participants tracked;
- full body, with full hand/finger detail;
- minimal interface burden for users – neither suits nor markers.

4 The Kinect Motion Sensing Device and Multi-Kinect Body Tracking

The Kinect One is, to date, the latest version of the revolutionary body sensing device developed by Microsoft in collaboration with PrimeSense. Designed for the Xbox One game console, it is also available for Windows 8+-based computer with a USB 3.0 compatible connection at the only additional cost of an adapter.

The Kinect is the acknowledged forefather of a family of devices called Natural User Interface (NUI) that allow users to interact with applications (videogames, interactive video-walls, virtual reality, etc.) through gestures and movements in a contactless manner.

The concept underlying the naturalness is that users need not to dress up/wear any sensor or sensor transponder/marker/reflector, so that he/she can enter into the tracking area with no burden of interface device set up and can start interacting immediately with an application.

In the Kinect suite of sensors, the IR depth camera returns a metric depth map of the pointed frustum of the environment. By leveraging depth data, a model-based analysis done by the Microsoft Kinect SDK (v2.0) is able to return 6-DoF tracking data of 25-joint skeleton bodies of up to six human figures at a sustained rate of 30 Hz. Additionally, color data by the RGB camera can be optionally mapped to body figures' 3D points for interesting mixed reality use scenarios.

However, a single Kinect sensor, whose sensing frustum is 70° H-FoV by 60° V-FoV in the distance range of 0.5–4.5 m from the unit, is suited for almost-frontal person tracking within an experimentally found angular tolerance of ±30°. Nevertheless, a wider area/angular coverage can be accomplished by using multiple units: a minimally optimal configuration is a circular arrangement of ~ 5 m diameter with a 60° angular displacement between adjacent units, for a total number of #6 Kinects units. In order to minimize mutual occlusions among participants, and to reduce the risk of mutual IR-light interference, in our setup the Kinect units have been placed at a height of 2.3 m, looking downward by 30–35° (Fig. 2).

Whatever fusion strategy of data from multiple Kinects, it will rely on a sensor co-registration, leading to a common reference system. For co-registration and real-time streaming of Kinect data, we have relied on the excellent work by Kowalski et al. [14], which have also made the related client-server software LiveScan3D publicly available. As to their description, in a LiveScan3D setup each computer runs a client application that is connected to a server, which collects all of the sensors data.

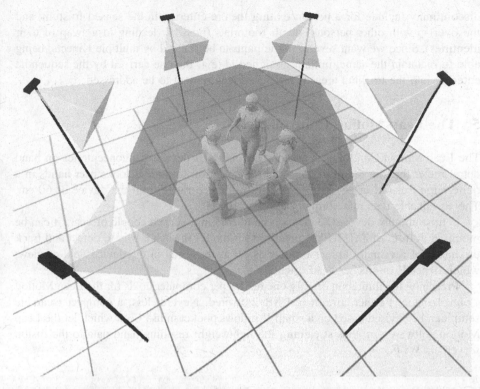

Fig. 2. A 3D graphical representation of the proposed multiple Kinect setup. The evidenced polyhedron in the center is the common sensed volume (average diameter: ~3 m).

The server allows the user to perform calibration, filtering, synchronized frame capture, and to visualize the acquired point cloud live. The poses of each single Kinect device are estimated in a two-step calibration procedure: the first step performs a rough estimation using a commonly viewed, A4-printed visual marker, the second step uses Iterative Closest Points [15] to refine the resulting poses.

Once co-registered, multiple Kinect data could be fused either at raw data level (fusion of co-registered depth maps, then extract body-tracking data from such a 3D richer dataset) or at high-level data, i.e. by fusing co-registered body tracking data out of each unit. By being the Microsoft Kinect (v2.0) SDK tied to a single-unit data, the former, promising approach could have only been pursued by calculating body-tracking data in a separate way than the official SDK support. Instead, the latter approach can leverage the calculation of the body-tracking data by means of the Microsoft Kinect (v2.0) SDK client-side, then sending skeleton data to the fusion server, which actually co-registers, filters, and fuses bodies' data.

Some considerations must be done on multiple body tracking and their identification. The MS Kinect SDK does associate a numeric, sequential id to each of the max #6 bodies it can locate and track, yet it cannot ensure to be able to keep the same id to the body it was assigned to earlier. Major factors influencing such identification discontinuity include for a person exiting then re-entering in the sensed frustum, and the overlap with other persons' depth footprints (possibly leading to a swap of their identities). Since we want several participants to be tracked by multiple Kinects, being able to maintain the same, initially assigned id (e.g. the one derived by the sequential entering into the tracking area) is a derived requirement to be addressed.

5   The Leap Motion Controller

The Leap Motion Controller is another popular NUI device that concentrates on hand detail rather than on the full body. The Leap Motion Controller looks user hands in a quite large frustum of $\sim 135° \times 115°$ in a distance range from the device of 60 cm. The sustainable data rate normally exceeds 100 Hz.

Whilst initially devoted to desktop hand tracking, since a couple of years it can be mounted in front of a HMD/VR headset (VR mode) in such a way to detect and track the hands of a visually immersed user as far as these fall in the device field-of-view, which depends on his/her head orientation.

Presently, the limitation of only one device per computer holds for the Leap Motion Controller too. Furthermore, it is USB 2.0-wired. Nevertheless, a compact wearable setup can be devised based on a small Windows pocket mini-PC on which let the Leap Motion software run, thus streaming the lightweight resulting hand data to the fusion server via Wi-Fi.

6   NUI Data Fusion System for Multi-person, Wireless, Markerless Area Tracking

This chapter introduces the multi-NUI device system architecture and gives details of the various modules implementing the key fusion functions in a flow we suppose to be the optimal one.

By referring to Fig. 3, each participant headset is composed by a HMD with a position-orientation (6-DoF) tracking system and a front-mounted Leap Motion Controller (VR mode, in the Leap Motion terminology). Whilst reported in the architectural scheme for completeness, the dashed parts have not yet been implemented in our system to date.

The first fusion in the step sequence is one among a suite of homogeneous Kinect sensors, each physically attached to a dedicated client computer. As already mentioned, we adopted the LiveScan3D client-server system of [14] so the Kinect client is just constituted by the plain LiveScan3D client with minimal interventions.

The multi-Kinect fusion server is based on the LiveScan3D server, majorly extended with the multi-body, multi-unit fusion techniques described in the specialized sections in the following chapters.

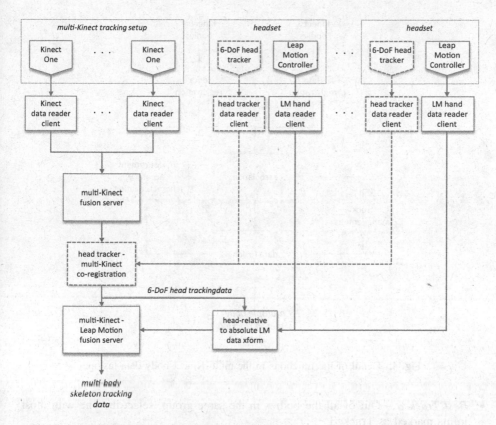

Fig. 3. Architecture of the multi-person tracking system based on multiple NUI devices.

6.1   Multiple Kinect Body Data Fusion

This module collects the various bodies coming from each single Kinect unit. In particular, it reads up to six body skeleton datasets from each Kinect in the pool and is committed to fuse corresponding bodies at its best.

Association

Since each Kinect assigns its own indices to the bodies detected in its view field, we have to assure correct mapping that each body corresponds to the same physical person. We do this by assigning all the bodies whose two or three spine joints are contemporarily within a short, predefined distance, to the same person into the scene. Then, all of the bodies assigned to the same group represent the same person and the count of groups represents the total count of people identified by all Kinects (Fig. 4).

Body Tracking Data Fusion

To obtain the final joint coordinates of a single person skeleton, we need to fuse all the bodies identified as belonging to the same group into one single skeleton. We implemented three different fusion techniques:

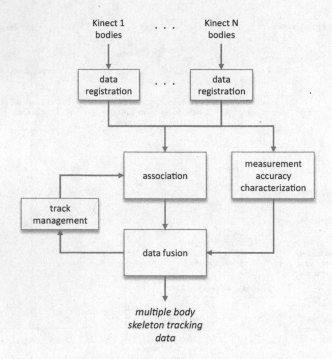

Fig. 4. Detail of the functions in the multi-Kinect body data fusion.

- *Best Tracked* – Out of all the bodies in the same group, select the one with most joints marked as Tracked.
- *Weighted Average* – The final coordinates of a joint are calculated as a weighted average of the coordinates of the same joint taken from each body within the same group. Separate weights are assigned depending on the tracking status of the joint: tracked, inferred or not tracked. The final coordinate component is calculated using the following formula:

$$\vec{x} = \frac{\sum_{i=1}^{N} w_i \vec{x}_i}{\sum_{i=1}^{N} w_i}$$

- *Kalman Filtering* – The final coordinates of a joint are obtained by applying a Kalman filter (based on a model of constant velocity motion of the joints) to all the coordinates of the same joint taken from the available sensors (see next chapter).

$$\begin{bmatrix} x_{k+1} \\ \dot{x}_{k+1} \end{bmatrix} = \begin{bmatrix} 1 & T \\ 0 & 1 \end{bmatrix} \begin{bmatrix} x_k \\ \dot{x}_k \end{bmatrix}$$

$$[\tilde{y}_k] = [1 \quad 0] \begin{bmatrix} x_k \\ \dot{x}_k \end{bmatrix}$$

In the previous system of equations, the variable T is used to represent the sample time, while x represents the position of the joint in one dimension and $\dot{x}$ its derivative which is constant between two time instants. The variable $\tilde{y}_k$ represents the measures provided by the Kinect units that track this joint.

Body Data Fusion by Kalman Filtering

Different strategies of sensor fusion among measurements provided by multiple Microsoft Kinect units at the same time have been proposed in literature in order to have a better estimation of each joint position. In [17], the authors proposed an interesting comparison between performances of EKF and Particle Filter, based on a "constant velocity" kinematic model. Considering that the aim of the present paper is the definition of a system able to track multiple targets in the scene with several Kinect devices, we have preferred to use a Kalman filter for sensor fusion, because of its more limited computational burden than the particle filter. This choice is also justified by the comparable accuracy offered by these two strategies and by the linearity of both prediction and output equations. Moreover, we preferred to implement one-dimensional Kalman filters (i.e. three independent filters working separately on the three-dimensional coordinates of the joints) based on a constant velocity kinematic model. The constant velocity model is applicable if considering that human motion to be captured for VR applications is relatively slow for a 90–100 Hz filter prediction frequency based on a 30 Hz measurement update frequency.

Since the Kinect SDK doesn't provide an estimation of measurements accuracy (they only provide an information about the joint status: tracked, not tracked, inferred) we decided to set the value of the measurement covariance matrix, at each update step, depending on the number of tracked joints by each device. Such logic aims at assigning a better reliability to measurements provided by units having a better view of the target person. Specifically, we assigned greater reliability to measurements if the device, which has provided them, tracks more than 20 joints. Inferred joints are ignored in the updating step (in this case, the logic assigns a very big value of the measurement covariance matrix in order to automatically discharge their measurements). Specifically, we set equal to 0.06 m^2 the variance for measurements related to a tracked joint provided by a device that tracks more than 20 joints, while we set equal to 0.6 m^2 the variance for measurements related to a tracked joint provided by a device that tracks less than 20 joints. Finally, we set equal to 100 m^2 the variance for measurements related to an inferred joint.

6.2   Multiple Kinects vs Head Tracker Co-registration

Assumed that the head tracking system's frame of reference be unique for all the participants' HMDs, this function is committed to put both the multiple Kinect system and the HMD tracking one in a common coordinate reference system. The assumption can be considered true e.g. in the case of the HTC Vive since it actually depends on the disposition in the room space of a single pair of Lighthouses for multiple HMD units (a common emitter system for one or more receivers).

The strategy behind such co-registration is to employ three persons for which both the systems return head tracking positions (direct measurement for the HMD head tracking system, and the Head node of the three bodies detected by the multi-Kinect tracking system). Once the HMD head positions have been transformed in the corresponding Kinect's Head position, the registration task is a best fitting alignment of the two resulting triangles in the 3D space. The found transformation will be applied to bring one coordinate system into the other's reference one, or vice-versa.

6.3   Kinect – Leap Motion Fusion

When a Leap Motion Controller is VR-mounted, its device-centered coordinate reference system is head-relative. This means that, in principle, LM data should be transformed by the 6-DoF matrix of the head node in order to be brought to a common reference ground for applying whatever combination strategy with Kinect skeleton data. In a physical environment with several tracked persons this relies on being able to put multi-Kinect bodies and LM units in a reliable correspondence (the mth body must correspond to the mth Leap Motion installed on his/her headset), yet this cannot be guaranteed by the *Association* function of the multi-Kinect fusion module for several reasons.

A better, more general approach is to check for the best match between the bodies' arm-hand position data and the LMs' forearm-hand coordinates once transformed by

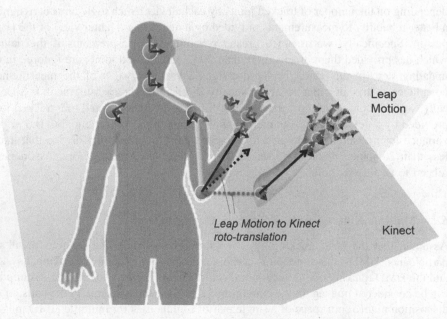

Fig. 5. Leap Motion to Kinect forearm-hand relocation by roto-translation to the Kinect elbow-forearm.

the head tracking 6-DoF data. Since the several device data-reading clients for both head trackers and the Leap Motion Controllers can be given assigned ids, they make the final association process deterministic, leading to a finally reliable identification of body skeletons put out by the complete fusion system.

Regarding how to combine the 3D forearm-hand data of the two sources, the proposed fusion strategy is a geometric-only one leveraging the commonality between the forearm starting/ending joints, which are actually tracked in both systems. Generally the two pairs of corresponding joints (elbow and wrist, for left and right forearms) do not coincide, mainly due to the different technologies and approaches employed for the detection and tracking of the anthropomorphic parts within the Kinect and the Leap Motion depth maps. In order to maintain an anthropometric coherence in the final body skeleton, it is somehow better to move the Leap Motion-sensed forearm-hand systems (left, right) to make them to coincide to the corresponding Kinect body forearm positions. In particular, it is desirable to make a LM forearm-hand system to be rigidly roto-translated in order to be aligned to the corresponding Kinect forearm, rooted in the elbow joint of the latter, yet retaining the rest of the LM joints after the transformation (Fig. 5).

7 Preliminary Results

The setup realized include a system of #5 Kinect units over the #6 of the complete system as ideally designed, for an actual circular coverage of 300° out of 360°, and a couple of Leap Motion Controllers for two participating users. VR HMDs havenot been introduced yet in the physical CVE to date, so the Kinect-head tracker co-registration has not been experimented yet.

To have a preliminary validation of the proposed approach to multiple-Kinects body fusion, we have carried out several simulation in Matlab/Simulink using data registered by two Kinect units.

In Fig. 6 the result of the sensor fusion is reported in blue, while in red and green the skeletons obtained by each one of the devices. The result of the sensor fusion offers a better estimation of the real pose of the target; in fact, the green skeleton has an unrealistic length of the right foot and of the femur.

Figure 7 reports the number of joints tracked by each device for each time instant. In the time interval 178 to 228 s. the second device has a better view of the target. This is confirmed by the unrealistic pose assumed by the target and the length of various parts, obtained using measurements provided by the first Kinect (red skeleton in Fig. 6).

In Figs. 8, 9 and 10 we have reported the time histories for the three coordinated of the SpineMid joint (numbered as 1) as put out by the two Kinect and by the Kalman filter. The arithmetic mean between the two sensors has also been reported, as comparison, in the case of the Z coordinate. By referring to Fig. 9, it is interesting to note how the results of sensor fusion are closer to measurements provided by the second Kinect in the time range 178 to 228 s, as a demonstration of the fine work of the filter and the related logic to set values of the measurement covariance matrix (the blue skeleton in Fig. 12). Indeed, the length of the legs and the feet, associated with the

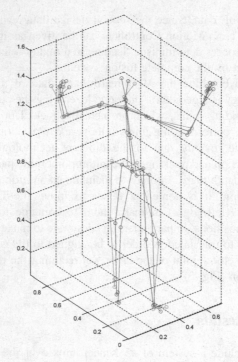

Fig. 6. Comparison among the measures provided by two Kinect units and the results of the multi-Kinect body fusion. (Color figure online)

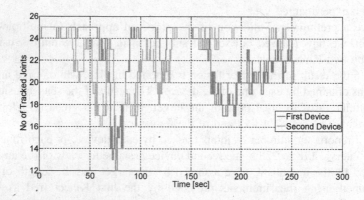

Fig. 7. Number of joints tracked by each of the two Kinect.

correct position of the Head joint, show that the results provided by the sensor fusion are much better than the measurements provided by each Kinect used standalone (the blue skeleton in Fig. 12) (Fig. 11).

Since we didn't set up any VR HMD tracker in our experimental setup, our only experimentations in fusing Kinect and Leap Motion data as described at chapter 5.3 have relied on head data supplied by the multi-Kinect fusion system. Kinect's head data

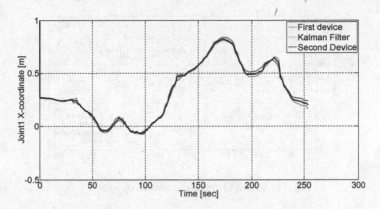

Fig. 8. X-coordinate of the joint n.1.

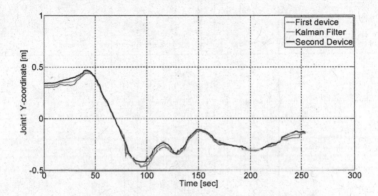

Fig. 9. Y-coordinate of the joint n.1.

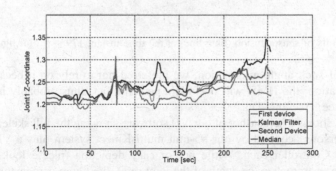

Fig. 10. Z-coordinate of the joint n.1.

are not as rich as other skeleton data in what it is a "terminal" body joint, for which no heading information is supplied by the Microsoft Kinect SDK v2. While, in principle, the Hi-Res Face Tracking data of the SDK v2 could have been used for compensating

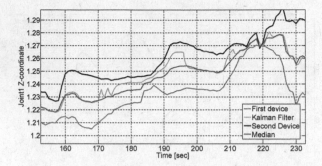

Fig. 11. Zoom of the Z-coordinate of joint n.1.

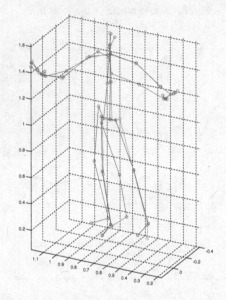

Fig. 12. Results of sensor fusion (blue line) at the time instant 179 s. (Color figure online)

for the lack of such angle information, we preferred not to rely on it because, in the final configuration, the HMD will occlude a person's face thus probably invalidating the Kinect Face Tracking data.

Figure 13 shows a screenshot of our VR software showing the full skeletons of two interacting persons acquired by our #5-unit multi-Kinect system plus a VR-mounted Leap Motion Controller each. While not of easy depiction (please look at ground shadows in order to realize the depth of the joint refs), the figure demonstrates that the preliminary heterogeneous system is already able to feed tracking data to VR apps using them at an interactive rate. In fact, the Predictor module of the multi-Kinect fusion system can be made running at multiples of the base Kinect body tracking data rate of 30 Hz, e.g. 60–90 Hz, while a normal data rate for the Leap Motion hand data is 100 Hz. The latency introduced by the multi-stage fusion has not yet been measured, yet it is not expected to invalidate the system usability for VR.

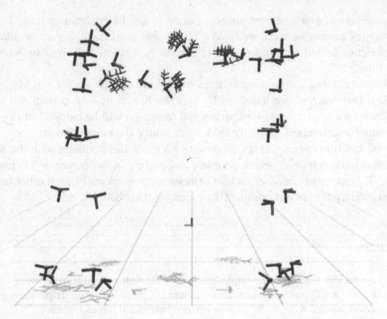

Fig. 13. Results of the merge of Kinect skeletons (large refs) and Leap Motion hand data (small refs) for two cooperating persons.

8 Conclusions

While based on largely preliminary results and with some parts not yet implemented (e.g. the HMD-based head tracking is a missing tile of the whole system mosaic), the proposed multi-NUI device system for full-body, wireless markerless tracking system supporting multiple persons in a CVE showed us encouraging results. The prospective final system promises even better precision and more tolerance to badly tracked poses by the single base NUI devices.

The system which has been set up in our institution's VR Lab has already proven to be a flexible hardware and software framework for experimenting with different co-registration and fusion techniques and data combination strategies. New data sources are expected to complete the sensor suite and to better validate the effectiveness of the proposed sensor ensemble. The cooperation between same-type sensors (multiple Kinect units) enhances the quality and the reliability of body tracking data, while the integration with complementary sensors (head trackers, Leap Motion Controllers) adds missing details (hands and fingers) in a coherent common space.

9 Future Works

As future development of the system, we might implement the use of an anthropo-metric coherence in the body fusion phase of the algorithm, in terms of three-dimensional physical constraints between the joints of the skeleton (for example, the distance between two nearby joints – bones – shall be constant in time, a/o some relative angles cannot be exceeded). We might also implement a particle filter as a further skeleton fusion technique, and test its extrapolation performance versus the Kalman filter.

Furthermore, since all the three sources of tracking data (Kinect, Leap Motion, and the HMD 6-DoF tracker) are based on IR light, each with its own emitter and with its own characteristics, an extensive experimental campaign will be carried out in order to assess mutual interferences possibly leading to source data degradation.

We will hold on looking at a Collaborative Virtual Environment with the shortest path to immersion possible, where people collaborating in the common VE just put a wireless VR "extended" headset on and start interacting naturally each other and with by directly manipulating environment's objects by their bared hands.

References

1. Microsoft Kinect for Windows. https://developer.microsoft.com/en-us/windows/Kinect
2. A State of the Art Report on Kinect Sensor Setups in Computer Vision. http://www.grk1564.uni-siegen.de/sites/www.grk1564.uni-siegen.de/files/inm2013/kinect-star.pdf
3. Khoshelham, K., Elberink, S.O.: Accuracy and resolution of kinect depth data for indoor mapping applications. Sensors **12**, 1437–1454 (2012)
4. Ye, M., Wang, X., Yang, R., Ren, L., Pollefeys, M.: Accurate 3D pose estimation from a single depth image. In: Proceedings of the IEEE International Conference on Computer Vision, Barcelona, Spain, pp. 731–738, 6–13 November 2011
5. Weiss, A., Hirshberg, D., Black, M.J.: Home 3D body scans from noisy image and range data. In: Proceedings of the IEEE International Conference on Computer Vision, Barcelona, Spain, pp. 1951–1958, 6–13 November 2011
6. Shotton, J., Sharp, T., Kipman, A., Fitzgibbon, A., Finocchio, M., Blake, A., Cook, M., Moore, R.: Real-time human pose recognition in parts from single depth images. Commun. ACM **56**, 116–124 (2013)
7. Grest, D., Krüger, V., Koch, R.: Single view motion tracking by depth and silhouette information. In: Ersbøll, B.K., Pedersen, K.S. (eds.) SCIA 2007. LNCS, vol. 4522, pp. 719–729. Springer, Heidelberg (2007). doi:10.1007/978-3-540-73040-8_73
8. Wei, X., Zhang, P., Chai, J.: Accurate realtime full-body motion capture using a single depth camera. ACM Trans. Graph. **31**, 1–12 (2012)
9. Gao, Z., Yu, Y., Zhou, Y., Du, S.: Leveraging two kinect sensors for accurate full-body motion capture (2015). http://www.mdpi.com/1424-8220/15/9/24297/htm
10. Liu, Y., Stoll, C., Gall, J., Seidel, H.-P., Theobalt, C.: Markerless motion capture of interacting characters using multi-view image segmentation. http://ieeexplore.ieee.org/abstract/document/5995424/
11. Leap Motion Controller VR Development. https://developer.leapmotion.com/windows-vr
12. Marin, G., Dominio, F., Zanuttigh, P.: Hand gesture recognition with leap motion and kinect devices. http://ieeexplore.ieee.org/abstract/document/7025313/
13. Craig, A., Krishnan, S.: Fusion of leap motion and kinect sensors for improved field of view and accuracy for VR applications
14. Kowalski, M., Naruniec, J., Daniluk, M.: LiveScan3D: a fast and inexpensive 3D data acquisition system for multiple kinect v2 sensors. In: 2015 International Conference on 3D Vision (3DV), Lyon, France (2015). http://ieeexplore.ieee.org/document/7335499/

15. Besl, P.J., McKay, N.D.: A method for registration of 3-D shapes. IEEE Trans. Pattern Anal. Mach. Intell. **14**(2), 239–256 (1992)
16. Kopniak, P.: Motion capture using multiple Kinect controllers (2015). http://www.pe.org.pl/articles/2015/8/7.pdf
17. Morato, C., Kaipa, K.N., Zhao, B., Gupta, S.K.: Toward safe human robot collaboration by using multiple Kinects based real-time human tracking. J. Comput. Inf. Sci. Eng. **14**(1), 011005-01–011005-10 (2014). doi:10.1115/1.4025810
18. Satyavolu, S., Bruder, G., Willemsen, P., Steinicke, F.: Analysis of IR-based virtual reality tracking using multiple Kinects. https://www.researchgate.net/publication/241628899_Analysis_of_IR-based_virtual_reality_tracking_using_multiple_Kinects

Safety Training Using Virtual Reality:
A Comparative Approach

Giovanni Avveduto[✉], Camilla Tanca, Cristian Lorenzini, Franco Tecchia,
Marcello Carrozzino, and Massimo Bergamasco

Scuola Superiore Sant'Anna, Pisa, Italy
g.avveduto@santannapisa.it

Abstract. Virtual Reality is widely regarded as an extremely promising
solution for industrial training purposes, as it allows to perform simulated hands-on activities in a controlled and safe environment. In this
paper we present a Virtual Reality system aimed at providing a training
solution for safety inside a generic power plant environment. The system
includes several scenarios in order to offer a wide range of tasks and situations. We have tested the system with a sample of users in order to
compare the effectiveness of traditional training against our system in
terms of theoretical and practical learning. We carried on our study with
questionnaires and observing the behaviour of all the users inside the
Virtual Environment. We also studied the involvement of trainees and
sense of presence generated by the system, as it is an important driver of
user engagement and, consequently, impacts on motivation and training
efficacy.

Keywords: Virtual environments · Virtual Reality · Training · Safety

1 Introduction

Education in industrial process is fundamental for any form of industry. Whenever new employees are introduced on a workplace, they have to be trained so
they can learn what to do inside the workplace in order to carry out their activities. Training commonly involves new workers (or experienced workers that have
to face new procedures) and progressively decreases throughout their careers.

Another important skill that workers need to develop is how to do their job
inside the workspace in safety using the correct procedures. Studies demonstrate
that workers are more likely to be exposed to health and safety risks when they
underestimate risk due to the confidence on their work environments [4]. All
workers must be aware of the safety procedures needed to correctly perform
their jobs without risks, not only new employees. As a matter of fact, the risk
perception of a worker decreases when the experience increases [21]; routine in
fact can lead to underrate threats. For this reason, even experienced workers
needs to be updated and regularly reminded about the safety procedures.

© Springer International Publishing AG 2017
L.T. De Paolis et al. (Eds.): AVR 2017, Part I, LNCS 10324, pp. 148–163, 2017.
DOI: 10.1007/978-3-319-60922-5_11

Current industrial safety training methods generally rely on repetitive classroom-taught lessons integrated by directions given in the physical workplace, followed by on the job training [16]. These lectures sometimes end up being not so engaging or even boring, so exploring alternative or supplementary ways to improve the workers awareness and compliances to the safety procedures is fundamental. Nonetheless finding a more effective way to transfer the knowledge and improving the information retention would be extremely useful.

2   VR and Training

In recent years, VR has been increasingly used in a wide range of applications, including education, science, health and military. One of the most important applications of VR is to provide training solutions in a variety of industries and fields (military, medicine, power generation, aircraft, etc.). Immersive VR (IVR), in particular, allows to realize simulators that enable an effective transfer of the skills acquired in the virtual context. To this purpose realistic sensorial feedback and natural interaction must be provided so as to match as close as possible real-life conditions. There are many kinds of IVR systems [3,18]. CAVE-like system are rooms where users are surrounded by large screens onto which a nearly continuous virtual scene is projected in stereoscopy. Interacting with own body inside a CAVE system can lead to body/projection occlusion problems, so it is not the most suitable IVR system when a natural interaction is of primary importance. CAVE like systems are also expensive and not portable. Recently, cheap fully immersive Head Mounted Displays (HMDs) have appeared on the market. HMDs solutions are traditionally more portable. Being the user's vision completely demanded to the HMD, the user cannot see the real environment surrounding. Providing a digital reconstruction of the users bodies, animated according to their movements, must be provided in order to allow own perception. Immersive VR systems are commonly able to trigger high levels of presence, a subjective sensation usually correlated with engagement and involvement not easily defined and measured [16,17]. Presence is therefore an important driver of user engagement and, consequently, impacts on motivation and training efficacy. This is one of the reasons why VR is becoming an important and powerful training tool, as it allows to perform simulated hands-on operations in a controlled and safe environment, reducing costs and risks associated to these activities.

This considerations are especially important when it comes to training for safety. The idea is to challenge operators with dynamic cases in order to train them to respond quickly in unusual situations, thus enabling them to effectively recognize and recover anomalies and malfunctions [14]. When placed in a virtual environment, users can explore all the solutions and the effects of their actions, including potentially dangerous ones, inside a virtual workplace. A learning experience can be developed offering a virtual experience in place of or after a classroom-taught lesson on safety. In case of experienced workers this solution is most usable. A virtual experience could in fact improve the attention or the awareness on safety, hence the users can be exposed to virtual risks without the dangers of "real-life" experiences. For all workplaces, it is possible to recreate the risk conditions where workers are subjected to. VR applications for safety have been already used in some fields. Van Wyk and De Villiers [19] studied how VR applications could help miners to improve their safety in South African mines, using all the peculiarity of the natural environment. Miners work in confined areas, in steeply inclined excavations, using handling heavy material and equipment and in the proximity of moving machinery. The virtual environment that they reconstruct reproduces these conditions. Previous studies where the VR is applied to the power production fields exists [5]. Power electric systems require continuous maintenance in order to maintain public safety, emergency management, national security and business continuity. These companies extensively use 2D diagrams as support for servicing activities. For this reason, often operator have difficulties in matching the provided information to the real world machinery in order to carry on the maintenance. VR simulators instead allow to model real objects according to their dimensions, appearance and features. A user trained using VR systems could easily recognize the real scenario allowing for an easier knowledge transfer.

3   The VR Safety Trainer

An industrial Virtual Safety Trainer simulator have been developed in collaboration with a power production company, in order to explore new ways to improve the adherence of workers behaviours to the standard safety procedures. The simulator consists of a set of real case scenarios, where workers can be trained in performing exercises, inspections or maintenance procedures. All the procedures have been designed in collaboration with and validated by experts in the field. The virtual environment have been logically modelled to simulate the real counterpart and respond to the users actions as it would do in real life. It is therefore possible for the trainee to experience, in a safe way, the outcomes of wrong actions when performing dangerous procedures. Accidents due to incorrect procedures or lack in observing safety rules are simulated: electrical short-cuts, explosions, burning and electric arcs are reproduced. Providing this kind of feedback in real-life training sessions is not possible or too dangerous for the trainee. Using VR, workers can be therefore safely practice procedures using a learning-by-doing paradigm, and recognize and recover anomalies and malfunctions.

The simulated scenarios include maintenance or securing procedures of low and medium voltage apparatus, inspections of confined spaces, and maintenance or securing of mechanical parts. Figure 1 shows an example of scenario. For each procedure a work plan describing the exercise to be performed is provided. Each scenario starts in a dress room where the worker can read the work plan, wear the Personal Protection Equipment (PPE) and choose all the tools needed to perform the task. A lift placed in a corner of each room allows the user to move across different rooms.

The simulator allows one or more trainee and trainers to communicate verbally and also to share the virtual experience. The system can be used both as

Fig. 1. A picture of a scenario containing low- and medium-voltage apparatus.

a training tool, as well as a validation tool. During a validation case the worker is asked to perform a specific procedure while the supervisor can see what the user is doing inside the VE.

3.1 Technological Setup

In order to guarantee a complete immersion of the user in the VE, the system exploits the use of HMDs, tracking systems and joypads. Each user wears a HMD and grab two tracked controllers with the hands. The first version of the system exploits an Oculus DK2 HMD, two Nintendo Wii controllers and an Optitrack tracking system. The recently available HTC Vive HMD is a cheaper but still effective solution that have been integrated. The user is free to move in a VE as he/she would do in real life, and the simplified tracking of the hands allows to naturally interact with the virtual objects.

The typical tracked area of the Vive systems is a 4 by 4 meters square. The virtual scenarios have been designed to match this size. However, it is possible to track bigger spaces according to own needs by using other tracking systems - like the Optitrack one. Figure 2 shows a user seen from the outside while using the system and a display presenting what the user is seeing.

The simulator have been developed using the Unreal Engine 4 framework[1] integrated with custom modules that handle different tracking systems and input/output devices.

A plugin for the engine to allow an effective integration of external tracking systems (like the Optitrack) with the system has been developed. The module performs implement sensor fusion [8] and calibration techniques to allow to track

---

[1] www.unrealengine.com.

Fig. 2. A picture showing a user interacting with the VE seen from the outside.

a wide area thanks to the optical external tracker while maintaining the near zero-latency accurate rotational tracking provided by the inertial sensors embedded in the HMDs. A second plugin to allow the use of the bluetooth Nintendo Wii controllers have been developed.

A framework to ease the development of industrial scenarios have been developed as well. The framework consists of a collection of reusable components with pre-defined behaviours allowing for an easier and higher-level development of new scenarios. These components reproduce many standard actual objects (like valves, physics handles, tools, personal protection equipments etc.). Furthermore the framework provides a set of base class and interfaces to easily implement logic and behaviour of generic components (like components that can be grabbed and manipulated, static components, objects that can be damaged and replaced, components that can be attached to the user or to other objects and so on). Mechanisms to define rules and logic of the tasks that users are required to perform have been defined. The infringement of the defined rules could lead to predefined outcomes and feedbacks to the user (like explosions, electric short-cuts, alarms etc.). Finally a mechanism to allow users to move across different scenarios based on a elevator metaphor have been implemented.

4   Method

In order to evaluate the effectiveness of using VR systems for safety training, we first reviewed the literature about evaluation methods of general training practice [7]. Kirkpatrick developed one of the most used models for measuring the effectiveness of a training procedure [1, 9–11] and provide guidelines for designing effective training. The model defines four levels of evaluation: reaction, learning, behaviour and results.

1. *Reaction level* rates what the participant though and felt about the training session and gives a measure of the user's satisfaction. Reaction level is measured collecting questionnaire, interviews and surveys after the learning session and analysing the verbal reactions of the users.
2. *Learning level* measures knowledge and/or skills increase. This level can be estimated during the training session through a knowledge demonstration or a test. More in details, pre-post knowledge questionnaire and performances tests can be used. Predetermined scoring and coherence between methods of evaluation and training targets can help to minimize risks of inconsistency of results.
3. *Behaviour level* measures the degree to which participants apply what they learned during training on the job and their changes in attitudes. This measurement can be, but is not necessarily, a reflection of whether participants actually learned. For example, the failure of behavioural change can be due to other circumstances such as individual's reluctance to change. The evaluation involves both pre- and post-event measurement of the learner's behaviour.
4. *Results level* seeks to determine the tangible results of the training such as: reduced cost, improved quality and efficiency, increased productivity, employee retention, increased sales and higher morale.

Some authors suggest to add a 5th level in order to measure the return on investment as evaluation parameter [15]. The power of the model is its simplicity and its ability to help people think about training evaluation criteria.

The power producer company – we worked in collaboration with to carry out this tool – currently utilize a traditional training approach. The knowledge transfer is achieved through classroom lecture, manuals and in-loco practice on real machinery. Physical practice with real equipment cannot be easily replaced by VR practice due to factors as a still inadequate haptic feedback. However the theoretical knowledge some practical skills could take advantage of the virtual approach.

In order to evaluate effectiveness of VR training in comparison with a traditional learning methodology an experiment have been conducted. The subject of the training session is to instruct users how to correctly perform inspections of confined spaces focusing on the adherence to the safety procedures. In order to perform the comparison two groups have been formed: the Control Group (CG) and the VR Group (VRG). The control group has been taught using only traditional techniques. Part of the lectures of the second group have been conducted in a VE.

We have followed the guidelines provided by Kirkpatrick to evaluate the training, in particular the first two steps and part of the third of his model. The experiment have been conducted on workers which have no previous experience on the job, so the last step and the change in attitudes of the third step of the Kirkpatrick's model doesn't apply to our case.

A strong sense of presence has proved to carry the potential to aid training transfer [12,13,16]. We used the Witmer And Singer Presence Questionnaire (PQ) [20] in order to estimate the sense of presence perceived by users during the VR evaluative session. Control, Sensory, Distraction and Realism are the main factors of the sense of presence.

4.1 Procedure

The simulator provides several scenarios where to perform different procedures. Among these, we choose the inspection of a confined space as test scenario for evaluating the impact of the system on the effectiveness of the training session.

The participants to the experiment have been recruited among colleagues and student with no previous experience on the subject of the training. A total of 24 subjects, aged between 24 and 46 (31.36 ± 6.3) took part to the evaluation, 12 for each of the two groups.

The training sessions of both groups have started with a traditional classroom lecture. The trainer instructed the workers about general safety rules that have to be observed when performing any job inside the power plant. During this lesson slides have been shown and commented by the trainer. The lecture explained the importance Personal Protective Equipment (PPE), and the correct procedures and tools needed to operate both in voltage risk environments and in confined spaces. Additional information were provided, as law references, the importance of reading the work plan and of a clean workspace.

After the first common lecture, each group have been taught how to perform an inspection of a confined spaces with different approaches. The control group watched a video of an expert performing the inspection in the correct way: the operations to undertake to accomplish the task and safety rules that need to be respected. The VR group users have been instructed by a trainer about the same procedure while immersed in the VE. The video watched by the CG users consisted in a screen capture of an expert conducting the inspection in the VR simulator, allowing the CG users to familiarize with the VE too. In order to evaluate differences in learning between the two approaches, two different criteria have been adopted: an evaluation based on pre-training (PreQ) and post-training questionnaires (PostQ) and an evaluation of the user's behaviour while performing the procedure in VR. The experiment have been therefore split in two phases, conducted on different days.

During the first phase, users first have answered the PreQ, then have taken part to the two lectures, and finally have answered the PostQ. Comparing the pre- and post-training questionnaires is a classical way – suggested also by Kirkpatrick and widely adopted in different fields – to measure the effectiveness of a training session. During this phase "reactions" [11] of the users have been collected.

The second phase of the evaluation took place 5 days after. Each subject have been asked to perform the inspection procedure using the VR simulator without any aid of the trainer. The experimenters have therefore observed and collected all the actions performed by the trainees and the adherence to the safety procedures. Finally, the presence questionnaire have been presented to the users.

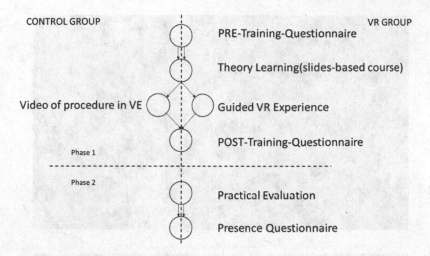

CONTROL GROUP

VR GROUP

PRE-Training-Questionnaire

Theory Learning(slides-based course)

Video of procedure in VE   Guided VR Experience

POST-Training-Questionnaire

Phase 1

Phase 2

Practical Evaluation

Presence Questionnaire

Fig. 3. Scheme of the experiment procedures adopted tor the two groups.

A scheme of the procedure adopted for the evaluation is shown in Fig. 3.

The inspection procedure taught during the course took place in a furnace room (see Fig. 4a), while the evaluative inspection took place in a condenser room (see Fig. 4b). Despite of the different scenario, the task to be performed and the safety procedures to respect are the same. As usually happens in real life training session, the workers are trained on procedures which are generally valid for a variety of scenarios.

4.2   Metrics

The pre- and the post-training questionnaires are composed by the same 42 true-false questions on the contents of the courses. When evaluating the results, to each question is assigned a score of 1 point if correctly answered and 0 points if not. In this way the total score of the PreQ and PostQ can be directly compared in order to evaluate the level of the knowledge transfer obtained by the two training approaches.

Questions about the pertinence of the questions to the contents taught in the course, the involvement and the perceived effectiveness of the courses have been added to the PostQ. These questions aim at collecting the "reactions" of the users in a 6-point Likert scale.

Similarly, a score is assigned to each action performed during the evaluative inspection procedure. One point is assigned for each correct PPE worn by the user and for each tool correctly used. One point is assigned to each correct step performed by the user to accomplish the inspection task. In this way it is possible to have a second comparison of the two different teaching approaches in terms of practical knowledge transfer. While the questionnaires' comparison aims at evaluating a more theoretical knowledge transfer, the second approach is closer to a practical evaluation of the training approach.

(a)

(b)

Fig. 4. The furnace (a) and the condenser (b) confined space scenarios.

All the collected scores have been normalized on the maximum score, and are presented as a percentage score. PQ results have been normalized on the maximum score, and are presented as a percentage score.

5 Training Results

Aim of the work is to compare the effectiveness of VR for safety training in comparison with a traditional classroom-based approach. In order to evaluate the differences in learning – both on theory and when performing an actual procedure in VR – we have asked the subject to answer questionnaires and have collected their behaviours. To statistically compare the differences both in questionnaires and in the collected scores the Wilcoxon signed-rank test have been used.

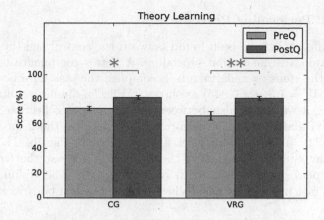

Fig. 5. Theory learning results for both groups. Bars reports 25th and 75th percentiles. *$p \leq 0.05$, **$p \leq 0.01$.

5.1 Part 1: Learning the Theory

As shown in Fig. 5, significant differences have been found between the PreQ and the PostQ for both the control and the VR groups. Knowledge of the users improved after attending the course for both groups (CG: $W = 10.00, p = 0.022$; VRG: $W = 0.00, p = 0.003$).

The base knowledge of the users before the training was the same for the two groups. As shown in Fig. 6 no relevant differences in the PreQs between the control and the VR groups have been found ($W = 22.5, p = 0.19$). Similarly, according to the PostQ results, no relevant differences in learning have been found between the control and VR group, meaning that both the teaching methods have resulted to be equally effective ($W = 23.5, p = 0.68$).

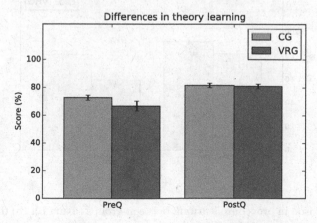

Fig. 6. Comparison between groups in theory leaning according to PreQ and PostQ. Bars reports 25th and 75th percentiles.

5.2   Part 2: Performing Procedures

Significant differences have been found between the control and the VR groups during the evaluative inspection procedure. A better compliance to the safety rules and to the steps to undertake to accomplish the task have been obtained by the VRG ($W = 1.5, p = 0.005$) as shown in Fig. 7a. Similar results have been obtained even if we distinguish between the equipment collection task ($W = 1.5, p = 0.004$) and the actions performed to a perform the inspection ($W = 10.0, p = 0.022$). Individual statistics are presented in Fig. 7b. Those findings agree with the embodied cognition theories which suggest that memory can be aided by performing actions with own body [2,6]. The training in VR is performed in fact by the user naturally using his/her own body as in real life.

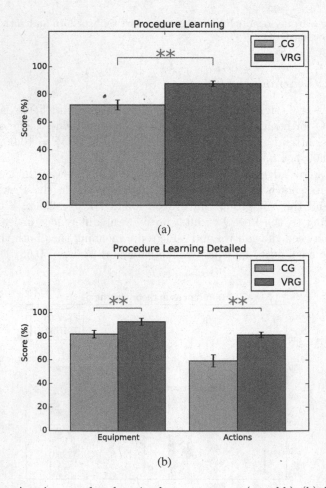

Fig. 7. Comparison in procedure learning between groups (a and b). (b) distinguishing between collection of the equipment and actions performed. Bars reports 25th and 75th percentiles. **$p \leq 0.01$.

5.3   Trainee Involvement

An important factor to be taken into account when evaluating a training course is the overall involvement of the trainees. Both the groups have first taken a classroom course on general safety rules, and then a second course on a specific procedure (different methods for the two groups). Both groups indeed have shown a greater involvement in the second part of the course: video watching for CG ($W = 0.0, p = 0.002$) and VR simulation for the VRG ($W = 0.0, p = 0.004$) as shown in Fig. 8 shows the difference.

Furthermore, as shown in Fig. 9, a very significant difference have also been registered between the two courses on the procedure taken by the two groups. The VR experience resulted in a greater involvement of the trainees with respect to watching the video (W = 4.0, p = 0.03), meaning that the VR course have resulted to be much more engaging.

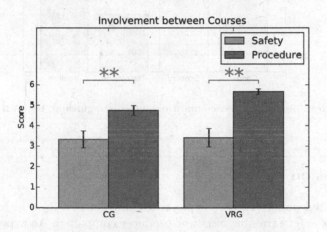

Fig. 8. Trainee's involvement between the two parts of each course. $**p \leq 0.01$.

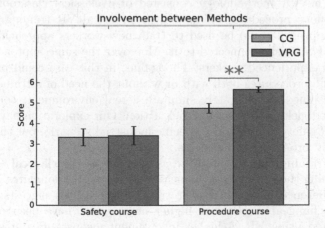

Fig. 9. Comparison of trainee's involvement between the two groups. $**p \leq 0.01$.

5.4   Sense of Presence in VR

Presence Questionnaire results are shown in Fig. 10. The positive factors have obtained high scores (Control: $80.61 \pm 10.05\%$; Sensory: $82.70 \pm 12.17\%$; Realism: $72.04 \pm 12.67\%$), while the negative Distraction factor have obtained a low score $(33.00 \pm 18.54\%)$.

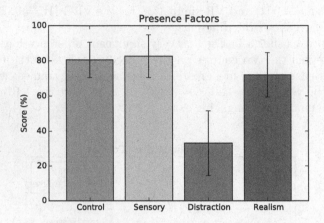

Fig. 10. Results of the presence questionnaire distinguishing between factors.

6   Discussion

In the presented paper, we have explored the impact of VR on learning, in the context of the safety training of power producer companies. An experiment aim at comparing the VR training with a traditional classroom training have been conducted. The VR methodology consisted of a classical classroom teaching on general safety procedures followed by a practical VR training on specific tasks. This approach could be used to train new workers approaching the job to understand the risks connected to it. Moreover the same approach could be useful also to experienced workers. The trainee in this case could practice and remind specific procedures both with or without the need of a trainer. The VR simulator, designed to accurately simulate a real environment, could provide immediate feedback to the user for each action. Our exploration have validated the use of VR safety training in a specific industrial scenario, but the approach could be easily brought to other fields.

The VR training turned out to be as effective as the classical approach in terms of learning the theory directly measurable with questionnaires. The lack of significant differences between the two training approaches suggests that methods are interchangeable. However higher involvement have been reported by users instructed using VR. A higher involvement means a greater engagement and user satisfaction. Therefore even if the two methods are similar in terms of knowledge transfer, the newer approach is preferable due to the better user involvement. An high level of sense of presence have been registered during the evaluative VR sessions for both groups. A strong sense of presence has proved to carry the potential to aid training transfer.

Furthermore, when the evaluation criteria take in consideration the workers behaviour of the user performing the procedure, the VR training resulted to be significantly much more effective than the traditional approach. The users performed better both in terms of adherence to the safety rules and in terms of correctly performing the assigned tasks. VR training could indeed raise the level of reception and memorization of physical procedures. Two variables should be taken into account when evaluating the practical performance: effect on memory and knowledge transfer. How much the improvement of the VR training are due to a better memorization? How much to a better knowledge transfer? In the experiment conducted it is not possible to distinguish between the contributions of the two factors, because we have only observed the combined results after some days. Thus, could be interesting to evaluate separately the two effects. In order to decouple the contributions we would like to conduct further experiments varying the amount of time between the training and evaluative sessions. In this way it should be possible to isolate the impact on memory and consequently the impact on knowledge transfer. The relation between gesture memorization and the body execution of it, is a known topic among embodied cognition theories [2,6]. The better performances registered in the evaluative phase could be justified by these theories.

According to the results we think that the introduction of VR as training methodology could lead to better knowledge transfer as well as guarantee a more pleasant and engaging learning experience.

7 Conclusions and Future Work

In the presented paper, we have explored the impact of using VR on learning in the context of safety training of power production companies. A VR Safety Trainer have been presented. An experiment aiming at comparing the VR approach with a traditional classroom-based approach have been conducted. Results suggests that replacing or supporting the traditional classroom-based training approach with a VR-based one lead to better knowledge transfer. VR training demonstrated to be more effective in terms of practical learning while equally effective in terms of theory learning. Furthermore, using VR systems in safety training improves workers involvement, engagement and therefore enjoyment.

The model adopted to evaluate the training session is inspired to the Kirkpatrick's one. However only the first two levels and part of the third of the model have been investigated by this evaluation. Studies can be conducted on real companies with workers specialized in the job in order to be able to evaluate also the behavioural change and the tangible outcomes of this kind of training. It would also be interesting to evaluate the long term impact of those new learning paradigms in comparison to the actual adopted system.

References

1. Alliger, G.M., Janak, E.A.: Kirkpatrick's levels of training criteria: thirty years later. Pers. Psychol. **42**(2), 331–342 (1989)
2. Barsalou, L.W.: Grounded cognition. Annu. Rev. Psychol. **59**, 617–645 (2008)
3. Biocca, F., Delaney, B.: Immersive virtual reality technology. In: Communication in the Age of Virtual Reality, pp. 57–124 (1995)
4. Bryson, A.: Health and safety risks in Britain's workplaces: where are they and who controls them? Ind. Relat. J. **47**(5–6), 547–566 (2016)
5. Cardoso, A., Prado, P.R., Lima, G.F.M., Lamounier, E.: A virtual reality based approach to improve human performance and to minimize safety risks when operating power electric systems. In: Cetiner, S.M., Fechtelkotter, P., Legatt, M. (eds.) Advances in Human Factors in Energy: Oil, Gas, Nuclear and Electric Power Industries. AISC, vol. 495, pp. 171–182. Springer, Cham (2017). doi:10.1007/978-3-319-41950-3_15
6. Chao, K.-J., Huang, H.-W., Fang, W.-C., Chen, N.-S.: Embodied play to learn: exploring kinect-facilitated memory performance. Br. J. Educ. Technol. **44**(5), E151–E155 (2013)
7. Gavish, N., Gutiérrez, T., Webel, S., Rodríguez, J., Peveri, M., Bockholt, U., Tecchia, F.: Evaluating virtual reality and augmented reality training for industrial maintenance and assembly tasks. Interact. Learn. Environ. **23**(6), 778–798 (2015)
8. He, C., Şen, H.T., Kim, S., Sadda, P., Kazanzides, P.: Fusion of inertial sensing to compensate for partial occlusions in optical tracking systems. In: Linte, C.A., Yaniv, Z., Fallavollita, P., Abolmaesumi, P., Holmes, D.R. (eds.) AE-CAI 2014. LNCS, vol. 8678, pp. 60–69. Springer, Cham (2014). doi:10.1007/978-3-319-10437-9_7
9. Kirkpatrick, D.L.: Evaluation of Training. McGraW-Hill, New York (1967)
10. Kirkpatrick, D.L.: Evaluating Training Programs. Tata McGraw-Hill Education, San Francisco (1975)
11. Kirkpatrick, D.L.: Techniques for evaluating training programs. Train. Dev. J. 78–92 (1979)
12. Li, H., Daugherty, T., Biocca, F.: Impact of 3-d advertising on product knowledge, brand attitude, and purchase intention: the mediating role of presence. J. Advert. **31**(3), 43–57 (2002)
13. Lombard, M., Ditton, T.: At the heart of it all: the concept of presence. J. Comput. Mediat. Commun. **3**(2) (1997). doi:10.1111/j.1083-6101.1997.tb00072.x, ISSN 1083-6101
14. Manca, D., Brambilla, S., Colombo, S.: Bridging between virtual reality and accident simulation for training of process-industry operators. Adv. Eng. Softw. **55**, 1–9 (2013)
15. Phillips, J.J.: How much is the training worth? Train. Dev. **50**(4), 20–25 (1996)
16. Sheridan, T.B.: Musings on telepresence and virtual presence. Presence Teleoper. Virtual Environ. **1**(1), 120–126 (1992)
17. Slater, M., Frisoli, A., Tecchia, F., Guger, C., Lotto, B., Steed, A., Pfurtscheller, G., Leeb, R., Reiner, M., Sanchez-Vives, M.V., et al.: Understanding and realizing presence in the Presenccia project. IEEE Comput. Graph. Appl. **27**(4), 90–93 (2007)
18. Tecchia, F., Avveduto, G., Brondi, R., Carrozzino, M., Bergamasco, M., Alem, L.: I'm in VR! using your own hands in a fully immersive MR system. In: Proceedings of the 20th ACM Symposium on Virtual Reality Software and Technology, pp. 73–76. ACM (2014)

19. Van Wyk, E., De Villiers, R.: Virtual reality training applications for the mining industry. In: Proceedings of the 6th International Conference on Computer Graphics, Virtual Reality, Visualisation and Interaction in Africa, pp. 53–63. ACM (2009)
20. Witmer, B.G., Singer, M.J.: Measuring presence in virtual environments: a presence questionnaire. Presence Teleoper. Virtual Environ. **7**(3), 225–240 (1998)
21. Zohar, D., Erev, I.: On the difficulty of promoting workers' safety behaviour: overcoming the underweighting of routine risks. Int. J. Risk Assess. Manag. **7**(2), 122–136 (2006)

Robots Coordinated Control for Service Tasks in Virtual Reality Environments

Esteban X. Castellanos, Carlos García-Sánchez,
Wilson Bl. Llanganate, Victor H. Andaluz[(⊠)],
and Washington X. Quevedo

Universidad de las Fuerzas Armadas ESPE, Sangolquí, Ecuador
{excastellanos, cagarcia, wbllanganate, vhandaluz1,
wjquevedo}@espe.edu.ec

Abstract. The work presented below, involves creating a virtual environment with which you can test the main controllers for robot. There are three controllers considered, the point-point control that takes the robot from a starting point to another point with a defined orientation; tracking trajectory which has a position and orientation in a defined time and path following that is not parameterized in time. It is proposed a selector control in order to perform complex tasks in the field of industrial robotics and service.

Keywords: Simulator 3D · Virtual reality simulator · Unity3D-MATLAB · Robot controllers

1 Introduction

Industrial robotics is set as the main axis of which are born robots themselves [1, 2]; It involves elements that allow to do repetitive tasks in which the operator is excluded due to the complexity or the degree of danger while improving production characteristics [3]. Nowadays, the focus of robotics takes place at performing non-repetitive tasks to improve the quality of life, meaning the rise of service robotics [4]; this subdivision is directed towards an area where daily tasks are instituted within a logical order to be properly executed by a robot; applications ranging from security systems in homes, robots aimed to help elderly people or those with disabilities, to defense and rescue systems used by organized armies, among others [5–9].

There are robotic arms that can reach a certain position following a path, this implies objects evasion and the determination of the best trajectory to the desired point [10]. In [11] the various ways to handle a path including heuristics and meta-heuristics techniques like genetic algorithms, optimization of swarm particles or even optimization ant colony [8, 12, 13] can be appreciated. Hence, it seeks to optimize the path that the robot should make with the purpose of providing adequate performance while avoiding the excessive spend of computational resources [14].

In both service and industrial robotics, the requirements presented in a task increase according to its complications, so a single control technique becomes inefficient, all of

© Springer International Publishing AG 2017
L.T. De Paolis et al. (Eds.): AVR 2017, Part I, LNCS 10324, pp. 164–175, 2017.
DOI: 10.1007/978-3-319-60922-5_12

these three control techniques can be executed according the time and need by a selector algorithm with which the task is efficiently achieved regardless of its complexity [15].

To solve the problem in both robotic (industrial and service) fields on how to control robots, we propose the implementation of a virtual reality environment in which highly complex tasks are developed by merging three control techniques based on the model and kinematic characteristics of the robot; besides a selector that allows the change of technique according the task requires it. Tasks can arise in two ways: when they require only manipulation, where the arm is used clearly since the task is inside the workspace, or, when the task requires additional locomotion, then a robot is used to facilitate the scope of the requested task. Through the controller, problems such as redundancy with the null space are solved and allow secondary objectives to be completed such as maximum manipulation, obstacle avoidance and stability points, among others. Virtual reality allows, through the creation of environments with a huge similarity with real environments, to train robots in situations with eminent risks or, the evaluation of models that want to work in a given environment. In addition, the possibility of testing through a virtual environment allows avoiding accidents that can occur in real form when a model is created and is implemented experimentally without having first tested for sustainable stability and performance. In fact, virtual reality welcomes and introduces the user partially or totally in the structured environment, allowing to improve the results of the tests since they are obtained with a great per- centage of confidence [16, 17].

The work is divided into 5 sections including the introduction. In Sect. 2, the algorithm design is presented. Then in Sect. 3, the kinematic model and control is performed. The results obtained are presented in Sect. 4 and finally, in Sect. 5 the conclusions of the work developed are presented.

2 Algorithm Design

Movement problems that have autonomous robots are solved through three clearly defined methods: Point-point Control, Trajectory Tracking and Path Following.

Point-Point Control. This type of control involves stabilizing the interest point of the robot to a desired point with a given orientation, where position is defined as $h_d(t, s, h) = h_d$ which is a constant, then, the velocity required is defined as $v_{hd}(t, s, h) = \dot{h}_d \equiv 0$. Thus, the control law that feedback the system is presented as $v_{ref}(t) = f(\tilde{h}(t))$.

Trajectory Tracking. This type of control is based on tracking a path dependent of time $y_d(t)$ with their respective derivatives $\dot{y}_d(t)$, $\ddot{y}_d(t)$ that describe the velocity and acceleration that is required to run the task. The desired trajectory does not depend on the instantaneous position of the robot, but is defined solely by the profile over time of the trajectory. Then it should be found control actions based on the robot control errors, both in position and in orientation, while the velocity for the interest point is defined as $v_{ref}(t) = f(\tilde{h}(t, s), \dot{h}_d(t, s))$.

Path Following. In the case of path following, the controller must be able to reduce to zero first, the distance from the robot to a point on the road and, secondly, the angle between the velocity vector of the robot and the tangent to the path desired at a specific point. The desired position depends only on the current location of the robot and path, having no time as influent in this type of control. Furthermore, the interest point velocity is defined as a tangent vector to the required path on a specifically desired P point. To implement this control in the robot is necessary that the desired path is inside the same workspace of the robot, moreover, the velocity module is defined for point of interest. Thus, it requires a control law $\mathbf{v}_{\mathrm{ref}}(t) = (s, v, \rho, \tilde{\beta})$ that feedback the system [18].

Figure 1 shows the scheme that governs the operation of the proposed control system. A switching control is presented where the different control techniques are applied based on a single control law independently of the complexity of the required task.

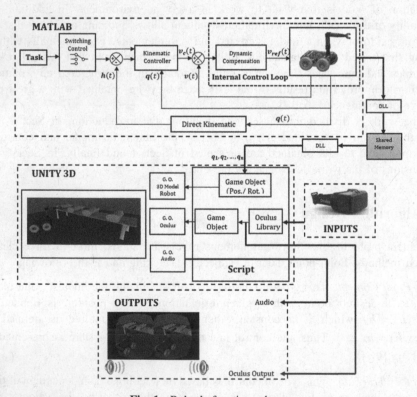

Fig. 1. Robot's function scheme

As shown in Fig. 1, at the Unity stage, a 3D environment is presented with virtual objects that interact with each other, the behavior of these objects and robots is programmed via scripts in C#. The actions of the robot act upon the velocities obtained as a result of the switching controller developed in MATLAB.

The transmission of the variables from MATLAB script to Unity is done using shared memory, which has the ability to exchange variables between two different applications. Therefore, applications run in parallel and data are shown in real-time simulation.

3 Kinematic Model and Control

3.1 Kinematic Model

The kinematic model of a robot provides de location of the end-effector h as function of the configuration of the robot whether it is a robotic arm or a mobile manipulator as shown in Fig. 2.

$$f : n_a \times m_p \to m \tag{1}$$

$$(q_p, q_a) \to h = f(q_p, q_a) \tag{2}$$

where n_a represents the configuration space of the robotic arm and m_p denotes the operational space of the mobile manipulator. The robot uses a configuration based on the vector $q = [q_1 \quad q_2 \quad \ldots \quad q_n]^T = [q_p^T \quad q_a^T]^T$ with n independent coordinates. Having $n = n_p + n_a$ where both terms represent the dimensions of the platform and the robotic arm, the same control law can be functional for any of those two individual configurations by nullifying either n_p or n_a and consequently its respective q vector.

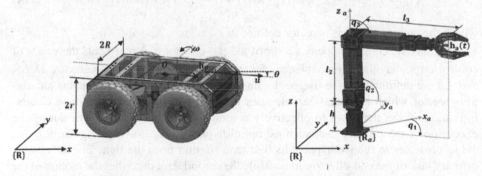

Fig. 2. Parameters of the kinematic model of the robot

The instantaneous kinematic model of a robot provides the derivative of its end-effector position as function of the individual derivatives of the robot components locations

$$\dot{h}(t) = J(q)v(t) \tag{3}$$

where $\dot{h} = \begin{bmatrix} \dot{h}_1 & \dot{h}_2 & \dots & \dot{h}_m \end{bmatrix}^T$ represents the vector of the end-effector velocity and $v = \begin{bmatrix} v_1 & v_2 & \dots & v_{\delta_n} \end{bmatrix}^T = \begin{bmatrix} v_p^T & v_a^T \end{bmatrix}^T$ is the vector which denotes the robot velocities where v_p contains the angular and linear velocities of the mobile platform and v_a contains the joint velocities of the robotic arm.

The matrix $J(q)$ is the Jacobian matrix that defines a linear mapping between the vector $\dot{h}(t)$ and the vector $v(t)$. Its size may differ according to the configuration of the robot having a square matrix if the robot is a robotic arm, and a matrix with different sizes of columns and rows if the robot is a mobile manipulator. An aspect which needs to be considered are the configurations where $J(q)$ is rank-deficient that are known as singular kinematic configurations. Finding the robot singularities is a critical factor in the development of the mobile manipulator model because they represent configurations where the mobility of the robot is reduced, and because in its surroundings small velocities in the operational space may produce lager velocities in the q space.

3.2 Kinematic Controller

The proposed controller can be applied to solve any motion problem which needs to be executed according the position $h_d(t, s, h)$ and velocity $v_{hd}(t, s, h)$ references. The design of the kinematic controller is based on the kinematic model of the robot so, the control law proposed is presented in the Eq. 4 that was implemented based on a minimal norm solution, meaning that the robot will reach its target with the smallest number of possible movements [18, 19].

$$v_c = J^+ \left(v_{hd} + L_k \tanh\left(L_k^{-1} K \tilde{h} \right) \right) + (I - J^+ J) L_D \tanh\left(L_D^{-1} D v_0 \right) \tag{4}$$

where the control action is a vector defined as $v_c = \begin{bmatrix} u_c & \omega_c & \dot{q}_{1c} & \dot{q}_{2c} & \dots & \dot{q}_{nac} \end{bmatrix}^T$; v_{hd} contains the chosen velocity vector of the end-effector h; $\tilde{h}$ represents the vector of control errors having an equivalence of $\tilde{h} = h_d - h$; I is an identity matrix; K, D, L_K, and L_D are definite positive diagonal gain constant matrices; and v_o contains an arbitrary vector which encloses the velocities associated to the robot. This type of configuration allows the robot to effectively accomplish secondary objectives during the execution of the primary task such as: optimize performance, avoid singularities, and avoid obstacles in the workspace. Its first term starting from the right side defines the primary task of the end-effector, meanwhile the second term describes the motion of the robot where the matrix $(I - J^+ J)$ protects the vector v_0 in the null space of the robot Jacobian so that the secondary control objectives don't interfere the execution of the primary control task of the robot.

The design of the switching control is based on a previous analysis of the task that the end effector needs to perform. If the path is extracted from an image, the first stage of the process requires a digital treatment which vectorizes the image to the convert it into a matrix containing the contour coordinates extracted from it. On the other hand if the route is obtained from a specific function no digital treatment is needed.

The resulting matrix is analysed with a statistical algorithm that determines the mean and standard deviation of the conformant points, allowing the switching controller to determine if the distance between two points is an outlier or not, deciding thus when to use position tracking to reach the more distant points.

3.3 Switching Control

A switching control which can allow the robot to execute structured and non structured tasks is proposed in order to accomplish any kind of chore that is required to be done as shown in Fig. 3. The first stage of the controller determines whether the main strategy of control needs to be path following or trajectory tracking, returning as result of the analysis a vector that contains the distances among the coordinates which follow the task route. The resulting vector is analysed with a statistical algorithm that determines the mean and standard deviation of the conformant points, allowing the switching controller to determine if the distance between two points is an outlier or not, deciding thus when to use point-point control to reach the more distant points.

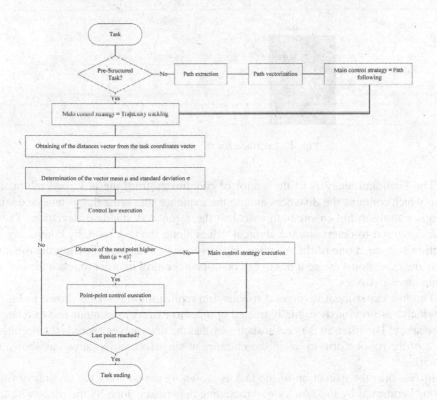

Fig. 3. Flow diagram of the switching control

4   Results

The total controller implemented is based on a previous analysis of the task that the end effector needs to perform. If the path is extracted from an image, the first stage of the process requires digital treatment to convert it into a vector containing the contour coordinates extracted from it with the help of the interface developed for image analysis shown in Fig. 4, and path following is set as main control strategy. On the other hand if the route is obtained from a specific function no digital treatment is needed, and trajectory tracking is set as main control strategy.

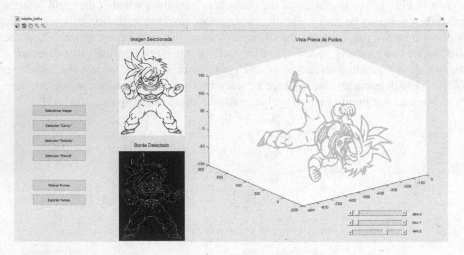

Fig. 4. Interface for the image analysis

The Euclidian analysis of the vector of coordinates from the task road returns an array which contains the distances among the sequence, the same that is analysed with a statistical algorithm in order to calculate the mean and standard deviation. These values are used to determine the atypical values along the task road, by comparing its addition with each one of the members in the vector of distances allowing the robot to know the exact point where it has to use point-point control in order to reach the further points among strokes.

The first experiment involves a robotic arm replicating the image shown in Fig. 5 (a) which was previously digitally treated in order to extract its contour and to rotate it in the space. The rotation is done in such way that the draw never exceeds the operative space of the robotic arm to avoid the entrance in singular configurations as shown in Fig. 5(b).

In Fig. 6(a) the execution of the task is shown, demonstrating the accuracy of the actions performed by the arm by overmounting the strokes done by the robot with the required path. The final outcome from the actions implemented by the arm are shown un Fig. 6(b) where it can be clearly appreciated that the final draw has a high degree of truthfulness with the original image, with its control errors shown in Fig. 6(c).

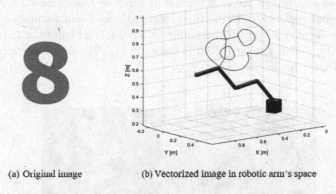

(a) Original image   (b) Vectorized image in robotic arm's space

Fig. 5. Digital treatment of the image selected for the task

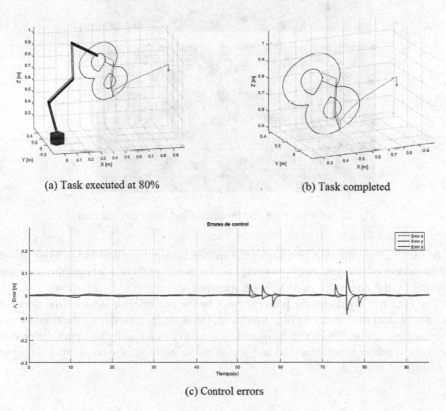

(a) Task executed at 80%   (b) Task completed

(c) Control errors

Fig. 6. Task being developed by the robot

The second experiment involves the use of a mobile manipulator's robotic arm in an exhaust pipes welding task, in which required speed and accuracy. The mobile manipulator is located in front of the muffler in a predefined industrial environment as shown in the Fig. 7(b). The weld path is shown in Fig. 7(a) which corresponds to the contour of the rear muffler cover.

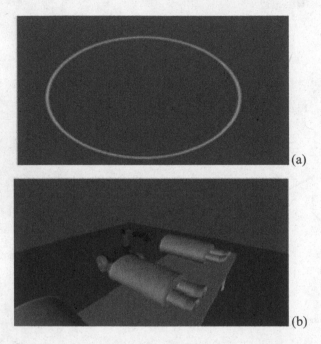

(a)

(b)

Fig. 7. (a) Weld path. (b) Predefined industrial environment

In the Fig. 8(a) the start position of the mobile manipulator arm and in Figs. 8(b–d) the sequence of images corresponding to the weld path that obeys the variables obtained by the controller in MATLAB executed simultaneously are shown.

The Fig. 9(a) highlights the path executed by the end effector in which the electrode does not contact the surface in pink and in red the welding path during the first test run. Additionally, in Fig. 9(b) it can be observed similarly in a highlighted pink the process where the welding is not executed and a path red to highlight the solder resulting from an additional test path.

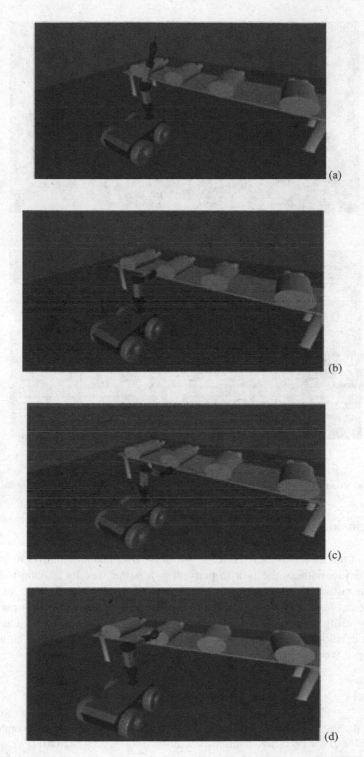

Fig. 8. (a) Starter position. (b) Beginning of the path. (c) Half path followed. (d) End of the path

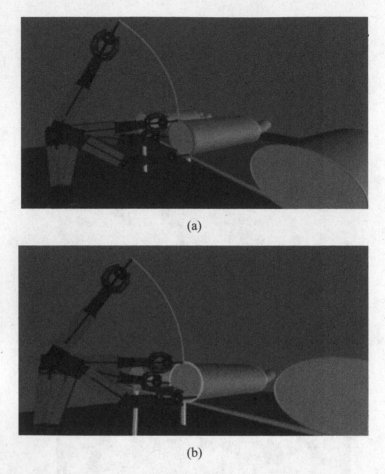

(a)

(b)

Fig. 9. (a) Resulting path of test one. (b) Resulting path of test two. (Color figure online)

5 Conclusions

The result of the tests was an interface in which the user had a high level of immersion allowing him to witness the task to perform in a better way by making him able to move in the virtual environment and receive sonorous stimulation in 360°. In addition, in the different tests analyses, the smooth execution of both programs in parallel was verified by using shared memories, opening up new possibilities for simulation of algorithms developed mathematically that allow the developer to interact virtually with his developed work.

References

1. Paik, J.K., Shin, B.H., Bang, Y., Shim, Y.B.: Development of an anthropomorphic robotic arm and hand for interactive humanoids. J. Bionic Eng. **9**, 133–142 (2012)

2. De la Casa Cárdenas, J., García, A.S., Martínez, S.S., García, J.G., Ortega, J.G.: Model predictive position/force control of an anthropomorphic robotic arm. In: Industrial Technology (ICIT), Seville (2015)
3. Pillajo, C.: Calculation of SCARA manipulator optimal path subjects to constraints. In: II International Congress of Engineering Mechatronics and Automation (CIIMA), Bogotá (2013)
4. Silva, R., Marcelino-Aranda, M., Silva, G., Hernández, V., Molina-Vilchis, M., Saldana-Gonzalez, G., Herrera-Lozada, J., Olguin-Carbajal, M.: Wheeled mobile robots: a review. IEEE Lat. Am. Trans. 10(6), 2209–2217 (2012)
5. Jayawardena, C., Kuo, I.H., Unger, U., Igic, A., Wong, R., Watson, C.I., Stafford, R.Q., Broadbent, E., Tiwari, P., Warren, J., Sohn, J., MacDonald, B.A.: Deployment of a service robot to help older people. In: 2010 IEEE/RSJ International Conference on Intelligent Robots and Systems (IROS), Taipei (2010)
6. Pan, Z., Polden, J., Larkin, N., Van Duin, S., Norrish, J.: Recent progress on programming methods for industrial robots. Robot. Comput. Integr. Manuf. 28(2), 87–94 (2012)
7. Lasota, P., Rossano, G., Shah, J.: Toward safe close-proximity human-robot interaction with standard industrial robots. In: 2014 IEEE International Conference on Automation Science and Engineering (CASE), Taipei, Taiwan (2014)
8. Zhao, Y.M., Lin, Y., Xi, F., Guo, S.: Calibration-based iterative learning control for path tracking of industrial robots. IEEE Trans. Ind. Electron. 62, 2921–2929 (2015)
9. Doriya, R., Chakraborty, P., Nandi, G.C.: Robotic services in cloud computing paradigm. In: International Symposium on Cloud and Services Computing (ISCOS) (2012)
10. Paulin, S., Botterill, T., Lin, J., Chen, X., Green, R.: A comparison of sampling-based path planners for a grape vine pruning robot arm. In: 6th International Conference on Automation, Robotics and Applications (ICARA), Queenstown (2015)
11. Savsani, P., Jhala, R.L., Savsani, V.J.: Optimized trajectory planning of a robotic arm using teaching learning based optimization (TLBO) and artificial bee colony (ABC) optimization techniques. In: IEEE International Systems Conference (SysCon), Orlando, Florida (2013)
12. Ostafew, C., Schoellig, A., Barfoot, T.: Visual teach and repeat, repeat, repeat: iterative learning control improve mobile robot path tracking in challenging outdoor environments. In: Intelligent Robots and Systems (IROS), Tokyo (2013)
13. Hwang, C.-L., Fang, W.-L.: Global fuzzy adaptive hierarchical path tracking control of a mobile robot with experimental validation. IEEE Trans. Fuzzy Syst. 24(3), 724–740 (2016)
14. Nakamura, T.: Real-time 3-D path generation method for a robot arm by a 2-D dipole field. In: 2013 IEEE/ASME International Conference on Advanced Intelligent Mechatronics, Wollongong (2013)
15. Gomez-Balderas, J., Flores, G., García, L., Lozano, R.: Tracking a ground moving target with a quadrotor using switching control. J. Intell. Robot. Syst. 70(1), 65–78 (2013)
16. Andaluz, V.H., Quevedo, W.X., Chicaiza, F.A., Varela, J., Gallardo, C., Sánchez, J.S., Arteaga, O.: Transparency of a bilateral tele-operation scheme of a mobile manipulator robot. In: De Paolis, L.T., Mongelli, A. (eds.) AVR 2016. LNCS, vol. 9768, pp. 228–245. Springer, Cham (2016). doi:10.1007/978-3-319-40621-3_18
17. Andaluz, V.H., Chicaiza, F.A., Gallardo, C., Quevedo, W.X., Varela, J., Sánchez, J.S., Arteaga, O.: Unity3D-MatLab simulator in real time for robotics applications. In: De Paolis, L.T., Mongelli, A. (eds.) AVR 2016. LNCS, vol. 9768, pp. 246–263. Springer, Cham (2016). doi:10.1007/978-3-319-40621-3_19
18. Andaluz, V., Roberti, F., Toibero, J., Carelli, R.: Adaptive unified motion control of mobile manipulators. Control Eng. Pract. 20(12), 1337–1352 (2012)

RRT* GL Based Path Planning for Virtual Aerial Navigation

Wilbert G. Aguilar[1,2,3(✉)], Stephanie Morales[2], Hugo Ruiz[1,4],
and Vanessa Abad[5]

[1] Dep. Seguridad y Defensa, Universidad de las Fuerzas Armadas ESPE,
Sangolquí, Ecuador
wgaguilar@espe.edu.ec
[2] CICTE Research Center, Universidad de las Fuerzas Armadas ESPE,
Sangolquí, Ecuador
[3] GREC Research Group, Universitat Politècnica de Catalunya,
Barcelona, Spain
[4] PLM Research Center, Purdue University, Lafayette, IN, USA
[5] Universitat de Barcelona, Barcelona, Spain

Abstract. In this paper, we describe a path planning system for virtual navigation based on a RRT combination of RRT* Goal and Limit. The propose system includes a point cloud obtained from the virtual workspace with a RGB-D sensor, an identification module for interest regions and obstacles of the environment, and a collision-free path planner based on Rapidly-exploring Random Trees (RRT) for a safe and optimal virtual navigation of UAVs in 3D spaces.

Keywords: Path planning · RRT · Point cloud registration · 3D modeling · Mobile robotics · RGB-D segmentation · Computational geometry

1 Introduction

Virtual Navigation is an useful alternative for several system with high risk as UAVs (Unmanned Aerial Vehicle), that require expert pilots in order to perform different functions like surveillance [1], filming [2–4], search and rescue, and military task [5], etc. Autonomous navigation [6] is an alternative for solving this issue and depends on perception and motion estimation algorithms to obtain the workspace and the pose of the vehicle in the workspace. Additionally, path planning and optimization are required for connecting the start with the goal point in the workspace. Other application of path planning is the orientation for a user who is navigating in a unknown environment. In this way, A RRT based path planner obtains a solution path in the workspace [7, 8] that will be followed by the user. There are several versions of the RRT developed to improve the solution path cost, hence we compared the RRT with the RRT* algorithm and two additional variations using the path cost as evaluation metrics.

Techniques for navigation like 3D perception and mapping based on RGB-D cameras [9], laser range scanners [10] and stereo cameras [11]. The Kinect was released on November 2010 as an RGB-D commercial camera, and after that, several

© Springer International Publishing AG 2017
L.T. De Paolis et al. (Eds.): AVR 2017, Part I, LNCS 10324, pp. 176–184, 2017.
DOI: 10.1007/978-3-319-60922-5_13

applications on robotics and simulation appeared such as on [12, 13]. Segmentation and object recognition are fundamental algorithms for vision applications. In [14] a color and depth segmentation is proposed to detect objects of an indoor environment by finding boundaries between regions based on the norm of the pixel intensity. A novel technique for depth segmentation uses the divergence of a 2D vector field to extract 3D object boundaries [15]. For path planning, the Ant Colony Algorithm based on the behavior of ants searching for food is used on many research projects due to its global optimization performance in multi goal applications [16]. Others use neural networks to give an effective path planning and obstacle avoidance solution that leads the UAV to the target position [17, 18]. Some strategies use behavior-based navigation and fuzzy logic approaches [19].

We use a probabilistic path planning algorithm. Several optimizations have been developed on this area like the RRT-Connect approach [20] that uses a simple greedy heuristic. Other variants have been presented in [21, 22]. Our contribution is focus on the overall system of an optimal UAV path planner, comparing the resulting paths of two variants of the RRT algorithm. The paper is organized as follows: The next Sections is focused on a brief description of virtual workspace. In Sects. 3 and 4 we introduce RRT path planning methods. Finally, experimental results and conclusions are presented the last two Sections.

2 Virtual Workspace

The virtual workspace is obtained by using the proposal of Hatledal [23] and a Kinect [24]. We obtain the colored point cloud in millimeters from the RGB-D sensor using [23], and align the point cloud relative to the Kinect to the virtual workspace coordinate frame by Iterative Closest Point (ICP), a registration method. The objective of regis-tration is the matching of two sets of points by estimation of the transform that maps one point set to the other [25, 26]. ICP assigns correspondence based on the nearest distance criteria and the least-squares rigid transformation giving the best alignment of the two point sets [27, 28].

Assuming that the point set $\{m_i\}$ and $\{d_i\}$, $i = 1 \ldots N$ are matched and related by (1), R is a 3×3 rotation matrix, T is a 3D translation vector and V_i is a noise vector [29, 30], for obtaining the optimal transformation that maps the set $\{m_i\}$ to $\{d_i\}$, we minimize the least-square error (2).

$$d_i = Rm_i + T + V_i \tag{1}$$

$$\Sigma^2 = \sum_{i=1}^{N} \left\| d_i - \widehat{R}m_i - \widehat{T} \right\|^2 \tag{2}$$

After obtaining a suitable UAV coordinate frame, we segment the image into regions. Each region is defined as a homogenous group of connected pixels respect to a selected interest property such as color intensity or texture [31, 32]. In our case, color threshold [33, 34] is an effective approach for segmenting, but the input image is generated from the point cloud, so each pixel has a corresponding xyz coordinate. The threshold values [35] are locally obtained by selecting a target region pixel:

$$g(u,v) = \begin{cases} 1, & \begin{aligned} p_R - s &\leq f(u,v) > p_R + s \\ p_G - s &\leq f(u,v) > p_G + s \\ p_B - s &\leq f(u,v) > p_B + s \end{aligned} \\ 0, & otherwise \end{cases} \tag{3}$$

Where p_R, p_G, p_B are the manually-selected pixel color components, s is the sensibility, $f(u,v)$ is a set of pixels from the input image, $g(u,v)$ is the output binary image (binarization) and t is the threshold value (a threshold value is needed for each color channel).

A binary mask is obtained and undesired noise and holes are removed by morphological operations (Dilatation, Erosion, Opening and Close). All of them depend on a structuring element [36]. The next step is the representation where adjacent pixels of the same class are connected to form spatial sets $s_1 \dots s_m$. For the representation of our binary image we use the blob detection method of Corke [37]. Blob is a contiguous spatial region of pixels. Property like area, perimeter, circularity, moments or centroid coordinates are used to identify these regions. We identify our interest regions filtering the blobs based on their position and area in order to simplify the problem. Knowing the boundaries of the virtual workspace and the minimum and maximum size of the target circles, we obtained the interest blobs and their centroid coordinates.

3   RRT Algorithms

RRT is a widely used algorithm in the literature for solving the motion planning because provides an efficient solution for the travelling salesman problem. However, there are several variation of the RRT proposed to optimized the solution path, i.e., a collision free-path that starts in X_{init} and ends in X_{goal}. The optimization problem is focused on a reliable path with minimal cost.

For explaining the RRT, be: X is a bounded connected open subset of $\mathbb{R}^d$ where $d \in \mathbb{N}$, $d \geq 2$. $G = (V, E)$ is a graph composed by a set of vertexes V and edges E. X_{obs} and X_{goal}, subsets of X, are the obstacle region and the goal region respectively. The obstacle free space $X \backslash X_{obs}$ is denoted as X_{free} and the initial state x_{init} is an element of X_{free}. A path in X_{free} should be a collision-free path. The RRT standard algorithm starts in the initial state. Then the graph incrementally grows by sampling a random state x_{rand} from X_{free}, and connects $x_{nearest}$ with this x_{rand}.

The RRT* algorithm has two additional optimization than the standard RRT. The first one is done after the addition of the new vertex to the tree. The connection between the new and each returned vertex with lowest cost functions is saved and the others are deleted. The second optimization procedure, if the cost function from x_{init} to each near vertex through x_{new} is less, a rewire procedure is executed. Both optimization procedures are included in the RRT* shown on the Algorithm 1.

Algorithm 1: Extended Function of the RRT* algorithm

1. $V' \leftarrow V; E = E';$
2. $x_{nearest} \leftarrow Nearest(G, x);$
3. $x_{new} \leftarrow Steer(x_{nearest}, x);$
4.   if $ObstacleFree(x_{nearest}, x_{new})$ then
5. $V' = V' \cup \{x_{new}\};$
6. $x_{min} \leftarrow x_{nearest};$
7. $X_{near} \leftarrow NearVertices(G, x_{new});$
8.   for all $x_{near} \in X_{near}$ do
9.   if $ObstacleFree(x_{near}, x_{new})$ then
10. $c' \leftarrow Cost(x_{near}) + Cost(Line(x_{near}, x_{new}));$
11.   if $c' < Cost(x_{near})$ then
12. $x_{min} \leftarrow x_{near};$ //Choose new parent for x_{new}
13. $E' = E' \cup \{(x_{min}, x_{new})\};$
14.   for all $x_{near} \in X_{near} \backslash \{x_{min}\}$ do
15.   if $ObstacleFree(x_{near}, x_{new})$ then
16. $c' \leftarrow Cost(x_{new}) + Cost(Line(x_{near}, x_{new}));$
17.   if $c' < Cost(x_{near})$ then
18. $x_{parent} \leftarrow Parent(x_{near});$ //Rewire
19. $E' \leftarrow E' \backslash \{(x_{parent}, x_{near})\};$
20. $E' \leftarrow E' \cup \{(x_{new}, x_{near})\};$
21.   return $G' = (V', E')$

---

4   RRT* GL

In order to decrease the time necessary for finding a reliable solution, accelerating the rate of convergence and optimization, we proved two variations of the RRT*. The modifications are on the Sample function, changing the probability of the generated random node. We have called these version RRT* Goal (Algorithm 2), RRT* Limits (Algorithm 3) and the combination of both RRT*GL.

For the RRT* Goal, we guide the exploration of the tree in the way of the goal region. We give a probability of 50% for sampling the goal region. The other 50% returns an identically distributed sample from X_{free}.

Once the reliable path is found, we increase the probability of the random sample in a specific space for the RRT* Limits. This accelerates the rate of convergence to an optimal low cost path. We obtain the uniform distributed random sample by delimiting the random range to the minimum and maximum coordinates (x, y, z) of the found path. This increases the density of random samples at the path surroundings, avoiding unnecessary optimizations for other sections of the tree.

Algorithm 2: Sample Function of the RRT* Goal algorithm

---

1. $if\ (i\ MOD\ 2 = 0)\ OR\ (feasible\ Path\ is\ TRUE)$
2. $x_{rand} \leftarrow random(X_{free});$
3. $else$
4. $x_{rand} \leftarrow X_{goal};$
5. $return\ x_{rand}$

Algorithm 3: Sample Function of the RRT* Limits algorithm

---

1. $if\ feasible\ Path\ is\ TRUE$
2. $minL\ = min(V)$
3. $maxL\ = max(V)$
4. $x_{rand} \leftarrow random(X_{free}, [minL, maxL]);$
5. $else$
6. $x_{rand} \leftarrow random(X_{free});$
7. $return\ x_{rand}$

---

5   Results and Discussion

The system was implemented in a laptop with the following characteristics: Processor Intel Core i7-4500 @1.90 GHz and 8.00 GB RAM. Real 3D image captured by a Kinect V2, in a zenith perspective, was processed off-line for three different scenes on the virtual workspace. The method used for the point cloud alignment was registration of two data sets. We rotated the Kinect for testing the transformation matrix effect on the original point cloud, calculate the average error percentage as the error of the virtual workspace plane on the robot coordinate frame related to the Kinect pose, and obtain the location on millimeters of five circle centroids recognized with the algorithm on the xy plane and the corresponding error percentage. The error was also calculated with respect to the robot virtual workspace seen by the Kinect (Table 1).

Table 1. Target points recognition

	p1		p2		p3	
	X	Y	x	y	x	Y
Real	252.2	300.1	497.9	151.2	988.52	208.37
Calculated	249.6	299	497	152.8	985.3	205.7
Error %	0.16	0.26	0.06	0.38	0.20	0.64

Each algorithm was tested ten times with 300 for obtaining the mean cost, number of segments in the resulting path, the time for locating the target point and the execution time. These comparative results are shown on the following Tables 2, and Figs. 1 and 2.

Table 2. Comparative results between RRT algorithms and our proposal.

Obstacles	Algorithm	Total cost	# segments	Goal time	Total time
1	RRT*	1431.8	25	5.55	61.57
	RRT* Goal	1289.9	26	0.86	54.73
	RRT* Limits	1455.2	27	17.7	60.73
	RRT* GL	1308.7	27	0.86	66.99
2	RRT*	1433.7	25	2.49	66.4
	RRT* Goal	1366	28	1.47	46.27
	RRT* Limits	1512	31	7.86	56.19
	RRT* GL	1359.6	28	1.19	65.4
3	RRT*	1331.1	23	4.59	44.42
	RRT* Goal	1065.5	20	1.21	60.28
	RRT* Limits	1156.9	25	6.06	65.4
	RRT* GL	1040.2	21	1.43	91.58

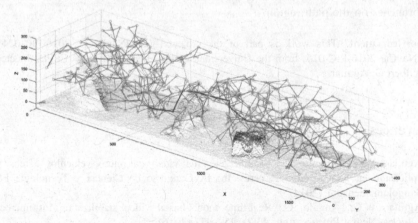

Fig. 1. Solution path with RRT*.

As we can see on the results tables, the RRT* Goal algorithm decreases the computational cost for finding a reliable solution, and the RRT* Limits algorithm increases the density of the tree branches around the path. The combination of both methods produces a faster and optimal path without increases the number of iterations.

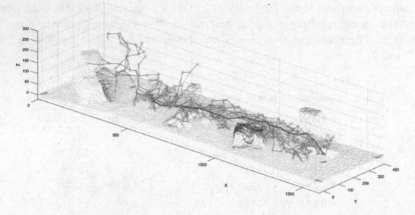

Fig. 2. Solution path with RRT* GL.

6 Conclusions

The system was experimentally tested, and has shown flexibility given by the automatic alignment of the point cloud to the robot coordinate frame based on ICP.

Our proposal, RRT* GL, achieves a fast and optimal path between the start and goal point because of RRT* Goal reduces the time required for finding a reliable solution and RRT* Limits improves the optimization by increasing the density of the tree branches on the path region.

Acknowledgement. This work is part of the projects VisualNavDrone 2016-PIC-024 and MultiNavCar 2016-PIC-025, from the Universidad de las Fuerzas Armadas ESPE, directed by Dr. Wilbert G. Aguilar.

References

1. Aguilar, W.G., Angulo, C.: Estabilización de vídeo en micro vehículos aéreos y su aplicación en la detección de caras. In: IX Congreso de Ciencia y Tecnología ESPE, Sangolquí, Ecuador (2014)
2. Aguilar, W.G., Angulo, C.: Real-time model-based video stabilization for microaerial vehicles. Neural Process. Lett. **43**(2), 459–477 (2016)
3. Aguilar, W.G., Angulo, C.: Real-time video stabilization without phantom movements for micro aerial vehicles. EURASIP J. Image Video Process. **1**, 1–13 (2014)
4. Aguilar, W.G., Angulo, C.: Robust video stabilization based on motion intention for low-cost micro aerial vehicles. In: 11th International Multi-Conference on Systems, Signals & Devices (SSD), Barcelona, Spain (2014)
5. Koren, Y.: Robotics for Engineers (1998)
6. Aguilar, W.G., Angulo, C., Costa, R., Molina, L.: Control autónomo de cuadricópteros para seguimiento de trayectorias. In: IX Congreso de Ciencia y Tecnología ESPE, Sangolquí, Ecuador (2014)

7. Vasishth, O., Gigras, Y.: Path planning problem. Int. J. Comput. Appl. **104**(2) (2014)
8. Cabras, P., Rosell, J., Pérez, A., Aguilar, W.G., Rosell, A.: Haptic-based navigation for the virtual bronchoscopy. In: 18th IFAC World Congress, Milano, Italy (2011)
9. Henry, P., Krainin, P., Herbst, E., Ren, X., Fox, D.: RGB-D mapping: using depth cameras for dense 3D modeling of indoor environments. In: The 12th International Symposium on Experimental Robotics (ISER) (2010)
10. Thrun, S., Burgard, W., Fox, D.: A real-time algorithm for mobile robot mapping with applications to multi-robot and 3D mapping. In: IEEE International Conference on Robotics and Automation, San Francisco (2000)
11. Gutmann, J.-S., Fukuchi, M., Fujita, M.: 3D perception and environment map generation for humanoid robot navigation. Int. J. Robot. Res. **27** (2008)
12. Oliver, A., Kang, S., Wunsche, B., MacDonald, B.: Using the kinect as a navigation sensor for mobile robotics. In: Conference on Image and Vision Computing New Zealand (2012)
13. Benavidez, P., Jamshidi, M.: Mobile robot navigation and target tracking system. In: The 6th International Conference on System of Systems Engineering, Albuquerque (2011)
14. Rao, D., Le, Q., Phoka, T., Quigley, M., Sudsang, A., Ng, A.Y.: Grasping novel objects with depth segmentation. In: IEEE/RSJ International Conference on Intelligent Robots and Systems (IROS), Taipei (2010)
15. Ali Shah, S.A., Bennamoun, M., Boussaid, F.: A novel algorithm for efficient depth segmentation using low resolution (kinect) images. In: IEEE 10th Conference on Industrial Electronics and Applications (ICIEA), Auckland (2015)
16. Liu, J., Yang, J., Liu, H., Tian, X., Gao, M.: An improved ant colony algorithm for robot path planning. Soft. Comput. **21**, 1 11 (2016)
17. Glasius, R., Komoda, A., Gielen, S.C.A.M.: Neural network dynamics for path planning and obstacle avoidance. Neural Netw. **8**(1), 125–133 (2000)
18. Xin, D., Hua-hua, C., Wei-kang, G.: Neural network and genetic algorithm based global path planning in a static environment. J. Zhejiang Univ. Sci. A **6**(6), 549–554 (2005-2006)
19. Seraji, H., Howard, A.: Behavior-based robot navigation on challenging terrain: a fuzzy logic approach. IEEE Trans. Robot. Autom. **18**(3), 308–321 (2002)
20. Kuffner, J.J., LaValle, S.M.: RRT-connect: an efficient approach to single-query path planning. In: IEEE International Conference on Robotics and Automation, San Francisco (2000)
21. Devaurs, D., Siméon, T., Cortés, J.: Efficient sampling-based approaches to optimal path planning in complex cost spaces. In: Akin, H.L., Amato, N.M., Isler, V., Stappen, A.F. (eds.) Algorithmic Foundations of Robotics XI. STAR, vol. 107, pp. 143–159. Springer, Cham (2015). doi:10.1007/978-3-319-16595-0_9
22. Gammell, J.D., Srinivasa, S., Barfoot, T.: Informed RRT*: optimal sampling-based path planning focused via direct sampling of an admissible ellipsoidal heuristic. In: IEEE/RSJ International Conference on Intelligent Robots and Systems (IROS 2014) (2014)
23. Hatledal, L.I.: Kinect v2 SDK 2.0 – Colored Point Clouds, 15 August 2015. http://laht.info/kinect-v2-colored-point-clouds/
24. Fankhauser, P., Bloesch, M., Rodriguez, D., Kaestner, R., Hutter, M. Siegwart, R.: Kinect v2 for mobile robot navigation: evaluation and modeling. In: 2015 International Conference on Advanced Robotics (ICAR), Istanbul (2015)
25. Myronenko, A., Song, X.: Point set registration: coherent point drift. IEEE Trans. Pattern Anal. Mach. Intell. **32**(12), 2262–2275 (2010)
26. Karaman, S., Frazzoli, E.: Incremental sampling-based algorithms for optimal motion planning. Int. J. Robot. Res. (2010)

27. Lachat, E., Hélene, M., Tania, L., Pierre, G.: Assessment and calibration of a RGB-D camera (Kinect v2 Sensor) towards a potential use for close-range 3D modeling. Remote Sens. **7**(10) (2015)
28. Pagliari, D., Pinto, L.: Calibration of kinect for xbox one and comparison between the two generations of microsoft sensors. Sensors **15**(11) (2015)
29. Eggert, D.W., Lorusso, A., Fisher, R.B.: Estimating 3-D rigid body transformations: a comparison of four major algorithms. Mach. Vis. Appl. **9**, 272–290 (1997)
30. Sreedhar, K., Panlal, B.: Enhancement of images using morphological transformations. Int. J. Comput. Sci. Inf. Technol. (IJCSIT) **4**(1) (2012)
31. Aguilar, W.G., Angulo, C.: Compensación y aprendizaje de efectos generados en la imagen durante el desplazamiento de un robot. In: X Simposio CEA de Ingeniería de Control, Barcelona, Spain (2012)
32. Aguilar, W.G., Angulo, C.: Compensación de los efectos generados en la imagen por el control de navegación del robot Aibo ERS 7. In: VII Congreso de Ciencia y Tecnología ESPE, Sangolquí, Ecuador (2012)
33. Navon, E., Miller, O., Averbuch, A.: Color image segmentation based on adaptive local thresholds. Image Vis. Comput. **23**, 69–85 (2005)
34. Aguilar, W.G., Angulo, C.: Estabilización robusta de vídeo basada en diferencia de nivel de gris. In: VIII Congreso de Ciencia y Tecnología ESPE, Sangolquí, Ecuador (2013)
35. Sahoo, P.K., Soltani, S., Wong, A.K.C.: A survey of thresholding techniques. Comput. Vis. Graph. Image Process. **41**, 233–260 (1988)
36. The MathWorks, Inc.: Pcregrigid Documentation (2015). http://www.mathworks.com/help/vision/ref/pcregrigid.html. Accessed 24 Feb 2016
37. Corke, P.I.: Robotics, Vision & Control: Fundamental Algorithms in MATLAB. Springer, Heidelberg (2011)

Virtual Reality System for Training in Automotive Mechanics

Washington X. Quevedo[✉], Jorge S. Sánchez, Oscar Arteaga,
Marcelo Álvarez V., Víctor D. Zambrano, Carlos R. Sánchez,
and Víctor H. Andaluz

Universidad de las Fuerzas Armadas ESPE, Sangolquí, Ecuador
{wjquevedo,jssanchez,obarteaga,rmalvarez,vdzambrano,
crsanchez9,vhandaluz1}@espe.edu.ec

Abstract. This article describes a virtual training system for recognition and assembly of automotive components is proposed. The system consists of a virtual reality environment developed with Unity 3D graphics engine, the same one that allows the user to have greater immersion in the teaching-learning process in order to optimize materials, infrastructure, time resources, among other benefits. The proposed system allows the user to select the work environment and the level of difficulty during the training process. The experimental results show the efficiency of the system generated by the man-machine interaction oriented to develop skills in the area of automotive mechanical.

Keywords: Automotive mechanics · Training system · Virtual reality · Unity3D · Modelling 3D

1 Introduction

Currently, the planning, definition, design, development and support processes of products in automotive area has evolved, in this way it has been necessary to improve the efficiency in each level of manufacturing vehicle's components [1]. Virtual reality is a technological tool with great potential in the automotive industry, allows the development of new prototypes in virtual environments, optimizing the resources of manufacturing companies. [2, 3]. The systems design that make up a vehicle such as: body car, cabin, power train, suspension, steering, brakes, to be simulated in virtual reality improves the productivity of the company, will allow to offer a system of training and efficient interactive training for after-sales staff [4]. Additionally, virtual reality can be taken to the commercial sector, where the customer can personalize vehicle in a virtual environment allowing to know the result of them acquisition [5].

The software CAD, CAM and CAE, used for the design and optimization of mechanical elements, are essential tools for engineering activities, because with them you can develop parts and components complex geometric with special specifications also simulate their behavior when are subjected to stresses and displacements of operation, which is necessary to determine its manufacturing process and actual application [6, 14, 16]. While these computational tools can predict the behavior of the different components that wish to make today there are proposals related to the area of

© Springer International Publishing AG 2017
L.T. De Paolis et al. (Eds.): AVR 2017, Part I, LNCS 10324, pp. 185–198, 2017.
DOI: 10.1007/978-3-319-60922-5_14

Virtual Reality, VR, which allows active interaction between people and three-dimensional media, which will get a better study of parts designed [7, 8].

The Virtual Reality area has many applications focused on entertainment, education, graphic design, communication, medicine, automotive processes, aerospace engineering, among others [9, 15]; the training for the improvement of technician's skills in the maintenance and assembly area in the industry is fundamental to improve the technical capacities of operators [6, 10]. Through Unity 3D tool, which is software for creating 3D virtual environments [11], combining the Virtual Reality with the design software of the automobile's mechanical components, creates a virtual environment that allows to interact with new prototypes in which you can check designs and specifications.

In some institutions of higher as the University of Warwick in England education they have implemented interactive technologies such as virtual reality in vocational training, which has yielded great results in the teaching-learning process as it turns out to be an attractive alternative for students engineering undergraduate and graduate [12, 13].

In this context, the present article shows the development of a virtual reality application for the recognition and assembly of vehicle components, with the aim of creating a virtual environment as close to reality that facilitates the teaching learning process optimizing resources, for the Automotive Engineering students. To develop the proposal is used mechanical CAD design software, to model in 3D the internal components of the engine and the appropriate environment, in such a way that the environment is similar to an automotive workshop, to model the internal components of the engine in 3D, and the right environment, in this way the environment be as real as possible an automotive workshop, additionally the process results of identification and assembly of the engine components seen from the application of virtual reality are presented.

The work is organized into 6 sections including the Introduction. Section 2 presents a problem formulation in the manufacturing processes of the automotive area; the export of the mechanical components developed in CAD software to virtual reality are presented in Sect. 3. Section 4 develops the virtual environment that allows a user immersion in automotive training and learning processes. The experimental results are presented in Sect. 5; while the conclusions are shown in Sect. 6.

2 Problem Formulation

Actually, the automotive industry for vehicle development involves the following levels of processes; definition and planning of the project, definition of specifications, conceptual design, product development and product support; in the fifth level of the process is the support level to the product in which other phases such as: supplier support, maintenance, customer support and manufacturing and assembly support; the main objective of this level is to provide the necessary assistance to the product developed in this case to the manufactured vehicle and is used by the customer through a suitable after-sales service with maintenance programs that allow to optimize the characteristics of the vehicle.

This paper aims to identify the components and facilitate learning both the assembly and operation of the various components that make up the vehicle, both from their external systems and internal elements, in a virtual reality environment [19]; which will allow students to increase their theoretical and practical skills, achieving learning outcomes in an interactive way that will be put into practice in their professional life, in this way contributes to solve problems in the maintenance area contributing to the product support level, the manufacture processes of a product aligned to the automotive industry are shown in Fig. 1.

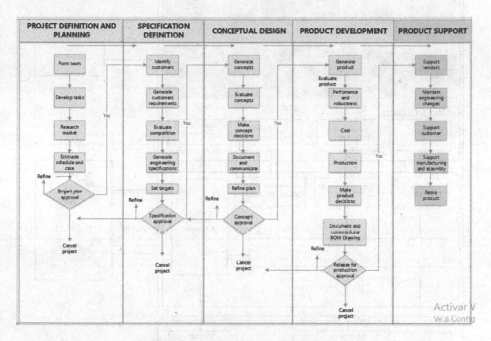

Fig. 1. Diagram of design process [17]

The application will allow to work in any of the vehicle's mechanical systems, such as: body car, cabin, power train, suspension, steering, brakes; allowing an interactive innovation of virtual reality in the manuals of technical service, which would allow the technicians to solve problems in a more efficient way, in the after-sales process.

The virtual reality area in the automotive manufacturing industry, can be included in the other levels of the process as: conceptual design and product development, with the help of tools as CAD, CAM, CAE and virtual environments, would optimize processes by reducing design times [6].

3 System Structure

The scripts of control are developed, to respond to the operation of different process associated to the virtual device in the Unity environment, Fig. 2.

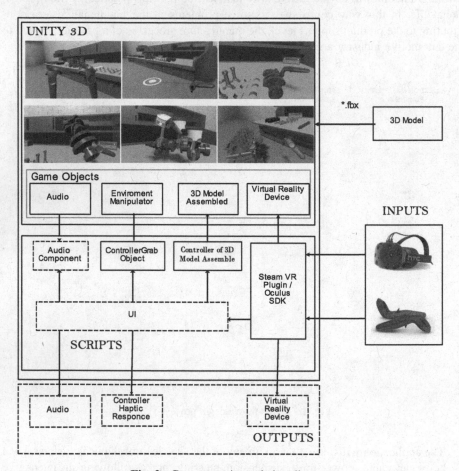

Fig. 2. Component interrelation diagram

The simulation phase of the scene, contains all virtual reality programming, where the components of the 3D model and the assembly controller used are linked, in this phase it's found the necessary configuration as the physical and coupling properties that simulates an assembly process identical to the real.

In the input and output phase can be considered several devices that allow to observe the virtual environment as: helmets of virtual reality (Oculus Rift, HTC VIVE and GearVR) and haptic input controls that allow to interact with the environment within which it can be considered the novint falcon, tracking hands devices (Leap Motion, Manus VR, Myo Armband, HTC VIVE). The use of different input and output devices in the desired application requires that the code structure be general, so that it is compatible on several platforms, without the need to reconstruct the project, and automatically detect the aforementioned devices.

The SCRIPTS stage manages communication with each of the input and output devices, providing the virtual environment with the functionality required, Additionally, to implementing the interface where the user is allowed different ways of interacting with the application, showing the different levels of difficulty in which the subroutine of the controller can be used to manipulate the objects of the environment with a sound response, using the algorithm based on the model's component hierarchy. Finally, the output stage provides the user surround audio 360, haptic response to the inputs, and visual feedback to the tracking of user movements within the virtual environment.

4 Machine Virtualization

The design of any equipment or element starts in a CAD software, this software is a parametric tool of solid modeling based on operations that takes advantage of the facility of learning of the graphical interface. For example, SolidWorks is a tool that allows you to create 3D solid models, in which you can see in detail its shape and its component parts, in addition that allows to realize kinetic analysis of the forces that interact in the created models [19].

In this paper, we propose a multi-layer scheme for the development of applications in virtual environments in order to provide a greater immersion to users in training tasks in the area of automotive mechanics. (i) Layer 1: Is responsible for importing 3D models created in CAD software; (ii) Layer 2: in this layer is determined from the reference system and establishes the hierarchies of each of the parts of the 3D model; and finally, (iii) Layer 3: the interaction between the virtual input devices and the environment where the application is executed. In addition, the evaluation phase of the training performed by the user is implemented in order to evaluate the knowledge and skills acquired with the application developed, see Fig. 3.

To import the 3D models developed in a CAD software to the Unity3D graphics engine it is necessary to previously use the software 3ds MAX, in order to establish the hierarchy of the parts of the model [18]. The hierarchies are established according to the assembly of the machine or modeling equipment, it also depends on the number of elements and the position constraints of each element according to the model. For the orientation and location of the parts of the model, the reference points (Pivot) are determined; At the end of this process you get a *.fbx file compatible with Unity3D in which the virtual environment application will be developed.

While in Layer 3, the configuration of inputs for the interaction of the moving parts that make up the 3D model and the user interface using HTC VIVE and Gear VR devices, is performed by using functions of OnTriggerEnter, OnTriggerStay, OnTriggerExit. For the manipulation of the object (moving part of the model) the GRIP or TRIGGER button is considered, emphasizing the collider of the object. While for the user's movement in the virtual environment, "teleportation" is implemented, which

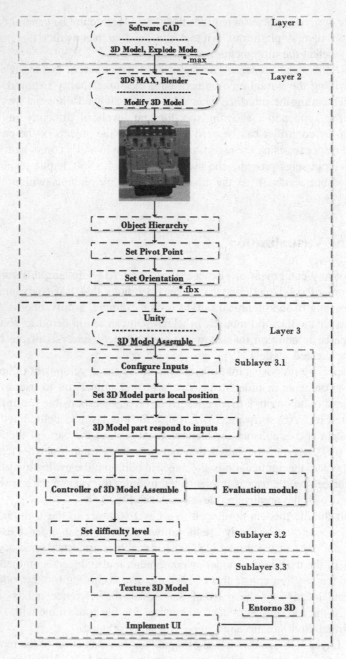

Fig. 3. Virtualization model

Fig. 4. Use of teleportation

consists in pointing a reference point on the surface for the purpose of transferring a desired point to the user, see Fig. 4.

In the second sublayer, the local position of each of the parts and pieces is recorded in relation to the original 3D model, in order to make a comparison between the correct position and the position in which the user locates the object. In case that the manipulation of the object is nearby of the correct position, an outline is shown for the purpose of guiding the user in the assembly process. For gripping the object, you must configure the response that each object will have to the input stimulus already configured previously, when the input device collides with a GameObject, *i.e., a*sks if your tag is of type "objects" the material of the object changes to a material that denotes selection (white body and blue outline), see Fig. 5.

In the third sub-layer the application drivers are developed, starting with the control of assembly of the 3D model. For the assembly, the original model of the object is used which makes its components invisible - with the function MeshRenderer, allows to activate again according to the correct position of the object manipulated by the user, see Fig. 6. This controller interacts with the evaluation module, designed to weight the test result, considering the following variables: time, difficulty, and correct positioning of objects (in this case, the outline help is disabled in the correct position of the object). The difficulty level selector edits the assembly controller parameters in order to vary the strength of the test.

Finally, the last sublayer focuses on the development of the virtual application environment and the texturing of each object considering the real characteristics, e.g., Color-texture-rigorousness of the object through albedo, metallic, normal and height map, obtained from an original image. In case it is not possible to obtain textures directly from the actual model, it is recommended to use Substance Painter to approximate the texture to a real state of the model. In order to allow a greater immersion of the user in the virtual environment, an environment according to the task to be executed is developed, compatible with the mobility and movement of the user

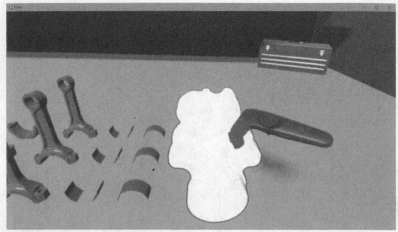

(a) Select object

(b) Object grip

Fig. 5. Handle object (Color figure online)

Fig. 6. Control assembly

(configured in the input of the devices) as tele-transportation and walking in the case of HTC VIVE, in which also sound response is added in each GameObject considering type of material when colliding: metallic, plastic, concrete, and feedback in the assembly and in the user interface.

5   Results and Discussion

In this section, we present an immersive virtual environment, see Fig. 7, of a workshop of automotive mechanics, in which a dynamic environment is developed so that the user can interact in a more real way with the proposed application.

Fig. 7. Virtual environment of the automotive workshop

Fig. 8. Test vehicle

The application allows assembly of the entire vehicle Fig. 8, according to the level of knowledge of the user, the application has different modules or assembly sections of the mechanical part e.g. transmission, brake and motor; in a similar way has different levels of difficulty depending on the number and detail of the parts being considered for a specific test e.g. bolts, nuts and bolts.

For this work is considered an internal combustion motor and ignited provoked, of the vehicle Suzuki Forsa, Fig. 9, of three-cylinder in line, the elements considered for the present project are, mobile components: camshaft, crankshaft, valves, pistons, connecting rods, wheels; fixed components such as the engine crankcase.

Initially an environment is shown where the motor is disarmed and the parts and pieces that make up it are on a work table, Fig. 10.

The main objective is to assemble the motor in an orderly manner, placing the available parts in the correct position. For this, the PC platform and the HTC VIVE device are used with their controls. The first step is to access the application and perform a recognition of the place and the input methods designed. To get close to a nearby place, walk to the desired place, if you want to reach an end of the room you need to press the touchpad of the remote and choose the desired location using the pointer that moves on the floor.

To select a part, simply carry a control to the desired object, in response you will get a color change that confirms that we are enabled to choose that part, to take the selected piece the TRIGGER button, as a visual response, there is the color change of the piece to its original texture as indicated in Fig. 5. To move from one place to another, the TRIGGER button is held down, to release the part at the desired location, the TRIGGER button is depressed (Press Up). It is advisable not to release the part if it is colliding with another. To select the correct part location, in the engine assembly,

Fig. 9. Motor model used in the application.

Fig. 10. Virtual work table

proceed to search for an approximate location until a outline that has the shape of the piece in the correct location, The system will accept the embedding of the part regardless of whether the part does not have the correct rotation or orientation at the time of detection, see Fig. 11.

Fig. 11. Assembly of connecting rod to crankshaft.

Fig. 12. Final motor assembly.

The user has the option of taking the motor assembly and rotating it or locating it according to its criterion to facilitate the embedding of parts. While running the test, it is possible to teleport with one control, while with the other you can hold the part or assembly of the motor. At the time of completing the motor assembly Fig. 12. you can see the statistics: time used, correct position of the pieces, difficulty level chosen and the option to redo the task.

6   Conclusions

In this paper, a virtual training system for automotive mechanics is proposed. The system consists of a virtual reality environment developed with graphic engine in Unity 3D. The same that allows the user to have a greater immersion during the teaching-learning process in order to optimize material resources, infrastructure, time and other benefits. The experimental results obtained show the efficiency of the system generated by the human-machine interaction oriented to develop skills and abilities in the area of automotive mechanics.

References

1. Nee, A.Y.C., Ong, S.K., Chryssolouris, G., Mourtzis, D.: Augmented reality applications in design and manufacturing. CIRP Ann.-Manuf. Technol. **61**(2), 657–679 (2012)
2. Reinhart, G., Patron, C.: Integrating augmented reality in the assembly domain-fundamentals, benefits and applications. CIRP Ann.-Manuf. Technol. **52**(1), 5–8 (2003)
3. Lehner, V.D., DeFanti, T.A.: Distributed virtual reality: Supporting remote collaboration in vehicle design. IEEE Comput. Graph. Appl. **17**(2), 13–17 (1997)
4. Borsci, S., Lawson, G., Broome, S.: Empirical evidence, evaluation criteria and challenges for the effectiveness of virtual and mixed reality tools for training operators of car service maintenance. Comput. Ind. **67**, 17–26 (2015)
5. Regenbrecht, H., Baratoff, G., Wilke, W.: Augmented reality projects in the automotive and aerospace industries. IEEE Comput. Graph. Appl. **25**(6), 48–56 (2005)
6. Gavish, N., Gutiérrez, T., Webel, S., Rodríguez, J., Peveri, M., Bockholt, U., Tecchia, F.: Evaluating virtual reality and augmented reality training for industrial maintenance and assembly tasks. Interact. Learn. Environ. **23**(6), 778–798 (2015)
7. Webel, S., Bockholt, U., Engelke, T., Gavish, N., Olbric, M., Preusche, C.: An augmented reality training platform for assembly and maintenance skills. Fraunhofer IGD, Germany, Ort Braude College, Israel. German Aerospace Center (DLR), Institute of Robotics and Mechatronics, Germany (2012)
8. Cheng, T., Teizer, J.: Real-time resource location data collection and visualization technology for construction safety and activity monitoring applications. School of Civil and Environmental Engineering, Georgia Institute of Technology, 790 Atlantic Drive N.W., Atlanta, GA 30332-0355, United States, October 2012
9. Farkhatdinov, I., Ryu, J.H.: Development of educational system for automotive engineering based on augmented reality. In: International Conference on Engineering Education and Research (2009)
10. Lisboa, H.B., de Oliveira Santos, L.A.R., Miyashiro, E.R., Sugawara, K.J., Miyagi, P.E., Junqueira, F.: 3D virtual environments for manufacturing automation. In: 22nd International Congress of Mechanical Engineering (COBEM 2013), 3–7 November 2013, University of São Paulo, Ribeirão Preto, SP, Brazil (2013)
11. Wang, S., Mao, Z., Zeng, C., Gong, H., Li, S., Chen, B.: A new method of virtual reality based on Unity3D. IEEE In International Conference on Geoinformatics, pp. 1–5 (2010)
12. Abulrub, A.H.G., Attridge, A.N., Williams, M.A.: Virtual reality in engineering education: the future of creative learning. In: IEEE Global Engineering Education Conference, pp. 751–757 (2011)

13. Anastassova, M., Burkhardt, J.M.: Automotive technicians' training as a community-of-practice: implications for the design of an augmented reality teaching aid. Appl. Ergon. **40**(4), 713–721 (2009)
14. Ong, S.K., Yuan, M.L., Nee, A.Y.C.: Augmented reality applications in manufacturing: a survey. Int. J. Prod. Res. **46**(10), 2707–2742 (2008)
15. Andaluz, V.H., et al.: Immersive industrial process environment from a P&ID diagram. In: Bebis, G., et al. (eds.) ISVC 2016. LNCS, vol. 10072, pp. 701–712. Springer, Cham (2016). doi:10.1007/978-3-319-50835-1_63
16. Vignais, N., Miezal, M., Bleser, G., Mura, K., Gorecky, D., Marin, F.: Innovative system for real-time ergonomic feedback in industrial manufacturing. Appl. Ergon. **44**(4), 566–574 (2012)
17. Ullman, D.G.: The Mechanical Design Process. McGraw-Hill, New York (2010)
18. Andaluz, V.H., et al.: Unity3D virtual animation of robots with coupled and uncoupled mechanism. In: Paolis, L.T., Mongelli, A. (eds.) AVR 2016. LNCS, vol. 9768, pp. 89–101. Springer, Cham (2016). doi:10.1007/978-3-319-40621-3_6
19. Serbest, K., Cilli, M., Yildiz, M.Z., Eldogan, O.: Development of a human hand model for estimating joint torque using MATLAB tools. In: IEEE International Conference on Biomedical Robotics and Biomechatronics, pp. 793-797 (2016)

Math Model of UAV Multi Rotor Prototype with Fixed Wing Aerodynamic Structure for a Flight Simulator

David Orbea[2], Jessica Moposita[2], Wilbert G. Aguilar[1,3,4(✉)],
Manolo Paredes[3], Gustavo León[5], and Aníbal Jara-Olmedo[5]

[1] Dep. Seguridad y Defensa,
Universidad de las Fuerzas Armadas ESPE, Sangolquí, Ecuador
wgaguilar@espe.edu.ec
[2] Dep. Energía y Mecánica,
Universidad de las Fuerzas Armadas ESPE, Sangolquí, Ecuador
[3] CICTE Research Center,
Universidad de las Fuerzas Armadas ESPE, Sangolquí, Ecuador
[4] GREC Research Group,
Universitat Politècnica de Catalunya, Barcelona, Spain
[5] CIDFAE Research Center, Fuerza Aérea Ecuatoriana FAE, Ambato, Ecuador

Abstract. This article presents the math modeling of a fixed wing Unmanned Aerial Vehicle (UAV) for a flight simulator, using a numerical method. The UAV is controlled through radio control or mission plan. The mathematical model contains a numerical approximation considering multiple Single Input Single Output (SISO) systems that related altitude, pitch, roll and yaw angle as an input parameters and yaw speed, x, y, z axis speed as output parameters.

The signal analysis shows unpredictable behavior during manual controlled flight, but an acceptable stable group of data in controlled mission.

Keywords: Unmanned Aerial Vehicle · UAV · Vertical take off and landing · VTOL · Multi rotor · Hybrid aircraft · Fixed wing · Surveillance · Math model

1 Introduction

Numerical analysis is an important aspect of applied mathematics. Some equations can be solved using exact techniques, but more complicated ones need to be solved using numerical estimation techniques [1–5]. Numerical simulation of the aircraft dynamics is the most important tool in the development and verification of the flight control laws and equations of motion for Unmanned Aircraft Vehicles (UAV) [6].

In the last years, UAV applications were growing for control, navigation and guidance, supporting the armed forces [6–10]. Rotary wing UAVs offer stability and simplicity in handling, but their flight time is limited. Fundamental limitation of micro-UAVs arises from on-board power operation, detection and calculation, which can be insubstantial for power requirements [11].

© Springer International Publishing AG 2017
L.T. De Paolis et al. (Eds.): AVR 2017, Part I, LNCS 10324, pp. 199–211, 2017.
DOI: 10.1007/978-3-319-60922-5_15

This prototype pretends to combine both platforms, in order to increase the flight time of a quad copter by implementing an aerodynamic fixed wing structure which supports the multi rotor propulsion system, in addition to performing a controlled take-off and landing.

The influence of this project is found in the mathematical analysis of new designs that allow to combine different aerodynamic configurations in order to obtain improvements in the flight time and flight versatility in aerial prototypes.

2   Related Works

Internationally, there are several approaches related with the analysis of combined systems of UAV multi rotor and fixed wing [12]. There are few ways the model could be solved. For example, Euler's method [13, 14] or Newton equations [15]. The quadrotor is commonly represented as a rigid body mass with inertia and autogyroscopics, acted upon by gravity and control torques [16]. A limitation of the numerical analysis techniques is the farther away from the initial value point the farther the approximation is from the actual value [13]. PID control is mostly used in aviation because is the better option for 3D systems [17], however, there are another control techniques such as Linear Quadratic (LQ) [18]. IAI Heron is an UAV developed by Malat, division of Israel Aerospace Industries which uses a PID control to stabilize the flight, however, system is controlled by a human pilot [17]. There is a work [19] that uses a similar numerical method to obtain the dynamic model of the drone in order to obtain parameters for autonomous navigation.

3   Math Model

Our quadrotor aircraft analysis considers a rigid cross frame equipped with four rotors [20], the up and down motion is achieved by increasing or decreasing the total thrust while maintaining an equal individual thrust. Meanwhile the left, right, forward, backward and yaw motions are achieved through a differential control strategy of the trust generated by each rotor [20]. Modeling this kind of aircraft is not an easy task because of its complex structure [21, 22], taking into account also the changing aerodynamic interference patterns between the rotors [22].

Instead of modeling the drone like a standard quadrotor helicopter considering its propeller speeds as inputs and angles as outputs, model can consider the internal controller, which is able to set and keep the desired angles and vertical speed without complexity of the drone model [19].

To obtain the math model we use a numerical approximation considering multiple SISO systems, linear single input single output control systems [23] that relate x-axis speed vs pitch angle, y-axis speed vs roll angle, z-axis speed vs altitude and yaw-speed vs yaw angle. Data is obtained with a mission plan at low speed previously configured drawing a rectangular trajectory. Figure 1 shows the mission plan with 6 waypoints at 5 m/s x/y cruise speed. Table 1 shows waypoints and parameters of mission.

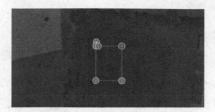

Fig. 1. Mission plan realized in QGroundControl v3.0.2 at Universidad de las Fuerzas Armadas – ESPE

Table 1. Waypoints and parameters of mission plan

Symbol	Name	Altitude difference (m)	Distance from previous point (m)
H	Auto home	0	0
T	Take off	5	1.62
2	Waypoint	0	22.9
3	Waypoint	0	16.97
4	Waypoint	0	22.9
L	Landing	−4.9	15.27

3.1 Data Obtained

The results obtained from MavLink Telemetry log are shown in Fig. 2. During the flight, the mission was executed three times to obtain better results. Then, replicating the mission with radio controller in stabilized mode.

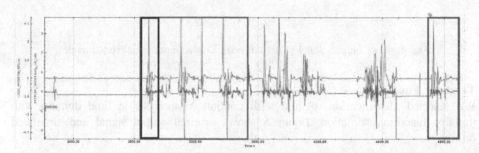

Fig. 2. Y-axis speed vs Roll telemetry log graph realized in APM planner 2.0.24 with marked regions of interest. Executed missions (Gray section), RC stabilized replicated mission (Red section), chosen mission region (Black section). (Color figure online)

The chosen region (black) has more stable data because of the wind conditions. Next analysis are based in this region of the graph. Figure 3 shows the coordinated axes of the prototype considering orientation of Inertial Measurement Unit (IMU).

Fig. 3. Coordinated axes (X-axis, Y-axis, Z-axis) of the prototype

3.2 X-axis Speed vs Pitch Angle

X-axis speed and pitch angle are main variables in forward flight because of the direct relation with cruise speed. In order to analyze parameters, Fig. 4 shows input and output signal data.

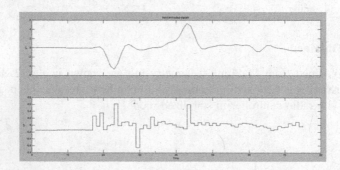

Fig. 4. Top: output signal (X-axis speed). Down: input signal (pitch angle).

Transfer Function

We selected identification method with continuous analysis in time domain with transfer function estimation. Figure 5 shows original output signal and simulated output.

$$Tf = \frac{0.2101s^2 - 0.005987s + 0.0144}{s^6 + 0.3859s^5 + 0.4872s^4 + 0.0995s^3 + 0.05612s^2 + 0.003729s + 0.001127} \quad (1)$$

Figure 6 shows the output (x-axis speed) and x-axis acceleration behavior for pulse train input.

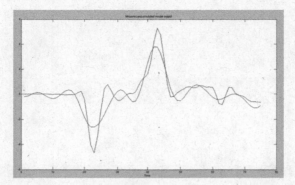

Fig. 5. Measured (black) and simulated (blue) model output X-axis speed (Color figure online)

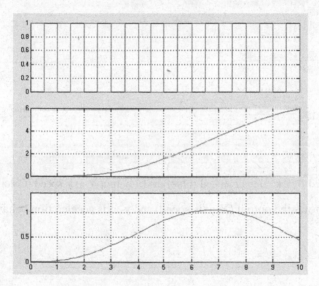

Fig. 6. Top: input signal pitch pulse rain (10 Hz, amplitude: 1, 50% pulse width). Middle: X-axis speed. Down: X-axis acceleration

3.3 Y-axis Speed vs Roll Angle

Y-axis speed and roll angle are related with lateral stability of the system. In order to analyze parameters, Fig. 7 shows input and output signal data.

Transfer Function
Figure 8 shows original output signal and simulated output.

$$Tf = \frac{-0.1079s^2 + 0.02002s - 0.003025}{s^6 + 0.2433s^5 + 0.4292s^4 + 0.0531s^3 + 0.0459s^2 + 0.00071s + 0.0005716} \quad (2)$$

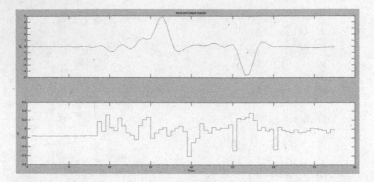

Fig. 7. Output signal (Y-axis speed). Down: input signal (roll angle).

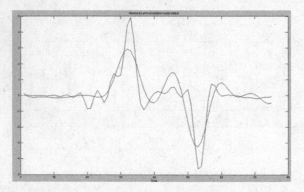

Fig. 8. Measured (black) and simulated (blue) model output Y-axis speed (Color figure online)

Figure 9 shows the output (Y-axis speed) and y-axis acceleration behavior for pulse train input.

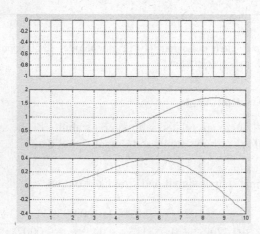

Fig. 9. Input signal roll pulse train (10 Hz, amplitude: 1, 50% pulse width), Y-axis speed, Y-axis acceleration

3.4   Z-axis Speed vs Altitude

In order to analyze parameters, Fig. 10 shows input and output signal data.

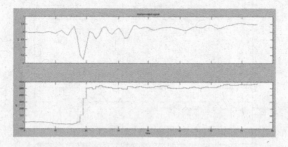

Fig. 10. Top: output signal (Z-axis speed). Down: input signal (altitude).

Transfer Function

Figure 11 shows original output signal and simulated output.

$$Tf = \frac{-0.0007482s^5 - 0.000002615s^4 - 0.00005317s^3 + 0.000008268s^2 + 0.000001498s + 0.0000002481}{s^5 + 5.45s^4 + 1.758s^3 + 0.6638s^2 + 0.1224s + 0.0000002109}$$

$$(3)$$

Figure 12 shows the output (z-axis speed) and z-axis acceleration behavior for step input.

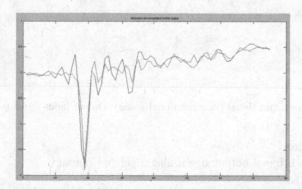

Fig. 11. Measured (black) and simulated (purple) model output Z-axis speed (Color figure online)

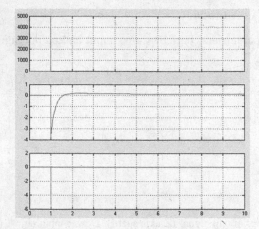

Fig. 12. Input signal altitude step (amplitude: 5000), z-axis speed, z-axis acceleration

3.5   Yaw Rotational Speed vs Yaw Angle

In order to analyze parameters, Fig. 13 shows input and output signal data prepared for analysis.

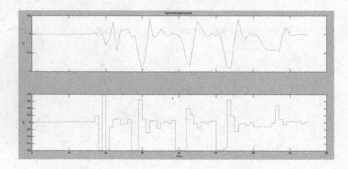

Fig. 13. Top: output signal (yaw rotational speed). Down: input signal (yaw angle).

Transfer Function

Figure 14 shows original output signal and simulated output.

$$Tf = \frac{-0.02006s^5 + 2.828s^4 - 3.956s^3 + 5.646s^2 - 0.8336s + 0.6348}{s^5 + 2.571s^4 + 7.109s^3 + 4.159s^2 + 1.061s + 0.5744} \quad (4)$$

Figure 15 shows the output (yaw rotational speed) and yaw rotational acceleration behavior for pulse train input

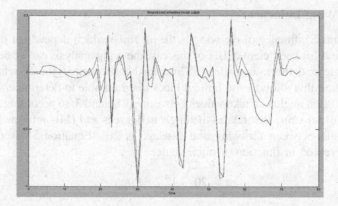

Fig. 14. Measured (black) and simulated (blue) model output yaw rotational speed (Color figure online)

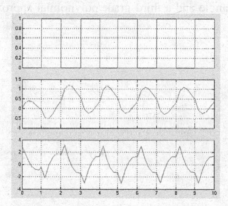

Fig. 15. Input signal yaw rate pulse train (10 Hz, amplitude:1, 50% pulse width), yaw speed, yaw acceleration.

Figure 16 shows output X-axis speed, Y-axis speed, Z-axis speed data according to the information of the IMU for the analyzed region of the mission.

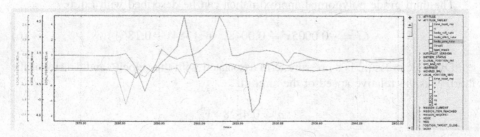

Fig. 16. Axis speed data. X-axis speed (Red), Y-axis speed (Blue), Z-axis speed (Green) for chosen mission region (Color figure online)

3.6   Fixed Wing Influence

The aerodynamic influence of the wing is the lift force which depends of the dynamic pressure (q) and lift coefficient (Cl). For this case the wing analysis can be dependent of the pitch angle and the x-axis speed. This variables were previously related with a transfer function that allows us to build a block diagram able to determine the value of lift force (L). Pitch angle can take values between −3.86 and 3.86 according to the IMU data. The constant value that relates the angle in degrees and IMU information is 12.2. Incidence angle between the wing and fuselage is 20°. Equation 5 describes attack angle (x) expressed in function of pitch angle.

$$x = 20 - 12.2 * Pitch \tag{5}$$

Lift Coefficient (Cl) is a dimensionless aerodynamic coefficient that refers to dynamic lift characteristics of a two-dimensional foil section considering the foil chord [24]. Figure 17 shows the characteristic curve for FX63-120 airfoil that relates Lift coefficient with attack angle and a third grade polynomial approximation.

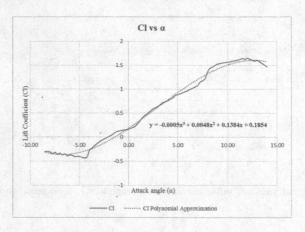

Fig. 17. Lift coefficient vs attack angle for FX63-120 airfoil (Blue), third grade polynomial approximation (Red). (Color figure online)

The third grade polynomial approximation can be described with Eq. 6.

$$Cl = -0.0005x^3 + 0.0048x^2 + .1384x + 0.1854 \tag{6}$$

Dynamic pressure is a pressure term associated with the velocity and density of the fluid. V is the relative speed of the aircraft.

$$q = 0.4328 * v^2 \tag{7}$$

Lift force relates dynamic pressure, lift coefficient and wing surface. For this case wing surface is 0.24 m^2 because of a 1.2 m wing span and 0.20 m chord.

$$L = 0.24 * q * Cl \tag{8}$$

Figure 18 shows the block diagram of the lift force analysis considering previous equations with pitch angle as an input and lift force as an output.

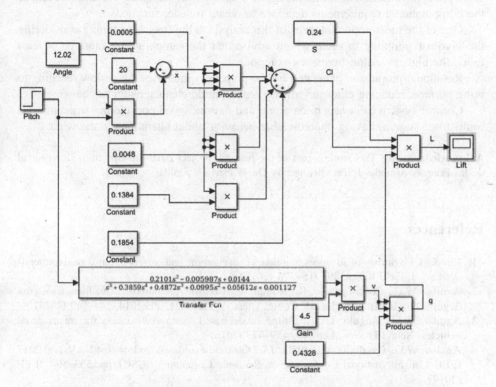

Fig. 18. Block diagram of the lift force analysis. Transfer function was obtained in Eq. 1 and relates pitch angle with X-axis speed. Forward flight speed affects the value of dynamic pressure (q) in Eq. 7.

Figure 19 shows the lift force transitory answer to a step input of pitch angle.

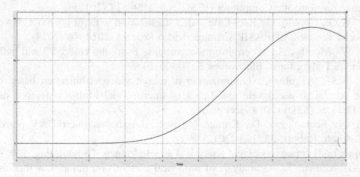

Fig. 19. Lift force transitory answer to step input of pitch angle

4   Conclusions

A mathematical modeling allows the use of available computational tools in modeling correctly. It lets us solve the problem by proven reliable computational approach using software applications. The initial parameters were got in stationary conditions because the computational requirements decrease to obtain transfer functions.

One of the most important steps of the analysis is the frequency tuning considering the Nyquist sampling theorem which advise that the sampling rate must be at least twice the highest analog frequency component.

Rotational propulsion generated by the propellers interferes the airflow reaching to wing surface, reducing efficiency of the aerodynamic characteristics of the wing.

Control system calibrates pitch angle and motors speed considering structure as a multi rotor system, having unpredictable behavior under alterations in the wind.

Acknowledgement. This work is part of the research project 2016-PIC-024 from Universidad de las Fuerzas Armadas ESPE, directed by Dr. Wilbert G. Aguilar.

References

1. Kendoul, F.: Survey of advances in guidance, navigation, and control of unmanned rotorcraft systems. J. Field Robot. **29**, 315–378 (2012)
2. Aguilar, W.G., Costa-Castelló, R., Angulo, C.: Control Autónomo de Cuadricopteros para Seguimiento de Trayectorias. IX Congr. Cienc. y Tecnol. ESPE **2014**, 144–149 (2014)
3. Aguilar, W.G., Angulo, C.: Real-time model-based video stabilization for micro aerial vehicles. Neural Process. Lett. **43**, 459–477 (2016)
4. Aguilar, W.G., Casaliglla, V.P., Pólit, J.L.: Obstacle avoidance for low-cost UAVs. In: 2017 IEEE 11th International Conference on Semantic Computing (ICSC), pp. 503–508. IEEE (2017)
5. Aguilar, W.G., Casaliglla, V.P., Pólit, J.L.: Obstacle avoidance based-visual navigation for micro aerial vehicles. Electronics **6**, 10 (2017)
6. Ładyżyńska-Kozdraś, E.: Modeling and numerical simulation of unmanned aircraft vehicle restricted by non-holonomic constraints. J. Theor. Appl. Mech. **50**, 251–268 (2012)
7. Aguilar, W.G., Luna, M.A., Moya, J.F., Abad, V., Parra, H., Ruiz, H.: Pedestrian detection for UAVs using cascade classifiers with meanshift. In: 2017 IEEE 11th International Conference on Semantic Computing (ICSC), pp. 509–514 (2017)
8. Aguilar, W.G., Angulo, C.: Real-time video stabilization without phantom movements for micro aerial vehicles. EURASIP J. Image Video Process. **2014**, 46 (2014)
9. Aguilar, W., Morales, S.: 3D environment mapping using the kinect V2 and path planning based on RRT algorithms. Electronics **5**, 70 (2016)
10. Aguilar, W.G., Angulo, C.: Optimization of robust video stabilization based on motion intention for micro aerial vehicles. In: 2014 International Multi-Conference on Systems Signals Devices (SSD) (2014, accepted)
11. Michael, N., Scaramuzza, D., Kumar, V.: Special issue on micro-UAV perception and control. Auton. Robots. **33**, 1–3 (2012)
12. Quadcopter body frame model and analysis. Fascicle Manag. Technol. Eng. **120**, 3–6 (2016)
13. Mullen, T., Mullen, T.: An analysis of numerical methods on traffic flow models (2015)

14. Xu, Y., Tong, C., Li, H.: Flight control of a quadrotor under model uncertainties. Int. J. Micro Air Veh. **7**, 1–19 (2015)
15. Mokhtari, A., Benallegue, A.: Dynamic feedback controller of Euler angles and wind parameters estimation for a quadrotor unmanned aerial vehicle. In: Proceedings of the 2004 IEEE International Conference on Robotics and Automation ICRA 2004, vol. 3, pp. 2359–2366 (2004)
16. Pounds, P., Mahony, R., Corke, P.: Modelling and control of a quad-rotor robot. In: Proceedings of the 2006 Australasian Conference on Robotics and Automation, pp. 1–26 (2006).
17. Garijo Verdejo, D., López Pérez, J.I., Pérez Estrada, I.: Control de un vehículo aéreo no tripulado (2009)
18. Bouabdallah, S., Noth, A., Siegwart, R., Siegwan, R.: PID vs LQ control techniques applied to an indoor micro quadrotor. In: IEEE/RSJ International Conference on Intelligent Robots and Systems, vol. 3, pp. 2451–2456 (2004)
19. Krajník, T., Vonásek, V., Fišer, D., Faigl, J.: AR-drone as a platform for robotic research and education. In: Obdržálek, D., Gottscheber, A. (eds.) EUROBOT 2011. CCIS, vol. 161, pp. 172–186. Springer, Heidelberg (2011). doi:10.1007/978-3-642-21975-7_16
20. Tayebi, A., McGilvray, S.: Attitude stabilization of a VTOL quadrotor aircraft. IEEE Trans. Control Syst. Technol. **14**, 562–571 (2006)
21. Erginer, B., Altug, E.: Modeling and PD control of a quadrotor VTOL vehicle. In: 2007 IEEE Intelligent Vehicled Symposium, pp. 894–899 (2007)
22. Krajník, T., Vonásek, V., Fišer, D., Faigl, J.: Unmanned aircraft systems. In: Obdržálek, D., Gottscheber, A. (eds.) EUROBOT 2011. CCIS, vol. 161, pp. 172–186. Springer, Heidelberg (2011). doi:10.1007/978-3-642-21975-7_16
23. Goodwin, G.C., Graebe, S.F., Salgado, M.E.: Control systems design. Int. J. Adapt. Control Signal Process. **16**, 173–174 (2002)
24. Abbott, I.H., Von Doenhoff, A.E.: Theory of Wing Sections: Including a Summary of Airfoil data. Press, 11, 693 (1959)

Exploiting Factory Telemetry to Support Virtual Reality Simulation in Robotics Cell

Vladimir Kuts[1(✉)], Gianfranco E. Modoni[2], Walter Terkaj[3],
Toivo Tähemaa[1], Marco Sacco[3], and Tauno Otto[1]

[1] Department of Mechanical and Industrial Engineering,
Tallinn University of Technology, Tallinn, Estonia
vladimir.kuts@ttu.ee
[2] Institute of Industrial Technologies and Automation,
National Research Council, Bari, Italy
gianfranco.modoni@itia.cnr.it
[3] Institute of Industrial Technologies and Automation,
National Research Council, Milan, Italy
walter.terkaj@itia.cnr.it

Abstract. Significant efforts of the current manufacturing companies are devoted to the implementation of the full synchronization between the real world at the shop-floor level and its digital counterpart (so-called Digital Twin). Indeed, a true reflection of the real factory can be exploited to monitor and simulate the factory performance, allowing to adjust and optimize processes, anticipate failures and also investigate problems. One of the major challenge to be tackled in order to realize the Digital Twin is the handling of the factory telemetry, which can track the evolution of the objects in the real world. This paper investigates the potential of an application for supporting and handling the factory telemetry, thus allowing to create a snapshot of the real system that can dynamically augment and enhance the data-driven simulation applications supporting the manufacturing execution phase. As a proof of concept of the architecture, a prototype has been developed in the field of robotics. In such context, the proposed architecture is on the basis of a Virtual Reality tool to simulate human presence for development of safety systems in robotic cells.

Keywords: Digital Twin · Factory telemetry · Robotic cell · Virtual Reality

1 Introduction

The concept of Digital Twin (DT) is creating and maintaining a digital representation of the real world of the factory and supporting its management and reconfiguration by the means of optimization and simulation tools, which are fed with real and updated factory data. This concept is not new as it was first used by NASA research in 1957, when the satellite Vanguard was sent into orbit [1]. More than half a century later, recent advances in ICT are offering new opportunities to fully exploit the potential of the DT in the manufacturing field. Such a potential has been recently analyzed in many articles and publications [2, 3]. Specifically, a DT based approach is described in [4] to enable a new strategy for taming organization complexity and simulating various

© Springer International Publishing AG 2017
L.T. De Paolis et al. (Eds.): AVR 2017, Part I, LNCS 10324, pp. 212–221, 2017.
DOI: 10.1007/978-3-319-60922-5_16

outcomes across the whole product lifecycle. In [5], the authors leveraged the digital model of the factory provided by the DT to conceive a new generation of autonomous manufacturing systems, that can execute high-level tasks without detailed programming and without human control. Another research work proposed a model for enhancing data exchange between different systems included in a Cyber Physical System and that are connected with the DT [6].

An effective DT implementation asks for:

- a data model to represent the evolution of the objects by integrating streams of data coming from different sources, e.g. monitoring systems (i.e. a real history), production-planning methods (i.e. a planned history), performance evaluation tools (i.e. a simulated history) [7];
- the acquisition and validation of data via an appropriate monitoring system to enable the synchronization between the real and digital factory [8]. This paper will focus on this aspect in particular;
- setting the level of detail (LoD) of the DT in order to make it effective and efficient while meeting specific goals.

One the technologies that can benefit from the DT is Virtual Reality (VR), which provides a virtual and realistic view of the environment where the flow of real-time and historical data is integrated with the human presence. In particular, if VR is integrated and connected with the DT, it can be exploited to:

- evaluate possible system reconfigurations via simulation (passive mode);
- remotely control the system (active mode).

The aim of this research project is investigating the potential of an approach to connect VR applications with the DT in the specific domain of industrial robotics and collaborative robots. All these enabling technologies are particularly relevant in the modern factories, as their inclusion in the scope of Industry 4.0 [9] can demonstrate. Equally important it is their integration. In this regard, the herein introduced approach combines VR with an enabler of the DT, the Factory Telemetry (FT), i.e. the data acquired by means of sensors distributed across the plant and then exploited by specific applications to monitor ongoing processes [10].

FT can be consumed by the VR applications under the form of a real time stream of data or as historical data. Real-time telemetry allows to acquire live data from the properly configured components (e.g. sensors, etc.) distributed across the whole factory network. In the scope of the DT, it allows to combine and overlap real and virtual processes that can be executed at the same time, thus giving an amount of additional functions for monitoring, analysis, learning. On the other hand, historical telemetry gives the opportunity to save data related to the real process execution and use it in order to simulate new configurations (e.g. new layouts) of the manufacturing line.

Usage of FT can bring several benefits during various stages of the factory lifecycle. In the field of robotics, it can dynamically augment and enhance the data-driven simulation applications supporting engineers in the development and programming of robotic cells. The novelty of the approach consists of the combination of the telemetry (historical and live) and the VR simulation tools, since a current state of the art shows a lack of solutions for synchronizing the digital and real environments [10]. Furthermore, a hardware and software configuration integrated into a whole "ready to use" system is designed to test the connection of the real and digital environments. Finally, with reference to this configuration, a case study is developed to show how the collaboration between two different geographic locations can be enabled by sharing the DT model. The remainder of this paper is structured as follows. Section 2 presents the benefits of an approach based on the DT, while Sect. 3 envisions an application supporting DT, eliciting their requirements. Section 4 illustrates the conducted experiments. Finally, Sect. 5 draws the conclusions, summarizing the major findings.

2   The DT Approach

One goal of this study is creating a digital clone of a system so that it is possible to remotely monitor and control the real existing facilities via its virtual twin. Regarding this, the synchronization between the real and virtual worlds can contribute to its implementation. Making a digital copy of an existing real manufacturing system or sub-system (e.g. a robotic cell) gives the ability to control both the real and virtual environment with the same system controller, thus allowing to apply corrective decisions to the real system based on the information the virtual system receives and analyses. As seen in Fig. 1, the system controller gathers all data from sensors and sends them to the virtual system in order to synchronize digital and real worlds. According to received information, virtual system processes data also based on some simulation application and then gives the feedback to main controller, which in turn sends commands to the real system, thus implementing the closed loop between the virtual and real factory.

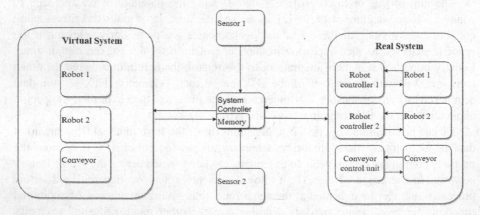

Fig. 1. Virtual and real world synchronization

Leveraging the digital clone, it is possible to support the simulations of different system configurations (see Fig. 2), thus helping optimize the production processes. A snapshot of the system can be taken by elaborating the flow of real data. Starting from the snapshot of the system, one or more simulations can be run to generate and playback a flow of simulated data. After the analysis of simulated data, reconfigurations or planning decision can be taken, creating a flow of data from the virtual world to

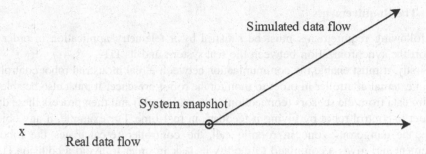

Fig. 2. Data flow – real and historical cut-off (time is on the x-axis)

reality. Historical data can be used in the virtual simulations to check how the real system can be better optimized or reprogrammed from the exact step of the process flow. This way, the idle time of the robot or other manufacturing system components can be reduced while they are being optimized or re-programmed. Moreover, the historical data can be used as an input of prediction tools, in order to foresee the behavior of robots, machines, and other equipment of a manufacturing context.

Another interesting aspect of the DT is that it enables an efficient interaction between smart objects and its surrounding environment, thus making the overall system smarter. For example, a robot, acting as a consumer of telemetry, can get data from sensors and according to this information may change its behavior. If a human being enters a dangerous zone, then the robot will stop and generate a new path around or proceed with the next task, exploiting a simulation of the safety system. Moreover, the co-work between multiple robots or components in the system can be improved. For example, one robot could ask for the position of another robot and based on this information the path of a second robot can be generated. This can be particularly relevant if different types and brands of robots are involved (e.g. ABB, Universal Robot, Kuka, Fanuc, MIR or others).

The DT cannot be realized without the development of a digital model of the environment, which must be as precise and detailed as its real twin in order to execute accurate simulations and evaluations [7]. Under these conditions, it is essential to represent the characteristics, behavior and relations of the system components like operators, products, resources, transporters, sensors. For instance, the kinematics of a robot must be properly modeled. However, the digitalization of the system and its components can be fully exploited only if a proper software application is able to handle the telemetry data, integrating the latter with other digital tools. The next section delves into the main characteristics of such a telemetry-based application.

3 Overview of the Envisioned Application Supporting FT

The approach introduced in this section is agnostic to the application domain but from this point onward we'll focus on the case study of a robotic cell, which helps to elicit the requirements of the analyzed application. Behind this case study, there is the need to enhance the DT through a system of synchronization similar to the one in Fig. 1.

3.1   The Requirements

The following requirements must be satisfied by a telemetry application in order to support the synchronization between the real system and its DT.

Firstly, it must enable the communication between a real industrial robot controller and an external controller in order to monitor the robot presence. It must also be able to acquire data from the sensors (connection to the real world) and then process these data in order to control robot by giving it feedback in real-time. For example, if any object enters the dangerous zone in robotic cell, the controller re-calculates the robot's movement and gives a command to modify its task in order to avoid a collision [11]. Also, in order to enable the communication between a generic virtual system and the external controller, proper protocols and command signals should be used.

Finally, a data storage should be used to collect all data mentioned above, also under the form of Big Data, in order to save historical points of the manufacturing line working process. Regarding this, in order to take the snapshot of the current robot's task and path data, it is needed to take into consideration different static and dynamic robot conditions (see Fig. 3). Moreover, all the handled data must be expressed in the same format in order to guarantee the digital continuity and support the semantic interoperability [12, 13].

Saved historical data	
Static	- Static object coordinates (tables, walls) - moment position coordinates of each movable part (each robot arm)
Dynamic	- Speed of the movable parts of the system - robot arm axis - External factors - operator, loader route - Movement vector of the movable parts - manufacture device program step, when moment saved

Fig. 3. Static/dynamic data for enabling historical data flow

3.2   The Implementation

An implementation of the envisioned application should provide two complementary ways to handle the telemetry data:

One is real time and exploits a binary protocol in order to be optimized for high performance. This solution allows various connected and enabled devices to receive real time data stream from the sensors. A specific study will investigate which is the best protocol and libraries to be used in order to support such as solution. In this regard, the UDP [14] protocol is faster than TCP [14], but UDP is unreliable without any acknowledgment, while TCP is a reliable three-way handshaking protocol. For streaming data, the UDP protocol is more suitable, as it represents a trade-off between speed and reliability.

Moreover, a Multicast transmission of the data over the factory network allows the software application (telemetry consumers) to receive the telemetry regardless of the PC where the software application runs, as long as it is connected to the network and enabled [15].

The second is Web service-oriented and allows to persist the data on the database. Since this solution does not have to support real time process, we could handle more data (both in Volume and Velocity) than through the solution 1. Under these conditions, we could say that solution 2 allows to visualize more data than solution 1 since it can support higher rates or even a higher number of sensors, which are instead limited due within solution 1 due to the real time requirements

Both the solutions provide proper connectors towards the telemetry consumers (e.g. simulator packages, VR tools and robots). A proper API (Application Programming Interface) should guarantee the access to telemetry data, enabling data analysis in external tools. In this regard, simulator packages, VR tools and robots can act as telemetry consumers.

Figure 4 shows the three steps through which data flow from the real system to the virtual system and back:

1. Data flow from real to virtual system;
2. Persistence of the real-time data into the data storage;
3. Integration of the optimized data in the virtual system, which was based on the historical data.

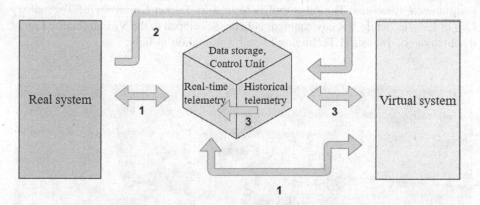

Fig. 4. Data flows between virtual and real system

A valid starting point for the implementation of both the options is represented by the OPC Unified Architecture [16], which in its transport layer defines two different mechanisms for data communication (factory telemetry): a TCP protocol for communication at high performance and a protocol based on the Web Services for communication Internet firewall-friendly. It will be also essential to exploit the new generation of storage systems which can run on distributed eventually cloud-based cluster system (e.g. Hadoop, Database sharding, NoSQL databases, etc.).

4   The Experiment: VR – Human Presence Simulation

The case of a measurement robot cell has been considered to test the ongoing developments related to the approach presented in the previous sections. The DT in robotics field can be applied within different use cases, bringing several benefits such as the following:

- decrease of safety errors and mishaps;
- improvements in run-time efficiency;
- improved accurateness of traceability;
- compression of lead time in production.

One significant use case is to foresee the response of a robot to human interaction and uncover previously unknown issues before they become critical in the real environment by comparing predicted and current responses.

In the presented experiment, the real system (see Fig. 5) consists of one industrial robot with attached 3D laser scanner probe and camera. The machine vision camera is used for detection of movement and shape of the static and dynamic objects in the cell. A robot controller is also a part of the robotics cell. Moreover, the robotic cell includes two laser sensors, which are rotating on 360° and map the room on the exact set up range, so they can detect changes in the environment and give the signals to the controller, when interferences are detected. A common table is used to place object for the inspection [17], as the main purpose of the presented robotic cell is to perform 3D scanning on site. The presented experiment is ongoing and involves two different geographical locations. The robot cell is located in Tallinn University of Technology Lab in Estonia, while VR environment is being developed at the Virtual Reality Lab of the Institute of Industrial Technologies and Automation in Italy.

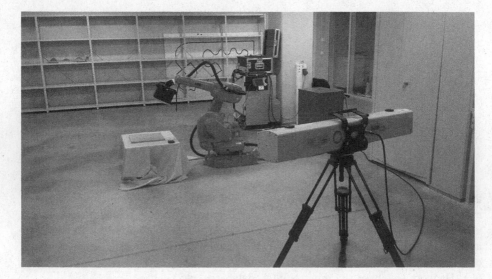

Fig. 5. Robot cell in real world

The digital model of the robotic cell was developed using Unity software tool (Fig. 6). The main components of the real environment were reproduced in the digital model while considering a proper scale of the room and of the related equipment. In order to be able to run experiments which involve human/object presence simulations and to not interrupt the real system sensors work, perception components are simulated as a triggers in the virtual environment and configured as their real counterparts. Input for the movement of the camera is gathered from the keyboard, joysticks or from the VR headsets with the usage of the generic avatar, which have the solid mesh for simulation of the person presence in the digital world.

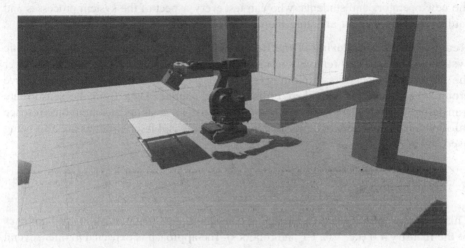

Fig. 6. Robot cell in virtual world

In order to enable an accurate simulation process, the movement of the robot and presence of the objects are modeled in the virtual. Regarding the data feedback, axis speed and placement of the robot in the real room are automatically sent by the external software Robot Operating system (ROS) [18] which is integrated into the external controller. Moreover, the ROS integration is important in order to use historical data for furthers simulations in the virtual environment and to send the feedback to the real system after processing the data.

4.1   Two Preliminar Experiments with VR Tools in the Robotic Cell

The virtual system developed in Unity can be used to run the two following experiment.

Human Presence Simulation to Test the Safety System in the Robotic Cell. The ISO/TS 15066:2016 [19] standard regulates the presence of human beings in a robot cell while it is working. The safety system in robotic cell, described above, can be tested in the VR environment by means of an avatar. In this way it can be avoided that an operator enters a dangerous zone for validation purposes. Sensors simulated in the virtual system react onto the avatar, which is being controlled by the operator with VR headset and give feedback to the external controller.

Moreover, the interaction with the historical data can be evaluated. Indeed, avoiding to interrupt the real process but using the persisted historical data, it is possible to interact with all simulated manufacturing line aspects and see how the system reacts. For example, it can be exploited to evaluate how operator takes raw material away from the conveyor and see how the system equipment reacts. Overall, this approach gives many options for simulations of the real processes without any risk to damage human health or expensive equipment, while giving an educational value for the new operators and students, who can test every aspect of the system processes and faults reactions without affecting the real environment.

Remote Online Monitoring of the Robot Cell. Leveraging the VR tools, the robotic system can be accessed remotely from any geographical point, giving the control over the processes. Operators exploiting clothes/glasses/tools RFID sensors can move around the robot cell with their ordinary daily routine. Data from the sensors are transferred towards the VR environment. In order to have an update about the presence information of the operators, machine vision cameras and laser scanners are also being used.

5   Conclusion

This paper has introduced an approach to combine three different enabling technologies of the Industry 4.0 (i.e. VR, FT and robotics). The approach is expected to offer several benefits regarding the quality of monitoring and simulation process in the manufacturing. Some preliminary experiments have been conducted in the specific domain of industrial robotics and collaborative robots. These experiments are ongoing and involve two different labs in Estonia and in Italy. However, the presented work is only a first step of a larger research agenda aiming at realizing a full synchronization between the real world of the plant and its virtual clone.

Future developments will address two main goals. First of all, it will be essential to evaluate the quality of service in terms of scalability and performance of the solution proposed, in order to verify its capability to support situations of intensive Big data. The second goal will regard the evaluation of the approach in various domains different from robotics.

Acknowledgments. The research was supported by I4MS project SmartIC Robotics - Regional Digital Innovation Hub in Robotics in Estonia.

Authors are grateful to the Integrated Engineering students of Tallinn University of Technology – Vladislav Minakov, Mohammad Tavassolian, Aleksei Tanjuhhin and Tengiz Pataraia helping in experiments and simulations.

The research was partially funded by the project "Smart Manufacturing 2020" within the "Cluster Tecnologico Nazionale Fabbrica Intelligente".

References

1. Computers in Spaceflight: The ŃASA Experience. http://history.nasa.gov/computers/Ch8-2. html. Accessed 23 Feb 2017
2. Grieves, M.: Digital twin: manufacturing excellence through virtual factory replication (2014). http://www.apriso.com/library/. Accessed 23 Feb 2017
3. Fritz, R., Kohlhoff, S.: Integration of Virtual and Physical Production Connection of Engineering Design with the Shop Floor (2015). Accessed 23 Feb 2017
4. Grieves, M., Vickers, J.: Digital twin: mitigating unpredictable, undesirable emergent behavior in complex systems. In: Kahlen, F.-J., Flumerfelt, S., Alves, A. (eds.) Transdisciplinary Perspectives on Complex Systems, pp. 85–113. Springer, Cham (2017). doi:10.1007/978-3-319-38756-7_4
5. Rosen, R., von Wichert, G., Lo, G., Bettenhausen, K.D.: About the importance of autonomy and digital twins for the future of manufacturing. IFAC-PapersOnLine **48**(3), 567–572 (2015). ISSN 2405-8963. http://dx.doi.org/10.1016/j.ifacol.2015.06.141
6. Schroeder, G.N., Steinmetz, C., Pereira, C.E., Espindola, D.B.: Digital twin data modeling with automationML and a communication methodology for data exchange. IFAC-PapersOnLine **49**(30), 12–17 (2016). ISSN 2405-8963. http://dx.doi.org/10.1016/j.ifacol. 2016.11.115
7. Terkaj, W., Tolio, T., Urgo, M.: A virtual factory approach for in situ simulation to support production and maintenance planning. CIRP Ann.- Manuf. Technol. **64**(1), 451–454 (2015)
8. Kádár, B., Lengyel, A., Monostori, L., Suginishi, Y., Pfeiffer, A., Nonaka, Y.: Enhanced control of complex production structures by tight coupling of the digital and the physical worlds. CIRP Ann. – Manuf. Technol. **59**(1), 437–440 (2010)
9. Brettel, M., Friederichsen, N., Keller, M., Rosenberg, M.: How virtualization, decentralization and network building change the manufacturing landscape an industry 4.0 perspective. Int. J. Mech. Ind. Sci. Eng. **8**(1), 37–44 (2014)
10. Modoni, G.E., Sacco, M., Terkaj, W.: A telemetry-driven approach to simulate data-intensive manufacturing processes. Procedia CIRP **57**, 281–285 (2016)
11. Cherubini, A., Passama, R., Crosnier, A., Lasnier, A., Fraisse, P.: Collaborative manufacturing with physical human–robot interaction. Robot. Comput.-Integr. Manuf. **40**, 1–13 (2016)
12. Modoni, G.E., Doukas, M., Terkaj, W., Sacco, M., Mourtzis, D.: Enhancing factory data integration through the development of an ontology: from the reference models reuse to the semantic conversion of the legacy models. Int. J. Comput. Integr. Manuf. (2016). Taylor & Francis
13. Capozzi, F., Lorizzo, V., Modoni, G., Sacco, M.: Lightweight augmented reality tools for lean procedures in future factories. In: De Paolis, L.T., Mongelli, A. (eds.) AVR 2014. LNCS, vol. 8853, pp. 232–246. Springer, Cham (2014). doi:10.1007/978-3-319-13969-2_18
14. Forouzan, B.A.: TCP/IP Protocol Suite. McGraw-Hill, Inc., New York City (2002)
15. Modoni, G.E., Veniero, M., Sacco, M.: Semantic knowledge management and integration services for AAL. In: Cavallo, F., Marletta, V., Monteriù, A., Siciliano, P. (eds.) ForItAAL 2016. LNEE, vol. 426, pp. 287–299. Springer, Cham (2017). doi:10.1007/978-3-319-54283-6_22
16. Mahnke, W., Leitner, S.H., Damm, M.: OPC Unified Architecture. Springer Science & Business Media, Heidelberg (2009)
17. Kuts, V., Tähemaa, T., Otto, T., Sarkans, M., Lend, H.: Robot manipulator usage for measurement in production areas. J. Mach. Eng. **16**(1), 57–67 (2016)
18. ROS documentation. http://wiki.ros.org/. Accessed 7 Mar 2017
19. ISO/TS 15066:2016 Robots and robotic devices – Collaborative robots

A VR-CAD Data Model for Immersive Design
The cRea-VR Proof of Concept

Pierre Martin[1,2], Stéphane Masfrand[2], Yujiro Okuya[1], and Patrick Bourdot[1(✉)]

[1] V&AR VENISE Group, LIMSI-CNRS, Orsay, France
`patrick.bourdot@limsi.fr`
[2] PSA Peugeot Citroën, Velizy-Villacoublay, France

Abstract. This work focuses on direct and interactive modifications of CAD objects in Virtual Reality (VR). Usually, CAD software requires some skills (experience and knowledge), on its functionalities and representations, as well as on the design history of CAD objects. On the other side, VR brings new paradigms for 3D interaction, and one needs intelligent middleware to manage CAD objects in any immersive Virtual Environment (VE). Previous work proposed a mechanism allowing implicit edition of the Construction History Graph (CHG) of CAD objects, based on the direct manipulation of their 3D visual representations. A labelling technique of the Boundary Representations (B-Rep) elements, coupled with an inference engine, provided a backward chaining of B-Rep elements towards the operators of a customized CHG. In this paper we propose a generalization of this approach to apply it to any CAD system based on B-Rep and CHG models. Firstly, several encapsulations structures are defined, to manage CHG nodes as well as the B-Rep components. Secondly the labelling, now attached to the encapsulations of the B-Rep elements, has been extended to a multi-labelling. This solves the issue of the B-Rep elements which are the result of several CHG operators, and more generally allows that several parameterizations of a CAD object may be proposed for its shape modification, when selecting any B-Rep element. These improvements make it possible direct and interactive modifications of CAD objects previously designed, by parsing native CHG of a given CAD system, to fill our structures with useful data for their 3D edition during a VR session. Moreover the multi-labelling mechanism grants the manipulation of CAD objects to non-experts through the inference engine. As a proof of concept we present cRea-VR, our VR-CAD model applied to CATIA.

1 Introduction

Computer-Aided Design (CAD) systems now play a central role in design and manufacturing industries. Thanks to continuous improvements and technological breakthroughs, these strategical tools have been integrated in the Product Lifecycle Management (PLM). The use of CAD tools, providing 3D digital mockup (DMU) functionalities, have particularly reduced the design time, optimizing the data flow between product development and the visualization stages. The

© Springer International Publishing AG 2017
L.T. De Paolis et al. (Eds.): AVR 2017, Part I, LNCS 10324, pp. 222–241, 2017.
DOI: 10.1007/978-3-319-60922-5_17

combination of DMUs with the feature-based parametric models increases the productivity of the design phases.

Although the use of CAD tools brings positive points such as easy visualization and simulation of new ideas, improving creativity or facilitating communication with colleagues, the mastery of CAD skills remains complex and time-consuming. Moreover, CAD tools are far from intuitive. Actually, most of the commands of these systems are made through WIMP interfaces (Windows, Icons, Menus, Pointing devices), or other classical desktop (2D) interfaces like mouse or keyboard, which may induce cognitive load and lower productivity. Many works concluded that changing the way users interact with CAD systems could improve productivity.

It is now fully admitted that the use of Virtual Reality (VR) has led to an acceleration of the design process. VR technologies provide new paradigms of 3D interaction, such as immersion and multi-sensorimotor perception, allowing to study CAD models at full scale (1:1) and interact in an intuitive way. A number of research have been conducted to link VR and CAD in order to enhance user interaction as well as object perception: this field is called Virtual Reality Aided Design (VRAD). But although VR technologies have been exploited by industries for twenty years, they are not yet fully integrated in the design process.

The use of VR in Industry allows users to work with virtual prototypes (digital mockups) and to quickly achieve design reviews. But VR-CAD integration still suffers from some identified drawbacks, and especially data interoperability between VR and CAD systems. In existing immersive project reviews conducted in industrial environments, CAD data have to be prepared to be imported in VR systems. In addition to the problems that conversions can raise, the main disadvantage of CAD-to-VR conversion is the loss of semantical information intitially contained by CAD objects. This makes it impossible to reflect in real-time modifications on CAD object that were decided during the review in a Virtual Environment (VE). This can only be achieved after the immersive session, in offline mode. Moreover, most of the time, CAD systems (desktop environments) are physically distant from VR systems, increasing the delay between stages of the design process. Thus a major technical issue is the complete integration of CAD with VR, in order to maintain semantical information and to allow direct and real-time modifications of CAD objects. To achieve such a VR-CAD integration, one has to exploit the persistent naming of the feature-based parametric CAD systems. Some previous research have been made in this direction, but all were CAD system dependent.

This paper presents an architecture based on a VR-CAD data model to fully integrate CAD objects, especially those coming from commercial CAD systems, within any VE platform. Whatever the industrial CAD system is, data conversion must be avoided to easily switch from one platform to another (e.g. from a desktop-CAD to a VR-CAD environment) and reuse the same CAD objects. In Sect. 2 we review most of the existing immersive modeling applications and VR-CAD work. Then we present the basic concepts of our approach in Sect. 3. In Sect. 4 we detail our data model and how the direct modification of CAD objects is supported. As a proof of concept, we present an implementation based on the commercial CAD system CATIA[1] and examples of modifications, in Sect. 5. Finally we conclude and give some of our perspectives in Sect. 6.

2   Related Work

Many researches in VR-CAD integration tried to enhance visualization and manipulation of CAD objects. The corner stone of these approaches is to convert and import CAD objects previously built in a CAD system, within a VE platform in order to provide a better perception of the model. Manipulations of objects and/or virtual assemblies, as well as navigation are often available, but one of the main limitations in the conversion/import approach lies on the impossibility to directly create or modify CAD models in the VE. That is why lots of work have been focusing on *immersive modelling*.

2.1   Sketching and Drawing in Virtual Environments

A first category of immersive modelling is dedicated to sketching and drawing. Some of them focused on immersive surface modelling. Fiorentino et al. [6] with SpaceDesign is a good example of free form design and sketching in immersive environments. Another example is the hybrid modelling environments proposed by Stark et al. [14] which is making possible to sketch objects in immersive environments and to integrate them in CAD/PDM systems. However, one of the limitations of immersive free-form modelling is that the accuracy of 2D interaction can not be easily replicated with 3D interactive paradigms based on VR technologies, except for some promising work using haptic devices (see for instance [1,13]).

2.2   Immersive Solid Modelling

Many authors have proposed solutions for immersive solid modelling. For instance, Trika et al. [16] developed a VR system integrating the TWIN modeler, whose the main interest is to maintain the knowledge representation of the parts (i.e. the adjacency information, and the polyhedric approximation of design features). Gao et al. [8] proposed an extended solid model for constraint-based solid modelling in a semi-immersive VR environment, where users can manipulate primitives through added data (control points and constraints). Ye et al. [20] worked on the LUCID system which provides to users new interaction paradigms to create, modify, visualize and feel CAD objects in a desktop environment (e.g. two hands interaction combining mouse and haptic devices). To ensure the genericity of the VR-CAD integration, lots of researches have been conducted using two popular geometric kernels: ACIS[2] (such as [6]) and OpenCascade[3] [7,9,18].

---

[1] CATIA: www.3Ds.com/fr/products/catia/.
[2] www.spatial.com/products/3D-acis-modeling.
[3] www.opencascade.org/.

In all of these works, there is no direct link with an actual CAD system: users have to convert geometries, created/modified in immersive sessions, into standard formats such as STEP or IGES for using them in a CAD system. From an industrial point of view, this means an increase of the design time. Moreover, the main CAD systems use a Construction History Graph (CHG) – also called design history graph [3,19] or feature dependency graph – to store the information—operators, parameters, transformation matrices, etc.—which fully describes the design history of CAD objects. Most of the time, information about construction history and modifications is lost when objects are converted across format.

To solve this issue Meyrueis et al. [12] conceived a method to deform the mesh of 3D objects previously created in a CAD system. They store the deformation information in a specific CHG they manage on the VR system side, to reconstruct the surfaces and merge the modifications with the original object in the CAD system after the immersive session. But immersive modifications of existing operators and their parameters are not possible. Another CAD system dependent approach has been conducted by Toma et al. [15] with the Solidworks[4] software thanks to the VRSolid module which provides a VR interface for this CAD system.

To conclude, comparison of the desktop and VR environments gives the main following results: the VR interface is more intuitive than the desktop one but is more physically demanding, but 2D desktop interfaces are preferred for the creation of parts. So, one of the most promising ways to reduce the design time, especially in industry, remains the direct modification of the CHG of CAD objects by simple interactions on their shapes: we talk about *implicit edition*.

2.3   Implicit Edition of the CHG

The lack of direct modification of the CHG of CAD objects fom VR interactions on their shapes can be explained by a series of obstacles [14]: (i) the usability of current VR-based user interfaces for CAD systems is limited; (ii) 2D interaction techniques of current CAD systems cannot be transferred one-to-one to VR systems; (iii) the accuracy of the modelling operations cannot be guaranteed in VR. In addition, direct modification of complex objects could introduce lag due to big updates, which deteriorates the real-time experience generally expected in VR. But the major issue to overcome for a real and efficient VR-CAD integration is the ability to use/reuse the persistent naming associated to a given CAD system: one has to gain access to the core of CAD systems (geometric kernels) with the help of application programming interfaces (API).

Ma et al. [10,21] have designed a constraint-based and hierarchically structured data model for solid modeling in VR environment. The model is composed of three layers: a constraint-based model for manipulation and modification, an hybrid home-made B-Rep/CSG representation of CAD objects, and their polyhedral representation for real-time visualization and interaction. The B-Rep and

---

[4] www.solidworks.com/.

the polyhedral models are linked through cross-references, and basic geometric operations are applied thanks to the ACIS kernel. An experimental implementation has been developed with the Division Reality[5] software.

Wang et al. [17] presented a CAD linked VR environment. They conceived an interesting hybrid data structure to support parametric design modifications. The VR system (immersive desktop) and the CAD system are linked, but run in two separate processes. Semantical information of CAD models is extracted during the creation of the VR environment, and each modification is directly reflected in the CAD system thanks to the introduction of the persistent naming mechanism in the VR-CAD integration.

In previous work, Bourdot et al. presented a VR-CAD integration [2,4]. A CAD model has been designed to ensure the implicit edition of the CHG. This model is based on a persistent naming system that creates and maintains permanent link between elements of B-Rep (Boundary Representation) and the CHG structures. As a proof of concept, the VRAD demonstrator has been implemented with OpenCascade. In order to apply this approach to an industrial context, some elements to interface it with CATIA were sketched, but their actual applicability was not demonstrated.

3   Basic Concepts

3.1   General Overview

We propose hereafter a generalization of our previous VR-CAD integration approach [2,4] in order to adapt it to an industrial context. To this end, we have designed a middleware architecture based on a VR-CAD data model (Fig. 1) for making this approach applicable to commercial software of CAD system which are generally preferred to be used in industry.

As the previous work, the principle of the implicit edition mechanism still aims at making possible a backward chaining of B-Rep elements towards the operators of a CAD model described by a CHG. It is also still based on a labelling technique of B-Rep elements coupled with inference procedures (Fig. 2). Such a mechanism allows to modify parameters of operators in the CHG, depending on the B-Rep element (vertice, edge or face) that have been selected by the user.

Our work extends the labelling technique to a *multi-labelling* (described and discussed in Subsects. 3.3 and 3.4), which is required for any B-Rep element that is the result of several CHG operators. A major consequence of the multi-labelling is that several parameterizations of a CAD object may be inferred and so proposed to the users, when selecting any B-Rep element. This wildly enhances the backward chaining with the CHG: a B-Rep element presents a greater number of links with the CHG nodes, so that users have more possibilities for direct modifications.

To support this approach in a more generic way, we designed a VR-CAD data model. This model is composed of several encapsulations (described in

---

[5] www.ptc.com.

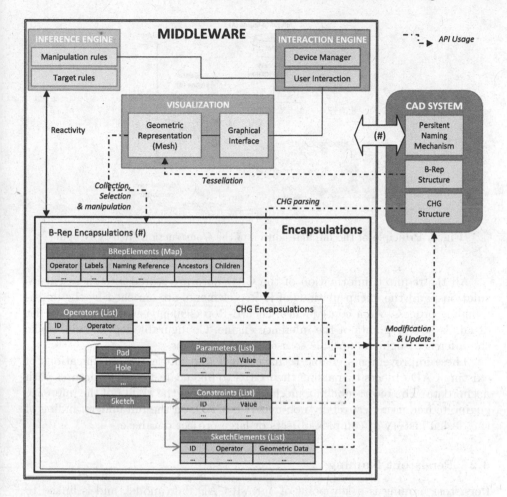

Fig. 1. VR-CAD data model for immersive and intuitive design - some useful information on the CHG & B-Rep entities of the target CAD system are stored within a number of permanent encapsulation structures.

Subsect. 4.1) to manage all necessary CHG structures (operators and their parameters, constraints and 2D elements of sketches) as well as B-Rep elements, which are dependent on the target CAD system. This concept of encapsulation structures relies on the ability to access to core functionalities of CAD systems through dedicated API. This makes this VR-CAD model generic, but one implementation with a specific CAD system will be different from another system because functions provided by API may not be exactly the same. Moreover, theses structures (especially B-Rep encapsulations) can be kept up-to-date thanks to the use of a persistent naming mechanism. Then, a major preliminary issue has been to decide with which persistent naming mechanism it was better to work; this choice is discussed in the next Subsection.

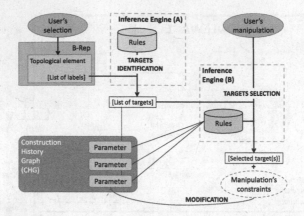

Fig. 2. Principle of the implicit edition of the Construction History Graph.

All the required information of the CAD data are stored into these encapsulations, and the encapsulations of B-Rep elements are enriched by the multi-labelling process. As a consequence, each B-Rep element is associated to a list of labels—entry points of the inference engine. Configurable logical rules make the inference engine adaptable to user needs and skills.

These improvements enable to have direct and interactive modifications of existing CAD objects by parsing their CHG to fill encapsulation structures with useful data. The multi-labelling mechanism reinforces the ability of the inference engine to free users, especially non-expert in CAD, on the full understanding of the design history of complex objects or large project database.

3.2   Persistent Naming

Persistent naming is a key point of our VR-CAD data model, and is linked to the encapsulation of B-Rep elements we propose.

In common feature-based parametric CAD systems, any feature operator is applied to one or several topological entities that are thus referenced by this operator. These references on the B-Rep elements have to be maintained to be able to modify and re-evaluate the CHG. An example is given in Fig. 3: when the slot is modified (2a to 2b), the solid is reevaluated to apply the edge fillet. The final result can be different from a CAD system to another (3b or 3c). So topological element may appear or disappear when operators are modified. To ensure a valid reevaluation of the CHG, one has to uniquely and persistently name B-Rep elements and keep theses associations up-to-date. This is the *persistent naming* mechanism, integrated into main commercial CAD systems.

We integrated the persistent naming of the target CAD system within our middleware data structures. This is a key issue regarding commercial CAD systems, whose mechanisms are generally only accessible through "black boxes". Accessing to core functions of CAD systems thanks to their API does not mean that any information is provided on how these naming mechanisms work. Our

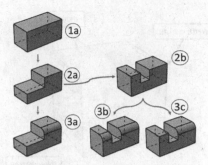

Fig. 3. Example of the persistent naming problem. A solid is built: A sketch is extruded (1a), then a slot (2a) and an edge fillet (3a) are applied. When the slot is modified (2b), the solid is reevaluated. Two results (3b) and (3c) are possible, depending on the CAD system.

approach does not require any knowledge on how these mechanisms behave, since there is a way to integrate them into our reactivity process with one of the encapsulation structures we present in this paper.

3.3 Labelling Mechanism

Basic Definition. A label is attached to each B-Rep element and can be seen as a direct link between this element and a CHG node. A label depends on the nature of the operator that has generated the B-Rep element, and so for the targets of a label, that are the CHG node information accessible from a label. Targets can be, for example, a parameter of the generating operator, a sketch constraint or a sketch element.

The standard form of a label is:

$$\text{NAME}(\text{ID}_{skel}, \text{ID}_{op}) \text{ or } \text{NAME}(\text{ID}_{op})$$

NAME is the name of the label: VSK for a point of a sketch (Vertex SKetch), or VPT for a vertex of the top face of an extrusion (Vertex Pad Top). We then have two forms which differ by having one (ID_{op}) or two (ID_{skel} and ID_{op}) identifiers. The identifier ID_{op} is always present and refers to the identifier of the operator that generates the B-Rep element. The identifier ID_{skel} refers to the identifier of a sketch element: ID_{pnt} for a point, ID_{crv} for a curve, etc.

Multi-labelling. A major issue of our previous approach [2,4] is that each B-Rep element was only associated to a single label depending on the operator that generated this element, which was inducing a fairly limited range of action. Users were accessing to a very narrow choice of modifications within the design tree, a label pointing only at a certain level of this tree.

To overcome this limitation, our VR-CAD data model is extending the labelling mechanism to a *multi-labelling*, and the encapsulation of a B-Rep element manages a list of labels to support this extension. Figure 4 especially shows

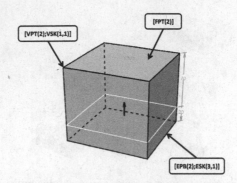

Fig. 4. Example of multi-labelling and potential targets. The final object is the result of the extrusion ($ID_{op} = 2$) of a sketch ($ID_{op} = 1$) colored in white. Three B-Rep elements are explicited. The top face of the extrusion ($ID_{op} = 2$) is labelled with FPT(2). The edge is labelled with ETB(2) and ESK(3,1): it belongs to the bottom face of the extrusion ($ID_{op} = 2$) and comes from the element ($ID_{crv} = 3$) of the sketch ($ID_{op} = 1$). Finally, the vertex is labelled with VPT(2) and VSK(1,1): it belongs to the top face of the extrusion ($ID_{op} = 2$) and comes from the element ($ID_{pnt} = 1$) of the sketch ($ID_{op} = 1$).

multi-labelling, where the vertex and the edge, given as examples, have each a list of two labels.

A first benefit is that several labels can now be created for a single B-Rep element related to a given CHG operator, in order to better target the different operator parameters that the users want to access while modifying this element. To decide if additional labels are necessary for a B-Rep element related to a given operator, we process as follow: if the operator is defined with several parameters, one label for each parameter is required and then created. So, after the selection of a B-Rep element, user can interact separately on each one, or in a combined way (with specific logic rules).

The second and major benefit of multi-labelling is to take into account the full history of B-Rep elements. One has to remember that the encapsulation of a B-Rep element contains a list of its ancestors (which are older B-Rep elements). We use this list to collect the labels of each ancestor. So, in addition to the main labels of a B-Rep element (related to the operator which generated this element), the final list of labels also contains the labels of all the ancestors of this element. Thus, all the CHG operators historically involved in the definition of a B-Rep element are represented by specific labels, and so, users can now access to each parameter of these CHG nodes (as a consequence of the first benefit).

3.4   Conceptual and Technical Remarks

Please note that persistent naming and multi-labelling are two different but complementary mechanisms (see Fig. 5). The first one (green arrows) describes links between similar elements which are persistent within different B-Rep graphs, each of these graphs corresponding to a state of the 3D object shape. The sec-

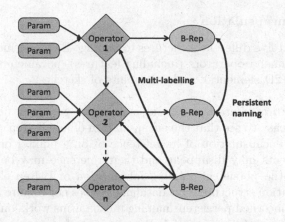

Fig. 5. Persistent naming vs. Labelling mechanisms. (Color figure online)

ond one (red arrows) provides direct links from a given B-Rep element toward a number of CHG nodes. That can be all the nodes which contributed to define the shape of this element, or a subset of these nodes, depending on the implementation choices related to the real user needs.

Although the persistent naming describes the historical affiliations between B-Rep elements of several versions of a 3D object, such a mechanism may be a black box in a number of CAD systems as we noticed in subsect. 3.2—for instance by keeping confidential the naming syntax. In that case, the CAD system API must at least provide functions allowing to determine the immediate ancestor of any B-Rep element. Once this multi-labelling is computed during the preparation of data (cf. parsing and encapsulation), one obtains a powerful way to implicitly edit the CHG: a large number of shortcuts to have a direct access to CHG nodes is provided when user needs to modify data from simple interactions with the B-Rep elements of the 3D objects.

4   Core System Architecture

This section details the middleware architecture which supports our VR-CAD model for interacting in VR with the native data of any CAD system based on CHG and B-Rep structures. Apart the description of the encapsulation structures for CAD data representations, we explain the parsing processes for creating and updating them. Then we focus on target identification using this multi-labelling and an inference engine. Targets are the data of the CHG nodes that users will be able to modify via direct selection/interaction on B-Rep elements. And finally, we discuss on parsing strategies to update during the working session the encapsulations of our VR-CAD data model.

4.1   Object Encapsulation

We have designed five different structures to manage B-Rep elements, and some CHG entities, namely: operators (including features), parameters of operators, sketch elements (2D elements), and constraints of sketches.

B-Rep Element Encapsulation — Having in mind the persistent naming problem (see Fig. 3), it is easy to see that the encapsulation of any B-Rep element cannot only rely on the encapsulation of its reference or on a pointer on this element: topological elements may disappear and their reference may be NULL. So the idea is to store the persistent naming information of B-Rep elements in the related encapsulation structure. Our data model does not require any knowledge about how the concerned persistent naming mechanisms work, only a process to retrieve the naming information of B-Rep elements from their encapsulations. Of course, a necessary condition for the proper functioning of our VR-CAD data model is that the API of the CAD system provides such possibility—the main computations being made by the targetted CAD system.

A B-Rep encapsulation typically contains: a pointer on the BRep element object, a pointer on the encapsulaton of its generating operator, a list of labels, a list of pointers on the encapsulation structures of B-Rep ancestors and B-Rep children, the persistent naming information, a pointer to the B-Rep (i.e. the full B-Rep, including all elements), and the functions for labelling, searching ancestors and creating visual representations. The lists of ancestors and children will be used by our labelling mechanism, which is different from the native persistent naming of the CAD system, as we will underline later on.

Operator Encapsulation — The encapsulation of CHG operatorsis is clearly less complex than B-Rep ones. It contains at least: a unique ID, a pointer on the operator object (which is valid until the operator is deleted), a type, a list of pointer to encapsulations of parameters and functions to update the concerned data. As for the different B-Rep encapsulations, the behavior of some functions may differ according to the type of operator (e.g. update processes). The updates and modifications of parameters are directly controlled by the related operator's encapsulation.

Parameter Encapsulation — Parameters are what users want to access during modifications of CAD models (e.g. the depth of a hole, the length of an extrusion, etc.). In our approach, links are made between the B-Rep elements visualized by users and parameters of operators which are not visible on the user interface. Parameter's encapsulation is simple: a unique ID and the type, the name, and the value of the parameter.

Constraint Encapsulation — Constraints can be considered as parameters, but are, in a number of CAD systems, related to sketches. That is why we designed a specific structure containing: a unique ID, a type, a pointer on the constraint object, a name, a value, and the list of the names of the elements linked to this constraint. The behavior of these encapsulations is almost the same as the behavior of parameter encapsulation. For now, only numerical constraints (length, distance, radius, etc.) are taken into account because such constraints are subject to be modified.

Sketch Component Encapsulation — 2D geometry represent all elements composing sketches (point, line, curve, etc.). We designed sketch component encapsulations containing: a unique ID, the type of the element, the list of constraints' name linked to this element, a pointer on the sketch element object and a pointer on the encapsulation of the sketch containing the element. Only names of constraints are stored within these encapsulations because constraint encapsulations are already included in the concerned sketch operator.

4.2   Parsing of Construction History Graph

It has been observed that designers prefer creating CAD object on desktop environments rather than in immersive ones [15]: time completion is approximatively the same but movements are more physically stressful due to higher distances. Moreover, the accuracy of classical 2D interactions is hardly reachable with free hand movements, except if they aim at changing values of existing parameters, where some virtual guides can especially be used to increase the 3D interaction accuracy. Based on this important observation—form modification is preferable to form creation in immersive environment—we consider the parsing of existing CHG as a necessary procedure to include in our middleware. The aim of the parsing process is to store all the existing necessary data of the CAD object, into our encapsulation structures.

CHG parsing is done at the beginning of each immersive session, and after each update of the modified object. If the modification of an operator leads to the deletion or the creation of topological elements (see Fig. 3), then all the CHG is parsed from the level of the modified operator to the newest elements (the last operator in the CHG), because the persistent naming information in our encapsulation structures would otherwise be obsolete. If the modification only consists in changing some parameters values of existing operators without deleting or creating B-Rep elements, then no complete update is needed.

The parsing process is decomposed in three steps:

Step 1: Operators and Parameters — The first step concerns the main elements of the CHG: the operators. Only operators containing interesting parameters (defined by users depending on their needs) are stored. All the operator's parameters are encapsulated at this step.

Step 2: Sketches, 2D Geometric Elements and Constraints — This step consists in retrieving all the sketches of the model. Depending on the CAD system, 2D elements can be embedded in operators (sketches), or can be fully described outside operators in the design tree. In the former case, the sketch operators are firstly retrieved and encapsulated, then the 2D elements are encapsulated with the constraints of the sketch operators. Otherwise, 2D elements are directly retrieved from the design tree.

Step 3: B-Rep Elements — The final step retrieves all the topological (B-Rep) elements and interesting data through three main stages. The first stage integrates the persistent naming information of the CAD system into our data structure, to allow direct access to the B-Rep element. Of course, this assumes that the API of this CAD system is providing functions for consulting the persistent naming data. The second stage concerns the labelling of B-Rep elements. The final stage is based on the search of the ancestors (B-Rep elements previously created) which are involved in the construction of a B-Rep element. Accessing to these ancestors allows to collect their labels, which are some major components to construct the multi-labelling of a considered B-Rep element (see Sect. 3.3). Finally, the outcome of this step 3 is the creation of three structures gathering the encapsulations of B-Rep elements depending on their dimensionality.

4.3   Target Selection

Our middleware is composed of an "intelligent" engine, called *inference engine* which helps users to choose the targets they may edit within the design tree. This is the *targets identification* process (part A of the inference engine in the Fig. 2). In classical CAD systems, editing nodes of the design tree is based on a number of user interactions with the full 2D representation of the CHG. Thanks to the targets identification process, users can now interact directly on the 3D shapes of the B-Rep elements of the CAD object, which is especially useful for immersive situations.

General Principle. The target identification is the process that chooses the targets the system has (may have) to implicitly edit within the CHG [2]. This identification is made thanks to a configurable inference engine based on Prolog rules. A rule associates parameters to a label, whose the generic form is:

$$\texttt{targ\_([listofparameters], label)}.$$

Then the principle is quite simple: when a user select a B-Rep element, we get the *labels* of this element (see Fig. 4) and we send it to the inference engine. Prolog rules are interactively executed and we retrieve a list of targets of the CHG. These rules have to be set up according to the user needs.

A novelty brought by our VR-CAD data model is to take into account the history of B-Rep element. Thus, users can directly and intuitively interact with a visible elements, on different levels of the CHG (and not only on the last level that generates this element).

Targets Identification Process. Our VR-CAD data model truly takes into account the full design history of each B-Rep element. This exhaustivity of information coming from the parsing of the CHG is not an end in itself. It allows to increase the possibilities of interaction, or, in other words, to have more degrees of freedom to configure interaction to the user needs. Nevertheless this increase in the number of possibilities makes more complex their management.

Thus, our inference engine consists of two differents parts, A and B (see Fig. 2), each representing a stage in the process of targets determination. The first stage has been described above, the *targets identification*. The second stage chooses among the potential targets those which have to be activated.

Presently, the choice among the potential targets is not made through an "intelligent component" like the first stage. All the potential targets are gathered into a single list and will be managed quite simply. Targets are ordered by their original label, from newest to oldest. Then, users will select in a sequential manner the target they want to activate, and deeper they run through this list, deeper will be the CHG modification (see Fig. 6).

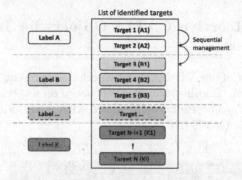

Fig. 6. List of targets identified by the part A of the inference engine.

4.4 Encapsulations Update

To maintain a real-time interaction is an important issue since CHG parsing is performed not only during the setup of the immersive session, but also after each modification of the CAD object. Particularly, more complex the CAD object is, the bigger is the number of B-Rep elements which have to be processed. This could lead to insufferable latencies. Optimizing this process must be considered.

In fact, there are two options regarding this parsing process: processing all the B-Rep elements from the beginning of the CHG (Global Update) or processing only interesting B-Rep elements (only the visible/pickable elements) that users will see and interact with (Local Update).

Global Update may need the longer setup time, and we may have to manage a massive amount of data, but the elements are definitely encapsulated for further interactions (modifications and updates). Only the new elements created by a modification stage will have to be parsed. The idea of the Local Update is to parse only interesting (visible) B-Rep elements. The launch of the session is faster, and we have to manage a smaller amount of data. But the amount of data to manage is not the most important issue. During the encapsulation of each B-Rep element, we have to retrieve its ancestors. This step will be completely different depending on the chosen option. Most of time, ancestors are not visible (they belong to a previous geometric result). With the Global Update, all the B-Rep elements will be encapsulated (visible and invisible ones). With the Local Update, each time a new element is created, all its ancestors which have not yet been parsed (and recursively, the ancestors of these ancestors) must be retrieved for being encapsulated too. This process may be complex and time-consuming, and it could bring important latencies, in particularly during the update.

We preferred the Global Update. Then, after each interactive modification during the session, and apart the encapsulation of the new B-Rep elements, the full parsing is used again, but only for the actualisation of the persistent naming information, and for creating the few necessary links on the new ancestors.

5   cRea-VR: Reactive CATIA Objects for Intuitive Modifications

As a proof of concept of our VR-CAD data model, we present and detail here the different features of our middleware cRea-VR based on a specific implementation with the CATIA V5 geometric kernel, coupled with a rendering system allowing immersive sessions in CAVE-like systems.

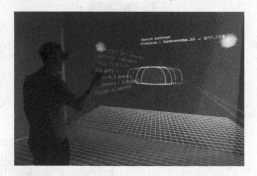

Fig. 7. Immersive session with cRea-VR.

5.1   cRea-VR Set-Up

We chose an implementation of our VR-CAD data model with the CATIA V5 geometric kernel in order to fit with the industrial needs, in particular the automotive industry. It is also designed to work with CAVE-like system as well as workstation. The CAVE-like system has 4 screens (ground, left, face and right), one cluster PC (Windows 7 Professional 64 bits, with Nvidia Quadro FX 5800 graphic cards) and one 3D projector with active-stereo (allowing stereoscopic visualization thanks to shutter glasses) are set for each screen. Users can interact with a 6dof device (Flystick) and its movements (head and hands) are tracked by an ART system. As a clustering rendering system, we used DRS (Distributed Rendering System) [5] in order to render a deformable object over a PC cluster.

5.2   Immersive Modification Process

The process of the immersive deformation of CAD object is described as below.

Preparing the CAD Object. Interesting parts of the CAD model that users want to access during immersive sessions have to be indicated. As we can see in the image 1 of Fig. 8, users have to check what are the different parameters they want to modify, and in which part of the CHG they are stored. Finally, names of interesting parts are stored in a configuration file. One has to notice that by default, our VR-CAD model will take into account all the data of the entire CAD model. With the specification of the interesting parts of the CAD models, we optimize the data management.

Creating the VR Session. User loads the original file. Then the CHG is parsed, and all the needed data are encapsulated in our VR-CAD data structures. When all necessary data are gathered, B-Rep elements are labelled. The graphical representations of the CAD object are computed while encapsulating the B-Rep elements. At the end of this process, users can see and manipulate the CAD object in the immersive environment, as shown in the Fig. 7.

Interacting in the VR Session. Users can have different interactions to manipulate CAD objects in VR: *exploration phase*, by pointing elements, or *modification phases* by selecting elements and doing some actions.

Image 2 of Fig. 8 shows the exploration of a CAD object. When users point elements (colored in green), information are displayed on the left panel, especially the kind of topological element and the targets—modifiable parameters—of the CAD models.

To modify the CAD object, users have to select a graphical element (colored in red, image 3 of the Fig. 8). By default, when several targets are reachable from this element, the first one is activated. Then information about the current modification and parameter are displayed (in white) on the top right. Users can then easily modify the current parameter by doing some 3D interactions, or can choose to switch to another reachable parameter.

When users modify a parameter of a CAD object, as shown in image 4 of the Fig. 8, the value ameter being updated is displayed on the top right. While the modificated part is highlighted (in this case, the modified sketch is displayed in green dotted line), the part of the CAD object not directly impacted becomes transparent (see Fig. 7). When modification is achieved and validated, the CAD object is updated and fully displayed.

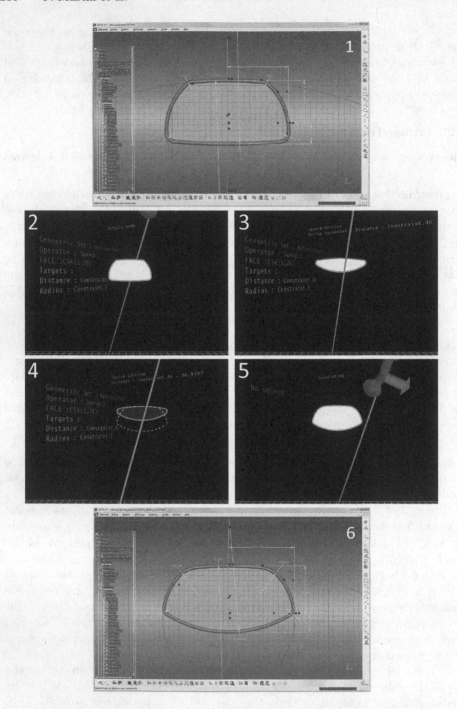

Fig. 8. Example of cRea-VR session. (1) Rear-view mirror designed in CATIA V5. (2) Object exploration. (3) Topological selection. (4) Distance modification. (5) Save/exit. (6) Check of modified CAD object reloaded in CATIA. (Color figure online)

At the end of the immersive session users can save the CAD object in its original format. Then, modified objects can be reloaded without any data conversion in the original CAD system (image 6 of Fig. 8).

5.3   First Feedback of Users

Industrial users highly request to visualize CAD objects at scale 1:1, and to evaluate them with a perspective point of view (adaptative stereoscopy depending on the tracked point of view). Senior CAD engineers of PSA have highlighted the following strengths of cRea-VR: real-time visualization of modifications, deep access to the parameters of CATIA objects, conversion-free immersive project reviews. But they converged on the fact that interactions need to be improved to become more natural and/or more intuitive.

Currently, we are designing a user study which evaluate the efficiency of the deformation task and user's preference between in the immersive system (cReaVR) and on workstation (CATIA interface) in order to analyze the effect of cReaVR on CAD deformation.

6   Conclusion and Future Work

In this paper, we have presented a VR-CAD data model for immersive and intuitive design. We have set up an architecture that gives users the possibility to directly interact and modify objects of common CAD systems based on CHG and B-Rep representations in the immersive environments.

We proposed a set of data structures to deal with existing representations (CHG and B-Rep) of common CAD systems. This is an important point considering the industrial context: engineers want to work with their existing tools and systems. Accessing to the API of the targetted CAD system makes that no conversion of data is required, either at the beginning or at the end of the immersive work session.

The reactivity scheme applied on our VR-CAD data model allows direct and simple access to the parameters of the CHG of CAD objects. Moreover, the multi-labelling increases the number of potential modifications from the selection of a single B-Rep element. Nevertheless, the management of all the possibilities has to evolve. For now, users can switch sequentially from a parameter to another, but we can easily imagine than another "intelligent component" could help the user to choose between all the available parameters. The design of the second part of the inference engine is one of our current priority.

User interface is also a part that we can now enhance. As we have previously demonstrated, multimodal interactions [2,11] are an interesting way to offer intuitive CAD interactions. Moreover, we will integrate some of our haptic work to improve the accuracy and to help users in the selection and modification tasks.

Finally, from an industrial point of view, this work has to be scaled to the industrial needs. The proof of concept based on CATIA has been tested on "simple" objects, far from the complex mock-ups we can find in industries. This scalability could be a great opportunity to test, validate and consolidate our approach.

Acknowledgements. This research has been supported by PSA Peugeot Citroën thanks to ANRT CIFRE French government PhD fundings, and by equipement grants from the same national government through the ANR Equipex DIGISCOPE project.

References

1. Bordegoni, M., Cugini, U.: Haptic modeling in the conceptual phases of product design. Virtual Reality **9**(2–3), 192–202 (2006)
2. Bourdot, P., Convard, T., Picon, F., Ammi, M., Touraine, D., Vézien, J.M.: VR-CAD integration: multimodal immersive interaction and advanced haptic paradigms for implicit edition of CAD models. Comput. Aided Des. **42**(5), 445–461 (2010)
3. Cicirello, V.A., Regli, W.C.: Resolving non-uniqueness in design feature histories. In: Proceedings of the fifth ACM Symposium on Solid Modeling and Applications, pp. 76–84. ACM (1999)
4. Convard, T., Bourdot, P.: History based reactive objects for immersive CAD. In: Proceedings of the Ninth ACM Symposium on Solid Modeling and Applications, SM 2004, pp. 291–296. Eurographics Association, Aire-la-Ville (2004)
5. Convard, T., Bourdot, P., Vézien, J.-M.: Managing deformable objects in cluster rendering. In: Sunderam, V.S., Albada, G.D., Sloot, P.M.A., Dongarra, J.J. (eds.) ICCS 2005. LNCS, vol. 3515, pp. 290–297. Springer, Heidelberg (2005). doi:10.1007/11428848_36
6. Fiorentino, M., de Amicis, R., Monno, G., Stork, A.: Spacedesign: a mixed reality workspace for aesthetic industrial design. In: Proceedings of the 1st International Symposium on Mixed and Augmented Reality, ISMAR 2002, pp. 86–94. IEEE Computer Society, Washington, DC (2002)
7. Foursa, M., d'Angelo, D., Wesche, G., Bogen, M.: A two-user framework for rapid immersive full cycle product customization. In: Shumaker, R. (ed.) VMR 2009. LNCS, vol. 5622, pp. 566–575. Springer, Heidelberg (2009). doi:10.1007/978-3-642-02771-0_63
8. Gao, S., Wan, H., Peng, Q.: An approach to solid modeling in a semi-immersive virtual environment. Comput. Graph. **24**(2), 191–202 (2000)
9. Ingrassia, T., Cappello, F.: VirDe: a new virtual reality design approach. Int. J. Interact. Des. Manuf. (IJIDeM) **3**(1), 1–11 (2009)
10. Ma, W., Zhong, Y., Tso, S.K., Zhou, T.: A hierarchically structured and constraint-based data model for intuitive and precise solid modeling in a virtual reality environment. Comput. Aided Des. **36**(10), 903–928 (2004)
11. Martin, P., Tseu, A., Férey, N., Touraine, D., Bourdot, P.: A hardware and software architecture to deal with multimodal and collaborative interactions in multiuser virtual reality environments. Proc. SPIE **9012**, 901209-1–901209-16 (2014). doi:10.1117/12.2042499
12. Meyrueis, V., Paljic, A., Fuchs, P.: D 3: an immersive aided design deformation method. In: Proceedings of the 16th ACM Symposium on Virtual Reality Software and Technology, pp. 179–182. ACM (2009)
13. Owada, S., Nielsen, F., Nakazawa, K., Igarashi, T.: A sketching interface for modeling the internal structures of 3D shapes. In: ACM SIGGRAPH 2007 Courses, p. 38. ACM (2007)
14. Stark, R., Israel, J.H., Wöhler, T.: Towards hybrid modelling environments - merging desktop-CAD and virtual reality-technologies. CIRP Ann.-Manuf. Technol. **59**(1), 179–182 (2010)

15. Toma, M.I., Gïrbacia, F., Antonya, C.: A comparative evaluation of human interaction for design and assembly of 3D CAD models in desktop and immersive environments. Int. J. Interact. Des. Manuf. (IJIDeM) **6**(3), 179–193 (2012)
16. Trika, S.N., Banerjee, P., Kashyap, R.L.: Virtual reality interfaces for feature-based computer-aided design systems. Comput. Aided Des. **29**(8), 565–574 (1997)
17. Wang, Q.H., Li, J.R., Wu, B.L., Zhang, X.M.: Live parametric design modifications in CAD-linked virtual environment. Int. J. Adv. Manuf. Technol. **50**(9–12), 859–869 (2010)
18. Weidlich, D., Cser, L., Polzin, T., Cristiano, D., Zickner, H.: Virtual reality approaches for immersive design. Int. J. Interact. Des. Manuf. (IJIDeM) **3**(2), 103–108 (2009)
19. Wu, J., Zhang, T., Zhang, X., Zhou, J.: A face based mechanism for naming, recording and retrieving topological entities. Comput. Aided Des. **33**(10), 687–698 (2001)
20. Ye, J., Campbell, R.I., Page, T., Badni, K.S.: An investigation into the implementation of virtual reality technologies in support of conceptual design. Des. Stud. **27**(1), 77–97 (2006)
21. Zhong, Y., Ma, W., Shirinzadeh, B.: A methodology for solid modelling in a virtual reality environment. Rob. Comput.-Integr. Manuf. **21**(6), 528–549 (2005)

Motion Style Transfer in Correlated Motion Spaces

Alex Kilias[1] and Christos Mousas[2]([⊠])

[1] School of Engineering and Digital Arts, University of Kent,
Canterbury CT2 7NT, UK
`alexk@kent.ac.uk`
[2] Department of Computer Science,
Southern Illinois University, Carbondale, IL 62901, USA
`christos@cs.siu.edu`

Abstract. This paper presents a methodology for transferring different motion style behaviors to virtual characters. Instead of learning the differences between two motion styles and then synthesizing the new motion, the presented methodology assigns to the style transformation the motion's distribution transformation process. Specifically, in this paper, the joint angle values of motion are considered as a three-dimensional stochastic variable and as a set of samples respectively. Thus, the correlation between three components can be computed by the covariance. The presented method imports covariance between three components of joint angle values, while calculating the mean along each of the three axes. Then, by decomposing the covariance matrix using the singular value decomposition (SVD) algorithm, it is possible to retrieve a rotation matrix. For fitting the motion style of an input to a reference motion style, the joint angle orientation of the input motion is scaled, rotated and transformed to the reference style motion, therefore enabling the motion transfer process. The results obtained from such a methodology indicate that quite reasonable motion sequences can be synthesized while keeping the required style content.

Keywords: Character animation · Motion style · Style transfer

1 Introduction

Animated virtual characters can be met in various applications of virtual reality, such as in video games, in films and so on. Those characters should be able to provide realistically each different motion that is performed, such as enabling a human like way for representing each action. Hence, even if the well-known key framing techniques are able to provide an intuitive way for animating a virtual character, since these are always dependent on the developer's technical and artistic skills, it still may not be possible to generate highly realistic character motion. Due to these shortcomings, motion capture technologies were developed in order to enhance the naturalness of the virtual character's motion. With

© Springer International Publishing AG 2017
L.T. De Paolis et al. (Eds.): AVR 2017, Part I, LNCS 10324, pp. 242–252, 2017.
DOI: 10.1007/978-3-319-60922-5_18

these technologies, it is possible to capture the required motion sequences, by simply capturing real humans performing the required motions. Then, by using motion retargeting techniques [1], those motion sequences can be transferred to any character. Moreover, these motion sequences can be interpolated [2], blended [3] and so on, therefore providing to the developer the ability to reuse the motion data, as well as input into the motion data the new spatial and temporal characteristics of a new animated sequence.

Among others, the requirement of transferring the style behavior of a motion sequence to another has attracted the research community. Generally, the techniques that have been proposed during the past years are based on the ability to learn the style content of a motion by using various methodologies related to statistical analyses and syntheses of human motion data. However, less attention has been given to methodologies that are able to transfer the required style by simply transferring the distribution of character's joint angles to a reference distribution that represents the motion style. The main advantage of such a methodology is its ability to treat each character's joint separately, allowing a partial motion style to be mapped to the original motion. Yet, it is required that the reference style motion be similar in content to the input motion. For example, it is not possible to transfer a motion style from locomotion to a non-locomotion sequence, and vice versa. Hence, in conjunction with the presented statics-based motion style transfer methodology, a simple extension that provides the partial motion style transfer is introduced.

Based on the aforementioned explanation, this paper presents a novel methodology for transferring a motion style of a motion sequence to any other motion sequences. The presented methodology is achieved by assigning the motion distribution transfer process to a linear transformation methodology. Based on this methodology, different examples are implemented and presented in this paper where either the whole body or the partial body motion of a character is enhanced with style content. The remainder of the paper is organized in the following sections. In Sect. 2 related work on motion synthesis techniques for transferring the motion styles is presented. The problem statement and the methodology's overview of the proposed methodology are presented in Sect. 3. The proposed methodology that is used for transferring the motion style of an input to a reference motion is presented in Sect. 4. The results obtained from the implementation of the proposed methodology are presented in Sect. 5. Finally, conclusions are drawn and potential future work is discussed in Sect. 6.

2   Related Work

Among others, data-driven techniques for animating virtual characters are the most popular. Those techniques are responsible for synthesizing new motion sequences by using existing motion data. The most popular approach is the motion graphs [4–7], which allows transitions between poses or footprints [8–10] where the locomotion of a character is synthesized by following the footprints placed in the 3D environment. However, the main drawback of those techniques is that it does not allow generalization of the motion data, such as allowing new styles to be synthesized.

While the ability to edit or synthesize new motion sequences by keeping the style variations of existing sequences is required, methodologies that are related to transferring the motion styles of one motion to any other have been previously proposed. The parameterization process for the motion data can be quite powerful in cases that require the prediction of a new motion style from existing motion data. In general, dimensionality reduction techniques, such as principal component analysis (PCA) [11,12] and Gaussian process models (GPMs) [13], as well as probabilistic models, such as the hidden Markov model [14,15], or other machine learning methods, such as the well-known radial basis function (RBF) [16,17], can be quite beneficial in cases that require a learning process to distinguish separate different motion styles. In the following paragraphs, methodologies that are responsible for synthesizing style variations from human motions are presented.

Urtasun et al. [12] used PCA to train a large motion capture dataset with variations in locomotion style sequences. Using PCA coefficients, they synthesized new motions with different heights and speeds. Cao et al. [18] used independent component analysis (ICA) to automatically determine the emotional aspects of facial motions and edit the styles of motion data. In addition, Shapiro et al. [19] used ICA to decompose each single motion into components, providing the ability to select the style component manually. Torresani et al. [20] proposed a motion blending-based controller, where the blending weights were acquired from a large dataset of motion sequences of which the motions' styles had been labelled by specialists. Liu et al. [21] constructed a physical model using an optimization approach to generate motions with learned physical parameters that contained the style aspects. Another solution proposed by Elgammal and Lee [22] assigned style properties to time-invariant parameters and used a decomposable generative model that explicitly decomposed the style in a walking motion video.

On the other hand, statistics have been used extensively in character animation [23–25]. Generally statistical models are also able to provide quite reasonable results. Specifically, Hsu et al. [26] proposed a style transfer methodology that learns linear time-invariant models by comparing the input and output motions in order to perform style translation. Brand and Hertzmann [15] used Markov models to capture the style of training motion, which were archived in order to synthesize new motion sequences while the style variations of the motion were transferred. Moreover, Gaussian process latent variable models (GPLVM) have been used to synthesize stylistic variations of human motion data. Generally, GPLVM can enable the probabilistic mapping of non-linear structure in human motion data from the embedded space to the data space. Methodologies such as those proposed by Grochow et al. [27] can be used for motion editing while maintaining the original style by adapting a Gaussian process latent variable models with the shared latent spaces (SGPLVM) model. Methodologies such as those proposed by Wang et al. [28] can be used to separate different style variations.

Interpolation and motion blending methodologies can also provide the desirable results. Therefore, Kovar and Gleicher [29] proposed a denser sampling methodology for the parameter space and applied blending techniques in order to generate new motion sequences. Rose et al. [16] used an interpolation method based on RBF to generate motions based on "verb" and "adverb" parameters. They constructed a "verb graph" to create smooth transitions between different actions.

By using signal processing related techniques it is possible to transfer a motion style to another motion sequence. Specifically, Unuma et al. [30] proposed a method that uses Fourier techniques to change the style of human gaits in a Fourier domain. Using this method, the motion characteristics based on the Fourier data could be extracted. Bruderlin and Williams [31] edited the stylistic motions by varying the frequency bands of the signal. Perlin [32] added rhythmic and stochastic noise functions to a character's skeletal joints in order to synthesize motion sequences with personality variations.

In the proposed methodology we try to transfer a motion style by aligning the distribution of two corresponding motion styles for each of the character's joint angle orientations. Based on this linear transformation process, the presented methodology succeed in synthesizing a style motion in a well manner.

3   Overview

In the following two subsections we present the problem statement of motion style transfer, and the methodology that is used in this paper for approaching this problem.

3.1   Problem Statement

This motion style transfer process problem is the requirement for finding a continuous mapping such as the input motion m_{in} to be represented as $t(m_{in})$, fulfilling the form $m_{in} \rightarrow t(m_{in})$, where $t(m_{in})$ denotes the target distribution of the reference style motion m_{ref}. Finally, having aligned the corresponding motion sequences, a decomposition process that is responsible for synthesizing the input motion and fulfilling the target style content is required. This transformation process in mathematic literature is known as the mass preserving transport problem [33–35]. Figure 1 shows a simple example of this problem.

3.2   Motion Representation

In the presented methodology, each joints' angle value of the character's motion is considered as a three-dimensional stochastic variable, and the motion data as a set of sample (postures), and therefore the correlation between three components can be measured by covariance. The presented approach changes motion style through a series of transformations of the mean and covariance related to

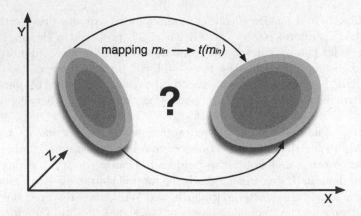

Fig. 1. The distribution transfer problem requires finding a mapping $m_{in} \rightarrow t(m_{in})$ between the input motion m_{in} and a reference motion style m_{ref}.

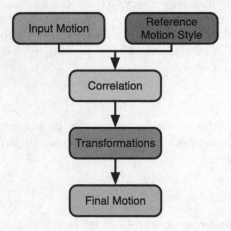

Fig. 2. The pipeline of the presented methodology.

translation, scaling, and rotation. Hence, the resulted motion succeeds in keeping the required components of the reference style motion. A simple graphical explanation of the presented methodology is shown in Fig. 2.

It should be noted that in the presented methodology the motion sequences are represented as $M = \{P(t), Q(t), r_1(t), ..., r_n(t)\}$ where $P(t)$ and $Q(t)$ represents the position and the orientation of the character's root in the $t-th$ frame, and $r_i(t)$ for $i = 1, ..., n$ is the orientation of the $i-th$ joint of the character in the $t-th$ frame. It should also be noted that the character's root position is executed by this process. Based on this representation, the necessary components of the character's joint angles are computed. Then by using the aforementioned methodology the transfer of the required style content to an input motion is achieved.

4   Methodology

In this section we present the methodology that was used for transferring a reference motion style to an input motion. In the presented methodology this is achieved by developing a statistics-based method that provides the feasibility of the transformation process in the joint angles orientation space by just utilizing the mean and the covariance matrix of the input motion. In the remainder of this section we introduce the methodology that was used for achieving this transformation.

4.1   Motion Style Transfer

Firstly, for both the input motion and the reference motion style, the mean angle orientation of joint angles along the three axes as well as the covariance matrix between the three components in the Euler space are computed. Thus for the joint angle values of the input motion M_{in} we have $M_{in} = (\bar{X}_{in}, \bar{Y}_{in}, \bar{Z}_{in})$ and for the reference motion style M_{ref} we have $M_{ref} = (\bar{X}_{ref}, \bar{Y}_{ref}, \bar{Z}_{ref})$, while we also have the covariance matrices represented as C_{in} and C_{ref} respectively.

Now it is possible to decompose the covariance matrixes using the singular value decomposition (SVD) methodology as presented in Konstantinides and Yao [36]:

$$C = U \Lambda V^T \tag{1}$$

where U and V are orthogonal matrices and are compressed by the eigenvectors of C. Moreover, $\Lambda = diag(\lambda^X, \lambda^Y, \lambda^Z)$ where λ^X, and λ^Z are the eigenvectors of C. U is employed in the next step as a rotation matrix to manipulate the joint angles of the style motion. Finally, the following transformation is used:

$$M = T_{ref} \cdot R_{ref} \cdot S_{ref} \cdot S_{in} \cdot R_{in} \cdot T_{in} \cdot M_{in} \tag{2}$$

where $M = (X, Y, Z, 1)^T$ and $M_{in} = (X_{in}, Y_{in}, Z_{in}, 1)^T$ denote the homogeneous coordinates of a joint angle orientation in Euler space for the output and the input motion respectively. Moreover, T_{ref}, T_{in}, R_{ref}, R_{in}, S_{ref}, and S_{in} denote the matrices of translation, rotation and scaling derived from the reference style and the input motion respectively. The definition of each aforementioned component is given in Appendix.

Based on this methodology, the key component of this transformation is its ability to transform an ellipsoid in order to fit another one. Thus, the two ellipsoids fit separately the joint angle orientation of the reference style and the input motion in the Euler angle space. The fitting of the ellipsoid functions as an extension to the method of fitting an ellipse in the two-dimensional space as proposed by Lee [37] and involves computing the mean and the covariance matrix. While the mean denotes the center coordinates of an ellipsoid, the eigenvalues and eigenvectors of the covariance matrix indicate the length and orientation of the three aces of the ellipsoid. The transformations act on all of the character's joint angles in the input motion and move them in the appropriate position in the Euler space. Results of the presented motion style transfer process are shown in Fig. 3 as well as at the accompanying video.

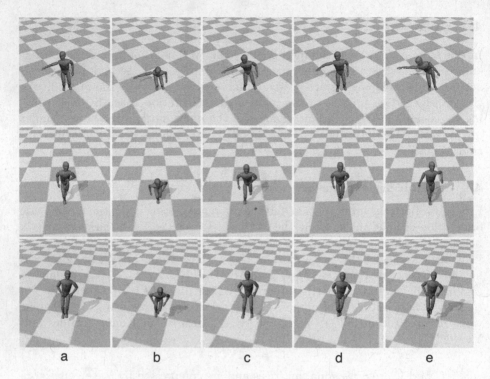

Fig. 3. Examples of motions s with the proposed methodology. The input motion (a), and the synthesized styles (b)–(e).

5   Implementation and Results

For the implementation of the proposed solution we asked an experienced designer to provide motion sequences with style content which are related to happy, angry, sad, tiered, proud, sneaky, cat walking, crab walking, lame walking and many more (see Fig. 4). On average, those motion sequences are not greater that 100 frames. Hence, based on the aforementioned methodology we

Fig. 4. Example postures of the different reference motion styles that used in the presented. methodology.

use various input motion-sequence themes provided by the CMU motion capture database [38] along with various synthesized example motions. Additional examples are presented in the accompanying video. It should be noted that the aforementioned methodology that maps the input motion to the reference motion style was generated off-line. However, the motion synthesis process is generated in real-time. Hence, by using an Intel i7 at 2.2 GHz with 8 GB memory, the presented methodology succeeds in providing the new motion on average of 45 frames per second.

6 Conclusions and Future Work

In this paper, a novel methodology for transferring the motion style of a reference motion to an input one was presented. The proposed methodology succeeds in transferring a motion style by aligning the corresponding motion spaces and by aligning the distribution and the centre of each joint angle orientation values. However, the presented method can provide quite reasonable results only while the motion sequences that are used correspond to the same content (i.e., to transferring a locomotion style to another locomotion sequence). Hence, for enhancing the motion style transfer process we assumed that a partial motion style transfer could be quite beneficial. Thus, we implemented a simple methodology that allows the partial motion transfer. On the other hand, the motion style transfer is quite a complex process. We assume that methodologies that synthesize motion sequences to contain specific stylistic content by aligning the distributions are a quite promising research area. Therefore, in our future work we would like to extend the presented methodology by developing enhanced methodologies that will enable a generalized motion style transfer process.

Appendix

Here the definition of the components used in Eq. 2 is presented. Specifically, the matrices of T_{ref}, T_{in}, R_{ref}, R_{in}, S_{ref}, and S_{in} denote the translation, rotation and scaling derived from the reference style and the input motion respectively. They are solved as:

$$T_{ref} = \begin{bmatrix} 1 & 0 & 0 & \bar{X}_{ref} \\ 0 & 1 & 0 & \bar{Y}_{ref} \\ 0 & 0 & 1 & \bar{Z}_{ref} \\ 0 & 0 & 0 & 1 \end{bmatrix} \tag{3}$$

$$T_{in} = \begin{bmatrix} 1 & 0 & 0 & -\bar{X}_{in} \\ 0 & 1 & 0 & -\bar{Y}_{in} \\ 0 & 0 & 1 & -\bar{Z}_{in} \\ 0 & 0 & 0 & 1 \end{bmatrix} \tag{4}$$

$$S_{ref} = \begin{bmatrix} \bar{\lambda}^X_{ref} & 0 & 0 & 0 \\ 0 & \bar{\lambda}^Y_{ref} & 0 & 0 \\ 0 & 0 & \bar{\lambda}^Z_{ref} & 0 \\ 0 & 0 & 0 & 1 \end{bmatrix} \tag{5}$$

$$S_{in} = \begin{bmatrix} 1/\sqrt{\bar{\lambda}^X_{in}} & 0 & 0 & 0 \\ 0 & 1/\sqrt{\bar{\lambda}^Y_{in}} & 0 & 0 \\ 0 & 0 & 1/\sqrt{\bar{\lambda}^Z_{in}} & 0 \\ 0 & 0 & 0 & 1 \end{bmatrix} \tag{6}$$

$$R_{ref} = U_{ref} \tag{7}$$

$$R_{in} = U_{in}^{-1} \tag{8}$$

References

1. Gleicher, M.: Retargetting motion to new characters. In: Annual Conference on Computer Graphics and Interactive Techniques, pp. 33–42 (1998)
2. Mukai, T., Kuriyama, S.: Geostatistical motion interpolation. ACM Trans. Graph. **24**(3), 1062–1070 (2005)
3. Kovar, L., Gleicher, M.: Flexible automatic motion blending with registration curves. In: ACM SIGGRAPH/Eurographics Symposium on Computer Animation, pp. 214–224 (2003)
4. Arikan, O., Forsyth, D.A.: Interactive motion generation from examples. ACM Trans. Graph. **21**(3), 483–490 (2002)
5. Kovar, L., Gleicher, M., Pighin, F.: Motion graphs. ACM Trans. Graph. **21**(3), 473–482 (2002)
6. Lee, J., Chai, J., Reitsma, P.S., Hodgins, J.K., Pollard, N.S.: Interactive control of avatars animated with human motion data. ACM Trans. Graph. **21**(3), 491–500 (2002)
7. Safonova, A., Hodgins, J.K.: Construction and optimal search of interpolated motion graphs. ACM Trans. Graph. **26**(3), 106 (2007)
8. van Basten, B.J., Peeters, P.W.A.M., Egges, A.: The step space: example-based footprint-driven motion synthesis. Comput. Animat. Virtual Worlds **21**(3–4), 433–441 (2010)
9. Mousas, C., Newbury, P., Anagnostopoulos, C.: Footprint-driven locomotion composition. Int. J. Comput. Graph. Animat. **4**(4), 27–42 (2014)
10. Mousas, C., Newbury, P., Anagnostopoulos, C.: Measuring the steps: generating action transitions between locomotion behaviours. In: International Conference on Computer Games: AI, Animation, Mobile, Interactive Multimedia, Educational & Serious Games, pp. 31–35 (2013)
11. Chien, Y.-R., Liu, J.-S.: Learning the stylistic similarity between human motions. In: Bebis, G., Boyle, R., Parvin, B., Koracin, D., Remagnino, P., Nefian, A., Meenakshisundaram, G., Pascucci, V., Zara, J., Molineros, J., Theisel, H., Malzbender, T. (eds.) ISVC 2006. LNCS, vol. 4291, pp. 170–179. Springer, Heidelberg (2006). doi:10.1007/11919476_18
12. Urtasun, R., Glardon, R., Boulic, R., Thalmann, D., Fua, P.: Style-based motion synthesis. Comput. Graph. Forum **23**(4), 799–812 (2004)

13. Ma, X., Le, B.H., Deng, Z.: Style learning and transferring for facial animation editing. In: ACM SIGGRAPH/Eurographics Symposium on Computer Animation, pp. 123–132 (2009)

14. Tilmanne, J., Moinet, A., Dutoit, T.: Stylistic gait synthesis based on hidden markov models. EURASIP J. Adv. Sig. Process. **1**, 1–14 (2012)

15. Brand, M., Hertzmann, A.: Style machines. In: 27th Annual Conference on Computer Graphics and Interactive Techniques, pp. 183–192 (2000)

16. Rose, C., Bodenheimer, B., Cohen, M.F.: Verbs and adverbs: multidimensional motion interpolation. IEEE Comput. Graph. Appl. **18**(5), 32–40 (1998)

17. Song, J., Choi, B., Seol, Y., Noh, J.: Characteristic facial retargeting. Comput. Animat. Virtual Worlds **22**(2–3), 187–194 (2011)

18. Cao, Y., Faloutsos, P., Pighin, F.: Unsupervised learning for speech motion editing. In: ACM SIGGRAPH/Eurographics Symposium on Computer Animation, pp. 225–231 (2003)

19. Shapiro, A., Cao, Y., Faloutsos, P.: Style components. In: Graphics Interface, pp. 33–39 (2006)

20. Torresani, L., Hackney, R., Bregler, C.: Learning motion style synthesis from perceptual observations. In: Advances in Neural Information Processing Systems, pp. 1393–1400 (2007)

21. Liu, C., Hertzmann, A., Popović, Z.: Learning physics-based motion style with nonlinear inverse optimization. ACM Trans. Graph. **24**(3), 1071–1081 (2005)

22. Elgammal, A., Lee, C.: Separating style and content on a nonlinear manifold. In: IEEE Conference on Computer Vision and Pattern Recognition, pp. 478–485 (2004)

23. Mousas, C., Newbury, P., Anagnostopoulos, C.N.: Evaluating the covariance matrix constraints for data-driven statistical human motion reconstruction. In: Spring Conference on Computer Graphics, pp. 99–106 (2014)

24. Mousas, C., Newbury, P., Anagnostopoulos, C.-N.: Data-driven motion reconstruction using local regression models. In: Iliadis, L., Maglogiannis, I., Papadopoulos, H. (eds.) AIAI 2014. IAICT, vol. 436, pp. 364–374. Springer, Heidelberg (2014). doi:10.1007/978-3-662-44654-6_36

25. Mousas, C., Newbury, P., Anagnostopoulos, C.-N.: Efficient hand-over motion reconstruction. In: International Conference on Computer Graphics, Visualization and Computer Vision, pp. 111–120 (2014)

26. Hsu, E., Pulli, K., Popović, J.: Style translation for human motion. ACM Trans. Graph. **24**(3), 1082–1089 (2005)

27. Grochow, K., Martin, S.L., Hertzmann, A., Popović, Z.: Style-based inverse kinematics. ACM Trans. Graph. **23**(3), 522–531 (2004)

28. Wang, J.M., Fleet, D.J., Hertzmann, A.: Multifactor Gaussian process models for style-content separation. In: International Conference on Machine learning, pp. 975–982 (2007)

29. Kovar, L., Gleicher, M.: Automated extraction and parameterization of motions in large data sets. ACM Trans. Graph. **23**(3), 559–568 (2004)

30. Unuma, M., Anjyo, K., Takeuchi, R.: Fourier principles for emotion-based human figure animation. In: Annual Conference on Computer Graphics and Interactive Techniques, pp. 91–96 (1995)

31. Bruderlin, A., Williams, L.: Motion signal processing. In: Annual Conference on Computer Graphics and Interactive Techniques, pp. 97–104 (1995)

32. Perlin, K.: Real time responsive animation with personality. IEEE Trans. Vis. Comput. Graph. **1**(1), 5–15 (1995)

33. Evans, L.C.: Partial differential equations and monge-kantorovich mass transfer. In: Current Developments in Mathematics, pp. 65–126 (1999)
34. Gangbo, W., McCann, R.J.: The geometry of optimal transportation. Acta Mathe. **177**(2), 113–161 (1996)
35. Villani, C.: Topics in Optimal Transportation, vol. 58. American Mathematical Society (2003)
36. Konstantinides, K., Yao, K.: Statistical analysis of effective singular values in matrix rank determinatio. IEEE Trans. Acoust. Speech Sig. Process. **36**(5), 757–763 (1988)
37. Lee, L.: Gait analysis for classification. Ph.d. thesis, Department of Electrical Engineering and Computer Science, Massachusetts Institute of Technology (2002)
38. Carnegie Mellon University, Motion capture database. http://mocap.cs.cmu.edu/

Pixel Reprojection of 360 Degree Renderings for Small Parallax Effects

Joakim Bruslund Haurum[1](✉) [iD], Christian Nygaard Daugbjerg[1] [iD],
Péter Rohoska[1] [iD], Andrea Coifman[1] [iD], Anne Juhler Hansen[2] [iD],
and Martin Kraus[2] [iD]

[1] School of Information and Communication Technology,
Aalborg University, Aalborg, Denmark
{jhauru13,cdaugb13,prohos13,acoifm16}@student.aau.dk
[2] Department of Architecture, Design and Media Technology,
Aalborg University, Aalborg, Denmark
{ajha,martin}@create.aau.dk

Abstract. By using 360° renderings, it is possible to create virtual reality experiences without having to render potentially complex 3D geometry with complex shading for every frame. Applying pixel reprojection to the 360° renderings can enable 3D movement of the user, which introduces motion parallax effects. The proposed pixel reprojection method employs nine camera views that are used to reconstruct an output from an arbitrary camera position within the space between the nine cameras. Each of the nine camera is supplied with a unique 360° rendering, generated from the position of the camera. Thereafter no 3D geometry is needed. Two variations of the algorithm are proposed. Evaluation of the two variations showed that only considering the four closest cameras resulted in a shorter render time, but also more visible errors in the reprojected image, when compared to considering all nine cameras.

Keywords: Pixel reprojection · Parallax effects · 360° renderings · Virtual reality

1 Introduction

In this paper, we discuss the use of pixel reprojection to calculate the output image for a virtual camera with an arbitrary orientation and a position that is constrained to the volume of a cube. The cube is formed by a set of known camera positions, and their output images including per-pixel depth information.

The intention with the produced algorithm is to introduce parallax in a 3D scene constructed from a set of pre-rendered cubemaps. We want to introduce a small parallax effect, i.e. objects close to the viewer appear to move more than objects far away when the viewer moves, as this has been found to be an important visual cue in the process of determining depth [6, p. 221]. This kind of parallax is known as motion parallax. Stereo parallax can also be introduced for Virtual Reality (VR) systems with pixel reprojection by rendering a separate

© Springer International Publishing AG 2017
L.T. De Paolis et al. (Eds.): AVR 2017, Part I, LNCS 10324, pp. 253–262, 2017.
DOI: 10.1007/978-3-319-60922-5_19

output image for each eye. In this case the users will experience a parallax effect by observing two images which are rendered from positions slightly apart from each other.

The proposed approach uses pixel reprojection based on nine cameras, each with a separate 360° rendering, in the form of a cubemap. Eight cameras are positioned at the corners of a cube, which the user can move within, while the ninth camera is at the cube's center. It is hypothesized that the algorithm will be faster than if the system has to render the output image directly from a complex 3D scene, as there is no geometry in the scene that has to be processed.

Applications of the proposed algorithm include photorealistic VR visualizations of e.g. architectural designs. This would, ideally, be computationally efficient compared to rendering complex 3D geometry with complex shader calculations for each frame. Furthermore, it could allow VR experiences based on real life images, as long as the depth information for each pixel is known. This would be possible with e.g. the Nokia Ozo [4].

2   Related Work

Our work is primarily inspired by the work of Kang [2] and the work of Hansen et al. [1]. Kang covers the use of *epipolar constraints*, which describes the link for a point between two or more cameras and their images. The constraint specifies that a point in a 2D image will correspond to a line through a 3D space, which the point in the image must lie on. The line can be projected onto the image of another camera and the search for the original point can be constrained to the line, see Fig. 1. This can significantly reduce the search time for the corresponding point, as the entire image no longer needs to be searched. Furthermore, Kang states that *"If the depth value at each pixel is known, then the change in location of that pixel is constrained in a predictable way"* [2, p. 344]. It is therefore essential that the depth of the images used in the pixel reprojection is available.

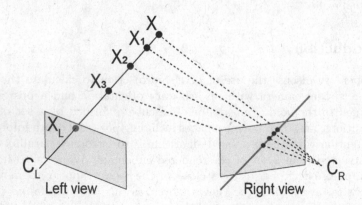

Fig. 1. Illustration of the epipolar constraints. The point X_L is a point on the image for camera C_L, but viewed as a line on the image of camera C_R

Hansen et al. cover the use of pixel reprojection for rendering the output for a light field Head-Mounted Display (HMD) with 8 × 15 lenses. This was achieved by rendering the view from the corner lenses, and calculating the rest by reprojecting the corner cameras' views to the lens' position in a fragment shader. The depth information was stored in the alpha channel of the camera's render texture. The reprojected pixel was chosen based on its proximity to the investigated pixel and depth.

Hansen et al.'s approach had a few constraints. Firstly, incorrect pixel intensities occur if a point in the scene is occluded for all four corner cameras. Secondly, all of the cameras must lie on the same plane, and the viewing direction of the cameras must be perpendicular to this plane.

Nehab et al. [3] and Sitthi-amorn et al. [5] solve a similar problem, i.e. they re-use pixels between frames, to reduce the amount of shader computations. This is achieved by using the spatio-temporal information between frames to determine the new location of a pixel.

3   Methods

In this section the different parts of our pixel reprojection algorithm are discussed. The different steps describe the setup of the cameras, the selection of pixel candidates and our proposed pixel reprojection approach.

3.1   Virtual Cameras

The first step is to setup the virtual cameras needed for the algorithm. We label the cameras which observe the virtual scene as the *pre-computed cameras* and the camera which the algorithm reprojects to as the *reprojected camera*. The pre-computed cameras are placed in the corners of a cube, and a single camera in the center of the cube.

All pre-computed cameras are rotated to the same orientation as the reprojected camera. Then each pre-computed camera renders a view based on a pre-computed cubemap (one for each pre-computed camera), where the corresponding depth information is stored in the alpha channel, as suggested by Hansen et al. [1]. The section of the cubemap which is rendered by a pre-computed camera, is saved in a render texture and supplied to the pixel reprojection algorithm.

3.2   Choosing Pixel Candidates

The candidates tested in the pixel reprojection algorithm are found by utilizing the epipolar constraint described by Kang [2].

For each pixel on the output texture of the reprojected camera, we want to determine a vector, which describes the epipolar line of the pixel. This is achieved by utilizing the near and far clipping plane of the camera. The vector is obtained by first determining the intersection points of the epipolar line with the near and far clipping planes.

Assuming that the target pixel that we want to determine the epipolar line for is represented with an x and y value between 0 and 1, then the intersection point on the clipping plane can be computed as in Eqs. 1 to 3.

$$\mathbf{q}_x = \mathbf{t}_x w_{\text{plane}} - \frac{w_{\text{plane}}}{2} \tag{1}$$

$$\mathbf{q}_y = \mathbf{t}_y h_{\text{plane}} - \frac{h_{\text{plane}}}{2} \tag{2}$$

$$\mathbf{q}_z = d_{\text{plane}} \tag{3}$$

where $\mathbf{q}$ is the intersection point in view space, $\mathbf{t}$ is the target pixel in texture coordinates and w, h and d are the width, height and distance to the clipping plane respectively.

These intersection points are transformed to world space by multiplying with the reprojected camera's inverse view matrix and then to the screen space of each pre-computed camera, where the unit vector between the two points is calculated. If one or both of the transformed points are located outside the image, the intersections between the epipolar line and the borders of the image is calculated. If an intersection with the image is found, then the relevant clipping point(s) are set to the found intersection point(s).

The pixels in the pre-computed camera's output texture, which lie along the epipolar line, as described by the unit vector, are then considered as candidates for the pixel reprojection algorithm. Only the pixels between the two clipping points are investigated, as every other point would be outside the reprojected camera's view frustrum.

3.3 Pixel Reprojection

The pixel reprojection algorithm can be summarized as having to transform a pixel from one of the pre-computed camera's output texture's screen space to world space, and then to the reprojected camera's screen space. For this reprojection, a set of requirements are checked to determine its accuracy.

First, the position $\mathbf{p}_{\text{s,PC}}$ of a pixel candidate in one of the pre-computed camera's output textures is chosen, as a possible candidate for the position $\mathbf{t}_{\text{s,R}}$ of the target pixel in the reprojected camera's output texture. The pixel candidate is then converted from screen space, to normalized device coordinates (NDC), with Eq. 4.

$$\mathbf{p}_{\text{n,PC}} = K^{-1}\mathbf{p}_{\text{s,PC}} \tag{4}$$

where $\mathbf{p}_{\text{n,PC}}$ and $\mathbf{p}_{\text{s,PC}}$ are the NDC and screen space coordinates of the pixel with respect to the pre-computed camera, and K is the pre-computed camera's viewport matrix. The components of $\mathbf{p}_{\text{s,PC}}$ are based on the choice of pixel candidate to be investigated. The pixel candidate is a pixel in the pre-computed camera's render texture. The x and y components of $\mathbf{p}_{\text{s,PC}}$ is the x and y components of the candidate pixel, while the z coordinate of $\mathbf{p}_{\text{s,PC}}$ is the alpha component of the candidate pixel.

The NDC are then converted to clip space. This requires that the perspective division (see Eq. 5) is inverted. However, this cannot be performed directly, as the w coordinate of the clip space is divided by itself during the perspective division, resulting in the loss of the necessary information.

$$n = \frac{c}{c_w} \tag{5}$$

where n and c are the NDC and the clip coordinates of a pixel. The conversion from NDC to clip coordinates, and to world coordinates, can nonetheless still be performed by applying Eq. 6. The equation can be derived by considering how the NDC and the clip coordinates are calculated, and the constraint that the w coordinate in world space has to be 1 for a point.

$$P_{world} = \frac{(PV)^{-1}p_{n,PC}}{((PV)^{-1}p_{n,PC})_w} \tag{6}$$

where P and V are the projection and view matrices of the pre-computed camera, and p_{world} is the world coordinate representation of the point.

The pixel, represented in world coordinates, can then be transformed into the screen space of the reprojected camera by multiplying with the reprojected camera's view and projection matrices, performing the perspective division and multiplying with the viewport matrix of the reprojected camera.

When the screen coordinates with respect to the reprojected camera, $p_{s,R}$, are obtained, a set of requirements needs to be checked. The Euclidean distance between $p_{s,R}$ and $t_{s,R}$ is determined. The distance should be within a threshold, initially set to 0.5 pixels, and which is updated during runtime. A 0.5 pixels offset is added to the threshold due to potential rounding errors. If $p_{s,R}$ is within the threshold, the depth value of $p_{s,R}$ is compared to the current best pixel's depth value. If the depth of $p_{s,R}$ is lower, then $p_{s,R}$ is saved as the current best match. Furthermore, the distance threshold is only updated if the calculated distance between $p_{s,R}$ and $t_{s,R}$ is below the current threshold without the 0.5 pixel offset. This is to avoid accumulating possible rounding errors. If no good match is found, an average of the pixel values at position $t_{s,PC}$ for all of the considered pre-computed cameras, is used.

3.4   Considered Pre-computed Cameras

If every single pixel candidate in all of the pre-computed cameras is analyzed, theoretically the best possible reconstruction should be obtained. It is, however, a slow process as a lot of unnecessary pixels have to be considered. This process can be sped up by limiting the number of cameras which are considered, but at a potential reduction in the reprojection accuracy. By only investigating the center pre-computed camera and the three pre-computed cameras closest to the reprojected camera, a tetrahedral subspace of the cube defined by the selected pre-computed cameras can be created, as shown in Fig. 2. This subspace always contains the reprojected camera.

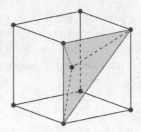

Fig. 2. Subspace created when considering the 3 closest pre-computed cameras and the center pre-computed camera

4   Results

The algorithm explained in Sect. 3 was implemented in a fragment shader, using the Unity3D game engine (version 5.4.3) running OpenGL 4.5. All cameras were initialized in such a way that the projection and viewport matrices were the same for all cameras.

Two different variations of the pixel reprojection algorithm were tested and compared. One method utilized all nine pre-computed cameras, while the other only utilized the four closest to the reprojected camera. These variations were compared to the directly observed 3D geometry, which served as a baseline. The scene used for testing consisted of four copies of the Utah teapot, with different scaling and textures applied. The system was evaluated in two ways:

– Evaluating the reconstruction errors produced in the reprojected images, by comparing them to images taken from a reference camera in the same position.
– Evaluating the render time per frame of the system.

As it was not possible to create cubemaps with a high enough precision to store the depth information in Unity, only the system performance test utilized the cubemaps. For the evaluation of reconstruction errors, the pixel reprojection algorithm was based on images, where the pre-computed cameras rendered the 3D geometry directly, and inserts the depth information into the alpha channel.

4.1   Errors in Reprojected Images

The accuracy of the pixel reprojection algorithms was analyzed by taking 30 screenshots, where the reprojected camera was placed and oriented differently in each image. The reprojected images were then compared to a reference image by subtracting the images from one another. An example of this is shown in Fig. 4, where the reprojection algorithm variations try to reconstruct Fig. 3. The images have been enhanced to increase readability.

The difference images were analyzed in two ways: By calculating the root mean square error (RMSE) of each color channel and calculate the mean value, and by visual inspection. It was found that in 27 of the images the reprojection with four pre-computed cameras had the lowest RMSE. The difference in

RMSE between the two methods were however quite small. Furthermore, when visually inspecting the images, the variation with all nine pre-computed cameras generally looked better.

Fig. 3. Reference image for the reprojected images in Fig. 4

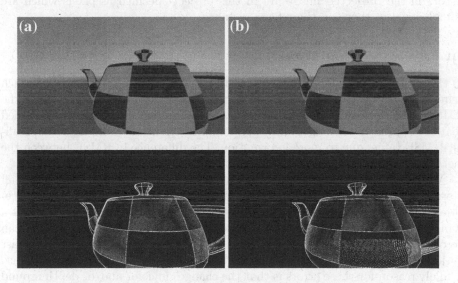

Fig. 4. (a) 9 Pre-computed Cameras (b) 4 Pre-computed Cameras

4.2   Render Time

The performance of the system was evaluated by measuring the time it took to render each frame, while the reprojected camera moved along a predefined path for 10 s. The test was performed five times for each variation, with a screen resolution of 1280 × 720. A baseline was also obtained, by observing the geometry directly. The mean render time and how it differs from the baseline can be observed in Table 1. The test was performed on a VR ready desktop computer with a Intel Quad Core i7-4790K at 4.0 GHz, a MSI GeForce GTX 980 and 16GB DDR3 ram at 1600 MHz:

Table 1. Results of mean render time per frame

Method	Render time
Baseline	16.6 ms
9 pre-computed cameras	206.2 ms
4 pre-computed cameras	85.8 ms

5   Discussion

In the best case scenario, the reprojected image would look identical to a reference image taken from a camera with the same position, orientation and settings. Errors in the projected image are in this project specified as pixels which are not identical to those on the reference image.

5.1   Reconstruction Errors

In the results, it can be observed that in 27 out of 30 test images the approach using the four closest pre-computed cameras, performed better when using the RMSE as the measuring metric. This result was unexpected as it was assumed that the approach utilizing all nine pre-computed cameras would have the smallest RMSE value, due to more information. The difference in RMSE between the methods was however, in most cases, not large.

When inspecting the images, it was observed that the approach using all nine pre-computed cameras resulted in images where the errors were less noticeable, than the reprojected images from the four cameras approach. In Fig. 4 a comparison between the two variations of the algorithm is shown. Here it can be observed that the edges of the objects and edges on the textures in the vast majority of the cases produce an error, for both of the reprojection variations. A likely reason for these errors is that the changes in color and/or depth around an edge and texture edge is relatively large, making accurate reprojection more difficult, as a slight pixel reprojection error can cause a large error in color value.

Both of the variations have small errors covering most of the teapot surface, and in the four camera variation the errors in the bottom are more frequent than the rest. When looking at the reprojected image in Fig. 4(b), it can be observed that parts of the teapot are visibly lacking, resulting in a light blending effect with the background. This only occurs near the handle in the reprojected image using all nine pre-computed cameras, as observed in Fig. 4(a), and in a less noticeable way. The cause for many of the errors occurring on the teapot surface could be that the surface is curved, resulting in a slight change in depth from pixel to pixel. The depth determines how much the pixel should move in the camera view, and the small changes would make the reprojection more prone to errors, as every pixel should move slightly different distances. The slight depth changes might also be smaller than the resolution of the saved depth buffer, which can cause reprojection errors. These types of errors occur in all 30 test images.

5.2   Render Time

The results from the performance test clearly show that neither of the pixel reprojection variations managed to match or outperform the baseline, as the time to render a frame in average took 189.7 and 69.2 ms longer than the baseline. This indicates that while some computation power is saved by not having to render the 3D geometry, it is outweighed by the added computations in the pixel reprojection. This could however potentially be counteracted if the algorithm can be more thoroughly optimized. The difference should also be reduced if more models were introduced into the scene, as the baseline would then have to spend additional time on rendering these, while the reprojection algorithm's performance should not be affected. It was also found that the variation which only considers the four closest pre-computed cameras, had a lower render time per frame than when all nine pre-computed cameras are considered, as expected.

6   Conclusion

We proposed a reprojection algorithm, which is able to reconstruct camera views with an arbitrary position and rotation, within a three dimensional space defined by nine pre-computed cameras rendering cubemaps or 3D geometry.

The accuracy and render time per frame were tested for two versions of the algorithm. The versions differ in whether they considered four or nine pre-computed cameras. The tests showed that the four camera approach more often had a lower RMSE, and always had the lowest render times. However, when inspecting the reprojected images the errors were often more noticeable compared to the nine cameras approach.

Despite these problems, the proposed system introduces a novel approach to introducing small parallax effects in a VR environment based on 360° renderings.

7   Future Work

Future development on the system should be focused on optimizing the algorithm, with regards to reprojecting pixels on curved surfaces. This could potentially be achieved by adding a second term to the distance threshold in the pixel reprojection algorithm, where the gradient of the depth information in the pre-computed cameras is utilized. Pixels on the edges of an object should however be handled with care, as these will result in a large gradient, which would result in an incorrect pixel reprojection.

The render time per frame of the algorithm could potentially be improved by trying to minimize the set of possible pixel candidates. This could potentially be achieved by moving the near clipping plane further away from the camera, reducing the amount the near clipping point moves when transformed into the screen space of a pre-computed camera.

Furthermore, it could be interesting to investigate how the parallax effect introduced with the proposed algorithm, affects the depth perception of user when compared to other VR environments. It would especially be interesting to see how it compares to VR environments based on 3D geometry and VR environments based on static 360° renderings.

Acknowledgments. The authors would like to thank the Utzon Center in Aalborg, Denmark, for giving us access to their 3D model assets from the Fatamorgana exhibition, and for providing us with access to the museum at any time needed.

References

1. Hansen, A.J., Klein, J., Kraus, M.: Light field rendering for head mounted displays using pixel reprojection. In: Proceedings of the 12th International Joint Conference on Computer Vision, Imaging and Computer Graphics Theory and Applications, vol. 1, pp. 27–36, VISIGRAPP, Porto (2017). doi:10.5220/0006091100270036
2. Kang, S.B.: Geometrically valid pixel reprojection methods for novel view synthesis. ISPRS J. Photogrammetry Remote Sens. **53**, 342–353 (1998). doi:10.1016/S0924-2716(98)00018-5
3. Nehab, D., Sander, P.V., Lawrence, J., Tatarchuk, N., Isidoro, J.R.: Accelerating real-time shading with reverse reprojection caching. In: Segal, M., Aila, T. (eds.) Proceedings of the 22nd ACM SIGGRAPH/EUROGRAPHICS symposium on Graphics hardware, pp. 25–35, Eurographics Association, Aire-la-Ville (2007). doi:10.2312/EGGH/EGGH07/025-036
4. Nokia: Nokia Ozo Camera (2017). https://ozo.nokia.com/eu
5. Sitthi-amorn, P., Lawrence, J., Yang, L., Sander, P.V., Nehab, D., Xi, J.: Automated reprojection-based pixel shader optimization. ACM Trans. Graph. **27**(5) (2008). doi:10.1145/1409060.1409080. Article 127 . ACM, New York
6. Snowden, R.J., Thompson, P., Troscianko, T.: Basic vision: an introduction to visual perception. OUP Oxford (2012). ISBN: 978-0-19-957202-1

Immersiveness of News: How Croatian Students Experienced 360-Video News

Mato Brautović[1(✉)], Romana John[1], and Marko Potrebica[2]

[1] University of Dubrovnik, Dubrovnik, Croatia
{mato.brautovic,romana.john}@unidu.hr
[2] University of Mostar, Mostar, Bosnia and Herzegovina
mpotrebicadbk@gmail.com

Abstract. More and more media companies are experimenting with virtual reality (VR) news and at the same time new VR technology products are available and affordable to a wider audience. This paper examines the concept of immersiveness in journalism based on 360-video content, probing the main components that are prerequisites to an immersive experience: flow, cognitive absorption, and presence. The research was conducted using a questionnaire from the work of Jennett et al. (2008) which was adapted for 360-video news.

The main results from this initial phase of research showed that participants experienced two out of three main components for total immersion, but authors are drawing attention to the fact that VR content is a good way for engaging with news and triggering empathy.

Keywords: Virtual reality · Immersiveness · Journalism · 360-video news · Presence

1 Introduction

In the past few years the development of new technologies has remarkably changed the way people can perceive, comprehend, and experience virtual reality. The use of simple goggles or modern VR headsets, three-dimensional representation of real events, but in the virtual world, is available to everybody who possesses a mobile phone with a good screen and processing power. As it is stated in the IAB Report [1], 2016 can be considered a historic year because virtual reality started to achieve mass scale; the VR experience that was reserved for gaming enthusiasts is now enabled on a daily basis to all mobile and computer users. There is still an ongoing debate on clarifying the definition of virtual reality. The main differentiation in explaining VR and other similar, but not the same terms that appear, such as augmented reality, interactive reality, and mixed reality lies in immersion, or even better to say in *immersiveness*. The definition of immersion is wide and variable, but at its core it means to become or make somebody completely involved in something [2], and in the VR context it is an experience that allows the user to interact and gives a sense of presence in an unreal/alternative environment. Jennett et al. [3] investigated how immersion can be measured and how it affects users. One of the key findings was that immersion can be measured subjectively, using questionnaires. Using that cognition and with the recent

L.T. De Paolis et al. (Eds.): AVR 2017, Part I, LNCS 10324, pp. 263–269, 2017.
DOI: 10.1007/978-3-319-60922-5_20

trend of immersive storytelling in journalism, this paper focuses on investigating the immersive experience of news.

2 Immersive Storytelling and Immersive Experience in Journalism

One of the authors whose name is directly connected with virtual reality and immersive journalism in the past few years is Nonny de la Peña, whose first research on the concept and implications of immersive journalism was published in 2010. De la Peña et al. [4] defined "immersive journalism as production of news in a form in which people can gain first-person experiences of the events or situation described in news stories, and the fundamental idea of it is to allow the participant to actually enter a virtually recreated scenario representing the news story. The sense of presence obtained through an immersive system affords the participant unprecedented access to the sights and sounds, and possibly feelings and emotions, that accompany the news."

Owen et al. [5] in their report about VR in journalism explain that VR as an emerging medium presents new technical and narrative forms, and at the same time raises questions on the relationship and position of journalists and audience. Users now have control over what, in a scene, they'll pay attention to, but journalists still decide how they will construct the story. It changes how audiences engage with journalism, bringing them into stories in a visceral, experiential manner that creates a feeling that a user is really "there", so-called social presence, which strengthens the empathy for the subject much more than it was possible in other media. Authors Slater and Sanchez-Vives [6] are on the same path claiming that the "goal is to give people experiential, non-analytic insight into events, to give them illusion of being present in them. That presence may lead to another understanding of the event, perhaps an understanding that cannot be well expressed verbally or even in pictures. It reflects the fundamental capability of what you can experience in VR – to be there and to experience a situation from different perspectives."

The past two years were challenging in terms of VR for most media outlets that decided to introduce new technology to their audience. There is still no unique point of view in defining whether immersive journalism and VR storytelling will become the usual way of presenting news to a mass audience, and to be added there is still no unique and ambiguous definition of virtual reality and its characteristics. But there are some common points which can be found in different articles, reports, and other publications regarding VR.

"One of the most remarkable aspects of immersive virtual environments is that people tend to respond realistically to virtual situations and events even though they know that these are not real. Even more surprisingly, this response-as-if-real (RAIR) occurs even though the level of fidelity with respect to everyday physical reality is severely reduced" [4].

According to Slater and Sanchez-Vives [6] presence is a subjective correlate of immersion. "If a participant in VR perceives by using her body in a natural way, then the simplest inference for her brain's perceptual system to make is that what is being perceived is the participant's actual surrounding. This gives rise to subjective illusion that is referred to in the literature as presence – the illusion of "being there" in the environment depicted by VR displays – *in spite of the fact that you know for sure that you are not actually there* (…) This fundamental aspect of VR to deliver an experience that gives rise to illusory sense of place and illusory sense of reality is what distinguishes it fundamentally from all other types of media."

Some findings from recent experiments in news organisations done by the Knight Foundation [7] confirm that statement: "Early tests of experiences have yielded deeper, more immersive stories that people enjoy and stay with longer than a traditional video or article. Feedback is characterised by more visceral and emotional reactions, and people say that VR brings them closer to the events and breaks down barriers inherently raised by a reporter or correspondent."

3   Characteristics of Immersiveness

For Owen and associates [5] immersion and presence are two VR concepts of particular relevance to journalism, and the core value of VR for journalism lies in this possibility for presence that can engender an emotional connection to a story and place, and also give the audience a greater understanding of stories when the spatial elements of a location are key to comprehending the reality of events. As it was explained by Jennet et al. [3] and considering other literature in the area, there are three main ideas that describe an engaging experience: *flow* as the process of optimal experience, when a person is completely involved in an activity and nothing else matters – which is almost the same definition as immersion itself; *cognitive absorption* as a person's attitude and reaction towards information technology; and the abovementioned idea of *presence* (although they believe that presence is possible without immersion in a gaming experience).

Components of flow [8] that are in direct connection with this topic are: intense and focused concentration; merging of action and awareness, a loss of reflective self-consciousness, and a distortion of temporal experience. Cognitive absorption also has foundations in components [3] like temporal dissociation, attention focus, heightened enjoyment, curiosity (one example of motivation), and control which is also one of the factors (along with sensory distraction and realism) of the third engaging idea - presence. To be noted, one component to CA was added - a question concerning motion sickness, because it was proved earlier that VR can cause this type of cognitive disconnection or conflict, "when your visual sense perceives that you are in motion, but your ears and other sensory systems perceive that you are stationary" [9].

From previous we derived the following hypothesis: participants who access VR news (360-video reports) experienced high levels of immersion.

4   Method

The original questionnaire coined by Jennet and associates [3] was adapted so it refers to VR news content, and consisted of 27 questions instead of original 31. There were forty participants involved in the study, and the sample was assured through an opportunity sample similar to Jennet et al. [3]. The sample consisted of 13 male and 27 female students coming from undergraduate and graduate journalism programmes at the University of Dubrovnik.

The procedure included accessing two 360-video reports: Hajj 360 - experience the journey to Mecca in 360° (2015) by Al Jazeera English (7.38 min long) and Beginning - A Pencils of Promise Virtual Reality Film (2016) by Pencils of Promise and USA Today (1.54 min long). The selection of 360-video was made from a selection of the best VR news examples by Nicklas Ben Rasmussen [10]. After watching the videos the participants were asked to fill in the immersion questionnaire. The videos were access via the DISCOVRY virtual reality headset combined with iPhone 6 smartphone in January 2017.

5 Result

The high number of participants stated that the seen reports held their attention (31 of 40) and focus (30 of 40). For the participants watching 360-videos didn't require any or little effort (24 of 40) and a majority of them reported that sense of being in the report was stronger than sense of being in the real word (21 of 40), they felt as they were moving through the story (17 of 40), and making progress towards the end (22 of 40) (Table 1).

Table 1. Flow

Flow	1	2	3	4	5	Median	SD
To what extent did the report/story hold your attention (1-Not at all; 5-A lot)	0	1	8	18	13	4	0.7
To what extent did you feel you were focused on the report/story (1-Not at all; 5-A lot)	0	3	7	15	15	4	0.9
How much effort did you put into watching the report/story (1-Very little; 5-A lot)	2	6	8	12	12	4	1.1
Did you feel that you were trying your best (1-Not at all, 5-Very much so)	1	7	8	17	7	4	1
To what extent was your sense of being in the report/story environment stronger than your sense of being in the real world (1-Not at all; 5-Very much so)	3	6	10	18	3	4	1
To what extent did you feel as though you were moving through the report/story according to you own will (1-Not at all; 5-Very much so)	4	7	12	12	5	3	1.1
To what extent did you feel you were making progress towards the end of the story/report (1-Not at all; 5-A lot)	2	3	13	15	7	4	1

Almost half of the participants lost track of time (18 of 40) and didn't want to stop watching and see what was happening around them (27 of 40). The watched 360-videos were not challenging, easy to use (23 of 40) and the participants didn't want to give up (19 of 40). The majority of participants felt motivated (26 of 40) and emotionally attached (26 of 40) while watching.

The participants were interested to see how the story's events would progress (27 of 40), and they enjoyed the graphics (19 of 40) and the news (26 of 40). The high number of participants reported they would like to watch the 360-videos again (25 of 40).

Only a few participants felt some level of nausea and dizziness while watching (6 of 40) (Table 2).

Table 2. Cognitive absorption

Cognitive absorption	1	2	3	4	5	Median	SD
To what extent did you lose track of time (1-Not at all; 5-A lot)	6	6	10	8	10	3	1.3
Did you feel the urge at any point to stop watching and see what was happening around you (1-Not at all; 5-Very much so)	18	9	5	4	4	2	1.3
To what extent did you find the report/story challenging (1-Not at all; 5-very difficult)	6	11	7	12	4	3	1.2
Were there any times during the report/story in which you just wanted to give up (1-Not at all; 5-A lot)	13	6	7	8	6	3	1.4
To what extent did you feel motivated while watching (1-Not at all; 5-A lot)	3	4	7	16	10	4	1.1
To what extent did you find the report/story easy to use (1-Not at all; 5-Very much so)	0	1	6	13	20	4.5	0.8
To what extent did you feel emotionally attached to the report/story (1-Not at all; 5-A lot)	6	4	12	13	5	3	1.2
To what extent were you interested in seeing how the report/story's events would progress (1-Not at all; 5-A lot)	1	5	7	13	14	4	1.1
To what extent did you enjoy the graphics and the imagery (1-Not at all; 5-A lot)	1	3	17	11	8	3	0.9
How much would you say you enjoyed watching the news (1-Not at all; 5-A lot)	0	5	9	11	15	4	1.0
Would you like to watch the report/news again (1-Definitely not; 5-Definitely yes)	4	4	7	9	16	4	1.3
To what extent did you feel nausea/dizziness/etc. (1-Not at all; 5-A lot)	22	6	6	4	2	1	1.2

While watching 360-videos the majority of participants felt consciously aware of being in the real world (21 of 40) and surroundings (23 of 40), but they forgot about their everyday concerns (23 of 40). A half of the participants were noticing events around them (21 of 40) but a third of them were not (12 of 40).

A high number of participants felt they were interacting with the story (19 of 40), they were separated from the real world (19 of 40), and the 360-videos were something that they were experiencing (24 of 40). The participants didn't forget the controls (15 of 40) (Table 3).

Table 3. Presence

Presence	1	2	3	4	5	Median	SD
To what extent did you feel consciously aware of being in the real world whilst watching (1-Not at all; 5-Very much so)	3	3	13	**16**	5	4	1
To what extent did you forget about your everyday concerns (1-Not at all; 5-A lot)	6	4	7	**12**	11	4	1.3
To what extent were you aware of yourself in your surroundings (1-Not at all; 5-Very aware)	3	8	7	**17**	5	4	1.1
To what extent did you notice events taking place around you (1-Not at all; 5-A lot)	1	**11**	6	**13**	9	4	1.1
To what extent did you feel that you were interacting with the report/story environment (1-Not at all; 5-Very much so)	1	5	15	**14**	5	3	0.9
To what extent did you feel as though you were separated from your real-world environment (1-Not at all; 5-Very much so)	3	7	11	**15**	4	3	1
To what extent did you feel that the report/story was something you were experiencing, rather than something you were just doing (1-Not at all; 5-Very much so)	2	3	11	**16**	8	4	1
At any point did you find yourself become so involved that you were unaware you were even using controls (1-Not at all; 5-Very much so)	5	**10**	16	6	3	3	1

6 Discussion

From the above results, we identified that the majority (>80%) of the participants experienced intense and focused concentration with a moderate loss of reflective self-consciousness, and a distortion of temporal experience which means that flow was achieved.

The participants were motivated (67.5%) and emotionally attached (65%) to the watched VR content with high enjoyment (65%); according to that, the main components of cognitive absorption were achieved.

The presence is only partially recorded. The participants were aware of the events around them and they were not separated from the real-world environment. Hence the hypothesis was only partially confirmed because the participants experienced two out of the three main components for total immersion.

Based on the presented results we can emphasise that virtual reality content is a good way for engaging with news and especially because it can result in a high level of empathy. Users can connect with other people or events in the news/reports and experience places/situations which are normally inaccessible.

7 Limits of Research

The research limits come from selection of the VR head-mounted display device which does not enable sound isolation, and which influenced our results in achieving presence and total immersion. Another limitation comes from the 360-videos we selected for participants and in future research the selection should be more diverse and of higher quality. In future research we plan to examine how different types of content, its length, and device selection will influence immersiveness of VR news, information recall, and empathy towards the story presented in the VR news. The plan is also to have a more representative sample.

References

1. The Interactive Advertising Bureau (IAB), Report: Is Virtual the New Reality? A Market Snapshot of VR Publishing and Monetisation (2016). https://www.iab.com/insights/virtual-reality/. Accessed 18 Dec 2016
2. Oxford Advanced Learner's Dictionary. http://www.oxfordlearnersdictionaries.com/definition/english/immerse. Accessed 10 Jan 2017
3. Jennett, C., et al.: Measuring and defining the experience of immersion in games. Int. J. Hum.-Comput. Stud. **66**, 641–661 (2008)
4. De la Peña, N., et al.: Immersive journalism: immersive virtual reality for the first-person experience of news. Presence **19**, 291–301 (2010)
5. Owen et al.: Virtual Reality Journalism. Tow Centre for Digital Journalism, Columbia Journalism School. http://towcenter.org/research/virtual-reality-journalism/. Accessed 10 Jan 2017
6. Slater, M., Sanchez-Vives, M.V.: Enhancing our lives with immersive virtual reality. Front. Robot. AI **3**, 1–47 (2016)
7. Doyle, P., Gelman, M., Gill, S.: Viewing the Future? Virtual Reality in Journalism. Knight Foundation. https://medium.com/viewing-the-future-virtual-reality-in-journalism. Accessed 5 Jan 2017
8. Nakamura, J., Csikszentmihályi, M.: Flow theory and research. In: Handbook of Positive Psychology, pp. 195–206. Oxford University Press (2001)
9. The Interactive Advertising Bureau (IAB), Report: Is Virtual the New Reality?: A Market Snapshot of VR Publishing and Monetisation (2016). https://www.iab.com/insights/virtual-reality/. Accessed 29 Dec 2016
10. Rasmussen, N.B.: 10 Great Examples of VR Media in Modern Journalism (2016). https://vrtodaymagazine.com/10-great-examples-of-vr-media-in-modern-journalism/. Accessed 10 January 2017

Interactive 3D Symphony in VR Space

Yanxiang Zhang[1(✉)], Clayton Elieisar[1],
and Abassin Sourou Fangbemi[2]

[1] Department of Communication of Science and Technology,
University of Science and Technology of China, Hefei, Anhui, China
petrel@ustc.edu.cn, claytone@mail.ustc.edu.cn
[2] School of Software Engineering,
University of Science and Technology of China, Hefei, Anhui, China
abassino@mail.ustc.edu.cn

Abstract. 3D music could bring brand new immersive experience to the users; it is becoming a very important and unique aspect in VR technologies. And as the concert of vocal or instrumental music, symphony also have 3D characteristic in the arrangement of music instruments. This paper develops a technology to turn the traditional symphony into interactive 3D symphony in VR space by arranging the virtual music instruments on a sphere in VR space while the users virtually sit at the center of the sphere; then users could interactively change the sound effects of the symphony by rotating or resizing the sphere, and could also interactively change the position of instruments on the sphere; users could even define their own instruments set to play the interactive 3D symphony, thus achieve superlative music experience.

Keywords: Interactive · 3D symphony · VR space

1 Introduction

3D sound is responsible for a very important part of the immersive experience found in VR applications such used in video games. With 3D sounds, audiences hear and interact with objects within virtual space in real-time as though they are in a new world [1].

Traditional symphony also have 3D characteristics in the arrangement of music instruments as in Fig. 1. But in a traditional symphony, all the music instruments are arranged on a 2D stage, and the audience are always seated in front of the orchestra. So under physical limitations, it is impossible for a traditional symphony to have 3D arrangement on music instruments even if new arrangement may mean better music effects.

On the other hand, different people have different personal music preference, some people may have more interest in certain music instruments in a symphony than others, if they could reposition the music instruments in a symphony, they could personalize symphonies and get a much better music experience. Also allowing users to interact with a symphony will make symphonies more enjoyable to listeners.

© Springer International Publishing AG 2017
L.T. De Paolis et al. (Eds.): AVR 2017, Part I, LNCS 10324, pp. 270–278, 2017.
DOI: 10.1007/978-3-319-60922-5_21

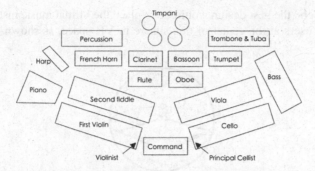

Fig. 1. Arrangement of music instruments in traditional symphony

How will the experience be if all the music instruments in a symphony are arranged around the audience? We can imagine this scenario easily and it must be a superlative immersive music experience. But actually it is almost impossible for all the music instruments in a symphony to surround an audience due to physical limitations, or it will be very expensive to realize this configuration. But with the help of virtual reality and 3D sound technology, we could realize this scenario in virtual space.

2 Literature Review

Most of the research on VR users experience focuses on visual system, however very few researches focus on 3D music in VR environment.

Allosphere in UCSB could allow users to experience 3D music in a fully Immersive environment in real space [3], but it is a unique scientific instrument for research purposes and not for normal audiences. Some works allow users to interact with virtual music instrument by using gesture [4], or interact with a 3D music system to experience immersive audio from various directions in a VR environment [5].

Industrial 3D sound technologies also provided software and hardware to create and experience 3D sound in VR space such as Realspace 3D [6] and Oculus [7].

Although many current technologies and researches focus on providing the interactive and immersive 3D music experience to users, however there is still no technology to allow audiences to experience immersive symphonies interactively in 3D VR space.

3 Design and Implementation

3.1 System Design

In traditional symphonies, all the music played by different instruments reaches the audiences at almost the same time, in 3D VR space, the distance between instruments and users should also be similar so that they could reach the users synchronously just as that in traditional symphonies. While we hope the virtual music instruments should surround the users, the best design would be to place the virtual music instruments on a sphere and the users at the center of this sphere in VR space, as shown as Fig. 2.

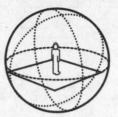

Fig. 2. System design

3.2   Technical Implementation

Deconstruction of Symphonies

In order to place different music instruments of a symphony onto a VR sphere, the music score of the symphony is first deconstructed into separate parts.

We can separate music scores for all music instruments from a symphony. In this paper, we utilize Standard MIDI files of symphonies and import them into a DAW program to modify each instruments, render each track into individual audio files and then import the instruments into Realspace 3D plug-in in Unity 3Dto build 3D symphony, as shown in Fig. 3.

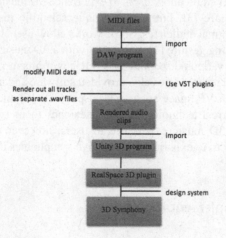

Fig. 3. Overview of steps to 3D symphony

MIDI Files

Standard MIDI files (".MID" or SMF) contain all MIDI instructions for music notations, songs, sequences, volume, tempo, and other audio effects [8]. So, a MIDI file of a symphony contains MIDI sequenced tracks of music scores with musical notations, tempo, volume and so on for each music instruments. With a MIDI file of a symphony, we directly utilize its MIDI data to provide a framework of instrumentations and focus more on modifying each music instruments within a Digital Audio Workstation (DAW).

DAW& VST Plug-Ins

Digital Audio Workstation (DAW) is a bundle of music-based programs combined into one powerful software used for recording, producing, mixing and mastering music. Its many built-in audio interfaces include a MIDI sequencer and a music notation editor which allows MIDI files to be recorded, mixed, and edited. [10] Though DAW programs provide a library of sounds from a variety of music instruments, we chose to utilize VST plug-ins also to provide more sounds to choose from for our 3D symphony instruments.

Virtual Studio Technology (VST) programs contain sound libraries of different kinds of music instruments, MIDI sound effects and other audio samples [9]. VST plug-ins generally run with DAW programs and will be used as a plug-in within a DAW program to provide best quality sounds for our music instruments. We modify the instruments by loading the VST instrument into the MIDI channels of each instrument and switching out the original sound with a different instrument sound. After we modify each instruments, we render out all audio tracks of each music instruments into individual music clips, and then we import these clips into 3D unity to construct a 3D symphony sphere in VR space (Fig. 4).

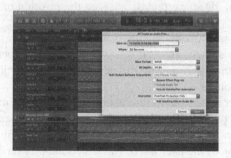

Fig. 4. Screenshot of rendering out each tracks from the DAW after modifications to instruments.

Unity 3D & Realspace 3D Plugin

Following the design of the system (Fig. 2), we carry its implementation within the Unity 3D game engine. Unity 3D is a software used for developing games for tablets, phones and other platforms [11]. Unity's audio interface features include 3D spatial sound, audio mixers for mixing and mastering and more [12]. In order to label and distinguished each instrument that is part of a 3D symphony, we create a 3D cube game object to which we attach the corresponding texture of the instrument it symbolizes. Additionally, we created a script that displays the name of the instrument whenever the user placesthe mouse over the cube and make rotate automatically the cube in order to provide a better sense of depth of the cube (Fig. 5).

Fig. 5. A 3D cube representing "French Horns" instrument.

Once an instrument is created with a 3D cube object, we can attach to it 3D audio source which will be generating the sound of the instrument. Though it is possible to audio in Unity 3D space through the "Spatial Blend" attribute of Unity original Audio Source component, we choose to use instead RealSpace's 3D Audio plugin for unity to provide the user a better 3D audio immersion. RealSpace is a plugin software developed for Unity 3D. It specializes in providing a 3D spatial sound solution for video games, movies and virtual reality [13].

After adding an audio source to the instrument (3D cube) and assigned the corresponding instrument track of the symphony, we created a script as shown below in order to move the instrument around in 3D space by dragging it with the left-click button of the mouse.

With the ability of dragging a selected instrument around, the user experiences a different sound effect in 3D space that depends on the position of the cube relatively to the user's position.

After creating the instrument and assigning to it the correspondent components (dragging script, audio source, etc....), we save it as a Unity prefab so that it can be used to create various that representing different instruments by just changing the cube texture and its audio source.

In order for the user to be able to interact with it environment, we used the original First-person controller provided by the standard unity asset to embody the user while locking the controller translation movements and allowing it to only look around in 3D. Hence, with the position of the user fixed, we created another script that allows him/her to pull toward or push away a selected instrument by pressing either the "R" key or the "F" (Fig. 6).

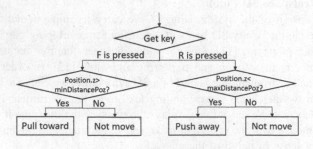

Fig. 6. "Pull" and "push"

By defining a maximum value (maxDistancePoz) above which the instrument cannot be pushed further, and a minimum value (minDistancePoz) below which the instrument cannot be pulled further, both in the Z axis, we create a virtual sphere space in which the instrument can be moved, dragged, pulled and pushed (Fig. 7).

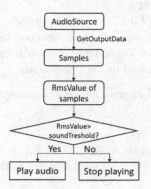

Fig. 7. Calculate the RMS value.

In order to allow the user to identify the instruments that are currently emitting sound, we calculate the root-mean-square value (RMS) as shown in the code below by allocating a float array and passing it to GetOutputData function of Unity to get the output data of the audio source. Then we sum all squared sample values, calculate the average and get its square root; that value is the used as a threshold based on which a particle effect is generated around an instrument if that instrument currently produces sound (Fig. 8).

Fig. 8. Particles generated around an instrument that is currently emitting sound.

Finally, through a "drag-all-script", we were able to control the rotational movement of all the cubes together and at once around the player in case he/she desires to control all of them together instead of moving them one by one. Such functionality, though limited to an orbital movement of the whole orchestra around the user, create an immense variation of the symphony in 3D space when performed.

Interactivity

We designed two kinds of interactions for users to experience the 3D symphony:

1. Interactive placement of virtual music instruments on the 3D symphony sphere in VR space, including randomly placement of all the virtual music instruments in a symphony on the sphere, select certain virtual music instrument and move it to another position on the sphere.
2. Interactive transformation of the 3D symphony sphere, including rotating the sphere which will lead to the change of angle between users' ears and virtual music instruments, and resizing of the sphere which will lead to the change of distance between users' ears and virtual music instruments.

   Any above interaction will directly affects and changes the 3D sound effects of the 3D symphony.

3D Symphony Output

If we use virtual music instruments A, B, C, D, E, F..., which has an angle of a, b, c, d, e, f ...to users ear plane, then the final sound comes to the center point of ear will be:

$$A \times \sin(a) + B \times \sin(b) + C \times \sin(c) + D \times \sin(d) + E \times \sin(e) + F \times \sin(f) + ...$$

Then by HRTF (A head-related transfer function) method and algorithms, 3D sound could be calculated and outputted.

3D Symphony could be output to two kinds of devices:

1. Headphone output. In this mode, it is necessary for users to interact with the 3D symphony sphere in VR space by mouse on PC or by touch on tablet.
2. Oculus output. In this mode, users could wear the oculus and rotate their head to rotate the 3D symphony sphere in VR space to achieve a more immersive experience.

4　Result

We realized a 3D symphony VR environment, in which users could interact with virtual music instruments. As shown in Fig. 9, cubes representing all different instruments that compose a particular symphony positioned around the user position so that he/she can interact (drag, pull, push) with each of them.

Presently, 3D symphony has 6 classical music that a user can choose from and interacting with different musical instruments, which is: Johann Sebastian Bach – "Air"; Johann Pachelbel – "Canon in D minor"; Joseph Hayden - "Farewell"; Wolfgang Mozart - "Jupiter"; Ludwig Van Beethoven – "Symphony No.5"; Franz Shubert – "Ave maria".

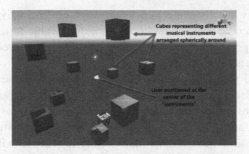

Fig. 9. Perspective view of 3D symphony configuration within Unity 3D.

By using the four options on the side bar, (from top to bottom) a user can restart a track or change symphonies using the green arrows. In addition to that, when users change a symphony, the background of each scene also change to give each symphony a different feeling thus enhancing the visual experience for the user.

5 Users Feedback

We made a investigate on this system with 11 users, the following is the questions and responses:

QUESTION 1: "Between traditional orchestra and 3d symphony, which one do you prefer?"
3 out of 11 participants chose traditional orchestra. While the remaining 8 chose 3D symphony. Therefore, the results tells us that more people preferred 3D symphony over traditional orchestra.

QUESTION 2: "What do you like most about our system?"
2 out of 11 participants liked the 'Functionality' of 3D symphony. While 2 out of 11 participants liked the 'Design' of 3D symphony. And the remaining 7 chose 'User interaction'. Therefore, the results tells us that more people like interacting with the music instruments within 3D symphony.

QUESTION 3: "Do you have suggestions on how we can improve 3D symphony?"
"improve design" were suggested 9 times in the suggestions made by the participants. While "more symphonies" were suggested 3 times and "add other features" 2 times. The results tells us that users would like to see more interaction with 3D symphony.

6 Conclusion

By bringing interaction and 3D surround sound experience to traditional orchestra, it is possible to create new innovative experiences for the user such as the ones described in this paper. While traditional orchestra performances rarely allow interaction between musicians and the audience, this paper introduces a novel way for users to interact with musical instruments while listening to a symphony. An interactive experience to the traditional orchestra could make symphonies more enjoyable to users of all ages and especially younger generations hence leading to a deep appreciation for musical instruments and orchestral music in general.

Further work will take into account more features such as a time indicator bar so users can know the length of a symphony or skip through any point of a symphony; more dynamic features can be implemented to the individual cubes such as a 'mute' or a 'solo instrument' option, so users can choose which instrument(s) to listen to in a symphony; User can also 'save arrangement' of the interaction within the system and export the exact experience out as an audio file to listen to on their various devices and more. Though our system mainly focuses on classical music at the moment, the system, can support other music genres such as Rock, R&B, Hip Hop and so on thus appealing to a larger audience with different personal musical preferences [14], and bringing new experiences for the user to interact with music instruments for all musical genres.

References

1. Arhippainen, L., Pakanen, M., Hickey, S.: Designing 3D virtual music club spaces by utilizing mixed UX methods: from sketches to self-expression method. In: Proceeding of the 16th International Academic MindTrek Conference (MindTrek 2012), pp. 178–184. ACM, New York (2012)
2. Amatriain, X., Höllerer, T., Kuchera-Morin, J.A., Pope, S.T.: Immersive audio and music in the allosphere. In: International Computer Music Conference, ICMC 2007, UC Santa Barbara, United States, pp. 276–283 (2007)
3. Rodrigue M, Waranis A, Wood T, Höllerer T.: Mixed reality simulation with physical mobile display devices. In: 2015 IEEE Virtual Reality (VR), 23–27 March 2015, pp. 105–110
4. Marshall, M.T., Malloch, J., Wanderley, M.M.: Gesture control of sound spatialization for live musical performance. In: Gesture-Based Human-Computer Interaction and Simulation, International Gesture Workshop, GW 2007, Lisbon, Portugal, 23–25 May 2007, pp. 227–238 (2009). Revised Selected Papers
5. Valbom, L., Marcos, A.: WAVE: sound and music in an immersive environment. Comput. Graph. **29**(6), 871–881 (2005)
6. RealSpace™ 3D Audio. http://realspace3daudio.com/. Accessed 24 June 2016
7. 3D Audio Spatialization. https://developer.oculus.com/documentation/audiosdk/latest/concepts/audio-intro-spatialization/. Accessed 24 June 2016
8. All about MIDI files. https://www.midi.org/articles/about-midi-part-4-midi-files
9. What is a VST? https://www.thoughtco.com/what-are-vst-plug-ins-1817748
10. What is a DAW? http://www.thedawstudio.com/what-is-a-daw/
11. Unity. https://en.wikipedia.org/wiki/Unity_(game_engine)
12. Unity Audio manual. https://docs.unity3d.com/Manual/Audio.html
13. RealSpace3D. http://realspace3daudio.com/
14. Personal music preferences. https://en.wikipedia.org/wiki/Psychology_of_music_preference

Virtual Bodystorming: Utilizing Virtual Reality for Prototyping in Service Design

Costas Boletsis[1]([✉]), Amela Karahasanovic[1], and Annita Fjuk[2]

[1] SINTEF Digital, Forskningsveien 1, 0373 Oslo, Norway
{konstantinos.boletsis,amela.karahasanovic}@sintef.no
[2] Telenor Research, Fornebu, Norway
annita.fjuk@telenor.com

Abstract. The paper describes our ongoing work on a new prototyping method for service design, Virtual Bodystorming. Virtual Bodystorming utilizes Virtual Reality (VR) and enables the user to role-play the service scenario in a fully immersive and collaborative VR environment. In this environment, various service-related areas and objects can be recreated with 3D graphics, while distant service users, providers, designers, and facilitators can communicate and collaborate. Virtual Bodystorming aims to minimize the gap between the actual service environment and its prototype by contributing to the development of fully immersive and highly-engaging service simulations. To illustrate the practical implementation of Virtual Bodystorming, we describe its main characteristics and present a first prototype version of the method. The method was evaluated by three experienced service designers, who highlighted the strengths of Virtual Bodystorming for service prototyping, regarding immersion and engagement, while emphasizing the service designer's significant role in directing the user interactions of the VR scene. The method was considered to be suitable for prototyping services that include human interaction and/or spatial aspects.

Keywords: Bodystorming · Service design · Service prototyping · User experience · Virtual Reality

1 Introduction

Service design is a young discipline, which departs from the standard managerial perspectives and focuses on the interactional experience of services [10]. Services consist of hundreds or thousands of components that are often not physical entities, but rather are a combination of processes, people skills, and materials that must be appropriately integrated to result in the "planned" or "designed" service [6].

A service prototype is "a simulation of a service experience" [20] and an important service design tool for making services visible and helping communicate service concepts at the early stages of the new service development process [1]. Service prototyping contributes to the service design process by (i)

© Springer International Publishing AG 2017
L.T. De Paolis et al. (Eds.): AVR 2017, Part I, LNCS 10324, pp. 279–288, 2017.
DOI: 10.1007/978-3-319-60922-5_22

defining the service design problems to be solved, (ii) evaluating the usability and effectiveness of a service concept, and (iii) enabling collaboration between different actors (e.g. users, stakeholders, service providers) [19]. The most crucial factor in the service prototyping process is the ability to create a realistic sensation for the users and immerse them in the service experience [9,19].

However, conventional service prototyping methods, such as scenarios, videos, cardboard, role-playing, storyboards, and others, are limited in their ability to relay information associated with specific service periods and interactions with users at touchpoints [8,9]. The need for new service prototyping methods that could offer more realistic simulations has been reported. The use of virtual elements for developing new service prototyping environments has been suggested as a way to address the limitations of the conventional methods and optimize the service prototyping process [9,13,19]. Virtual Reality (VR) can fulfill the conceptual framework for service experiences, as well as overcome the limitations of conventional simulation methods by simulating visual, audio, and haptic interaction [9,18]. Virtual settings have already been used to analyze and evaluate services in a more realistic environment, as these technologies could "minimize the gap between the practical and service prototyping test environments" [9]. These virtual environments for service prototyping have been under development at the laboratories of Fraunhofer IAO's "ServLab" [13], KITECH's "s-Scape" [9], and University of Lapland's "SINCO" [14,19].

Nevertheless, the utilization of VR in service prototyping faces certain issues. Primary obstacles include the high development cost of the earlier VR systems and their resource-demanding or even limited networking capabilities [5,9,11]. Furthermore, there have been difficulties in connecting the service prototyping method with the underlying VR technology. Establishing a VR system that supports design, realization, evaluation, optimization, and detailed management procedures for service prototyping processes is a challenge [9]. Because of those issues, VR implementation in service prototyping has not matured enough to reach the theoretically praised, fully immersive and collaborative VR capabilities that would allow for a higher degree of realism in the simulation of service environments [9,13].

Over the last few years, major changes in the VR technology field have taken place, allowing the development of affordable, high-quality, immersive, and collaborative 3D virtual environments. This opens the way for the use of fully immersive, collaborative VR in service prototyping [7,9,11]. Naturally, the level of immersion and interaction in a VR environment directly affects user engagement [4,16]. Therefore, it can be hypothesized that a fully immersive VR environment with collaborative aspects could minimize the gap between the actual service environment and its prototype, thus allowing the user to have a more representative and complete service experience and, consequently, enable the service designer to extract high-quality user feedback. Based on this hypothesis, we address the need for a new, fully immersive and collaborative VR-enabled service prototyping method.

1.1   Virtual Bodystorming, Contribution, and Paper Organization

In this ongoing work, we propose a new service prototyping method, "Virtual Bodystorming", and we present its first, prototype version. Virtual Bodystorming is based on the popular service prototyping method of bodystorming, also known as service role-play [20].

Fig. 1. An example of a bodystorming session, role-playing the service scenario in a simulated service environment, using props and mock-ups (image under CC BY-SA 2.0 license by Unsworn Industries) [21].

Bodystorming enables the user to enact and role-play the service scenario in various prototyping environments (Fig. 1), such as the original service location (high-fidelity prototyping), a similar service location (medium-fidelity prototyping), or an office/lab space equipped with mock-ups (low-fidelity prototyping) [3,15,17]. Overall, bodystorming attempts to "place" the user in the service environment, empathize with the user, and get valuable feedback about the experience [15,17,19]. Due to its theatrical nature, experiential and spatial qualities, bodystorming can provide the infrastructure and the management procedures from which a new, VR-enabled service prototyping method can be built.

Virtual Bodystorming utilizes fully immersive, collaborative VR technology that enables the user to role-play the service scenario in a VR environment. In that environment, various service-related areas and objects can be recreated with 3D graphics, while distant service users, providers, designers, and facilitators can communicate and collaborate.

The goal of Virtual Bodystorming is to improve service prototyping by creating an affordable, collaborative, and highly engaging method. The method is destined to enable agile development of medium-to-high fidelity prototypes and easier involvement from different user groups. The first version of Virtual Bodystorming is developed to exclusively support service design by targeting to recreate the experiential representations necessary for successfully conveying an experience with a service.

The contribution of this work is summarized as follows:

- Introduce a new experience prototyping method for service design, utilizing a fully immersive, collaborative VR environment to implement and advance the related literature's theoretical suggestions regarding the use of VR for service prototyping.
- Describe the implementation of the fully immersive, collaborative VR system for service prototyping, analyze its attributes, and demonstrate its suggested use, thus enabling researchers to reproduce it and potentially build on its implementation.
- Assess the user experience with the first version of a new VR service prototyping method through a preliminary expert evaluation.

The rest of the paper is organized as follows. Section 2 presents the main requirements on which we based the development of the prototype version of Virtual Bodystorming. Section 3 describes the prototype, focusing on the hardware/software aspects, networking attributes, VR maps, and proposed user roles and interactions. At the end of Sect. 3, the expert evaluation of the Virtual Bodystorming prototype is presented. The paper concludes in Sect. 4.

2   Virtual Bodystorming Requirements

The design of Virtual Bodystorming should satisfy established bodystorming principles (cf. [3,15,17,19]) combined with our objectives for an affordable, engaging, and agile tool for creating medium-to-high fidelity prototypes. Therefore, we pose the following requirements for the Virtual Bodystorming method:

- *The method should enable the user to explore and experience the service scenario, while role-playing and interacting with the virtual artifacts and other users.* This requirement is in line with the main properties of bodystorming [3,15,17], as implemented in a virtual environment.
- *The method should technically support all the user roles of a bodystorming session, such as service users, service providers, et. al.* Bodystorming is a process that involves various user types for the service scenario to be better enacted and for the feedback to be useful [15,19]. Moreover, Virtual Bodystorming, due to its technical nature, demands the additional role of the VR system operator, i.e. an experienced programmer who handles the VR-related technical aspects and supports the agile development of the process.
- *The method should enable direct communication and collaboration to promote participatory design.* Bodystorming is inherently a participatory and collaborative method since it is based on role-playing, simulating multi-user service environments, and establishing meaningful collaborations between users, service providers, and stakeholders [3,15,17]. For Virtual Bodystorming, communication and collaboration are translated into a virtual networking element where distant bodystorming users log into the virtual environment and experience the service scenario together.

- *The method should enable the agile development and editing of the virtual environment and its contents.* Prototype development agility is a crucial property of experience prototyping; it enables flexibility to modify the service experience and rapid visualization of user feedback [19]. In the case of Virtual Bodystorming, large 3D asset libraries and of an experienced VR system operator are of the essence for ensuring the agility of the process and the fidelity of the visualized service.
- *The method should be affordable (low-to-medium cost) and user-friendly.* Because Virtual Bodystorming depends on VR technology, there is the need for a VR platform that is easy to access and does not burden users with high costs. The fact that VR recently became more accessible to the average consumer [7] can help fulfill this requirement.

3   Prototyping Virtual Bodystorming

To better illustrate the implementation of Virtual Bodystorming, we develop a prototype version of the method based on the requirements above.

3.1   User Roles

At first, we define the core roles and interactions for users of the Virtual Bodystorming session based on the main user roles and interactions in typical service design cases:

- *Service designer:* the designer is responsible for organizing the Virtual Bodystorming sessions. The designer assigns service users to their role-playing characters, provides ideas and suggestions on the acting, and collects the feedback from the users and the service provider.
- *Service users:* the end users of the service, who, in the Virtual Bodystorming session, role-play the service scenario in the virtual environment, while communicating and collaborating with other service users. Service users provide the service designer with feedback about the service prototype and their experience.
- *Service provider:* the provider supplies the designer with service design tasks and problems and observes the Virtual Bodystorming sessions in the virtual environment, as a spectator, communicating feedback about the service prototype and the way users respond to it to the service designer.
- *VR system operator:* the system operator is responsible for developing the virtual environment and making changes to it according to the service designer's feedback. The system operator also participates in Virtual Bodystorming as a spectator, looking for usability flaws of the system while in use.

Naturally, other user roles can be added, such as service and product developers, service managers, stakeholders, and third-party businesses. In the first version of Virtual Bodystorming, the core users are described, bearing in mind

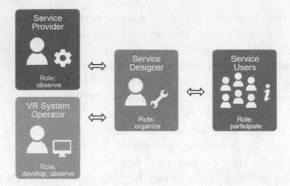

Fig. 2. The core user roles and interactions (visualized as arrows) in virtual bodystorming.

that additional user types may be covered by the existing core roles (e.g. the service provider). Moreover, Fig. 2 makes clear that the service designer plays a central role in Virtual Bodystorming, since the designer mediates the process and elicits service users' feedback, which will consequently drive the service provider's decisions.

3.2 VR Development

The choice of Virtual Bodystorming software and hardware was based on facilitating the agile development of VR environments and offering robust networking and easy access to end users while maintaining the costs at a low-to-medium level (following the requirements of Sect. 2).

VR Hardware and Game Engine: The VR prototype of Virtual Bodystorming was developed using the Unreal Engine game engine by Epic Games and the HTC Vive VR headset. The interaction utilized the HTC Vive controllers and the teleportation VR locomotion technique was implemented [2]. HTC Vive (*vive.com*) is a medium-cost VR headset that is designed to utilize "room scale" technology for turning a room into 3D space via sensors. Unreal Engine supports our future plan of designing and exporting the VR scenes to Google Android smartphones, thus enabling users with a low-cost, generic VR headset, a Bluetooth controller (for navigation purposes), and an Android smartphone to access the virtual environment.

Networking: The use of the Unreal Engine also allowed us to create a multi-user VR environment since the networking functionality is an intrinsic feature of the game engine. Users can navigate through the VR environment, represented as avatars; they can see each other, and communicate via audio chat. The system also supports spectators, i.e. users overlooking the VR environment and observing other users navigating and interacting.

Asset Library: A low-cost, large 3D asset library was built to facilitate the creation of various VR service environments. Naturally, VR environments will

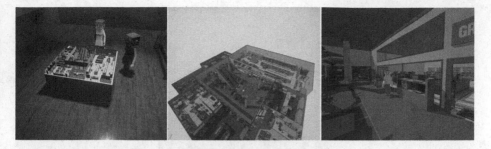

Fig. 3. Prototype screenshots (*left to right*): the Lobby level, the map of the service level where virtual bodystorming takes place, and meeting another user while navigating the service level.

be created and edited ad hoc, depending on the service scenario, user feedback, and progress of the Virtual Bodystorming session.

3.3   Virtual Environment

The virtual environment of the Virtual Bodystorming prototype is divided into two levels: the Lobby Level and the Service Level (Fig. 3). The Lobby Level is a virtual meeting room for discussion and feedback. At this Level, the service designer welcomes users in the VR space, presents the service scenario, explains the goals of the session, assigns the role-playing characters, collects and discusses user feedback, and provides an overview of the Service level. The Service Level is the main level of the Virtual Bodystorming where the service prototyping takes place. Naturally, each cycle of the service prototyping process requires going back and forth between the Lobby and the Service Level, while the presence of users at the Lobby Level gives the VR system operator time to prepare the next iteration of the Service Level, based on the user feedback.

3.4   Expert Evaluation

As a preliminary evaluation of the Virtual Bodystorming method and its virtual environment, we conducted an expert evaluation with three service designers (Fig. 4). The use of expert designers for the preliminary evaluation would allow us to utilize their experience in dealing with service prototyping methods for reliably identifying the pros and cons of Virtual Bodystorming, as well as receiving useful feedback about future improvements and potential. The aim of this evaluation was to assess overall user experience, reveal possible problems with the method, and gather recommendations for its further development. We used a cognitive walkthrough method followed by semi-structured interviews [12]. All the experts had more than ten years' experience in Human-Computer Interaction and more than five years' experience in service design.

A service scenario was presented to the participants. The service scenario was exploring the idea of attracting newspaper subscriptions, using a new service

Fig. 4. Evaluating the virtual bodystorming prototype.

path in a shopping mall. At first, the participants acquired the role of service users, while one of the authors acquired the role of the service designer. Other users were represented by virtual agents. Then, the participants began to go through the service scenario, starting from the Lobby Level. At that stage, the service prototyping goal was presented, bodystorming properties were defined, and preliminary ideas were introduced (e.g. placing a digital newspaper stand by the grocery store of the shopping mall). One of those ideas was implemented at the Service Level, where participants could navigate as spectators, witnessing the interactions. Each session lasted between 35 to 40 min. At this stage, the networking/collaborative element, even though implemented, was not evaluated due to the small sample size and the limited number of user roles.

At the end of the session, the semi-structured interviews were conducted. Participants were asked about: (i) their overall experience, focusing on the elements of positive/negative affection, engagement, and immersion, (ii) problems they might have experienced during the session or potential issues of the method, and (iii) their recommendations about future development and application of the method, focusing on how they would improve the method and what kind of applications they foresee for it.

The participants' overall impression was that the interaction and the navigation in the VR environment were user-friendly, and that the two-level structure of the method was useful. The method achieved a satisfying level of immersion, while the design of the VR environment elicited positive feelings.

- *"It gives you a feel of space which is better than seeing photos or projections ... it is more like being there."*
- *"It has a game-like feeling that makes it more attractive and engaging."*

However, participants also stated that the service designer should have an active role in controlling the game-like feeling coming from the environment and that being immersed in the VR environment for a long period of time may lead to cognitive overload.

- *"Specific task-related guidelines and directing the VR scene are necessary since users may play around in the VR environment, instead of focusing on the task."*
- *"It is too immersive and I would definitely need a break after using it for some time."*

Participants considered Virtual Bodystorming to be ideal for prototyping services that include human interaction (human touchpoints) as well as services that take place in open spaces (e.g. public transport, airports, warehouses, etc.) As for the future, participants suggested focusing more on telepresence features (e.g. users creating customized avatars) and ensuring that the method is technically robust enough to support a large number of users and efficiently handle fail states.

4   Conclusion

In this work, we introduced a prototyping method for service design which applies the bodystorming concept in fully immersive VR settings. The method aims at optimizing the service prototyping process by contributing to the development of high-fidelity service prototyping environments, which can offer better service simulations, high user engagement and, ultimately, lead to useful, high-quality feedback.

The presentation of the Virtual Bodystorming method focuses on covering the method's main infrastructure (bodystorming, design requirements, user roles) and the enabling technology (VR hardware/software, networking, VR environment, 3D asset library). Expert evaluation of the prototype helped us concretize the strengths of the method, discover potential pitfalls, and plan the next step in its development phase.

The current work and the introduction of Virtual Bodystorming provide the opportunity for organizations, businesses, designers, and researchers to reproduce and further advance the method. Furthermore, we hope that this work will trigger a discussion around the potential of VR in service design, which, so far, is an under-researched field [9].

Future work will focus on: (i) iteratively refining the method based on experts' and users' comments, (ii) testing its performance through case studies, (iii) measuring user experience and engagement while using the method, and (iv) comparing the method with other widely-used service prototyping methods.

Acknowledgements. We would like to thank Antoine Pultier for his VR development work. This research is funded by the Norwegian Research Council through the Centre for Service Innovation (*csi.nhh.no*).

References

1. Blomkvist, J., Holmlid, S.: Existing prototyping perspectives: considerations for service design. In: Nordic Design Research Conference, Nordes 2011, Nordes, pp. 1–10 (2011)

2. Bozgeyikli, E., Raij, A., Katkoori, S., Dubey, R.: Point & teleport locomotion technique for virtual reality. In: Proceedings of the 2016 Annual Symposium on Computer-Human Interaction in Play, CHI PLAY 2016, pp. 205–216. ACM (2016)
3. Burns, C., Dishman, E., Verplank, W., Lassiter, B.: Actors, hairdos & videotape - informance design. In: Conference Companion on Human Factors in Computing Systems, CHI 1994, pp. 119–120 ACM (1994)
4. Dede, C.: Immersive interfaces for engagement and learning. Science **323**(5910), 66–69 (2009)
5. Funkhouser, T.A.: Network topologies for scalable multi-user virtual environments. In: Proceedings of the IEEE 1996 Virtual Reality Annual International Symposium, pp. 222–228, VRAIS 1996. IEEE (1996)
6. Goldstein, S.M., Johnston, R., Duffy, J., Rao, J.: The service concept: the missing link in service design research? J. Oper. Manag. **20**(2), 121–134 (2002)
7. Hilfert, T., König, M.: Low-cost virtual reality environment for engineering and construction. Vis. Eng. **4**(1), 1–18 (2016)
8. Holmlid, S., Evenson, S.: Prototyping and enacting services: Lessons learned from human-centered methods. In: Proceedings from the 10th Quality in Services Conference, QUIS 2007, vol. 10 (2007)
9. Jung Bae, D., Seong Leem, C.: A visual interactive method for service prototyping. Managing Serv. Qual. **24**(4), 339–362 (2014)
10. Khambete, P., Roy, D., Devkar, S.: Validation of a service design pattern language as an effective framework for multidisciplinary design. In: Proceedings of the 7th International Conference on HCI, IndiaHCI 2015, pp. 1–9, ACM (2015)
11. Koutsabasis, P., Vosinakis, S., Malisova, K., Paparounas, N.: On the value of virtual worlds for collaborative design. Des. Stud. **33**(4), 357–390 (2012)
12. Lazar, J., Feng, J.H., Hochheiser, H.: Research Methods in Human-Computer Interaction. Wiley, Hoboken (2010)
13. Meiren, T., Burger, T.: Testing of service concepts. Serv. Ind. J. **30**(4), 621–632 (2010)
14. Miettinen, S., Rontti, S., Kuure, E., Lindström, A.: Realizing design thinking through a service design process and an innovative prototyping laboratory - introducing Service Innovation Corner (SINCO). In: Proceedings of the conference on Design Research Society, DRS 2012 (2012)
15. Oulasvirta, A., Kurvinen, E., Kankainen, T.: Understanding contexts by being there: case studies in bodystorming. Pers. Ubiquit. Comput. **7**(2), 125–134 (2003)
16. Psotka, J.: Immersive training systems: virtual reality and education and training. Instr. Sci. **23**(5–6), 405–431 (1995)
17. Schleicher, D., Jones, P., Kachur, O.: Bodystorming as embodied designing. Interactions **17**(6), 47–51 (2010)
18. Seth, A., Vance, J.M., Oliver, J.H.: Virtual reality for assembly methods prototyping: a review. Virtual Reality **15**(1), 5–20 (2011)
19. Simo, R., Miettinen, S., Kuure, E., Lindström, A.: A laboratory concept for service prototyping - Service Innovation Corner (SINCO). In: Proceedings of the 3rd Service Design and Service Innovation Conference, pp. 229–241. No. 067 in ServDes 2012. Linköping University (2012)
20. Stickdorn, M., Schneider, J.: This is Service Design Thinking: Basics, Tools, Cases. Wiley, Hoboken (2012)
21. Industries, U.: Bodystorming (2011). https://www.flickr.com/photos/unsworn/6070125919, image used without modifications, licensed under the Creative Commons BY-SA2.0 license. Accessed 29 Mar 2017

Capturing Reality for a Billiards Simulation

Fuche Wu$^{(\boxtimes)}$ and Andrew Dellinger

Providence University, 200, Sec. 7,
Taiwan Boulevard, Shalu District, Taichung City 43301, Taiwan
fcwu@pu.edu.tw

Abstract. A mixed reality platform for a billiards simulation was implemented. For a better training experience, the system uses a natural and tangible user interface as input. The system will capture the reality of user manipulations, including the ball motion, observer position, and gesture. The primary input sensor is an RGB-depth camera. With the help of depth information, the capturing process becomes more robust and efficient. In this physical mini-pool table, an inexperienced user can pick a cue and hit a ball easier to get practical training in a game of billiards. However, distance perception is very critical in training. The display simulating the motion parallax effect is helpful for the user to perceive the distance and orientation in a virtual simulation. For convenience, the system allows a natural gesture to interact with the system. With this system, we demonstrate that capturing reality bring real experiences into the virtual world.

Keywords: Augmented reality · Virtual reality · Mixed reality · Motion parallax

1 Introduction

Virtual, Augmented, and Mixed Reality (VR, AR, and MR, respectively) related research has become very vigorous in recent years, especially in the medical, training, and games areas. After visualization of a person, object, or system, the subsequent data processing needed to interact with different types of display devices has a broad range of research [1]. When the user interacts with the virtual object, the system still has many challenges. One challenge is that although keyboard and mouse are conventional input devices, they are not suitable for an inexperienced user to perform three-dimensional manipulation. Another challenge is the rendering of a virtual object in relation to the real environment; there are many details of this relationship which need improvement. Especially, the perceptual distance may have inconsistencies between the virtual and the real world. This difference may not be a serious issue for a game. But it will be a huge barrier for health- and training-related applications. Thus, how to capture reality becomes a critical issue in VR/AR and MR application.

Billiards is an entertaining game. Alves et al. [12] used a projector to project a guide line in order to teach the user how to hit the ball. However, their table was huge and may be not suitable to use in the home. We also can create the game as a video game playing in a virtual space. However, it may lack the feeling of hitting the ball.

© Springer International Publishing AG 2017
L.T. De Paolis et al. (Eds.): AVR 2017, Part I, LNCS 10324, pp. 289–298, 2017.
DOI: 10.1007/978-3-319-60922-5_23

Alternatively, we can use a small piece of a real table, cue stick, and ball, and place the rest of the huge table in virtual space. The user is playing with the real ball, called a mother ball, which can interact with the other balls in virtual space. As we know, when playing billiards, the most important technique is to determine the trajectory of the mother ball. To provide an accurate sense of space and distance, and to transfer the experience of training in the virtual space into a real, full-size billiards table is a big challenge. We not only need the mother ball to interact with the virtual balls; we need the user to participate in the virtual environment. When the user's head or the location of the eyes change, the system must provide the corresponding view. So just like the real scene, a player can perceive the relative relationship among the balls on the table. For simulating the user walking around the table, the system also provides the ability to recognize the gesture. The user can use his hand to rotate around the ball to find a suitable target to hit. Hammond [17] has mentioned a similar idea. But he just focuses on the motion detection of the ball with the image processing technique. Our system configuration is as follows. A mini pool table setup in front of television (Fig. 1).

Fig. 1. System configuration

On the table, the mother ball is always located at a fixed position. The Intel Realsense camera (SR300) is used as the primary sensor. Its Software Development Kit (2016 R3 SDK) provided the face and gesture recognition modules, which makes system integration easier. The depth camera will continually monitor the physical environment and capture any particular event, transferring it into the virtual space to display the corresponding view for the user.

Virtual space is flexible. Physical space is natural for the user. Chapoulie et al. [11] also found that the operation of physical devices implemented in virtual spaces is efficient. Thus, it is convenient to use a natural and tangible user interface as a primary input. But there is a gap between the virtual and physical worlds, in which a critical issue is the sense of distance. Therefore, to correct the perception in VR/AR applications, depth clues by motion parallax is crucial. Thus, we are going to construct a mixed reality platform for a game of billiards to observe the impact of motion parallax on the depth perception in this platform.

2 Related Works

The development of mixed realities has a long history, and Bjork et al. [2] have reviewed different types of games, including AR2 Hockey, RV-Border Guards, and AquaGauntle. These games integrate virtual and real environments, and were created by the Mixed Reality Systems Laboratory. Pan et al. [3] also presents a lot of learning systems through VR/MR, such as virtual bowling. Kuo et al. [4] also made a virtual bowling game through magnetic bombs. However, in their systems mainly focus on interactive ability more than the motion accuracy. In our experiments, we want to pay a attention to a virtual training platform.

We believe that the value of a virtual training system relies on the perceived realness of distance and orientation. Van Veen's [5] research had the same conclusion. The research on a virtual autopsy used data from a body after a CT or MRI scan. The research allowed a mobile device to be placed at different positions. At each different position, Van Veen tried to provide a corresponding view of the body. One conclusion was that motion parallax will help improve depth and distance observations, thereby enhancing efficiency.

Many factors may produce an incorrect perception of distance and orientation. Steinicke et al. [6] explored the effects of projection angles. Perspective projections of virtual environments on a computer screen are affected by the interplay between the geometric field of view and the field of view provided by the display. Langbehn et al. [7] also analyze the impact of the visual blur effects on the depth of field and analyze motion blur in terms of their effects on distance and speed estimation in immersive virtual environments.

Dey et al. [8] also pointed out in their study that in hand-held AR devices, the perception of distance is often incorrect, including egocentric and exocentric depth perception. Egocentric depth perception refers to the distance to an object perceived from the observer's viewpoint; exocentric depth perception relates to the distance between two objects in the view.

Depth judgment is subject to the subtle properties of the surrounding environment and is not always accurate even in the real world. Thus, use of visualizations for occluded objects improves depth perception akin to non-occluded objects. Also, a larger display screen is helpful. And motion parallax provides an important clue to depth perception. According to Palmer [9], Read [10] and Teittinen [16], people's judgment of depth depends on several different factors, some of which are physiological, and some which are psychological. These factors are presented below in Sect. 2.1.

2.1   Physiological Factors of Depth Perception

(1) binocular parallax:
As the eyes are horizontally displaced (average 65 mm), we see the world from two slightly different viewpoints. The visual fields of the two eyes overlap in the central region of vision, but points that are not on the so-called horopter (Panum's fusional area) fall onto different retinal positions. This lateral displacement which is relative to the fixation point is called binocular disparity.

(2) Accommodation:
Accommodation is the tension of the muscle that changes the focal length of the lens of the eye. Thus it brings into focus objects at different distances. This depth cue is quite weak, and it is effective only at short viewing distances (less than 2 m) with other cues.

(3) Motion parallax:
If we close one of our eyes, we can perceive depth by moving our head. This happens because the human visual system can extract depth information in two similar images sensed after each other, in the same way, it can combine two images from different eyes.

(4) Convergence of Parallels:
When watching an object close to us, our eyes point slightly inward. This difference in the direction of the eyes is called convergence. This depth cue is effective only at short distances (less than 10 m).

2.2   Depth Perception of Psychological Hints

(1) Size (Relative Size, Linear Perspective)
When looking down a straight level road, we see the parallel sides of the road meet in the horizon. This effect is often visible in photos, and it is an important depth cue. It is called linear perspective.

(2) Familiar Size: When the real size of the object is known, our brain compares the sensed size of the object to this real size, and thus acquires information about the distance of the object.

(3) Texture Gradients: The closer we are to an object the more detail we can see of its surface texture. So objects with smooth textures are usually interpreted being farther away. This is especially true if the surface texture spans the entire distance from near to far.

(4) Shading and Shadows: When we know the location of a light source and see objects casting shadows on other objects, we learn that the object shadowing the other is closer to the light source. As most illumination comes downward, we tend to resolve ambiguities using this information. The three-dimensional looking computer user interfaces are a nice example on this. Also, bright objects seem to be closer to the observer than dark ones.

(5) Air Perspective (Aerial Perspective): The mountains in the horizon always look slightly bluish or hazy. The reason for this is small water and dust particles in the air between the eye and the mountains. The farther the mountains, the hazier they look.

(6) Edge Interpretation/Overlapping:
When objects block each other out of our sight, we know that the object that blocks the other one is closer to us. The object whose outline pattern looks more continuous is felt to lie closer.

3   Implementation

Our development tool is in Unity. The tool provides the basic rendering capability and a physics engine for interaction calculation among ball collisions. Our system consists of three main parts: Pre-calibration stage, physical event capturing, and pool game simulation. We will discuss them in sequence.

3.1   Pre-calibration Stage

Integration of real objects into a virtual space needs to let them be in the same coordinate system. Finding out the relationship between the two worlds is imperative. Traditionally in robot systems, this is called hand-eye calibration, which can be divided into arm correction, camera correction, hand-eye correction, and platform correction. A related technique has been developing for decades. Hu et al. [13] used a hand-held laser while solving arm, platform, and camera correction problems. But when the human is involved, the issue of correction becomes more difficult. It is not easy to correct the human eye. We can estimate the location of the human eye, but it is hard to determine the focal length for individual users. To solve this problem, we try to establish a personal adjustment of the human eye correction system.

The dimension of a standard surface for a pool table is 2.84 m by 1.42 m. For convenience of use, the unit of the model is scaled as 10 cm in Unity. We place the location of the mother ball as the original point in the virtual coordinates. On the real table, we also set up the mother ball at the original position. For calibrating the position of the camera, the calibration process was done with OpenCV. But we found that if we sample some points with the calibrated parameters in three-dimensional space, there is a little shift with the depth data captured by the camera, as Fig. 2 shows. To fix this error, we re-estimate the camera position by assuming the table top is a plane and find out the transform between the depth data and the calibrated x-y plane.

Ponto et al. [14] have shown that in the VR environment, the judgment of depth and shape perceptions has significant differences from the real world. Part of the reason is derived from the estimation error of the eye's position, which is wider and deeper than previously thought. This situation makes operating in VR not as efficient as in the real world. We can alleviate this problem by sensing corrections. We can place a box in front of the screen and also render the same size virtual box on the screen close to the physical one. The correction method is to compare the edge of the two boxes and see if

Fig. 2. Camera calibration with OpenCV and the shift difference between the captured depth and the calibrated estimation.

the edge is straight or not with a stick. Half of the straight line renders on the screen, and half is in the physical world. If all the parameters are well estimated, the line, even crossing the boundary, should still be a straight line. If not, the location of the observation point may not be determined correctly.

3.2 Physical Event Capturing

To simulate the real ball rolling into the virtual environment, we must detect the trajectory of the ball first. Because we set the ball in a fixed position, when it leaves its place, we can begin to check the movement of its trajectory and its movement speed. Having the direction and speed, then, we can simulate the real ball rolling into the virtual environment. To track the motion of ball and also to keep the performance in real-time, we will try to avoid using an algorithm that is too complex. Since the platform is well calibrated, the size of the mother ball is known, and the mother ball is placed in a fixed position, we can check the ball's region. First, the Canny filter detects the edge. Then, pixels located between the boundaries can be selected to perform the Circle Hough Transform. Figure 3 shows the input region from the depth map and the resulting renders in three-dimensional space. Where the white pixels are the input

(a)　The green region is the input pixels　　　　(b) result

Fig. 3. Input region and its result renders in 3D (Color figure online)

pixels, the red ball is at the estimated location. The Circle Hough Transform only checks the plane which parallels the table top and the center of the ball pass. In the first run, we will check with different heights to make sure the size is correct. Figure 4 are the results in various planes. The physical radius is 19 mm, which has the maximum value.

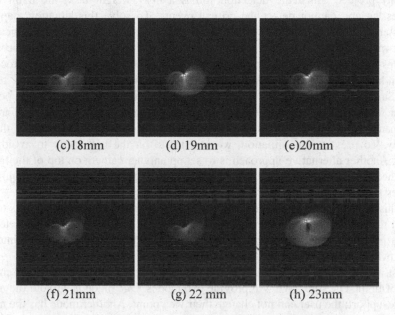

(c)18mm   (d) 19mm   (e)20mm

(f) 21mm   (g) 22 mm   (h) 23mm

Fig. 4. Circle Hough Transform estimated in different planes.

Radkowski and Oliver [15] tried to have a real scene, allowing the user to have the feeling of moving parallax. For simulating the moving parallax effect, the system has to track the position of the head and the eye's motion. They use the OpenCV Haar classifier to find the location of the face and the ARtoolkit to track its location. Since the Realsense SDK's face module already has this function, that makes things easier. However, its result is not stable because of noise. Thus, we use the Kalman filter to provide a smooth estimation.

For simulating the user walking around the table, the system needs to recognize hand gestures. Realsense SDK provides the hand tracking module for gesture detection. To avoid misevaluation of the event, a user should raise their palm first to confirm preparation to get into the gesture recognition mode. The system will provide a handle for grasping. The user can move their index finger toward the palm center just like seizing the handle. Then, the user can move their hand toward their right side to simulate walking around the table in a counterclockwise direction, or vice versa by moving toward the left side as walking in a clockwise direction.

4   Result

The physical event capturing process consists of ball tracking, eye tracking, and hand tracking. All are implemented in C++. The main program is developed in Unity for visualization and user interface. Original, the capture function is applied as a plugin for the Unity project. Since the detection job is a heavyweight task, the main thread becomes lag and cannot detect the critical events. To solve this situation, capturing process and Unity process are two separated process and each one communicates to another with a named pipe. With this configuration, the frame rate of Unity process can be 50 fps for rendering at a resolution of 1920 × 1080. For the capturing process, it also can keep about 10 to 30 fps when with eye tracking and without a case, respectively. Since only one camera is used, it should cover the head pose and ball position together. Thus, making the detection of the ball position harder in such a small area. Its performance should be pretty good otherwise it cannot detect the motion of the ball correctly. To prevent this situation, we will try to hit the ball softly to avoid rapid motion. Another alternative approach is to set up another camera on top of the table to detect the movement of the ball only. It will make thing easier, but an extra equipment becomes necessary.

In this project, what we want to know is how useful the motion parallax is to help the user realize the distance and orientation in a virtual environment, and to determine whether or not this platform can become an efficient training platform. We intend to design two experiments as follows:

First, we prepare a fixed layout of the ball and ask the user to hit the ball into the pocket with the cue stick. We will provide two modes. One mode is without the motion parallax support; the user can not change their viewpoint. Another mode has the motion parallax function; the user can alter their viewpoint by moving their head. We will divide participants into two groups which are without or with motion parallax function mode respectively. Mainly, we will compare their performance by counting their failure rate.

Second, we will verify whether such a platform is an excellent training tool or not. The participants also will be divided into two groups. They will pass a test on a real table to compare their performance. One group can practice in our platform before the testing. Another group will not allow practicing.

After the experiment, all participants will provide feedback about their satisfaction. We want to figure out that in the personal view of users whether the moving parallax is helpful or not, and if it is an efficient training platform or not.

At the initial trial, we find that the performance will be dominated by their experience and the system still not easy let the user hit the ball into the pocket right now. Thus, we adjust the performance comparison in an individual base. Each one will compare the performance by their self. And, if the mother ball can hit the ball then we will count it as a success event. In the beginning, the view direction of the display camera is parallel with the table surface. The user is not easy to hit the ball. After changing the view angle turns to look down at the front of the table. Without motion parallax function mode, users only 30% can hit the ball. And, most of the success event the ball is in front of the mother ball. With motion parallax function the success rate is more than 70%. With motion parallax function, the system can provide a more realistic position for the user to aim.

Our experiment runs on a Microsoft Surface Pro tablet. For measuring the exact angle for each shot, an angle measurement sheet place on the table. The system also will show the best angle as a hint to lead user how to hit the mother ball. For emulating a motion parallax effect, the different views based on different observing position are shown in Fig. 5.

Fig. 5. Different views from different observing position

5   Future Work and Conclusion

Right now, the system just can be an auxiliary training platform. There are some situations which need more study.

First, the reaction among balls and the table top is not real enough. The friction coefficient and the collision coefficient between the balls and the table are not calculated from the real world. We may need to consider more experiments to capture the real behavior to determine the right coefficient and let the behavior be closer to the real reaction.

Currently, the mother ball is at a fixed position, and only the ball can go into the virtual world to be active with other balls. But in a real situation, the virtual ball also has the possibility to enter the actual area. Maybe we can recreate the layout from the virtual world to solve this problem. In future, we may add a projector to help mark the location of the ball from the virtual position into the physical desktop. Then, the platform could go beyond a training platform. It could become a real game. The users can play together or through the internet.

The system does not monitor the various ways of the ball rolling. It just simulates a follow shot. In general techniques, it may also be a back shot or a stop shot. Additionally, for the purpose of enhancing the training, we may display some guidance information to help user how to aim the target.

A physical system has the natural benefits of being limited by its physics. The virtual world has its flexibility but lacks the real sensory input. How to capture the reality to construct a better simulation in this project is a good beginning.

References

1. Kersten-Oertel, M., Jannin, P., Collins, D.L.: The state of the art of visualization in mixed reality image guided surgery. Comput. Med. Imaging Graph. **37**(2), 98–112 (2013)
2. Bj, S., et al.: Designing ubiquitous computing games - a report from a workshop exploring ubiquitous computing entertainment. Pers. Ubiquitous Comput. **6**(5–6), 443–458 (2002)
3. Pan, Z., et al.: Virtual reality and mixed reality for virtual learning environments. Comput. Graph. **30**(1), 20–28 (2006)
4. Kuo, H.-C., et al.: GaussMarbles: spherical magnetic tangibles for interacting with portable physical constraints. In: Proceedings of the 2016 CHI Conference on Human Factors in Computing Systems, pp. 4228–4232. ACM, Santa Clara (2016)
5. van Veen, R.: Real-time self-generated motion parallax on a personal mobile display (2016)
6. Steinicke, F., Bruder, G., Kuhl, S.: Realistic perspective projections for virtual objects and environments. ACM Trans. Graph. **30**(5), 1–10 (2011)
7. Langbehn, E., et al.: Visual blur in immersive virtual environments: does depth of field or motion blur affect distance and speed estimation? In: Proceedings of the 22nd ACM Conference on Virtual Reality Software and Technology, pp. 241–250. ACM, Munich (2016)
8. Dey, A., Sandor, C.: Lessons learned: Evaluating visualizations for occluded objects in handheld augmented reality. Int. J. Hum.-Comput. Stud. **72**(10), 704–716 (2014)
9. Palmer, S.E.: Vision Science: Photons to Phenomenology. The MIT Press Cambridge (1999)
10. Read, J.: Early computational processing in binocular vision and depth perception. Progress Biophys. Mol. Biol. **87**(1), 77–108 (2005)
11. Chapoulie, E., et al.: Finger-based manipulation in immersive spaces and the real world. In: 2015 IEEE Symposium on 3D User Interfaces (3DUI). IEEE (2015)
12. Alves, R., Sousa, L., Rodrigues, J.: PoolLiveAid: augmented reality pool table to assist inexperienced players (2013)
13. Hu, J.S., Chang, Y.J.: Automatic calibration of hand-eye-workspace and camera using hand-mounted line laser. IEEE/ASME Trans. Mechatron. **18**(6), 1778–1786 (2013)
14. Ponto, K., et al.: Perceptual calibration for immersive display environments. IEEE Trans. Vis. Comput. Graph. **19**(4), 691–700 (2013)
15. Radkowski, R., Oliver, J.: Simulation of motion parallax for monitor-based augmented reality applications. In: ASME 2013 International Design Engineering Technical Conferences and Computers and Information in Engineering Conference. American Society of Mechanical Engineers (2013)
16. Teittinen, M.: Depth cues in the human visual system. http://www.hitl.washington.edu/scivw/EVE/III.A.1.c.DepthCues.html
17. Hammond, B.: A computer vision tangible user interface for mixed reality billiards. In: 2008 IEEE International Conference on Multimedia and Expo, Hannover, pp. 929–932 (2008)

Operating Virtual Panels with Hand Gestures in Immersive VR Games

Experiences with the Leap Motion Controller

Yin Zhang and Oscar Meruvia-Pastor[✉]

Department of Computer Science, Memorial University of Newfoundland,
St Johns, NL A1B 3X7, Canada
oscar@mun.ca
http://www.cs.mun.ca/~omeruvia/research

Abstract. Portable depth-sensing cameras allow users to control interfaces using hand gestures at a short range from the camera. These technologies are being combined with virtual reality (VR) headsets to produce immersive VR experiences that respond more naturally to user actions. In this research, we explore gesture-based interaction in immersive VR games by using the Unity game engine, the LeapMotion sensor, a laptop, a smartphone, and the Freefly VR headset. By avoiding Android deployment, this novel setup allowed for fast prototyping and testing of different ideas for immersive VR interaction, at an affordable cost. We implemented a system that allows users to play a game in a virtual world and compared placements of the leap motion sensor on the desk and on the headset. In this experimental setup, users interacted with a numeric dial panel and then played a Tetris game inside the VR environment by pressing the buttons of a virtual panel. The results suggest that, although the tracking quality of the Leap Motion sensor was rather limited when used in the head-mounted setup for pointing and selection tasks, its performance was much better in the desk-mounted setup, providing a novel platform for research and rapid application development.

1 Introduction

Virtual Reality (VR) gaming platforms have become quite popular, with VR headsets such as the Oculus Rift [22], HTC Vive [15], PlayStation VR [25] and Samsung Gear VR [23] being released recently. In spite of their novelty, these devices are not part of the first wave of attempts to bring VR into the consumer market. Back in 1995, the Virtual Boy [8], released by Nintendo, stands out as one of the exemplars of the first wave of commercial virtual reality devices, which did not manage to establish a permanent market for the technology. Some of the reasons for the failure of earlier waves to establish permanent markets include a lack of usability, reduced user adoption, and the high cost of earlier VR technologies.

The most recent rising of commercially available Virtual Reality owes credit in part to Palmer Luckey [7] who founded Oculus back in 2012.

© Springer International Publishing AG 2017
L.T. De Paolis et al. (Eds.): AVR 2017, Part I, LNCS 10324, pp. 299–308, 2017.
DOI: 10.1007/978-3-319-60922-5_24

Fig. 1. Experimental setup for operation of virtual panels through hand gestures.

His Oculus VR headsets set off a new wave of interest in Virtual Reality which continues until today. In the meantime, Apple [29], Samsung and HTC helped popularize the modern smartphone with high-resolution screens, accurate motion (and other) sensors and compact form factors that made them an appropriate fit to the technology required to make convincing VR.

As Google Cardboard [10] first illustrated in 2014 and later Samsung with the Gear VR in 2015, a low-cost, affordable and more casual form of VR using Smartphones is possible. By sliding a smartphone into a head-mounted display, users can get access into relatively simple virtual worlds. In addition to this, there was another significant development in the hardware that contributed to a more complete and affordable VR experience: portable, short-range depth sensing cameras [2]. Portable and short range depth sensors allow computing devices such as PCs, laptops and smartphones to capture its immediate environment as well as help identify a user's hands and/or face in the proximity of the devices [13,21,24,28].

In this work, we use the Leap Motion as the depth sensing camera and as a gesture recognition device. As shown in Fig. 1, the Leap Motion controller is originally designed to be placed on a physical desktop, facing upward, or it can also be mounted on a VR headset for first-person interaction [1]. The device uses three LED emitters to illuminate the surrounding space with IR light, which is reflected back from the nearby objects and captured by two IR cameras [18]. The device's software installed on the connected PC will analyze the captured images in real-time, determine the position of objects, and perform the recognition of users' hands and fingers. Its suitability for a variety of tasks has been the focus of recent research [1,3,12,27].

The motivation of this research is to explore VR gesture control with a low-cost combination of equipment, including a smartphone, an infrared controller and a VR headset, to address implementation challenges and propose solutions to overcome the major barriers to being able to control, with hand motions and gestures, a simple VR game. In this research, we tested our software with four users, who tested the system under the 4 conditions described below (2 hardware setups X 2 applications) and provided unstructured feedback on their experience. Through the implementation of this project, we show how a low cost solution to develop VR applications using a laptop, Unity, a VR Headset, an Android phone and the Leap Motion controller can be used to address existing limitations and suggest solutions to usability issues in these platforms.

2 Implementation

2.1 Project Setup

This research is implemented in Unity 5.3 on OS X El Capitan system on a MacBook PRO. In addition, we have the Leap Motion SDK_Mac_2.3.1, Splashtop Streamer [26], as well as Leap Motion Core Asset 2_3_1 [19] package installed in the Unity engine. Meanwhile, the Samsung S5 phone is equipped with the Splashtop Streamer client and is inserted in the Freefly VR [9] headset.

The Leap Motion SDK connects the Leap Motion controller to the computer, allowing the captured data from the Leap motion to be delivered to the analyzing software on the computer in real-time (see Fig. 2). The Leap Motion Core Asset package, which is imported into the Unity engine, will function as the connector between the Unity engine and the Leap Motion analyzing software, which translates the input data from the analyzing software as a control signal and generate the corresponding hand model and gestures. The Splashtop Streamer mirrors the PC screen onto any mobile devices with the Splashstop client installed and in the same network. This novel setup allows us to avoid Android depolyment, as the program executes dircclty from the laptop to the HMD. This makes development much faster than the process of deploying an executable for the HMD (an Android phone) oach time the source code changes. A prototype in development can be tested using the actual HMD rather than on a software android simulator running on the laptop.

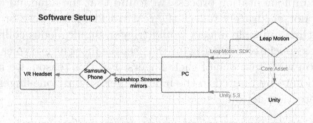

Fig. 2. Software setup flow chart.

As for the Hardware part, the Leap Motion sensor is always connected to the PC through the USB port, whereas the Samsung phone is wirelessly connected, mirroring the PC screen. The Samsung Phone is slid into the Free Fly VR headset and calibrated for horizontal and vertical axis with the help of the Free Fly VR SDK (see Fig. 3). In this research, we tested two conditions with regards to the location of the Leap motion controller, either horizontally placed on the desk with the device looking up (referred to as "desk-mounted") or mounted on top of the VR headset facing away from the user's head (or "head-mounted").

Fig. 3. Hardware setup.

2.2 Applications

Dial Panels. To explore the experience of point touch accuracy using the Leap Motion gesture controller, we simulated the dial panel with 9 number buttons and two symbol buttons: # and * (see Fig. 4). The button's color will change in response to users' actions upon detection of a collision with the toggle buttons of the panel. A box collider component placed on each button allows buttons to react to a virtual collision with the hand model generated by the Leap Motion SDK. Multiple canvas layers on each button work under the button color changing script, allowing it to change colour when it is picked by the hand model to provide a clear visual feedback.

Shadow casting has been previously found useful to localize objects in virtual environments [6,11,16]. In our system, a shadow of the controlling hand is cast along with the hand model on a panel plane beneath the buttons layer, to provide a sense of the distance between the hand and the panel through visual feedback.

During the implementation process, we found that the hand model generated sometimes did not accurately reflect the real world's hand pose or position. In addition, sometime multiple fingers would trigger simultaneous collisions on the panel. This was especially confusing for the user, as most users typically intended to push a button with just one of their fingers. For this reason, we modified the collision detection to be limited to the index finger, so only one finger can trigger the collision detection action.

Games. We also implemented the well-known Tetris game [20], which is displayed within the VR environment (see Fig. 8). The game is controlled by the user through a control panel which is placed besides the falling blocks. The user then moves his or her hand around and presses on the buttons that will control whether the falling block is displaced to the left or right, sped towards the bottom, or rotated around. For the implementation of the game control, we built a game control engine. The game control functions described above are triggered by detecting the collision between the buttons in the control panel and the hand model (see Fig. 5).

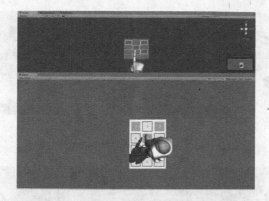

Fig. 4. Dial panel.

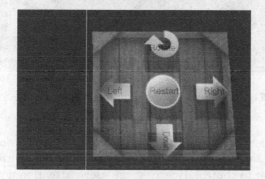

Fig. 5. Tetris control panel.

Comparison Between Head-Mounted and Desk-Mounted Leap Motion Placement. Both the implementation of the dial panel and the Tetris game are compared under head-mounted and desk-placed conditions. The leap motion is horizontally placed on the desk in the desk-placed condition, whereas it is mounted on to the top of the VR headset facing outside away from the user's head in the head-mounted situation (see Fig. 6). The complete setup with the four experimental conditions is shown in the accompanying video available at our website.

3   Results and Evaluation

When testing the implementation of the dial panel we obtained a stable result where users can predict the placement of the hand using the shadow effect and easily choose the button using the output information provided by the visual feedback (see Fig. 7).

As for the implementation of the Tetris game, the control panel can be difficult to operate during play. As a result of various evaluation sessions, we figured out several modifications on the gaming control panel regarding the size,

Fig. 6. Leap motion positon comparison.

Fig. 7. Screen capture of dial panel simulation.

transparency, shadow effects and the visual feedback on collision, with the goal of improving the user experience. Eventually, the game's control panel became reachable and easier to control. However, the user's attention needed to correctly operate the panel was still causing some distraction when trying to control the blocks. Overall, the control panel did not feel as comfortable as using a regular keyboard, from the point of view of the gaming experience (see Fig. 8). This is in line with Barret and Krueger [4], who found that typing performance suffers when applying keystrokes on planar surfaces when compared to keystrokes on actual physical keys that displace upon typing. We hypothesize that the lack of haptic feedback on a planar virtual keyboard further reduces the user's performance.

With regards to the comparisons of the head-mounted versus desk-mounted conditions for the location of the Leap Motion controller, the head-mounted version more closely resembles the original setup of the Oculus Rift combined with the Leap Motion sensor, as used in most head-mounted setups [5,14]. This eliminated the dependency between the user's hand and the placement of the sensor on the table or desk. However, we noticed that the Leap Motion controller did not behave as effectively as when placed on the desk and so the hand tracking was not as stable as in the desk-placed configuration. We hypothesize this is mainly because the user's hand orientation when pointing out was somewhat parallel to the line of sight of the Leap Motion controller, making it especially challenging for the internal Leap Motion algorithms to estimate the correct hand pose.

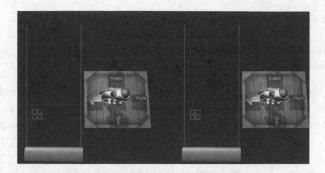

Fig. 8. Screen capture of tetris game.

We found that the lack of haptic feedback in the prototype developed caused some sensory confusion. It was hard for users to figure out the depth of the panels containing the buttons to be clicked. Through the whole implementation of this research, we found out that achieving stable tracking and making sure the control panel was reachable and usable were the most challenging aspects of this work.

3.1 Motion Sensor Limitations

It has been reported that the Leap Motion controller does not perform in a way that can be reliably used as a professional tracking system [12] and that its performance as an input device for everyday generic computer pointing tasks is rather limited when compared with standard input devices [3]. In addition, we have found that the current version of the Leap Motion controller and the Leap Motion SDK provides at times unsatisfactory tracking results, in part due to the following technical limitations:

– The LeapMotion SDK doesn't produce an RGBD depth map, so it limits the general tracking of objects in 3D and the general usability of the controller when compared to other depth-sensing controllers that provide an RGBD image, such as Intel's RealSense [17] and Occipital's Structure sensor [21].
– Other items within the neighborhood of the hand (such as a piece of paper behind the hand) can cause the system to loose track of the hand altogether.
– The SDK's ability to correctly estimate the hand pose seem to vary, depending on where the controller is placed (desk- vs head-mounted). In particular, the current version of the Leap Motion SDK produces reduced tracking quality in the head-mounted configuration, especially when the user is making a fist, with hand poses where the fingers are pointing towards the depth-direction and parallel to the device's line of sight, and when the user has a single finger extended with the rest as a fist.

4   Insights on Interaction Improvement

After the implementation of the applications mentioned above, we came up with several suggestions for improving the interaction:

- Providing visual feedback by means of projecting a shadow of the hand model on the control panels made a positive contribution for users trying to assess how far to move their hand to press on the buttons of the panels. This was even more relevant the first time users were interacting with the system, as it was the time when they were forming a mental map of the relationship between their own hand movements and the representation of the hand model shown within the VR environment.
- A more natural choice for an application like the Tetris game would be the swipe gesture, where the blocks are displaced to the left or to the right by a physical waving of the hand within the VR scene.
- The lack of haptic feedback was disconcerting for most users, since it was easy for the hand controller to pass through the button and past the back of the virtual panel, making it hard to know when the button was clicked. For this reason, an additional controller, such as a joystick, or the hand-held button clicker device provided by the Freefly VR, might be better able to indicate the button click operation rather than using a pressing motion of the fingers to indicate a button click.
- Providing auditory feedback by having the users hear a sound when a button is clicked would help users to become certain that the button click operation was successfully registered.
- Current technologies can already bring users to experience an immersive VR experience at a low cost, but more reliable gesture controllers and better depth-sensing SDK's are still needed.

5   Conclusions

The built-in Leap Motion hand detection system presents some limitations in estimating the pose of a user's hand in the real world, but it still constitutes a workable device for rapid prototyping of real world gaming environment conditions, particularly when the controller is placed on the desk. At times, the lack of stability of the controller prevented the users from concentrating on playing the game itself. The low-cost smartphone used as a VR display, with the support from a simple and lightweight VR headset and a desk-placed depth sensor constitutes a convenient and affordable method for VR development for people who want to try the technology at early stages of development. Any game or similarly suitable type of application can be directly mirrored from the laptop to the proposed configuration, allowing for fast development of prototypes for research and evaluation of new ideas. We plan to expand this work with a user study where we compare the performance outcomes of people using the Leap Motion in the desk-mounted setup versus the head-mounted configuration across a variety of tasks within the VR environment.

References

1. Adhikarla, V.K., Sodnik, J., Szolgay, P., Jakus, G.: Exploring direct 3d interaction for full horizontal parallax light field displays using leap motion controller. Sensors 15(4), 8642–8663 (2015)
2. Arthur, K.W.: Effects of field of view on performance with head-mounted displays. Ph.D. thesis, University of North Carolina at Chapel Hill (2000)
3. Bachmann, D., Weichert, F., Rinkenauer, G.: Evaluation of the leap motion controller as a new contact-free pointing device. Sensors 15(1), 214 (2015). http://www.mdpi.com/1424-8220/15/1/214
4. Barret, J., Krueger, H.: Performance effects of reduced proprioceptive feedback on touch typists and casual users in a typing task. Behav. Inf. Technol. 13(6), 373–381 (1994). http://dx.doi.org/10.1080/01449299408914618
5. Beattie, N., Horan, B., McKenzie, S.: Taking the leap with the oculus HMD and CAD - plucking at thin air? In: Proceedings of The 1st International Design Technology Conference, DESTECH2015, vol. 20, pp. 149–154. Elsevier (2015). http://www.sciencedirect.com/science/article/pii/S2212017315002029
6. Besacier, G., Tournet, J., Goyal, N., Cento, F., Scott, S.D.: Object and arm shadows: Visual feedback for cross device transfer. In: CHI 2014 Extended Abstracts on Human Factors in Computing Systems, pp. 463–466, CHI EA 2014. ACM Press, New York (2014) http://doi.acm.org/10.1145/2559206.2574832
7. Clark, T.: How Palmer Luckey created Oculus rift, November 2014. http://www.smithsonianmag.com/innovation/how-palmer-luckey-created-oculus-rift-180953049/?no-ist/
8. Edward, B.: Unraveling the enigma of Nintendo's virtual boy, 20 years later, August 2015. http://www.fastcompany.com/3050016/unraveling-the-enigma-of-nintendos-virtual-boy-20-years-later/
9. FreeflyVR: Freefly VR: how does it work, the complete guide (2014). https://www.freeflyvr.com/freefly-vr-how-it-works/
10. Google Inc.: Google cardboard Google VR (2016). https://www.google.com/get/cardboard/
11. Greene, E.: Augmenting visual feedback using sensory substitution. Master's thesis, University of Waterloo (2011). https://uwspace.uwaterloo.ca/bitstream/handle/10012/6161/Greene_Eugene.pdf
12. Guna, J., Jakus, G., Poganik, M., Tomai, S., Sodnik, J.: An analysis of the precision and reliability of the leap motion sensor and its suitability for static and dynamic tracking. Sensors 14(2), 3702 (2014). http://www.mdpi.com/1424-8220/14/2/3702
13. Higuchi, M., Komuro, T.: [Paper] robust finger tracking for gesture control of mobile devices using contour and interior information of a finger. ITE Trans. Media Technol. Appl. 1(3), 226–236 (2013)
14. Hilfert, T., König, M.: Low-cost virtual reality environment for engineering and construction. Vis. Eng. 4(1), 1–18 (2016). http://dx.doi.org/10.1186/s40327-015-0031-5
15. HTC Corporation: Vive - Home (2016). https://www.htcvive.com/ca/
16. Hu, H.H., Gooch, A.A., Thompson, W.B., Smits, B.E., Rieser, J.J., Shirley, P.: Visual cues for imminent object contact in realistic virtual environment. In: Proceedings of the Conference on Visualization 2000, pp. 179–185, VIS 2000. IEEE Computer Society Press, Los Alamitos (2000). http://dl.acm.org/citation.cfm?id=375213.375238

17. Intel Corp.: Intel RealSense Technology. http://www.intel.com/content/www/us/en/architecture-and-technology/realsense-shortrange.html (2016)

18. Leap Motion Inc.: How Does the Leap Motion Controller Work? (2016). http://blog.leapmotion.com/hardware-to-software-how-does-the-leap-motion-controller-work/

19. Leap Motion Inc: Leap motion developers (2016). https://developer.leapmotion.com/unity/

20. Noobtuts.com: Unity 2D Tetris Tutorial (2012). http://noobtuts.com/unity/2d-tetris-game/

21. Occipital, Inc.: Structure Sensor - 3D scanning, augmented reality, and more for mobile devices (2016). http://structure.io/

22. OculusVR: Oculus (2016). https://www.oculus.com/en-us/

23. Samsung Corporation: Samsung gear VR - the official Samsung galaxy site (2016). http://www.samsung.com/global/galaxy/wearables/gear-vr/

24. Sharp, T., Keskin, C., Robertson, D., Taylor, J., Shotton, J., Kim, D., Rhemann, C., Leichter, I., Vinnikov, A., Wei, Y., Freedman, D., Kohli, P., Krupka, E., Fitzgibbon, A., Izadi, S.: Accurate, robust, and flexible real-time hand tracking. In: Proceedings of CHI, the 33rd Annual ACM Conference on Human Factors in Computing Systems. ACM Press, April 2015. http://research.microsoft.com/apps/pubs/default.aspx?id=238453

25. Sony Interactive Entertainment: PlayStation VR (2016). https://www.playstation.com/en-ca/explore/playstation-vr/

26. Splashtop Inc.: Top-performing remote desktop and remote support (2016). http://www.splashtop.com/

27. Weichert, F., Bachmann, D., Rudak, B., Fisseler, D.: Analysis of the accuracy and robustness of the leap motion controller. Sensors **13**(5), 6380 (2013). http://www.mdpi.com/1424-8220/13/5/6380

28. Welch, G., Bishop, G.: Scaat: Incremental tracking with incomplete information. In: Proceedings of the 24th annual conference on Computer graphics and interactive techniques, pp. 333–344. ACM Press/Addison-Wesley Publishing Co. (1997)

29. Whitwam, R.: How Steve Jobs killed the stylus and made smartphones usable, October 2011. http://www.extremetech.com/computing/98923-how-steve-jobs-killed-the-stylus-and-made-smartphones-usable/

Virtual Reality Toolset for Material Science: NOMAD VR Tools

Rubén Jesús García-Hernández[1]([✉]) and Dieter Kranzlmüller[1,2]

[1] Bavarian Academy of Sciences, Munich, Germany
{garcia,kranzlmueller}@lrz.de
[2] Ludwig-Maximilians-Universität, Munich, Germany

Abstract. We describe a free-software virtual reality system which provides material scientists with a tool to more easily study simulations of chemical systems at the atomic and molecular levels, and which is compatible with the NOMAD infrastructure (an international, open repository which is developing advanced analysis techniques and contains millions of materials). The system runs on multiple virtual reality hardware, from CAVE-like ($CAVE^{TM}$ is a trademark of the University of Illinois Board of Trustees. We use the term CAVE to denote the both the original system at Illinois and the multitude of variants developed by multiple organizations.) to phone-based. Informal talks with non-domain experts showed positive responses, and a user study was used to confirm the usefulness of the new system by domain experts.

Keywords: Portable VR · CAVE · User study · Material science · CaO · LiF

1 Introduction

In this paper we describe a collection of virtual reality tools for analyzing chemical systems in the context of material science. Materials are becoming more complex as user try to optimize for particular properties needed in industrial applications. Supercomputer-based simulations are used to investigate the characteristics of the material and its interaction with other chemicals. In order to effectively visualize the results of the simulations, 3D visualization is becoming a must. In the future, we expect the use of virtual reality techniques to prove invaluable for the study of especially complex materials.

The paper is structured as follows: The next section introduces NOMAD, a framework and database which produces an unified view on materials. Then, some related work in the virtual reality field regarding material science is presented. Section 2 introduces the hardware and SDKs which support our targeted systems. Section 3 describes in some detail two materials which we have used as test cases. Afterwards, Sect. 4 indicates the steps required to transform the datasets commonly used in material science for their use in our virtual reality framework, and provides an overview of the developed software. Finally, Sect. 5

L.T. De Paolis et al. (Eds.): AVR 2017, Part I, LNCS 10324, pp. 309–319, 2017.
DOI: 10.1007/978-3-319-60922-5_25

details a user study being performed with domain experts and presents preliminary results regarding the advantages of the system with respect to classical software. Section 6 concludes the paper.

1.1   NOMAD

The NOMAD repository [14] is an open database of materials (currently hosting more than three million entries), which accepts computer simulations using the most common software packages (called *codes* in the material science parlance).

On top of the repository, the center of excellence [13] is preparing an homogeneous and normalized database. Forty *codes* are supported, and development continues. An encyclopaedia allowing complex searches regarding the materials stored is being created. Big data analytics will also allow the discovery of descriptors which can be used to find the best material for a given use case lessening the need for expensive computer simulations of million of chemical compounds. Computations-on-demand are also envisioned. Within this project, advanced graphics (both remote visualization and virtual reality environments) will be used to provide better insights into the materials and their properties.

1.2   Virtual Reality in Material Science

Virtual Reality provides an immersive virtual world which allows users to enjoy a different reality. 3D glasses and tracking hardware transfer the user to a computer-generated environment, which they can explore and interact with in an intuitive manner. High quality visual and auditive stimuli make the user feel the virtual world as real, commonly also including subconscious responses. The environment can be used for gaming (most commonly), but also for learning, training, research or even for medical treatment of illnesses such as phobias.

In the material science field, Dobrzanski and Honysz [7] describes a virtual laboratory where users can perform experiments, to be used to practice before using real laboratory equipment, where mistakes can be very expensive. Other similar systems in the experimental chemistry field also exist, e.g. Chemistry Lab VR [16].

In contrast, the work presented here presents the user with the result of three-dimensional simulations of materials at the atomic scale, effectively shrinking the user to the femtometric scale.

There are some virtual reality viewers of chemical reactions, mostly used for educational purposes. For example, alcohol metabolism is explored by Yang et al. [17]. Our work instead provides a general framework for any chemical reaction, and is focused towards research and industry applications.

Fig. 1. CAVE-like system (left), HTC Vive (center) and Samsung GearVR (right)

2 Targeted APIs and Systems

See Fig. 1 for an overview of the systems targeted. We are supporting the OpenVR[1] and Oculus Mobile[2] SDKs, which while they have been optimized to target specific hardware at the moment (HTC Vive and Samsung GearVR respectively), they are designed to support additional hardware for multiple vendors. OpenVR also supports Oculus Rift.

For the CAVE-like environment at the Leibniz Supercomputing Centre of the Bavarian Academy of Sciences (LRZ), we use an in-house set of libraries which take care of synchronization among the nodes and the projectors.

The system (Fig. 1, left) is composed of a cubic, five-wall installation with 2.7 m sides. Each side is back-projected using two full-HD stereo projectors which are handled by one rack-mounted PC each. Mirrors are used to reduce the space needed. One extra computer is used for control, tracking and synchronization.

We use tracking hardware from Advanced Realtime Tracking (ART) [4]: a Flystick 3 and tracked stereo glasses. Although only one person can be tracked at a time, we have found collaboration with up to three people is quite comfortable, with users looking from behind the tracked users's elbows and obtaining an almost-correct perspective.

In order to have portable tools, we need to ensure that device-independent code can be shared among the different devices. However, due to the lower processing power of mobile devices, we are forced to use a simplified rendering algorithm and to limit the size of the datasets in some cases. The input interface layer must also be tailored for each device.

3 Use Cases

We have chosen two use cases: a chemical reaction (4D dataset, space + time) and exploration of excitons (6D dataset, 3D electron density for each 3D electron hole position) The 6D dataset is especially interesting for virtual reality, as it is unfeasible for exploration in a normal monitor and it decomposes nicely into two 3D subdomains in virtual reality.

---

[1] https://github.com/ValveSoftware/openvr.
[2] https://developer.oculus.com/mobile.

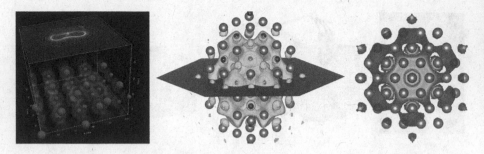

Fig. 2. Adsorption of CO_2 on CaO(001) surface, using the Paraview software [1] (left), and exciton in LiF, shown in 3D (center) or 2D (right), using the Vesta software [12]

3.1 Adsorption of Carbon Dioxide on a Calcium Oxide surface

Carbon dioxide is used in many industrial applications for a variety of purposes. Activation of carbon dioxide is an important step for a further catalytic conversion of CO_2 to useful chemicals (e.g., methane) to make renewable fuels. In addition, carbon dioxide capture and storage [9] is also one of the techniques proposed to mitigate global warning. Calcium oxide based materials are used for this purpose. Therefore, finding materials which can be used to bind carbon dioxide optimally is of great interest both in the scientific and industry communities.

Our first use case is a molecular dynamics simulation of a molecule of CO_2 (3 atoms) on a CaO (001) surface (32 atoms), using a total of 35 atoms for 423 timesteps spanning 6752 fs (see Fig. 2, left). From the simulation, we can learn how electron density and vibrational energy redistribute upon adsorption of CO_2 on CaO at a finite temperature. A series of such simulations would allow us to choose a better material for CO_2 capture and conversion.

Interface. In the case of the GearVR, swiping up and down change the timestep, while swiping forward and backwards allows the user to fly in the gaze direction. The back button cycles among the isosurfaces, atoms, and everything.

In the Vive, the triggers allow smooth movement in space and time, while the side buttons move the current isosurface and timestep in discrete steps.

In the CAVE, the joystick allows you to move and rotate the object, while the buttons move you in time. The trigger can be used to cycle the isosurfaces.

3.2 Excitons in Lithium Fluoride

Excitons are bound states of an electron and an electron hole, created when a sufficiently energetic photon interacts with an electron and makes the electron move to a different energy level. They influence the behavior of a material on absorption and emission of light, and are important in opto-electronic applications such as solar cells and lighting devices. Photocathalysis and water splitting are other applications. Excitons in lithium fluoride are a very well studied phenomena [10] so the study of this system with virtual reality tools provides a good baseline to compare against classical tools.

Our second use case is a simulation of the electron density around 344 Lithium and 342 Fluor atoms in a cubic crystal structure, performed for each hole position (see Fig. 2, center and right; in 90% of the cases, researchers are using 2D slices).

Interface. The hole positions are indicated by a cube of dots located above the controller. One of the dots is marked to indicate the current hole position, and the points are colour coded according to the maximum density at that position. The current hole position can be changed by clicking the controller while pointing it in the direction desired.

The other controller (for the Vive) shows the available isosurfaces. Two buttons can be used to discard non-required isosurfaces and to choose the current isosurface. In the case of the CAVE, the trigger can be used to select whether the isosurface or the hole changes.

4   Data Preparation and Developed Software

In the following sections, we describe the input, processing and output of the pipeline used to prepare the data for our VR software, and the software itself.

4.1   Input

We use as input a collection of gaussian cube files [5], which contain a discretized, volumetric representation of electron densities, and a user selection of isovalues.

In the case of the $CaO+CO_2$ reaction, each of the cubes represent one timestep of the reaction. The resolution is $101 \times 101 \times 184$ for the full density simulation and $51 \times 51 \times 97$ for the relative density simulation. In both cases, 423 timesteps were simulated. Isovalues at 0.85, 2.00, 3.95 and 18.36 were chosen for the demo which was shown to non-expert users, as these can be used to highlight the chemical bond. For domain experts, we used 0.01, 0.05, 0.1, and 0.5 for the full densities and 0.1, 0.05, 0.025, 0.01 (both positive and negative) for the relative densities. These values were requested by a domain expert.

Respectively for the LiF excitons, each of the cubes represent the electron density for a given position of the hole. The resolution is 81^3 and the hole position was selected from an 11^3 grid, resulting in 1331 input files. As the electron density depends strongly on the distance between the hole position and the atom positions, we chose isosurfaces as a percentage of maximum densities for this demo. In a first step, isosurfaces from 10% to 80% at 10% intervals were used to find the most interesting hole positions and density levels. Then, after discovering that the region around 20% was to be studied in more detail, isosurfaces from 14% to 26% at 2% intervals were chosen by a domain expert.

4.2 Processing

The cube files had to be extended by one unit in each direction to allow the correct extraction of isosurfaces in the case of periodic data, using a python script. Paraview with python scripting was used to export vrml [2] for each isosurface and for the atoms. MeshLab [6] was used to port these vrml files to ply, and for mesh simplification in the case of the first demo. LODs at 50%, 25%, 6% and 2% were used.

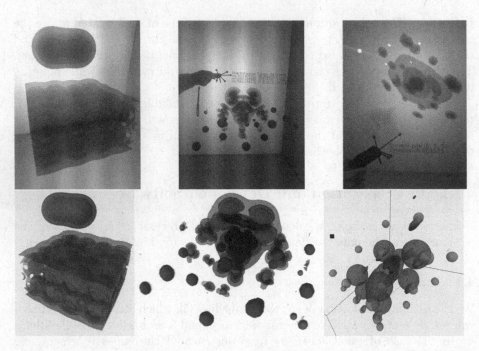

Fig. 3. Top: LRZ CAVE-like environment. Bottom: HTC Vive. CO_2+CaO(001), full densities (left), relative densities (center). LiF exciton (right)

4.3 Developed Software

For the chemical reaction, we have developed a viewer which allows us to move in space and in time, and to show isosurfaces and atoms using isosurface transparency to simulate volumetric rendering. In the case of the GearVR, a low-cost, order-independent additive blending [15] is used. In the other systems, a higher quality depth peeling algorithm [8] is used instead. Isosurfaces and atoms can also be shown as opaque surfaces when needed. Some more details about the adaptations of the interface for the specific usecases can be seen in Sect. 3.

In the case of the GearVR, memory limitations force us to show only half the timesteps for the CO_2+CaO full densities demo. In the case of the LiF demo, we have encountered a GCC bug [11] which we are investigating how to mitigate.

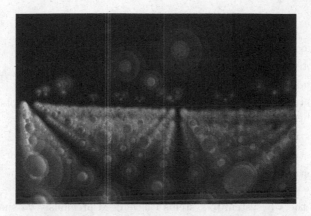

Fig. 4. CO_2+CaO(001), full densities (left), 7×7 repetitions using LOD simplification

Images of the software in action can be seen in Fig. 3. The software produced will be distributed as free software under the Apache 2.0 license [3].

5   User Study and Discussion

We did not try to distinguish which of the supported systems was better. The optimal system depends on the needs and budget of each organization, with the CAVE-like system allowing easy collaboration among multiple researchers (at a much higher cost), while the GearVR can provide a quick overview of the system at a moderate cost; the Vive system is a compromise solution. We think having a portable system which runs on multiple architectures and having users choose the hardware in accordance with their needs is a more user-friendly approach. Therefore, the purpose of the user study is to compare the systems to the classical, non-immersive PC solutions commonly used in material science.

We have presented an early prototype of the system running on HTC Vive (see Fig. 4) to non-domain experts in various public events. The responses were positive, but we did not do a formal user study.

After we prepared demos using isovalues selected by experts on the relevant systems, other experts were shown the systems on the different supported architectures and asked to perform a post-questionnaire using both a 7-point Likert scale and textual answers (questionnaire in Table 1). We distinguish between domain experts and students to assert whether the tool can also be used in teaching and to take into account the fact that domain experts have years of experience using the classic systems, while they very often have not used virtual reality hardware before. We currently are in the process of data collection. Our null hypothesis is that the answer to the questions is 4 (neutral towards the system). The preliminary data analysis of the 15 participants yields a statistically significant advantage (at 95% confidence level, critical value 2,145) of the VR system for questions 1 $(4,67 \pm 2,23, t = 2,32)$, 3 $(5,20 \pm 2,41, t = 3,85)$, 4

Table 1. Post-questionnaire

1	I find navigating the VR system easier
2	I find interacting with the VR system easier
3	I find understanding the visualization in the VR system easier
4	I think students will have an easier time understanding concepts by the use of the VR system
5	I think students will find navigating the VR system easier
6	I think students will find interacting with the VR system easier
7	I think students will find understanding the visualization in the VR system easier
8	I prefer the VR system to systems I have used previously for similar tasks
9	In general, do you think the use of VR in this specific example is positive or negative?
10	Can you foresee having an easier time discovering new phenomena by using VR systems like this?
11	Can you think of any study which can be performed more easily on the VR than in classic systems?
12	Can you think of any study which can be performed more easily on the classic systems?
13	Can you think of any additional benefits of the VR representation?
14	Can you think of any additional drawbacks of the VR representation?

$(5,40 \pm 2,37,$ t $= 4,58)$, and 7 $(5,00 \pm 2,39,$ t $= 3,24)$. We report the 95% interval as $\mu \pm 2\sigma$.

Interaction (questions 2 and 5) and navigation (question 6) at $4,40 \pm 2,11$, t $= 1,47$, $4,33 \pm 2,69$, t $= 0,96$, and $4,27 \pm 3,34$, t $= 0,62$, respectively, are only found to be slightly easier in the VR system, and the results for these questions are not significant. More work needs to be done to provide an easier-to-use system. Question 8 $(4,20 \pm 2,64,$ t $= 0,59)$ indicates a non-significant, slight preference for VR use.

A general view was used by averaging the answers to questions 1–8. The result is $4,683 \pm 1,997$, t $= 2,65$: slight, but significant, preference for the VR system.

Users provided in questions 9–14 valuable input about their views on the advantages, disadvantages and application areas of the system. In general, the answers to question 9 were positive towards the VR system, while 10 had 6 positive and 3 negative answers. The many possible studies mentioned in question 11 and 12 show that both VR and classical software systems will coexist with each providing advantages in different scenarios. Textual comments by users follow:

With respect to new discoveries using VR (question 10), VR can provide new insight for the following reason: Manual inspection of large datasets is impossible, i.e. the person who has carried out the calculation would need to screen every electron/hole combination to get the full picture. While this is still possible for simple systems like LiF, it is not feasible for complex materials. Also, with the VR tools in hand, this knowledge is accessible to a larger community.

The following studies were presumed to be performed more easily in VR (question 11): Cosmology/star formation studies, 4D systems like time evolution, space-time systems, trajectories, dynamical phenomena, chemical reactions, Complicated systems with a lot of detail, and some tasks within certain studies.

On the contrary, some studies are perceived to be easier to perform on classical systems (question 12): 3D excitons, Rayleigh-Jeans instability, where you usually represent your results with a single slice through the volume, 2D visualizations allow for plots that are more easily analyzed at the PC and presented in talks or publications, 3D visualizations without VR, which allows for projections along different crystal axes (giving insights into the symmetry of the wavefunction). In the case of simple systems, non-VR is also preferred.

The advantages of the system (question 13) are: providing a better representation and understanding of the spatial extension/distribution of phenomena, more complete understanding of the problem, allowing the user to directly interact with the representation, powerful visualization tools for specific excitations where the real-space character is of particular interest, such as charge-transfer excitons (helping understand the influence of the wavefunction on both hole and electron position), and scanning for interesting configurations could be easier. In particular, rotating a complex 3D system using the traditional 2D display is hard, and there is potential to become easier than an equivalent 2D system. It is much easier to focus on certain parts of a complicated system. It is also an attractive educational instrument for young students, and allows broader outreach to the non-scientific audience.

With respect to drawbacks (question 14): there is a possibility of over-interpretation of the visual data, as the interpretation of the 6D wavefunction is –in principle– highly non-trivial and its determination requires a careful calculation with extensive tests and convergence checks. Multiple users mentioned the need for extra hardware, the lack of availability of VR infrastructure, its cost and difficulty of setup, or logistics problems. The technology is under development and specialized, and often single-user. Some users found it cumbersome, harder to navigate, tiring for daily work, or requiring too much effort compared to the benefits for the specific example. In particular, the system is very sensitive to the quality of the loaded data, and the data volume is high.

6   Conclusions and Future Work

We have developed a virtual reality viewer for material science simulations and compared it to the classical software used in the field. Although the system is still an early prototype, domain experts consider that it can be useful in a variety of tasks and think that it is a valuable addition to their tools; however, the state of the technology is still seen as experimental, unavailable, costly or difficult to setup by end users. A small, albeit statistically significant, advantage of the

VR system with respect to traditional tools is confirmed by the user study. More work needs to be done, though, to easen interaction and navigation in the virtual world and to add more functionality to the system.

For future work, we would like to use real-time volume rendering to provide higher-quality visuals and to avoid the pre-selection of isosurfaces. We would also like to investigate ways to present the exciton datasets in the GearVR, and to increase the functionality of the demos. We must also work on generalizing the demos to work in other types of datasets and to integrate them with the NOMAD encyclopaedia. Additional functionality from the classical tools used in material science should be ported to the VR system as well, under guidance from domain experts. Finally, we would like to also target other VR devices.

Acknowledgements. The project received funding from the European Union's Horizon 2020 research and innovation program under grant agreement no. 676580 with The Novel Materials Discovery (NOMAD) Laboratory, a European Center of Excellence. The CO_2+CaO datasets were provided by Sergei Levchenko (Max Planck Society), and the LiF datasets by Caterina Cocci (Humbolt Universität zu Berlin). Figure 2, center and right were provided by Dima Nabok (Humbolt Universität zu Berlin). We would also like to thank the participants in the user study.

References

1. Ahrens, J., Geveci, B., Law, C.: ParaView: an end-user tool for large data visualization. In: Visualization Handbook. Elsevier, January 2005
2. Ames, A., Nadeau, D., Moreland, J.: The VRML 2.0 Sourcebook. No. Bd. 1 in The VRML 2.0 Sourcebook. Wiley (1996)
3. Apache License Version 2.0 (2004). https://www.apache.org/licenses/LICENSE-2.0
4. ART Advanced Realtime Tracking. http://www.ar-tracking.com/home/. Accessed 22 Feb 2017
5. Bourke, P.: Gaussian Cube Files (2003). http://paulbourke.net/dataformats/cube/. Accessed 22 Feb 2017
6. Cignoni, P., Callieri, M., Corsini, M., Dellepiane, M., Ganovelli, F., Ranzuglia, G.: MeshLab: an open-source mesh processing tool. In: Scarano, V., Chiara, R.D., Erra, U. (eds.) Eurographics Italian Chapter Conference. The Eurographics Association (2008)
7. Dobrzanski, L., Honysz, R.: The idea of material science virtual laboratory. J. Achiev. Mater. Manuf. Eng. **42**(1–2), 196–203 (2010)
8. Everitt, C.: Interactive order-independent transparency (2001). http://www.nvidia.com/object/Interactive_Order_Transparency.html. Accessed 23 Feb 2017
9. Kheshgi, H., de Coninck, H., Kessels, J.: Carbon dioxide capture and storage: seven years after the IPCC special report. Mitig. Adapt. Strat. Glob. Change **17**(6), 563–567 (2012)
10. Kunz, A.B., Miyakawa, T., Oyama, S.: Electronic energy bands, excitons, and plasmons in lithium fluoride crystal. Physica Status Solidi (b) **34**(2), 581–589 (1969)
11. Mirzayanov, M.: 60766 - [4.7 regression] wrong optimization with $-O2$ (2014). https://gcc.gnu.org/bugzilla/show_bug.cgi?id=60766. Accessed 23 Feb 2017

12. Momma, K., Izumi, F.: VESTA3 for three-dimensional visualization of crystal, volumetric and morphology data. J. Appl. Crystallogr. **44**(6), 1272–1276 (2011)
13. Home - NOMAD (2015–2017). https://www.nomad-coe.eu/. Accessed 22 Feb 2017
14. The NOMAD Repository was established to host, organize, and share materials data. NOMAD Repository 2015-2017. http://nomad-repository.eu/cms/. Accessed 22 Feb 2017
15. Sellers, G.: Order independent transparency - OpenGL SuperBible (2013). http://www.openglsuperbible.com/2013/08/20/is-order-independent-transparency -really-necessary/. Accessed 23 Feb 2017
16. Smith, C.: Chemistry Lab VR (2016). Submitted to SB Hacks II. https://devpost. com/software/chemistry-lab-vr. Accessed 06 Mar 2017
17. Yang, M., McMullen, D.P., Schwartz-Bloom, R.D., Brady, R.: Dive into alcohol: a biochemical immersive experience. In: 2009 IEEE Virtual Reality Conference, pp. 281–282, March 2009

Measuring the Impact of Low-Cost Short-Term Virtual Reality on the User Experience

Mario Alaguero[1], David Checa[1], and Andres Bustillo[2](✉)

[1] Department of History and Geography, University of Burgos, Burgos, Spain
{malaguero,dcheca}@ubu.es
[2] Department of Civil Engineering, University of Burgos,
Avda Cantabria s/n, Burgos, Spain
abustillo@ubu.es

Abstract. The continuous innovation of new affordable hardware and software over recent years is leading to a surfeit of Virtual Reality (VR) applications in the entertainment industry. However, the abundance of VR applications is unfortunately not matched by case studies and evaluation methods related to low-cost Virtual Reality experiences. A gap in the literature exists, where the utility of VR to display narrative stories could be studied, due to the sensations of amazement, astonishment, and excitement that it awakens. This research reports the steps taken to create a low-cost VR experience designed to transmit a single concept. The key aspects of the experience may be summarized as follows: a short duration, the selection of an evocative scenario limited to a single storyline, short animation of 3D-models selected to produce intense visual impacts with minimal modelling and animation and the collaborative participation of undergraduate students in the development of the VR environment. Members of the public were invited to trials of this VR experience portraying a Nativity scene over the 2016/17 Christmas Season in Burgos (Spain). The user experience was evaluated through surveys administered to numerous final-users immediately after the 3D-experience. The results showed very high levels of satisfaction, even though the 3D-experience for around half of the viewers was not their first one. In a few rare cases, sickness effects were reported. Viewers identified the movement of light as one of the most impressive aspects and considered the duration reasonable, with few or no suggestions for improvement.

Keywords: Short experiences · Low-cost · Virtual Reality · Oculus Rift · Blender

1 Introduction

The expansion of Virtual Reality (VR) over recent years, prompted by the surfeit of new and affordable hardware and software applications has produced technological innovations that are not often placed in the public domain, nor are they sufficiently well implemented and integrated in educational processes and narrative storylines [1]. One

© Springer International Publishing AG 2017
L.T. De Paolis et al. (Eds.): AVR 2017, Part I, LNCS 10324, pp. 320–336, 2017.
DOI: 10.1007/978-3-319-60922-5_26

barrier to the integration of these technologies in learning environments is the scarcity of studies on the advantages and drawbacks of the development of Virtual Reality environments that combine technological and pedagogical perspectives for varied purposes [2]. This limitation should be overcome as soon as possible, to bring home the potential reality of VR that can present almost any learning concept in an interactive scenario at first hand; an approach to which young people are invariably more receptive [2, 3], because VR environments stimulate sensations of amazement, astonishment, and excitement in users [4].

VR applications for learning purposes can follow many different strategies depending on the final use of the VR environment. For example, cultural heritage learning requires very detailed environments built with high resolution textures and 3D-models [2], while Engineering [5] and Computer Science learning [6] call for simpler and more geometrical components with plain colors. The final devices that show the VR environment also play a central role in the selected strategy, depending on their computing capabilities: the experience of a smartphone mounted on cardboards differs from the experience of Oculus Rift Head Mounted Displays (HMD) connected to a workstation. The same may likewise be said of the two most popular game engines: Unity and Unreal Engine.

The challenges that VR opens to teaching and storytelling activities have opened a very interesting and active line of research. Many VR teaching applications are related to Engineering topics: Concentrating Solar Power [7] and the operation of a power plant in the city of Piestany (Slovakia) [8] are two examples. Besides, there are also examples of its use for 3D modeling and animation teaching [9], learning a second language [10], explaining Cultural Heritage to the general public, whether it is the Jing-Hang Grand Canal in China [11] or medieval European villages [12] and cities [13].

Most of these applications face a major problem, due to cost constraints on the project. Although the budgets for major exhibitions may be reasonable, small-scale exhibitions and locally developed classroom applications have to be more resourceful. Some recent works report the development of software tools, hardware and methods especially designed for this type of low-cost project. First, automatic and semi-automatic tools for 3D-model construction have been validated in studies on medieval churches [14, 15]. Second, low-cost 3D displays and tactile devices have been developed in various VR learning environments [16–18]. Third, optimized methodologies for both 3D-modelling [2] and virtual reality integration [12, 19] have been presented to reduce computing and human effort in VR projects related to medieval churches [19] and villages [12].

Besides the project costs, the limitations of hardware on the real-time rendering of 3D models often limits interactivity between the end user and the virtual models [20], thereby reducing the impact of VR and potential learning [2, 4]. However, the launch of low-cost, high-fidelity HMDs over the past two years, such as Oculus Rift™, have opened new horizons for the application of 3D-immersive environments, although modeling, integration in the game engine and the simplification of storylines still need to be optimized to assure low-cost short-term VR experiences.

This paper reports the design of an ad-hoc low-cost method to generate VR experiences that may represent an initial point-of-contact for the general public with these technologies and especially with high-quality HMDs such as Oculus Rift; Oculus

Rift combined with workstation processing capabilities is a high-quality HMDs in comparison with smartphones mounted in cardboards. The idea of this design is to measure the impact of low-cost short-term Virtual Reality on the user experience. The proposed method is based on: (i) a short duration, both to reduce costs and avoid simulator-sickness problems reported with such devices in previous works [12]; (ii) the selection of a powerful storyline in only one scenario; (iii) low-level animation of 3D-models with little effort required for modeling and animation that impact on visual perception; and, (iv) cooperation with graduate students in the development of the VR environment. Following these guidelines a VR environment was produced and tested: the design of a Nativity scene in the Christmas Season in Burgos (Spain), from the 23 December 2016 to the 8 January 2017; the user experience was evaluated with numerous members of the public. The evaluation gathered information that might answer some of the questions in relation to Oculus Rift and high quality yet affordable HMD in the context of storytelling, and in a more general view, for teaching purposes: can the HMD generate an acceptable degree of immersivity? Does this HMD induce physical discomfort? [21].

The remaining of this paper is structured as follows: Sect. 2 describes the process to recreate the virtual environments and discusses its real implementation in a study case: the design of a Nativity scene over the 2016–17 Christmas Season in Burgos (Spain); Sect. 3 evaluates the results of the experience from the surveys administered to the visitors. Finally, Sect. 4 presents the conclusions and future lines of work.

2 Development of the VR Experience

The production tasks of a VR experience may be grouped into three main stages: pre-production, 3D model generation and integration in the game engine.

2.1 Pre-production

First, the identification of the main objectives of the VR experience was done. The objectives relate to two different categories: end-user and technical objectives. The objectives in relation to the viewers are to generate entertainment that includes the narration of the story of the birth of Jesus Christ and the visit of the three Kings from the Orient. It is an initial point-of-contact with virtual environments for the general public that may never have used them. Its duration and design avoids sickness effects. From a technical point of view, the objective was to develop a VR experience at a low cost, considering that two Oculus Rift HMDs and the corresponding work stations were available for this experience without it implying any extra cost.

The VR experience designed to achieve these objectives, fulfilled the following criteria: first, a short duration (between 1 and 2 min), performed only in one environment, although slight movements of the viewer position may help to generate the effect of motion. Some animations were included to intensify this effect and the main animation was related to the story, but, as anthropomorphic movements are very time consuming tasks, they were reduced as much as the storyline would allow, making extensive use of lighting animation (from day to night, stars and sunset, flickering lamps and fires in villages lighting up and extinguished…). Animated lighting has the extra advantage of producing strong 3D effects, because it changes the shadow lines of the objects in the environment. This strategy strikes a balance between entertainment and cost reduction. Along the same lines of cost reduction, the 3D-modeling was performed in a 3D-marathon, reinforced by a seminar of low poly-modelling techniques to which the undergraduate students studying for the Degree in Communications Media at the University of Burgos were invited, after their standard course in 3D-modelling. While learning to optimize 3D-model geometries, they prepared, in a collaborative way, most of the 3D-models that will be used in the VR environment. Figure 1 shows a scheme of the decisions over the design of the VR experience and its objectives.

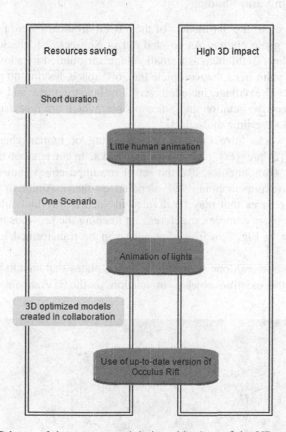

Fig. 1. Scheme of the strategy and design objectives of the VR experience

This strategy has two disadvantages; first, the VR experience should be very short, the story to be narrated should be very simple and, better still, well-known to the viewer, so that a number of the details may be omitted, and the duration should be limited to less than 2 min. Hence the choice of the nativity scene, the birth of Jesus Christ and the visit of the three Kings from the Orient that forms a cornerstone of Spanish culture, especially during the Christmas season. The second disadvantage is that the interactivity of the VR environment with the user should be negligible to reduce costs, a decision that can influence perceptions of amazement and astonishment in the viewer. At the same time, the reduction of interactivity might imply a lower learning rate [22]; although this is not a critical issue in the selected VR experience, it can be very important in later teaching experiences of similar characteristics. This short VR experience is designed for viewers as an initial point-of-contact with a VR environment and is not expected to have a significant effect on viewer satisfaction.

2.2 3D-Modelling and Shading

In the second stage, all the 3D-models of the VR environment were prepared for their integration in the game engine. As pointed out in Subsect. 2.1, the layout of the VR environment displays Bethlehem as a small village surrounded by a low-lying hills and desert with a few palm trees that complete the 360° space, leaving no plain horizons to bore the viewers. The village included very similar structures and objects, such as houses, stalls, streets, vegetation and a few people, which are repeated throughout the scene, in order to save time and effort.

As previous works have outlined, 3D-modeling of human characters [23] and texture mapping [2] are very time-consuming tasks. In an attempt to simplify these tasks, some basic componentes, like the set of modified cubes shown in Fig. 2, was modeled and the texture mapping was prepared on them. Although basic structures, these objects have faces that may be divided in such a way that subsequent modifications can create more complex structures, but keeping the previous mapping process, so that, as shown in Fig. 2, a 32-vertex cube can be transformed into a 121-vertex one-level house.

These processes were done with four basic templates that should be used for each classification of the existing objects, in relation to the UVmapping characteristics:

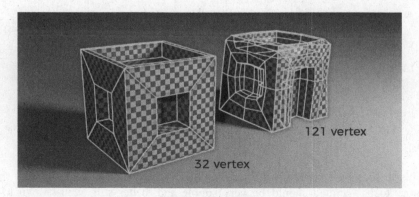

Fig. 2. Examples of a 32-vertex and a 121-vertex template for texture mapping

houses, characters, vegetation and complements. Each template includes all the images and materials necessary to map at least one object of the four families of objects. Figure 3 shows two of these templates including four houses (first) and three human characters (second).

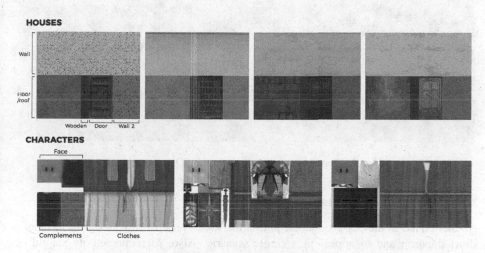

Fig. 3. Examples of the texture templates of the houses and the human characters

Once the first objects had been modeled and textured, they were then modified to create new ones. These objects were related to another texture image, made with the same template, so that all the models in the scene were made from just a few basic models. Figure 4 shows four village houses modeled from the same basic 3D model and textured with the house template shown in Fig. 3.

Fig. 4. Different buildings created from the same basic 3D model and texture template

Finally, Fig. 5 shows the general layout of the 3D-environment; although it is easy to detect the 3D-models that are duplicated, this fact is not so easily detected by the viewers in the VR experience, as the results included in Sect. 3 will outline.

Fig. 5. Top view of the village in the 3D-environment.

2.3   Integration in the Game Engine

As mentioned in the pre-production phase, the VR experience was designed to be of a short duration and to appear in a single scenario. Also, user interactivity should be limited to reduce costs. With this in mind Unreal Engine 4 was selected as the game engine, because of its ease at achieving photorealistic results and its visual programming system.

Once the game engine was selected, this third phase, in which the virtual experience is created, can be divided into three tasks: the generation of the scene, the illumination and the depiction of events of the experience, and the programming of the cinematic sequence.

Firstly, the scene is created inside the game engine. As expected, this phase requires a good amount of time to import and to organize the assets inside the game engine in comparison with previous works of similar characteristics [12]. This phase also includes the task of generating the project and the editor set-up, as well as correct classification of the sources to speed up the last two tasks of this phase. Once all the assets are well organized, the objects are placed in the scene, as shown in Fig. 6. At this point, the virtual world is also scaled, to create an optimal sensation of immersivity for the viewer: in this case, the sensation of observing a mock-up of a nativity scene.

In the second task, the illumination and the generation of the events in the VR environment were completed; these may be considered artistic tasks that include subtasks involving material design and the illumination of the environment. It is integrated with the generation of events and simultaneous changes of lighting during the experience. Costs were further reduced in this task, with the help of the Unreal Engine visual scripting system (Blueprints), a semi-automated day-to-night system, as in Fig. 7. With the preset skysphere material included in the game engine, the designer can automatically switch from daylight to nighttime illumination, merely by changing the orientation of our light source. So, a blueprint that manages this orientation and the

Fig. 6. Basic scene created inside the game engine.

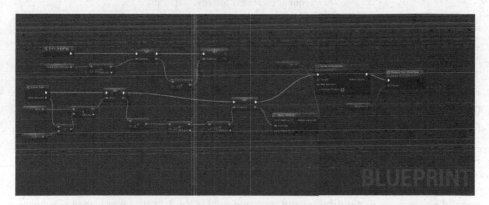

Fig. 7. The Blueprint created for the effect of daylight to nighttime.

time that passes between sunset and sunrise was programmed. This automation is a crucial time-saving device.

Other events created for this experience include the supplementary illumination that complements the main lighting at key points such as the portal. Some loop animations, which reduce the overall costs, were also included for more than one asset.

Finally, most of the time is spent on the creation and the optimization of the cinematic sequence stage. This task is critical otherwise motion sickness may be induced due to incorrect optimization of the VR experience [12]. The optimization includes subtasks such as instantiation of objects, for example plants or animals, which once again can be repeated, to save processing loads. Also, the optimization of assets depending in its distance from the character, and baking light in the scene to balance the visuals with performance, guaranteeing the necessary 90 fps. Lastly, a cinematic sequence was created with the sequencer tool of Unreal Engine 4, in this way the position of the viewers is easily defined, and music and narration can be synchronized with user viewing (Fig. 8).

Fig. 8. Sequence created for this experience.

3   Evaluation of the Effect of the VR Experience

The VR experience was installed in a civic center close to the center of the city of Burgos from the 23 December 2016 to the 8 January 2017, Fig. 9. During this 2-week period, 980 viewers had the opportunity to test the VR experience. After the experience, the viewers were asked to fill in a short survey.

The survey was filled in by 306 people with a gender distribution of 115 men (38%) and 191 women (62%) and an age distribution of 32% children (5–12 old years), 6% teenagers (13–17 years old), 53.5% adults (18–65 years old) and 8.5% older men. The survey consisted of six questions. The first four questions had between two and five possible responses depending on the question, while the last two were open questions. The questions were designed to evaluate all the proposed objectives of the VR experience.

First the viewer was asked about previous experience with Virtual Reality, Fig. 10 (Have you experienced a VR experience before?). Surprisingly, it was only the first VR experience for 44% of the viewers. A result that may be explained by the inclusion of cardboards and short demo-games in different-nature goods purchased over the year 2016 in Spain. Even if this is the reason, final viewer satisfaction with the VR experience will not be reduced by previous VR experiences, maybe because there is a notable difference between the VR experience with cardboards and Oculus Rift. Regarding gender differences, women formed the main group without previous VR experience, unlike men whose experience was more varied. This difference might be

Fig. 9. Members of the public testing the VR experience during the Christmas Season.

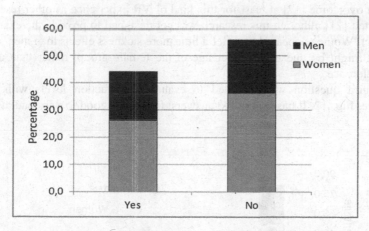

Fig. 10. Novelty of the VR experience for the viewers (question 1).

due to the lower usage of new technologies among women in Spain, although the survey results are by no means conclusive on that point. In any case, considering the rapid development of these technologies, within a couple of years there will be very few members of the European public without direct experience of VR.

Simulation sickness in reaction to the VR Experience was addressed in the second question, Fig. 11. The question had 4 optional responses: from no-sickness to strong sickness effects. The great majority had never suffered simulation sickness at all (87%),

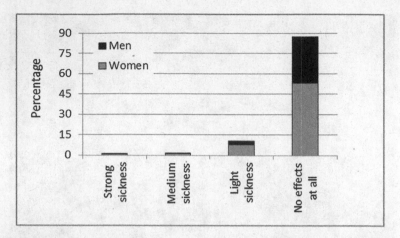

Fig. 11. Sickness effects during the VR experience (question 2).

while only 2% suffered medium or strong effects. A short VR experience certainly helps to keep the sickness rate low and, unlike other VR experiences [12, 13], the one in this study was designed without a need for the viewer to change location during the experience, an option that can also help lower sickness rates. In any case, the simulation sickness problems reported in the first version of Oculus Rift HMD appear to have been overcome [12] at least for this kind of VR experience as other research has also reported [21] although this research was not designed to provide the exact reason for this fact. Women appeared to suffer a little more sickness effects than men, although this result might be due to the older age of the female group, rather than an actual gender difference.

The third question was included to evaluate satisfaction levels with the VR Experience, Fig. 12. It has 4 possible answers: from very good to very bad avoiding a

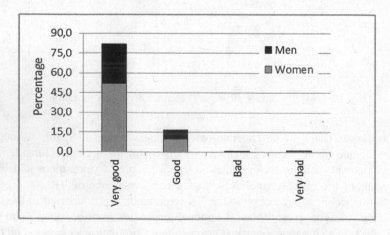

Fig. 12. Satisfaction with the VR experience (question 3).

mid-way value to assure that the viewers provide a well-defined answer. The great majority (82%) really enjoyed the experience, while only 1.7% considered it bad or very bad. This reduced rate of dissatisfaction is very significant for two reasons: first the percentage of viewers with sickness effects was higher than 1.7% (2%) and it would be reasonable to expect that when affected by sickness, the viewers would also find the experience unsatisfactory, and second that the low-cost design of the VR experience might imply that some viewers find it too simple or uninteresting. Therefore the VR experience can be considered a success from the point of view of viewer satisfaction. No gender-based differences were noted in the answers.

As is clear, the duration of the VR experience may affect sickness levels and viewer satisfaction, and therefore the fourth question inquired into the viewer's perception of its duration. The question has 3 possible answers: short, sufficiently long and too long. In this case a middle value was included because it is not a neutral answer to the question. Viewer opinions, Fig. 13, were mainly divided between the viewers who found the duration acceptable (55.2%) and the viewers who found it too short (42.5%). This result is of interest, because it showed that almost half of the viewers would have preferred a longer experience but, in any case, they were satisfied (Question 3) and, therefore, the short duration of the VR experience will not penalize the satisfaction level; a worse result might have arisen if the viewers had found the duration sufficient and the satisfactory level had been low, because in this case the experience would have been incorrectly designed or the decision to keep it very short would weigh too much on the satisfaction level of the viewers. In any case, almost all the viewers were not tired, because only 1.9% found it too long, an expected percentage considering that 2% suffered sickness effects during the experience. Again, no gender differences were identified in the answers to this question.

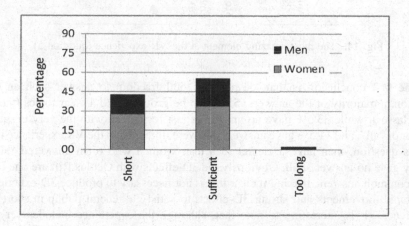

Fig. 13. Perception of the duration of the VR experience (question 4).

In the fifth question the viewer was asked to identify the most amazing element/s in the VR experience, to identify the elements that leave a stronger impression on the viewers, and therefore to give a higher priority to those elements in future projects,

Fig. 14. The viewer has in this case an empty space to answer freely. The answers were grouped into 7 categories:

- "animation and lights": the answers are related to the movement of objects or to the changes in lighting
- "3D-effects": the answers are connected to 3D sensations
- "storyline": the answers are related to the story itself
- "Any specific 3D-model": the viewer identifies a specific 3D-model (the buildings, the stars, the Kings…)
- "All": the answer was just this word or any synonymous
- Other: for some very rare cases that refer to the event organization, place…
- NA: the viewers that write no answer at all.

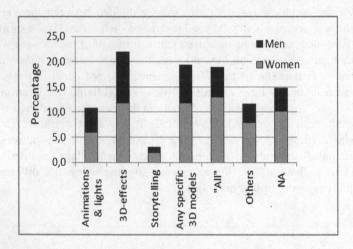

Fig. 14. The most amazing element in the VR experience (question 5).

The first conclusion is that, despite the total freedom to answer such an open question, a majority of the answers, 55%, can be grouped into 4 clear topics (the first four classes), while 33.5% gave no answer or just responded with the very unspecific answer of "all", and 11.5% gave answers that were unrelated to the VR experience itself. In this question, men have a clearer idea than women who often answered "all" or simply gave no answer at all. Obviously the 3D-effects with Oculus Rift are one of the most common answers, making it clear that is not necessary to produce 3D-experiences with rapid movements and strong 3D-effects to satisfy a general public in short-term experiences. It is interesting to note that, although the experience includes very few animations, they appear astonishing to the viewers, who especially cited the flickering of lights, and dawn and sunset; the reason might be the vivid sensation of a 3D nature of the environment, due to the oblique lights that reproduce dawn and sunset, swiftly changing the dimensions of the shadows. Finally, it is interesting to note that viewers try to perceive a limited number of objects and, therefore, there is a significant group of answers that refers to a specific object as the most amazing element; this answer might facilitate the future development of scenarios with a very limited number of well-defined objects and a low-quality background, as in the case of Cultural Heritage VR experiences [12].

Finally, the last question was again an open question with an undirected answer on what would they change in the VR experience, Fig. 15. The answers were grouped into 8 categories: more animations, more objects and scenarios, more definition of the 3D-models, a longer experience, a better or just-a-different story, other answers not included in previous categories, the answer "nothing" and the viewers who left this question empty (NA). Almost 40% of responses were "nothing", an answer that might mean that they are very satisfied with the experience, in line with the results of Question 3, or that they have not identified any special issue that should be improved. It is interesting to note that only 20.8% would improve the number of objects or its definition and movements, the most complex tasks in terms of resources consumption. In any case, as noted in previous responses to the questions, there is no clear weak point for the viewers in the VR experience. Finally, it was not possible to extract any clear conclusion or difference in terms of gender behavior.

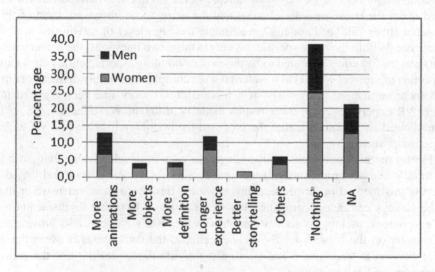

Fig. 15. The most amazing element in the VR experience (question 6).

4 Conclusions and Future Works

The recent release of Oculus Rift and similar high-quality head mounted displays are leading to a surfeit of Virtual Reality applications for their core sector: the entertainment industry. But, in many cases, methodologies and best practice for low-cost applications of such devices need to be developed, for both simple concepts and well-known storylines. This research has focused on the development of such a methodology for a balanced case between entertainment and cost reduction. The methodology identifies some key elements for the reduction of resource consumption: a short duration (between 1 and 2 min), a limited number of scenes, a very limited number of animations, mainly intensified by the movement of light, 3D-modeling completed in a collaborative 3D-modeling marathon, an array of low poly modelling techniques including standardized UV-maps and textures templates and the use of the Unreal Engine 4 game engine with the Blueprints scripting system for a semi-automated day-to-night lighthing changes.

This methodology has been tested by designing the Nativity scene during the Christmas Season in Burgos (Spain), Christmas 2016–17, and the effect of the experience was evaluated among numerous final-users (306) by filling-in a 6-question survey. The results of a survey show firstly that half of the viewers have enjoyed some previous VR experience, although this previous experience might be related to low-cost hardware like cardboards and mobile phones, because they have no influence on the levels of surprise and amazement that the VR experience provokes. Second, sickness effects were very rarely detected, due to the improvements of earlier Oculus Rift versions and the absence of any need for the viewer to move during the VR experience. Third, most of the viewers really enjoyed the experience and affirmed that its duration was either right or a little too short, while less than 2% considered it too long, clearly reflecting the number of viewers who suffered sickness effects. When the viewers were asked about the most amazing element and the items to be improved, most of them answered either "all" or "nothing", reaffirming the high level of satisfaction with the experience. Within the more specific answers to these two questions, the movements of lights and the 3D effect appeared to be the most astounding aspects, while only a minor proportion of viewers would have preferred more complex and highly defined scenarios with more animations. Obviously, if a more complex story had been narrated in a longer VR experience, then these results might be different. Nevertheless, the results have allowed us to conclude that the proposed methodology for low-cost VR experiences is satisfactory.

Further research will focus on including some easy-to-develop interactivity with the 3D-models and scenario to extend the time duration of the experience and the adaptation of this method to further teaching activities. Besides, a more extensive analysis of the surveys can detect correlation between sickness effects and disatisfaction with the experiment, as long as its correlation with the user's age can also provide new information on the reasons for the sickness effects; the correlations between the different answers to questions 5 and 6 will also provide further insight into the viewers perceptions and expectations.

Acknowledgments. This work was partially supported by the Program "Impulso de la Industria de Contenidos Digitales desde las Universidades" and the Project Number RTC-2016-4851-7 of the Spanish Ministry of Industry, Tourism and Commerce.

References

1. Tsaramirsis, G., Buhari, S.M., Al-Shammari, K.O., Ghazi, S., Nazmudeen, M.S., Tsaramirsis, K.: Towards simulation of the classroom learning experience: virtual reality approach. In: Proceedings of the 10th 2016 3rd International Conference on Computing for Sustainable Global Development, INDIACom 2016, art. no. 7724484, pp. 1343–1346 (2016)

2. Bustillo, A., Alaguero, M., Miguel, I., Saiz, J.M., Iglesias, L.S.: A flexible platform for the creation of 3D semi-immersive environments to teach cultural heritage. Digit. Appl. Archaeol. Cult. Herit. **2**, 248–259 (2015)

3. Korakakis, G., Pavlatou, E.A., Palyvos, J.A., Spyrellis, N.: 3D visualization types in multimedia applications for science learning: a case study for 8th grade students in Greece. Comput. Educ. **52**, 390–401 (2009)

4. Hupont, I., Gracia, J., Sanagustín, L., Gracia, M.A.: How do new visual immersive systems influence gaming QoE? A use case of serious gaming with oculus rift. In: 2015 Seventh International Workshop on Quality of Multimedia Experience (QoMEX), pp. 1–6 (2015)

5. Menezes, P., Chouzal, F., Urbano, D., Restivo, T.: Augmented reality in engineering. In: Auer, M.E., Guralnick, D., Uhomoibhi, J. (eds.) ICL 2016. AISC, vol. 545, pp. 221–228. Springer, Cham (2017). doi:10.1007/978-3-319-50340-0_18

6. Grivokostopoulou, F., Perikos, I., Hatzilygeroudis, I.: An innovative educational environment based on virtual reality and gamification for learning search algorithms. In: Proceedings - IEEE 8th International Conference on Technology for Education, T4E 2016, art. no. 7814804, pp. 110–115 (2016)

7. Ritter III, K.A., Chambers, T.L., Borst, C.W.: Work in progress: networked virtual reality environment for teaching concentrating solar power technology. In: ASEE Annual Conference and Exposition, Conference Proceedings, June 2016

8. Hain, V., Löffler, R., Zajíček, V.: Interdisciplinary cooperation in the virtual presentation of industrial heritage development. Procedia Eng. **161**, 2030–2035 (2016)

9. Villagrasa, S., Fonseca, D., Redondo, E., Duran, J.: Teaching case of gamification and visual technologies for education. J. Cases Inf. Technol. **16**(4), 38–57 (2014)

10. Reitz, L., Sohny, A., Lochmann, G.: VR based gamification of communication training and oral examination in a second language. Int. J. Game-Based Learn. **6**(2), 46–61 (2016)

11. Chen, S., Pan, Z., Zhang, M., Shen, H.: A case study of user immersion based systematic design for serious heritage games. Multimedia Tools Appl. **62**(3), 633–658 (2013)

12. Checa, D., Alaguero, M., Arnaiz, M.A., Bustillo, A.: Briviesca in the 15th c.: a virtual reality environment for teaching purposes. In: Paolis, L.T., Mongelli, A. (eds.) AVR 2016. LNCS, vol. 9769, pp. 126–138. Springer, Cham (2016). doi:10.1007/978-3-319-40651-0_11

13. De Paolis, L.T.: Walking in a virtual town to understand and learning about the life in the middle ages. In: Murgante, B., Misra, S., Carlini, M., Torre, C.M., Nguyen, H.-Q., Taniar, D., Apduhan, B.O., Gervasi, O. (eds.) ICCSA 2013. LNCS, vol. 7971, pp. 632–645. Springer, Heidelberg (2013). doi:10.1007/978-3-642-39637-3_50

14. Martin Lerones, P., Llamas Fernandez, J., Melero Gil, A., Gomez-Garcia-Bermejo, J., Zalama Casanova, E.: A practical approach to making accurate 3D layouts of interesting cultural heritage sites through digital models. J. Cult. Herit. **11**, 1–9 (2010)

15. Alaguero, M., Bustillo, A., Guinea, B., Iglesias, L.: The virtual reconstruction of a small medieval town: the case of Briviesca (Spain). In: CAA 2014 21st Century Archaeology, Concepts, Methods and Tools. Proceedings of the 42nd Annual Conference on Computer Applications and Quantitative Methods in Archaeology, pp. 575–584. Archaeopress (2015). ISBN 978-1-78491-100-3

16. Gelsomini, M.: An affordable virtual reality learning framework for children with neurodevelopmental disorder. In: ASSETS 2016 - Proceedings of the 18th International ACM SIGACCESS Conference on Computers and Accessibility, pp. 343–344 (2016)

17. Sanna, A., Lamberti, F., Bazzano, F., Maggio, L.: Developing touch-less interfaces to interact with 3D contents in public exhibitions. In: Paolis, L.T., Mongelli, A. (eds.) AVR 2016. LNCS, vol. 9769, pp. 293–303. Springer, Cham (2016). doi:10.1007/978-3-319-40651-0_24

18. Lupu, R.G., Ungureanu, F., Stan, A.: A virtual reality system for post stroke recovery. In: 2016 20th International Conference on System Theory, Control and Computing, ICSTCC 2016 - Joint Conference of SINTES 20, SACCS 16, SIMSIS 20 - Proceedings, art. no. 7790682, pp. 300–305 (2016)

19. Bruno, F., Bruno, S., De Sensi, G., Luchi, M.L., Mancuso, S., Muzzupappa, M.: From 3D reconstruction to virtual reality: a complete methodology for digital archaeological exhibition. J. Cult. Herit. **11**, 42–49 (2010)

20. Wu, H.K., Wen-Yu Lee, S., Chang, H.Y., Liang, J.C.: Current status, opportunities and challenges of augmented reality in education. Comput. Educ. **62**, 41–49 (2013)

21. Chessa, M., Maiello, G., Borsari, A., Bex, P.J.: The perceptual quality of the oculus rift for immersive virtual reality. In: Human-Computer Interaction, pp. 1–32 (2016, article in press)

22. Jang, S., Vitale, J.M., Jyung, R.W., Black, J.B.: Direct manipulation is better than passive viewing for learning anatomy in a three-dimensional virtual reality environment. Comput. Educ. **106**, 150–165 (2017)

23. Guinea, B., Alaguero, M., Melgosa, F., Bustillo, A.: Using a short video animation to assist with the diagnosis of sleep disorders in young children. In: Paolis, L.T., Mongelli, A. (eds.) AVR 2016. LNCS, vol. 9769, pp. 13–29. Springer, Cham (2016). doi:10.1007/978-3-319-40651-0_2

Augmented and Mixed Reality

Making the Invisible Visible: Real-Time Feedback for Embedded Computing Learning Activity Using Pedagogical Virtual Machine with Augmented Reality

Malek Alrashidi[1(✉)], Khalid Almohammadi[2], Michael Gardner[1], and Victor Callaghan[1]

[1] School of Computer Science and Electronic Engineering, University of Essex, Colchester, UK
{mqaalr,mgardner,vic}@essex.ac.uk
[2] Computer Science Department, Community College, University of Tabuk, Tabuk, Kingdom of Saudi Arabia
kalmohammadi@ut.edu.sa

Abstract. In today's digital world, the use of diverse interconnected physical computer-based devices, typified by the Internet-of-Things, has increased, leaving their internal functionalities hidden from people. In education, these hidden computational processes leave learners with a vagueness that obscures how these physical devices function and communicate in order to produce the high-level behaviours and actions they observe. The current approach to revealing these hidden worlds involves the use of debugging tools, visualisation, simulation, or augmented-reality views. Even when such advanced technologies are utilised, they fail to construct a meaningful view of the hidden worlds that relate to the learning context, leaving learners with formidable challenges to understanding the operation of these deep technologies. Therefore, a pedagogical virtual machine (PVM) model was employed to evaluate the learning effectiveness of the proposed model. We presented the experimental evaluation of the PVM model with AR that concerned students learning to program a desk-based robot (which is used as an example of an embedded computer) and reveal the learning effectiveness of using PVM with AR compared to traditional engineering laboratory methods. Overall, the PVM with AR improved learning and teaching, as compared to traditional environments, and learners preferred the use of the PVM with AR system for doing similar activities.

Keywords: Educational robotics · Augmented reality · Pedagogical virtual machine · Human factors · User evaluation · Embedded computing

1 Introduction

In today's digital world, the use of diverse interconnected physical computer-based devices, typified by the Internet-of-Things, has increased, leaving their internal functionalities hidden from people. In education, these hidden computational processes leave learners with a vagueness that obscures how these physical devices function and

© Springer International Publishing AG 2017
L.T. De Paolis et al. (Eds.): AVR 2017, Part I, LNCS 10324, pp. 339–355, 2017.
DOI: 10.1007/978-3-319-60922-5_27

communicate in order to produce the high-level behaviours and actions they observe. The current approach to revealing these hidden worlds involves the use of debugging tools, visualisation, simulation, or augmented-reality (AR) views. Even when such advanced technologies are utilised, they fail to construct a meaningful view of the hidden worlds that relate to the learning context, leaving learners with formidable challenges to understanding the operation of these deep technologies.

The use of AR technology in education shows a positive impact on learning and teaching, especially when exploring and visualising abstract concepts. However, the challenge is bigger for students working on laboratory-based activities, especially in areas that involve physical entities, as much of the important system functionality and processes are invisible. This can make a barrier to learning and requires a lot of effort from learners to understand the system activities and processes. In a previous paper [1], we proposed a pedagogical virtual machine (PVM) model that aims to link physical object activity with learning activity and reveal the related educational value from the physical object. The use of AR, and its ability to reveal deep technologies, further improves the effectiveness of the PVM framework introduced above by superimposing data, in real-time, concerning the invisible computational processes being explored by the learners. The PVM is composed of four main layers: the data layer, aggregation layer, pedagogical layer, and the user interface layer. The data layer is responsible for sniffing any data that is being transmitted on the embedded computing. Then, the aggregation layer collects this data and produces a more meaningful representation. The pedagogical layer takes the aggregated data and maps it to the learning activities based on the preset learning design. Finally, the user interface layer is where learners visualise and view the workflow of the learning activities using AR with information from the other PVM layers (data to pedagogical layers). In addition, the learner can track their progress and obtain instant feedback based on their performance in the learning activity.

In this paper, we present the experimental evaluation of the PVM model with AR that concerned students learning to program a desk-based robot (which is used as an example of an embedded computer), and reveals the learning effectiveness of using PVM with AR compared to traditional engineering laboratory methods. The experiment examines three research questions:

1. Does PVM with AR reduce the time for solving a learning activity task and with fewer trials compared to the traditional approach of programming?
2. Does PVM with AR reduce the load in learning compared to the traditional approach?
3. Does PVM with AR assist students effectively while solving the learning activity task compared to the traditional approach?
4. Do students prefer the use of PVM with AR over the traditional approach?

The paper starts by stating related work (Sect. 2), and then describes the experimental design used to gather evidence of the value of the concepts proposed in the model (Sect. 3). After that, the paper presents the experimental results (Sect. 4) and concludes by discussing the findings of the study and their broader values for the research area (Sect. 5).

2   Background and Related Work

Several possibilities can be realised by using AR in education [2]. Wu et al. [2] provide the advantages of AR in education. First, AR makes it possible to visualise relationships that are complex and concepts that are hard to understand [3, 4]. Second, AR can facilitate the timely presentation of information at the right place, contributing to reducing time searching for such information, reducing errors, and improving the ability to memorise and recall information [5, 6]. Additionally, by using AR, there is the possibility of experiencing phenomena that may not be experienced in real-world situations [6, 7].

Dünser and Billinghurst [8] indicated that through AR, complex phenomena can be easily understood. This is because AR provides unique visual and interactive experiences that integrate both virtual and real information and, thus, facilitates the communication of abstract concepts to learners. This capability allows the superimposition of virtual graphics over real objects by designers, thus making it possible to manipulate digital content in a physical manner and interact with it. As such, spatial and temporal concepts are demonstrated more effectively in addition to the relationship between virtual and real objects. For example, through reading in combination with a 2D picture, a student can theoretically understand the position of the earth relative to that of the sun. A much better and practical understanding can be gained by using a 3D visual system. AR has made it possible to animate dynamic processes to provide a direct, tangible interaction that makes it possible for learners to interact intuitively with digital content.

One further element of AR affordance is the ability to facilitate the visualisation of invisible events or concepts through superimposing virtual information or objects onto physical environments or objects [3, 9]. Essentially, when taking this into account, AR systems could provide students with support and assistance in terms of enabling and helping them visualise unobservable phenomena or abstract scientific concepts through the adoption of virtual objects, including—but not limited to—molecules, symbols, and vectors. For instance, through the application of augmented chemistry, students are able to choose chemical elements, add them into a framework of a 3D molecular model, and revolve and pivot the model [10].

Another example of the AR in education is the use of tangible interfaces and AR models of 3D objects [11]. In the tangible interfaces, physical objects are coupled to a digital source of information. The AR models are used in engineering courses containing graphics so as to promote the students' understanding of the relationship that exists between 3D objects and their projection. The tangible interfaces system was tested with 35 students who were majors in engineering. From the tests, the students' performance and ability to transfer 3D objects into 2D projections significantly improved. Higher rates of engagement with the AR models were also realised.

Andujar et al. [12] considered a digital control system design based on a field-programmable gate array (FPGA) development board. Here, AR is used to demonstrate how the various activities carried out in the lab can be performed in the same way it is done in the workplace. The system provides physical contact and, thus, reduces cases of student discouragement because of a lack of it. The study used 10 teachers and 36 students in evaluating the system. For both the students and teachers, there was higher engagement, greater motivation, and significant improvement in learnability of abstract concepts when compared to the traditional learning methods. In this AR prototype and many others, designers focused on the visual aspects of embedded electronics.

Onime and Abiona [13] built an augmented reality mobile system to handle practical laboratory experiments in science, technology, and engineering. The system replicated existing hands-on experiments using photographic markers of laboratory kits. The researchers examined the system based on two learning scenarios in the field of microelectronic and communication engineering. In the engineering scenario, they used an Arduino-compatible board called Seeding Stalker v2, which has embedded sensors for the hands-on experiment. The learning goal was to connect the resistor and light emitting diode (LED) to the board and to pulsate the LED. They used a low-cost 2D photographic mock-up of the same hardware board as a photo-realistic marker for the augmented reality mobile experiment. They built a 3D virtual object for the LED and the resistor and produced step-by-step instructions to connect them to the board using the aid of AR. In the communication scenario, they introduced three types of antennae communication, and learners were asked to establish bi-directional wireless radio links. In contrast, the AR version involved three mock-up marker objects for all antennae, and when the learner pointed at the marker, the radiation appeared in 2D or 3D mode. In the scenarios, 148 students participated in both experiments. After finishing the experiment, they stated that the augmented reality mobile application made a positive impression and was helpful for learning and grades compared to the existing hands-on experiment.

AR has been used so as to assist the users in seeing the complicated information in robotic systems. Freund et al. [14] developed a state oriented modelling method that incorporated virtual reality words. This enabled users to see 3D state data regarding autonomous systems. The AR was also used by Daily et al. [15] to visualise data from the distributed robot swarms. These robots pass information and work in cooperation so as to alert when there are intruders. The users use AR to collect and pass data from each robot and also to show the quickest way to the intruder.

In addition, Chen et al. [16] proposed a system that makes it easier for researchers to visualise and interpret complex robot data by augmenting the robot's information (such as sensor map and task-relevant data) with the real-world environment, maximising the shared perceptual space between the user and the robot. Thus, AR technology can assist humans not only in testing robots' systems but also in understanding complex robot information and improving human-robot interaction.

It has been stated by Collett and MacDonald [17] that the mobile robot programming is lacking the necessary tools to help developers in the debugging process. Robots communicate with the environment and that makes programming very challenging. This communication with the environment complicates the process in such a way that the programmers have to first know what information the robot is receiving. Thus, they developed an AR debugging tool that supports the programmers' perception of the robots world instead of using a simulated world by developers, augmented reality allows them to view the robot world with additional virtual objects in the real environment. Thus, developers do not need to shift between the real environment and the robot world because augmented reality brings the robot data into the real-world context. One benefit of this method is that it assists developers in identifying the source of the errors in the robot application. The disadvantage of this study, however, is that they employed AR as visualisation tools represent the robot data in 3D and 2D-only graphical views. The system is lacking text support such that, if it was present, it would be more likely to see the errors and the bugs.

Magnenat et al. [18] argue that AR and the visual feedback improve the ability of high-school learners to comprehend event-handling concepts in computer science. They proposed an AR system with incorporated visual feedback that overlay robot's events in real time. The system gives a timeline that gives the location and the time of execution of the robot events. This assists the learners in knowing what the robot is doing and, thus, assisting the learners to know where the program is. The AR system enabled learners to identify errors in their programs quicker and reduce the time between runs.

Likewise, Lalonde et al. [19] proposed a predictor for programming mobile robots known as robot observability. This predictor serves the purpose of diagnostic transparency by making sure that the incremental procedure of building and debugging robot programs is made available. This is an essential tool students can use in the diagnosis of a misbehaving robot. Students, by audio feedback, are capable of creating a tool that enhances the predictor performance through identification of the robot's internal state evolution. The robot, for example, is capable of speaking its action and stating its purpose. Furthermore, the authors stated that 86% of learners thought that data logging and visual interfaces are valuable tools for debugging. However, the study had not taken into consideration the broader implication in the use of AR as a visual interface capable of guiding students and revealing the procedures of internal communication, which in real time are taking place within the physical objects.

Based on the literature, creating an AR interactive learning environment that can help students in understanding invisible entities while performing laboratory learning activities using instant feedback has not been looked at, especially in providing a pedagogical explanation framework for real-time computational activities. This can enable learners to construct a meaningful view of the physical objects related to learning and teaching. Especially, the focus is on revealing the abstract concepts learners encounter when dealing with computational objects. Therefore, this study tries to close the gap by evaluating the proposed PVM model and reveal its effectiveness in learning and teaching.

3 Materials and Methods

3.1 Experimental Design

The experiment evaluated two educational learning approaches (PVM with AR, and a traditional approach) to be used by students for solving a learning activity based on a modularised educational robot called BuzzBot [20]. The type of approach (PVM with AR, traditional) was used as an independent variable in the experiment. A between-subjects design was used to examine the AR and TR systems. This was used to avoid knowledge transfer which might result in making it more difficult to identify the effectiveness of the approach used. Nonetheless, a within-subjects design was also used to gather participants' opinions regarding both approaches.

The learning activity required students to design a behaviour-based robot that follows a wall and avoids obstacles. This behaviour is widely known in the robotics field [21, 22]. However, to minimise the complexity of the task, students were given a programming source code to edit and modify according to task requirement instead of making the programming code from scratch. The given source code was designed to make the robot misbehave at runtime, and students were asked to solve the problem based on the assigned approach (PVM with AR or TR). The programming source code was written using object-oriented style, which makes code easy to read, understand and modify, especial for small programmes [23]. A complete list of robot classes was given and made available to use for modifying or replacing functions in the code. Both approaches (PVM with AR and TR) required students to use Python programming language to edit and debug the given programming code for the mobile robot.

3.2 Participants

Twenty students from the School of Computer Science and Electronic Engineering (CSEE), University of Essex were invited to take part in the experiment. The students were divided into two groups, AR and TR, with 10 students in each group. The sample formed 75% male compared to 20% female and 5% preferred not to say. At the time of the experiment, the level of study for all participants was 100% postgraduate (master and PhD), with 85% doing computer science and 15% doing engineering. 55% of participants stated their computer expertise level as expert, against 45% who stated their level as intermediate. In addition, 50% of participants expressed their computer programming skills as intermediate, compared to expert (45%) and beginner (5%).

65% of participants declared that they had studied during their degree at least one of the following modules: embedded systems, robotics, artificial intelligence, digital electronics, and communications engineering, compared to 35% who had not studied any of these. 90% of participants stated that they had been involved in practical activities or assignments in science or engineering labs, against 10% who had not participated in lab activities. After completing lab activities or assignments, 55% of participants stated that they felt good in relation to achieving the activity/assignment learning objective, compared to very good (10%), average (30%), and bad (5%). In relation to the assessment, 55% of participants depended on the teacher or instructor to assess their lab activity/assignment work, as compared to those who relied on an educational software tool (10%) or themselves (35%).

All participants (100%) had completed a programming assignment as part of their course. When participants discovered that the program was not behaving as expected, 40% of them said they would look at the source code, 30% said they would add a print statement inside the program, and 30% stated they would use a debugging tool (Fig. 1).

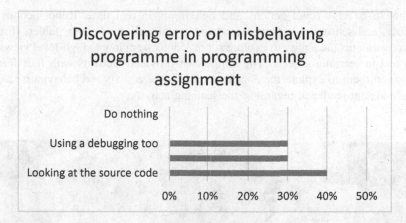

Fig. 1. Discovering error or misbehaving programme in programming assignment

3.3 Procedure

The procedure of the experiment was divided into three phases: before, during, and after.

1. Before the experiment. Participants were provided with a link to an online questionnaire to gather demographic information and their familiarity with computing, programming, and embedded system learning activity and assessment. On the day of the experiment, participants were informed about the experiment aim, phases, and procedure, and signed a consent form.
2. During the experiment. Participants were provided with the learning activity instruction and robot material, such as classes and functions. They then logged into Raspberry Pi and used Geany IDE to start working on the assigned programming task. A tablet-holder desk stand was used to support the AR group to allow them to work hands-free. Time and debugging times were observed during the experiment by the instructor.
3. After the experiment. Participants were provided with an online questionnaire to gather information about their experience on the approach used (TR or AR). Lastly, participants were asked to experience the other approach (swapping from AR to TR or vice versa). Another survey link was provided to gather user opinion on both approaches and to evaluate the AR system.

3.4 Educational Learning Approach

3.4.1 PVM with AR Approach

The first approach was using the AR technique. An AR application was designed to visualise and analyse robot actions and states and produce pedagogical feedback based on the learning activity. This approach followed the PVM model for structuring a learning activity and analysing computational objects in terms of pedagogy [1]. Once students debugged or executed the source code, they could point their tablet's camera at the robot to overlay robot actions and behaviours in real time. Robot actions and behaviours and sensors' values were updated in real time on students' tablets (Fig. 2). This gave students the ability to explore robot actions from low to high-level views that correspond to learning objects. The application provided students with four features that allowed them to explore the construction of robot actions and behaviours, as well as obtain instant feedback regarding the learning activity.

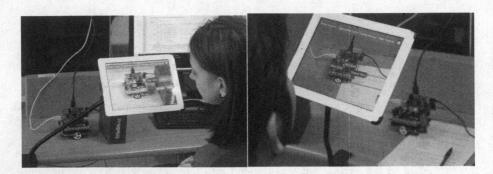

Fig. 2. Students using PVM with AR application

The PVM with AR application was developed with the Unity 3D game engine (https://unity3d.com) using the Vuforia Augmented Reality Software Development Kit (https://developer.vuforia.com). Then, the application was built and run on an IOS apple tablet using the Apple Integrated Development Environment Xcode (https://developer.apple.com). Programming the robot was done with Raspberry Pi (https://raspberrypi.org) using the Geany text editor (www.geany.org).

3.4.2 Traditional Approach

The second approach was the conventional approach for debugging and executing programming code in computer and engineering science. This approach allowed students to execute code and examine the robot without visualisation help; instead, robot outputs (actions) were represented on the tool's console (log file) in real time (Fig. 3). A print statement was added to robot classes in order to print robot states and actions on the tool's console. This was added to assist student understanding of robot programme behaviour. It was noted by Ahmadzadeh et al. [24] that a print statement is used in programming code as a debugging strategy to find errors. In addition, it helps in examining particular programme behaviours and revealing values of interest [25]. Thus, during runtimes, students were able to see robot actions in abstract meanings such as *Left Motor Move Forward, Object Near:09.* In both approaches, the low-level data representations were the same but the appearance was different, being visualised in AR, and log file text in the traditional approach. In both approaches, students were allowed to debug the programming code many times until the task learning objectives were achieved.

Fig. 3. Students using traditional approach

3.5 Measurements

Qualitative and quantitative data were collected to evaluate the learning effectiveness and pedagogical value of the PVM using AR, as compared to TR. The research instruments consisted of three questionnaires for participants and participants' observations. The first questionnaire collected general demographic information and preliminary knowledge on evaluated topics, such as computing and programming experience, and a computing system assessment to establish the participant's background. The second questionnaire was given to participants after they finished the learning activity, and divided into two parts. The first part measured the effectiveness of the approach used for the learning activity task. This part was designed using 5-Likert scales ranging from "strongly disagree" at one end to "strongly agree" at the other, with "Neutral" in the middle. The second part measured cognitive workload when doing the learning activity. The cognitive workload was based on NASA-TLX (Task Load Index) that was used to assess the overall workload of the learning activity task [26]. To measure the workload experience, six rating scales were used: mental demand, physical demand, temporal demand, performance, effort and frustration. Participants rated each of these scales on a Likert scale, ranging from low to high. The third questionnaire gathered participants' opinions after experiencing both approaches (AR and TR). This questionnaire was short and designed using a combination of open and closed questions. Closed questions were utilised to gather the participants' feedback using Likert scales whilst open questions were used to give participants the opportunity to state their views about the preferred approach. Participants were observed while performing the activity and two constructs were recorded. The first construct was the time taken to complete the task, and the second was the amount of debugging time it took to solve the task. These were observed to measure the effectiveness of each approach (AR and TR) in terms of time and number of trials. Data were anonymised and analysed using the statistical program SPSS (Statistical Package for the Social Science).

4   Experiment Results

4.1   Task Performance

Throughout the experiment, the completion time for the learning activity was measured to define the amount of time required for participants to solve the task. In addition, the number of trials (debugging) was counted to indicate the number of debugging participants required to solve the task. A t-test was performed to test whether there was a statistically significant difference in mean Time and mean Debugging Times between the AR and TR groups. The test revealed a significant difference in mean Time and mean Debugging Times between students using AR and students using TR, $p < .01$. The test results are reported in Table 1. From the table, the mean Time and mean Debugging Times for the AR students were significantly lower than those for the TR students, indicating that the PVM with AR reduced the time for solving a learning activity task and with fewer trials. These results supported research question 1.

Table 1. Independent samples t-test findings for time and debugging times, grouped by approach

	Group statistics				Independent samples test	
	AR		TR			
	M	SD	M	SD	T	Sig.
Time	08:50	01:25	14:13	03:44	−4.252	.001
Debugging times	4.30	.949	8.10	1.663	−6.275	.000

4.2   Cognitive Overload

The cognitive overload questionnaire was used to assess students' workload given the methods used to achieve the learning activity. There are six subscales that calculate the overall workload. Results from two independent t-tests revealed that students who used AR with a PVM for solving programming activity had a lower mean in the overall cognitive workload than those students who used the conventional approach. This indicated a significant difference between both groups, $t = -5.052, p = .001$ (Table 2). In relation to the subscales, the test revealed that the AR group found the task did not require mental effort, as compared to the hands-on group, which was statically different $(t = -3.398, p = .007)$. In terms of physical effort, there was no significant difference between the groups $(t = -1.573, p = .143)$. In addition, the group that used the AR application had a lower time pressure than the control group $(t = -2.939, p = .014)$. The control group students were not satisfied with their task performance as the approach used influenced them significantly $(t = -4.034, p = .002)$. During the task, the AR group was less frustrated than the control group $(t = -4.572, p = .001)$. After completing the task, the control group students revealed they had found it hard to accomplish the learning task, which was significantly different from the AR group $(t = -5.903, p = .001)$. These results supported research question 2.

Table 2. Cognitive workload for controlling the mobile robot

	Group statistics				Independent samples test	
	AR		TR			
	M	SD	M	SD	T	Sig.
Mental demand	3.40	1.430	9.90	5.877	−3.398	**.007**
Physical demand	2.90	1.969	5.70	5.272	−1.573	.143
Temporal demand	3.50	1.509	8.20	4.826	−2.939	.014
Performance	2.30	1.767	8.80	4.789	−4.034	**.002**
Effort	2.80	1.549	11.60	4.452	−5.903	**.001**
Frustration	1.50	1.080	8.50	4.720	−4.572	**.001**
Cognitive workload	2.73	.778	8.78	3.70	−5.052	**.001**

4.3 Learning Approach Effectiveness

After completing the activity, participants were asked to rate the approach used in a subjective questionnaire. A t-test was performed to study the differences between the two groups of students with respect to their responses to the post-questionnaire items. The test revealed that there was statistically significant differences in the mean scores of both groups' students, $p < .001$. The findings are reported in Table 3. From Table 3, it can be stated that the PVM with AR was a more effective tool for assisting learning while performing the learning activity compared to traditional approach and this finding support research question 3.

Table 3. Independent-samples t-test findings for experiment post questionnaire items

Questionnaire	Group statistics				Independent samples test	
	AR		TR			
	M	SD	M	SD	T	Sig.
1. Discovering bugs and errors took a lot of effort	1.30	.483	3.50	.850	−7.117	<.001
2. This approach helped me to discover and correct the bugs and errors very quickly	4.80	.422	2.70	.483	10.357	<.001
3. By using the available tools, I was able to understand the robot behaviour	4.80	.422	2.50	.972	6.866	<.001
4. By using the available tools, I was not able to deconstruct and examine the robot behaviour in more detail	1.50	.707	3.40	.966	−5.019	<.001
5. By using the available tools, I was able to know if I had accomplished the learning objective	4.80	.422	3.00	1.155	4.630	<.001
6. When I debugged the robot, I found it difficult to keep track of the robot and to look at the robot output at the same time	1.40	.516	4.10	.876	−8.399	<.001
7. Knowing why the robot was misbehaving while the robot was running in real time was very challenging	1.30	.483	3.50	1.080	−5.880	<.001

Table 4. Independent-samples t-test findings for user post opinions

Opinion	Group statistics				Independent samples test	
	AR		TR			
	M	SD	M	SD	t	Sig.
1. I think the use of AR has a significant advantage over traditional methods for discovering and revealing errors and bugs in embedded computing activities	4.90	.316	4.50	.707	1.633	.127
2. I think that the use of AR is not suitable for assisting students' learning activities	1.60	.699	1.90	1.197	−.684	.503
3. I think the use of AR allows me to get a deeper understanding of how things work and communicate more than TR for computer science and engineering activities/assignments	4.40	.516	4.40	.516	.000	1.000
4. I don't see that AR application makes any difference	1.30	.483	1.40	.516	−.447	.660

4.4 Subjective User Experience

After experiencing both approaches, participants were asked to state their view in a short questionnaire. Additionally, a t-test was performed to study differences between both groups of students with respect to their opinions (Table 4). The test revealed no significant differences between students of both groups, $p > .05$. That is, students who used AR and those who used TR thought that the use of AR had a significant advantage over traditional methods for discovering and revealing errors and bugs in embedded computing activities, and that the use of AR allowed them to get a deeper understanding of how things work and communicate more than TR for computer science and engineering activities/assignments. On the other hand, students from both groups did not think that the use of AR was not suitable for assisting students' learning activities and they disagreed that the AR application made no difference.

4.4.1 Groups' Approach Preferences

Moreover, participants were then asked which approach they preferred for doing the activity. 95% of participants stated their preferences for the use of a PVM with AR system for practising and carrying out similar activities, whereas only one participant preferred TR. Additionally, participants were asked to state the reason for their choice and some of the participants' statements were:

"AR makes a real difference in the way code is debugged, changing stressful and laborious work into a fun, engaging, and enjoyable experience. Using this approach in assignments would definitely simplify things and have a great impact on the quality of the work submitted" (Participant 3 in the AR group).

"I am not experienced with programming robots, so I found this approach really useful as it clearly explains how everything is connected" (Participant 4 in the AR group).

"Seeing in real time how my action translates to the robot behaviour was beneficial. I was able to quickly detect what went wrong when the code is running and didn't have to spend much time debugging" (Participant 9 in the AR group).

"I would rather know what the robot is doing at a higher level when I am first learning to use it. And I believe AR will allow students to progress in their understanding of the low-level instructions of the robot" (Participant 2 in the TR group).

"As the number of rules gets larger, it becomes increasingly difficult to track the robot's responses to different sensory input. The AR method provides pictures and high-level linguistic descriptions for monitoring the robot. This would be useful for debugging the code and varying the rules" (Participant 4 in the TR group).

"I can see the use of this technology in robotics but its use in other domains will need further study. It had a lot of expressiveness which is not possible on a whiteboard" (Participant 6 in the TR group).

"I'm more used to TR and for such a simple task, it is easier to stick to already learned behaviour" (Participant 8 in the TR group).

From these comments, it is possible to see that the majority of participants thought the PVM with AR gave extra value to the activity, helping them to obtain a clear picture of the things that were happening in hidden worlds. This supported research question 4.

5 Discussion and Conclusion

This study presented and evaluated an AR learning application that uses the PVM explanation framework for constructing pedagogical meaningful information of computational objects. The study compared the PVM with AR application with its equivalent traditional approach to studying its learning effectiveness on students' performance in solving problem tasks, especially with real-time systems. Both applications were designed to provide the same information and workflow capabilities. The main findings and their implications are discussed below.

An important aspect of the PVM computational model proposed was assisting learners to assist students solving the task more quickly and with fewer trails, as proposed in research question 1. The completion time and debugging time were calculated to see how long it took participants to complete the activity. The result showed that the PVM with AR system enabled learners to find misbehaving actions faster and with less debugging time than the traditional approach. It reduced the time taken to complete a complex task, such as solving behaviour-based robotics and reduced the number of trials that learners needed to fix the problem. Comparison of this finding with those of other studies [17–19] confirms the benefits of using a visual interface for debugging, as this assists learners and developers in identifying errors faster and minimises the time between runs.

An important angle for the PVM model proposed was the requirement of providing learners with assistance during learning in order to reduce the task workload, as proposed in research question 2. The reason for this measurement was to ensure that the PVM model, as a learning environment, does not add more complexity for learners. The cognitive workload was evaluated by obtaining learners' views on the learning activity workload in terms of mental demand, physical demand, temporal demand, performance, effort, and frustration. Based on feedback from learners, the analysis showed that cognitive overload was lower in the PVM with AR than with the traditional approach. These results agree with the findings of other studies, in which users in the AR condition had a lower task workload [27–29]. In a more in-depth analysis of cognitive workload subscales, the use of a traditional programming environment to debug the robot and find misbehaving actions was complex and required more effort than the use of a PVM with AR system. Moreover, the traditional programming method increased learners' frustration during the task, and traditional learners rated their performance lower than those in the PVM with AR group. It is worth noting that the primarily demographic results revealed that all learners, in both groups, have programming skills; thus, these results did not relate to learners' programming skills ability. It seems possible that these results are because of learners who use a traditional programming environment seeing both worlds (robot and environment) and trying to figure out the cause of the problem, whereas those who were using a PVM with AR were immersed in both worlds. This could be additional evidence in support of research question 1, that states that AR with PVM learners solve learning activity faster and with fewer trials. Both groups agreed that an editing embedded computing programming task did not require physical activity. It may be that these learners are used to practical tasks that involve programming in their studies.

The strategy to evaluate learners' preference was to ask participants to experience both learning environments. Based on learner feedback, the analysis showed that a large majority of participants preferred using a PVM with AR to do embedded computing laboratory practical work. Learners thought a PVM with AR had a significant advantage over traditional methods for discovering and revealing errors and bugs in embedded computing activities and that it enabled them to acquire a deeper understanding of how things work and communicate than the traditional approach. Additionally, they considered that a PVM with AR was a suitable tool to aid them during the activity and guide them in achieving the learning objectives. This result is consistent with the comments provided by participants who stated that a PVM with AR keeps the focus on the learning context, making it easy to observe and visualise phenomena. Another comment stated the usefulness of a PVM with AR in regard to the deconstruction and construction mechanism in explaining the components of physical objects (e.g., software and hardware). Holding attention, usefulness, being exciting, offering greater learning speed, and saving time are among other reported comments that might provide evidence for participants' choice of a PVM with AR. One interesting comment made by one of the participants who preferred the traditional approach to using a PVM with AR was that he/she would do a simple learning activity in the environment already learnt. A possible explanation for this claim may be related to the computing and programming skills the participant has. Radu [30] indicates that AR technology may not be an effective learning approach for some students. It could also be related to the design of the learning activity, as this was not proposed for solving complicated embedded computing problems. However, it can be concluded that this finding supports research question 4, that states that a PVM with AR would be preferred to traditional methods, which is also supported by the research outcome of Sayed et al. [31].

One aspect that was not addressed in this evaluation, because of time limitations, is related to comparing the PVM with AR application to other forms of learning technology that utilise the principle of the PVM framework (e.g., web-based, virtual environments). It is, therefore, worth considering this aspect when employing a PVM framework in other studies. This could help in identifying whether the information provided by the PVM influences learners to gain knowledge regardless of the technology being used. Ibáñez et al. [32] compared AR learning to web-based applications and found that the AR group performed better than the web-based group.

The study took into consideration learners' prior knowledge to ensure the validity of the sample, whereas other learner characteristics (e.g., gender, age difference, level of computer expertise, level of study) were not examined. Squire and Jan [33] found older students are different to younger students in terms of making arguments and integrating pieces of evidence in AR-related science learning. In addition, O'Shea et al. [34] found that a male group had better conversations during the process of the activity than a female group and related this to the male gaming experience. Additionally, Cheng and Tsai [35] suggested considering presence in AR environments as an important learner characteristic, which indicates to what degree learners feel immersed within the AR learning environments. Another aspect not addressed relates to AR displays. A tablet was used as a visual interface for the AR learning environment, whereas a head-mounted display and glasses were not employed. In addition, a technical evaluation for measuring network and system latency between the AR display and physical objects was not considered; it would be beneficial if this were applied to indicate the accuracy of synchronisation when overlaying information from a real-time system.

References

1. Alrashidi, M., Callaghan, V., Gardner, M.: An object-oriented pedagogical model for mixed reality teaching and learning. In: 2014 International Conference on Intelligent Environments (IE), pp. 202–206 (2014)
2. Wu, H.-K., Lee, S.W.-Y., Chang, H.-Y., Liang, J.-C.: Current status, opportunities and challenges of augmented reality in education. Comput. Educ. **62**, 41–49 (2013)
3. Arvanitis, T.N., et al.: Human factors and qualitative pedagogical evaluation of a mobile augmented reality system for science education used by learners with physical disabilities. Pers. Ubiquit. Comput. **13**(3), 243–250 (2007)
4. Shelton, B.E.: Using augmented reality for teaching Earth-Sun relationships to undergraduate geography students. In: The First IEEE International Augmented Reality Toolkit Workshop, ART 2002 (2002)
5. Cooperstock, J.R.: The classroom of the future: enhancing education through augmented reality. In: Proceedings of HCI International 2001 Conference on Human-Computer Interaction, pp. 688–692 (2001)

6. Neumann, U., Majoros, A.: Cognitive, performance, and systems issues for augmented reality applications in manufacturing and maintenance. In: Proceedings of the Virtual Reality Annual International Symposium, Washington, DC, USA, p. 4 (1998)
7. Klopfer, E., Squire, K.: Environmental detectives—the development of an augmented reality platform for environmental simulations. Educ. Technol. Res. Dev. 56(2), 203–228 (2007)
8. Dünser, A., Billinghurst, M.: Evaluating augmented reality systems. In: Furht, B. (ed.) Handbook of Augmented Reality, pp. 289–307. Springer, New York (2011)
9. Dunleavy, M., Dede, C., Mitchell, R.: Affordances and limitations of immersive participatory augmented reality simulations for teaching and learning. J. Sci. Educ. Technol. 18(1), 7–22 (2009)
10. Kotranza, A., Lind, D.S., Pugh, C.M., Lok, B.: Real-time in-situ visual feedback of task performance in mixed environments for learning joint psychomotor-cognitive tasks. In: 2009 8th IEEE International Symposium on Mixed and Augmented Reality, pp. 125–134 (2009)
11. Chen, Y.-C., Chi, H.-L., Hung, W.-H., Kang, S.-C.: Use of tangible and augmented reality models in engineering graphics courses. J. Prof. Issues Eng. Educ. Pract. 137(4), 267–276 (2011)
12. Andujar, J.M., Mejias, A., Marquez, M.A.: Augmented reality for the improvement of remote laboratories: an augmented remote laboratory. IEEE Trans. Educ. 54(3), 492–500 (2011)
13. Onime, C., Abiona, O.: 3D mobile augmented reality interface for laboratory experiments. Int. J. Commun. Netw. Syst. Sci. 9(4), 67 (2016)
14. Freund, E., Schluse, M., Rossmann, J.: State oriented modeling as enabling technology for projective virtual reality. In: Proceedings of 2001 IEEE/RSJ International Conference on Intelligent Robots and Systems, vol. 4, pp. 1842–1847 (2001)
15. Daily, M., Cho, Y., Martin, K., Payton, D.: World embedded interfaces for human-robot interaction. In: Proceedings of the 36th Annual Hawaii International Conference on System Sciences, p. 6–pp (2003)
16. Chen, I.Y.H., MacDonald, B., Wunsche, B.: Mixed reality simulation for mobile robots. In: 2009 IEEE International Conference on Robotics and Automation, pp. 232–237 (2009)
17. Collett, T.H.J., MacDonald, B.A.: An augmented reality debugging system for mobile robot software engineers. J. Softw. Eng. Robot. 1(1), 18–32 (2010)
18. Magnenat, S., Ben-Ari, M., Klinger, S., Sumner, R.W.: Enhancing robot programming with visual feedback and augmented reality. In: Proceedings of the 2015 ACM Conference on Innovation and Technology in Computer Science Education, New York, USA, pp. 153–158 (2015)
19. Lalonde, J., Bartley, C.P., Nourbakhsh, I.: Mobile robot programming in education. In: Proceedings 2006 IEEE International Conference on Robotics and Automation, ICRA 2006, pp. 345–350 (2006)
20. Callaghan, V.: Buzz-boarding; practical support for teaching computing, based on the internet-of-things. In: 1st Annual Conference on the Aiming for Excellence in STEM Learning and Teaching, Imperial College, London & The Royal Geographical Society, pp. 12–13 (2012)
21. Arkin, R.C.: Motor schema—based mobile robot navigation. Int. J. Robot. Res. 8(4), 92–112 (1989)
22. Pfeifer, R., Scheier, C.: Understanding Intelligence. MIT Press, Cambridge (1999)
23. Wiedenbeck, S., Ramalingam, V.: Novice comprehension of small programs written in the procedural and object-oriented styles. Int. J. Hum.-Comput. Stud. 51(1), 71–87 (1999)

24. Ahmadzadeh, M., Elliman, D., Higgins, C.: An analysis of patterns of debugging among novice computer science students. In: Proceedings of the 10th Annual SIGCSE Conference on Innovation and Technology in Computer Science Education, New York, USA, pp. 84–88 (2005)

25. Li, X., Flatt, M.: Medic: metaprogramming and trace-oriented debugging. In: Proceedings of the Workshop on Future Programming, New York, USA, pp. 7–14 (2015)

26. Hart, S.G., Staveland, L.E.: Development of NASA-TLX (Task Load Index): results of empirical and theoretical research. In: Meshkati, P.A.H.N. (ed.) Advances in Psychology, vol. 52, pp. 139–183. North-Holland, Amsterdam (1988)

27. Medenica, Z., Kun, A.L., Paek, T., Palinko, O.: Augmented reality vs. street views: a driving simulator study comparing two emerging navigation aids. In: Proceedings of the 13th International Conference on Human Computer Interaction with Mobile Devices and Services, pp. 265–274 (2011)

28. Tang, A., Owen, C., Biocca, F., Mou, W.: Comparative effectiveness of augmented reality in object assembly. In: Proceedings of the SIGCHI Conference on Human Factors in Computing Systems, New York, USA, pp. 73–80 (2003)

29. Tang, A., Owen, C., Biocca, F., Mou, W.: Experimental evaluation of augmented reality in object assembly task. In: Proceedings of the 1st International Symposium on Mixed and Augmented Reality, p. 265 (2002)

30. Radu, I.: Augmented reality in education: a meta-review and cross-media analysis. Pers. Ubiquit. Comput. **18**(6), 1533–1543 (2014)

31. Sayed, E., et al.: ARSC: augmented reality student card–an augmented reality solution for the education field. Comput. Educ. **56**(4), 1045–1061 (2011)

32. Ibáñez, M.B., Di Serio, Á., Villarán, D., Delgado Kloos, C.: Experimenting with electromagnetism using augmented reality: impact on flow student experience and educational effectiveness. Comput. Educ. **71**, 1–13 (2014)

33. Squire, K.D., Jan, M.: Mad city mystery: developing scientific argumentation skills with a place-based augmented reality game on handheld computers. J. Sci. Educ. Technol. **16**(1), 5–29 (2007)

34. O'Shea, P.M., Dede, C., Cherian, M.: Research note: the results of formatively evaluating an augmented reality curriculum based on modified design principles. Int J Gaming Comput. Mediat. Simul. **3**(2), 57–66 (2011)

35. Cheng, K.-H., Tsai, C.-C.: Affordances of augmented reality in science learning: suggestions for future research. J. Sci. Educ. Technol. **22**(4), 449–462 (2012)

ARSSET: Augmented Reality Support on SET

Andrea Sanna[1(✉)], Fabrizio Lamberti[1], Francesco De Pace[1],
Roberto Iacoviello[2], and Paola Sunna[2]

[1] Dipartimento di Automatica e Informatica, Politecnico di Torino,
c.so Duca degli Abruzzi 24, 10129 Torino, Italy
{andrea.sanna,fabrizio.lamberti}@polito.it, depazz91@gmail.com
[2] RAI, Centro Ricerche e Innovazione Tecnologica, via Cavalli 6, 1038 Torino, Italy
{roberto.iacoviello, paola.sunna}@rai.it

Abstract. The preparation of a set for a television production is a complex work; usually, several objects have to be manually placed in the environment and the configuration might be changed many times before finding the final set up. This configuration phase can be expensive and time consuming when large and heavy objects have to be moved. In order to tackle this issue, virtual sets allow the director of production to create virtual scenes before placing real objects. This paper proposes an alternative approach based on augmented reality technologies: objects of the scene are computer generated assets, which can be placed and manipulated in a real environment. With respect virtual sets, the proposed solution allows the director to move in a real scene enriched by computer-generated objects to be placed in the environment. The user wears an AR headset and manipulates objects by a tablet. The proposed system was evaluated by a group of 9 testers, which had to create an augmented TV set. Subjective and objective parameters have been used to assess the system usability.

1 Introduction

The set up of a television set is a time consuming and expensive job. A crew has to manually place the objects in the environment. Unfortunately, several different object placements have to be tried before achieving the right configuration.

For this reason, producers soon realized the advantages of creating *Virtual Sets*. A Virtual Set (VS) is a television studio that allows the real-time combination of people or other real objects and computer generated elements. A proper VS should have at least these properties: people and real objects have to be integrated in the virtual set, 3D models must be rendered in real time during the shooting and there must be coherence between real and virtual, also when cameras are moving. According to this definition, if only pre-rendered images are used or there are not camera movements (e.g., in weather forecasts), a proper VS is not implemented.

There are different ways to create a set nowadays, from the traditional way to the virtual approach. Each of them has advantages and drawbacks. With the traditional approach, the director works with real objects in the real environment;

© Springer International Publishing AG 2017
L.T. De Paolis et al. (Eds.): AVR 2017, Part I, LNCS 10324, pp. 356–376, 2017.
DOI: 10.1007/978-3-319-60922-5_28

in this way, a very precise idea of what will appear on the screen can be obtained. On the other hand, this approach is very expensive in terms of resources, since different configurations have to be usually tried. By using virtual studios, the above mentioned problems can be avoided, but the director works in a fictitious environment and it is not possible to walk through the environment before the shooting. As the consequence, the director can only imagine how the scene will appear on the screen. This last issue is very important: the storyboard can in part avoid this type of problems. On the other hand, it is clear that having full access to the completed mixed set during the pre-visualization phase is much more effective. For instance, the storyboard presents a given view of the set and does not allow a full 3D immersion in the set in order to try different views.

Nowadays it is possible to recreate the entire set on a mobile device and manipulate all the elements that compose it. The ShotPro application (http://www.shotprofessional.com/) for iPad is a system that allows a director to see the entire set realized in computer graphics and manipulate it. Another example is FrameForge (http://www.storyboardbetter.com/): a software that helps film makers to pre-visualize their work by creating an optically correct Virtual Film on the computer.

The type of approach described above solves some of the problems of the traditional set creation: now directors can really see the entire set and they can have a good idea of what will appear on the screen. Unfortunately, this interaction is still mediated by the screen device and directors cannot move around in the real environment. Moreover, directors are not really "there", thus they can only see what is displayed on the device screen.

Thanks to the recent introduction in the market of low cost stereoscopic displays, such as Oculus Rift, it is now possible to experience a new virtual paradigm. With such devices, the user can really move around the 3D environment and this enhances a lot the interaction with the 3D models. Video games have been one of the first fields of application of these devices, which are now used also in the pre-production phase of film making [13].

One of the big issues related to the head-mounted devices with a closed view (that is, the user can only view the virtual environment) is that they cannot be used for a long time since they might cause symptoms such as: general discomfort, headache, stomach awareness, nausea, vomiting, etc. There are some researches that study this kind of physical problem. In [3] it is emphasized that symptoms can occur if the user wear a head-mounted display for more then 20–30 min; moreover, these problems occur also during adaptation and they persist also after having used the device.

The user can experience postural instability since the sensory and motor systems of the user "work" in different spaces and this may cause incongruities among the respective inputs. In fact, the ability to maintain posture is based on predictable relations among visual, vestibular and somatosensory sensations. When these relations change, the resulting sensory conflict creates a need for adaptation and the posture control systems are temporarily disturbed [9]. Moreover, these physical problems are related to the user's age and to the past experience with immersive devices [4].

These problems suggest that using a head-mounted device to create a set in a virtual reality environment might still be not appropriate, since normally the preparation of a set takes plenty of time, much more than 20–30 min. Furthermore, a completely virtual approach needs to have all the set modeled in computer graphics and this might require a lot of resources in terms of time, computational power and financial investment.

The work presented in this paper tries to find an alternative solution using Augmented Reality (AR) technologies. As AR consists in a mix between the real world and the 3D environment, it benefits from all the positive features of the approaches described before (e.g., i provides users an immersive experience) but, at the same time, AR allows users to maintain a link with the real world. Moreover, computer-generated contents are used but in a smaller amount, because also the real environment is visible and it has not to be modeled.

The paper is organized as follows: Sect. 2 reviews how AR has been used for cinema and TV productions, whereas Sect. 3 presents functional requirements that guided the design and the development of ARSSET. Section 4 shows both the hardware and the software system architecture, whereas Sect. 5 presents the multimodal UI. Finally, results and their analysis are presented in Sect. 6.

2   AR in Cinema and Television Productions

An important field of application for AR technologies (readers can refer to [14] for a survey of AR applications) is cinema and television production. Computer animation, starting from pioneering work in 1940s and 1950s, has become increasingly more important in enriching the video content by adding computer generated elements. After the first examples in the 1960s, computer graphics has made great strides and nowadays it is very often quite difficult to understand which elements are real or not.

An use of AR according the definition provided in [12] has been made in TV sport productions; in particular, the first examples of AR appeared as annotations of live camera footage during sports events: the virtual lines in American football matches as well as the offside lines in soccer, which are superimposed to help the audience to understand actions. This first simple annotations have evolved a good deal and the technique is now employed to add virtual overlays in most sport events [1]. Since the live action is usually captured by tracked camera, interactive viewpoint changes are in principle possible albeit not under the viewer's control.

Virtual annotations have soon moved beyond sport information and are now ubiquitous in television programs. It is also quite common to present TV scenes in virtual settings, by filming the real people using tracked cameras in front of a green screen and then adding the virtual rendering of a studio. Another area, where AR can play an important role is the pre-production phase. Virtual Reality can partially support this phase; however, the problems related to a virtual reality-based approach have been mentioned above: huge use of resources and the discomfort caused by a prolonged use of head-mounted devices.

The AR can provide several benefits with respect to a pure virtual reality implementation as real life sets can be completed by computer generated features, thus allowing users to benefit for a real-time interactive set-up. The difference between traditional film methods and using a pre-visualization tool based on AR can be summarized in this claim: a director can achieve a realistic picture of what the scene should look like. All the people involved in the production process could have access to the same visualization, thus preventing the errors related to the use of a traditional paper-based storyboard, where some amount of interpretation is unavoidable. Moreover, it would greatly speed up the production process.

For instance, MR-PreViz [5] makes it possible to merge real backgrounds and computer-generated contents (humans and creatures) in an open set at an outdoor location. Methods for the composition of real backgrounds and computer graphics images using chroma-key or rotary encoder are already available in shooting studios. However, they are limited to indoor use. Some techniques of composition by mixed reality have also been proposed. The MR-PreViz system aims to realize indoor-outdoor systems to pre-visualize the movie scene with the dedicated camera for film-making.

A method presented in [6] uses AR techniques to shot scenes without using real actors. As a substitute for real actors, virtual ones are superimposed on a live video in real-time according to a real camera motion and the illumination. The insertion of the virtual objects into the real world is achieved by two key techniques: real-time estimation of camera and environmental lighting and rendering virtual actors according to these estimations. To obtain the real-time pose estimation of a camera, the authors utilize a pre-defined 3D environment model. The geometric registration is the basic technique: the pose of a camera is estimated from each video frame in real-time. The estimation of the camera pose and the modeling of the environment have been separated. Finally, to improve the realism, photometric registrations have been used to cast shadows.

An augmented virtuality pre-visualization system in presented in [16]: the pre-visualization is done on a mobile platform that is usable in the on-set production environment. The system's software infrastructure is primarily built using the Unity 3D game engine and some plugins provided by the Google's Project Tango. The Unity game engine has been used to link the virtual environment and the user interface. The Project Tango combines 3D motion tracking with depth sensing to give the device the ability to know its location and how it is moving through space, thus providing a correlation between a real camera and a virtual scene camera. By utilizing real-time rendering, the application provides users a live preview of how a final rendering could look like from a preliminary perspective.

Ncam (http://www.ncam-tech.com/) consists of a multi-sensor camera bar and a tethered server system. The camera bar attaches to any type of camera quickly and simply, whether hand-held, Steadicam, dolly or crane mounted. It takes minimal alignment times, and it is scalable to work simultaneously over multiple cameras. Ncam does not require any special fiducial or tracking marker as it automatically tracks the environment. This means that there are no modifications required to the set to allow Ncam to work properly. It can be used everywhere both in out-door or in-door locations, since it is quite flexible and highly mobile. Ncam provides complete position and rotation information as well as focal length and focus; therefore, it can be used by directors and directors of photography to add in real time virtual objects during the shooting.

3   Functional Requirements

The project described in this paper has been proposed by the Italian television broadcaster RAI - Radiotelevisione Italiana. The basic idea it to support the production director during the set up of a television studio by means of an augmented reality application. The application has to enable the director to insert and manipulate a set of computer-generated 3D models previously loaded in an object library.

The user has to be able to freely move in the real environment; for this reason an AR HMD has been chosen as display device. In particular the Epson Moverio BT-200 has been used. From the input point of view, the native interface of the AR glasses is not intuitive and user friendly. In order to tackle this issue, the input interface has been separated from the visualization one, thus following the approach proposed in [11] where a tablet is used to manipulate virtual objects.

In order to define the application requirements form the point of view of the end-user, a RAI's director (Ariella Beddini) helped software designers in identifying basic tasks to be accomplished during real shootings related to the pre-visualization of:

- different shots taken by different cameras with different fields of view;
- crane camera's movements and related shadows;
- focus/out-of-focus elements;
- the entire set with the possibility to walk freely around.

The first two points are directly linked: knowing the position of the crane allows a director to take the appropriate shot without having any kind of shadow issue in the shot. During this work, crane platforms have not been considered due to the difficulties to simulate their movements and the high computational power necessary to simulate real-time shadows. In addition, the selected AR glasses have only a camera and its movements are the movements of the user. Changes of focal lens have been simulated by using different fields of view on the same camera. The possibility to focus/defocus has been simulated by introducing a special object called *focus point*, discussed later in detail. The last requirement is the main goal of this work: creating a AR system such that a director can have access to a library of 3D objects that can be placed on the set and then manipulated, while the director can still walk around freely in the augmented environment.

4   System Architecture

In this section the system architecture including hardware and software elements is presented.

4.1   Hardware Architecture

Both the number of actions to be performed to complete the assigned task and the difficulty of each action strongly influence the system usability. According to [11], the separation of the input from the data visualization seems to be a proper way to interact with 3D contents. Moreover, due to the fact that a desirable feature is to see directly what is on the set, an AR see-through device has been selected; in particular, a commercial Android tablet as input device and the Epson Moverio BT-200 as a see-through device for the visualization have been adopted.

The tablet works as a proper joystick and it communicates with the AR glasses via Wi-Fi. Both the devices have to be connected in the same LAN. The last element of the scene is a target (marker): it is an image printed on a sheet format A0. When the application detects it, the system can obtain some essential information (such as distance from the camera and orientation) necessary to place computer-generated assets correctly aligned in the real environment. The target is also essential to define one of the two reference systems used by the system (the World Coordinate System - WCS). The WCS, is fixed in the environment and it is placed at the center of the target.

4.2   Software Architecture

The software architecture is divided in two parts: one for the tablet and the other one for the Moverio glasses. The Moverio's software has been developed by using Vuforia, Unity3D and Android. The main role of Vuforia is to recognize and track the image target. Thanks to Vuforia, all the 3D models are correctly placed in the real environment. On the other hand, Unity3D is able to manage 3D objects and the developed application can be directly converted into an APK for the Android tablet.

The tablet application has been developed by using CMU Sphinx, Android Studio and Android. Sphinx is an external library that has been chosen to manage the speech recognition-based input interface (see Sect. 5). This library has been imported in Android Studio. Android Studio is the well-known IDE used to develop applications for all the Android devices. It has been used to create the tablet application and its main role is to manage the user's touch input.

Each system uses two different threads: the Main Thread to manage the user inputs and to update the UI and a Secondary Thread to manage the network connection and the data transfer. Figure 1 shows the system behavior at the bootstrap. The main activity of the tablet's application, that is running on the Main Thread, is to create a socket with the IP address and the port number of the Moverio glasses on a Secondary Thread using an AsynkTask. If the Application

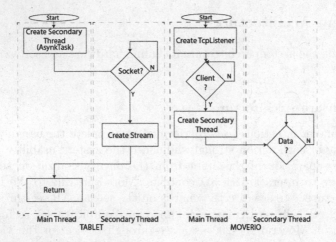

Fig. 1. Creation of the threads at the bootstrap.

on the Moverio is not running, the AsynkTask waits for a connection; otherwise, it creates a socket connection and, consequently, it connects to the Moverio glasses, thus creating also a stream where to write the future data. After this initialization step, the control moves back to the Main Thread.

The behavior of the application for the Moverio glasses is similar: at the system bootstrap, the Main Thread creates a TcpListener that waits for a Tcp-Client. When it connects, a Secondary Thread is created and it is waiting for incoming data. When the application for the tablet detects a user input, it creates new data on the Main Thread and then it sends these data to the Moverio application by using the Stream previously created in the Secondary Thread. Moreover, the tablet interface is updated on the Main Thread. In the application for the Moverio glasses, the Secondary Thread is waiting for incoming data. When data are received, they are passed to the Main Thread for updating the UI (for example, to translate a 3D model to a new position). Figure 2 shows this situation: Data sent from the Tablet to the Moverio are organized in a JSON message, which contains 5 fields: category, id, pos (posX, posY, posZ), rot(rotX, rotY, rotZ) and scale. The *category* field is an integer value that represents the object's type (e.g., "Chair", "Table", and so on), the *id* field is an integer value that represents an object inside a category, the other fields contain float values that are used to translate, rotate and scale the selected 3D model. The *scale* field contains only one value as the scaling factor is considered homogeneous on the three axes. This data structure is used for each operation, from the selection of an object to its manipulation.

4.3 Functionalities

From the functional point of view, the main features of the system are the following:

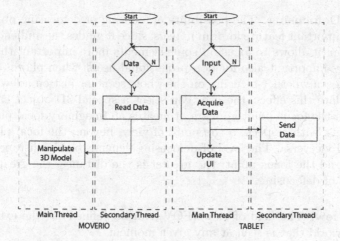

Fig. 2. Workflow of the threads.

- manipulating all the degrees of freedom (also resetting and deleting);
- changing of the reference system (from WCS to local and viceversa);
- focusing/defocusing;
- changing the field-of-view;
- saving objects positions and scaling factors.

Each of them is presented in the following sections.

Manipulation. By the tablet, the user can choose the objects of the set from a list of elements previously loaded; objects can be viewed and placed in the real world. This system allows the user to control 7 degrees of freedom (DOF) of 3D objects:

- 3 for translation;
- 3 for rotation;
- 1 for scaling;

The user can reset all of them at the same time or each of them individually.

Change of the Reference System. In the proposed system, when manipulating objects, two distinct reference systems are present at the same time and the user can choose which one to use for a given manipulation: the WCS, fixed into the environment, and the local system, centered into the object origin. X and Y axes of the WCS are aligned with the target sides, whereas the Z-axis orthogonal to the target.

Focusing/Defocusing. The possibility of focusing or defocusing objects is an extremely important feature for film makers, since it guides the audience through the narration, it allows to focus on some elements more important than others. It is actually important also for non-professional users: when photos are taken, it can be chosen whether focusing on the whole scene or just on a few elements.

To simulate this effect, the user can select a special 3D object called *focus point*. When the focus point appears, it creates an imaginary focal plane: every object that is, with respect to the point of view, beyond the focal plane is out of focus and viceversa. The level of defocusing depends on the distance between the object and the focus point: the greater is the distance, the greater will be the amount of defocusing.

Field of View. The field of view (FOV) can be defined as "the extent of the observable world that is seen at any given moment".

Normally each lens has its own FOV and for this reason, if the camera-subject distance is kept constant, each lens sees a different portion of the scene: from the ultra-wide-angle (114°/84° FOV) to super telephoto (less than 1° FOV). Typically, a director uses different cameras with different lenses, depending on the scene: for instance, a wide-range angle could be used to obtain a long shot or a super telephoto to emphasize a detail. To emulate this behavior, the user can choose another special object, called *mask*. By the mask, the dimension of the shot can be changed, thus seeing in real-time what it would be viewed from different cameras.

Save Option. The manipulation is a very important feature for a virtual set, but it would be useless if the user had to keep in mind the position of every object that has been placed in the set. In order to help the director to keep track of the set up that has been arranged, the possibility to save into a XML file the position and the scaling factor of all the 3D models has been added. Positions are given in the world reference system, which is centered on the target image.

5   The Multimodal System Interface

This section presents the multimodal user interface, that is the different ways the user can interact with this system.

5.1   Input Interface

The system provides the user several functionalities; the user can: manipulate all the DOF, reset them individually or all at the same time; the reference system and the FOV can be changed. Moreover, the user can focus/defocus the objects in the scene and save their position/scaling data. In order to simplify user interaction, a hybrid interface composed by touch and voice interaction has been implemented. By this hybrid interface, the user can accomplish a lot of tasks in a simple and very intuitive way, without being forced to use complex gestures.

The Touch Interface. 2D touch interfaces are widespread as smartphones and tablets are of common use in everyday life. For the app developed for the tablet, the relationship between gesture and action is as follows:

- tap on the icons: the user can select objects/functionalities to use;
- long-click (on the 3D object's icon): a pop-up menu appears and shows the list of the instances of the model selected;
- double-tap: the user can reset position/rotation/scaling at the same time;
- pinch: the user can both scale the 3D model and change the FOV;
- drag: the user can move and rotate objects in the 3D environment.

The Vocal Interface. By this interface, the user can change the reference system and delete objects. The speech recognition engine is always listening to the "special" sentence: *activate voice*. If it does not recognize this sentence, the interface remains in a wait state. When the user speaks the special sentence (and this is recognized), to the state where a command is expected. When the speech recognition engine recognizes a command, the command itself is sent to the Moverio and a new state is reached. In this new (third) state, the interface waits for a confirmation: YES or NO. When the confirmation is detected, a message is sent to the glasses and the interface returns to initial state, thus waiting for the activation phrase. The voice commands can be:

- *rotation*: the rotation is reset and the selected 3D object turns back to the original orientation;
- *position*: the position is reset and the selected 3D object turns back to the original position (0,0,0 in the WCS);
- *scaling*: the scaling factor is reset and the selected 3D object turns back to the original scaling factor;
- *local*: the reference system changes from WCS to local;
- *world*: reference system changes from local to WCS;
- *delete*: the selected 3D model is canceled.

5.2   The Output Interface

Since this system is composed by two different devices, each of them has its graphical interface.

The Tablet Interface. The aim of the tablet is to allow users an easy manipulation of the 3D objects displayed on the Moverio glasses. The manipulation of a 3D model using a 2D interface is still an open problem.

Inspired by the interface used to guide the well-known Parrot Drone (https://www.parrot.com) and by the metaphor of the cube in [2], an interface has been designed mixing both concepts. Figure 3 shows the tablet interface. As the tablet acts like a joystick, it is natural to use it in landscape mode, hence a portrait version of the layout has not been implemented. The *Dowload* (1) button saves

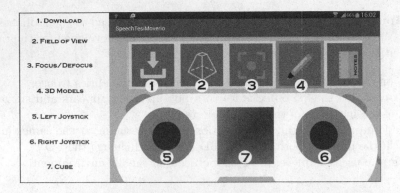

Fig. 3. The tablet interface.

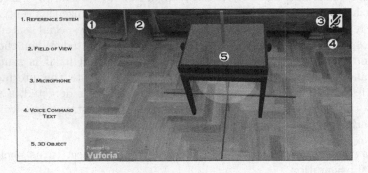

Fig. 4. The Moverio's interface.

the XML file where positions and scaling factors of the objects are saved. The *Field of View* (2) button allows the user to change the FOV of the camera, thus emulating different lenses. The *Focus/Defocus* (3) button lets the user to place the special object *focus point*. With the *Objects* (4) button, a 3D model can be chosen and manipulated. In general, there are many other objects available in the system, not just the pen and the notebook shown in Fig. 3: the list can slide horizontally. The *Left-joystick* (5) and the *Right-joystick* (6) are the "proper joystick", with the Left-joystick the user can move the models on the XY plane, whereas with the Right-joystick the user can move the models along the Z-axis. Finally, the *Cube* (7) button manages the rotation: the rotation applied to the cube is directly applied to the selected 3D model.

The Moverio BT-200 Interface. Since the Epson Moverio BT-200 has a small FOV, a limited amount of information is presented on its interface. Its interface has to be simple and clear to allow the best vision of the scene (Fig. 4). The *Reference System* (1) label refers to the reference system that is currently selected. The *FOV* (2) label shows to the user the actual FOV. When the *Microphone* (3) icon is barred, as shown in Fig. 4, the user cannot employ voice commands. When voice commands are enabled, the microphone is ready to listen to the commands The *Voice Command Text* (4) label displays the command spoken from the user and a question in order to verify if the command acquired from the system is actually the one meant by the user.

6   The Usability Test

In order to assess the system usability, some tests have been organized at Polytechnic of Turin; these tests allow system designers to evaluate different types of parameters [7, 10] and to assess the system usability.

Being interested in analyzing both objective and subjective parameters, an heterogeneous set of KPIs has been chosen. In particular, time necessary for task completion, number of interactions and subjective user's feedback (gathered by a questionnaire) are used to evaluate the system usability.

A group of people with different grades of familiarity with AR technologies was involved in the test. Testers were students and members of the computer science department at Polytechnic of Turin; the group was composed by nine people: 8 men and 1 woman. Partecipants' ages ranged from 25 to 36 (the average equal to 27.6). All participants volunteered their time and were not compensated for their participation. All participants but one, had some knowledge of Augmented Reality. Six of them had already employed AR applications, whereas 3 testers had never used any AR application. All of them had some knowledge of computer science, but with different levels of expertise: 1 PhD student, 1 Research Assistant, 1 Assistant Professor and 6 students of Computer Engineering.

A rectangular room with an artificial lighting suitable for visualizing 3D models using optical see-through devices has been used for the test. The participants had to recreate as faithfully as possible an augmented set according to several reference images. In particular, they had to place six 3D models, using translation, rotation and scaling functions. Moreover, they were enabled to use vocal commands (by a bluetooth microphone) to change the reference system (global to object and viceversa) and to reset the 3D objects' parameters.

Figure 5 shows the room with the position, orientation and scaling of the 3D objects. A sheet of paper representing the target image (format A0) was placed in the middle of the room and the testers had to place the 3D models all around the real environment. Testers had to manipulate six 3D models: 1 piano, 1 stool, 2 chairs, 1 table and 1 notebook. These 3D models have been chosen to verify if the manipulation of different objects of different sizes can be easily accomplished using the proposed tool. The piano had to be placed at the top-right corner without rotating it and its stool in front of it, with a rotation of 90° with respect the initial object orientation (all inserted objects are initially displayed over the target image).

The table had to be placed on the left side, rotating it of 90°. The two chairs had to be positioned near the piano, applying a rotation between 30° and 90°; the first chair had to be manipulated without scaling it, whereas the second chair

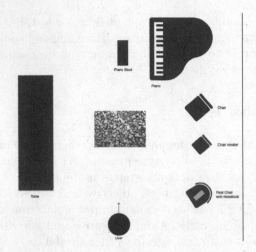

Fig. 5. A top view of the test room.

had to be scaled down. Finally, the notebook had to be placed on the top of a real chair, positioned close to the smallest 3D model chair.

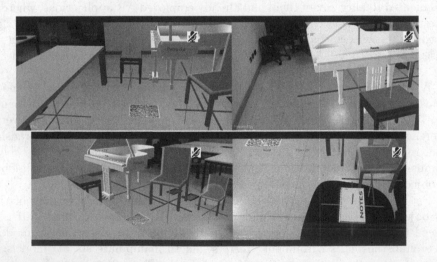

Fig. 6. Some pictures representing the augmented set to be recreated by the testers.

A real small plastic bottle has been positioned where the piano had to be placed (the bottle acted as reference point). In addiction, testers had some support pictures representing the augmented set that they were supposed to recreate (Fig. 6). Before starting the task, the testers were individually introduced to the Multimodal Interface, thus explaining them how to use the translation, rotation and scaling system during a training section; in particular, each tester had

2 min. to try these functions using a medium size object (the chair model). After completing the training section, the participants had to accomplish the assigned task. They were placed in front of the Image Target (see Fig. 5): in this way, they were aligned with the World Coordinate System (WCS). They were aware to be able to move freely in the environment and they could switch between WCS and the local reference system of each object if necessary. A log file kept track both of the completion time and performed instructions. After the test, each participant filled a questionnaire; the questionnaire contained 26 questions (Fig. 7).

GENDER		When moving around, the system was stable and clear	(SA)
AGE		When moving around, it was uncomfortable to interact with the system	(SA)
Do you know what AR is?		The Tablet's User Interface was easy to understand	(SI)
Have you ever used an Augmented Reality application?		The Tablet's User Interface was appropriate to accomplish the task	(SI)
The working of the system was easy to understand	(SI)	It was frustrating using the Tablet's User Interface	(SA)
The system understood my selections	(SI)	The rotation system behaved as I expected	(RE)
The system was slow and sluggish in responding to my selections	(SA)	The transaltion system behaved as I expected	(RE)
The system behaved as I expected	(RE)	The scaling system behaved as I expected	(RE)
I found the system easy to understand	(SI)	The touch User Interface was appropriated to accomplish the task	(RE)
Using the system, it was easy to accomplish my task	(SI)	Did you usually use applications controlled by vocal commands?	
It was frustrating interacting with the system	(SA)	Did you use vocal commands in this test?	
It was satisfying interacting with the system	(SA)		

Fig. 7. An excerpt of the questionnaire.

6.1 Results

The scores coming from the questionnaire (ranging in a scale from 1 to 5: 1 equal to 'no', 2 equal to 'more no than yes', 3 equal to 'neutral', 4 equal to 'more yes than no' and 5 equal 'yes') have been grouped in three categories: *Satisfaction* (SA), *Simplicity* (SI) and *Reliability* (RE) (see Fig. 7). For each sample, the outcomes in every category have been averaged in order to obtain a score for the category. In Table 1, parameters for all the nine testers are listed. In particular:

- *time*: completion time in seconds;
- *rot*: number of rotations;
- *joyL*: number of interactions with the left joystick;
- *joyR*: number of interactions with the right joystick;
- *scal*: the number of scaling interactions;
- *SA*: the Satisfaction score;
- *SI*: the Simplicity score;
- *RE*: is the Reliability score.

6.2 Result Analysis

The validity of the presented study is limited by the fact that the evaluation was conducted with a low number of participants (9); moreover, all participants

Table 1. Objective and subjective values.

Tester	time	rot	joyL	joyR	scal	SA	SI	RE
1	291.8	165	1028	70	162	3	3.67	2.8
2	332.6	374	1352	377	157	3.17	3.5	4.2
3	281.4	216	1057	558	115	4.33	4.83	4.8
4	223.1	480	551	302	188	3.17	4.33	3.8
5	277.3	149	700	185	178	3	3.83	3.6
6	359.9	513	1157	29	28	3.67	4.33	4.2
7	313.5	221	1042	67	43	3.17	4.67	4
8	228.1	183	1237	67	65	4.33	4.5	4.8
9	250.6	403	552	90	295	4.67	4.67	4.6

had a computer science background and they were not experts in the application domain. On the other hand, this study is suitable to establish the basic functionality and usability of the application.

As already mentioned above, the interpupillar distance (IPD) of the Moverio glasses cannot be adapted to the user's needs. A non-matching IPD between user and glasses can cause eye fatigue and image doubling in some conditions. A few of the testers felt this issue, which is related to the hardware and may be avoided by employing glasses with tunable IPD. Another issue is related to the limited field of view of the glasses: testers complained about the impossibility of watching large objects without moving away, thus forcing them to change the point of view. This is a limitation of most see-through devices nowadays available, and only a step forward in the see-through devices technology will be able to overcome it.

The Vocal Command Interface was not used by any tester, who preferred to use the double-tap gesture to reset object positions and never felt the necessity of changing the reference coordinate system. This can be explained by considering the mental workload necessary to activate the vocal interface (a set of phrases and commands has to be remembered) with respect the intuitiveness provided by the touch interface. As mentioned above, testers had only a short briefing of two minutes to become familiar with the system. Due to the lack of vocal interactions, the number of questions analyzed has been reduced to the pertinent ones (17), that is the list shown in Fig. 7.

The statistical analysis of the data is divided in two parts: in the first one, a standard analysis based on mean value and standard deviation is performed, whereas the Principal Component Analysis is applied to search for correlation and significativeness of selected parameters in the second part of analysis.

Standard Analysis. Mean values and standard deviations for all the samples given in Table 1 are listed in Table 2.

Table 2. Average scores and standard deviations for all the Categories taken into account during the test. The last column contains the fraction of the mean value represented by the standard deviation.

Categories	Mean	Stand.Dev.	Stand.Dev./Mean (%)
Time (sec)	284.3	46.2	16.3
Rotation (NI)	300.4	142.2	47.3
JoystickLeft (NI)	964.0	293.9	30.5
JoystickRight (NI)	193.9	181.5	93.6
Scaling (NI)	136.8	84.2	61.5
Satisfaction	3.61	0.66	18.3
Simplicity	4.26	0.48	11.3
Reliability	4.09	0.64	15.6

As a general comment, it can noticed that nine samples are not sufficient to have strong statistical significance and any remark derived from the data should be taken as indicative.

First of all, it is apparent from the data that in the subjective (*Satisfaction, Simplicity, Reliability*) and objective (completion time) categories the standard deviation represents a small fraction of the mean value. This means that the mean values in those categories have been obtained averaging similar values: most testers employed a similar time to complete the task and had a similar appreciation of the system. Standard deviations are slightly larger for the *Rotation* and *JoystickLeft* (translation along (X,Y)) categories and definitely larger for the *Scaling* and *JoystickRight* (translation along Z) categories. These categories are related to the manipulation of the 3D objects and some dependences of the user skill can be expected. However, it seems that distances along the vertical direction are more difficult to estimate: this issue might be alleviated by adding in the user's view a reference scale or a numerical label for vertical distances.

In order to rate the proposed system, a reference metric should be available. This is not possible for the objective parameters without external information (e.g., evaluations of similar systems). For instance, the time of completion is difficult to assess as a reference value about the "right time for completion" is missing. For the subjective parameters, the intermediate score (3, on a scale from 1 to 5) can be used as the reference as the "neutral" value indicates neither dislike nor appreciation. The three average scores of *Satisfaction, Simplicity* and *Reliability* are all larger than the central value. Although, as mentioned above, the low number of samples suggests some care in drawing conclusions, the data hints a general appreciation of the system. The slightly lower score in the *Simplicity* category might suggest that a longer training phase is necessary to assimilate system functionalities.

Principal Component Analysis. When data related to several heterogeneous categories are analyzed, it could be difficult to identify a possible correlation among the considered parameters. A method to standardize usability metrics into a single score is proposed in [15], where the Principal Component Analysis (PCA) [8] is used to analyze data. The PCA is employed in situations where many of the measured events are correlated and provide redundant information. The PCA tries to extract out of the original variables (e.g., the selected *Categories*) a smaller set of uncorrelated variables that represents most of the original information.

A brief sketch of the procedure applied to the selected *Categories* is provided. The first step of the procedure switches to standardized variables: each variable is replaced by its standard form:

$$x_i \rightarrow z_i = \frac{x_i - \bar{x}}{\sigma},$$

where $\bar{x}$ is the mean value and σ the standard deviation. Starting from Table 1, it is possible to get a standardized version (see Table 3). The data in each column have mean value zero and variance 1. Standardized data are used to compute the covariance matrix and then eigenvalues and eigenvectors of the covariance matrix. The outcome for the standardized Table 3 is displayed in Table 4.

Table 3. Standardized data from the results of Table 1.

Tester	time	rot	joyL	joyR	scal	SA	SI	RE
1	0.163	−0.952	0.218	−0.683	0.300	−0.927	−1.228	−2.010
2	1.047	0.517	1.320	1.009	0.240	−0.670	−1.583	0.173
3	−0.062	−0.594	0.316	2.007	−0.259	1.087	1.191	1.109
4	−1.325	1.262	−1.405	0.596	0.609	−0.670	0.148	−0.451
5	−0.151	−1.065	−0.898	−0.049	0.490	−0.927	−0.895	−0.762
6	1.638	1.494	0.657	−0.909	−1.293	0.087	0.148	0.173
7	0.633	−0.559	0.265	−0.699	−1.114	−0.670	0.857	−0.139
8	−1.216	−0.826	0.929	−0.699	−0.853	1.087	0.503	1.109
9	−0.729	0.721	−1.402	−0.573	1.880	1.602	0.857	0.797

The first row in the Table contains the eigenvalues, one for each one of the new PCA variables (labeled as PC1, ..., PC8). The sum of all the eigenvalues is equal to the total variance of the original variables (8, since there are 8 standardized variables), so each eigenvalue corresponds to the amount of variance accounted for each new variable. They are written in order of decreasing eigenvalue and, hence, of decreasing importance. The column of each eigenvalue contains the components of the corresponding eigenvector in terms of the original variables. The idea behind the PCA is of keeping only the new variables that are considered "important". There are different criteria to determine which components to retain:

Table 4. Eigenvalues and eigenvectors of the covariance matrix.

	PC1	PC2	PC3	PC4 ·	PC5	PC6	PC7	PC8
	2.69	2.10	1.13	1.08	0.54	0.33	0.10	0.03
time	−0.353	−0.384	0.385	−0.032	−0.071	−0.746	0.116	0.062
rot	0.112	0.001	0.897	0.065	0.089	0.368	−0.184	−0.032
joyL	−0.222	−0.576	−0.125	−0.184	−0.362	0.288	−0.326	−0.499
joyR	0.133	−0.016	0.009	−0.904	0.344	−0.060	−0.170	0.117
scal	0.169	0.573	0.142	−0.215	−0.482	−0.289	0.000	−0.511
SA	0.538	−0.174	−0.032	0.065	−0.460	−0.172	−0.454	0.477
SI	0.494	−0.189	−0.068	0.268	0.512	−0.307	−0.217	−0.490
RE	0.484	−0.355	0.069	−0.146	−0.177	0.124	0.751	−0.061

- **Kaiser's Rule**: keep only the Principal Components (PC's) with eigenvalue larger than 1;
- **Scree Plot Test**: plot the fraction of total variance accounted for by each eigenvalue and keep only those present in the initial steep part of the plot;
- **Cumulative Variance**: stop retaining when the cumulative variance of the PC's reaches a predetermined value (at least 50%, preferably 70% or more).

Table 4 shows that the first 4 eigenvalues satisfy Kaiser's Rule; Fig. 8 shows the Scree Plot: a clear plateau is not reached, but the steepest part corresponds to the first 3 eigenvalues; the first eigenvalue alone represent about the 74% of the total variance. The first three PCA variables can be kept and considered as new and independent variables. The interpretation of their meaning can be done using the relative weight of the original components in each eigenvector. As in [15], only the components larger in absolute value that 0.3 will be considered important. Looking at the PC1 column in Table 4, it can be seen that the relevant components are: *time, Satisfaction, Simplicity* and *Reliability*. All the subjective components enter roughly with the same weight and their sign is opposite to the one of the time component. This means that the subjective categories are correlated with each other and anti-correlated with the completion time. This finding is in accord with the claim: it is natural for the user to be more satisfied if the time spent to complete a task is lower. It is then natural to consider the PC1 variable as a new parameter summarizing the 4 original categories: an appropriate name for it might be *Usability*. Of the two other PCA variables, PC3 shows a high correlation between number of rotations and time of completion, which is again rather intuitive. On the other hand, PC2 does not show any consistent pattern.

PC1 exhibits the qualitative features expected for a usability score. In order to simplify calculations, the "important" components of PC1 are kept, thus reducing the eigenvector dimensions to 4. A standardized score can be obtained by multiplying the 4 components of PC1 by the corresponding components of the standardized samples of Table 3 and summing the intermediate results; in this

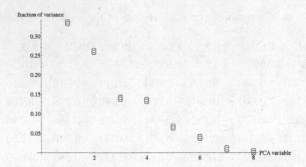

Fig. 8. Scree plot of the eigenvalues of the test data set.

way, standardized scores of this new category (the rows from 1 to 9 in the "raw" column of Table 5) are obtained. These scores have mean value zero and variance close to its eigenvalue (the eigenvalue obtained considering the entire eigenvector would be 2.29). These reference values are standardized using mean values and standard deviations of the performed test; then they have been multiplied by the weights of the *Usability* variable. The outcome is a *Reference Score* of "−2.62", to be compared to the mean value of "0" of the samples. Since it appears more natural to have the reference score set to zero, in such a way to have good scores with positive values and bad scores with negative ones, all the values are added to +2.62, thus obtaining "0" as the *Reference Score* (see Table 5). In other words, positive values indicate good usability and negative scores bad usability.

Table 5. Standardized scores for the *Usability* category.

Tester	Usability (raw)	Usability (normalized)
1	−2.14	0.48
2	−1.43	1.19
3	1.73	4.35
4	−0.04	2.58
5	−1.26	1.36
6	−0.37	2.25
7	−0.23	2.39
8	1.80	4.42
9	1.93	4.55
Average	0	2.62
Reference	−2.62	0

7 Conclusion

A new approach to support directors in cinema and television productions is presented in this paper. An AR-based tool allows directors to overlap computer generated assets to the real stage. The augmented set is displayed on a AR glasses, whereas the object interaction is performed by a tablet. Objects can be added, placed in the environment and scaled. Positions, rotations and scale factors can be saved to reproduce next the selected set configuration.

A deep usability analysis has been also carried out. This analysis shows how users appreciate the proposed tool. Moreover, also a real TV director both provided functional requirements and tested the developed tool by providing useful suggestions to complete the development process.

Major drawbacks are due to technological constraints as the selected visualization device provides a narrow field of view, thus increasing the distance between the user and large objects to be placed in the environment. Future work will be also aimed to investigated the implementation of real time shadows, which are necessary to better understand the impact of lights and moving objects.

References

1. Cavallaro, R., Hybinette, M., White, M., Balch, T.: Augmenting live broadcast sports with 3D tracking information. IEEE Multimedia **18**(4), 38–47 (2011)
2. Cohé, A., Deècle, F., Hachet, M.: tBox: a 3D transformation widget designed for touch-screens. In: Proceedings of the ACM SIGCHI Conference on Human Factors in Computing Systems, pp. 3005–3008 (2011)
3. Hakkinen, J., Vuori, T., Puhakka, M.: Postural stability and sickness symptoms after HMD use. In: Proceedings of the 2002 IEEE International Conference on Systems, Man and Cybernetics, pp. 147–152 (2002)
4. Hupont, I., Gracia, J., Sanagustin, L., Gracia, M.A.: How do new visual immersive systems influence gaming QoE? A use case of serious gaming with Oculus Rift. In: Proceedings of the 7th International Workshop on Quality of Multimedia Experience (QoMEX), pp. 1–6 (2015)
5. Ichikari, R., Tenmoku, R., Shibata, F., Ohshima, T., Tamura, H.: Mixed reality previsualization for filmmaking: on-set camera-work authoring and action rehearsal. Int. J. Virtual Reality **7**(4), 25–32 (2008)
6. Ikeda, S., Taketomi, T., Okumura, B., Sato, T., Kanbara, M., Yokoya, N., Chihara, K.: Real-time outdoor pre visualization method for videographers real time geometric registration using point-based model. In: Proceedings of IEEE International Conference on Multimedia and Expo (ICME), pp. 949–952 (2008)
7. Isenberg, T., Isenberg, P., Chen, J., Sedlmair, M., Moller, T.: A systematic review on the practice of evaluating visualization. IEEE Trans. Vis. Comput. Graph. **19**(12), 2818–2827 (2013)
8. Jolliffe, I.T.: Principal Component Analysis. Springer, Secaucus (2002)
9. Kennedy, R.S., Berbaum, K.S., Lilienthal, M.G.: Disorientation and postural ataxia following flight simulation. Aviat. Space Environ. Med. **68**(1), 13–17 (1997)
10. Lam, H., Bertini, E., Isenberg, P., Plaisant, C., Carpendale, S.: Empirical studies in information visualization: seven scenarios. IEEE Trans. Vis. Comput. Graph. **18**(9), 1520–1536 (2012)
11. Lopez, D., Oehlberg, L., Doger, C., Isenberg, T.: Towards an understanding of mobile touch navigation in a stereoscopic viewing environment for 3D data exploration. IEEE Trans. Vis. Comput. Graph. **22**(5), 1616–1629 (2016)

12. Milgram, P., Kishino, A.F.: Taxonomy of mixed reality visual displays. IEICE Trans. Inf. Syst. **77**(12), 1321–1329 (1994)
13. Ramsbottom, J.: A virtual reality interface for previsualization. Honours report, University of Cape Town (2015)
14. Sanna, A., Manuri, F.: A survey on applications of augmented reality. Adv. Comput. Sci.: Int. J. **5**(1), 18–27 (2016)
15. Sauro, J., Kindlund, E.: A method to standardize usability metrics into a single score. In: Proceedings of the SIGCHI Conference on Human Factors in Computing Systems, pp. 401–409 (2005)
16. Stamm, A., Teall, P., Benedicto, G.B.: Augmented virtuality in real time for previsualization in film. In: Proceedings of the 2016 IEEE Symposium on 3D User Interfaces (3DUI), pp. 183–186 (2016)

Overcoming Location Inaccuracies in Augmented Reality Navigation

Christian A. Wiesner[1($\boxtimes$)] and Gudrun Klinker[2]

[1] Robert Bosch GmbH, Leonberg, Germany
christian.wiesner@de.bosch.com
[2] Faculty of Computer Science, Technische Universität München, Munich, Germany
http://www.bosch.com

Abstract. One of the major opportunities of Augmented Reality (AR) is supporting drivers in wayfinding. In order to correctly display AR visualisations in the environment, accurate global localisation as well as precise mapping of the environment is necessary. As a first step we assessed the positioning error of current Global Navigation Satellite Systems (GNSS) sensors and found that the accuracy of current GNSS sensors is not high enough to correctly position AR visualisations at intersections. Based on these results, we developed a novel visualisation which does not require precise localisation and still provides drivers with the impression that it is part of their environment. We implemented this novel visualisation along with a traditional AR visualisation in a car prototype in order to compare them in a user study. Overall, the novel visualisation was preferred over the traditional visualisation without adding additional workload on drivers or decreasing the usability of the visualisation.

Keywords: Augmented Reality · Navigation · GNSS accuracy · Automotive

1 Introduction

The Head-Up-Display (HUD) projects virtual information onto the windshield, enabling the driver to perceive important information, without having to take the gaze off the road. It therefore has the potential to increase safety, as shown by Medenica et al. [10] using a driving simulator. As the information is displayed in the area where the street is visible, the opportunity arises to use the HUD in conjunction with Augmented Reality (AR).

A common problem with path finding is that it is problematic to figure out which turn to take, as numeric distance depictions are difficult to relate to actual distances. This is especially the case if several intersections are close to each other. As identified by Gabbard et al. [5] AR can help the driver in these cases in choosing the correct turn.

For displaying an AR navigational visualisation at the correct position in the environment, accurate knowledge of the vehicle's global position is needed. The

© Springer International Publishing AG 2017
L.T. De Paolis et al. (Eds.): AVR 2017, Part I, LNCS 10324, pp. 377–388, 2017.
DOI: 10.1007/978-3-319-60922-5_29

global position is determined by the use of a Global Navigation Satellite System (GNSS). Examples for GNSS systems are the American GPS or the Russian GLONASS system. Pfannmüller et al. evaluated in [11] that a global deviation of 6 m led to higher navigation errors when used with an AR visualisation. In their work the AR visualisation was a three-dimensional arrow at an intersection.

In a first step we measured the actual error of nowadays GNSS sensors in cars. This measurement was performed to assess the quality of a car's GNSS sensor for using it in conjunction with AR. As the GNSS error was higher than 6 m, we developed a new AR visualisation, which takes the positional error into account. We developed the visualisation in a way, it does not require a precise localisation and still conveys to the driver it is registered in three dimensions and correlates with the environment.

We implemented this visualisation in a car prototype equipped with a prototypical version of an HUD. We also implemented the traditional three-dimensional arrow in the prototype. With these two visualisations we performed a user study in our engineering process, as suggested by Gabbard and Swan [4]. The user study was performed to investigate the effect of the visualisations on the drivers in actual traffic situations. It should be noted that we used a GNSS system with a high accuracy to focus on the perception of the visualisations.

2   Related Work

Tönnis et al. distinguished between primary, secondary and tertiary tasks [12]. Navigational information is usually displayed mainly in the area of the tertiary tasks, which leads to a relatively high distraction. Displaying and conveying the navigational information in the area of the primary tasks, where the display area of the HUD is located, has the potential to decrease inattention by the driver.

Wayfinding and navigational aids are opportunities for AR, as identified by Gabbard et al. [5]. However, localising the absolute position and the orientation of the car remains a major challenge.

Different visualisations for AR wayfinding have already been proposed. Examples include a three-dimensional arrow [13] of which we implemented a similar version in our car prototype. Kim and Dey described a navigation visualisation which was implemented in a car simulator [9]. This visualisation shows the route on a two-dimensional map which merged into a three-dimensional representation of the road. Although this visualisation significantly reduced the number of navigational errors, it would need a much bigger field of view than currently available in HUDs. Bolton et al. compared, using a driving simulator, conventional navigation hints with an AR arrow visualisation and an AR highlighting of landmarks in the real environment (e.g. a public house) [1]. The AR visualisation outperformed the conventional navigation hints, but the proposed AR landmark visualisation performed best. As these studies showed an improvement in the navigational task, we implemented our visualisation in a real car prototype to investigate the effect on drivers under real traffic situations.

Tönnis et al. identified common principles for presenting information in HUDs [14]. They classified them in dimensions and used pair-wise combinations of these to illustrate examples. One of the examples was the comparison between contact-analog (i.e. correctly world-registered) and an unregistered representation. As they pointed out, AR visualisations should never be distorted, but correct registration is not always necessary. Pfannmüller et al. analysed the needed GNSS accuracy for displaying an arrow correctly on the road and its effect on users' ability to successfully navigate through traffic [11]. They concluded a positional error of 6 m led to significantly higher errors in navigation. We developed an AR navigational visualisation which is not registered in the world environment to deal with localisation inaccuracies.

3   GNSS Analysis

Global Navigation Satellite Systems (GNSS) is a general term for a satellite based positioning system. Examples for GNSS systems are the American GPS system and the Russian GLONASS system. We first analysed the accuracy of nowadays GNSS systems. For this purpose we identified a route which consisted of usual aspects of a common route, such as highways, country and city roads. The driving time was about 10 min long. We first measured the route with a high-precision differential GPS (dGPS). A dGPS enhances the precision of GPS receivers through the support of precisely known ground stations. These ground stations can measure the current atmospheric delay of the satellite signal and broadcast it to receivers in the area. In Europe the EGNOS system has been in operation since October 2009. The EGNOS system consists of three geostationary satellites and a network of ground stations [3].

The first measurement served as a reference for testing another high-precision GNSS system. After we established the accuracy of the second device, we used it as an internal reference for measuring the accuracy of the car's built-in navigation system. By employing these steps we are able to assess the accuracy of a car's GNSS system.

3.1   First Measurement with Differential GPS

The first measurement was performed using a dGPS system by JAVAD. For increasing the position accuracy it uses the Real-Time Kinematic (RTK) technology. RTK works on the principle of having stationary broadcast stations, whose precise positions are known. The station measures the time required for the signal to travel from the satellite to the station. As the position of the station is known beforehand, the delay of the signal due to current atmospheric circumstances can be calculated. This delay is then distributed to GNSS sensors in the region which can use these correction factors to improve their position.

The result of this measurement was a precise measurement of the reference route, which can be seen in Fig. 1.

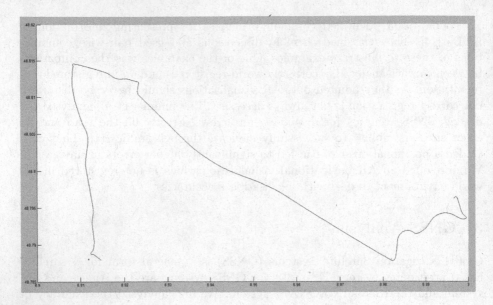

Fig. 1. Measured route (x-axis: longitude, y-axis: latitude)

3.2   Second Measurement

For the second measurement we used the Racelogic VBSS100_V3, which also uses the RTK technology. We recorded at the same time the measurement of the car navigation system. After completion we compared the Racelogic VBSS100_V3 with the previously recorded route with the JAVAD system, to investigate its validity of serving as an internal reference.

In order to compare the measurements we needed to have an equal number of data points. As described by [8] it is advisable to interpolate the dataset with higher number of data points to the number of points in the smaller dataset.

Because these were two separate measurements, the minimal distance for each data point of the VBSS100_V3 dataset had to be calculated to all data points in the JAVAD dataset. The root mean square (RMS) error for the minimal distances was $2.84\,\mathrm{m}$ (mean $= 2.4\,\mathrm{m}$, std. dev. $= 1.52\,\mathrm{m}$).

As the route was not exactly the same in the two measurements, due to small deviations while driving the route a second time, therefore the VBSS100_V3 measurement was considered to be precise enough to serve as a reference for the car's navigation system.

3.3   Comparison to the Conventional Car GPS

As the last step we compared the measurement of the Racelogic VBSS100_V3 with the vehicle's navigation system. As the measurements were taken simultaneously we could measure the distance between two data points with the same timestamp. We interpolated the dataset with the higher number of data points

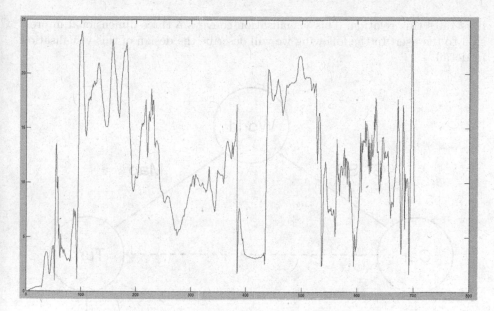

Fig. 2. Positional error between the VBSS100_V3 and the car's navigation system

to match the number of data points in the smaller dataset. We found the RMS error of the distances to be 16.13 m (mean = 14.92 m, std. dev. = 6.14 m) (Fig. 2).

According to [11] the RMS error of 16.13 m of the vehicle's navigation system would not allow an accurate display of a three-dimensional arrow correctly at an intersection, so that the driver is still able to successfully navigate through traffic.

Even with perfect GNSS localisation, a recognition of the environment is also necessary to correctly place the three-dimensional arrow at an intersection. This environment recognition is necessary to account for slopes of the terrain.

Our results show that the accuracy of current navigation systems is not sufficient to robustly display AR visualisation correctly at an intersection. For this reason we developed a new visualisation to overcome this lack of accuracy.

4   Navigation Concept

We developed a visualisation, which is able to cope with the GNSS inaccuracy and does not require terrain detection. We call this visualisation the Sails visualisation. The visualisation is not shown continuously, instead the Sails are appearing and disappearing as the vehicle moves through the intersection. The visualisation is only dependent on the distance to the turn. Very importantly, the visualisation is registered with respect to the car coordinate system rather than with respect to the world coordinate system, giving the user the impression the visualisation is part of the vehicle. The spatial relationship graph (SRG) in Fig. 3

illustrates this relation. This visualisation conveys a three-dimensional impression to the user. In the following we will describe the design of this visualisation in detail.[1]

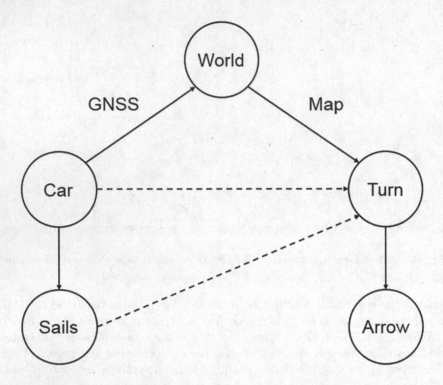

Fig. 3. Spatial relationship graph for sails/arrow representation.

When the car is approaching the intersection the Sails appear on the side opposite to the turning direction. As the car further advances towards the intersection, the Sails are spreading out and bending in a curve to convey to the driver in which direction and when to turn the car. Once the car reaches the intersection, the Sails are fully bent. At the exact location of the intersection the Sails change their colour to convey to the driver the exact moment of the turn. This is especially important if there are several intersections next to each other. In a last step the Sails disappear to the side opposing the turning direction, giving the driver the impression of driving past them.

We implemented this visualisation in our car prototype, which is equipped with a prototypical version of an AR HUD. We also implemented a rather traditional AR visualisation, a three-dimensional arrow, in our car prototype to compare it against our novel visualisation. The two different visualisations can be seen in Fig. 4. These two visualisations were compared in a user study which is described in the next section.

---

[1] Filed for patent.

(a) A 3D arrow located at the intersection pointing to the left.

(b) Sails representation, where the
sails are pointing to the right.

Fig. 4. The two visualisations shown in the Head-Up-Display.

5 User Study

In the user study we compared the novel Sails representation to a rather traditional three-dimensional arrow on the road. We implemented both visualisations
in our car prototype which is equipped with a prototypical HUD to investigate
the effect on users in actual traffic situations.

5.1 Setup of the User Study

The users were asked to drive a predefined route three times. The test route
consisted of six right turns and one left turn. Furthermore the route included a
roundabout and two successive turns to investigate the effect of the visualisations
in these cases.

5.2 Participants

We conducted the user study with 16 test subjects, 10 of whom were male and
6 were female. The age stretched from 23 to 45 with an average age of 32.4 years
(standard deviation of 6.0). All of the participants were familiar with a car
navigation system and 8 of the participants had driven a car equipped with a
HUD before.

5.3 Test Procedure

The test route was about 10 min long. In the first test drive the visualisations
were disabled to give users the opportunity to familiarise themselves with the
car and the route to investigate the effect of the visualisations on the users. The
users then drove the same route with one of the visualisations enabled and the
second time with the remaining visualisation. The order of the visualisations was
equally distributed amongst the test subjects. After each test drive there was a
short break, in which participants filled out the questionnaires.

Following the test drives, we conducted a qualitative interview to record
feedback from the test subjects on their perception of the two visualisations and
how they could be improved.

5.4 Independent Variables

The independent variable in this within-subjects design was the visualisation. All participants drove without the visualisation, as well as with the "Arrow" and the "Sails" visualisation.

5.5 Dependent Variables

We used the NASA Task Load Index (NASA-TLX) [6] in our user study. The NASA-TLX gives an indication of the perceived workload. The NASA-TLX was filled out after all three test drives. As a further measure we used the System Usability Scale (SUS) [2] to indicate the perceived usability of the visualisation.

A popular used measure in industrial design is the AttracDiff. [7] The AttracDiff measures the hedonic and the pragmatic quality of an application. The pragmatic quality describes how helpful an application is in supporting a user pursuing their tasks. The hedonic quality describes how stimulating it is to use an application and how much the user identifies with the application. To develop an attractive product both dimensions should be maximised. The SUS and the AttracDiff were only filled out by the participants after a test drive with a visualisation, as they can only be judged on an application.

Table 1. Overview of the SUS and TLX scores

Rating	SUS		TLX	
	Mean	Std. dev	Mean	Std. dev
None	-	-	16.51	12.93
Arrow	76.875	17.26	17.15	8.78
Sails	77.03	20.05	19.49	11.77

6 Results and Discussion

In this section we present the results of the user study. The results for the SUS and the TLX scores can be seen in Table 1. As the SUS scores were not normally distributed, we performed a paired signed-rank Wilcoxon test and did not find significant differences ($p\text{-}value = 1$). As the TLX scores were not normally distributed, we performed a Friedman's test and did not find significant differences ($\chi^2 = 2$, $p\text{-}value = 0.3679$) between the two visualisations. These results show that the new Sails visualisation does not increase the workload on the participants and is similar to the traditional visualisation in terms of usability.

Figure 5 shows the mean values for the AttracDiff where the rectangles depict the confidence intervals for the visualisations. Overall, the Sails representation scored a higher hedonic quality, whereas the arrow scored a higher pragmatic quality. The results for each individual dimension can be seen in Fig. 6.

Portfolio-presentation

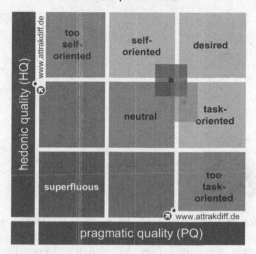

Fig. 5. The results of the AttracDiff. Orange depicts the "Arrow" visualisation and blue the "Sails" visualisation. (Color figure online)

The arrow's higher score in the pragmatic quality can be interpreted as that the visualisation was perceived as an easier way of route guidance. In both hedonic dimensions the Sails scored higher which means users identified themselves more with this visualisation and it was more stimulating to use. Overall, the attractiveness, i.e. how much people desire a product, was higher of the Sails representation.

We observed an overall preference for the Sails representation. Results of the subjective preference can be seen in Table 2. In the interview three subjects mentioned that the Sails can be distracting due to its relatively complex animation. However, seven of the participants mentioned that the arrow representation is not always visible, this is especially the case while stopping at an intersection. This is due to the limited field of view (FoV) of the HUD. Inspite of using a high-precision GNSS system, four participants nevertheless noted that the arrow is not steadily attached to the road.

Table 2. Preference of the visualisations

Preference	No. of people	Percentage
Sails	9	56.25%
Rather sails	1	6.25%
Rather arrow	0	0%
Arrow	5	31.25%
None	1	6.25%

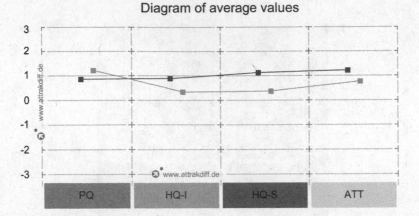

Fig. 6. The results for each dimension of the AttracDiff. Orange depicts the "Arrow" visualisation and blue the "Sails" visualisation (PQ = pragmatic quality, HQ = hedonic quality, I = identification, S = stimulation, ATT = attractiveness). (Color figure online)

Overall, the Sails representation was perceived as more capturing and the arrow visualisation as more simplistic. This interpretation correlates with the outcome of the AttracDiff. The Sails representation was therefore the preferred visualisation, without adding extra workload or being less usable as indicated by the TLX and SUS scores.

7   Conclusion and Future Work

In this study, we described the development of a navigational AR visualisation which overcomes the global positioning error of current navigation systems. Our visualisation is only dependent on the distance to the next turn.

In a first step we assessed the GNSS accuracy of current navigation systems. We found the RMS error to be 16.13 m. This deviation is certainly too high to correctly position a three-dimensional arrow at an intersection, as reported by [11], where a deviation of 6 m led to a higher number of navigational errors.

For this reason we developed an AR visualisation, which is only dependant on the distance to the next turn. The visualisation does not require a high GNSS accuracy and yet gives the user the impression the visualisation is occurring in her/his environment. For displaying an AR visualisation in the world's coordinate system the localisation needs to be very precise. As shown the current state of nowadays GNSS systems of cars are not accurate enough to do so. Our visualisation is registered to the vehicle's coordinate system and therefore does not need to compensate for fast movements of yawing or pitching of the vehicle.

We implemented the proposed AR visualisation and the traditional three-dimensional arrow in our car prototype. Then we compared the two visualisations in a user study. We measured usability, workload and pragmatic and hedonic quality. There was no significant difference in usability and workload. The arrow visualisation scored in a higher pragmatic quality and the Sails visualisation achieved a higher hedonic quality.

For the user study we chose a high-precision GNSS system to concentrate on the perception of the visualisations. Even though the three-dimensional arrow's location was much more precise than a conventional GNSS system, the sails representation was still the preferred visualisation. Hence this visualisation is one necessary step closer in integrating AR visualisations into series-production vehicles.

In future work we would like to investigate the visualisations' behaviour in environments where it becomes more challenging for the visualisations to correctly display AR visualisations. As an example, we would conduct a user study through a road consisting of cobble stone and analyse the effect of the visualisations on the user.

Acknowledgements. The authors wish to thank the members of the Fachgebiet Augmented Reality at the TU Munich, who contributed in giving advice towards setting up the user study. The authors would also like to thank the software development team in Leonberg for helping to prepare the prototype. This project was made possible in the environment provided by the Robert Bosch GmbH.

References

1. Bolton, A., Burnett, G., Large, D.R.: An investigation of augmented reality presentations of landmark based navigation using a head-up display. In: Proceedings of the 7th International Conference on Automotive User Interfaces and Interactive Vehicular Applications - AutomotiveUI 2015, pp. 56–63 (2015)
2. Brooke, J.: SUS - a quick and dirty usability scale. Usability Eval. Ind. **189**, 4–7 (1996)
3. EGNOS. http://www.esa.int/Our_Activities/Navigation/EGNOS/What_is_EGNOS
4. Gabbard, J.L., Swan, J.E.: Usability engineering for augmented reality: employing user-based studies to inform design. IEEE Trans. Vis. Comput. Graph. **14**, 513–525 (2008)
5. Gabbard, J.L., Fitch, G.M., Kim, H.: Behind the glass: driver challenges and opportunities for AR automotive applications. Proc. IEEE **102**, 124–136 (2014)
6. Hart, S.G., Staveland, L.E.: Development of NASA-TLX (Task Load Index): results of empirical and theoretical research. Adv. Psychol. **52**, 139–183 (1988)
7. Hassenzahl, M.: The interplay of beauty, goodness, and usability in interactive products. Hum. Comput. Interact. **19**, 319–349 (2004)
8. Huber, M., Schlegel, M., Klinker, G.: Temporal calibration in multisensor tracking setups. In: Science and Technology Proceedings - IEEE 2009 International Symposium on Mixed and Augmented Reality, ISMAR 2009, pp. 195–196 (2009)
9. Kim, S., Dey, A.K.: Simulated augmented reality windshield display as a cognitive mapping aid for elder driver navigation. In: Proceedings of the 27th International Conference on Human Factors in Computing Systems - CHI 2009 (2009)
10. Medenica, Z., Kun, A.L., Paek, T., Palinko, O.: Augmented reality vs. street views: a driving simulator study comparing two emerging navigation aids. In: Proceedings of the International Conference on Human-Computer Interaction with Mobile Devices and Services (MobileHCI 2011), pp. 265–274 (2011)

11. Pfannmüller, L., Walter, M., Bengler, K.: Lead me the right way?! The impact of position accuracy of augmented reality navigation arrows in a contact analogue head-up display on driving performance, workload, and usability. In: Proceedings of the 19th Triennial Congress of the International Ergonomics Association (IEA) 2015 (2015)

12. Tönnis, M., Broy, V., Klinker, G.: A survey of challenges related to the design of 3D user interfaces for car drivers. In: Proceedings - IEEE Virtual Reality (2006)

13. Tönnis, M., Klein, L., Klinker, G.: Perception thresholds for augmented reality navigation schemes in large distances. In: Proceedings - 7th IEEE International Symposium on Mixed and Augmented Reality 2008, pp. 189–190 (2008)

14. Tönnis, M., Klinker, G., Plavšic, M.: Survey and classification of head-up display presentation principles. In: Proceedings of the International Ergonomics Association (IEA) (2009)

The Use of Augmented Reality Glasses for the Application in Industry 4.0

Roberto Pierdicca[1(✉)], Emanuele Frontoni[2], Rama Pollini[2], Matteo Trani[3], and Lorenzo Verdini[3]

[1] Department of Civil Engineering, Building and Architecture, Universitá Politecnica delle Marche, Via Brecce Bianche 12, 60131 Ancona, Italy
r.pierdicca@univpm.it
[2] Department of Information Engineering, Universitá Politecnica delle Marche, Via Brecce Bianche 12, 60131 Ancona, Italy
{e.frontoni,r.pollini}@univpm.it
[3] INTERMAC: Machines for Glass, Stone and Metal Processing, Via dell'Economia, 40, 61122 Pesaro, PU, Italy
{Matteo.Traini,Lorenzo.Verdini}@intermac.com

Abstract. In nowadays Industrial environment, the fast changes of machine components and the growing need of specialised worker claims an evolution. In the towards of this direction, the Industry 4.0 paradigm seems to play a pivotal role, because is aimed at making industrial production entirely automated and interconnected. Augmented Reality (AR) is one of the nine pillar of the new Industry environments and is still considered and is a real solution for several purposes, first of all production environments. In this article we propose a case study of a *training-on-the-job* application through the use of glasses for AR, using Unity framework and Vuforia libraries. The goal is to develop an AR android application that allows to assist the operator during the assembly phase of an object composed of numerous components that must be assembled in a precise order and together with a final verification measurements on some parts of the final object. This work poses considerable attention to the usability of the HDM device and the readability of the information. The application has been validated after a number of practical tests carried out by specialized technicians who normally perform this type of assembly. The description of the applied procedure and the assessment are presented.

Keywords: Augmented reality · Glasses · Industry 4.0 · Training on the job · Human-computer interaction

1 Introduction

Recent technological advances in different domains allowed the paradigm of *Industry 4.0* to become paramount at a worldwide scale. The fourth industrial revolution, stemmed through the union of various skills, is aimed at making

© Springer International Publishing AG 2017
L.T. De Paolis et al. (Eds.): AVR 2017, Part I, LNCS 10324, pp. 389–401, 2017.
DOI: 10.1007/978-3-319-60922-5_30

industrial production entirely automated and interconnected. This revolution is divided into nine pillars of enabling technologies. (i) The manufacturer advanced solutions ensures effective interconnection between machines. (ii) Additive Manufacturing allows the connection between digital 3d printers and software development, (iii) Augmented Reality applied to support manufacturing processes, (iv) Simulation allows to optimize the machines testing them in real time, (v) Horizontal/Vertical Integration ensures integration of data and systems across the value chain, (vi) Industrial IoT, the set of technologies that interconnects devices, (vii) Cloud manages and stores data on the network, (viii) Cybersecurity protects the systems and the network from potential threats, (ix) big data and Analytics allows the collection and analysis of a large number of data from different sources to support decision making. In line with the recent research trends, Augmented Reality (AR) is one of the emerging technologies involved in the new Industry environments. Despite AR is still considered an emerging technology, have proved to be a valuable solution for several purposes: cultural heritage [6], environmental monitoring [15], medicine [7] just to mention some. Nowadays, it has reached a degree of maturity that make it ready for being used within the production environments. The production processes may generate problems which make the operations less efficient and potentially dangerous for the technicians during their work. The main problems are: (i) Human error: even the most experienced workers can make mistakes due to the high number of procedures to be remembered and the difficulty in identifying the precise points of intervention. (ii) Inefficiencies: due to inadequate training received by engineers and poor access to statistics on the operations carried out. Also very often paper manuals used for training are not updated, thus creating further confusion. (iii) Costs: errors and inefficiencies involving higher personnel costs, longer execution times, recurring errors and accidental damage to components due to incorrect execution of the procedures.

Potential uses of AR are various and can be potentially applied in all activities taking place in the companies. The main usage scenarios can be summarized as follows:

- **Production**: any operation which provides step by step procedures can benefit from the use of AR; installations and assemblies are just few examples where the AR can make a difference by making the fourth-generation factory.
- **Quality control**: with the AR support in quality control processes, you can check whether the objects are produced according to the standards of production.
- **Safety management**: AR makes available the tools needed to manage the risks and the safety of workers and goods inside the factories.
- **Maintenance and remote assistance**: maintenance activities require the allocation of significant human and financial resources to ensure the effectiveness and efficiency of operations. In this context, AR would ensure the reduction of the execution time and human errors.
- **Training**: the use of augmented reality can be very effective for the companies in which the training processes involve a large number of technical

geographically dispersed over a vast territory pier. The benefits are both on new staff and technical experts to form in new tasks.
- **Logistics**: AR tools can improve the efficiency of store management during indoor navigation and picking.
- **Design**: AR provides instruments able to improve the prototyping and visualization in the design phase.

Given the above, in this article we propose a case study of a *training-on-the-job* application through the use of glasses for AR. This work was done in collaboration with INTERMAC company, the Biesse Group company specialized in glasses, stone and metal processing technologies. The goal of this joint venture is to develop an AR application (Android based) that allows to assist the operator during the assembly task by replacing the printed manual. Through the use of the head-mounted display (HMD), the user receives step-by-step instructions to assembly the object. The application drives the operator thanks to the aid of both textual information and 3D models of the components overlapping to the real scene. This work poses considerable attention to the usability of the HDM device and the readability of the information and paves the way towards new forms of *training-on-the-job*, to be used in advanced industrial scenario.

The remainder of this paper is organized as follows: Sect. 2 is an overview of the existing approach of augmented reality applied in industry, a description of the principal HMDS and a description of the approach used to improve the legibility of the RA operations; Sect. 3 describe in detail the methodology used to develop the application; Sect. 4 is reserved to describe the results obtained from the tests using the application by specialized operators (in the laboratory) and non-specialists (through a special survey); concluding remarks, together with the limitation of the system and future research directions, are outlined in Sect. 5.

2   Background

Related Works

AR is a technology that is gaining considerable successes in the field of maintenance task [11]. Several subcategories can be identified as servicing, installation, repair, assembly, testing, but one of the categories of greatest interest is that of 'assemblage'. In their works [18, 19], the authors have empirically demonstrated that the use of instructions in AR (using monitor-based display or head-mounted display) in a sequence of assembling (assembly task) significantly reduces the percentage of errors rather than using a printed manual. In [12] the authors demonstrate improved speed and accuracy in the assembly of Psychomotor Phase of Procedural Tasks than when using 3D-graphics-based assistance presented on a stationary LCD. From their studies is showed that the user's mental effort is lower because part of the work is performed by the AR system. In literature there are many cases of AR applied to the maintenance through the use of hand-held display; in [2] is described an assembly system in AR overlapping images and simple 3D objects to interact with. In [16], a similar approach is used in the medical field by displaying pre-rendered animations on hand-held display to describe an anesthesia machine. While [13] conducted an experiment comparing the use of AR with and without feedback showing that that AR + feedback significantly improves the user experience during the task performance. The work of [14] proposes an alternative solution using a large projection screen. The use of head-mounted display is minor compared to the hand-held display but is spreading in recent years with the advent of new devices. One of the first uses that can be found in literature is the work performed to facilitate the operations in aircraft manufacturing [5]. In [17], the authors use the monocular optical see-through assembly to the doorlock into a car door. In [20] the user is guided step-by-step through the furniture assembly process in a very intuitive and proactive way. In [1] the authors realize a framework to self-supplied that generated all the necessary data for user intervention and use a robust marker-less tracking. In [9] was proposed a model general assembly in order to define a standardization of performance metrics applicable in various fields. Zheng et al. [21] have made a comparison between Eyewear-Peripheral e Eyewear-Central conditions. Eyewear-Central was faster than Eyewear-Peripheral. In [10] a comparison has been made among tablet, hmd, in-situ projection and paper, discovering, unlike what has been said above, that HMD is the slowest. On the contrary of [21], central Eyewear is less powerful because it blocks their field of view. In both works, it is noticed that the participants used the tablet or paper instruction with both hands, thus interfering in the assembly task.

Display Devices

There are three different types of technologies: Video see-through, Optical see-through [4] and Projective based. The video see-through is closer to virtual reality (VR), the virtual environment is replaced by a digital video of the physical world and the virtual content is superimposed on the video frame. The optical see-through allows to have a greater perception of the real world, contents in AR are superimposed through mirrors and transparent lenses. The projection based technology allows to project the digital content directly on the real object.

Video See-Through. Video see-through is the most economical technique and offers many advantages; (i) The devices that use this technique may be HMD or mobile device (smartphone or tablet); (ii) the current environment is digitized (via video) and it is easier to interact with the real world by superimposing virtual objects; (iii) the brightness and contrast of the virtual objects can be easily adapted in the real world; (iv) it is possible to match the perception of delay between the real and the virtual environment. The main disadvantages are: (i) the low resolution of the camera; (ii) the limited field of view; (iii) in many devices the focus distance can not be adjusted; (iv) In HMD devices, the user may be disoriented because the camera is near the eye positioning.

Optical See-Through. Optical see-through technique is applied to the HMD devices, AR content is mirrored on a curved planar screen. The main advantages are: (i) the display is ideal for a long period of use as it does not create discomfort effects on the user and leave unchanged the real vision; (ii) the user has a direct, unmodified view to the real world, without any delays; the AR objects depend only by the resolution of the display. (ii) They have a low energy consumption compared with see-through video. The disadvantages are: (i) the projection of images on the lenses has a contrast and brightness reduced therefore are not suitable for outdoor use; (ii) The reduced field of view can lead to the leakage of the projection from the edges of the lenses; (iii) it requires difficult and time-consuming calibration (user- and session-dependent).

Projective. Projective technique is based on the projection of the digital content on real-world objects. The advantages are: (i) it does not require lenses to wear; (ii) it allows to cover large surfaces generating a wide field of vision. The main disadvantages are: (i) the headlamp shall be recalibrated if the surrounding environment or the distance from the projection surface changes; (ii) it can be only used in indoor environments because of the low brightness and contrast of the projected images.

Main Types of Available Devices

In the Table 1, some of the best known HDM devices for AR commercially available and that allow to develop custom solutions for are shown. The table shows the comparison of some of the major features available. In [3] was made a comparison between the google glass and the vuzix M100 (the device chosen for our experiment).

Table 1. Features of main HMDs

Model	Resolution	Field of view	Touch pad	Opt. See through	Gestures	Binocular	Stand-alone
XOne	/	/	X	/	X	X	V
Golden-i	800x600	32°	V	X	X	X	V
Google glass	640x360	12°	V	V	X	X	V
Vuzix M2000AR	1280x720	30°	X	V	X	X	X
Vuzix M100	400x240	14°	V	X	X	X	X
Vuzix Star 1200XLD	852x480	35°	V	V	X	V	X
Recon Jet	400x240	14°	V	X	X	X	V
Atheer One	1024x769	65°	X	V	V	V	X
Meta Pro	1280x720	40°	X	V	V	V	X
Epson Moverio	960x540	23°	V	V	V	V	V

3   Methodology

In this section are described the activities carried out to develop an augmented reality app for the task of assembling machine components, with a specific focus on the purposes of the app, on the main HW and SW components, beside a description of the layout design.

3.1   Objective of the Application

The purpose of this project is to test a real decrease in the execution time of a task rather than using a printed manual. The application allows to train and drive the user in real time during the assembly phase of an object composed of numerous components that must be assembled in a precise order and together with a final verification measurements on some parts of the final object. To facilitate the mounting operation we decided to create 3D virtual components with exactly the same shape and size of the actual components and for every task we superimposed the virtual component to the real object assembled (the mechanical component used for this test is showed in Fig. 1).

Fig. 1. Example of a real component used for the development of this showcase; in particular, the object is a cone that one have to mount over a machine for glass moulding.

Once completed, the application has been tested in the laboratory of Intermac, in order to receive feedback from experienced staff. The application was also tested by untrained personnel during two important fairs of the sector (namely Marmomac and Glasstech respectively held in Verona and Dusseldorf); in addition to test the application, users were interviewed in order to obtain further information on the application and on the difficulties encountered in the use. In the following, a brief description of each element is provided, together with the way in which they were used.

3.2 Hardware Components

After appropriate research among the available models we chose VuzixM100 device, which have the following hardware features: display with WQVGA resolution, 1 GHz dual core CPU, 1 GB RAM, 4 GB Internal Memory expandable up to 32 GB with an external slot, camera 5MP camera with 1080p video recording, 600 mAh battery, which you can connect an external battery of 3,800 mAh, ear speaker and noise canceling microphone, microUSB port, WI-FI and bluetooth 4.0 connectivity support. The device is equipped with 4 buttons, two for scrolling forward and back, one for selection and one for switching on and off. It has a voice recognition system using proprietary libraries but expandable via payment. The operating system is based on Android 4.0 Ice Cream Sandwich in which are installed the proprietary app. you can install your apps developed. Battery life is approximately 1–2 h when used.

3.3 Software Components

For the implementation of the AR experience, we used the Unity framework and Vuforia libraries.

Unity 3D Game Engine is a system that allows the development of multi-platform games developed by Unity Technologies that includes a game engine and an integrated development environment (IDE). Supported platforms include BlackBerry 10, Windows Phone 8, Windows, OS X, Linux (mainly Ubuntu), Android, iOS, Unity Web Player, Adobe Flash, PlayStation, Xbox and Wii. The development environment allows to create and manage 3D objects and create simple mobile application.

Vuforia AR SDK. Vuforia represents one of the most advanced solutions for the development of AR applications for mobile devices. Vuforia SDK is subdivided into two SDK dedicated to the development of Android and iOS platforms, respectively; Vuforia Unity Extension is also available that allows to use the Unity environment to manage advanced functions for creating augmented reality applications, and all the prefab objects useful for the creation of three-dimensional scene; also allows the release of apps for both Android iOS platforms. The strength of this SDK is given by the possibility of identifying and tracing different types of targets: (i) Image target consists of a simple two-dimensional color image; (ii) Cylinder Target (iii) Multi Target allows to track multiple targets (as long as a portion of the multi-target track is recognized for all others); (iv) Frame Markers are special markers that are identified by a unique code; (v) Object Recognition allows to recognize solid three-dimensional objects. Vuforia provides an online tool that allows to calculate the image quality to target and save it in a suitable format for use in RA. Finally it provides a cloud platform where target images can be saved (or can download directly on the device). Vuforia SDK is offered with a freemium mode, where you can use all the features in development mode but you have to buy a license if you want to market the application.

3.4 Application Workflow

The development of the application followed a strict pipeline, designed in a close cooperation with the worker and of the experts of Intermac, in order to fulfil with the foreseen expectations of the AR experience.

1. Installation of Unity (version 5.3.6) and importing Vuforia AR Extension (version 6.2).
2. Select the image to use as Target Image upon which the virtual elements will be superimposed with the same point of view of the user. Operators must carry out the assembly operation over a 30 cm × 30 cm sheet, which represents the marker to be recognized by the application. We chose to use an image rich of edges so as to make more robust the tracking phase; this was an obliged choice, given the presence of the physical components and the presence of the operator's hands.
3. Creating 3D models for each real component, keeping the same dimensions and shapes. The models were created using Unity and each one has a different color in order to be better identified (Fig. 2)
4. Creation of the sequence of operations to be performed in chronological order for the object assembling. At each assembly step, the position in which it will go to the real component, is superimposed augmented reality virtual object

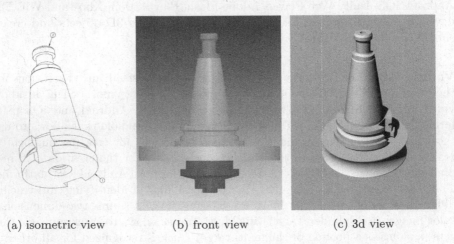

(a) isometric view   (b) front view   (c) 3d view

Fig. 2. Example of virtual component used during the assembly task.

by a short animation. Also appears a short text at the top describing the operation with keywords to play.

5. Creation of the sequence of operations to be performed in chronological order for the measurements to be performed on the object mounted.

The mobile application has been developed for Android S.O., according to the specifications of the VuzixM100 SDK. In order to switch from one task to the next we decided to use the select button on the device placed near the ear.

Usability and Legibility

In accordance with the guidelines defined in [8], we used the black text (without outline) over a white billboard because it is the combination that ensures readability. The font used is Roboto Regular, one of the standard android fonts. The background as well as being white is slightly transparent so you can use the large text without obstructing the operator's field of vision. In this way we are guaranteed a real good view of the object being assembled and virtual components overlay. The background has a red line at the top because red is a color that catches the eye's attention allowing you to direct the eye toward the text to read. We used the color red on animations that describe the steps to take on the real object (screw and measure) to make more explicit the manual operations to be played by the operator. All virtual components have different colors so they are easier to distinguish and then allow to decrease the execution time of the task. An example of the User Interface is showed in Fig. 3.

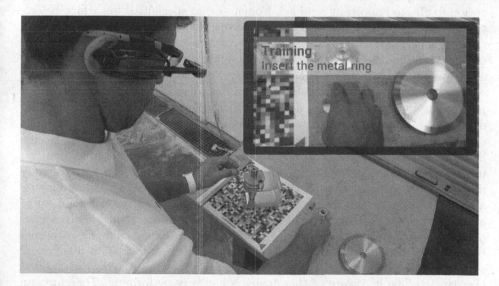

Fig. 3. Snapshot of the application running on the Vuzix M100 (Color figure online)

4   Results and Discussion

The application has been validated after a number of practical tests carried out by specialized technicians who normally perform this type of assembly. We also worked with the technicians during all phases of the application development, as well as to improve usability and build an application that meets the real needs of end users. In Fig. 4 is showed a specialist Intermac technician who performs a task assembly with the aid of the Vuzix M100.

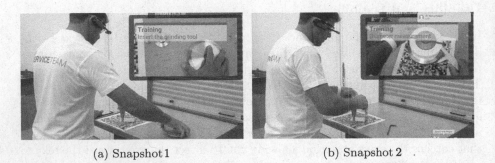

(a) Snapshot 1   (b) Snapshot 2

Fig. 4. Example of different tasks displayed by the application running on the devices

Nonetheless, it was also worth to test the application with not experienced users. During two industry trade fairs it has been asked users to test the application to obtain important feedback from users not specialized but which belong to the sector. From information gained during the development of the app and the feedback received from different types of users, we can affirm that the use of AR in the industry domain, especially in the branch of *training-on-the-job*, ensures a shorter execution time of a task. The use of a HMD guarantees the enormous advantage of being able to have both hands free, a key condition in performing manual tasks. The use of the Vuzix M100 has allowed us to quickly develop the application because it allows one to install Android native applications; The Vuzix also provides a SDK (not available for Unity) with specific libraries but most of the features are already exposed. For example, one can use the sensor of gestures, using predefined gesture because they are already mapped with Android basic actions (back button, etc.). Moreover, developing an Android app for the chosen devices can be compared to the development of an app for tablets or smartphones, of course taking into account different type of interaction between the user and the application. Even tough we witnessed to the aforementioned positive aspects, emerged different drawbacks that can be summarized as follows: (i) The Vuzix overheats and thus warms the area around the ear. (ii) The hardware of this device is not very performing. Therefore, an AR application can becomes slower, especially using the multi-target tracking or managing heavy 3d models. Hence, the camera allows the recognition of the target by only a limited distance (about 2 m). The same application running on a latest generation smartphone guaranteed a much faster and performing recognition thanks to a more powerful processor and a higher-resolution camera. Besides, the battery duration is very low (up to 1 h), this represent a great impediment for a daily usage of the device in normal operational conditions (iv). The video see-through display is too small, hence it has a limited field of view. This oblige the developer to find a right balance between the dimension of the text and the contents. The smaller is the text, the less the text is readable. All these aspects worsen the quality of the experience and may lead to a lengthening of the execution time of the task. However, the rapid development of technologies will allow to increase the quality of the hardware at the same cost providing enhanced performance.

5   Conclusion and Outlook

In this paper, a new Augmented Reality application based on the use of AR glasses was presented. The work was conducted within the activities of a joint venture between an academic institution and Intermac enterprise, giving an added value in terms of technological transfer. By testing the application in real case environment (with both experts and non experts users) we demonstrated how such application can really ease the operational task that field workers have to performing during their daily activities. The aid that AR can bring in the world of Industry 4.0 is invaluable. Bearing in mind the rapidity of changing of the mechanical components, as well as the necessity of delivering the assembling instruction all over the world, the potential of this kind of application is huge, since it can be uploaded on demand with respect to the specifications of each single enterprise. Actually, the training of the workers is made just with the aid of paper book or of long and expensive training courses. The use of AR applications instead will allow to overcome this issue, be replacing, or at least reducing, the time and the costs of training. This test was also useful as a benchmark for the research community, since we had the possibility to test with different users the weakness points of wearable devices that, due to the actual technological limitations, are many. The interaction with the UI is already not advanced and it requires more investigations in order to make the interaction touch less with the aid of sensors or input commands based on voice recognition. Moreover, the low performance of the camera do not allow to get a robust tracking of the scene. The use of QRcodes or artificial marker should be replaced with more advanced system of environmental interpretation and extended tracking. Finally, it is worth to note that human limitations arose, mainly due to the diopters and the ergonomic of the faces, different among different users. A closer investigation is required in this direction, in order to develop solutions that could fit to the majority of every worker.

Acknowledgments. The authors would like to thanks the Intermac team for putting at the disposal of the research team their laboratories and qualified staff. We also thanks Andrea Pantaloni, Tommaso Pantaloni and Michele Sasso, of 48h Studio for helping on the development of the application.

References

1. Alvarez, H., Aguinaga, I., Borro, D.: Providing guidance for maintenance operations using automatic markerless augmented reality system. In: 2011 10th IEEE International Symposium on Mixed and Augmented Reality. Institute of Electrical and Electronics Engineers (IEEE), October 2011. https://doi.org/10.1109%2Fismar.2011.6092385
2. Billinghurst, M., Hakkarainen, M., Woodward, C.: Augmented assembly using a mobile phone. In: Proceedings of the 7th International Conference on Mobile and Ubiquitous Multimedia - MUM 2008. Association for Computing Machinery (ACM) (2008). https://doi.org/10.1145%2F1543137.1543153
3. Brusie, T., Fijal, T., Keller, A., Lauff, C., Barker, K., Schwinck, J., Calland, J.F., Guerlain, S.: Usability evaluation of two smart glass systems. In: 2015 Systems and Information Engineering Design Symposium. Institute of Electrical and Electronics Engineers (IEEE), April 2015. https://doi.org/10.1109%2Fsieds.2015.7117000
4. Cakmakci, O., Rolland, J.: Head-worn displays: a review. J. Disp. Technol. 2(3), 199–216 (2006). https://doi.org/10.1109%2Fjdt.2006.879846
5. Caudell, T., Mizell, D.: Augmented reality: an application of heads-up display technology to manual manufacturing processes. In: Proceedings of the Twenty-Fifth Hawaii International Conference on System Sciences. Institute of Electrical and Electronics Engineers (IEEE) (1992). https://doi.org/10.1109%2Fhicss.1992.183317
6. Clini, P., Frontoni, E., Quattrini, R., Pierdicca, R.: Augmented reality experience: from high-resolution acquisition to real time augmented contents. Adv. Multimed. 2014, 18 (2014)
7. De Paolis, L.T., Ricciardi, F., Manes, C.L.: Augmented reality in radiofrequency ablation of the liver tumors. In: Computational Vision and Medical Image Processing V: Proceedings of the 5th Eccomas Thematic Conference on Computational Vision and Medical Image Processing (VipIMAGE 2015), Tenerife, Spain, 19–21 October 2015, p. 279. CRC Press (2015)
8. Fiorentino, M., Debernardis, S., Uva, A.E., Monno, G.: Augmented reality text style readability with see-through head-mounted displays in industrial context. Presence: Teleoper. Virtual Environ. 22(2), 171–190 (2013). https://doi.org/10.1162%2Fpres_a_00146
9. Funk, M., Kosch, T., Greenwald, S.W., Schmidt, A.: A benchmark for interactive augmented reality instructions for assembly tasks. In: Proceedings of the 14th International Conference on Mobile and Ubiquitous Multimedia - MUM 2015. Association for Computing Machinery (ACM) (2015). https://doi.org/10.1145%2F2836041.2836067
10. Funk, M., Kosch, T., Schmidt, A.: Interactive worker assistance. In: Proceedings of the 2016 ACM International Joint Conference on Pervasive and Ubiquitous Computing - UbiComp 2016. Association for Computing Machinery (ACM) (2016). https://doi.org/10.1145%2F2971648.2971706
11. Henderson, S., Feiner, S.: Exploring the benefits of augmented reality documentation for maintenance and repair. IEEE Trans. Vis. Comput. Graph. 17(10), 1355–1368 (2011). https://doi.org/10.1109%2Ftvcg.2010.245
12. Henderson, S.J., Feiner, S.K.: Augmented reality in the psychomotor phase of a procedural task. In: 2011 10th IEEE International Symposium on Mixed and Augmented Reality. Institute of Electrical and Electronics Engineers (IEEE), October 2011. https://doi.org/10.1109%2Fismar.2011.6092386

13. Liu, C., Huot, S., Diehl, J., Mackay, W., Beaudouin-Lafon, M.: Evaluating the benefits of real-time feedback in mobile augmented reality with hand-held devices. In: Proceedings of the 2012 ACM Annual Conference on Human Factors in Computing Systems - CHI 2012. Association for Computing Machinery (ACM) (2012). https://doi.org/10.1145%2F2207676.2208706

14. Patrick, E., Cosgrove, D., Slavkovic, A., Rode, J.A., Verratti, T., Chiselko, G.: Using a large projection screen as an alternative to head-mounted displays for virtual environments. In: Proceedings of the SIGCHI Conference on Human Factors in Computing Systems - CHI 2000. Association for Computing Machinery (ACM) (2000). https://doi.org/10.1145%2F332040.332479

15. Pierdicca, R., Frontoni, E., Zingaretti, P., Mancini, A., Malinverni, E.S., Tassetti, A.N., Marcheggiani, E., Galli, A.: Smart maintenance of riverbanks using a standard data layer and augmented reality. Comput. Geosci. **95**, 67–74 (2016)

16. Quarles, J., Lampotang, S., Fischler, I., Fishwick, P., Lok, B.: A mixed reality approach for merging abstract and concrete knowledge. In: 2008 IEEE Virtual Reality Conference. Institute of Electrical and Electronics Engineers (IEEE) (2008). https://doi.org/10.1109%2Fvr.2008.4480746

17. Reiners, D., Stricker, D., Klinker, G., Mueller, S.: Augmented reality for construction tasks: doorlock assembly. In: Proceedings of IEEE and ACM IWAR 1998 (1st International Workshop on Augmented Reality), San Francisco, pp. 31–46. AK Peters, November 1998

18. Tang, A., Owen, C., Biocca, F., Mou, W.: Comparative effectiveness of augmented reality in object assembly. In: Proceedings of the Conference on Human Factors in Computing Systems - CHI 2003. Association for Computing Machinery (ACM) (2003). https://doi.org/10.1145%2F642611.642626

19. Wiedenmaier, S., Oehme, O., Schmidt, L., Luczak, H.: Augmented reality (AR) for assembly processes design and experimental evaluation. Int. J. Hum. Comput. Interact. **16**(3), 497–514 (2003)

20. Zauner, J., Haller, M., Brandl, A., Hartman, W.: Authoring of a mixed reality assembly instructor for hierarchical structures. In: Proceedings of the Second IEEE and ACM International Symposium on Mixed and Augmented Reality. Institute of Electrical and Electronics Engineers (IEEE) (2003). https://doi.org/10.1109%2Fismar.2003.1240707

21. Zheng, X.S., Foucault, C., da Silva, P.M., Dasari, S., Yang, T., Goose, S.: Eye-wearable technology for machine maintenance. In: Proceedings of the 33rd Annual ACM Conference on Human Factors in Computing Systems - CHI 2015. Association for Computing Machinery (ACM) (2015). https://doi.org/10.1145%2F2702123.2702305

Augmented Reality Applications for Education: Five Directions for Future Research

Juan Garzón[1(✉)], Juan Pavón[2], and Silvia Baldiris[2]

[1] Catholic University of the East, Rionegro, Colombia
fgarzon@uco.edu.co
[2] Complutense University of Madrid, Madrid, Spain
jpavon@fdi.ucm.es, sbaldiris@gmail.com

Abstract. Augmented Reality (AR) systems have reached certain level of maturity in educational environments and their effectiveness has been widely proven. There are many literature review studies that have determined the trends, affordances and challenges of this emerging technology in educational settings. However, these studies do not propose practical solutions that aim to solve the challenges and issues found in AR systems. There are still some problems that need to be addressed in order to obtain the best of this technology and ensure the most appropriate integration of AR into education. There are still unexplored fields of application in which AR systems can help expand the possibilities and improve learning processes. This paper, proposes five directions for future research around possible solutions for some of the most important challenges of AR applications for education. These proposals are based on the findings of a literature review of 50 studies published between 2011 and 2017 in scientific journals. As a result, we provide a guideline for developers and practitioners to continue to expand the accurate integration of AR systems into educational environments.

Keywords: Augmented reality · Special education · Vocational education

1 Introduction

Augmented Reality (AR) technologies, have been studied and developed since the early 60s. However, it was not until 1994 that Milgran and Kishino [1], and then Azuma in 1997 [2], provided accurate definitions of this emerging technology. Prior to 2010, most AR applications were complex and expensive systems that were difficult to access because of their high costs and limited expansion [3]. Although there were some attempts to expand AR systems by creating some applications for education, it was not until the apparition of mobile devices such as smartphones and tablets, that AR systems gained the interest of the research community and expanded around the world along with the usage of mobile devices [4], to become an important tool that has taken root in educational environments.

Augmented Reality systems are present in many fields such as education, medicine, tourism, entertainment, and others [5]. Its efficacy has been widely demonstrated by

© Springer International Publishing AG 2017
L.T. De Paolis et al. (Eds.): AVR 2017, Part I, LNCS 10324, pp. 402–414, 2017.
DOI: 10.1007/978-3-319-60922-5_31

many studies, which have identified a large number of benefits that inclusion of these systems brings to every scenario where it is applied [6].

The integration of AR systems into mobile devices, led to an increase in the number of AR applications in particular as of 2010 [7]. Likewise, the number of studies related to the application of AR systems into education has increased significantly over the past seven years [3]. Most of these studies are based on qualitative and quantitative analysis of case studies, designed to validate an AR application. Moreover, there is large number of literature review studies, which aim to identify the trends, affordances and challenges of AR systems in education.

However, these literature review studies do not offer solutions to those detected challenges. This paper, proposes possible answers to some of the problems that need to be addressed in order to improve the experience of using AR systems in educational settings by suggesting five directions for future research: (1) Design of AR systems that consider special needs of particular users, (2) Integration of AR systems into unexplored fields of education, (3) Inclusion of AR systems into learning processes of unexplored target groups, (4) Integration of AR systems into business and industry, and (5) Design of pedagogically efficient AR systems.

The research was divided into four stages: at first, we selected the studies to be reviewed (including case studies and literature review studies). We then carefully read each study and identified the reported challenges. Third, we classified the challenges according to the five directions of investigation, and finally, we declared possible solutions for those challenges and documented the research.

The five directions for investigation proposed in this study, arose from the analysis of 50 research papers. We conclude that as AR systems continue to mature, most of the challenges that have been found in the studies will be solved and the benefits of their usage in educational environments will expand worldwide, enriching learning and teaching experiences.

The rest of the paper is structured as follows: Sect. 2 presents previous related studies. Section 3 presents the methodology implemented to develop the search. Section 4 presents the five directions of investigation for future research and finally, Sect. 5 concludes the paper.

2 Related Work

As stated before, literature review studies aim to define the trends, affordances and challenges of AR systems in education. As for the trends, these studies show that the number of research papers related to the application of AR in education has steadily increased in the last 6 years [8]. Most common target groups for AR applications are secondary school, Bachelor or equivalent level, and primary school; whilst most applications of AR are related to the broad field of Natural Sciences and Mathematics [9].

With regard to the affordances, these studies have demonstrated that the integration of AR systems into educational settings, brings a large number of benefits including academic performance improvement, attitude toward learning, and cost reduction. The most reported advantage of AR systems for education are "Learning gains" and "Motivation" [8]. Students felt more motivated when they learned using AR systems, which led then to acquire knowledge in a more significant way [10]. Improvement in the academic level of students, eventually reduces the costs associated with grade repetition and school or college dropout [11].

With reference to the challenges, most of these studies declare some limitations of this technology when applied in educational settings. These limitations include unexplored fields of application and unexplored target groups [9], technical difficulties, teacher resistance, and pedagogical issues. Table 1 summarizes the main challenges, problems and limitations of AR systems, reported in some literature review studies.

Table 1. Sumarize of challenges and directions for future research in literature review studies.

Study	Reported challenges	Future research
Carmigniani et al. [5]	Social acceptance. Privacy concerns. Ethical concerns. High costs. Tracking	Continue to monitor the impact of AR on society. Continue to explore how AR can best be applied to expand teaching and learning environments
Radu [12]	Attention tunneling. Usability difficulties. Ineffective classroom integration. Learner differences	Continue to design effective educational AR experiences.
Wu et al. [13]	Technological issues (mainly technical difficulties). Pedagogical issues (teacher resistance, lack of instructional design). Learning issues (cognitive overload)	Applications for unexplored broad fields of education. Use of design models to solve pedagogical issues. Identify curricular and technology characteristics that only AR system can provide
Bacca et al. [9]	Difficulties maintaining superimposed information. Paying too much attention to virtual information. Design for specific knowledge field. Teachers cannot create new learning content	Applications in *Early Childhood* and *Vocational Educational Training* target groups. Applications in the fields of, Health, Education, and Agriculture. Considerations of special needs of students
Diegmann et al. [6]	Every AR application must be designed to a specific context	Considerations of special needs of particular users
Akcayir et al. [3]	Pedagogical issues. Technical problems. Usability issues. Require more time. Not suitable for large groups. Cognitive overload. Ergonomic problems. Difficult to design	Use of design models to solve pedagogical issues. More studies related to the development and usability of AR systems. Considerations of special needs of particular users. More research to discard novelty effect

In addition to these, there are many studies that validated through the qualitative and quantitative analysis of case studies, the effectiveness of specific AR applications in educational settings. However, these studies do not offer possible directions or practical solutions to the challenges encountered. Thus, in this paper, we extract the main challenges reported in 50 studies, group them into categories, and define five directions for future research.

3 Methods

This section describes the process carried out to develop the search. At first, we describe the protocol for selecting the studies to be reviewed. We then explain the process undertaken to extract the data related to the reported challenges. After that, we explain the process of classifying the challenges in order to establish the five directions of investigation for future research.

3.1 Research Protocol

This protocol defines the strategy carried out to develop the search. In order to guarantee the quality of the studies and the updating of the data, we focused our research on scientific papers published in journals indexed in the Social Sciences Citation Index (SSCI) database between 2011 and 2017. We used the key words "Augmented Reality" + "Education" for the search and selected the most cited studies. Papers selected for the study accomplished the following criteria:

- Studies written in English.
- Studies published between 2011 and 2017.
- Studies focused on education.
- Case studies or literature review studies.
- Primary studies published in journals indexed in the SSCI database or the ConferenceProceedings Citation Index (CPCI).
- Studies that have been cited at least once.

Having into account that this research is focused on the challenges reported in scientific studies, we excluded papers that did not report any challenges for AR systems in education.

As a result, we elaborated a list with the 50 most cited papers that satisfied all the inclusion criteria; 40 of the papers corresponds to case studies and 10 to literature review studies. The average citation number received by the selected studies is 58.6. Moreover, all the studies appear in the first 100 results in Google Scholar (sorting by relevance) for the search of the terms "Augmented Reality" + "Education".

3.2 Data Extraction

Once the protocol was agreed, two of the researchers individually read each paper. Content analysis technique was applied to extract the data of each paper. We designed a data extraction form in which we recorded the data extracted from the papers. The document contained the following information: study name, year of publication, sample size, target group, reported disadvantages or challenges, and indications for future research.

3.3 Classification of the Challenges

After completing the data extraction form, we analyzed the reported disadvantages and challenges, and classified them in order to establish five different categories. Separately, we classified the indications for future research (of each paper) into the same five categories. From the analysis of this disadvantages and challenges, we propose the five directions for future research, which are described in the next section.

4 Five Directions of Investigation for Future Research

Although the number of reported disadvantages has decreased significantly by comparing the period of time 2011–2017, AR systems have still some problems to overcome when applied in educational settings. There are some technical and pedagogical specifications that need to be addressed. There are still unexplored target groups and unexplored fields of application of this emerging technology. Therefore, after analyzing the data reported in the selected studies, we proposed five directions of investigation for future research, which aim to solve some of the gaps, and the issues of this technology and thus enhance the affordances of AR for education.

4.1 Design of AR Systems that Consider Special Needs of Particular Users

Among the applications of AR used in the selected studies, just a single one, "HeartRun", includes aids for special needs of particular users [14]. It represents just 2.50% of the selected studies, which is obviously a very low percentage that must increase in order to guarantee access to all type of users. Moreover, some literature review studies have detected this situation, but have not proposed any practical solutions.

Teachers, developers and practitioners must ensure that future AR applications permit any student, regardless of their limitations and taking into account preferences and special needs, to study efficiently using these technologies [15]. Hence, this direction has to do with the need of addressing this significant gap of AR systems. There are some guidelines and standards that stakeholders may use, with the intention of creating *Accessible* AR applications. Next, we describe some of these guidelines and standards.

Ergonomics of Human-System Interaction. The International Organization for Standardization (ISO), provides the Software Ergonomics Standards. These standards establish design principles for multimedia user interfaces, promoting productivity, safety, and health; and outlines practices for improving accessibility.

Ergonomics of human-system interaction (ISO 9241-171:2008), provides ergonomic guidance and specifications for the design of accessible software for use at work, in home, in education and in public places [16]. This standard defines *Accessibility* as "usability of a product, service, environment or facility by people with the widest range of capabilities". This standard is applicable to any interactive system such as AR applications, and promotes the usability of systems for a wider range of users, including handicapped people, elderly people, temporally disable people, and people with cognitive limitations.

Web Content Accessibility Guidelines (WCAG) 2.0. These guidelines cover a wide range of recommendations for making multimedia content more accessible [17]. It is a technical standard (ISO/IEC 40500:2012) that includes 12 guidelines that seek to lead the practitioners to develop content accessible for a wider range of people with disabilities such as blindness, low vision, deafness, hearing loss, learning disabilities, and cognitive limitations. Mobile accessibility is covered by the WCAG and refers to making applications more accessible to people with disabilities when they are using their mobile devices.

The document "Guidance on Applying WCAG 2.0 to Non-Web Information and Communications Technologies (WCAG2ICT)" [18], describes how the WCAG 2.0, can be applied to non-web Information and Communications Technologies under the four principles of accessibility of software: perceivable, operable, understandable, and robust.

Perceivable principle, states that both the information and the components of the user interface must be presented to users so that they can be perceived. Operable principle, states that both, surfing and the components of the user interface must be operable. Understandable principle, states that both, surfing and the components of the user interface must be understandable. Robust principle, states that the content has to be interpreted by different user agents, including assistive technologies.

Universal Design for Learning (UDL). This is a scientifically valid framework for teaching and learning that seeks to address all the user needs and preferences. It helps educators address learner's special needs by suggesting flexible goals, methods, materials and assessments. The main objective of this framework, is to eliminate the barriers existing in curricula giving all learners equal opportunities to learn.

This framework consist of a set of guidelines that can assist anyone who wants to develop any kind of educative material, under three principles based on neuroscience research [19]:

- Principle 1: Provide multiple means of representation.
- Principle 2: Provide multiple means of action and expression.
- Principle 3: Provide multiple means of engagement.

4.2 Integration of AR Systems into Unexplored Fields of Education

Applications of AR systems in educational settings have gained acceptance from educators and learners due to their proven efficacy. This technology has been successfully integrated into many broad fields of education, achieving promising results [20].

Most applications of AR into education in the selected studies correspond to the broad field of *Natural Sciences, Mathematics and Statistics* (52.50%). *Social Sciences, journalism and information* (15%), *Arts and Humanities* (15%), and *Engineering, manufacturing and construction* (15%), are other common broad fields where AR is applied. Although there are no applications related to the broad field of *Health* among the selected studies, that is another important field of application of AR systems [21].

In contrast, there are fields of education where AR has not been applied, or at least, there is no evidence in the scientific literature. There are two broad fields of education that have not been benefited from AR systems among the selected studies: *Agriculture, forestry, fisheries and veterinary* and *Business, administration and law*.

Bacca et al. [9], conducted a literature review study in 2014, including 32 studies published between 2003 and 2013. While *Natural Sciences, Mathematics and Statistics* was the most explored broad field of education (40.6%), there were no applications related to the broad fields of *Agriculture, forestry, fisheries and veterinary*, or *Business, administration and law*.

Chen et al. [8], analyzed 55 studies published between 2011 and 2016, and found that, as well as in the study by Bacca et al., most AR applications were related to the Broad field of *Natural Sciences, Mathematics and Statistics* (40%). Likewise, they could not find any application related to the broad fields of *Agriculture, forestry, fisheries and veterinary*, or *Business, administration and law*.

In total, 127 AR systems from 2003 to 2017 (combining current study with the studies by Bacca et al. and Chen et al.) were analyzed and there was no evidence of applications related to the broad fields of *Agriculture, forestry, fisheries and veterinary*, and *Business, administration and law*.

Although AR systems have been proven to be more suitable to teach subjects such as Sciences and Engineering, there is a great opportunity for innovators to initiate the integration of AR into these unexplored broad fields of education. The importance of developing strategies for integrating AR systems into some unexplored fields of education is outlined below.

Agriculture and Forestry. Precision agriculture is a farming management concept, which integrates technology into agriculture with the intention of optimizing returns on inputs while preserving resources [22]. Issues such as climate change and a rapidly growing population around the world, brings new challenges to the farming processes. There is a clear need to develop more accurate farming methods, which provide opportunities for innovators to develop new technologies and techniques that help protect environment whilst increasing food production [23].

The most common technologies applied to precision agriculture are: precision positioning systems, automated steering systems, smart sensors, and integrated electronic communications. So far, AR systems have not been integrated into this vital field. This technology could be a useful and innovative tool that contributes to both precision agriculture and forestry. Hence, stakeholders have a great opportunity to begin exploring the possibilities that AR applications can provide to continue to enlarge the multiples benefits that technology can bring to agriculture development and forest conservation.

Business and Administration. Technology has important tangible and intangible effects on both business and administration. Technology plays an important role in some relevant aspects of business and administration, such as communication, efficiency of operations, information security, inventory management, business culture, and research capacity. Technology development has redefined business in ways that could not have been predicted. For example, the use of social networks has changed the way in which advertising is taken to customers. Internet, allows the exchange of information, databases, and possible money transferences, removing workplace boundaries, what enlarge the opportunities for expansion of enterprises and have increased the competitive nature of the business world [24].

Businesses have become so technology-dependent that if technology were taken away from companies, all business operations around the world would collapse. Having an efficient technology infrastructure allows administration systems to get more work done, faster, more efficiently, and more securely, which evidently improves business possibilities. In order to continue to expand business, and improve administration techniques, there is a need of continue to develop technological solutions. Hence, developers and practitioners can provide innovative and efficient AR systems that combined with business and administration theories can improve this type of processes.

4.3　Inclusion of AR Systems into Learning Processes of Unexplored Target Groups

Most common target groups for AR applications in the selected studies are *Secondary school* (35%), *Bacheloror equivalent level* (32.50%), and *Primary school* (25%). Oppositely, there are two target groups that have not been taken into account: *Post-secondary non-tertiary education* and *Short-cycle tertiary education*. These target groups corresponds to Vocational Education (VE), defined by the UNESCO as: "Education programmes that are designed for learners to acquire the knowledge, skills and competencies specific to a particular occupation, trade or class of occupations or trades" [25]. In VE, *Training*, is defined as "Education designed to achieve particular learning objectives".

The study by Bacca et al. [9], shows that only one study out of 32, focused on *Short-cycle tertiary education* astarget group. In addition, Chen et al., do not show any application that focuses on VE astarget group. In all, only one out of 127 AR applications, focused on Vocational Educations as target group (combining current study with the studies by Bacca et al. and Chen et al.).

Students in VE programmes, usually have completed secondary education, but due to different reasons, are not willing to enroll in a university. These students seek to prepare themselves to work in a trade, perhaps as a technician. This preparation includes training in manual or practical activities that are related to a specific occupation.

The inclusion of AR systems in training processes enriches the learning experience of students who can acquire knowledge on a more vivid way. However, the potential of this technology in VE has not been tapped, which means that innovators and stakeholders have a great opportunity to become leaders in this field.

4.4 Integration of AR Systems into Business and Industry

Although there is a notable reduction in the cost of AR systems, possibly due to the integration of this technology into mobile devices such as smartphones and tablets, a more significant participation of different economic sectors such as industry is needed. This with the intention of enlarging the investment for developing AR technologies, improve their affordances, and reduce final prices to the users.

A search for patents in two databases: the Global Patent Search Network (GPSN) of the United States Patent and Trademark Office (USPTO) [26] and Google Patents (GP), allowed us to identify that only a patent related to the AR technologies for education, has been registered in the last 10 years.

This apparent lack of interest in the industry for developing AR systems for education, may be due to entrepreneurs ignoring the good benefits that this emerging technology can bring to industrial processes. In addition, because researchers, developers and practitioners, have been unable to "sell the idea" to managers and policymakers within the industry.

With the purpose of integrating AR systems into industry, we propose two possibilities. The first has to do with the consideration of unexplored fields of application and the second has to do the consideration of unexplored target groups.

Unexplored Fields of Application. Companies related to agriculture are willing to invest money in new technologies that help improve farming processes [27]. The new technologies included in precision agriculture are drones, high precision position systems, smart sensors and aerial imagery. Data collected from these devices provides information to be used in machine learning and analytics software. The combination of these technologies with AR systems, could improve the monitoring, control, quality of predictive models in plant performance, and storage processes.

To make a difference in business, entrepreneurs have to be innovative, namely, to do things differently, cheaper, smarter, value added, or better quality. An important mechanism to be successful in business is to integrate new technologies into processes. Different studies have shown that organizations that have invested in technology (in the last two decades), have increased their market share, financial figures and overall competitiveness [28]. Augmented Reality holds the power to revolutionize the way we do business. It offers users graphical enhancements to the real environment that can be applied to marketing, sales, construction, communications and other forms of business that have not yet been deeply explored.

Unexplored Target Groups. The expansion of the global economy, has caused that labor market requires specific skills from workers, increasing the demand for vocational professionals. This have boosted the development of VE programs through publicly funded training organizations. However, the supply of these new required skills is not just responsibility of education or the government. Industry plays a central role in articulating the needed skills with the training curriculum [29].

Training processes in industry can be reinforced by the use of AR systems. This technology increases the depth of the instructions on even the more complex tasks. For example, AR overlaying make possible the illustration of step-by-step reparation processes of any machinery for inexperienced workers. Hence the integration of AR systems into business and industry, can be achieved by the inclusion of AR applications that are designed to support training processes for VE programs students.

4.5 Design of Pedagogically Efficient AR Systems

Sometimes, AR applications are evaluated only taking into account their technical efficacy. These applications are designed by professional programmers and consequently their quality in terms of technology is out of discussion [30]. Technical or technological issues reported in the studies have decreased in the last years. Most of the problems that used to present AR applications have been solved. This has to do probably with the fact that these applications have been widely integrated into mobile devices such as smartphones and tablets [31], which are mature technologies. However, these applications have to go beyond technical characteristics. What is important here, is not only that these systems work properly, but that satisfy the real purposes of education.

Engineers have abilities for technical issues such as designing, programming, assembling, among others. Nevertheless, these abilities are not sufficient when the purposes have to do with pedagogical issues. On the other hand, thematic and pedagogical experts such as teachers, may not have the capacity to develop these tools because they lack the programming and assembling skills.

So, how to design AR applications that are technically efficient and pedagogically accurate? As stated by Diegmann et al., AR applications are not magical bullets in educational environments. Every application is unique and has to be designed to be applied in a specific scenario [6]. We have to remember that as well as other technological applications, AR systems are merely pedagogical tools that have to be complemented by an appropriate pedagogical content, and their design and usage have to be guided by a thematic expert. Namely, the tool does not replace the teacher, it just complements the learning process.

Teachers and stakeholders with no programming experience, may use "Authoring Tools" to create their own AR applications. These intuitive interfaces permit the user to create learning environments without the necessity of using programming languages. Some of the most popular Authoring tools that can be accessed to create AR applications are ATOMIC, AMIRE, and ComposAR.

However, in order to ensure the quality of any Digital Educational Resource (DER), its development should involve the participation of an interdisciplinary group of professionals, each one of whom is responsible for developing a specific activity under the guidelines of an Instructional Design Model. Instructional Design models involve activities that are systematically related and seek to maximize the process of educational software development [32].

There are many Instructional Design models, which are composed mostly of five basic phases: Analysis, Design, Development, Implementation, and Evaluation. Due to its simplicity, versatility, linearity and other benefits, in this paper we recommend the Instructional Design Model "ADDIE" [33]. Figure 1 represents the interaction of each phase in the Instructional Design Model ADDIE.

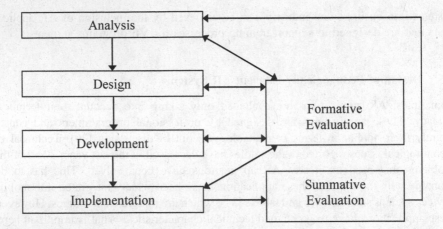

Fig. 1. Instructional design model

Analysis. The analysis phase is the basis for the remaining phases of the instructional design. In this phase, it is necessary to define the nature of the problem, identify its origin and propose some possible solutions. This phase may include specific research techniques such as user analysis, pedagogical context analysis, and analysis of specific needs. Some usual results of this stage are the Educational goals and a list of activities to be developed. These results are the inputs to the Design phase.

Design. This phase uses the results of the Analysis phase, to plan a strategy for developing the instruction. In this phase, it is necessary to establish some routes to reach the Educational Goals. Some elements of the Design phase include the objectives of the DER, the thematic contents, and the assessment instruments.

Development. This phase is based on the phases of Analysis and Design. Its purpose is to generate the structure of the instruction. All the pedagogical materials such as thematic content, activities, and assessment instruments are created. In this phase, programmers develop or integrate technologies.

Implementation. This phase refers to the delivery of the instruction. This is the start of the learning process, all the materials created in the Development phase are introduced to the target learners. It focuses on developing training for both educators and learners. This phase may include re-design work in order to correct found issues.

Evaluation. This phase measures the effectiveness of the instruction. The evaluation can be formative, within each phase of the process, or summative, at the end of the implementation of the instruction.

5   Conclusion

In this paper, we propose five directions for future research around practical solutions for some of the challenges of AR systems for education. We analyzed, classified and synthetized the challenges reported in 50 scientific papers that included case studies and literature review studies. The proposed directions have to do with the need of addressing special requirements of users, the opportunities for developing unexplored broad fields of education and unexplored target groups, and possible strategies to integrate AR into industry, looking to obtain funding for the development of this emerging technology. Despite its proven efficacy when applied in educational settings, AR systems still have some problems to overcome. In order to continue improving the possibilities and trying to extend its benefits to each educational scenario, stakeholders and practitioners must continue to address all gaps and develop strategies to solve challenges encountered.

References

1. Milgram, P., Kishino, F.: A taxonomy of mixed reality visual displays. IEICE Trans. Inf. Syst. 77(12), 1321–1329 (1994)
2. Azuma, R.: A survey of augmented reality. Presence Teleoperators Virtual Environ. 6(4), 355–385 (1997)
3. Akçayir, M., Akçayir, G.: Advantages and challenges associated with augmented reality for education: a systematic review of the literature. Educ. Res. Rev. 20, 1–11 (2017)
4. Dunleavy, M., Dede, C., Mitchell, R.: Affordances and limitations of immersive participatory augmented reality simulations for teaching and learning. J. Sci. Educ. Technol. 18(1), 7–22 (2009)
5. Carmigniani, J., Furht, B., Anisetti, M., Ceravolo, P., Damiani, E., Ivkovic, M.: Augmented reality technologies, systems and applications. Multimed. Tools Appl. 51(1), 341–377 (2011)
6. Diegmann, P., Schmidt-kraepelin, M., Van Den Eynden, S., Basten, D.: Benefits of augmented reality in educational environments – a systematic literature review. In: Wirtschaftsinformatik, vol. 3, no. 6, pp. 1542–1556 (2015)
7. Mekni, M., Lemieux, A.: Augmented reality: applications, challenges and future trends. In: Applied Computational Science, pp. 205–214 (2014)
8. Chen, P., Liu, X., Cheng, W., Huang, R.: A review of using augmented reality in education from 2011 to 2016. In: Popescu, E., et al. (eds.) Innovations in Smart Learning, pp. 13–18. Springer, Singapore (2017)
9. Bacca, J., Fabregat, R., Baldiris, S., Graf, S., Kinshuk: Augmented reality trends in education: a systematic review of research and applications. Educ. Technol. Soc. 17, 133–149 (2014)
10. Yilmaz, R.M.: Educational magic toys developed with augmented reality technology for early childhood education. Comput. Hum. Behav. 54, 240–248 (2016)
11. Martín-Gutiérrez, J., Fabiani, P., Benesova, W., Meneses, M.D., Mora, C.E.: Augmented reality to promote collaborative and autonomous learning in higher education. Comput. Hum. Behav. 51, 752–761 (2015)
12. Radu, I.: Why should my students use AR? A comparative review of the educational impacts of augmented-reality. In: 11th IEEE International Symposium on Mixed and Augmented Reality, ISMAR 2012, Science and Technology Papers, pp. 313–314 (2012)
13. Wu, H.K., Lee, S.W.Y., Chang, H.Y., Liang, J.C.: Current status, opportunities and challenges of augmented reality in education. Comput. Educ. 62, 41–49 (2013)
14. Schmitz, B., Klemke, R., Walhout, J., Specht, M.: Attuning a mobile simulation game for school children using a design-based research approach. Comput. Educ. 81, 35–48 (2015)

15. Vanderheiden, G., Treviranus, J.: Creating a global public inclusive infrastructure. In: Stephanidis, C. (ed.) UAHCI 2011. LNCS, vol. 6765, pp. 517–526. Springer, Heidelberg (2011). doi:10.1007/978-3-642-21672-5_57

16. ISO: Ergonomics of human-system interaction. International Organization for Standardization (2008)

17. ISO: Web Content Accessibility Guidelines. International Organization for Standardization (2012)

18. Vanderheiden, G., Korn, P., Martínez, L., Pluke, M., Snow-Weaver, A.: Guidance on applying WCAG 2.0 to non-web information and communications technologies. W3C Working Group Note (2013)

19. UDL: Universal Design for Language Guidelines (2011)

20. Bower, M., Howe, C., McCredie, N., Robinson, A., Grover, D.: Augmented reality in education-cases, places and potentials. EMI. Educ. Media Int. 51(1), 1–15 (2014)

21. Barsom, E.Z., Graafland, M., Schijven, M.P.: Systematic review on the effectiveness of augmented reality applications in medical training. Surg. Endosc. Other Interv. Tech. 30(10), 4174–4183 (2016)

22. Bongiovanni, R., Lowenberg-Deboer, J.: Precision agriculture and sustainability. Precis. Agric. 5(4), 359–387 (2004)

23. OECD: Adoption of Technologies for Sustainable Farming Systems. In: Wageningen Workshop Proceedings, p. 149 (2001)

24. Paul Drnevich, D.C.: Information technology and business-level strategy: toward an integrated theoretical perspective. Mis Q. 37(2), 483–509 (2013)

25. UNESCO: The International Standard Classification of Education (2011)

26. United States Patent and Trademark Office: Global Patent Search Network. http://gpsn.uspto.gov/. Accessed 22 July 2016

27. Technology Quarterly, the Future of Agriculture: The Economist (2016). http://www.economist.com/technology-quarterly/2016-06-09/factory-fresh. Accessed 23 Jan 2017

28. Afzal, A.: The role of information technology in business success (2015). https://www.linkedin.com/pulse/role-information-technology-business-success-abid-afzal-butt. Accessed 12 Feb 2017

29. Eichhorst, W., Rodríguez-planas, N., Schmidl, R., Zimmermann, K.F.: A road map to vocational education and training in industrialized countries. ILR Rev. 68(2), 314–337 (2015)

30. Livingston, M.A., Zanbaka, C., Swan, J.E., Smallman, H.S.: Objective measures for the effectiveness of augmented reality. IEEE Proceedings of Virtual Reality, VR 2005, vol. 2005, pp. 287–288 (2005)

31. Gervautz, M., Schmalstieg, D.: Anywhere interfaces using handheld augmented reality. IEEE Xplore Digit. Libr. 45(7), 26–31 (2012)

32. Gibbons, A.S., Boling, E., Smith, K.M.: Instructional design models. In: Spector, J.M., Merrill, M.D., Elen, J., Bishop, M.J. (eds.) Handbook of Research on Educational Communications and Technology, pp. 607–615. Springer, New York (2014)

33. Peterson, C.: Bringing ADDIE to life: instructional design at its best. J. Educ. Multimed. Hypermedia 12(3), 227–241 (2003)

Semantic Exploration of Distributed AR Services

Krzysztof Walczak(✉), Rafał Wojciechowski, and Adam Wójtowicz

Poznań University of Economics and Business,
Niepodległości 10, 61-875 Poznań, Poland
{walczak,rawojc,awojtow}@kti.ue.poznan.pl
http://www.kti.ue.poznan.pl/

Abstract. In this paper, we present a new approach to building large-scale ubiquitous augmented reality (AR) applications. Instead of fixed AR content, presented on specific places or objects, we propose the concept of a semantic network of distributed AR services contributed by different providers. These services have different roles and offer different content and functionality, but the synergy offered by such a diverse network of services opens new fields of application for AR systems. The services in our approach are modeled using well-established standards from the domain of business process modeling, but they are additionally annotated using semantic descriptions of the role and properties of particular services and their relationships, allowing meaningful selection of dynamic exploration paths by users with different interests, constraints and privileges. An indispensable element of such heterogeneous AR systems is proper consideration of security and privacy issues, which are also covered in this work.

Keywords: Augmented reality · Business process modeling · Security policies · Semantics

1 Introduction

The aim of this research work is to develop a model enabling dynamic ad-hoc secure exploration of distributed augmented reality (AR) services using high-level semantic descriptions. Current location-aware AR platforms such as *Layar* [10] and *Wikitude* [23] have a number of underlying problems with respect to these functionalities. First of all they lack support for business services. AR platforms are not connected to internal business processes of businesses offering the services. The services are vendor-specific and they are not interoperable. Creation and management of AR services is a complex process, which requires high expertise in computer programming and graphics design. New services are often designed from scratch, which is costly and time consuming. At the same time privacy remains a serious problem – the systems do not currently really support user privacy. One central service provider may have access to all user data, when – in reality – users may want to limit this by provider and/or location. Finally, access control for AR in physical locations is an issue, in particular, limited access control rights within digital augmented reality spaces as well as lack

© Springer International Publishing AG 2017
L.T. De Paolis et al. (Eds.): AVR 2017, Part I, LNCS 10324, pp. 415–426, 2017.
DOI: 10.1007/978-3-319-60922-5_32

of a model of rights management for physical spaces, i.e., anyone can augment any space without restrictions.

The model proposed in this paper addresses these problems by exploring how to:

1. Build a business service-oriented architecture that allows for the easy sharing of components and data between end-users and service providers, thus lowering development costs and improving interconnectivity between services.
2. Aggregate and link related business services offered by different providers to create composite services with a clearly added value for both the providers and the end-users.
3. Provide robust support for data privacy by allowing users to specify more accurately with whom, what and where they will share their data.
4. Support proper digital rights of service components, services, data and the physical environment.

In summary, the proposed model alters how location-aware AR services are delivered by combining a service oriented architecture with exploratory work on how to control digital and physical rights. This leads to lowered development costs, greater service integration and an improved ability to monetize the hybrid digital and physical space. This is complemented by a privacy approach that – in contrast to existing services – offers robust protection for both businesses and consumers. This is illustrated by use case examples.

2 State of the Art

A business process is defined as a sequence of activities that represent the steps required to achieve a business objective, such as providing a service, a product or other value for a customer. Business processes can be modeled, executed, and monitored using Workflow Management Systems (WfMS) [6], which are typically integrated in systems for Business Process Management (BPM) [9,22]. Currently, there are a variety of BPM products available on the market, both open source and commercially licensed. Examples are: *Intalio—BPMS* [8], *ActiveVOS BPM* [7], *JBoss jBPM* [17], *Activiti BPM Platform* [1], *Bizagi BPM* [3], and *Oracle BPM Suite* [16]. In the existing BPM systems, the workflow of business processes is defined with modeling tools using a graphical notation. Currently, the dominant graphical notation for modeling business processes is BPMN 2.0, which also standardizes an executable XML-based form of business process models [13].

As opposed to standard business services, AR business services are location-dependent – users may interact with the services at different locations and the location of users may influence the execution of the underlying business processes. Currently available standards for business process modeling do not take into account the spatial context, and need to be extended with new AR-specific elements, which would enable controlling the business process execution depending on the location of users and services. Business process modeling standards need also to be extended with new elements required for adequate presentation of user tasks and possible user interaction in AR environments.

Location-aware augmented reality has been an area of rapid development over recent years with platforms such as *StudierStube* [19] and *MORGAN* [14] being among the earliest to provide the core services, such as the registration of 3D graphics and audio relative to the users' position. However, these early AR platforms required that developers created independent applications that had to be downloaded and installed separately. More recent and commercially successful platforms, such as *Layar* [10] and *Wikitude* [23], offer more flexibility, but they have important limitations and are commercial products. In contrast, *Mixare* [11], although offering less functionality as compared to the commercial products, is an open-source alternative, which can be easily customized. Dynamic contextual AR systems based on semantic matching of user's context and the available services have been proposed in [18,20].

The currently available AR platforms are limited to presentation of location-based information services, which enable users to obtain basic information about the places located nearby, but do not allow them to execute business processes in AR environments. Moreover, creation and modification of services usually require involvement of highly qualified IT professionals, who are experts in the design and programming of complex interactive multimedia content. As a result, in most cases, end-users must use ready-made content, which is usually too simple and too static for real business scenarios. Therefore, new methods for flexible creation of AR services and complex business scenarios are needed.

Additionally, none of these platforms place any restrictions on what kind of content can be used for augmenting real-world locations or who can add content to a given location. This presents potentially a number of social and economic challenges for physical space owners over the coming years, as competitors could add content to their locations, while the possibility to lease physical space to augmented reality developers/providers could open new revenue streams. Furthermore, previous works in this field noted the potentially invasive impact augmented reality games can have in public spaces. For example, from a purely social level it may be desirable to restrict what people can do, e.g., not allowing game playing at a cemetery.

There are many techniques that aim at protecting multimedia data (particularly 3D models in AR systems). DRM (Digital Rights Management) is a technique to control access and usage of digital content, including multimedia data as described by Zeng et al. in [27]. Modern DRM techniques are designed to maintain control over the content during a large part of the content life cycle. However, constant progress in AR technology in conjunction with the development of ubiquitous infrastructures challenge the existing protection techniques in AR systems. In particular, content offered within AR services interacting dynamically with each other in a ubiquitous environment and created by distributed service providers cannot be sufficiently protected by current DRM systems. The most distinguished standardization effort in the domain of protecting the usage of multimedia content is MPEG-21 REL [21] – a rule-based access control language. Unfortunately, Digital Item representation, which is the base for this model, is not expressive enough to support interactive AR scenes with spatially-sensitive composite content provided by different service providers. Generic standards developed to allow modeling of rule-based access control, such as XACML [12], despite their usefulness in many multimedia protection scenarios, do not support spatial constraints. XACML has spatially-aware extension called GeoX-ACML [15], however, mainly due to its two-dimensional limitation and lack of AR interaction protection, GeoXACML is not sufficient for AR frameworks. The same applies to GEO-RBAC [4].

Data and service security in distributed VR/AR environments is a wide and growing topic. Fine-grained access control mechanisms designed for 3D collaborative environments that are based on analysis of the call graphs, such as proposed in [24] could set a base for further research. However, they cannot be applied directly, since they do not take into account the specificities of: augmented reality, mobile spatial interaction, and dynamic service composition. Similarly, security models for large-scale distribution of structured 3D content proposed in [25], that represent an attempt to mitigate the malicious host problem, cannot be applied directly.

There is also a need for AR-specific research on data security focused on users' privacy protection. Due to novelty of the problem, many articles only point at forthcoming research directions and do not present any solutions. An example is [5], in which OS-level access control to AR objects such as human face or skeleton is discussed. Other researchers focus on providing AR-specific location privacy [2], but they propose anonymization-based approach only. Finally, privacy-preserving frameworks for ubiquitous systems based on a trusted third party operating in a "security infrastructure as a service" model [26] could be an inspiration for AR-specific security infrastructure. Generally, in order to preserve users' privacy in AR systems, access to users' data can be limited by different techniques – separately or as their combinations:

- policy-based techniques, e.g., formalized XACML security policies,
- privacy-preserving database querying, e.g., based on data anonymization techniques,
- techniques dedicated to AR solutions, e.g., obfuscation of animation streams.

3   Proposed Approach

3.1   Architecture for Explorable AR Services

The goal of this work is to develop an open, dynamic and secure framework for building interactive and collaborative mobile business environments based on AR business services. The conceptual model of the proposed framework is presented in Fig. 1.

Within the framework, *Basic AR Business Services* are contributed by different *service providers* (businesses, administration or citizens) and are combined by *service aggregators* (ad-hoc or based on higher-level models) into *Aggregated*

AR Business Services, in which users interact with different services, and services also interact with each other to form more complex scenarios. The services (basic and aggregated) are formally specified through models of the underlying business processes. *Service models* and *aggregation models* are created by *AR service managers* and *aggregation managers*, accordingly, using BPM tools extended with AR-specific elements. Service managers define allowed usage of their services in *AR Service Policies*, taking into account inter-services interactions and spatial constraints.

The AR business service models are deployed to the *Server AR Platform*, which consists of the following components: *AR Service Catalogue*, *AR Service Execution Platform*, and *Security & Privacy Enforcement Platform*.

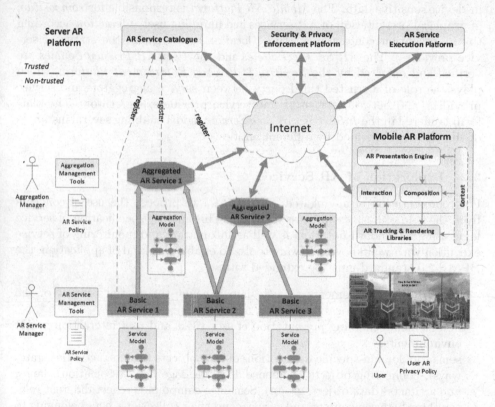

Fig. 1. Conceptual model of the proposed framework.

The *AR Service Catalogue* is used for registering AR business services in multi-dimensional context regions (with dimensions related to location, time, semantics, access rights, preferences, etc.). Therefore, the services can be discovered by users (implicitly or explicitly) depending on their current context. With AR business services, users can access up-to-date information related to their context and can execute actions. Since AR business services are formally modeled as business processes, which can access IT platforms of the service providers, the current status of the providers can be taken into account during aggregation and exploration of the services.

AR business services are accessed by the *Mobile AR Platform*, which enables discovering services of interest to a user, or requested by some other services, through the use of the *AR Presentation Engine*. AR business services – provided as a result of business processes run by service aggregators and service providers – are presented and interacted with using an AR interface in the form of multimedia widgets, which are connected through service-oriented interfaces to remote business logic of business processes running on the *AR Service Execution Platform*. *User AR Privacy Policies* allow users to define privacy settings (identity privacy, location privacy, path privacy) and access control settings related to in-device sensitive data. The *Mobile AR Platform* is responsible for *composition* of graphical presentation of AR services and handling user *interaction* according to the execution context (e.g., time, location, preferences, the status of service providers). The *AR Service Policies* and the *User AR Privacy Policies* are verified and enforced by the *Security & Privacy Enforcement Platform*, which plays the role of a trusted third party between service aggregators and service providers, and between end-users and service providers/aggregators. The platform is offered in the *Infrastructure as a Service* model enabling several instances of the platform provided by different entities.

3.2 Exploration of AR Services

For representation of aggregated AR services, we propose the use of concepts from the field of business process modeling. This enables specification of service logic using a standard notation as well as automation and monitoring of service execution with well-known software tools. To enable this kind of application, the BPMN 2.0 standard must be extended with:

- new AR-specific elements to take into account the spatial context of the service execution (location of users and services);
- new elements enabling presentation of user tasks and user interaction in AR environments;
- semantic domain-specific descriptions of flow objects (events, activities, gateways), connecting objects (sequence flow, message flow, association), lanes, and artifacts (data object, group). Semantic compounds reflect different relationships between content and services and their collections, e.g., belonging to the same class/category, similarity of meaning, location in space, availability in time, etc.

An aggregated AR service in the proposed approach is represented as semantically enhanced business process model, as presented in Fig. 2. Sub-services as well as connecting objects of the model are annotated with semantic descriptions. Different domain-specific ontologies can be used for creating the descriptions. For example, museum ontology, shopping ontology, nature monuments ontology,

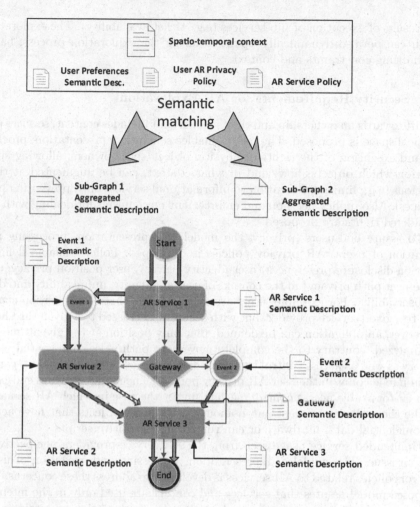

Fig. 2. An aggregated AR service.

can be used to describe services, while another set of ontologies, e.g., city exploration ontology, tourist agency ontology and history lesson ontology, can be used to describe connecting elements of the model.

When a user selects an aggregated AR service from the service catalogue, a service exploration graph is formed. The exploration graph is a subgraph of the AR service model adjusted to selected static elements of the user's context (e.g., preferences, privileges, device used). The exploration graph complies with given constraints and maximizes the value of a declared goal function based on semantic proximity.

Each exploration graph contains all possible exploration paths in the given preset context. Particular exploration paths that will be followed by a user depend on variable context elements (e.g., location and time), user interaction with the aggregated AR service (e.g., selecting an option in the user interface), and results of execution of sub-services (e.g., ticket availability). The exploration graph can be also dynamically updated during the exploration process, based on changing constraints and context.

3.3   Security Requirements for AR Exploration

A shift towards an ownership and rights model that includes content, services and physical space is proposed. The model enables semantic representation, processing and execution of the rights of physical object/space owners, allowing specification which objects, how, and in what context, can be augmented at their locations (e.g., limiting a location to informational services only, preventing paid services). Also, policy decision and enforcement mechanisms for dealing with the considered rights are proposed.

To assure end-users' privacy, the model of representation, processing and execution of users' AR privacy policies is developed. Policies enable defining location-disclosure preferences (user identity privacy, user position privacy, user movement path privacy) in the context of user anonymity, unlinkability and data unobservability. For example, users are able to define that their position can be sent to a given service provider, but with accuracy decreased to a given threshold. Moreover, an obligation can be defined, that only position at the given time can be analyzed, contrary to the complete movement path. Also, non-spatial usage history as well as access control to mobile device sensors and data sources can be taken into account in the user AR privacy policies. The model provides end-users with customizable access control mechanism for the case in which AR scenarios on the client device interact autonomously with other objects that have access to confidential data, hardware or can run security-sensitive scripts.

Unintended service usage seen from the AR service-providers perspective is also an issue. The model of representation, processing and execution of usage control policies related to AR services is developed to address these concerns. The proposed model assures that services and content are used only in the intended manner, taking into account mutual interactions and spatial constraints. For example, AR service providers are able to restrict who can use their AR services by defining spatial proximity requirements in order to prevent mass scale market-sensitive data harvesting. Another provider could restrict that only a given class of aggregators can aggregate their services, e.g., in connection with non-commercial services only. A mobile network operator could publish AR services for exclusive usage by their network clients.

AR service composition security can be seen also from the AR service aggregator perspective. The goal here is to give aggregators confidence that they can rely on AR service descriptions within the service aggregation process. A solution to this problem is a scheme for the proof of authenticity of the AR services descriptions that proves descriptions' consistency with their actual implementation and execution. It is possible due to introducing a trusted party – the *Security & Privacy Enforcement Platform* – that can fully control the *AR Service Execution Platform*, and therefore can examine the service execution process (the platforms are provided in the IaaS model enabling co-existence of independent and competing instances).

4   Application Domains of the Proposed Approach

Two application domains of the proposed approach are discussed below. The first is a network of touristic and cultural services offered in a city by different stakeholders. The second is a maintenance scenario, in which AR services offered by different providers are used by technicians during their routine work.

4.1   Touristic and Cultural AR Services

A prominent application domain of the proposed approach is access to cultural and touristic information and services. Augmented reality offers in this field clear advantages as it helps users to navigate in potentially unknown environments (e.g., a city visited by a user for the first time), and locate and identify specific points of interest. AR also helps to precisely explain meaning of specific elements (e.g., buildings or monuments), directly superimposing information on the view of the real environment.

In this domain, however, there is a variety of service providers and information sources, which must be properly amalgamated, taking into account security and privacy concerns. The first source of information may be municipal services providing maps and guidance through the city. Second are cultural heritage sites and museums, which offer information services on items both inside and outside the museums. Third are touristic agencies, which offer guiding and planning services that help users to properly organize their visit taking into account specific constraints (e.g., available time), preferences (e.g., interests in specific type of objects) and privileges (e.g., acquired access permissions).

A specific case, which demonstrates the importance of the proposed AR access control techniques, is a museum which would like to sell their own outdoor AR services, but prevent others from doing so at their site. They may, however, allow general tourist information and social networks AR services to remain active. It would allow for developing a marketplace within the AR area, similarly to existing environments in social spaces and games. The fundamental change here is that the rights are drawn not only on the ability to rent or own content and services, but also on aspects such as the underlying rights held by the property owners. This allows property owners to lease their space for use in AR, and service owners to lease their services to the physical space owners.

4.2   Maintenance AR Services

The proposed approach can be also applied in a use-case scenario in which AR services are used to support maintenance and monitoring work as well as training within existing and developing technical installations. AR technologies are used to provide maintenance, monitoring and training staff with up-to-date contextual information required or useful for their tasks. This information is displayed on multimedia mobile devices, such as smartphones, tablets or AR glasses, directly in the vicinity of the control and measurement points. In order to maximize service reliability in difficult weather or lightning conditions, visual identifying markers for particular installation elements can be used (e.g., QR codes) to support robust feature detection.

Content presented on mobile devices corresponds to interactive scenarios describing the operator's actions. These scenarios contain descriptions of tasks (manual activities, tools) as well as supporting information regarding maintenance procedures, parameters, technical conditions, safety standards, norms, repair manuals, etc. The different kinds of data are served by a number of distributed AR services offered by distinct service providers (e.g., technical, security and safety services), according to their AR business process definitions. On each level of the scenario execution, an operator receives instructions regarding tasks as well as contextual data containing, among others, current values of device's parameters. Instructions can have the form of animated graphical content, still images, text or audio/video sequences, superimposed directly on the view of selected infrastructure elements. Scenario progress is monitored at runtime by the system, so that warning messages can be generated in case of exceptional or dangerous situations. Moreover, automated verification of the task result's correctness can be performed, which is particularly useful in the training process. Functionality of the mobile AR application can support also collaborative scenarios with other users – local or remote.

Application of the proposed approach for such a use case scenario would directly influence the effectiveness, comfort, safety and security of maintenance works. Having access to the current context data directly in the workplace allows keeping proper order of the consecutive activities and allows employees to conveniently access data about particular elements of the specific installation (including dependencies between a given element and the state of other control elements), and therefore allows for faster and more accurate decision making. Consequently, applying the proposed approach would shorten the duration of tasks execution while increasing their safety. In turn, taking advantage of a context-based AR information system in the training domain would increase the effectiveness of the training process by providing trainees with access to data presented in the context of specific control points in a meaningful and intuitive manner and by decreasing the effort of the trainers by partial automation of the training process.

5   Conclusions

In this paper, we have presented an approach to building a new class of context-aware and secure AR services based on a high-level semantic model of a network of services offered by different providers. Any non-trivial application of AR to real-world problems, which is based on a sound business model, must take into account elements presented in this paper: diversity of sources, their relationships, context and preferences of users, and last but not least – security and privacy issues. Without these critical elements AR cannot be applied on a ubiquitous scale in serious applications.

Acknowledgments. This work was supported by the Polish National Science Centre (NCN) under Grant No. DEC-2012/07/B/ST6/01523.

References

1. Alfresco Software, Inc.: Activiti BPM Platform (2017). https://www.activiti.org/
2. Aryan, A., Singh, S.: Protecting location privacy in augmented reality using k-anonymization and pseudo-id. In: 2010 International Conference on Computer and Communication Technology (ICCCT), pp. 119–124. IEEE (2010)
3. Bizagi Lmtd.: Bizagi BPM (2017). http://www.bizagi.com/
4. Damiani, M.L., Bertino, E., Catania, B., Perlasca, P.: GEO-RBAC: a spatially aware RBAC. ACM Trans. Inf. Syst. Secur. **10**(1) (2007). http://doi.acm.org/10.1145/1210263.1210265
5. D'Antoni, L., Dunn, A.M., Jana, S., Kohno, T., Livshits, B., Molnar, D., Moshchuk, A., Ofek, E., Roesner, F., Saponas, T.S., et al.: Operating system support for augmented reality applications. In: HotOS, vol. 13, p. 21 (2013)
6. van Hee, K.: Workflow Management - Models, Methods, and Systems. The MIT Press, Cambridge (2004)
7. Informatica, LLC: ActiveVOS BPM (2017). http://www.activevos.com/products/activevos/overview
8. Intalio, Inc.: Business Process Management System (2015). http://www.intalio.com/products/bpms/overview/
9. Ko, R.K., Lee, S.S., Lee, E.W.: Business process management (BPM) standards: a survey. Bus. Process Manag. J. **15**(5), 744–791 (2009). http://dx.doi.org/10.1108/14637150910987937
10. Layar B.V.: Layar Creator (2017). http://www.layar.com/
11. Mixare Project (2017). https://code.google.com/archive/p/mixare/
12. OASIS Open: eXtensible Access Control Markup Language (XACML) Version 3.0 (2013). http://docs.oasis-open.org/xacml/3.0/xacml-3.0-core-spec-os-en.pdf
13. Object Management Group, Inc.: Business Process Model and Notation – Version 2.0 (2011). http://www.omg.org/spec/BPMN/2.0/
14. Ohlenburg, J., Herbst, I., Lindt, I., Fröhlich, T., Broll, W.: The Morgan framework: enabling dynamic multi-user AR and VR projects. In: Proceedings of the ACM Symposium on Virtual Reality Software and Technology, VRST 2004, pp. 166–169. ACM, New York (2004). http://doi.acm.org/10.1145/1077534.1077568
15. Open Geospatial Consortium: GeoXACML Implementation Specification (2011)
16. Oracle Corporation: Oracle Business Process Management Suite (2017). http://www.oracle.com/us/technologies/bpm/suite/overview/index.html
17. Red Hat, Inc.: JBoss jBPM - Open Source Business Process Management (2017). http://www.jbpm.org/
18. Rumiński, D., Walczak, K.: Semantic contextual augmented reality environments. In: Julier, S., Lindeman, R.W., Sandor, C. (eds.) 2014 IEEE International Symposium on Mixed and Augmented Reality (ISMAR) - Science and Technology, 12 September 2014, Munich, Germany, pp. 401–404. IEEE; IEEE Visualization and Graph Technical Communication; IEEE Computer Society, IEEE, New York (2014)
19. Schmalstieg, D., Fuhrmann, A., Hesina, G., Szalavári, Z., Encarnação, L.M., Gervautz, M., Purgathofer, W.: The studierstube augmented reality project. Presence: Teleoper. Virtual Environ. **11**(1), 33–54 (2002). http://dx.doi.org/10.1162/105474602317343640

20. Walczak, K., Rumiński, D., Flotyński, J.: Building contextual augmented reality environments with semantics. In: 2014 International Conference on Virtual Systems Multimedia (VSMM), pp. 353–361, December 2014

21. Wang, X., DeMartini, T., Wragg, B., Paramasivam, M., Barlas, C.: The MPEG-21 rights expression language and rights data dictionary. IEEE Trans. Multimedia **7**(3), 408–417 (2005)

22. Weske, M.: Business Process Management: Concepts, Languages, Architectures. Springer Publishing Company, Incorporated, Heidelberg (2010)

23. Wikitude GmbH: Wikitude Augmented Reality SDK (2017). https://www.wikitude.com/

24. Wójtowicz, A.: Secure user-contributed 3D virtual environments. In: Cellary, W., Walczak, K. (eds.) Interactive 3D Multimedia Content: Models for Creation, Management, Search and Presentation, pp. 171–193. Springer, London (2012)

25. Wójtowicz, A.: Security model for large scale content distribution applied to federated virtual environments. In: Franch, X., Soffer, P. (eds.) CAiSE 2013. LNBIP, vol. 148, pp. 502–511. Springer, Heidelberg (2013). doi:10.1007/978-3-642-38490-5_45

26. Wójtowicz, A., Wilusz, D.: Architecture for adaptable smart spaces oriented on user privacy. Logic J. IGPL **25**(1), 3–17 (2017)

27. Zeng, W., Yu, H., Lin, C.Y.: Multimedia Security Technologies for Digital Rights Management. Academic Press, Cambridge (2011)

Automated Marker Augmentation and Path Discovery in Indoor Navigation for Visually Impaired

Raees Khan ShahSani[✉], Sehat Ullah, and Sami Ur Rahman

Department of Computer Science & I.T., University of Malakand,
Chakdara, Pakistan
shahsani@uom.edu.pk

Abstract. The past two decades have seen abundance of applications of Augmented Reality (AR), from gaming to medical, engineering, and academic fields. Certain work has been done to employ AR techniques for assisting the blind and visually impaired people to navigate in large indoor environments. This research contributes to the existing solutions by providing a viable technique, using merely a mobile phone camera and fiducial markers. The markers are detected and connected to generate a floor plan with the help of our proposed automatic path generation algorithm. Similarly, path augmentation algorithm efficiently populate the generated path with auditory and textual information. The proposed solution also provides a way to edit an already stored path when we need to extend the floor plan for inclusion of additional paths. An android application is developed to implement these algorithms. Time benchmarking the system shows effective results in automatic path generation, path augmentation, and path extension processes.

Keywords: Augmented Reality · Indoor navigation · Visually impaired · Android · ARToolkit

1 Introduction

Augmented Reality and its applications have progressively achieved attention of both academia and industry, especially during the past two decades. It works by placing virtual information or objects over physical environment being captured with a video camera – leading to a mixed reality having both virtual and physical environments in a meaningful context [1]. Thus the environment surrounding the user gets interactive, which can be manipulated digitally using AR technology [2].

AR-based tracking can be broadly categorized into two groups, marker-based and marker-less tracking [3]. Marker-less tracking use feature based or model based approach for calculating camera's pose and orientation. While marker-based techniques employ fiducial markers positioned in a real environment and tracked with a camera. These are usually passive markers with no electro coating over them, and with a variety of different patterns printed on a plain paper. ARToolkit [4], ARToolkit Plus [5], and ARTag [6] are a few popular marker-based AR systems.

© Springer International Publishing AG 2017
L.T. De Paolis et al. (Eds.): AVR 2017, Part I, LNCS 10324, pp. 427–437, 2017.
DOI: 10.1007/978-3-319-60922-5_33

Indoor navigation has always been challenging for visually impaired people to carry out their routine tasks. According to World Health Organization's fact file, about 285 million people are facing problems in vision [7]. These include around 13% complete blind people and 87% being visually impaired. White cane stick and guide dogs have been affective in many scenarios for helping blind people in mobility. White cane stick works well with obstacles within its range, i.e. a meter away. Guide dogs can assist in already known places, which however are unacceptable in some societies [8].

Indoor positioning systems currently use various technologies for user's localization. Wireless methods are comprised of GPS-based [9–11], Infrared-based [8], NFC-based [12], Bluetooth-based [13, 14], and RFID-based [15, 16] techniques. Major drawback of these systems is that installation of physical infrastructure is required in the target environment, e.g. Wi-Fi routers, RFID sensors, and Bluetooth beacons [17]. Yet such solutions have a tendency of localization errors and inaccurate results [18]. In contrast, previous studies have shown that Computer Vision techniques may be effective in navigation systems and indoor positioning [19].

Despite of various approaches proposed by researchers; no existing applications help visually impaired people to navigate easily inside large indoor buildings. The primary objectives of this research are:

- An automated system for generating and augmenting path in an indoor environment using marker-based computer vision methods with the help of a smartphone camera.
- Development of an Android application to facilitate a visually impaired person to navigate easily in a large indoor environment using merely a smartphone device.

2 Related Work

For outdoor navigation, GPS has been an ideal and de facto solution for positioning and user tracking. However, for indoor environments no such unique technology has been developed so far to solve the problem. To address the challenge, various approaches have been proposed in the literature. Commercial solutions have also been introduced in the market, which utilize various sensors/hardware of the smartphone for user's current position localization. Such solutions include (a) *dead reckoning* systems which employ accelerometer, gyroscope, and magnetometer of the smartphone [20]; (b) *received signal strength indication* systems like Wi-Fi, Bluetooth, and RFID; (c) *computer vision-based* systems use the high computational capabilities and high performance cameras of smartphones in either marker-based or marker-less approaches for calculating user locality and orientation in indoor environments.

Authors in [21] have proposed a marker-based navigation system using ARToolkit markers, which uses images sequence to locate user position, and overlays user's view with location information. Video stream obtained from a camera mounted to the user's head and connected with the tablet, is transmitted wirelessly to a remote computer; which performs detection of ARToolkit markers, location recognition, and image sequence matching. This location information is then transmitted back the user's tablet. The system does not store any pre-defined map of the indoor environment, so the shortest path to the destination cannot be calculated. It heavily relies on Wi-Fi network infrastructure to be deployed in the building for connecting to the remote server. The image recognition process is also very slow as it tries to match an input image to a buffer of 64 images each time to calculate user location.

In [22], authors have deployed ARToolkit markers in various positions in an indoor environment, which are detected using a camera attached to a laptop device. The laptop displays a pre-defined 2D map of the indoor environment. A route planner algorithm is developed that calculates the current location of the user. The algorithm uses a pre-defined matrix, which represents the links between any two locations on the map. It assists the user with both an audio clip associated with the current location, as well as displaying navigational information over the video stream using AR technique. The route planner algorithm lacks the capability of calculating the shortest path. Moreover, user needs to carry a laptop with a camera being connected.

Subakti and Jiang in [23] have used a combination of different hardware and software for guidance and navigation system for fresh students to experience the indoor building of a university. They have used an HMD for augmented display, android application for guidance and navigation, microcontrollers deployed in the building for sensing light, temperature, and sound. BLE beacons are deployed at various locations in the building to propagate location packets for sensing in the android application. The system works in two mode – marker-based using location-aware QR codes, and with invisible markers using BLE packets for navigational purposes. Map of the building is created as graph of BLE beacons and QR codes in which shortest path can be calculated with Dijkstra's shortest path algorithm [24]. The system works well but its deployment is accompanied with complex BLE and microcontroller sensors infrastructure.

Yin et al. [25] proposed a peer-to-peer (P2P) based indoor navigation system that works with no aid from predefined maps or connectivity to a location service. Previous travelers record the path on which they navigate in a building and share it with other new travelers. The existing path is merged with Wi-Fi measurements and other key points like turns, stairs, etc. to create a consolidated path information. Smartphone application, *ppNav*, is developed to assist a new user in employing the path traces of the reference path, generated by previous users. [26] has used ultrasonic sensors and visual markers to assist a blind user navigation in indoor environments. Obstacles are sensed with ultrasonic modules connected to a pair of glasses. RGB camera is also attached with the glasses to detect markers in the environment. Map of the building is stored manually in the software, which makes it difficult to modify or edit paths.

Zeb et al. [8] have developed a desktop application using ARToolkit library to detect markers with the help of a webcam attached to a laptop. Markers are deployed inside a building and their connectivity is manually carried out using hardcoded entries in the application's database along with auditory information about each marker. A blind user can then navigate through the building by detecting the markers with a webcam, and getting response audio information using headphones. The solution well addresses the situation but needs the user to carry a laptop device. Moreover, hard-coding the path manually into the application makes it harder to extend/update the current path setup.

In [27], authors have developed an indoor navigation system with the help of a laptop attached to the back of the user, an HMD for displaying augmented information, a camera and an inertial tracker are attached to the user's head. A wrist-mounted touchscreen device is used to display a UI for application monitoring and tracking. ARToolkit markers are deployed in the building, which are tracked by the head mounted camera, and fed into the laptop for comparing to the pre-stored map of the building. The results are displayed on the HMD along with navigational aids using AR techniques. The system works well but is bulky and under low light conditions, it does not accurately identify the markers. Similarly, map generation and storage also requires manual coordinate editing.

Al-Khalifa and Al-Razgan in [28] have developed a system named *Ebsar*, which uses Google Glass connected to a smartphone to assist a visually impaired person in indoor navigation and positioning. The building is prepared with the help of a sighted person, called a map builder, who moves around the indoors of the building and explores different paths. The map builder marks every room, office, etc. with QR codes generated by Ebsar installed on a smartphone. Distance and direction between the QR codes is determined with the help of smartphone's accelerometer and compass sensors. All the information gathered is used to create a floor plan graph with each node representing a checkpoint in the building like a room, office, or stairs; and edges for number of steps and direction between the checkpoints. The map is then uploaded to some central web server, which is available to any user with *Ebsar* installed on smartphone. At the first entrance to the building, the Google glass worn by a visually impaired user detects the QR code, and the application automatically downloads the corresponding map file of the building to the user's phone. The user can then use voice commands for both input and output of information about the current location. The system is evaluated for performance and accuracy with several sighted and blind users yielding acceptable results. Although, it heavily relies on the smartphone's accelerometer that can cause certain margin of error in calculating the steps; and the user should constantly have to wear a Google glass connected via Wi-Fi to the phone.

Another research in [29] has developed an indoor navigation system using smartphone by utilizing custom 2D colored markers, and accelerometer for step detection. Colored markers printed on plain papers are displayed on the entrance and other key intersection points inside the building. However, the exact position of each marker in the building has to be recorded offline, i.e. it lacks the automatic buildup of indoor paths. Distance between the markers is measured with accelerometer of the phone. The system proves to be scalable and simple yet has several drawbacks like poor detection of colored markers in low light conditions, incapable of working with multiple-floors building, and inaccuracy found in measuring steps using accelerometer.

Authors in [30] propose an indoor navigation system using smartphone, a newer version of Bluetooth, known as Bluetooth Low Energy (BLE), and visual 2D markers. The building is split into multiple logical regions where each region is installed with a BLE beacon device. The visual markers, *ArUco* [31], are pasted on the floors of the building, which are then detected by a user with a phone camera pointed towards the floor. Location information decoded from the marker is used by the smartphone application along with the beacon's data to localize the user in the environment. Although the markers are not inter-related, they provide information about the current position only. The system provides an efficient and accurate positioning but requires beacons infrastructure to be deployed in the overall building, while no path calculation algorithm is proposed.

3 Proposed System

3.1 System Design

Indoor navigation system should be designed in manner to ease the path generation and path augmentation processes; as well as provide a robust and accurate user localization in the environment. Such a system should be flexible to assist in path editing and map extension.

With these goals in mind, we have designed a system thatautomatically detects fiducial markers and creates a floor plan, augments the markers with localization information; and at the same time providing an intuitive way to assist a visually impaired in indoor navigation.

The system's major function is to assist a visually impaired person in indoor navigation inside hospitals, universities, shopping malls, museums, and other large buildings. It would facilitate the navigation with auditory information to be augmented with the real-world video stream. We have used ARToolkit markers, which are printed on plain papers. These makers are capable of detection using an average quality camera under normal lighting conditions of an indoor environment [32]. The person has to carry a smartphone device, and headphones connected to the phone. The phone should have both the rear camera with a flashlight and the front facing camera. The phone is installed with our indoor navigation application developed using ARToolkit SDK (Fig. 1).

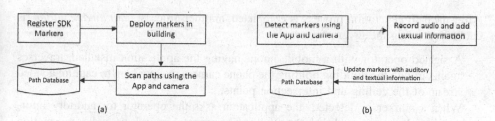

Fig. 1. (a) Path generation process. (b) Path augmentation process

3.2 Path Generation

The given steps are carried out for preparing markers to identify the paths inside a building.

- Path generation process starts with the step of registering ARToolkit markers in a library.
- The required number of markers is prepared for all of the possible paths in a single-floor or multiple-floor building.
- The markers are printed on plain paper, and pasted on ceilings of the identified paths inside the building, i.e., in front of each point of interest location like a room, office, lab, etc.
- When completed, the user with the help of the Android application on a smartphone starts to scan the building and detects each marker with phone camera.

– As a marker is detected, a node for it is created in a graph data structure storing information like marker unique identifier, andits direction.
– Upon detection of next marker, the application connects it to the previously detected marker using an adjacency matrix, using the given algorithm:
   • Suppose we have detected the first marker m_1 and created its node in the graph.
   • Upon the detection of next marker m_2, the application checks the angle θ between the y-axis of the camera and the y-axis of the marker.
   • If $\theta = 0°$, it means m_2 is in straight direction to the m_1.
   • If $\theta = 90°$, m_2 is to the right direction of m_1.
   • If $\theta = 180°$, m_2 lies behind m_1.
   • If $\theta = 270°$, m_2 is to the left direction of m_1.
   • We take a $\pm 45°$ range at each direction calculation, because the camera's y-axis does not have to be in precise angle along the marker's y-axis. For instance, connecting m_2 in straight direction to m_1, we consider angle range $45°$ to $-45°$ (i.e. $315°$).
   • Similarly, for connecting in right side direction we take range of $45°$ to $135°$.
– This way all of the hallways and corridors of the building are covered-up and a graph of the entire vicinity is build up in the application's database.

3.3 Path Augmentation

After the path generation process is completed, another process, *path augmentation*, is carried out using the given steps:

– A sighted operator with a mobile phone having the application installed, traverses again through the building holding the phone camera in a position to capture a video stream of the ceiling and intersection points.
– When a marker is detected, the application asks the operator for auditory information to be augmented with the marker. The operator records an audio information for the marker and its corresponding location inside the building like Room No. 4, Office, Lab, etc.
– Here the application also gives an option to add some textual information for the detected marker, which will be used to translate it into other languages by the application, when desired by the user.
– This way all of the hallways and corridors of the building are traversed and the application database is populated with the auditory and textual information about the entire markers.

4 Technical Assessment and Discussion

For testing the system and the proposed algorithms for path generation and path augmentation, we have designed several experiments. The experiments have been carried were on first floor of the Academic Block, University of Malakand. The actual floor plan of the selected building is Fig. 2.

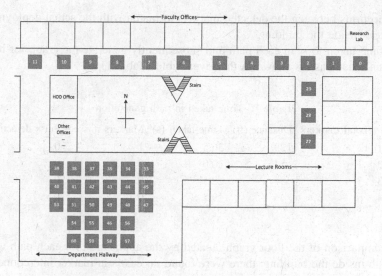

Fig. 2. Floor plan of the selected building and markers deployment

4.1 Path Selection

We selected four different paths for testing the path generation and the path augmentation algorithms. Here path 1 passes linearly across the corridor of CS department from Research Lab to the HOD office, while the other paths have been selected through the marker distribution in the department hallway as shown in Fig. 3.

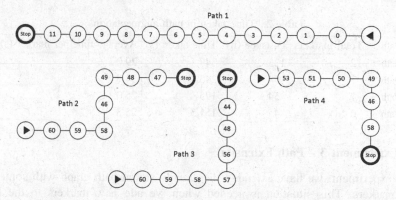

Fig. 3. Distribution of makers in the building and path directions

4.2 Experiment 1 – Path Generation

The primary objective of this experiment is to find out the average time taken to detect markers using smartphone camera, identify them, and connect them with each other to define a pathway in indoor of the building. We will also check the level of accuracy in interconnections between the detected markers to match with the actual deployment of the markers inside the building.

The time taken to scan each path and subsequently generate the graph for it in the application's database is shown in the given table (Table 1).

Table 1. Time taken in path generation

Path	Total markers	Distance (ft)	Time taken (s)	Markers missed	False detection
Path 1	12	123	36.5	1	0
Path 2	7	54	20.0	0	0
Path 3	7	54	22.5	0	0
Path 4	6	45	19.5	0	0

On comparison of the floor graph created by the application for each path with the actual path inside the building; there were found no errors in marker interconnections.

4.3   Experiment 2 – Path Augmentation

In this experiment, the time taken to augment the selected paths with auditory and textual information has been calculated. The average time taken by the application for this task, which is about half a minute, seems efficient. The results are shown in the given table (Table 2).

Table 2. Time taken in path augmentation

Path	Total markers	Distance (ft)	Time taken (s)	Average time per marker (s)
Path 1	12	123	347.5	29.0
Path 2	7	54	243	34.7
Path 3	7	54	175	25.0
Path 4	6	45	151.5	25.3

4.4   Experiment 3 – Path Extension

In this experiment, we have extended the already stored path graph with some additional markers. This situation is needed when we add new markers to the indoor building where we already have generated paths. Considering the Path-1 in the selected paths, we wish to extend the path and attach the markers having id: 29, 28, and 27; we start with selecting marker id: 2, and moving toward the new path, thus scanning with phone camera till the last marker (id: 27), the final path becomes (Fig. 4):

Fig. 4. Path-1 after extension to include new markers

5 Conclusion

After reviewing several proposals and implementations presented in various researches for assisting the visually impaired people in indoor navigation and localization, we have proposed a novel approach towards the same situation. The solution has been implemented as an Android application, and tested in an indoor environment for efficiency and effectiveness. It has a vital advantage over other solutions in that it requires only a smartphone with the application installed, and its camera features for detection and identification of plain markers – thus localizing the user inside an indoor environment. It presents an *automating path generation* algorithm that simplifies the creation of pathways inside the building by merely detection and connection of pre-deployed markers. Similarly, the *path augmentation* algorithm adds auditory and textual information to the path graph. Both algorithms have been tested in a real scenario and the experiments have shown comparatively acceptable benchmarks. We also have tested the *path extension* algorithm, with which we can efficiently extend the existing path graph to include newly deployed markers.

References

1. Dunleavy, M., Dede, C., Mitchell, R.: Affordances and limitations of immersive participatory augmented reality simulations for teaching and learning. J. Sci. Educ. Technol. J. Art. **18**(1), 7–22 (2009)
2. Aloor, J.J., Sahana, P.S., Seethal, S., Thomas, S., Pillai, M.T.R.: Design of VR headset using augmented reality. In: 2016 International Conference on Electrical, Electronics, and Optimization Techniques (ICEEOT), pp. 3540–3544 (2016)
3. Rabbi, I., Ullah, S., Alam, A.: Marker based tracking in augmented reality applications using ARToolkit: a case study. J. Eng. Appl. Sci. (JEAS), Univ. Eng. Technol. Peshawar **34**(1), 15–25 (2015)
4. ARToolkit. http://www.hitl.washington.edu/artoolkit/
5. Wagner, D., Schmalstieg, D.: ARToolKitPlus for pose tracking on mobile devices. In: 12th Computer Vision Winter Workshop (CVWW 2007), Sankt Lambrecht, Austria (2007)
6. Fiala, M.: ARTag, a fiducial marker system using digital techniques. In: 2005 IEEE Computer Society Conference on Computer Vision and Pattern Recognition (CVPR 2005), vol. 2, pp. 590–596. IEEE (2005)
7. Visual impairment and blindness – WHO, August 2014. http://www.who.int/mediacentre/factsheets/fs282/en/

8. Zeb, A., Ullah, S., Rabbi, I.: Indoor vision-based auditory assistance for blind people in semi controlled environments. In: 2014 4th International Conference on Image Processing Theory, Tools and Applications (IPTA), pp. 1–6 (2014)
9. Barnard, M.E.: The global positioning system. IEEE Rev. **38**(3), 99–102 (1992)
10. Abbott, E., Powell, D.: Land-vehicle navigation using GPS. Proc. IEEE **87**(1), 145–162 (1999)
11. Panzieri, S., Pascicci, F., Ulivi, G.: An outdoor navigation system using GPS and inertial platform. IEEE Trans. Mechatron. **7**(2), 134–142 (2002)
12. Ozdenizci, B., Ok, K., Coskun, V., Aydin, M.N.: Development of an indoor navigation system using NFC technology. In: 2011 Fourth International Conference on Information and Computing, pp. 11–14 (2011)
13. Blattner, A., Vasilev, Y., Harriehausen-Mühlbauer, B.: Mobile indoor navigation assistance for mobility impaired people. Procedia Manuf. **3**, 51–58 (2015)
14. Mahmood, A., Javaid, N., Razzaq, S.: A review of wireless communications for smart grid. Renew. Sustainable Energy Rev. **41**, 248–260 (2015)
15. Yelamarthi, K., Haas, D., Nielsen, D., Mothersell, S.: RFID and GPS integrated navigation system for the visually impaired. In: 2010 53rd IEEE International Midwest Symposium on Circuits and Systems, pp. 1149–1152 (2010)
16. Fallah, N., Apostolopoulos, I., Bekris, K., Folmer, E.: Indoor human navigation systems: a survey. Interact. Comput. **25**, 21–33 (2013)
17. Mautz, R.: Indoor positioning technologies. Doctoral dissertation, Department of Civil, Environment Geomatic Engineering, Institute of Geodesy Photogrammetry, ETH Zurich, Zurich (2012)
18. Levchev, P., Krishnan, M.N., Yu, C., Menke, J., Zakhor, A.: Simultaneous fingerprinting and mapping for multimodal image and WiFi indoor positioning. In: Proceedings of Indoor Positioning Indoor Navigation, pp. 442–450 (2014)
19. Abu Doush, I., Alshatnawi, S., Al-Tamimi, A.-K., Alhasan, B., Hamasha, S.: ISAB: integrated indoor navigation system for the blind. Interact. Comput. **29**(2), 181–202 (2016)
20. Yang, L., Dashti, M., Jie, Z.: Indoor localization on mobile phone platforms using embedded inertial sensors. In: 2013 10th Workshop on Positioning, Navigation and Communication (WPNC), pp. 1–5 (2013)
21. Kim, J., Jun, H.: Vision-based location positioning using augmented reality for indoor navigation. IEEE Trans. Consumer Electron. **54**(3), 954–962 (2008)
22. Huey, L.C., Sebastian, P., Drieberg, M.: Augmented reality based indoor positioning navigation tool. In: 2011 IEEE Conference on Open Systems, pp. 256–260 (2011)
23. Subakti, H., Jiang, J.R.: A marker-based cyber-physical augmented-reality indoor guidance system for smart campuses. In: 2016 IEEE 18th International Conference on High Performance Computing and Communications; IEEE 14th International Conference on Smart City; IEEE 2nd International Conference on Data Science and Systems (HPCC/SmartCity/DSS), pp. 1373–1379 (2016)
24. Dijkstra, E.W.: A note on two problems in connexion with graphs. Numer. Math. J. Art. **1**(1), 269–271 (1959)
25. Yin, Z., Wu, C., Yang, Z., Liu, Y.: Peer-to-Peer indoor navigation using smartphones. IEEE J. Select. Areas Commun. **35**(5), 1141–1153 (2017)
26. Simões, W.C.S.S., de Lucena, V.F.: Blind user wearable audio assistance for indoor navigation based on visual markers and ultrasonic obstacle detection. In: 2016 IEEE International Conference on Consumer Electronics (ICCE), pp. 60–63 (2016)
27. Kalkusch, M., Lidy, T., Knapp, N., Reitmayr, G., Kaufmann, H., Schmalstieg, D.: Structured visual markers for indoor pathfinding. In: Augmented Reality Toolkit, The First IEEE International Workshop, pp. 8–16. IEEE (2002)

28. Al-Khalifa, S., Al-Razgan, M.: Ebsar: indoor guidance for the visually impaired. Comput. Electr. Eng. **54**, 26–39 (2016)
29. Chandgadkar, A., Knottenbelt, W.: An indoor navigation system for smartphones. Imperial College London, London, UK (2013)
30. La Delfa, G.C., Catania, V.: Accurate indoor navigation using smartphone, bluetooth low energy and visual tags. In: Proceedings of the 2nd Conference on Mobile and Information Technologies in Medicine (2014)
31. Garrido-Jurado, S., Muñoz-Salinas, R., Madrid-Cuevas, F.J., Marín-Jiménez, M.J.: Automatic generation and detection of highly reliable fiducial markers under occlusion. Pattern Recogn. **47**(6), 2280–2292 (2014)
32. Rabbi, I., Ullah, S., Javed, M., Zen, K.: Analysis of ARToolKit Fiducial Markers Attributes for Robust Tracking (2017)

Virtual Product Try-On Solution
for E-Commerce Using Mobile Augmented
Reality

Anuradha Welivita[✉], Nanduni Nimalsiri, Ruchiranga Wickramasinghe,
Upekka Pathirana, and Chandana Gamage

Department of Computer Science and Engineering, University of Moratuwa,
Moratuwa, Sri Lanka
{anuradha.12,nanduni.12,ruchiranga.12,upekka.12,chandag}@cse.mrt.ac.lk

Abstract. Augmented Reality has opened doors to numerous ways of
enhancing human computer interaction. It has brought up opportunities to seamlessly improve user experience in e-commerce applications.
In this paper we describe an approach of building a mobile augmented
reality application that enables the users to virtually try out facial accessories such as eyewear. The application uses face tracking and head pose
estimation techniques in rendering virtual content realistically over the
human face in real-time.

Keywords: Augmented reality · E-commerce · Face tracking · Head
pose estimation

1 Introduction

Augmented Reality (AR) is a technology that superimposes computer generated
images and graphics onto visualizations of real world environments. It enhances
the user's perception of reality by combining real and virtual elements. From
early 2000 onwards, with the proliferation of mobile devices such as tablets
and mobile phones, AR has gained a perfect medium to reach consumers and
is becoming the next 'big thing' in technology. Mobile AR has further opened
up opportunities to seamlessly improve user experience in areas of retail, e-
commerce, marketing and advertising. Increasingly, companies are using AR
technology to reach out to customers to market their products by allowing
customers to virtually visualize product models of jewellery, eyewear etc. on
themselves.

We are in the process of developing a mobile application that allows users
to augment themselves and try out fashionable facial accessories without having
to visit the outlets. The main idea behind this application is to render virtual
accessories realistically on the human faces in real-time on a live video feed
captured in a mobile device. This application runs on the Unity3D platform
and has a pluggable virtual object pose estimation component integrated in. It

L.T. De Paolis et al. (Eds.): AVR 2017, Part I, LNCS 10324, pp. 438–447, 2017.
DOI: 10.1007/978-3-319-60922-5_34

uses face tracking and head pose estimation techniques in estimating the final object pose. The application can also connect to an online web portal so that the retailers can dynamically update available models of facial accessories, which the customers can try out whenever they are made available.

The motivation behind developing this mobile application is to build up a better customer engagement model which is accessible to the customers at their convenience through personal mobile devices. With this application, customers can experience an enhanced online shopping experience allowing them to try out items before actually purchasing them.

This paper first describes related work in the field. The next section discusses the methodology including the system architecture of the application in detail. The implementation details, challenges addressed and an evaluation of the application being developed are described in the subsequent sections. Finally the possible improvements and future work are discussed.

2   Related Work

Masquerade is a popular mobile application which has the ability to track the position and the orientation of the human face. This application is well known for its ability to put on various types of 3D masks and enhance the user's appearance in the live video feed. Still this application performs poor in identifying a face in instances where there is a strong light source visible to the camera closer to or behind the face of the user. Furthermore the application only focuses on entertainment purposes.

Snapchat is another image messaging software product that provides AR filters to create special graphical effects over the user's face. This application uses an Active Shape Model algorithm to estimate the positions of the features of interest in the human face. Snapchat AR filters are also only targeted at providing entertainment to the users.

TryLive is a 3D product visualization and a virtual try-on solution that provides the users with virtual shopping experience. It uses AR technology to provide immersive interaction with real time movements and also provides the ability to manually scale the rendered content. It has an inbuilt face tracking algorithm that detects the eyes and the mouth and has the ability to differentiate faces of children, adults, men or women. This also has a mobile version which is compatible with Android and iPhone mobile devices. Only the online PC version of the product is available for demonstration. Even though the online demo in general scenarios shows promisingly realistic results, the initialization takes a couple of seconds within which the user has to keep steady. If the user moves within that time, the accuracy of the face tracking significantly degrades. It also performs poorly in terms of face tracking when the user actually wears real glasses.

The significance of the proposed mobile application being developed lies in the fact that it primarily targets the e-commerce and retail industries. Its light-weight design and technical simplicity makes it possible to be run smoothly on a mobile device while maintaining its robustness at the same time. This application has the potential to make a remarkable impact on the business sector by bringing in novel means of interaction with the customers using AR.

3   Methodology

The virtual object pose estimation component acts as the main component of the application and performs the core face detection, facial feature extraction, face tracking and geometric pose estimation operations for determining the head pose and ultimately the pose of the virtual object to be rendered on the human face. The algorithms used in the implementation were chosen based on a comprehensive evaluation carried out on a PC prior to the mobile application development. The rationale behind the decisions of the final development methodology of the application is also discussed in Sect. 4.

3.1   System Architecture

The proposed application is designed to communicate with a backend system that holds a database of 3D models of facial accessories. The business owner can upload the 3D models of the designs available for sale and the users can then download them via the mobile application and try them out virtually. Furthermore if a user wishes to purchase a certain model, the application can again communicate with the backend server to notify the purchase request and forward the user to proceed with the necessary steps for checkout.

A detailed view of the application architecture is illustrated in Fig. 1. The proposed application consists of two main components, Application controller and the Object pose estimator. Application controller is responsible in reading frames one at a time from the mobile device camera as a 640×480 image and feeding it into the Object pose estimator component. The returned results are used in updating the pose of the 3D model used in terms of position, scale and rotation in a 3D world.

The Object pose estimation component acts as the core component that supports the main functionality of the system. Once an image frame is fed into this module by the Application controller, this component will first perform a face detection to see if the image contains a face or not. If a face is detected the algorithm will proceed with fitting a facial model to the face there by extracting four facial features, specifically the centers of the two eyes, the nose tip and the center of the mouth. Once all the four features are extracted successfully, the algorithm then proceeds with extracting feature points on the face that are suitable to be used with a point tracker. All the computations from this point onwards are done on a processed image obtained by applying a histogram equalization technique to compensate for unfavourable lighting conditions. The facial region extracted from the processed image is then used for feature extraction using a corner detection algorithm. The proposed application uses a threshold value on the number of extracted corner points to decide whether to proceed

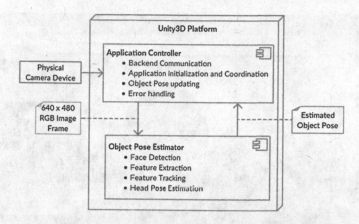

Fig. 1. The detailed architecture of the mobile application.

or not since a lower corner point count would significantly degrade the tracking and object pose estimation accuracies.

The extracted corner points in the facial region in the previous image frame are then fed into a point tracker along with the next image frame to estimate the positions of those corner points in that new image frame. Once the corresponding corner points set of the previous image frame and the next image frame are available the geometric transformation matrix between those two sets of points is computed. This transformation matrix models the movement of the corner points and it is then used to transform the feature points of the two eyes and the mouth forward. The position of the nose tip feature point in the next image frame is estimated separately using the same approach used in estimating the positions of the corner points i.e. by employing a point tracker. The reasons behind the decisions on different ways of tracking and estimation employed in the process are discussed in Sect. 4.

Once an estimation of the positions of the four facial features are available in each frame, a head pose estimation algorithm is employed in estimating the head pose and eventually the pose of the 3D object being rendered on top of the video feed.

3.2   Application Front-End

Figure 2 shows the tentative user interface of the application where the available 3D models of glasses are shown to the left and the selected model is rendered in the correct location and correct orientation over the user's face. The circles in red, blue and green represents the corner points, estimated facial feature points and the ground truth facial feature points respectively. In case the model is not shown in correct pose, apart from the automatic reinitialization procedure which is embedded into the application, the user is also given the option to manually reinitialize the algorithm.

Fig. 2. The GUI of the application.(Color figure online)

4   Implementation

4.1   Face Detection and Initialization

For the purpose of first checking whether the image contains a face or not and if it does, for further processing requirements, the Viola-Jones face detection algorithm [1] was used. Once a face is detected a shape model is fitted to the face to extract the main features of interest namely the two eyes, the tip of the nose and the center of the mouth. To compensate for low light conditions and irregular illumination of faces the Contrast Limited Adaptive Histogram Equalization was used.

4.2   Face Tracking Feature Estimation

For extracting good features to track, the Shi-Tomasi corner extractor [2] was used. The tracking of points across different consecutive frames were achieved with the use of a Kanade-Lucas-Tomasi (KLT) point tracker [3].

Finally, the estimation of the positions of the four facial feature points in each frame was achieved by computing the geometric transform between the matching corner point pairs in two consecutive image frames.

In determining the transformation matrix, two points from one set are chosen at random along with their corresponding points in the other set. Then those points are normalized so that the center of mass is at (0,0) and the mean distance from the center is $\sqrt{2}$. The normalized points are next used in generating a matrix which is then subjected to single value decomposition. The right most matrix out of the three resultant matrices is used in the final computation of the transform matrix. This obtained matrix is used again to evaluate how close the transformed points using that matrix are to the actual points and if the results are not good enough the same process is followed a certain number of times until satisfactory results are achieved. This algorithm is based on [4,5].

4.3 Head Pose Estimation

As suggested by Gee and Cipolla [6], head pose can be estimated geometrically by finding the facial normal of a given facial image considering the geometric distribution of the facial features. A modified version of their method is used in the proposed application.

The roll angle of the head is computed by taking into account the angle between the line connecting the pair of eyes and the horizontal axis. The computation of the pitch angle relies on the assumption that in an average human being the ratio between the lengths from the eye level to the base of the nose and to the center of the mouth stays roughly the same. In [6], the authors have proposed this ratio to be 0.6 and when the subject changes the pitch angle of the head, this ratio varies between 0 and 1. Hence the pitch angle can be calculated proportionately to the change in this ratio. Similarly the computation of the yaw angle relies on the assumption that the ratio between the length of the perpendicular drawn from the nose tip to the facial symmetrical axis (facial normal) and the length from the mid point between the eyes to the center of the mouth stays the same. When the yaw is 90^0, the authors of [6] have proposed this ratio to be 0.6. Hence the yaw can be calculated proportionately to the change in this ratio that lies between 0 and 0.6.

5   Evaluation Results

The accuracy of the estimated locations of the facial features and the head pose were evaluated against ground truth data obtained from the GI4E head pose database [7] that consists of videos obtained with a standard webcam for testing head tracking and pose estimation. The point to point root-mean-square (RMS) error was taken as a measure to determine the accuracy of the estimated locations of the four facial features, the pair of eyes, nose tip and the mouth. Figure 3 shows the point to point RMS errors obtained for five different videos of subject 1 in the GI4E database. The five videos were chosen to represent translation, roll, pitch, yaw and the scaling of the subject's head as indicated by different background colors in the graphs.

The actual and the estimated values of the head pose in terms of roll, yaw and pitch were also plotted as denoted in Fig. 4 to visualize the deviation of the estimated head pose angles from the ground truth angles in the GI4E database.

According to the results obtained, the point to point RMS error between the actual and the estimated facial feature points fluctuates between 2 and 8 pixel lengths which indicates that the facial feature point estimations are quite accurate.

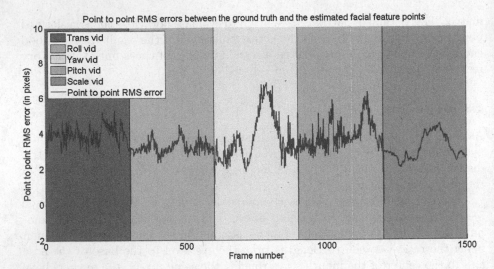

Fig. 3. Point to point RMS errors between the ground truth and the estimated facial feature points.(Color figure online)

When considering the head pose, the deviations between the actual and the estimated values of the roll angle are observed to be negligible. But noticeable deviations can be observed in the estimations of the yaw and pitch angles. The deviations of the pitch angle can be due to incorporation of a common face ratio rather than taking into account the actual face ratio of the subject in the video. The deviations of the estimated values of the yaw angle become larger as it takes higher values. This is due to the fact that the tracking accuracy of the tip of the nose drops as the yaw angle increases significantly. In such cases, the estimated position of the nose tip usually appears a bit closer to the center of the face away from the actual nose tip, giving a value that is bit less than the actual yaw angle.

When the application was tested on a PC with 1.80 GHz CPU and 4 GB memory, an average FPS of 60.3 was obtained. When it was tested on a mid-range Android smart phone having 1.2 GHz processor and 1 GB memory, an average FPS of 8.6 could be observed. Still, this frame rate could give satisfactorily smooth real-time performance in a normal usage scenario of the application. Better performance can be expected in devices with higher computation capabilities.

6   Subjective Evaluation

The virtual try-on solution was tested using the System Usability Scale (SUS) [8] and the User Experience Questionnaire (UEQ) [9] to collect subjective data in order to measure the user engagement.

Fifteen third party participants were asked to try-on various models of eyewear using the application and rate their experience. From the results obtained,

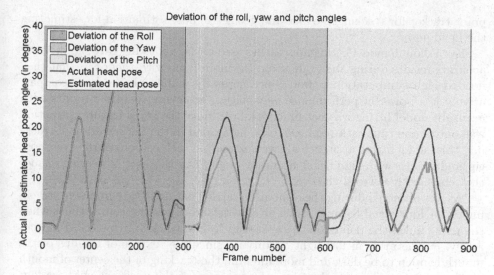

Fig. 4. Deviation of the roll, yaw and pitch angles.

an average SUS score of 78.93 out of 100 could be observed. This implies that the application usability is well above the average. Scores of 1.333, 1.731, 1.154, 1.154, 1.288 and 1.346 were obtained for the six UEQ scales attractiveness, perpicuity, efficiency, dependability, stimulation and novelty respectively. These were above average scores with respect to the benchmark values in UEQ.

The results imply that the participants preferred to use the mobile augmented reality try-on solution over physically visiting the eye-wear shops and that it is capable of enhancing customer engagement.

7   Discussion

Building this application becomes challenging due to the constraints of limited processing power and memory available in mobile devices. A proper balance between the accuracy and the speed of the application is required since the most accurate algorithms might not perform well with sufficient speed and vice versa. Hence the final decisions on the implementation approach of the mobile application were taken considering the results of various comparisons between algorithms and trial and error experiments. Prior to the implementation of the application to be run on a mobile platform, a comprehensive research was carried out on selecting out the suitable algorithms for the purpose from those that exist in the literature. Implementations of different algorithms for face detection, feature extraction, face tracking and head pose estimation were tried on a PC environment and comparisons between those algorithms were done to choose the best approach to follow.

Accordingly, it was decided to use a Viola-Jones face detection cascade for detecting faces, a model fitting approach for initial feature extraction, the KLT point tracker for tracking the face and geometric pose estimation for estimating the head pose.

Even though model fitting approaches used for face tracking gave significantly accurate results during the evaluation, the main issue with them was that they needed high computation power. Since normally mobile phones have comparatively less powerful performance capabilities, achieving real-time results with accurate model fitting was not practical. Still, since the facial feature extraction was only a one time task required to be performed in the initialization of tracking, this model fitting approach allowed extracting the positions of the eyes, nose tip and mouth with significant accuracy even when the user is wearing shades that completely covered the eyes.

As was observed during the evaluation carried out on PC environment, tracking of the four facial features alone gives satisfactory results. But at times when the user blinks, the points on the eyes tend to lose track or get tracked inaccurately. Furthermore in low light conditions, since the texture of the lips of the mouth happen to be dark and more uniform, the tracking of the center of mouth also seem to perform poorly. Since the accuracy of the positions of those four facial features is critical in computing the head pose and there by the object pose accurately, a better approach had to be followed.

Again as was tested in the evaluation carried out on PC environment, the approach of extracting a significant number of corner points in the facial region to be fed into the KLT point tracker and estimating the positions of the four facial feature points based on the geometric transform of the corner points across the frames became the solution to the aforementioned problem. Even though using this approach significantly improved the position estimations of the two eyes and the mouth, the position estimation of the nose suffered in terms of accuracy. A possible reason for that loss of accuracy would be the elevated location of the nose tip from the rest of the face. When the pose of the head changes, a point on the nose tip moves a slightly larger distance than a point on the mouth since it is having an elevated position closer to the camera than the mouth point. Since a majority of the corner points tracked are from areas around the nose, they fail to accurately estimate the position of the nose tip.

This problem was solved by following a hybrid approach where the tip of the nose is fed into a point tracker alone while the positions of the other three points, the two eyes and the mouth are being estimated from the movement of the detected corner points. As the eyes are not independently being tracked, this approach gave the added advantage of being able to perform the face tracking accurately even if the user is actually wearing glasses or shades on.

As was mentioned in Sect. 4, in order to deal with irregular and unfavourable lighting conditions a contrast limited adaptive histogram equalization was applied on the image frames. The ordinary histogram equalization performed poorly in this situation since in most cases the foreground in the image frames was brighter than the background. Even with this additional processing done on each image frame, the real-time performance of the application was not hindered since it is not a computationally expensive operation.

8   Conclusion

In this paper we discussed about a mobile augmented reality application which uses face detection, face tracking and head pose estimation techniques to estimate the pose of a virtual object to be realistically placed on a human face in real-time. This application would enhance the online shopping experience of customers as they can virtually try out models of eyewear before actually purchasing them. The specifics of the application development, system architecture and methodology were also presented. The challenges met in developing the application and how they were addressed were also discussed.

Currently the development of the core object pose estimation component of the application has been completed targeting trying out of virtual models of eyewear. Further improvements on the application that deals with communication with the business client's server and implementation of in-app online purchase functionality are yet to be done. The algorithm used for face tracking can also be improved to track the ears allowing users to try out earrings as well.

References

1. Viola, P., Jones, M.: Rapid object detection using a boosted cascade of simple features. In: IEEE Computer Society Conference on Computer Vision and Pattern Recognition, pp. 511–518. IEEE (2001)
2. Shi, J., Tomasi, C.: Good features to track. In: IEEE Conference on Computer Vision and Pattern Recognition, pp. 593–600. IEEE (1994)
3. Tomasi, C., Kanade, T.: Detection and Tracking of Point Features. School of Computer Science, Carnegie Mellon University, Pittsburgh (1991)
4. Hartley, R., Zisserman, A.: Multiple View Geometry in Computer Vision. Cambridge University Press, Cambridge (2003)
5. Torr, P., Zisserman, A.: MLESAC: a new robust estimator with application to estimating image geometry. Comput. Vis. Image Underst. **78**, 138–156 (2000)
6. Gee, A., Cipolla, R.: Determining the gaze of faces in images. Image Vis. Comput. **12**, 639–647 (1994)
7. Ariz, M., Bengoechea, J., Villanueva, A., Cabeza, R.: A novel 2D/3D database with automatic face annotation for head tracking and pose estimation. Comput. Vis. Image Underst. **148**, 201–210 (2016)
8. System Usability Scale (SUS) — Usability.gov. https://www.usability.gov/how-to-and-tools/methods/system-usability-scale.html
9. UEQ - User Experience Questionnaire. http://www.ueq-online.org

DyMAR: Introduction to Dynamic Marker Based Augmented Reality Using Smartwatch

Satyaki Roy, Pratiti Sarkar, and Surojit Dey[✉]

Design Programme, Indian Institute of Technology, Kanpur, India
{satyaki,pratiti,surojit}@iitk.ac.in

Abstract. With the new emerging technologies, many ways are being adopted to provide quality information and knowledge in the learning environment. The use of Augmented Reality (AR) technology is being widely accepted in various domains including the field of education and learning. AR applications are available as either marker-based or marker-less. This experience of AR is becoming easily available with the evolving mobile wireless devices. However, there is a huge scope of using wearables as a medium of AR. In this paper, we are proposing the use of smartwatch as a platform to introduce dynamic markers. With the help of voice recognition, Dynamic markers help in providing a platform with wide collection of markers that can be selected anywhere without the need to carry any related document as the target. Further the scope of application of Dynamic Marker based Augmented Reality (DyMAR) is discussed.

Keywords: Augmented Reality · Dynamic Marker · Smartwatch

1 Introduction

The world is now getting surrounded with the evolving technologies to provide the users with a comfortable, easy and seamless experience. Augmented Reality (AR) is one such technology. This technology has evolved over the years and is now becoming more and more powerful to create its impact in various domains. AR makes use of virtual information which is overlaid on top of the real world to give an interactive experience. The advent of portable wireless devices and wide use of internet are becoming the backbone of AR.

When it comes to learning and education, various technologies have been used and worked upon for enhancing the understanding skills and quick grasping of new concepts. Many researches and works have been done using AR as well to provide a better learning experience by using the digital medium in the normal daily life scenario. Currently, marker-based and marker-less AR systems are used which have been described in the following section. Through this work, we have tried to explore a new reach of marker-based AR with the introduction of Dynamic Markers with the use of the wearable – smartwatch, to provide the similar experience without the need of the physical presence of the target.

© Springer International Publishing AG 2017
L.T. De Paolis et al. (Eds.): AVR 2017, Part I, LNCS 10324, pp. 448–456, 2017.
DOI: 10.1007/978-3-319-60922-5_35

2 Background

2.1 Augmented Reality

Augmented Reality (AR) is a technology used to integrate virtual objects (generated by computer) in the live scenario. In AR one is always in direct contact with the nearby surrounding. It provides the required assistance and aid in getting virtual overlay of infographics, audio, video, etc. for different purposes. With the use of the overlaid virtual information, the surrounding space can be made more interactive and useful in several ways.

The research on Augmented Reality has been going from quite a long time. With the development in technologies and their usage, the use and power of AR is being realized and brought more and more into existence. As described by Azuma [1], the application of the same can be seen in various domains like medical, manufacturing and repair, visualization, education and learning, entertainment and many more. According to Azuma et al. [2], the AR systems overlay the layers of virtual objects and informations in real time on top of the real environment which makes it possible to provide the necessary and relevant information to the user at the right time. AR systems thus help in better learning and understanding as the actual interactive 3D visualization of a complex structure can be seen and related information can be observed, which is otherwise difficult to understand when explained only in words or in form of a 2D image.

2.2 How Augmented Reality Works

Augmented Reality superimposes the virtual objects in the real environment in real-time. According to Amin and Govilkar [3], the AR system works in three major steps i.e. Recognition, Tracking and Mix. Any object that is to be overlaid on the live environment is first identified using the device having a camera. Its spatial information is then tracked in real-time and finally the related virtual computer-generated information (graphic content, text, video, audio etc.) are superimposed in the actual live scenario.

In the present scenario, AR applications are available as either marker-based or marker-less as described by Johnson et al. [4]. In marker-based, the camera detects a pre-defined marker and augments the related information in the real world. The camera reads the image, recognizes its position, orientation and movement; and decodes it using image processing techniques to produce the related virtual object in the 3D form in the real-world environment. Marker-less AR on the other hand involves a device that uses GPS, compass and image recognition to overlay the virtual graphics in a live environment. There is no need of having a prior knowledge about the environment. The GPS feature helps in the tracking and identification of natural features in the surrounding to interact with the available augmented reality resources [5].

2.3 Scope of Smartwatch in Augmented Reality

With the expansion of internet usage, the system of AR is getting widely acknowledged. The electronic gadgets with internet connection and cameras like personal computers, smart phones, tablets etc. are making it as an easy mode of the availability of AR. Head Mounted Devices (HMD) as well as eyewear glasses with cameras and see-through screens are another means of using AR hands-free. Advance research is going on for bringing the AR experience in contact lenses [6].

According to International Data Corporation (IDC) [7], wearables are the near future. Smartwatch is one of the wearables that has come out way beyond a normal wrist watch. Other than showing time, the small device has the capability to show digital information on its small touchscreen. Now-a-days many companies are competing and working on developing the different prototypes of smartwatches to add more user-friendly features. This wide range of competition has also made it economically feasible for varied range of users to adapt the smartwatch in their daily lives. Various smartwatches are also being introduced for the education purposes for kids.

In this paper, we are showcasing another mode of implementing AR with the help of new type of markers i.e. dynamic markers using the smartwatch. Since smartwatch can be worn in hand and can be carried at all places without any burden, this will help in easily using the fed markers without the need of a target to be physically present.

2.4 Tangible User Interface

Tangible User Interface (TUI) helps to interact with the digital data using the physical entities (gestures, touch, speech, etc.) [8]. Kim and Woo [9] proposed a system to easily track the movement of the hand of a user in 6-DOF. This was done using Head Mounted Display to provide the Augmented Reality environment and a smartwatch with depth sensor is worn on wrist to determine the orientation of the hand. Fiorentino et al. [10] has used Augmented Reality for simplifying the drawing and navigation on CAD (Computer-Aided Design) system. Here the drawing itself acts as the tangible device which is used with gestures for the navigation functions. In another work, AR approach is used by combining with TUI so as to enable easy visual tracking of the AR objects on top of a table [11]. Thus, with the advancement in technology, TUI is emerging as one of the essential tools which brings up endless possibilities to easily interact with the digital platforms. This paper touches upon the use of TUI on smartwatch for enhancing the augmented reality experience.

3 Concept of DyMAR

DyMAR stands for Dynamic Marker based Augmented Reality. DyMAR uses the display of a smartwatch to show the marker which is to be scanned by an AR device. It can generate any number of markers on its screen. The information about the whole set of markers in a specific book can be easily downloaded and stored in the database so that the users don't have to carry the books along with them anymore. Whenever and wherever one wants to augment any object, the user will just have to speak the keywords related to that, based on which the marker will be generated automatically. In case a user is not carrying his books with him and instantly needs to see something in AR, DyMAR proves to be a very handy tool in such scenarios as he has the whole library of AR markers with him. This reduces the extra effort that the user had to put for getting the seamless AR experience to a great extent. The system is being implemented using ARToolKit and Android based smartwatch. The steps of the DyMAR system has been diagrammatically explained below.

3.1 Information Storage

In the online database, the information regarding the visual contents of different books is stored. For example, in the books of Biology there are a lot of diagrams and pictorial representations in the different chapters. For every diagram and picture there is a figure number, title and sometimes a brief description of the visual content so that students find it easier to correlate with the text content of the book. These metadata (figure number, title and brief description) are stored in the database maintained online. For each Graphic content there is an Augmented Reality marker tagged along with it which is used for initiating the augmentation when required (Fig. 1).

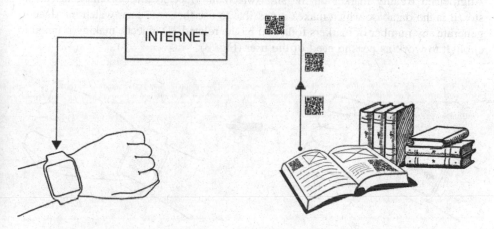

Fig. 1. The markers stored in the online database is extracted in the smartwatch

3.2 Taking the Input

The voice recognition feature of a smartwatch is being used for taking the inputs from the user. We are considering the fact, that the feature of voice recognition has greatly evolved over time and gives accurate results to a considerable extent. If the user wants to generate the marker for a specific article from his book, he has to speak out the title of the article or some keywords related to it. It is not really necessary to memorize the exact titles of the graphic contents of the book for successfully feeding the input. As DyMAR is designed in a way that it generates the relevant Augmented Reality markers based on the keywords needed as input by the user (Fig. 2).

Fig. 2. Voice input with keywords given to the smartwatch

3.3 Generating Dynamic Markers

After the smartwatch picks up the keywords from the input fed using voice recognition, it maps the keywords with the information of the Graphic contents stored into its database. Once it finds the appropriate target the user wants to see, it generates the Augmented Reality marker on the smartwatch interface. Numerous markers can be stored in the database which makes it possible to use the same smartwatch interface to generate any number of markers followed by the related 3D objects, making it tangible enough to work as per the need of the user (Fig. 3).

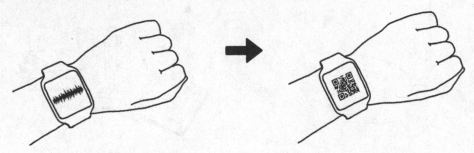

Fig. 3. Generation of appropriate marker by mapping keywords with related graphic content

3.4 Augmentation

Once the marker is generated on the smartwatch's display screen, the user just have to scan it with the AR device (in this case a mobile phone) connected via Bluetooth. On recognizing the marker the augmentation of the desired article starts. The marker gives the exact location in space to the AR device where it has to augment. Apart from giving the location it also provides features like zooming in or zooming out and rotation of the augmented form. The user need not carry any book anymore for getting the AR experience. Especially when there is inappropriate lighting or it is dark it becomes difficult to scan the markers on book but now when it is on the smartwatch's screen the user doesn't have to worry about that (Fig. 4).

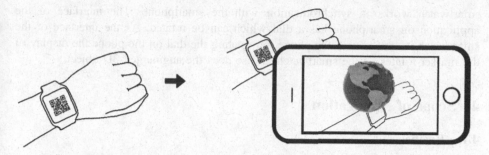

Fig. 4. Scanning of marker using smart phone to get the augmented object

3.5 Concept Prototyping and Testing

For the preliminary phase of prototyping, Android smartphone and smartwatch were used. Using the open source Google API, voice to text conversion was done. This text was matched with the name of the markers in the database which gets displayed on the smartwatch. For each of the marker, the corresponding 3D models were developed using blender. The .obj files of the rendered 3D objects were used in Unity 3D Game Engine to implement the overlaying of these objects onto the real world on the phone application on identifying the markers. The prototype was tested using 9 different markers with 12 users (8 males and 4 females). The list of 9 markers were given to them which were to be spoken randomly. The success rate was 88.9% where some of the voice inputs were not correctly recognized. However, gender was not a major factor in this (Fig. 5).

When the use of smartwatch is suggested as a platform for DyMAR, a major concern of 360° rotation of the smartwatch cannot be ignored. Human wrist can be rotated to some extent but there are limitations beyond which it cannot move freely. Due to this the user cannot see the 3D object from all the sides and angles. For addressing this issue the feature of rotation has been added to the application. The

Fig. 5. Preliminary prototyping

smartwatch works in synchronization with the smartphone. The interface of the application on smartphone has a dial which can be rotated. As the interface of the smartwatch is synced with the phone, on rotating the dial on the phone the display of the marker rotates on the smartwatch and so does the augmented 3D object.

4   Scope of Application

4.1   Engineering

In engineering textbooks especially in the disciplines of Mechanical and Civil a lot of pictorial representations are given to show a lot of different angles and structures. But when one gets to see the same thing in the laboratory or workshop, they often find it difficult to correlate. By using DyMAR one can easily augment those objects in classroom or workshops and get a better understanding. For example, if someone is unable to understand the different angles and parameters of the Machine Tool while working in mechanical workshop, the tool can easily be augmented using marker on the smartwatch. This enhances the practical understanding of the contents to a great extent.

4.2   Educational Trips

In schools, students are taken for educational trips for giving them a better learning experience. On those trips teachers explain a lot of things to them which they have studied in the classroom. In this way they can relate with the things practically. In our study we found that the students find it difficult to correlate the contents of the book with the real life experience because the figures and diagrams in the books are in two dimension. Although with the introduction of AR students can now see things in 3D which makes the contents more interesting for them. But on educational trips they cannot really roam around with their books in hand for using the markers for augmentation. In this case, the smartwatch can easily project the relevant marker from its library which can be used for augmentation. This makes it quite effortless for the students to experience the world of AR and learn things quickly in an interesting manner.

4.3   Classroom

In our study we observed that the quality of print in school textbooks is not uniform. In case of bad print quality it becomes difficult for the AR device to recognize the markers. DyMAR completely solves this problem as it generates the markers on the display of the smartwatch. This makes it very easy and flawless for the AR device to read it and give a smooth experience for the user. In case of low light, DyMAR proves to be a very efficient way to generate the marker for augmentation. The screen of the smartwatch has a good resolution with high contrast for the marker. Even in darkness the user can comfortably augment the required objects in space.

4.4 Manuals for Maintenance and Repair

In case of some breakdown in machineries the maintenance workers in a factory find it difficult to go through the manuals for the repair job. Using DyMAR one can store the diagrammatic information of the manuals in the database linked with markers. When required the relevant markers can be generated on the smartwatch by feeding the keywords as voice input. Using the markers the diagrams will be augmented in space along with the markings and information given in the manual. The scale of the augmented object can be changed as desired in space.

5   Conclusion

The current AR systems are either marker-based or marker-less. For the marker-based AR system, the camera of the AR device recognizes the marker and tracks the related digital data for 3D visualization and superimposes it on the real physical environment. In this paper we have taken the Marker-based AR system to the next level by introducing DyMAR i.e. Dynamic Marker based Augmented Reality. This is done using smartwatch wearable as the medium to generate the relevant markers using voice recognition on giving the input of related keywords. This does not require the physical presence of a target image, ultimately avoiding the need to carry any book or related documents to scan the markers related to the 2D content (diagrams, figures, etc.). We have also discussed the possible application areas where DyMAR can be used extensively for a better learning and working experience.

References

1. Azuma, R.T.: A survey of augmented reality. Presence: Teleoper. Virtual Environ. **6**(4), 355–385 (1997)
2. Azuma, R., Baillot, Y., Behringer, R., Feiner, S., Julier, S., MacIntyre, B.: Recent advances in augmented reality. IEEE Comput. Graph. Appl. **21**(6), 34–47 (2001). IEEE Computer Society
3. Amin, D., Govilkar, S.: Comparative study of augmented reality SDK's. Int. J. Comput. Sci. Appl. **5**(1), 11–26 (2015)
4. Johnson, L., Levine, A., Smith, R., Stone, S.: Simple augmented reality. In: The 2010 Horizon Report, pp. 21–24. The New Media Consortium, Austin (2010)
5. Marker vs Markerless AR. https://appreal-vr.com/blog/markerless-vs-marker-based-augmented-reality/
6. Contact Lenses for Superhuman Vision. http://www.engr.washington.edu/fac-research/high-lights/ee_contactlens.html
7. IDC, Worldwide Wearables Market Increases 67.2% Amid Seasonal Retrenchment. http://www.idc.com/getdoc.jsp?containerId=prUS41284516
8. Ishii, H., Ullmer, B.: Tangible bits: towards seamless interfaces between people, bits and atoms. In: Proceedings of the ACM SIGCHI Conference on Human Factors in Computing Systems, pp. 234–241. ACM (1997)

9. Kim, H.I., Woo, W.: Smartwatch-assisted robust 6-DOF hand tracker for object manipulation in HMD-based augmented reality. In: IEEE Symposium on 3D User Interfaces (3DUI), pp. 251–252. IEEE (2016)

10. Fiorentino, M., Uva, A.E., Monno, G., Radkowski, R.: Augmented technical drawings: a novel technique for natural interactive visualization of computer-aided design models. J. Comput. Inf. Sci. Eng. 12(2), 024503 (2012)

11. Kato, H., Billinghurst, M., Poupyrev, I., Imamoto, K., Tachibana, K.: Virtual object manipulation on a table-top AR environment. In: 2000 Proceedings of IEEE and ACM International Symposium on Augmented Reality, (ISAR 2000), pp. 111–119. IEEE (2000)

12. Rawassizadeh, R., Price, B.A., Petre, M.: Wearables: has the age of smartwatches finally arrived? Commun. ACM 58(1), 45–47 (2005)

13. Chuah, S.H.W., Rauschnabel, P.A., Krey, N., Nguyen, B., Ramayah, T., Lade, S.: Wearable technologies: the role of usefulness and visibility in smartwatch adoption. Comput. Hum. Behav. 65, 276–284 (2016)

14. Liarokapis, F., Anderson, E.F.: Using augmented reality as a medium to assist teaching in higher education, pp. 9–16 (2010)

15. Dey, S., Sarkar, P.: Augmented reality based integrated intelligent maintenance system for production line. In: 8th Indian Conference on Human Computer Interaction, pp. 126–131. ACM (2016)

16. Zhou, F., Duh, H.B.L., Billinghurst, M.: Trends in augmented reality tracking, interaction and display: a review of ten years of ISMAR. In: 7th IEEE/ACM International Symposium on Mixed and Augmented Reality, pp. 193–202. IEEE Computer Society (2008)

17. Lee, K.: Augmented reality in education and training. TechTrends 56(2), 13–21 (2012)

18. Henrysson, A., Ollila, M.: UMAR: ubiquitous mobile augmented reality. In: 3rd International Conference on Mobile and Ubiquitous Multimedia, pp. 41–45. ACM (2004)

The Smartkuber Case Study: Lessons Learned from the Development of an Augmented Reality Serious Game for Cognitive Screening

Costas Boletsis[1]([⊠]) and Simon McCallum[2]

[1] SINTEF Digital, Forskningsveien 1, 0373 Oslo, Norway
konstantinos.boletsis@sintef.no
[2] Norwegian University of Science and Technology,
Teknologivegen 22, 2815 Gjøvik, Norway
simon.mccallum@ntnu.no

Abstract. In this work, we present a case study, examining the design, development, and evaluation of an Augmented Reality serious game for cognitive screening (namely Smartkuber), which aims to provide reliable and motivating cognitive screening for the elderly. This case study can be of interest for the game designers and researchers, allowing them to build on previous experiences and lessons learned. Smartkuber's development process took place in four stages: (1) analysing the state of the art and defining characteristics, (2) setting up and examining the interaction method, (3) adding and evaluating the game content, and (4) evaluating cognitive screening performance and future direction. The "lessons learned" around the design and development of serious games for cognitive screening are discussed, with focus on Augmented Reality, interaction, test validity, and game motivation aspects.

Keywords: Augmented Reality · Cognitive screening · Elderly · Serious games

1 Introduction

Best practices in dementia care emphasise the importance of early detection; yet, cognitive impairment is still under-recognised and under-diagnosed [10, 30, 34]. Early diagnosis has many benefits, providing an explanation for changes in behaviour and functioning and allowing the person to be involved in future care planning [30].

Cognitive screening represents the initial step in a process of further assessment for dementia and can help identify potential cases for management, thus leading to early diagnosis. Screening for dementia is usually accomplished by means of a global cognitive scale through cognitive tests (such as the Mini-Mental State Exam [9] and the Montreal Cognitive Assessment [28]). However, the existing pen-and-paper screening tests present certain intrinsic limitations, i.e. culture, gender, and educational biases, long test-rest periods (usually one

© Springer International Publishing AG 2017
L.T. De Paolis et al. (Eds.): AVR 2017, Part I, LNCS 10324, pp. 457–472, 2017.
DOI: 10.1007/978-3-319-60922-5_36

month or more), "white coat" and learning effects and the user's potential lack of motivation [4, 30, 33].

Serious games for cognitive screening may be an alternative to traditional, pen-and-paper and computerised cognitive screening tests, potentially motivating and engaging the player to regularly perform cognitive screening tasks; thus, increasing the recognition of cognitive impairment, triggering referral for a more comprehensive assessment and leading to earlier detection [4, 36]. Taking as a prerequisite that the games' content consists of accredited cognitively stimulating exercises, serious games for cognitive screening can be validated against established tests used in clinical practice and provide the player with constant monitoring of his/her cognitive health [4, 23, 37].

In this work, we present a case study, examining the design, development, and evaluation of an Augmented Reality (AR) serious game for cognitive screening (namely Smartkuber), which commenced in 2012 and aims to provide reliable and motivating cognitive screening for the elderly. The case study describes in detail the software release life cycle of Smartkuber (Alpha, Beta, and Release Candidate version) and can be of interest for game designers, game developers, and researchers of the Serious Games and Augmented Reality fields, allowing them to build on previous experiences and lessons learned.

The Smartkuber's design, development and evaluation processes are described in the following sections (Sects. 2–6), leading to the "lessons learned" of Sect. 7.

2   Analysing the State of the Art and Defining Characteristics

The analysis of the state of the art was a significant, first step in order to identify the research gaps and best practices for us further defining the proper game characteristics, which the developed game should have in order to achieve the desired cognitive goals. A literature review of dementia-related serious games [25] and a taxonomy of serious games for dementia [26] (Fig. 1) took place, at that stage and several important observations were made, ranging from the *content* of the games (e.g. interaction methods and problems, platforms, cognitive tasks, et al.) to their *context*, thus to generic conclusions regarding the health functions and health uses that they serve (e.g. most games were serving preventative and rehabilitative cognitive purposes, less educative games, no assessing games).

Based on the findings, the project was decided to focus on the *cognitive* function of the players, serving *preventative* and *assessing* purposes and covering the preclinical stages of cognitive impairment. The technical details of the existing systems were documented and analysed in order to form the basis for chosing our system's interaction method [25].

3   Setting Up and Examining the Interaction Method

The interaction technique of the game was based on the examination of the state of the art, in combination and alignment with our desired goals. We required that

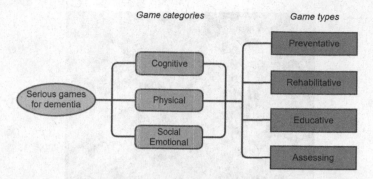

Fig. 1. The schematic of the "serious games for dementia" taxonomy, as published in [26].

the technical infrastructure of the game - supplementary to the game content - would be able to stimulate the elderly players cognitively, while taking into consideration their specific interaction needs [14,16,24].

After examining the related research, the interaction technique of the system was chosen to be based on the manipulation of tangible objects, i.e. cubes, and the use of the Augmented Reality (AR) as the underlying technology (i.e. Tangible Augmented Reality [2]). AR was utilised in the project since it can be beneficial for mental processes, supporting spatial cognition and mental transformation and reducing cognitive load by minimising attention switching. Moreover, AR can evoke the initial engagement of the player utilising the "wow effect" and utilise a variety of sensors, allowing the recording of valuable secondary data related to the users' motor skills. The cubes were chosen as an interaction component because of their properties as accredited assistive tools for occupational therapy [29], cognitive training [11,13], cognitive assessment [31], and motor rehabilitation [11]. The game element that is associated with the cube, makes them appealing to a wide target audience - ranging from children to elderly players [1,13,35]. In our case, the cubes provide also a promising platform for augmentation with various gaming "skins" [3].

The Alpha version of Smartkuber focused on interaction aspects and included two demo mini-games. The implemented interaction technique featured the player sitting at an office, playing the game on a tablet PC by manipulating AR cubes, which are placed on the actual desktop. The whole system was quite portable; it consisted of 9 cubes of 3.5 cm/edge, a tablet PC and a base stand, which the player could adjust according to his/her position, in order to have clear view of the desktop, where he/she would interact with the cubes using both hands (Fig. 2). In order to utilise and test the interaction technique, we developed two demo mini-games. Those games were designed so as to implement two different gaming and interaction styles, that would allow us to witness the player's performance under two different conditions. The first game was a word game, where the player should use 9 letters (displayed as 3D models on the cubes) to form as many words as possible within 5 min. The second game

Fig. 2. Testing the interaction technique of an early version of Smartkuber through a pilot study.

was a speed/shape-matching game, where the player should match simple shapes (cube, sphere et al.) of different colours as quickly as possible. The first game favoured a more focused and calm interaction, whereas the second game favoured fast movements [3].

A pilot study with the Alpha version of Smartkuber and regular players was conducted in order to study the interaction with the AR cubes, aiming at improving the system for later testing, thus safeguarding the elderly players [3]. The study was exploratory in nature, looking for interaction problems, specific user behaviours and it was based on direct observation and semi-structured, informal interviews. The study led to the discovery of several AR technology-related limitations, like the marker occlusion problem, AR lagging, losing depth perception, and dealing with limited 3D AR gaming space [3].

The technical issues would be addressed in the next version of the game, where the game content would also be added.

4   Defining System Requirements

The examination of Smartkuber's Alpha version gave us a better overview of the future technical and interaction needs of the system. Therefore, while started working on the Beta version and adding the game content, we considered the establishment of the system requirements to be an important and necessary action for guiding the following game design and development processes (Table 1). The system requirements originated from our observations and findings regarding the Alpha version of the game, as well as from the set project objectives: (1) the game should be an entertaining game that can stimulate the cognitive abilities of the players for screening purposes, (2) the game should target elderly players, and (3) the game should adopt the positive characteristics of the widely-used screening tests and address the negative ones.

Table 1. The usability, game design, and technical requirements for the cognitive screening game [5].

	Requirements
1.	Interface elements (e.g. menus) should be easy to understand
2.	The necessary information should be communicated across the expected range of user sensory ability (highlighting/differentiating elements, maximising legibility, et al.)
3.	The system should be simple to use, easy to learn and used individually by the player
4.	The interface actions and elements should be consistent, protecting the users from errors
5.	The screen layout, colours and interaction components should be appealing to the player
6.	The system should capture an instance of the player's cognitive status, addressing a wide range of cognitive and motor skills
7.	The system content should record the player's cognitive performance on a frequent/iterative basis
8.	The game content should be automatically or randomly generated in every gaming session
9.	The game should engage and entertain the player over time by utilising the appropriate game mechanics
10	Cross-platform (mostly Android, iOS) gaming should be supported

The establishment of the system requirements, very early in the Beta version of the game, facilitated the design of Smartkuber and served as a guide and a checklist, which we would use to stay "on target".

5 Adding and Evaluating the Game Content

Following the system requirements, the game content was added and the Beta version of Smartkuber (working title: CogARC) was developed and evaluated [5] (Fig. 3). A mini-game architecture was followed in order to address a spectrum of cognitive abilities. Six mini-games were designed and developed with the valuable help of the team's neuropsychologist (Table 2). The mini-games scoring computation formula was related to the successful completion of the cognitive task and inversely related to the level-completion time. Therefore, the player's game objective was to complete the cognitive tasks of the mini-game levels correctly and as fast as possible, to score more points. Leaderboards were also implemented to utilise the Competition game mechanic. Furthermore, the game mechanics of Challenges, Feedback and Rewards were also utilised, by using points (Reward), cognitively stimulating cognitive tasks as game levels (Challenges) and messages about the player's performance (Feedback). The levels of the mini-games were randomly generated to address and minimise the learning

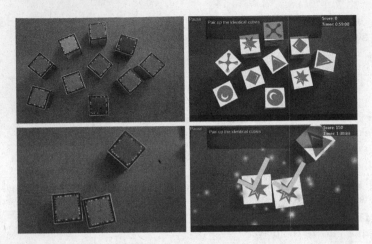

Fig. 3. The real world view (*left*) and the augmented view, as seen on the tablet PC screen (*right*). A screenshot from "Shape match" with all the cubes on scene (*upper part*) and a success message after a correct shape match (*lower part*).

Table 2. The characteristics of the game's Beta version and the cognitive abilities they address [5].

Title	Goal	Cognitive abilities
Shape match	Match same shapes	Perception, Attention, Executive functions: Flexibility, Response Inhibition
Colour match	Match one word's meaning to another word's colour	Perception, Visual Processing, Attention, Motor Skills, Executive functions: Flexibility, Response Inhibition
Sum tower	Use the numbers to create the desired total sum	Motor Skills, Executive functions: Problem Solving, Decision Making
Building blocks	Find the answer to simple arithmetic calculations	Motor Skills, Executive functions: Problem Solving, Decision Making
Pattern memory	Memorise a 3 × 3 matrix pattern of coloured tiles and recreate it	Attention, Visual and Spatial processing, Motor Skills, Executive functions: Working Memory
Word game	Use letters to form as many words as possible	Language Processing, Motor Skills, Executive functions: Problem Solving, Decision Making, Working Memory

effects. The difficulty level of the game tasks was uniform and at a moderate degree for all the mini-game levels, in order for the system to be able to establish a player-specific scoring baseline and detect changes in scores over time, for screening purposes. The user interface (UI) design of Smartkuber's Beta version was specifically designed for elderly players and was based on the principles of simplicity and intuitiveness [5].

A usability and game experience testing was conducted as part of the game's quality assurance process [5]. The testing was focused on qualitative observations, investigating the game experience that the Beta version of the game offered (using the in-Game Experience Questionnaire [18–20]), the usability of the system (using the System Usability Scale [8]), as well as on documenting the players' specific remarks (using open, semi-structured interviews). The goal of the usability and game experience testing was to identify any usability problems and determine the players' satisfaction with the game. A convenience sample of five healthy, older adults (n = 5, mean age: 67.6, SD: 5.77) participated in the testing. The results showed that some AR issues of the previous stage, such as the loss of the depth perception and lagging problems, remained. Furthermore, there was a mixed perception of the reality-virtuality space by the elderly players (i.e. perceiving the markers as AR game content), leading to confusion, and also three mini-games presented interaction and content issues. However, cubes were considered by the players to be a suitable component.

The outcomes of the testing would form the Release Candidate (RC) version of the game [7] (Fig. 4). Redefining the role of the utilised AR technology in the Reality-Virtuality spectrum and redesigning the game content were among the issues that were addressed. The Tangible Augmented Reality implementation - so far - was borrowing elements from Mediated Reality. The game interaction technology "moved" towards the Reality spectrum on the Reality-Virtuality Continuum [27] and the main part of Smartkuber's interaction and its game content were placed at the real world. Augmented Reality was utilised solely for real-world recognition and for verifying the correct, real-world game tasks.

The interaction technique and its components were also adjusted [7]. The RC version of Smartkuber utilised just 6 cubes of 4.4 cm/edge with game content on every side (e.g. letters, numbers, colours, faces, shapes) (Fig. 4). The tablet base stand was removed as an interaction component and the game tasks are

Fig. 4. The Smartkuber game setup [7].

performed by the player getting the instructions on the tablet PC and then leaving it aside to manipulate the cubes - using both hands - in order to form the right answer. The RC version followed a linear gameplay and two mini-games were "killed" since they did not perform well at the evaluation of the Beta version. A basic narrative was added for every game task. The mini-games of the RC version of Smartkuber are presented in Table 3 and can be seen in Fig. 5.

To evaluate the game experience that the RC version of Smartkuber offered, a game experience study was conducted utilising the in-Game Experience Questionnaire (iGEQ) [7]. The game was tested under realistic conditions, therefore the participants were allowed to take Smartkuber with them and play it at their own place of will (e.g. home, office, et al.), for as many sessions as they wanted, within a period of 6 weeks. Thirteen elderly players (n = 13, mean age: 68.69, SD: 7.24, male/female: 8/5) completed 244 Smartkuber gaming sessions

Table 3. The mini-games of Smartkuber (Release Candidate version) and the cognitive abilities they address [7].

Title	Goal	Cognitive abilities
Reconstruct the flag	The player has to memorise the flag and use the cubes to reconstruct it	Attention, Memory, Motor Skills, Executive functions: Working Memory, Flexibility, Response Inhibition
Reconnect old friends	The player has to memorise the friend's faces and use the cubes to form the right pair of friends	Attention, Memory, Motor Skills, Visual Processing, Executive functions: Working Memory, Flexibility, Response Inhibition
Repeat the pattern	The player has to memorize a shape pattern and use the cubes to form it	Attention, Memory, Motor Skills, Visual & Spatial Processing, Executive functions: Working Memory, Flexibility, Response Inhibition
Numerical calculation	The player has to do a numerical calculation and use the cubes to form the right answer	Attention, Memory, Motor Skills, Executive functions: Problem Solving, Decision Making, Working Memory, Flexibility, Response Inhibition
Find the word	The player is given a word quiz and uses the cubes to form the right answer	Attention, Memory, Motor Skills, Language, Executive functions: Problem Solving, Decision Making, Working Memory, Flexibility, Response Inhibition

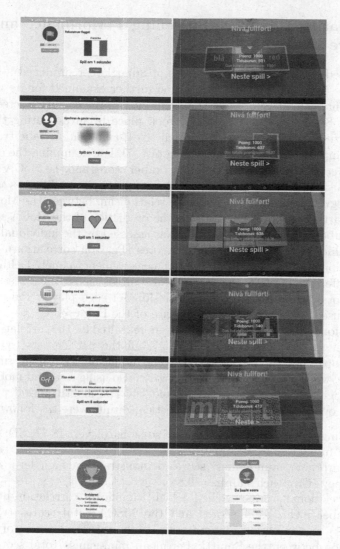

Fig. 5. The 5 mini-game levels of a Smartkuber gaming session (tablet PC view), their solutions (AR view), and the endgame screen - leaderboard (tablet PC view).

over the period of 6 weeks (mean number of sessions/player: 18.77, SD: 2.68). The measurements revealed a high level of players' cognitive involvement with Smartkuber. They also showed that the players felt skilful enough while playing Smartkuber, though the difficulty level may have needed further tweaking to challenge the players more. Finally, the players demonstrated high values of positive and low values of negative feelings, thus potentially highlighting the entertaining and motivating nature of Smartkuber and the suitability of its UI and interaction technique for the elderly players [7]. The same study also explored the test validity of the game, which is described in the following section.

6   Evaluating Cognitive Screening Performance and Future Direction

The described quality assurance process of Smartkuber produced a promising and valuable instrument, which should be further examined for its validity as an assessment tool. At this stage, the evaluation of the cognitive screening performance of Smartkuber (RC version) took place by investigating the game's construct, criterion (concurrent and predictive), and content validity, assessing its relationship with the MoCA screening test [7]. For examining the concurrent validity, the correlation between the Smartkuber scores and the MoCA scores was calculated (using the Pearson correlation). The predictive ability was assessed by the linear regression, which modelled the relationship between the MoCA scores and the Smartkuber scores, focusing on the prediction of the MoCA score using the Smartkuber score. Content validity was assessed by the individual Smartkuber mini-games scores with the MoCA scores (Pearson correlation), as well as the calculation of a learning-effect-related measurement, namely Delta score, i.e. the score difference between the mean total score of the 20% last sessions minus the mean total score of the 20% first sessions of each player. Paired samples T-test was used to evaluate the significance of the Delta score.

As mentioned above, 13 participants were recruited for the correlational study [7]. Regarding experience with technology, all the participants ($n = 13$) were using a laptop or desktop PC and at least one mobile device (tablet, smartphone, or e-reader), while 69.2% of them ($n = 9$) were also using a second mobile device.

All participants successfully completed the two-month period playing the game at an open and free rate. The statistical results were the following:

- 244 gaming sessions (mean number of sessions/player: 18.77, SD: 2.68) were recorded from the 13 participants.
- The Smartkuber mini-games' scores demonstrated a high level of internal consistency (Cronbach's alpha = 0.84).
- The correlational study revealed a high, significant correlation between the Smartkuber mean total scores and the MoCA total scores ($r[11] = 0.81$, $p = 0.001$) and it also demonstrated a high statistical power of 0.95. The correlation between the Smartkuber mean mini-games/total scores and the MoCA subtests/total scores are described in Table 4.
- Smartkuber mean total scores ($\beta = 0.007$, $p = 0.001$) were significant predictors of MoCA scores, explaining 62.1% of MoCA total score variance, when controlling for age, education, gender, frequency of technology use and video gaming ($S = 1.35$, $F[1,12] = 20.70$ with $p = 0.001$).
- The Delta score differences were not statistically significant ($p > 0.05$) for any of the players.

The correlational study provided important insights on the utilisation of the Smartkuber game as a cognitive health screening tool for elderly players [7]. The Smartkuber scores - both totally and individually - revealed significant correlations and high concurrent validity with the MoCA scores, while demonstrating a high value of internal consistency. The significant correlation between

Table 4. Correlations between the Smartkuber mini-games and MoCA total scores [7].

MoCA	#1: Reconstruct the flag	#2: Reconnect old friends	#3: Repeat the pattern	#4: Numerical calculation	#5: Find the word	Total score
Visuospatial	0.74**	0.73**	0.64*	0.54	0.49	0.63*
Naming	0.52	0.68*	0.82**	0.68*	0.79**	0.75**
Attention	0.54	0.64*	0.68*	0.56*	0.61*	0.64*
Language	0.61*	0.65*	0.52	0.67*	0.50	0.60*
Abstraction	0.34	0.47	0.61*	0.43	0.32	0.45
Del. recall	0.18	0.15	0.11	0.08	−0.04	0.08
Orientation	0.57*	0.68**	0.71**	0.79**	0.87**	0.78**
Total score	0.76**	0.85**	0.83**	0.79**	0.70**	**0.81**

$* \ p < 0.05, \ ** \ p < 0.01$

the Smartkuber total scores and the MoCA scores likely reflected the cognitive demand of the tasks, addressing the visuoperceptual, attention, working memory, language, motor and inhibitory response skills of the players and suggesting they tapped into the cognitive domains screened by the MoCA test. Regression results indicated that Smartkuber total scores were significantly predictive of MoCA total scores after adjusting for demographics. The Delta scores showed no significant difference in scoring between the first and the last players' sessions and all the players managed to demonstrate steady game performances. Therefore, the results revealed no learning effects during the Smartkuber game sessions, implying that the iterative gameplay of the cognitive screening game instrument did not rely on or affect the players' short-term memory.

The future direction of Smartkuber take many forms:

- The use of Smartkuber as the main part of a gaming system for cognitive screening and sleep duration assessment of the elderly is a direction which is currently under examination [6]. Smartkuber is used in combination with a smartwatch to record performances related to cognitive performance and sleep quality, which is another indicator of cognitive decline. A pilot study focusing on technical and usability issues has already been conducted, to that direction. The ultimate goal of this direction is a system that will triangulate its measurements (by measures of cognitive skills, motor skills, and sleep duration/stages) in order to trigger reliable referrals for a more comprehensive assessment [6].
- Another direction can be the development of the "Cognitive Passport" (coming from the concept of the Biological Passport [32]), i.e. a database where the game performance (and potentially the sleep stages, and the sleep duration measurements from the smartwatch device mentioned above) of each player is stored (Fig. 6). The database will constitute the players' user profiles with the player's cognitive-related measurements and performance, over time. The Cognitive Passport will set each player's baseline performance and

provides the opportunity to detect changes related to the individual performance, rather than just measuring performance against population means.
- A long-term direction is a Smartkuber game for kids targeting entertainment and learning, as well as a Smartkuber game of dual identity, targeting transgenerational play and grandparents playing along with their grandchildren.

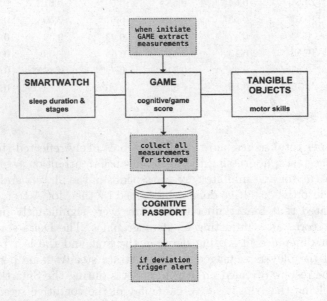

Fig. 6. The functionality of the Cognitive Passport database [6].

7   Lessons Learned

Through the Smartkuber project - and so far - we have learned a few valuable lessons, which could be generalised and be of use for serious game designers, AR developers, and researchers:

- Serious games have great potential as motivating, valid measures of cognitive performance and evaluating their test validity is a promising research field. In this context, test validity refers to the serious games being evaluated and developed with a combination of subjective assessments and correlational studies, which demonstrated that they successfully assess cognitive performance [22]. So far there are many works examining the experimental validity of serious games for cognitive training, referring to treatments or interventions that impact cognitive-related outcomes. The test validity of cognitive serious games can act supplementary to their experimental validity, thus creating a strong defence line against cognitive impairment. The examination of the state of the art [25,26] showed that there is a promising, unexplored, research space for serious games as entertaining, motivating, and valid measures of cognitive performance and this project demonstrated positive results about it.

- Tangible Augmented Reality is a technology that can be suitable for the elderly and can help bridging the technology gap between ICTs and the elderly users. The tangible, real artifacts add a level of familiarity and playfulness with the TAR interaction method and it empowers elderly users to comprehend what AR is, how it works, as well as how to use it effectively. Naturally, the implementation of the TAR technology should be based on many iterations and adhere to specific design guidelines related to the elderly users' target group, in order for it to be utilised properly.

- Testing a serious game under realistic conditions, at the player's place of will and for a long duration, can lead to better game-motivation analysis. Evaluating a serious game performance in laboratory settings can sometimes skew the results around the motivating power of the game. Allowing the player to play the game at a familiar environment of his/her choice, whenever he/she wants and for a long period of time, trully tests the motivation and the engagement that the game can offer.

- The Competition, Reward, and Feedback game mechanics can strongly motivate elderly players. The use of competition, challenges, performance feedback, and leaderboards can create a fun and entertaining environment with the elderly discussing and comparing their performances. The intrinsic motivation, coming from the sense of belonging to the "community" that plays the game, as well as from the players always wanting to perform better at the cognitive tasks, blends well with the extrinsic motivations of points, rewards, and rankings.

- Augmented Reality can be utilised in a meaningful way, within the context of a cognitive screening game. Many times in games, AR is used just to provide the "novel" label and to trigger the "wow effect". In cognitive screening games, AR can offer much more than just fascinating the player, since it can add an underlying level of cognitive complexity, which does not affect the game difficulty level and, at the same time, manages to stimulate the player cognitively and physically (motor skills). The challenging part of implementing AR in a cognitive screening context is finding the right balance between the utilised AR elements that could serve the game scenario and the ones serving screening process. In our project, we had to adjust the interaction method in order for AR to have meaningful presence and to be technically robust [5,7].

- The design and ethical guidelines around elderly users should be respected and implemented when designing serious games for such a sensitive and unique target group. Serious games for elderly players target a niche market and should be designed accordingly, thus catering to the special interaction needs of the elderly population [15,17,21]. Furthermore, all the safeguarding procedures and ethical guidelines should be applied, as well as many iterations and testings should take place, in order to confirm that the final product is not only entertaining, motivating, and effective, but also safe.

– A mini-game architecture can facilitate the cognitive screening performance of a serious game by addressing a spectrum of cognitive abilities. Mini-games can be a resource in their own right, incorporating different gameplay mechanics, and - when united - focusing on a single topic [12]. Furthermore, mini-games provide the opportunity for the player to explore various and different game scenarios and experience the motivating feeling of achievement that comes from the completion of a level or a mini-game, more frequently [4,12].

– Cubes can be a valuable tool for cognitive screening serious games and suitable for elderly players. The game element that is associated with the cubes, combined with the fact that they have been successfully used as assistive tools for cognitive training and cognitive assessment [11,13,31] can create a promising interaction component for cognitive screening serious games.

8   Conclusion

Serious games for cognitive screening is a promising subfield of the "serious games for health" domain, while Augmented Reality can be a suitable, enabling technology, with the proper adjustments. Our work on Smartkuber led to several findings that could be potentially generalised and benefit the Serious Games and Augmented Reality communities. Ultimately, through the project, we managed to show that, even though the field of cognitive screening serious games presents many unique, research challenges, it can highly contribute to the fight against cognitive impairment and dementia, in a meaningful and innovative way.

References

1. Barakova, E., van Wanrooij, G., van Limpt, R., Menting, M.: Using an emergent system concept in designing interactive games for autistic children. In: Proceedings of the 6th International Conference on Interaction Design and Children, IDC 2007, pp. 73–76 (2007)
2. Billinghurst, M., Kato, H., Poupyrev, I.: Tangible augmented reality. In: Proceedings of ACM SIGGRAPH Asia, pp. 1–10 (2008)
3. Boletsis, C., McCallum, S.: Augmented reality cube game for cognitive training: an interaction study. Stud. Health Technol. Inf. **200**, 81–87 (2014)
4. Boletsis, C., McCallum, S.: Connecting the player to the doctor: utilising serious games for cognitive training & screening. DAIMI PB **597**, 5–8 (2015)
5. Boletsis, C., McCallum, S.: Augmented reality cubes for cognitive gaming: preliminary usability and game experience testing. Int. J. Serious Games **3**(1), 3–18 (2016)
6. Boletsis, C., McCallum, S.: Evaluating a gaming system for cognitive screening and sleep duration assessment of elderly players: a pilot study. In: Bottino, R., Jeuring, J., Veltkamp, R.C. (eds.) GALA 2016. LNCS, vol. 10056, pp. 107–119. Springer, Cham (2016). doi:10.1007/978-3-319-50182-6_10
7. Boletsis, C., McCallum, S.: Smartkuber: a cognitive training game for cognitive health screening of elderly players. Games Health J. **5**(4), 241–251 (2016)

8. Brooke, J.: SUS-A quick and dirty usability scale. In: Usability Evaluation in Industry, pp. 189–194. Taylor & Francis (1996)
9. Cockrell, J.R., Folstein, M.F.: Mini-mental state examination (MMSE). Psychopharmacol. Bull. **24**(4), 689–692 (1988)
10. Connolly, A., Gaehl, E., Martin, H., Morris, J., Purandare, N.: Underdiagnosis of dementia in primary care: variations in the observed prevalence and comparisons to the expected prevalence. Aging Mental Health **15**(8), 978–984 (2011)
11. Correa, A., de Assis, G.A., Nascimento, M.d., Ficheman, I., de Deus Lopes, R.: GenVirtual: an augmented reality musical game for cognitive and motor rehabilitation. In: Virtual Rehabilitation, pp. 1–6 (2007)
12. Frazer, A., Argles, D., Wills, G.: Assessing the usefulness of mini-games as educational resources. In: ALT-C 2007: Beyond Control (2007)
13. Gamberini, L., Martino, F., Seraglia, B., Spagnolli, A., Fabregat, M., Ibanez, F., Alcaniz, M., Andres, J.M.: Eldergames project: an innovative mixed reality tabletop solution to preserve cognitive functions in elderly people. In: Proceedings of the 2nd Conference on Human System Interactions, pp. 164–169 (2009)
14. Gerling, K., Masuch, M.: When gaming is not suitable for everyone: playtesting Wii games with frail elderly. In: Proceeding of the 1st Workshop on Game Accessibility: Xtreme Interaction Design (FDG 2011), Bordeaux, France (2011)
15. Gregor, P., Newell, A.F.: Designing for dynamic diversity: making accessible interfaces for older people. In: Proceedings of the 2001 EC/NSF Workshop on Universal Accessibility of Ubiquitous Computing: Providing for the Elderly, WUAUC 2001, pp. 90–92 (2001)
16. Gregor, P., Newell, A.F., Zajicek, M.: Designing for dynamic diversity: interfaces for older people. In: Proceedings of the Fifth International ACM Conference on Assistive Technologies, ASSETS 2002, pp. 151–156 (2002)
17. Heller, R., Jorge, J., Guedj, R.: EC/NSF workshop on universal accessibility of ubiquitous computing: providing for the elderly event report. In: Proceedings of the 2001 EC/NSF Workshop on Universal Accessibility of Ubiquitous Computing: Providing for the Elderly, WUAUC 2001, pp. 1–10. ACM (2001)
18. IJsselsteijn, W., De Kort, Y., Poels, K.: The game experience questionnaire: development of a self-report measure to assess the psychological impact of digital games. Manuscript in preparation. FUGA technical report Deliverable 3.3 (2013)
19. IJsselsteijn, W., De Kort, Y., Poels, K., Jurgelionis, A., Bellotti, F.: Characterising and measuring user experiences in digital games. In: International Conference on Advances in Computer Entertainment Technology, vol. 2, p. 27 (2007)
20. IJsselsteijn, W., van den Hoogen, W., Klimmt, C., de Kort, Y., Lindley, C., Mathiak, K., Poels, K., Ravaja, N., Turpeinen, M., Vorderer, P.: Measuring the experience of digital game enjoyment. In: Proceedings of Measuring Behavior, pp. 88–89 (2008)
21. Ijsselsteijn, W., Nap, H.H., de Kort, Y., Poels, K.: Digital game design for elderly users. In: Proceedings of the 2007 Conference on Future Play 2007, pp. 17–22 (2007)
22. Kato, P.: What do you mean when you say your serious game has been validated? Experimental vs. Test Validity (2013). http://wp.me/p299Wi-dp. Accessed 8 Apr 2017
23. Manera, V., Petit, P.D., Derreumaux, A., Orvieto, I., Romagnoli, M., Lyttle, G., David, R., Robert, P.: 'Kitchen and cooking', a serious game for mild cognitive impairment and Alzheimer's disease: a pilot study. Front. Aging Neurosci. **7**(24), 1–10 (2015)

24. McCallum, S., Boletsis, C.: Augmented reality & gesture-based architecture in games for the elderly. In: pHealth, Studies in Health Technology and Informatics, vol. 189, pp. 139–144. IOS Press (2013)
25. McCallum, S., Boletsis, C.: Dementia games: a literature review of dementia-related serious games. In: Ma, M., Oliveira, M.F., Petersen, S., Hauge, J.B. (eds.) SGDA 2013. LNCS, vol. 8101, pp. 15–27. Springer, Heidelberg (2013). doi:10.1007/978-3-642-40790-1_2
26. McCallum, S., Boletsis, C.: A taxonomy of serious games for dementia. In: Schouten, B., Fedtke, S., Bekker, T., Schijven, M., Gekker, A. (eds.) Games for Health, pp. 219–232. Springer, Wiesbaden (2013). doi:10.1007/978-3-658-02897-8_17
27. Milgram, P., Kishino, F.: A taxonomy of mixed reality visual displays. IEICE Trans. Inf. Syst. **77**(12), 1321–1329 (1994)
28. Nasreddine, Z.S., Phillips, N.A., Bedirian, V., Charbonneau, S., Whitehead, V., Collin, I., Cummings, J.L., Chertkow, H.: The montreal cognitive assessment, MoCA: a brief screening tool for mild cognitive impairment. J. Am. Geriatr. Soc. **53**(4), 695–699 (2005)
29. Neistadt, M.: A critical analysis of occupational therapy approaches for perceptual deficits in adults with brain injury. Am. J. Occup. Ther. **44**(4), 299–304 (1990)
30. Scanlon, L., O'Shea, E., O'Caoimh, R., Timmons, S.: Usability and validity of a battery of computerised cognitive screening tests for detecting cognitive impairment. Gerontology **62**(2), 247–252 (2016)
31. Sharlin, E., Itoh, Y., Watson, B., Kitamura, Y., Sutphen, S., Liu, L.: Cognitive cubes: a tangible user interface for cognitive assessment. In: Proceedings of the SIGCHI Conference on Human Factors in Computing Systems, CHI 2002, pp. 347–354 (2002)
32. Sottas, P.E., Robinson, N., Rabin, O., Saugy, M.: The athlete biological passport. Clin. Chem. **57**(7), 969–976 (2011)
33. Tong, T., Guana, V., Jovanovic, A., Tran, F., Mozafari, G., Chignell, M., Stroulia, E.: Rapid deployment and evaluation of mobile serious games: a cognitive assessment case study. Procedia Comput. Sci. **69**, 96–103 (2015)
34. Waldemar, G., Phung, K., Burns, A., Georges, J., Hansen, F.R., Iliffe, S., Marking, C., Rikkert, M.O., Selmes, J., Stoppe, G., Sartorius, N.: Access to diagnostic evaluation and treatment for dementia in europe. Int. J. Geriatr. Psychiatry **22**(1), 47–54 (2007)
35. Zhou, Z., Cheok, A., Pan, J.: 3D story cube: an interactive tangible user interface for storytelling with 3D graphics and audio. Pers. Ubiquit. Comput. **8**(5), 374–376 (2004)
36. Zucchella, C., Sinforiani, E., Tassorelli, C., Cavallini, E., Tost-Pardell, D., Grau, S., Pazzi, S., Puricelli, S., Bernini, S., Bottiroli, S., et al.: Serious games for screening pre-dementia conditions: from virtuality to reality? A pilot project. Funct. Neurol. **29**(3), 153–158 (2014)
37. Zygouris, S., Giakoumis, D., Votis, K., Doumpoulakis, S., Ntovas, K., Segkouli, S., Karagiannidis, C., Tzovaras, D., Tsolaki, M.: Can a virtual reality cognitive training application fulfill a dual role? Using the virtual supermarket cognitive training application as a screening tool for mild cognitive impairment. J. Alzheimers Dis. **44**(4), 1333–1347 (2015)

Author Index

Printed in the United States
By Bookmasters